THE ASIAN TURN IN FOREIGN INVESTMENT

This collection critically discusses the increasing significance of Asian States in the field of international investment law and policy. Consisting of contributions authored by a leading team of scholars and practitioners of international investment law, this volume presents analyses of both national and multilateral investment law rule-making in Asia, including a critical discussion of certain States' approaches to balancing the different tensions between investment protection and the preservation of States' regulatory sovereignty. It also contains thematic chapters on cutting-edge developments which are of relevance to Asia as well as the global community, such as investors' obligations of due diligence, additional transparency in treaty-based investment arbitration responses by the Association of Southeast Asian Nations (ASEAN) Member States to trans-boundary haze pollution and the relevance of human rights obligations in international investment law. It also contemplates future possibilities for investor–State dispute settlement, including the use of investor–State mediation in view of the Singapore Convention on Mediation.

Mahdev Mohan is the global policy and standards lead for emerging markets at Google LLC and was formerly a faculty member at the Singapore Management University (SMU) School of Law, where he taught public international law and directed SMU's Asian Business and Rule of Law initiative. A former Nominated Member of Parliament of Singapore, he is the executive director of the Society of International Law Singapore, an editorial board member of the *Journal of East Asia and International Law* and *China and WTO Review*, and has written and practised in the fields of public international law, investment arbitration and human rights law in Asia. Mohan was an associate tenant of Temple Garden Chambers within its public international law practice group.

Chester Brown is Professor of International Law and International Arbitration at the University of Sydney Law School; a barrister at 7 Wentworth Selbourne Chambers, Sydney; and an overseas member of Essex Court Chambers, London. He teaches and researches in the fields of public international law, international dispute settlement, international investment law and international commercial arbitration. He also maintains a practice in these fields and has been involved as counsel in proceedings before the International Court of Justice, the Iran–United States Claims Tribunal, inter-State and investor–State arbitral tribunals, as well as in inter-State conciliation proceedings and international commercial arbitrations.

The Asian Turn in Foreign Investment

Edited by

MAHDEV MOHAN

Google, LLC

CHESTER BROWN

Univeristy of Sydney Law School

CAMBRIDGE
UNIVERSITY PRESS

CAMBRIDGE
UNIVERSITY PRESS

Shaftesbury Road, Cambridge CB2 8EA, United Kingdom

One Liberty Plaza, 20th Floor, New York, NY 10006, USA

477 Williamstown Road, Port Melbourne, VIC 3207, Australia

314–321, 3rd Floor, Plot 3, Splendor Forum, Jasola District Centre, New Delhi – 110025, India

103 Penang Road, #05–06/07, Visioncrest Commercial, Singapore 238467

Cambridge University Press is part of Cambridge University Press & Assessment, a department of the University of Cambridge.

We share the University's mission to contribute to society through the pursuit of education, learning and research at the highest international levels of excellence.

www.cambridge.org
Information on this title: www.cambridge.org/9781009457545

DOI: 10.1017/9781108675772

First published 2021
First paperback edition 2024

A catalogue record for this publication is available from the British Library

Library of Congress Cataloging-in-Publication data
NAMES: Mohan, Mahdev, editor. | Brown, Chester, 1972– editor.
TITLE: The Asian turn in foreign investment / edited by Mahdev Mohan, Chester Brown, University of Sydney.
DESCRIPTION: Cambridge, United Kingdom ; New York, NY : Cambridge University Press, 2021. | Includes index.
IDENTIFIERS: LCCN 2020035141 | ISBN 9781108426596 (hardback) | ISBN 9781108675772 (ebook)
SUBJECTS: LCSH: Investments, Foreign – Law and legislation – Asia. | Investments, Foreign – Law and legislation – European Union countries.
CLASSIFICATION: LCC KNC747 .A858 2021 | DDC 346.5/092–dc23
LC record available at https://lccn.loc.gov/2020035141

ISBN 978-1-108-42659-6 Hardback
ISBN 978-1-009-45754-5 Paperback

Contents

Figures

Tables

Contributors

Nadja Alexander is Professor of Law (Practice) at SMU School of Law and Director of the Singapore International Dispute Resolution Academy (SIDRA). She is conjoint Professor at Newcastle Law School, Australia, and Senior Fellow of the Dispute Resolution Institute at Mitchell Hamline School of Law, United States. She sits on mediation panels in Singapore, Hong Kong, Japan, India and Australia. Nadja is a foundation member of the International Advisory Board of the United Nations Office of the Ombudsman, which has oversight of the Global Mediation Panel. Nadja's books include *The Singapore Convention on Mediation: A Commentary* (with Shouyu Chong), *Global Trends in Mediation, Singapore Mediation Handbook, International Comparative Mediation* and *EU Mediation Law Handbook*.

Ei Ei Aung is Senior Associate and Head of the Corporate Practice at U Tin Yu & Associates, Yangon, Myanmar. Ei Ei received her Bachelor of Laws from Dagon University, Myanmar, and Master of Laws specializing in International Business Law from Assumption University in Bangkok, Thailand. She has experience advising on foreign direct investment trade mark registration and property law, and representing clients in dispute resolution. Together with Stephenson Harwood (U Tin Yu's associated international law firm), she jointly advises international companies on market entry, commercial arrangements, joint ventures and dealing with regulatory bodies in Myanmar, both in Yangon and Nay Pyi Taw.

Jessica Beess und Chrostin is Senior Associate at Covington & Burling LLP's office in New York. Ms. Beess und Chrostin represents clients in international commercial, investment treaty and intra-State arbitration, as well as in international disputes before US courts. She was formerly Adjunct Professor of Law at Vanderbilt Law School, where she taught investment arbitration, and is a frequent writer and speaker on topics relating to international arbitration. Beess und Chrostin holds a JD cum laude from Harvard Law School and a BA cum laude with honours from Columbia University.

Chester Brown is Professor of International Law and International Arbitration at the University of Sydney Law School. He is also a barrister at 7 Wentworth Selborne Chambers, Sydney, and an overseas member of Essex Court Chambers, London. He teaches and researches in the fields of public international law, international dispute settlement, international investment law and international commercial arbitration. He also maintains a practice in these fields and has appeared as counsel in proceedings before the International Court of Justice, the Iran–United States Claims Tribunal, inter-State and investor-State arbitral tribunals, as well as in inter-State conciliation proceedings and international commercial arbitrations.

N Jansen Calamita is Head of Investment Law and Policy, Centre for International Law, and Research Associate Professor (CIL), Faculty of Law, National University of Singapore. Prior to entering academia, Professor Calamita served in the Office of the Legal Adviser in the US Department of State and as a member of the UNCITRAL Secretariat. He began his career in private practice in New York. He is co-editor (with Loretta Malintoppi) of *International Litigation in Practice* (Brill) and a member of the editorial board of the *Yearbook of International Investment Law and Policy* (Oxford University Press).

Julien Chaisse is Professor at the City University of Hong Kong, School of Law. He is an award-winning scholar of international law with a focus on the regulation and development of economic globalization. He has published numerous well-regarded books and articles, and his scholarship has been cited by international courts/tribunals, as well as US courts. Julien served as a senior fellow at the World Trade Institute (Switzerland) and as a diplomat for the Embassy of France in New Delhi (India). He is also an experienced arbitrator and a sought-after consultant/expert to international organizations, governments, law firms and private investors.

Shouyu Chong is a PhD candidate and Visiting Lecturer at the Centre of Construction Law and Dispute Resolution, the Dickson Poon School of Law, King's College London. He is also a Research Fellow at the Singapore International Dispute Resolution Academy. He researches private international law and cross-border dispute resolution mechanisms, including litigation, arbitration and mediation. He is funded by the Centre of Construction Law and Dispute Resolution, as well as the Society of Construction Law, to conduct research on jurisdiction and arbitration clauses.

Ingrid Coinquet is the founder and managing director of Augmenta Group, which is a global connector for clients, investors, lawyers and experts for the recovery of distressed claims, offering dispute strategy and financing access until the actual recovery of the claim. Ingrid has more than fifteen years of extensive experience in cross-border disputes and distressed debt recovery, including ten years as general counsel for investment funds and third-party funders. She has also worked in the Disputes and Banking/Project Finance departments of top-tier law firms, including Baker & McKenzie, where she gained valuable experience in representing multinational companies in international disputes, as well as major financial institutions in banking and project finance. Ingrid is a qualified attorney in the State of New York, USA.

Antony Crockett is a senior consultant with international law firm Herbert Smith Freehills based in Hong Kong. Antony is an international dispute resolution specialist with expertise in international commercial arbitration, investment treaty arbitration and public international law. He is admitted to practice in Australia (Victoria), England and Wales and Hong Kong SAR. Antony holds the degrees LLB (Hons) and BSc (Environmental Science) from the University of Melbourne and an LLM (Dist.) from the London School of Economics and Political Science. An Australian national, Antony has lived and practised in Asia (Hong Kong, Jakarta and Singapore) for almost a decade.

Nguyen Manh Dzung is the founder of Dzungsrt & Associates LLC and an internationally recognized specialist in all areas of maritime law, commercial litigation and international arbitration in Vietnam. Dzung was the first ever Vietnamese member of the ICC Court, and he is also a panel member of the Vietnam International Arbitration Centre. He was a key contributing editorial member of the Drafting Committee of Law on Commercial

Arbitration and Decree on Commercial Mediation of Vietnam. He has presented and lectured extensively on ADR and international commercial arbitration at the Judicial Academy of the Ministry of Justice of Vietnam and the Diplomatic Academy of the Ministry of Foreign Affairs of Vietnam.

Dang Vu Minh Ha is a senior associate of Dzungsrt & Associates LLC. She focuses mainly on commercial arbitration and mediation. Minh Ha obtained her first degree in law with distinction and her LLM in International Commercial Law from the University of Leicester, United Kingdom. She is usually involved in drafting legal opinions in both Vietnamese and English; she assists clients in local courts and arbitration in relevant fields. Minh Ha is also co-author of a number of publications on arbitration such as the Vietnam chapter in the 'IBA Country Guides', *Young Arbitration Review*, *Global Arbitration Review*, and the *Vietnam National Report in the ICCA Handbook on Commercial Arbitration*.

Abhimanyu George Jain is a PhD candidate and research associate at the Graduate Institute of International and Development Studies in Geneva. He has been admitted to the practice of law in India and in England and Wales. He has previously worked as a management consultant, as a corporate lawyer and, most recently, as a member of the team of counsels representing India in two investment arbitration disputes.

Shotaro Hamamoto holds the degrees of LLB (Kyoto), LLM (Kyoto) and Docteur en droit (Paris II). He is Professor of the Law of International Organizations at the Graduate School of Law, Kyoto University. He is the Co-Chair of the International Law Association's Committee on Procedure of International Courts and Tribunals (2016–). He has served as counsel for Botswana in *Legal Consequences of the Separation of the Chagos Archipelago from Mauritius* (ICJ, Advisory Opinion, 2018–2019) and for Japan in the *Whaling in the Antarctic* (ICJ, *Australia* v. *Japan, New Zealand intervening*, 2010–2014), *Hoshinmaru* (ITLOS, *Japan* v. *Russia*, 2007) and *Tomimaru* cases (ITLOS, *Japan* v. *Russia*, 2007). He also served as the assistant for the Spanish government in *Fisheries Jurisdiction* (ICJ, *Spain* v. *Canada*, 1997–98). He is also the Japanese delegate to UNCITRAL (2010–).

Jie (Jeanne) Huang is an associate professor at the University of Sydney Law School in Australia. She teaches and researches in the fields of law for digital trade, private international law, international litigation and arbitration, international investment law and underwater cultural heritage protection. She has published four books and authored many articles in esteemed law journals, such as the *Journal of International Economic Law* and the *Journal of Private International Law*. Thirteen of her articles are indexed by SSCI. As a chief investigator, she has received funding from China National Social Science Fund (equivalent to the Australian Research Council), China's Ministry of Education, the China Law Society, the Shanghai Philosophy and Social Science Fund, and the Shanghai Government Development and Research Center Fund.

Aziah Hussin (LL.M., (University College London); Advocate & Solicitor (Singapore); Solicitor (Higher Courts, England & Wales), was an adjunct faculty member at the Singapore Management University School of Law, and an International Law Research Consultant for the Singapore International Dispute Resolution Academy where she led research on the Singapore Convention on Mediation.

Shreyas Jayasimha is a founding partner of Aarna Law, which has offices in Bangalore, Delhi and Mumbai, and an advocate, arbitrator and mediator with more than nineteen years of experience in domestic and international dispute resolution across various industry sectors. He has recently established Aarna ADR in Maxwell Chambers, Singapore. Shreyas is a member of the Foundation for International Arbitration Advocacy (FIAA), Geneva, since 2012, the national coordinator for the UNCITRAL National Coordination Committee of India (UNCCI) and a member of the Mumbai Centre for International Arbitration (MCIA) Council. He is also the only India-based representative of the ICC Fraudnet focused on asset tracing and recovery. He has also been the co-counsel for a State party in two significant investment treaty arbitrations.

Naazima Kamardeen is a professor in the Department of Commercial Law in the Faculty of Law, University of Colombo, Sri Lanka. She teaches and has published widely in intellectual property law, international trade and WTO law, international investment law, cultural property law and environmental law. She served on the National Committee that drafted the law on plant variety protection. She obtained her bachelor's degree in law from the University of Colombo, master of laws degree in international legal studies from Georgetown University and doctorate from the University of Colombo. She is also Attorney-at-Law of the Supreme Court of Sri Lanka.

Jaemin Lee is currently Professor of Law at School of Law, Seoul National University in Seoul, Korea. His major areas of teaching and research are public international law, international investment law and international trade law. Upon graduation from SNU College of Law in 1992, he joined the Korean Ministry of Foreign Affairs as a foreign service officer. Between 2000 and 2004, he practised law with Willkie Farr & Gallagher LLP (Washington, DC) as an associate attorney of the firm's international trade group. From 2004 to 2013 he taught international law at the School of Law, Hanyang University in Seoul, Korea.

Chin Leng Lim is the Choh-Ming Li Professor of Law at the Chinese University of Hong Kong. He practises as a barrister from Keating Chambers, London, where his work has included foreign investment and treaty matters. He is Honorary Senior Fellow of the British Institute of International and Comparative Law and a visiting Professor at King's College London. He was, recently, the inaugural Lionel A. Sheridan Visiting Professor at the National University of Singapore. His books include *Lim, Ho and Paparinskis, International Investment Law and Arbitration* (Cambridge, 2018), with a foreword by Gaillard, and the forthcoming *Cambridge Companion to International Arbitration*.

Aloysius Llamzon is a senior associate at King & Spalding's Washington, DC, and New York offices. He represents corporate and sovereign clients in inter-State, investment treaty and commercial arbitrations seated throughout the world. Llamzon was formerly Senior Legal Counsel at the Permanent Court of Arbitration in The Hague and has practised at leading law firms in Hong Kong and Manila. He holds LLM and JSD degrees from Yale Law School, and AB and JD degrees from the Ateneo de Manila University. His book *Corruption in International Investment Arbitration* (Oxford University Press, 2014) is a leading treatise on the subject.

Mark Mangan of Dechert LLP leads the firm's international arbitration practice in Singapore. He has been retained over the last eighteen years to help resolve disputes in Asia and elsewhere. Mark serves as both counsel (more than fifty cases) and arbitrator (more than fifteen arbitrations). As counsel, Mark represents clients in important and complex matters, often involving a government or political dimension, in the oil and gas, mining, finance, telecommunications, high technology, manufacturing, construction and sports sectors. As arbitrator, Mark has been appointed under the rules of arbitration of Singapore International Arbitration Centre (SIAC), International Chamber of Commerce (ICC), London Court of International Arbitration ('LCIA'), Stockholm Chamber of Commerce (SCC), and Korean Commercial Arbitration Board (KCAB), as well as an ad hoc arbitrator.

Robert McCorquodale is Professor of International Law and Human Rights at the University of Nottingham, a barrister at Brick Court Chambers, London, and the Principal of Inclusive Law, a consultancy on business and human rights. Robert has published extensively on many aspects of public international law, with his current focus being on business and human rights. He has also provided advice, capacity-building, legislative proposals and training to governments, corporations, international organizations, law firms and civil society around the world. He has appeared as an advocate before the International Court of Justice and the United Kingdom Supreme Court.

Mahdev Mohan is the global policy and standards lead for emerging markets at Google LLC and was formerly a faculty member at the Singapore Management University (SMU) School of Law, where he taught public international law and directed SMU's Asian Business and Rule of Law initiative. A former Nominated Member of Parliament of Singapore, he is the executive director of the Society of International Law Singapore, an editorial board member of the *Journal of East Asia and International Law* and *China and WTO Review*, and has written and practised in the fields of public international law, investment arbitration and human rights law in Asia. Mohan was an associate tenant of Temple Garden Chambers within its public international law practice group.

Luke Nottage is Professor of Comparative and Transnational Business Law and Associate Director of the Centre for Asian and Pacific Law at the University of Sydney. His publications include *International Arbitration in Australia* (2010), *Foreign Investment and Dispute Resolution in Asia* (2011) and *International Investment Treaties and Arbitration Across Asia* (2018). Luke has consulted for law firms, the EC, the OECD, the UNDP, ASEAN and the Japanese government, and for Australian parliamentary inquiries into investment treaty ratification. He is on the ACICA Rules committee and listed on the Panel of Arbitrators for AIAC, BAC, JCAA, KCAB, NZIAC, SCIA and TAI.

Dinusha Panditaratne is a specialist in Sri Lanka's foreign policy, with an academic background in international law. Currently the Non-Executive Director of the National Development Bank of Sri Lanka, she has served as head of the Lakshman Kadirgamar Institute of International Relations and Strategic Studies (LKI), the think tank of Sri Lanka's Ministry of Foreign Affairs, from 2015 to 2018. Prior to her role at LKI, Panditaratne was an assistant professor at the Faculty of Law at the Chinese University of Hong Kong and previously worked as a corporate finance lawyer in New York at Milbank, Tweed, Hadley & McCloy LLP. She received her undergraduate degree from Oxford University and her master's and doctorate in law from Yale Law School.

Xu Qian is Associate Professor and "Hundred Talents Program Fellow" at Guanghua Law School, Zhejiang University, with a research focus on alternative dispute resolution and economic, social and cultural rights. Dr QIAN's academic publications include the research monograph "*Water Services Disputes in International Arbitration*" published by Kluwer Law International in 2020. Her research articles have also been published both top-peer reviewed academic journals (*American Journal of International Law* (Unbound), *Asia Pacific Law Review, and Asian Journal of WTO and International Health Law and Policy*) and leading US law reviews (*UC Davis Business Law Journal*, *Wayne Law Review*, and *Georgia Journal of International and Comparative Law*).

Dr Prabhash Ranjan is a senior assistant professor at the Faculty of Legal Studies, South Asian University, India. He holds a PhD in law from King's College London. He was a visiting fellow at the Lauterpacht Centre for International Law, Cambridge University, and a visiting scholar at Brookings India. He has also been the Book Review Editor at the Indian Journal of International Law. He publishes and teaches in the area of international investment law and world trade law with a focus on India's bilateral investment treaties. His recent book *India and Bilateral Investment Treaties: Refusal, Acceptance, Backlash* was published by Oxford University Press in 2019.

Siraj Shaik Aziz is an advocate and solicitor of the Supreme Court of Singapore. He graduated with a Bachelor of Laws (Hons) from SMU in 2015 and was admitted to the Singapore Bar the following year. At the time of writing, Siraj was a research associate with the Asian Business & Rule of Law Initiative at the Centre for Cross-Border Commercial Law in Asia at SMU's School of Law with a research focus on international commercial arbitration and investor–state dispute settlement in the region. He has since returned to legal practice and is a CLAS (Criminal Legal Aid Scheme) Fellow with Pro Bono Services Office of the Law Society of Singapore.

Surya P Subedi, QC, DCL, OBE, obtained his DPhil in Law from the University of Oxford in 1993. Since then he has taught at five universities in the United Kingdom, the United States and the Netherlands. He has been Professor of International Law at the University of Leeds since 2004. He also practises law as a Barrister out of Three Stone Chambers, Lincoln's Inn, London. He was elected to the Institut de Droit International in 2011. He has advised a number of governments on international legal matters and acted as a counsel in cases before the International Court of Justice. He has been appointed to serve on the Panels of Arbitrators of ICSID, the Panels of the Dispute Settlement Body of the WTO and the Panels of International Investment Arbitrators of CIETAC.

Henry Winter is a senior associate in Hogan Lovells' Singapore office and specializes in international commercial and investor–State arbitration. Henry has experience sitting on both sides of the table, representing multinational corporations, foreign investors and governments in arbitrations under the SIAC, ICC, UNCITRAL and ICSID rules. He is also experienced in commercial litigation and investigations. He has experience dealing with a wide range of disputes, including corporations law, insolvency, financial services, resources, corporate fraud and white-collar crime, construction and antitrust. Henry is ranked as a 'next generation lawyer' by Legal 500 and a 'Future Leader' by Global Arbitration Review.

Dr Ewa Zelazna is a lecturer in law at the University of Leicester. Zelazna was a visiting research fellow at the Max Planck Institute for International Public Law and Comparative Constitutional Law in Heidelberg, Germany, and the Centre for the EU External Relations Law, T.M.C. Asser Institute in The Hague, the Netherlands. She was a research assistant at the British Institute of International and Comparative Law and completed traineeships at the Court of Justice of the European Union.

Zhang Sheng is Associate Professor of Xi'an Jiaotong University Law School. He is Deputy Secretary-General of the China International Investment Arbitration Forum and Director of the Chinese Society of International Economic Law. He is also an editor of the *Chinese Journal of Comparative Law*. He was a visiting fellow at the Lauterpacht Centre for International Law and a visiting PhD student at the Max-Planck Institute for Comparative and International Private Law. His research focus is on international investment law. He has published in journals such as the *European Journal of International Law*, *Journal of World Investment and Trade*, *ICSID Review*, *Columbia FDI Perspectives* and the *Chinese Journal of Comparative Law*.

Acknowledgements

The economies of China, India and ASEAN are, as a regional bloc, expected to grow at 6.3 per cent per year over the next five years, accounting for about one-third (or 32.1 per cent) of global economic growth. Australia is ranked as one of the world's top five capital-importing economies, with USD 5.1 billion worth of foreign direct investment inflows into the country. Foreign direct investment is at the heart of the Asian growth story. Nonetheless, there is an increased desire to balance this growth with the right of Asian States to set regulatory priorities and to protect legitimate public welfare objectives. Investor–State dispute settlement (ISDS) has stirred debate about the balance which should be struck between safeguarding the State's right to regulate in the public interest, on the one hand, and the need to ensure an adequate level of protection for foreign investment, on the other. There is also a call to reform the ISDS process to ensure consistency, accountability and transparency, which is evidenced in 'next generation' investment-related treaties to which certain Asian States adhere.

In this twenty-two-chapter book, expert contributing authors critically examine the pivot to Asia in foreign investment law and policy, which we term the 'Asian Turn'. We are confident that this volume will make a valuable contribution to the extant literature on the subject in Asia.

The editors acknowledge the funding from the Ministry of Education of Singapore Tier 1 'Category B' Grant Project entitled 'Investment Arbitration in Asia: Reflection, Review and the Regulatory Turn' administered by the SMU School of Law and from the SMU Centre for Cross-Border Commercial Law in Asia where the preparatory academic conferences took place. We are immensely grateful to our former students and research assistants from SMU School of Law and the University of Sydney Law School, who provided excellent support throughout the conception, drafting, editing and publication of this volume. In particular, we would like to thank Alexis Ang, Siraj Shaik Aziz, Rhys Carvosso, Peter Dougherty, Shalini Jayaraj, Jaya Anil Kumar, Claire Lim, Nicolette Oon, Wong Yan Yee, Kartik Singh, Brendan Yeo Yi Sheng, Anuki Suraweera, Chen Li Xin, Yvonne Guo and Aaron Yoong.

Finally, we would like to thank our respective families for their unstinting love and support: Mahdev expresses his sincere appreciation to Vinita and Sahana, and Chester also wishes to note his heartfelt gratitude to Catherine, Caroline and Andrew.

Table of Cases

DECISIONS OF INTERNATIONAL COURTS AND TRIBUNALS

Abaclat and others (formerly Giovanna a Beccara and others) *v.* Argentine Republic (ICSID Case No. ARB/07/5, Dissenting Opinion of Georges Abi-Saab of 28 October 2011)

Achmea B.V. (formerly Eureko B.V.) *v.* Slovak Republic [I] (PCA Case No. 2008–13, Final Award of 7 December 2012)

Adel A Hamadi Al Tamimi *v.* Sultanate of Oman (ICSID Case No. ARB/11/33, Award of 3 November 2015)

ADF *v.* United States of America (ICSID Case No. ARB (AF)/00/1, Final Award of 9 January 2003)

Alasdair Ross Anderson et. al. *v.* Republic of Costa Rica (ICSID Case No. ARB(AF)/07/31, Award of 29 May 2010)

Alps Finance and Trade AG *v.* Slovak Repubic, (UNCITRAL, Award of 5 March 2011)

Amco Asia Corporation and others *v.* Republic of Indonesia (ICSID Case No. ARB/81/1)

American Manufacturing and Trading Inc. *v.* Republic of Zaire (ICSID Case No. ARB/93/1)

Ansung Housing Co., Ltd. *v.* People's Republic of China (ICSID Case No. ARB/14/25)

Apotex Holdings Inc *v.* United States (Apotex III) (ICSID Case No ARB(AF)/12/1, Award of 25 August 2014)

Asian Agricultural Products Ltd (AAPL) *v.* Republic of Sri Lanka (ICSID Case No. ARB/87/3, Final Award of 27 June 1990)

ATA Construction, Industrial and Trading Company *v.* Hashemite Kingdom of Jordan (ICSID Case No. ARB/08/2, Award of 18 May 2010)

ATA Construction, Industrial and Trading Company *v.* Hashemite Kingdom of Jordan (ICSID Case ARB/8/02, Order Taking Note of the Discontinuance of the Proceeding of 11 July 2011)

Azurix Corp *v.* Argentine Republic (ICSID Case No. ARB/01/12, Award of 14 July 2006)

Bayindir Insaat Turizm Ticaret Ve Sanayi A.S. *v.* Islamic Republic of Pakistan (ICSID Case No. ARB/03/29, Award of 27 August 2009)

Beijing Urban Construction Group Co. Ltd. *v.* Republic of Yemen (ICSID Case No. ARB/14/30, Decision on Jurisdiction of 31 May 2017)

BG Group plc *v.* Argentine Republic (UNCITRAL, Award of 24 December 2007)

Biwater Gauff (Tanzania) Ltd. *v.* Tanzania (ICSID Case No. ARB/05/22, Procedural Order No. 3 of 29 September 2006)

Biwater Gauff (Tanzania) Ltd. *v.* United Republic of Tanzania (ICSID Case No. ARB/05/22, Award of 24 July 2008)

Cargill Inc. *v.* Mexico (ICSID Case No. ARB(AF)/05/2, Award of 18 September 2009)
Cargill, Incorporated *v.* Republic of Poland (ICSID Case No. ARB(AF)/04/2, Award of 5 March 2008)
CC/Devas (Mauritius) Ltd., Devas Employees Mauritius Private Limited, and Telcom Devas Mauritius Limited *v.* Republic of India (PCA Case No. 2013–09, Award on Jurisdiction and Merits of 25 July 2016)
Champion Trading Company and Ameritrade International, Inc. *v.* Arab Republic of Egypt (ICSID Case No. ARB/02/9, Award of 27 October 2006)
Churchill Mining PLC and Planet Mining Pty. Ltd. *v.* Republic of Indonesia (ICSID Case No. ARB/12/14 and 12/40, Decision on Jurisdiction of 24 February 2014)
Churchill Mining PLC and Planet Mining Pty. Ltd. *v.* Republic of Indonesia (ICSID Case No. ARB/12/14 and 12/40, Award of 6 December 2016)
Churchill Mining PLC and Planet Mining Pty. Ltd. *v.* Republic of Indonesia (ICSID Case No. ARB/12/14 and 12/40, Decision on Annulment of 18 March 2019)
CME Czech Republic B.V. (The Netherlands) *v.* The Czech Republic (UNCITRAL, Final Award of 14 March 2003)
CME Czech Republic B.V. *v.* Czech Republic (UNCITRAL, Partial Award of 13 September 2001)
CMS Gas Transmission Company v Argentine Republic (ICSID Case No ARB/01/8, Award of 12 May 2005)
Compañía de Aguas del Aconquija S.A. and Vivendi Universal S.A. *v.* Argentine Republic (ICSID Case No. ARB/97/3, Award of 20 August 2007)
ConocoPhillips and Perenco *v.* Vietnam (UNCITRAL)
Continental Casualty *v.* Argentine Republic (ICSID Case No. ARB/03/9, Award of 5 September 2008)
CSOB *v.* Slovakia (ICSID Case No. ARB/97/4, Decision on Jurisdiction of 24 May 1999)
Dangelas and others *v.* Vietnam (UNCITRAL)
Deutsche Bank AG *v.* Democratic Socialist Republic of Sri Lanka (ICSID Case No. ARB/09/02, Award of 31 October 2012)
Deutsche Telekom *v.* India (PCA Case No 2014–10, Interim Award of 17 December 2010)
DialAsie SAS *v.* Vietnam (UNCITRAL, Award of 17 November 2014)
Duke Energy Electroquil Partners and Electroquil S.A. *v.* Republic of Ecuador (ICSID Case No. ARB/04/19, Award of 18 August 2008)
EDF International S.A., SAUR International S.A. and León Participaciones Argentinas S. A. *v.* Argentine Republic (ICSID Case No. ARB/03/23, Award of 11 June 2012)
Ekran Berhad *v.* People's Republic of China (ICSID Case No. ARB/11/15)
El Paso *v.* Argentine Republic (ICSID Case No. ARB/03/15, Award of 31 October 2011)
Eli Lilly and Company *v.* Canada (ICSID Case No. UNCT/14/2, Notice of Intent to Submit a Claim to Arbitration under NAFTA Chapter Eleven of 7 November 2012)
Emilio Agustín Maffezini *v.* The Kingdom of Spain (ICSID Case No. ARB/97/7)
Enron Corporation and Ponderosa Assets LP *v.* Argentine Republic (ICSID Case No ARB/01/3, Award of 22 May 2007)
Eskosol SpA in Liquidazione *v.* Italian Republic (ICSID Case No. ARB/15/50, Procedural Order No 3 of 12 April 2017)
Ethyl Corporation *v.* The Government of Canada (UNCITRAL, Award on Jurisdiction of 24 June 1998)

EuroGas Inc. and Belmont Resources Inc *v.* Slovak Republic (ICSID Case No. ARB/14/14, Procedural Order No. 3 of 23 June 2015)
Feldman *v.* Mexico (ICSID Case No ARB(AF)/99/1, Award of 16 December 2002)
Flemingo Duty Free Shop Private Limited *v.* Republic of Poland (UNCITRAL, Award of 12 August 2016)
Fraport AG Frankfurt Airport Services Worldwide *v.* Republic of Philippines (ICSID Case No. ARB/11/12, Award of 10 December 2014)
Fraport AG Frankfurt Airport Services Worldwide *v.* Republic of Philippines (ICSID Case No. ARB/03/25, Award of 16 August 2007)
Fraport AG Frankfurt Airport Services Worldwide *v.* Republic of Philippines (ICSID Case No. ARB/03/25, Dissenting Opinion of Mr. Bernardo M. Cremades of 16 August 2007)
Glamis Gold *v.* United States of America (UNCITRAL, Award of 8 June 2009)
Gustaf F.W. Hamester GmbH & Co KG *v.* Republic of Ghana (ICSID Case No. ARB/07/24, Award of 18 June 2010)
Hela Schwarz GmbH *v.* People's Republic of China (ICSID Case No. ARB/17/19)
Hesham Talaat M. Al-Warraq *v.* Republic of Indonesia (UNCITRAL)
Hulley Enterprises (Cyprus) Limited, Yukos Universal Limited (Isle of Man) and Veteran Petroleum Limited (Cyprus) *v.* Russian Federation (PCA Case Nos. AA226-228, Final Awards of 18 July 2014)
Impregilo S.p.A. *v.* Argentine Republic (ICSID Case No. ARB/07/17, Award of 21 June 2011)
Inceysa Vallisoletana *v.* Republic of El Salvador (ICSID Case No. ARB/03/26, Award of 2 August 2006)
Indian Metals & Ferro Alloys Ltd (India) *v.* Republic of Indonesia (PCA Case No 2015–40, Award of 29 March 2019)
Inmaris Perestroika Sailing Maritime Services GmbH and others *v.* Ukraine (ICSID Case No. ARB/08/8, Award of 1 March 2012)
International Thunderbird Gaming *v.* Mexico (UNCITRAL, Award of 26 January 2006)
Ioan Micula and others *v.* Romania (ICSID Case No. ARB/05/20, Award of 11 December 2013)
Ioannis Kardassopoulos and Ron Fuchs *v.* Georgia (ICSID Case Nos. ARB/05/18 and ARB/07/15, Award of March 3, 2010)
Ioannis Kardassopoulos *v.* Georgia (ICSID Case Nos. ARB/05/18, Decision on Jurisdiction, of 6 July 2007)
Jan de Nul N.V. and Dredging International N.V. *v.* Arab Republic of Egypt (ICSID Case No. ARB/04/13, Award of 6 November 2008)
Joseph Charles Lemire *v.* Ukraine (ICSID Case No. ARB/06/18, Award of 28 March 2011)
Joseph Charles Lemire *v.* Ukraine (ICSID Case No. ARB/06/18, Decision on Jurisdiction and Liability of 14 January 2010)
Joy Mining Machinery Ltd. *v.* Arab Republic of Egypt (ICSID Case No. ARB/03/11, Award on Jurisdiction of 6 August 2004)
Les Laboratoires Servier, SAS., Biofarma, SAS., Arts et Techniques du Progres *v.* Republic of Poland (UNCITRAL, Award of 14 February 2012)
LG&E *v.* Argentine Republic (ICSID Case No ARB/02/1, Decision on Liability of 3 October 2006)
Louis Dreyfus Armateurs SAS *v.* The Republic of India (PCA Case No. 2014–26, Award of 11 September 2018)

Quasar de Valores SICAV *v.* Russia (SCC Case No. 24/2007, Award of 20 July 2012)
Quiborax S.A., Non Metallic Minerals S.A. and Allan Fosk Kaplún *v.* Plurinational State of Bolivia (ICSID Case No. ARB/06/2, Decision on Jurisdiction of 27 September 2012)
Raymond Charles Eyre and Montrose Developments (Private) Limited *v.* Democratic Socialist Republic of Sri Lanka (ICSID Case No. ARB/16/25, Procedural Order No. 1 of 1 June 2017)
Recofi SA *v.* Vietnam (UNCITRAL)
Romak SA (Switzerland) *v.* Uzbekistan (PCA Case No. AA280, Award of 26 November 2009)
Ronald S. Lauder *v.* Czech Republic (UNCITRAL, Final Award of 3 September 2001)
RosInvestCo UK Ltd. *v.* The Russian Federation (SCC Case No. V079/2005, Award on Jurisdiction of October 2007)]
RSM Production Corporation *v.* Grenada (ICSID Case No. ARB/05/14, Order of the Committee Discontinuing the Proceeding and Decision on Costs of 28 April 2011)
RSM *v.* Saint Lucia (ICSID Case No. ARB/12/10, Decision on Saint Lucia's Request for Security for Costs of 13 August 2014)
Rumeli Telekom A.S. and Telsim Mobil Telekomunikasyon Hizmetleri A.S. *v.* Republic of Kazakhstan (ICSID Case No. ARB/05/16, Award of 29 July 2008)
Rusoro Mining Ltd. *v.* The Bolivarian Republic of Venezuela (ICSID Case No. ARB(AF)/12/5, Award of 22 August 2016)
S.D. Myers Inc. *v.* Government of Canada (UNCITRAL, Partial Award of 13 November 2000)
Saba Fakes *v.* Republic of Turkey (ICSID Case No. ARB/07/20, Award of 14 July 2010)
Salini Costruttori S.p.A. and Italstrade S.p.A. *v.* Hashemite Kingdom of Jordan (ICSID Case No. ARB/02/13, Decision on Jurisdiction of 29 November 2004)
Salini Costruttori S.P.A. and Italstrade S.P.A. *v.* Kingdom of Morocco (ICSID Case No ARB/00/4, Decision on Jurisdiction of 16 July 2001)
Saluka Investments BV *v.* The Czech Republic (UNCITRAL, Partial Award of 17 March 2006)
Sanum Investments Limited *v.* Lao People's Democratic Republic (PCA Case No. 2013–13, Award on Jurisdiction of 13 December 2013)
Sempra Energy International *v.* Argentine Republic (ICSID Case No ARB/02/16, Award of 28 September 2007)
Señor Tza Yap Shum *v.* The Republic of Peru (ICSID Case No. ARB/07/6, Decision on Jurisdiction and Competence of 19 June 2009)
SGS Société Générale de Surveillance S.A. *v.* Islamic Republic of Pakistan (ICSID Case No. ARB/01/13)]
SGS Société Générale de Surveillance S.A. *v.* Republic of the Philippines (ICSID Case No. ARB/02/6, Decision on Jurisdiction of 29 January 2004)
Shin Dong Baig *v.* Vietnam (ICSID Case No. ARB(AF)/18/2)
Siemens A.G. *v.* Argentine Republic (ICSID Case No. ARB/02/8, Award of 6 February 2007)
South American Silver Limited (Bermuda) *v.* Bolivia (PCA Case No. 2013–15, Procedural Order No. 10 of 11 January 2016)
Spyridon Roussalis *v.* Romania (ICSID Case No. ARB/06/1, Award of 1 December 2011)
Técnicas Medioambientes Tecmed S.A. *v.* United Mexican States (ICSID Case No. ARB(AF)/00/2, Award of 29 May 2013)
Teinver S.A., Transportes de Cercanías S.A. and Autobuses Urbanos del Sur S.A. *v.* The Argentine Republic (ICSID Case No. ARB/09/1, Decision on Jurisdiction of 21 December 2012)

Decisions of Other International Courts and Tribunals

Pressos Compañía Naviera and Others *v.* Belgium (European Court of Human Rights App. No. 17849/91, Judgment of 20 November 1995)
Prince Hans-Adam II of Liechtenstein v Germany (Liechtenstein *v.* Germany) (European Court of Human Rights App. No. 42527/98, Judgment of 12 July 2001)
Pulp Mills (Argentina *v.* Uruguay) (Judgment) [2010] ICJ Rep 14
Slovak Republic *v.* Achmea B.V (Case C-284–16) (Court of Justice of the European Union, Judgment of 7 March 2018)
Social and Economic Rights Action Centre for Economic and Social Rights *v.* Nigeria (African Commission on Human and Peoples' Rights Communication No. 155/96, Decision of 27 May 2002)
Starrett Housing Corporation *v.* Islamic Republic of Iran (1983) 4 Iran-US CTR 122
Status of Eastern Carelia (Finland *v.* U.S.S.R) PCIJ Ser B (No. 5) (1923)
The Mayagna (Sumo) Awas Tingni Community *v.* Nicaragua (IACHR Series C No 79, Judgment of 31 August 2001)
Timurtas *v.* Turkey (European Court of Human Rights App. No. 23531/94, Judgment of 13 June 2000)
Tippetts, Abbett, McCarthy, Stratton and TAMS-AFFA Consulting Engineers of Iran *v.* Islamic Republic of Iran (1984) 6 Iran-US CTR 219
Vélásquez Rodriguez *v.* Honduras (1989) 28 ILM 294
Young, James and Webster *v.* United Kingdom (European Court of Human Rights, App. Nos. 7601/76 and 7806/77, Judgment of 13 August 1981)
Decisions of National Courts
AIG Capital Partners Inc & Anor. *v.* Kazakhstan [2005] EWHC 2239 (Comm)
Akai Holdings Ltd. *v.* Ho Wing On Christopher [2009] 5 HKLRD K2
Bayer Corporation *v.* Natco Pharma. Ltd (Intellectual Property Appellate Board of India, Order No. 45/2013 of 2013)
Bayer Corporation *v.* Union of India (Petition for Special Leave to Appeal (C) No. (S). 30145/ 2014, 12 December 2014)
Benvenuti and Bonfant Srl *v.* Banque Commerciale Congolaise (French Cour de cassation, Decision of 21 July 1987)
Cannonway Consultants Ltd *v.* Kenworth Engineering Ltd [1995] 1 HKC 179
Choc *v.* Hudbay Minerals Inc. 2013 ONSC 1414
Essar Oilfields Services Limited *v.* Norscot Rig Management Pvt Limited [2016] EWHC 2361 (Comm)
Excalibur Ventures LLC *v.* Texas Keystone Inc and others [2016] EWCA Civ. 1144
Geoffrey L Berman (In His Capacity as Trustee of The Lender Trust) *v.* Spf Cdo I, Ltd And Others[2011] 2 HKLRD 815
Government of the Lao People's Democratic Republic *v.* Sanum Investments Ltd [2015] SGHC 15
Liberian Eastern Timber Corp. *v.* Government of Republic of Liberia, 650 F.Supp. 73 (S.D. N.Y. 1986)
Otech Pakistan Pvt Ltd *v.* Clough Engineering Ltd [2007] 1 SLR (R) 989
Re Co. A [2015] HKEC 2089
Re Cyberworks Audio Video Technology Ltd [2010] 2 HKLRD 1137
Re Vanguard Energy Pte Ltd [2015] SGHC 156
Sanum Investments Limited *v.* The Government of the Lao People's Democratic Republic [2016] SGCA 57

Table of Treaties

BILATERAL INVESTMENT TREATIES

Additional Protocol Between the Government of the People's Republic of China and the Government of the People's Republic of Bulgaria concerning the Reciprocal Encouragement and Protection of Investments, signed 26 June 2007 (entered into force 10 November 2007) (China–Bulgaria Protocol)

Additional Protocol between the Government of the People's Republic of China and the Government of the Slovak Republic to the BIT signed in 2005 (China–Slovakia Protocol)]

Additional Protocol to the Agreement between the Government of the People's Republic of China and the Government of Romania on the Mutual Promotion and Protection of Investments signed in 2010) (China–Romania Protocol)

Agreement between Canada and Mongolia for the Promotion and Protection of Investments, signed 8 September 2016 (entered into force 24 February 2017) (Mongolia–Canada BIT)

Agreement between Canada and the Czech Republic for the Promotion and Protection of Investments, signed 6 May 2009 (entered into force 22 January 2012) (Canada–Czechia BIT)

Agreement between Canada and the Slovak Republic for the Promotion and Protection of Investments, signed 20 July 2010 (entered into force 14 March 2012) (Canada–Slovakia BIT)

Agreement between Japan and the Hashemite Kingdom of Jordan for the Promotion and Protection of Investment, signed 27 November 2018 (not yet in force) (Japan–Jordan BIT)

Agreement between Japan and the Islamic Republic of Iran on Reciprocal Promotion and Protection of Investment, signed 5 February 2016 (entered into force 26 April 2017) (Japan–Iran BIT)

Agreement between Japan and the Kingdom of Cambodia for the Liberalisation, Promotion and Protection of Investment, signed 14 June 2007 (entered into force 31 July 2008) (Japan–Cambodia BIT)]

Agreement between Japan and the Kingdom of Saudi Arabia for the Promotion and Protection of Investment, signed 20 April 2013 (entered into force 7 April 2017) (Japan–Saudi Arabia BIT)

Agreement between Japan and the Lao People's Democratic Republic for the Liberalisation, Promotion and Protection of Investment, signed 16 January 2008 (entered into force 3 August 2008) (Japan–Laos BIT)

Agreement between Japan and the Oriental Republic of Uruguay for the Liberalisation, Promotion and Protection of Investment, signed 26 January 2015 (entered into force 14 April 2017) (Japan–Uruguay BIT)

Agreement between Japan and the People's Republic of China concerning the Encouragement and Reciprocal Protection of Investments, signed 27 August 1988 (entered into force 14 May 1989) (China–Japan BIT)
Agreement between Japan and the Republic of Armenia for the Liberalisation, Promotion and Protection of Investment, signed 14 February 2018 (entered into force 15 May 2019) (Japan–Armenia BIT)
Agreement between Japan and the Republic of Colombia for the Liberalisation, Promotion and Protection of Investment, signed 12 September 2011 (entered into force 11 September 2015) (Japan–Colombia BIT)[
Agreement between Japan and the Republic of Kazakhstan for the Promotion and Protection of Investment, signed 23 October 2014 (entered into force 25 October 2015) (Japan–Kazakhstan BIT)
Agreement between Japan and the Republic of Peru for the Promotion, Protection and Liberalisation of Investment, signed 21 November2008 (entered into force 10 December 2009) (Japan–Peru BIT)
Agreement between Japan and the Republic of Uzbekistan for the Liberalisation, Promotion and Protection of Investment, signed 15 August 2008 (entered into force 24 September 2009) (Japan–Uzbekistan BIT)
Agreement between Japan and the Socialist Republic of Vietnam for the Liberalisation, Promotion and Protection of Investment, signed 14 November 2003 (entered into force 19 December 2004) (Japan–Vietnam BIT)
Agreement between Japan and the State of Iraq for the Promotion and Protection of Investment, signed 7 June 2012 (entered into force 25 February 2014) (Japan–Iraq BIT)
Agreement between Japan and the State of Kuwait for the Promotion and Protection of Investment, signed 22 March 2012 (entered into force 24 January 2014) (Japan–Kuwait BIT)
Agreement between Japan and the Sultanate of Oman for the Reciprocal Promotion and Protection of Investment, signed 19 June 2015 (entered into force 21 July 2017) (Japan–Oman BIT)
Agreement between Japan and the United Arab Emirates for the Promotion and Protection of Investment, signed 30 April 2018 (not yet in force) (Japan–UAE BIT)
Agreement between Japan and Ukraine for the Promotion and Protection of Investment, signed 5 February 2015 (entered into force 26 November 2015) (Japan–Ukraine BIT)
Agreement between the Argentine Republic and Japan for the Promotion and Protection of Investment, signed 1 December 2018 (not yet in force) (Japan–Argentina BIT)
Agreement between the Belgium-Luxembourg Economic Union and the People's Republic of China concerning the Encouragement and Reciprocal Protection of Investments, signed 6 June 2005 (entered into force 1 December 2009) (China–BLEU BIT (2005))
Agreement between the Czech Republic and the Kingdom of Saudi Arabia for the Encouragement and Reciprocal Protection of Investments, signed 18 November 2009 (entered into force 13 March 2011) (Saudi Arabia–Czechia BIT)
Agreement between the Czech Republic and the People's Republic of China on the Promotion and Protection of Investments, signed 8 December 2005 (entered into force 1 September 2006) (China–Czechia BIT (2005))
Agreement between the Czech Republic and the Republic of India for the Promotion and Protection of Investments, signed 11 October 1996 (entered into force 8 February 1998, terminated 25 April 2017) (India–Czechia BIT)

Agreement between the Government of Australia and the Government of the People's Republic of China on the Reciprocal Encouragement and Protection of Investments, signed 11 July 1988 (entered into force 11 July 1988) (China–Australia BIT)

Agreement between the Government of Barbados and the Government of the People's Republic of China for the Promotion and Protection of Investments, signed 20 July 1998 (entered into force 1 October 1999) (China–Barbados BIT)

Agreement between the Government of Canada and the Government of the Republic of Latvia on the Promotion and Reciprocal Protection of Investments, signed 5 May 2009 (entered into force 24 November 2011) (Canada–Latvia BIT)

Agreement between the Government of Canada and the Government of Romania for the Promotion and Reciprocal Protection of Investments, signed 8 May 2009 (entered into force 23 November 2011) (Canada–Romania BIT)

Agreement between the Government of Canada and the Government of the People's Republic of China for the Promotion and Reciprocal Protection of Investments, signed 9 September 2012 (entered into force 1 October 2014) (China–Canada BIT)

Agreement between the Government of Canada and the Government of Barbados on the Reciprocal Promotion and Protection of Investments, signed 29 May 1996 (entered into force 17 January 1997) (Canada–Barbados BIT)

Agreement between the Government of Chile and the Government of Uruguay on the Promotion and Reciprocal Protection of Investments, signed 25 March 2010 (entered into force 18 March 2012) (Chile–Uruguay BIT)

Agreement between the Government of Georgia and the Government of Greece on the Promotion and Reciprocal Protection of Investments, signed 9 November 1994 (entered into force 3 August 1996) (Georgia–Greece BIT)

Agreement between the Government of India and the Government of Nepal for the Promotion and Protection of Investments, signed 21 October 2011 (terminated 22 March 2017) (India–Nepal BIT)

Agreement between the Government of Japan and the Government of the Republic of Kenya for the Promotion and Protection of Investment, signed 28 August 2016 (entered into force 14 September 2017) (Japan–Kenya BIT)

Agreement between the Government of Japan and the Government of the Independent State of Papua New Guinea for the Promotion and Protection of Investment, signed 26 April 2011 (entered into force 17 January 2014) (Japan–Papua New Guinea BIT)

Agreement between the Government of Japan and the Government of the Republic of Mozambique on the Reciprocal Liberalisation, Promotion and Protection of Investment, signed 1 June 2013 (entered into force 29 August 2014) (Japan–Mozambique BIT)

Agreement between the Government of Japan and the Government of the Republic of the Union of Myanmar for the Liberalisation, Promotion and Protection of Investment, signed 15 December 2013 (entered into force 7 August 2014) (Japan–Myanmar BIT)

Agreement between the Government of New Zealand and the Government of the People's Republic of China on the Promotion and Protection of Investments, signed 22 November 1988 (entered into force 25 March 1989) (China–New Zealand BIT)

Agreement between the Government of the Czech Republic and the Government of the Kingdom of Cambodia for the Promotion and Reciprocal Protection of Investments, signed 12 May 2008 (entered into force 23 October 2009) (Cambodia–Czechia BIT)

Agreement between the Government of the Democratic Socialist Republic of Sri Lanka and the Government of the People's Republic of China on the Reciprocal Promotion and

Protection of Investments, signed 13 March 1986 (entered into force 25 March 1987) (China–Sri Lanka BIT)

Agreement between the Government of the Kingdom of Saudi Arabia and the Government of Malaysia concerning the Promotion and Reciprocal Protection of Investments, signed 25 October 2000 (entered into force 14 August 2001) (Malaysia–Saudi Arabia BIT)

Agreement between the Government of the Kingdom of Thailand and the Government of Romania for the Promotion and Protection of Investments, signed 30 April 1993 (entered into force 20 August 1994) (Thailand–Romania BIT)

Agreement between the Government of the Kingdom of Thailand and the Government of the Arab Republic of Egypt for the Promotion and Protection of Investments, signed 18 February 2000 (entered into force 27 February 2002) (Thailand–Egypt BIT)

Agreement between the Government of the Lebanese Republic and the Government of Malaysia for the Promotion and Protection of Investments, signed 26 February 1998 (entered into force 20 January 2002) (Malaysia–Lebanon BIT)

Agreement between the Government of the People's Republic of China and the Government of the Lao People's Democratic Republic concerning the Encouragement and Reciprocal Protection of Investments, signed 31 January 1993 (entered into force 1 June 1993) (China–Laos BIT)

Agreement between the Government of the People's Republic of China and the Government of the Kingdom of Sweden on the Mutual Protection of Investments, signed 29 March 1982 (entered into force 29 March 1982) (China–Sweden BIT)

Agreement between the Government of the People's Republic of China and the Government of the Republic of Korea on the Promotion and Protection of Investments, signed 7 September 2007 (entered into force 1 December 2007) (China–South Korea BIT (2007))]

Agreement between the Government of the People's Republic of China and the Government of the United Republic of Tanzania concerning the Promotion and Reciprocal Protection of Investments, signed 24 March 2013 (entered into force 14 April 2014) (China–Tanzania BIT)

Agreement between the Government of the People's Republic of China and the Government of the People's Republic of Bulgaria concerning the Reciprocal Encouragement and Protection of Investments, signed 27 June 1989 (entered into force 21 August 1994) (China–Bulgaria BIT)

Agreement between the Government of the People's Republic of China and the Government of Romania concerning the Encouragement and Reciprocal Protection of Investments, signed 12 July 1994 (entered into force 1 September 1995) (China–Romania BIT)

Agreement between the Government of the People's Republic of China and the Government of the Islamic Republic of Pakistan on the Reciprocal Encouragement and Protection of Investments, signed 12 February 1989 (entered into force 30 September 1990) (China–Pakistan BIT)

Agreement between the Government of the People's Republic of China and the Government of the Republic of Chile concerning the Encouragement and the Reciprocal Protection of Investments, signed 23 March 1994 (entered into force 1 August 1995) (China–Chile BIT)

Agreement between the Government of the People's Republic of China and the Government of the Republic of Peru concerning the Encouragement and Reciprocal Protection of Investments, signed 9 June 1994 (entered into force 1 February 1995) (China–Peru BIT)

Agreement between the Government of the People's Republic of China and the Government of the Republic of Iceland concerning the Promotion and Reciprocal Protection of Investments, signed 31 March 1994 (entered into force 1 March 1997) (China–Iceland BIT)

Agreement between the Government of the People's Republic of China and the Government of the Kingdom of Thailand for the Promotion and Protection of Investments, signed 12 March 1985 (entered into force 13 December 1985) (China–Thailand BIT)

Agreement between the Government of the People's Republic of China and the Government of Malaysia concerning the Reciprocal Encouragement and Protection of Investments, signed 21 November 1988 (entered into force 31 March 1990) (China–Malaysia BIT)

Agreement between the Government of the People's Republic of China and the Government of the Republic of the Philippines concerning Encouragement and Reciprocal Protection of Investments, signed 20 July 1992 (entered into force 8 September 1995) (China–Philippines BIT)

Agreement between the Government of the People's Republic of China and the Government of the Socialist Republic of Vietnam concerning Encouragement and Reciprocal Protection of Investments, signed 2 December 1992 (entered into force 1 September 1993) (China–Vietnam BIT)

Agreement between the Government of the People's Republic of China and the Government of the Kingdom of Cambodia for the Promotion and Protection of Investment, signed 19 July 1996 (entered into force 1 February 2000) (China–Cambodia BIT)

Agreement between the Government of the People's Republic of China and the Government of the Union of Myanmar on the Promotion and Protection of Investments, signed 12 December 2001 (entered into force 21 May 2002) (China–Myanmar BIT)

Agreement between the Government of the People's Republic of China and the Government of the Republic of France on the Encouragement and Reciprocal Protection of Investments, signed 26 November 2007 (entered into force 20 August 2010) (China–France BIT (2007))

Agreement between the Government of the People's Republic of China and the Government of the Republic of Uzbekistan on the Promotion and Protection of Investments, signed 19 April 2011 (entered into force 1 September 2011) (China–Uzbekistan BIT)

Agreement between the Government of the People's Republic of China and the Government of the Federal Republic of Nigeria on the Reciprocal Promotion and Protection of Investments, signed 27 August 2001 (entered into force 18 February 2010) (China–Nigeria BIT)

Agreement between the Government of the People's Republic of China and the Portuguese Republic on the Encouragement and Reciprocal Protection of Investments, signed 9 December 2005 (entered into force 26 July 2008) (China–Portugal BIT (2005))

Agreement between the Government of the People's Republic of China and the Government of the Republic of Singapore on the Promotion and Reciprocal Protection of Investments, signed 21 November 1985 (entered into force 7 February 1986) (China–Singapore BIT)

Agreement between the Government of the Republic of Colombia and the Government of the Republic of Peru on the Promotion and Reciprocal Protection of Investments, signed 26 April 1994 (entered into force 21 March 2004, terminated 30 December 2010) (Peru–Colombia BIT)

Agreement between the Government of the Republic of Finland and the Government of the Republic of Indonesia for the Promotion and Protection of Investments, signed 13 March 1996 (entered into force 7 June 1997, terminated 2 August 2008) (Indonesia–Finland BIT)

Agreement between the Government of the Republic of India and the Government of the Republic of Cyprus for the Mutual Promotion and Protection of Investments, signed 9 April 2002 (entered into force 12 January 2004, terminated 22 March 2017) (India–Cyprus BIT)

Agreement between the Government of the Republic of India and the Government of the Republic of Mauritius for the Promotion and Protection of Investments, signed 4 September 1998 (entered into force 20 June 2000, terminated 22 March 2017) (India–Mauritius BIT)

Agreement between the Government of the Republic of India and the Government of the Republic of Iceland for the Promotion and Protection of Investments, signed 29 June 2007 (entered into force 16 December 2008, terminated 21 July 2019) (India–Iceland BIT)

Agreement between the Government of the Republic of India and the Government of the Republic of Austria for the Promotion and Protection of Investments, signed 8 November 1999 (entered into force 1 March 2001, terminated 24 March 2017) (India–Austria BIT)

Agreement between the Government of the Republic of India and the Government of the Republic of the Philippines for the Promotion and Protection of Investments, signed 28 January 2000 (entered into force 29 January 2001) (India–Philippines BIT)

Agreement between the Government of the Republic of India and the Government of the Republic of Armenia for the Promotion and Protection of Investments, signed 23 May 2003 (entered into force 30 May 2006, terminated 22 March 2017) (India–Armenia BIT)

Agreement between the Government of the Republic of India and the Government of the Kingdom of Bahrain for the Promotion and Protection of Investments, signed 13 January 2004 (entered into force 5 December 2007, terminated 4 December 2017) (India–Bahrain BIT)

Agreement between the Government of the Republic of India and the Government of the People's Republic of Bangladesh for the Promotion and Protection of Investments, signed 9 February 2009 (entered into force 7 July 2011) (India–Bangladesh BIT)

Agreement between the Government of the Republic of India and the Government of the Republic of Belarus for the Promotion and Protection of Investments, signed 27 November 2002 (entered into force 23 November 2003, terminated 22 March 2017) (India–Belarus BIT)

Agreement between the Government of the Republic of India and the Belgium-Luxembourg Economic Union for the Promotion and Protection of Investments, signed 31 October 1997 (entered into force 8 January 2001, terminated 22 March 2017) (India–BLEU BIT)

Agreement between the Government of the Republic of India and the Government of the Republic of Bulgaria for the Promotion and Protection of Investments, signed 29 October 1998 (entered into force 23 September 1999, terminated 22 March 2017) (India–Bulgaria BIT)

Agreement between the Government of the Republic of India and the Government of the People's Republic of China for the Promotion and Protection of Investments, signed 21 November 2006 (entered into force 1 August 2007, terminated 3 October 2018) (India–China BIT)

Agreement between the Government of the Republic of India and the Government of the Arab Republic of Egypt for the Promotion and Protection of Investments, signed 9 April 1997 (entered into force 22 November 2000, terminated 29 March 2016) (India–Egypt BIT)

Agreement between the Government of the Republic of India and the Hashemite Kingdom of Jordan for the Promotion and Protection of Investments, signed 30 November 2006 (entered into force 22 January 2009) (India–Jordan BIT)

Agreement between the Government of the Republic of India and the Government of the Republic of Latvia for the Promotion and Protection of Investments, signed 18 February 2010 (entered into force 27 November 2010) (India–Latvia BIT)

Agreement between the Government of the Republic of India and the Government of Mongolia for the Promotion and Protection of Investments, signed 3 January 2001 (entered into force 29 April 2002, terminated 22 March 2017) (India–Mongolia BIT)

Agreement between the Government of the Republic of India and the Government of the Kingdom of Morocco for the Promotion and Protection of Investments, signed 13 February 1999 (entered into force 22 February 2001, terminated 22 March 2017) (India–Morocco BIT)

Agreement between the Government of the Republic of India and the Government of the Socialist Republic of Vietnam for the Promotion and Protection of Investments, signed 9 March 1997 (entered into force 1 December 1999, terminated 22 March 2017) (India–Vietnam BIT)

Agreement between the Government of the Republic of India and the Government of the Republic of Mozambique for the Reciprocal Promotion and Protection of Investments, signed 19 February 2009 (entered into force 23 September 2009) (India–Mozambique BIT)

Agreement between the Government of the Republic of India and the Government of the Sultanate of Oman for the Promotion and Protection of Investments, signed 2 April 1997 (entered into force 13 October 2000, terminated 22 March 2017) (India–Oman BIT)

Agreement between the Government of the Republic of India and the Government of Romania for the Promotion and Reciprocal Protection of Investments, signed 17 November 1997 (entered into force 9 December 1999, terminated 22 March 2017) (India–Romania BIT)

Agreement between the Government of the Republic of India and the Government of the Kingdom of Saudi Arabia concerning the Encouragement and Reciprocal Protection of Investments, signed 25 January 2006 (entered into force 20 May 2008, terminated 31 July 2019) (India–Saudi Arabia BIT)Agreement between the Government of the Republic of India and the Government of the Republic of Finland on the Promotion and Protection of Investments, signed 7 November 2002 (entered into force 9 April 2003, terminated 31 July 2019) (India–Finland BIT)

Agreement between the Government of the Republic of India and the Government of the Kingdom of Denmark concerning the Promotion and Reciprocal Protection of Investments, signed 9 September 1995 (entered into force 28 August 1996, terminated 13 May 2017) (India–Denmark BIT)

Agreement between the Government of the Republic of India and the Government of the Italian Republic on the Promotion and Protection of Investments, signed 21 November 1995 (entered into force 26 March 1998, terminated 23 March 2017) (India–Italy BIT)

Agreement between the Government of the Republic of India and the Government of the Republic of Senegal for the Promotion and Protection of Investments, signed 3 July 2008 (entered into force 17 October 2009) (India–Senegal BIT)

Agreement between the Government of the Republic of India and the Government of the United Arab Emirates on the Promotion and Protection of Investments, signed 12 December 2013 (entered into force 21 August 2014) (India–UAE BIT)

Agreement between the Government of the Republic of India and the Government of the State of Qatar for the Reciprocal Promotion and Protection of Investments, signed

7 April 1999 (entered into force 15 December 1999, terminated 22 March 2017) (India–Qatar BIT)

Agreement between the Government of the Republic of India and the Government of the Union of Myanmar for the Reciprocal Promotion and Protection of Investments, signed 24 June 2008 (entered into force 8 February 2009) (India–Myanmar BIT)

Agreement between the Government of the Republic of India and the Government of the Democratic Socialist Republic of Sri Lanka for the Promotion and Protection of Investment, signed 22 January 1997 (entered into force 13 February 1998, terminated 22 March 2017) (India–Sri Lanka BIT)

Agreement between the Government of the Republic of India and the Government of the United Mexican States on the Promotion and Protection of Investments, signed 21 May 2007 (entered into force 23 February 2008, terminated 30 July 2019) (India–Mexico BIT)

Agreement between the Government of the Republic of India and the Government of the Republic of Poland for the Promotion and Protection of Investments, signed 7 October 1996 (entered into force 31 December 1997, terminated 22 March 2017) (India–Poland BIT)

Agreement between the Government of the Republic of India and the Government of His Majesty the Sultan and Yang-Di-Pertuan of Brunei-Darussalam on the Reciprocal Promotion and Protection of Investments, signed 22 May 2008 (entered into force 18 January 2009) (India–Brunei BIT)

Agreement between the Government of the Republic of India and the Government of the Syrian Arab Republic on the Mutual Promotion and Protection of Investments, signed 18 June 2008 (entered into force 22 January 2009) (India–Syria BIT)

Agreement between the Government of the Republic of India and the Government of the Republic of Trinidad and Tobago for the Promotion and Protection of Investments, signed 12 March 2007 (entered into force 7 October 2007, terminated 15 August 2018) (India–Trinidad and Tobago BIT)

Agreement between the Government of the Republic of Indonesia and the Government of the People's Republic of China on the Promotion and Protection of Investments, signed 18 November 1994 (entered into force 1 April 1995, terminated 31 March 2015) (China–Indonesia BIT (1994))

Agreement between the Government of the Republic of Indonesia and the Government of the Kingdom of Denmark concerning the Promotion and Protection of Investments, signed 22 January 2007 (entered into force 15 October 2009) (Indonesia–Denmark BIT)

Agreement between the Government of the Republic of Indonesia and Government of the Argentine Republic for the Promotion and Protection of Investments, signed 11 October 2018 (not yet in force) (Indonesia–Singapore BIT)

Agreement between the Government of the Republic of Indonesia and Government of Serbia for the Promotion and Protection of Investments, signed 6 September 2011 (not yet in force) (Indonesia–Serbia BIT)

Agreement between the Government of the Republic of Indonesia and Government of the Argentine Republic for the Promotion and Protection of Investments, signed 7 November 1995 (entered into force 1 March 2001, terminated 19 October 2016) (Indonesia–Argentina BIT)

Agreement between the Government of the Republic of Indonesia and Government of the Republic of Malaysia for the Promotion and Protection of Investments, signed 22 January 1994 (entered into force 27 October 1999, terminated 20 June 2015) (Indonesia–Malaysia BIT)

Agreement between the Government of the Republic of Indonesia and Government of the Lao People's Democratic Republic concerning the Promotion and Protection of

Investments, signed 18 October 1994 (entered into force 14 October 1995, terminated 13 October 2015) (Indonesia–Laos BIT)

Agreement between the Government of the Republic of Indonesia and the Government of the Kingdom of Cambodia concerning the Promotion and Protection of Investments, signed 16 March 1999 (terminated 7 January 2016) (Indonesia–Cambodia BIT)

Agreement between the Government of the Republic of Indonesia and the Government of the Socialist Republic of Vietnam for the Promotion and Protection of Investments, signed 25 October 1991 (entered into force 3 April 1994, terminated 7 January 2016) (Indonesia–Vietnam BIT)

Agreement between the Government of the Republic of Kazakhstan and the Government of the Republic of Macedonia on the Reciprocal Promotion and Protection of Investments, signed 2 July 2012 (entered into force 21 May 2016) (Kazakhstan–North Macedonia BIT)

Agreement between the Government of the Republic of Korea and the Government of the Socialist Republic of Vietnam for the Promotion and Protection of Investments, signed 15 September 2003 (entered into force 5 June 2004) (Korea–Vietnam BIT)

Agreement between the Government of the Republic of Korea and the Government of the Republic of the Union of Myanmar for the Promotion and Protection of Investments, signed 6 June 2014 (entered into force 31 October 2018) (Korea–Myanmar BIT)

Agreement between the Government of the Republic of Korea and the Government of Japan for the Liberalisation, Promotion and Protection of Investment, signed 22 March 2002 (entered into force 1 January 2003) (Japan–South Korea BIT)

Agreement between the Government of the Republic of Korea and the Government of the Republic of Indonesia concerning the Promotion and Protection of Investments, signed 16 February 1991 (entered into force 10 March 1994) (Indonesia–South Korea BIT)

Agreement between the Government of the Republic of Singapore and the Government of the Republic of Colombia for the Promotion and Protection of Investments, signed 27 September 2010 (entered into force 16 June 2012) (Singapore–Russia BIT)

Agreement between the Government of the Republic of Singapore and the Government of the Republic of Colombia for the Promotion and Protection of Investments, signed 12 July 2013 (not yet in force) (Singapore–Colombia BIT)

Agreement between the Government of the Republic of Singapore and the Government of the Republic of Uzbekistan on the Promotion and Protection of Investments, signed 15 July 2003 (entered into force 23 November 2003) (Singapore–Uzbekistan BIT)

Agreement between the Government of the Republic of Singapore and the Government of Ukraine on the Promotion and Reciprocal Protection of Investments, signed 18 September 2006 (entered into force 14 July 2007) (Ukraine–Singapore BIT)

Agreement between the Government of the Republic of Turkey and the Government of the State of Kuwait concerning the Reciprocal Promotion and Protection of Investments, signed 27 May 2010 (entered into force 8 May 2013) (Kuwait–Turkey BIT)

Agreement between the Government of the Russian Federation and the Government of the Republic of India for the Promotion and Mutual Protection of Investments, signed 23 December 1994 (entered into force 5 August 1996, terminated 27 April 2017) (India–Russia BIT)

Agreement between the Government of the Slovak Republic and the Government of the Republic of Kenya for the Promotion and Reciprocal Protection of Investments, signed 14 December 2011 (not yet in force) (Kenya–Slovakia BIT)

Agreement between the Government of the Slovak Republic and the Government of Malaysia for the Promotion and Protection of Investments, signed 12 July 2007 (entered into force 5 February 2012) (Malaysia–Slovakia BIT)

Agreement between the Government of the State of Israel and the Government of the Republic of the Union of Myanmar for the Reciprocal Promotion and Protection of Investments, signed 5 October 2014 (entered into force 5 September 2017) (Myanmar–Israel BIT)

Agreement between the Government of the United Kingdom of Great Britain and Northern Ireland and the Government of the United Mexican States for the Promotion and Reciprocal Protection of Investments, signed 12 May 2006 (entered into force 25 July 2007) (UK–Mexico BIT)

Agreement between the Government of the United Kingdom of Great Britain and Northern Ireland and the Government of the Kingdom of Thailand for the Promotion of the Investment of Capital and for the Protection of Investments, signed 28 November 1978 (entered into force 11 August 1979) (UK–Thailand BIT)

Agreement between the Government of the United Kingdom of Great Britain and Northern Ireland and the Government of the Republic of Indonesia for the Promotion and Protection of Investments, signed 27 April 1976 (entered into force 24 March 1977) (UK–Indonesia BIT)

Agreement between the Government of the United Kingdom of Great Britain and Northern Ireland and the Government of the Democratic Socialist Republic of Sri Lanka for the Promotion and Protection of Investments, signed 13 February 1980 (entered into force 18 December 1980) (UK–Sri Lanka BIT)

Agreement between the Government of the United Mexican States and the Government of the People's Republic of China on the Promotion and Reciprocal Protection of Investments, signed 11 July 2008 (entered into force 6 June 2009) (China–Mexico BIT)

Agreement between the Government of the United Mexican States and the Government of the Republic of Iceland on the Promotion and Reciprocal Protection of Investments, signed 24 June 2005 (entered into force 28 April 2006) (Mexico–Iceland BIT)

Agreement between the Kingdom of Spain and the Russian Federation on the Promotion and Reciprocal Protection of Investments, signed 26 October 1990 (entered into force 28 November 1991) (Spain–Russia BIT)

Agreement between the People's Republic of China and the Federal Republic of Germany on the Encouragement and Reciprocal Protection of Investments, signed 1 December 2003 (entered into force 11 November 2005) (China–Germany BIT (2003))

Agreement between the People's Republic of China and the Kingdom of Spain on the Promotion and Reciprocal Protection of Investments, signed 14 November 2005 (entered into force 1 July 2008) (China–Spain BIT (2005))

Agreement between the People's Republic of China and the Republic of Finland on the Promotion and Reciprocal Protection of Investments, signed 15 November 2004 (entered into force 15 November 2006) (China–Finland BIT (2004))

Agreement between the Portuguese Republic and the Republic of India on the Mutual Promotion and Protection of Investments, signed 28 June 2000 (entered into force 19 July 2002, terminated 22 March 2017) (India–Portugal BIT)

Agreement between the Republic of Austria and the Republic of the Philippines for the Promotion and Reciprocal Protection of Investments, signed 11 April 2002 (entered into force 1 December 2003) (Philippines–Austria BIT)

Agreement between the Republic of Colombia and the Republic of India for the Promotion and Protection of Investments, signed 10 November 2009 (not yet in force) (India–Colombia BIT)

Agreement between the Republic of India and the Commonwealth of Australia for the Promotion and Protection of Investments (signed 26 February 1999, entered into force 4 May 2000) (India–Australia BIT)

Agreement between the Republic of India and the Commonwealth of Australia for the Promotion and Protection of Investments, signed 17 November 1992 (entered into force 29 July 1993) (Australia–Indonesia BIT)

Agreement between the Republic of India and the Federal Republic of Germany for the Promotion and Protection of Investments, signed 10 July 1995 (entered into force 13 July 1998, terminated 3 June 2017) (India–Germany BIT)

Agreement between the Republic of India and the Kingdom of Spain for the Promotion and Reciprocal Protection of Investments, signed 20 September 1997 (entered into force 15 December 1998, terminated 23 September 2016) (India–Spain BIT)

Agreement between the Republic of India and the Kingdom of the Netherlands for the Promotion and Protection of Investments, signed 6 November 1995 (entered into force 1 December 1996, terminated 1 November 2016) (India–Netherlands BIT)

Agreement between the Republic of India and the Republic of France for the Promotion and Protection of Investments, signed 2 September 1997 (entered into force 17 May 2000, terminated 15 April 2017) (India–France BIT)

Agreement between the Republic of India and the Republic of Hungary for the Promotion and Protection of Investments, signed 3 November 2003 (entered into force 2 January 2006, terminated 29 March 2017) (India–Hungary BIT)

Agreement between the Republic of India and the Slovak Republic for the Promotion and Reciprocal Protection of Investments, signed 25 September 2006 (entered into force 27 September 2007, terminated 22 March 2017) (India–Slovakia BIT)

Agreement between the Republic of India and the United Kingdom of Great Britain and Northern Ireland for the Promotion and Protection of Investments, signed 14 March 1994 (entered into force 6 January 1995, terminated 22 March 2017) (India–UK BIT)

Agreement between the Republic of Indonesia and the Federal Republic of Germany for the Promotion and Protection of Investments, signed 14 May 2003 (entered into force 2 June 2007, terminated 1 June 2017) (Germany–Indonesia BIT)

Agreement between the Republic of Indonesia and the Government of the Republic of India for the Promotion and Protection of Investments, signed 10 February 1999 (entered into force 22 January 2004, terminated 7 April 2016) (India–Indonesia BIT)

Agreement between the Republic of Indonesia and the Russian Federation for the Promotion and Protection of Investments, signed 6 September 2007 (entered into force 15 October 2009) (Indonesia–Russia BIT)

Agreement between the Slovak Republic and the Islamic Republic of Iran for the Promotion and Reciprocal Protection of Investments, signed 19 January 2016 (entered into force 30 August 2017) (Iran–Slovakia BIT)

Agreement between the State of Israel and Japan for the Liberalisation, Promotion and Protection of Investment, signed 1 February 2017 (entered into force 5 October 2017) (Japan–Israel BIT)

Agreement between the State of Kuwait and the Republic of India for the Encouragement and Reciprocal Protection of Investments, signed 27 November 2001 (entered into force 28 June 2003, terminated 27 June 2018) (India–Kuwait BIT)

Agreement between the Swiss Confederation and the Kingdom of Thailand on the Promotion and Reciprocal Protection of Investments, signed 17 November 1997 (entered into force 21 July 1999) (Thailand–Switzerland BIT)

Agreement between the Swiss Confederation and the Republic of India for the Promotion and Protection of Investments, signed 4 April 1997 (entered into force 16 February 2000, terminated 6 April 2017) (India–Switzerland BIT)

Agreement between the Swiss Federal Council and the Government of the People's Republic of China on the Promotion and Reciprocal Protection of Investments, signed 27 January 2009 (entered into force 13 April 2010) (China–Switzerland BIT (2009))

Agreement between the United Arab Emirates, on the one hand, and the Belgian–Luxembourg Economic Union, on the other hand, on the Reciprocal Promotion and Protection of Investments, signed 8 March 2004 (entered into force 22 November 2007) (BLEU–UAE BIT)

Agreement between the United States of America and the Oriental Republic of Uruguay concerning the Encouragement and Reciprocal Protection of Investment, signed 4 November 2005 (entered into force 31 October 2006) (US–Uruguay BIT)

Agreement on Economic Co-operation between the Government of the Kingdom of the Netherlands and the Government of the Kingdom of Thailand, signed 6 June 1972 (entered into force 3 March 1973) (Netherlands–Thailand BIT)

Agreement on Encouragement and Reciprocal Protection of Investments between the Government of the People's Republic of China and the Government of the Kingdom of the Netherlands, signed 26 November 2001 (entered into force 1 August 2004) (China–Netherlands BIT (2004))

Agreement on Encouragement and Reciprocal Protection of Investments between the Kingdom of the Netherlands and the Czech and Slovak Federal Republic, signed 29 April 1991 (entered into force 1 October 1992) (Netherlands–Slovakia BIT)

Agreement on Encouragement and Reciprocal Protection of Investments between the Kingdom of the Netherlands and the Czech and Slovak Federal Republic, signed 29 April 1991 (entered into force 1 October 1992) (Netherlands–Czechia BIT)

Agreement on the Encouragement and Reciprocal Protection of Investments between the Kingdom of the Netherlands and the Sultanate of Oman, signed 17 January 2009 (not yet in force) (Oman–Netherlands BIT)

Modification of the Agreement on the Promotion and Mutual Protection of Investments between China and Cuba, signed 20 April 2007 (entered into force 1 December 2008) (Modification to China–Cuba BIT)

Treaty between Thailand and the Federal Republic of Germany concerning the Promotion and Reciprocal Protection of Investments, signed 13 December 1961 (entered into force 10 April 1965, terminated 20 October 2004) (Germany–Thailand BIT)

Treaty with the Czech and Slovak Federal Republic concerning the Reciprocal Encouragement and Protection of Investment, signed 22 October 1991 (entered into force 19 December 1992, amended 1 May 2004) (US–Czechia BIT)

MULTILATERAL INVESTMENT TREATIES AND FREE TRADE AGREEMENTS

Agreement among the Government of Brunei Darussalam, the Republic of Indonesia, Malaysia, the Republic of the Philippines, the Republic of Singapore and the Kingdom of Thailand for the Promotion and Protection of Investments, signed 15 December 1987 (entered into force 2 August 1988)

Agreement between Japan and the Republic of Singapore for a New–Age Economic Partnership Agreement, signed 13 January 2002 (entered into force 30 November 2002) (Japan–Singapore EPA)

Agreement between New Zealand and Singapore on a Closer Economic Partnership, signed 14 November 2000 (entered into force 1 January 2001) (NZ–Singapore CEPA)

Agreement between New Zealand and the Territory of Taiwan, Penghu, Kinmen and Matsu on Economic Cooperation, signed 10 July 2013 (entered into force 1 December 2013) (ANZTEC)

Agreement between the Government of Japan and the Government of Malaysia for an Economic Partnership, signed December 2005 (entered into force 13 July 2006) (Japan–Malaysia EPA)

Agreement Establishing the Association of South–East Asian Nations (ASEAN)– Australia–New Zealand Free Trade Area, signed 27 February 2009, [2010] ATS 1 (entered into force 1 January 2010 for Australia, New Zealand, Brunei, Burma, Malaysia, the Philippines, Singapore and Vietnam; 12 March 2010 for Thailand; 1 January 2011 for Laos; 4 January 2011 for Cambodia) (ASEAN–Australia–New Zealand FTA)

Agreement on Investment Among the Governments of the Hong Kong Special Administrative Region and the Member States of ASEAN, signed 12 November 2017 (entered into force 17 June 2019) (ASEAN–Hong Kong Investment Agreement)

Agreement on Investment of the Framework Agreement on Comprehensive Economic Cooperation between China and the ASEAN, signed 15 August 2009 (entered into force 1 January 2010)(ASEAN–China Investment Agreement)

Agreement on Investment under the Framework Agreement on Comprehensive Economic Cooperation among the Governments of the Member Countries of ASEAN and India, signed 12 November 2014 (not yet in force) (ASEAN–India Investment Agreement)

Agreement on Investment under the Framework Agreement on Comprehensive Economic Cooperation among the Governments of the Member Countries of ASEAN and the Republic of Korea, signed 2 June 2009 (entered into force 1 September 2009) (ASEAN–Korea Investment Agreement)

Agreement on Trade and Economic Cooperation between the European Economic Community and the People's Republic of China, signed 21 May 1985 (entered into force 1 October 1985) (EU–China Trade and Economic Cooperation Agreement)

ASEAN–Japan Comprehensive Economic Partnership Agreement, signed 28 March 2008 (entered into force 1 December 2008) (Japan–ASEAN EPA)

ASEAN Comprehensive Investment Agreement, signed 26 February 2009 (entered into force 1 March 2012)(ACIA)

Canada–Colombia Free Trade Agreement, signed 21 November 2008 (entered into force 15 August 2011 (Canada–Colombia FTA)

Canada–Honduras Free Trade Agreement, signed 5 November 2013 (entered into force 1 October 2014) (Canada–Honduras FTA)

Canada–Panama Free Trade Agreement, signed 11 August 2009 (entered into force 1 April 2013) (Canada–Panama FTA)

Canada–Peru Free Trade Agreement, signed 29 May 2008 (entered into force 1 August 2009) (Canada–Peru FTA)

China–Australia Free Trade Agreement, signed 17 June 2015 (entered into force 20 December 2015)(China–Australia FTA)

China–Hong Kong Closer Economic Partnership Arrangement, signed 29 June 2003 (entered into force 29 June 2003) (China–Hong Kong CEPA)

China–Iceland Free Trade Agreement, signed 15 April 2013 (entered into force 2 July 2014) (China–Iceland FTA)

China–Korea Free Trade Agreement, signed 1 June 2015 (entered into force 20 December 2015) (China–Korea FTA)

China–New Zealand Free Trade Agreement, signed 7 April 2008 (entered into force 1 October 2008)(China–New Zealand FTA)

China–Pakistan Free Trade Agreement, signed 24 November 2006 (entered into force 1 July 2007) (China–Pakistan FTA)

China–Peru Free Trade Agreement, signed 28 April 2009 (entered into force 1 March 2010) (China–Peru FTA)

China–Singapore Free Trade Agreement, signed 23 October 2008 (entered into force 1 January 2009) (China–Singapore FTA)

China–Switzerland Free Trade Agreement, signed 6 July 2013 (entered into force 1 July 2014) (China–Switzerland FTA)

Colombia–Korea Free Trade Agreement, signed 21 February 2013 (entered into force 15 July 2016) (Colombia–Korea FTA)

Comprehensive and Progressive Agreement for Trans–Pacific Partnership, signed 8 March 2018 (entered into force 30 December 2018 for Australia, Canada, Japan, New Zealand, Mexico and Singapore; 14 January 2019 for Vietnam) (CPTPP)

Comprehensive Economic Cooperation Agreement between the Republic of India and the Republic of Singapore, signed 29 June 2005 (entered into force 1 August 2005) (India–Singapore CECA)

Comprehensive Free Trade Agreement for Closer Economic Partnership between Pakistan and Malaysia, signed 8 November 2007 (entered into force 1 January 2008) (Pakistan–Malaysia FTA)

Comprehensive Trade and Economic Agreement between Canada and the European Union, signed 30 October 2016 (provisionally entered into force 21 September 2017) (CETA)

Economic Partnership Agreement between the European Union and Japan, signed 17 July 2018 (entered in force 1 February 2019) (EU–Japan EPA)

Energy Charter Treaty, signed 17 December 1994, (1995) 34 ILM 381 (entered into force 16 April 1998)

European Union–Singapore Free Trade Agreement, signed 19 October 2018 (not yet in force) (EU–Singapore FTA)

European Union–Singapore Investment Protection Agreement, signed 19 October 2018 (not yet in force) (EU–Singapore IPA)

European Union–South Korea Free Trade Agreement, signed 15 October 2009 (entered into force 13 December 2015) (EU–Korea FTA)

European Union–Vietnam Free Trade Agreement, signed 30 June 2019 (not yet in force) (EU–Vietnam FTA)

European Union–Vietnam Investment Protection Agreement, signed 30 June 2019 (not yet in force) (EU–Vietnam IPA)

Framework Agreement on Comprehensive Economic Cooperation between the Governments of the Member States of ASEAN and the Government of the People's Republic of China, signed 4 November 2002 (entered into force on 1 January 2010) (ASEAN–China FTA)

Free Trade Agreement between Mexico and Central America, signed 22 November 2011 (entered into force 1 July 2013) (Mexico–Central America FTA)

Free Trade Agreement between the Islamic Republic of Pakistan and the Democratic Socialist Republic of Sri Lanka, signed 1 August 2002 (entered into force 12 June 2005) (Sri Lanka–Pakistan FTA)

Hong Kong–New Zealand Closer Economic Partnership Agreement, signed 29 March 2010 (entered into force 1 January 2011) (HK–NZ CEPA)

India–Japan Comprehensive Economic Partnership Agreement, signed 15 February 2011 (entered into force 1 August 2011) (India–Japan CEPA)

India–Korea Comprehensive Economic Partnership Agreement, signed 7 August 2009 (entered into force 1 January 2010 (India–Korea CEPA)

India–Malaysia Comprehensive Economic Cooperation Agreement, signed 18 February 2011 (entered into force 1 July 2011) (India–Malaysia CECA)

India–Sri Lanka Free Trade Agreement, signed 28 December 1998 (entered in to force 15 December 2001) (India–Sri Lanka FTA)

Indonesia–Australia Comprehensive Economic Partnership Agreement, signed 4 March 2019 (not yet in force) (IA–CEPA)

Indonesia–EU Comprehensive Economic Partnership Agreement (not yet signed) (IE–CEPA)

Investment Agreement for the COMESA Common Investment Area, signed 23 May 2007 (not yet in force) (COMESA Investment Agreement)

Investment Promotion and Protection Agreement between Japan, Republic of Korea and China, signed 13 May 2012 (entered into force 17 May 2014) (PRC–Japan–Republic of Korea Trilateral Investment Treaty)

Japan–Australia Economic Partnership Agreement, signed 8 July 2014 (entered into force 15 January 2015) (JAEPA)

Japan–Brunei Economic Partnership Agreement, signed 18 June 2007 (entered into force 31 July 2008) (Japan–Brunei EPA)

Japan–Chile Economic Partnership Agreement, signed 27 March 2007 (entered into force 3 September 2007)

Japan–Indonesia Economic Partnership Agreement, signed 20 August 2007 (entered into force 1 July 2008) (Japan–Indonesia EPA)

Japan–Malaysia Economic Partnership Agreement, signed 13 December 2005 (entered into force 13 July 2006)(Japan–Malaysia EPA)

Japan–Mexico Economic Partnership Agreement, signed 17 September 2004 (entered into force 1 April 2005) (Japan–Mexico EPA)

Japan–Mongolia Economic Partnership Agreement, signed 10 February 2015 (entered into force 7 June 2016) (Japan–Mongolia EPA)

Japan–Philippines Economic Partnership Agreement, signed 8 September 2006 (entered into force 11 December 2008) (Japan–Philippines EPA)

Japan–Switzerland Economic Partnership Agreement, signed 19 February 2009 (entered into force 1 September 2009) (Japan–Switzerland EPA)

Japan–Thailand Economic Partnership Agreement, signed 3 April 2007 (entered into force 1 November 2007) (Japan–Thailand EPA)

Japan–Vietnam Economic Partnership Agreement, signed 25 December 2008 (entered into force 1 October 2009) (Japan–Vietnam EPA)

Korea–Australia Free Trade Agreement, signed 8 April 2014 (entered into force 12 December 2016)(Korea–Australia FTA)[

Korea–Canada Free Trade Agreement, signed 11 March 2014 (entered into force 1 January 2015) (CKFTA)

Korea–Singapore Free Trade Agreement, signed 4 August 2005 (entered into force 2 March 2006) (Korea–Singapore FTA)

Korea–US Free Trade Agreement, signed 30 June 2007 (entered into force 1 March 2012) (KORUS FTA)

Korea–Vietnam Free Trade Agreement, signed 5 May 2015 (entered into force 20 December 2015) (VKFTA)

New Zealand–Malaysia Free Trade Agreement, signed 26 October 2009 (entered into force 1 August 2010) (NZ–Malaysia FTA)

North American Free Trade Agreement, signed 17 December 1992, United States–Canada–Mexico (1993) 32 ILM 289, 605 (entered into force 1 January 1994)

Protocol on Investment to the Australia–New Zealand Closer Economic Relations Trade Agreement, signed 16 February 2011 (entered into force 1 March 2013) (ANZCERTA Investment Protocol)

Singapore–Australia Free Trade Agreement, signed 17 February 2003 (entered into force 28 July 2003) (Singapore–Australia FTA)]

Singapore–Costa Rica Free Trade Agreement, signed 6 April 2010 (entered into force 1 July 2013) (Singapore–Costa Rica FTA)

Singapore–EFTA Free Trade Agreement, signed 26 June 2002 (entered into force 1 January 2003) (Singapore–EFTA FTA)

South African Development Community Protocol on Finance and Investment, signed 18 August 2006 (entered into force 16 April 2010)

Sri Lanka–Singapore Free Trade Agreement, signed 21 January 2018 (entered into force 1 May 2018) (Sri Lanka–Singapore FTA)

Thailand–Australia FTA, signed 5 July 2004 (entered into force 1 January 2005) (Thailand–Australia FTA)

Trans–Pacific Strategic Economic Partnership Agreement (Brunei Darussalam, Chile, New Zealand, Singapore), signed 18 July 2005 (entered into force 28 May 2006) (TPSEP)

United States–Chile Free Trade Agreement, signed 6 June 2003 (entered into force 1 January 2004) (US–Chile FTA)

United States–Colombia Trade Promotion Agreement, signed 22 November 2006 (entered in force 15 May 2012) (US–Colombia TPA)

United States–Dominican Republic–Central America Free Trade Agreement, signed 28 May 2004 (entered into force for the United States on 28 February 2006; El Salvador 1 March 2006; Honduras and Nicaragua 1 April 2006; Guatemala 1 July 2006; Dominican Republic 1 March 2007; Costa Rica 1 January 2009) (DR–CAFTA)

United States–Morocco Free Trade Agreement, signed 15 June 2004, entered into force 1 January 2006 (US–Morocco FTA)

United States–Peru Trade Promotion Agreement, signed 12 April 2006 (entered into force 1 February 2009) (US–Peru TPA)

United States–Singapore Free Trade Agreement, signed 6 May 2003 (entered into force 1 January 2004) (US–Singapore FTA)

OTHER INTERNATIONAL CONVENTIONS

Agreement on ASEAN Preferential Trading Arrangements, signed 24 February 1977 (entered into force 25 August 1977)

Agreement on the Common Effective Preferential Tariff Scheme for the ASEAN Free Trade Area, signed 28 January 1992 (entered into force 28 January 1992)

Agreement on Trade-Related Aspects of Intellectual Property Rights, opened for signature 15 April 1994, 1869 UNTS 299; 33 ILM 1197 (1994) (entered into force 1 January 1995) (TRIPS Agreement)

Agreement on Trade-Related Investment Measures, opened for signature 15 April 1994, 1868 UNTS 186 (entered into force 1 January 1995) (TRIMS Agreement)

American Convention on Human Rights, opened for signature 22 November 1969, 1144 UNTS 123 (entered into force 18 July 1978)

ASEAN Agreement on the Movement of Natural Persons, signed 19 November 2012 (entered into force 14 June 2016)

ASEAN Agreement on Transboundary Haze Pollution, opened for signature 10 June 2002 (entered into force 25 November 2003)

ASEAN Framework Agreement on Services, signed 15 December 1995 (entered into force 30 December 1998)

ASEAN Trade in Goods Agreement, signed 26 February 2009 (entered into force 17 May 2010)

Convention on Settlement of Investment Disputes Between States and Nationals of Other States, signed 18 March 1965, 4 ILM 532 (entered into force 14 October 1966) (ICSID Convention)

Convention on the Recognition and Enforcement of Foreign Arbitral Awards, signed 10 June 1958, 330 UNTS 38 (entered into force 7 June 1959) (New York Convention)

Declaration constituting an Agreement establishing the Association of South-East Asian Nations (ASEAN), opened for signature 8 August 1967, 1331 UNTS 235 (entered into force 8 August 1967) (ASEAN Declaration)

European Convention for the Protection of Human Rights and Fundamental Freedoms, opened for signature 4 November 1950, 213 UNTS 221 (entered into force 3 September 1953)

Framework Agreement on the ASEAN Investment Area, signed 7 October 1998 (entered into force 25 May 1999)

Framework Agreements on Enhancing ASEAN Economic Cooperation, signed 28 January 1992 (entered into force 28 January 1992)

General Agreement on Tariffs and Trade, opened for signature 15 April 1994, 1867 UNTS 190 (entered into force 1 January 1995) (GATT)

General Agreement on Trade in Services, opened for signature 15 April 1994, 1869 UNTS 183 (entered into force 1 January 1995) (GATS)

International Covenant on Civil and Political Rights, opened for signature 16 December 1966, 999 UNTS 171 (entered into force 23 March 1976) (ICCPR)

International Covenant on Economic, Social and Cultural Rights, opened for signature 19 December 1966, 993 UNTS 3 (entered into force 3 January 1976) (ICESCR)

Protocol to Amend the ASEAN Framework Agreement on Services, signed 2 September 2003 (entered into force on 31 December 2004)
Treaty Establishing the European Economic Community, signed 25 March 1957, 298 UNTS 3 (entered into force 1 January 1958) (EEC Treaty or Treaty of Rome)
Treaty of Amity and Cooperation in Southeast Asia, signed 24 February 1976, 1025 UNTS 317 (entered into force 26 April 2012)
Treaty of Lisbon, signed 13 December 2007, (2007) OJ C306 (17 December 2007) (entered into force 1 December 2009)
Treaty on the Functioning of the European Union (2010) OJ C83 (30 March 2010) (entered into force 1 December 2009)
Understanding on Rules and Procedures Governing the Settlement of Disputes, opened for signature 15 April 1994, 1869 UNTS 401 (entered into force 1 January 1995) (WTO DSU) United Nations Convention on International Settlement Agreements Resulting from Mediation, opened for signature 7 August 2019 (not yet in force) (Singapore Convention on Mediation)
United Nations Convention on Transparency in Treaty–based Investor–State Arbitration, opened for signature 17 March 2015 (entered in force 18 October 2017) (Mauritius Convention)
Vienna Convention on Consular Relations, opened for signature 24 April 1963, 596 UNTS 261 (entered into force 19 March 1967)
Vienna Convention on Succession of States in respect of treaties, opened for signature 23 August 1978, 1946 UNTS 3 (entered into force 6 November 1996)
Vienna Convention on the Law of Treaties, opened for signature 23 May 1969, 1155 UNTS 331 (entered into force 27 January 1980)

Abbreviations

AANZFTA	ASEAN - Australia - New Zealand Free Trade Agreement
ACIA	ASEAN Comprehensive Investment Agreement
ADB	Asian Development Bank
AIIB	Asian Infrastructure Investment Bank
ALF	Association of Litigation Funders
ASEAN	Association of Southeast Asian Nations
ATE	After the Event
BITs	bilateral investment treaties
BOI	Board of Investment of Sri Lanka
BRI	Belt and Road Initiative
CAFTA-DR	Dominican Republic–Central American–United States Free Trade Agreement
CEPEA	Comprehensive Economic Partnership for East Asia
CETA	EU–Canada Comprehensive Economic and Trade Agreement
CIETAC	China International Economic and Trade Arbitration Commission
CIFC	Colombo International Financial City
CJEU	Court of Justice of the European Union
CL	compulsory licenses
COMESA	Common Market for Eastern and Southern Africa
CPC	Ceylon Petroleum Corporation
CPC (2015)	Civil Procedure Code (2015) (Vietnam)
CPTPP	Comprehensive and Progressive Agreement for Trade-Pacific Partnership
CSOB	Ceskoslovenska Obchodni Banka AS
CSP	Australia-Singapore Comprehensive Strategic Partnership
DIFC	Dubai International Financial Centre
DSB	Dispute Settlement Body
DSMs	dispute settlement mechanisms
DSU	WTO Dispute Settlement Understanding
EAFTA	East Asia Free Trade Area
EC	European Commission / European Community
ECJ	European Court of Justice
ECT	Energy Charter Treaty
ECtHR	European Court of Human Rights
EKCP	East Kutai Coal Project

EPA	Economic Partnership Agreement
EU	European Union
EUSFTA	European Union–Singapore FTA
EUSIPA	European Union–Singapore Investment Protection Agreement
EVFTA	EU–Vietnam Free Trade Agreement
EVIPA	European Union–Vietnam Investment Protection Agreement
F&N	Fraser & Neave
FCT	treaties of Friendship, Commerce and Navigation
FDI	foreign direct investment
FET	fair and equitable treatment
FIL	Foreign Investment Law
FTAs	free trade agreements
FTAAP	Free Trade Area of the Asia-Pacific
G20	Group of Twenty
GATS	General Agreement on Trade in Services
GATT	General Agreement on Tariffs and Trade
GCC	Gulf Cooperation Council
GDP	gross domestic product
GOI	Government of Indonesia
HCCCA	Hague Convention on Choice of Court Agreements
HKAB	Hong Kong Advisory Body
IA-CEPA	Indonesia–Australia Comprehensive Economic Partnership
IBA	International Bar Association
ICAC	Independent Commission Against Corruption
ICCA-QMUL	International Council for Commercial Arbitration–Queen Mary University of London
ICCPR	International Covenant on Civil and Political Rights
ICESCR	International Covenant on Economic, Social and Cultural Rights
ICS	Investment Court System
ICSID	International Centre for Settlement of Investment Disputes
IIAs	international investment agreements
iMSAs	international mediated settlement agreements
IPR	intellectual property rights
ISA	investor-State arbitration
ISDS	investor-State dispute settlement
IT	information technology
ITA	investment treaty arbitration
ITS	Investment Tribunal System
JIS	joint interpretive statements
KORUS	U.S.–Korea Free Trade Agreement
LCA (2010)	Law on Commercial Arbitration (2010) (Vietnam)
LCI Report	Law Commission of India in a report on the 2015 Draft Model
LCIA	London Court of International Arbitration
LDA	Louis Dreyfus Armateurs
LTTE	Liberation Tiger of Tamil Eelam
MAI	Multilateral Agreement on Investment
MBL	Myanmar Brewery Ltd

MCIL	Myanmar Citizens Investment Law
MFIL	Myanmar Foreign Investment Law
MFN	most-favored nation
MIC	Myanmar Investment Commission / multilateral investment court
MIL	Myanmar Investment Law
MOFCOM	Ministry of Commerce (China)
MOJ	Ministry of Justice (Vietnam)
MPoI	Minimum Platform on Investment
MST	Minimum Standard of Treatment
MTF	moving treaty frontier
NAFTA	North American Free Trade Agreement
NGOs	non-governmental organisations
NT	National Treatment
NTBs	Non-Tariff Barriers
OECD	Organisation for Economic Cooperation and Development
OFDI	outward foreign direct investment
OSS	online one stop shop
PCA	Permanent Court of Arbitration
PRC	People's Republic of China
PT ICD	PT Indonesian Coal Development
RCEP	Regional Comprehensive Economic Partnership
REIO	regional economic integration organisation
SADC	Southern African Development Community
SAFTA	Singapore–Australia Free Trade Agreement
SAR	special administrative region
SCC	Stockholm Chamber of Commerce
SGCA	Singapore Court of Appeal
SIAC	Singapore International Arbitration Centre
SICC	Singapore International Commercial Court
SIMC	Singapore International Mediation Centre
SOEs	State-owned enterprises
STP	Sondong, Tampubolon & Partners
SWIFT	Single Window Investment Facilitation Taskforce
TFEU	Treaty on the Functioning of the European Union
TIPs	Treaties with Investment Provisions
TIRPA	Transfer of Immovable Property Restrictions Act 1987
TPF	third-party funding
TPP	Trans-Pacific Partnership
TRIMs	Agreement on Trade-Related Investment Measures
TRIPS Agreement	Agreement on Trade-Related Aspects of Intellectual Property Rights
TTIP	Trans-Atlantic Trade and Investment Partnership
UAE	United Arab Emirates
UDHR	Universal Declaration of Human Rights
UK	United Kingdom
UMEHCL	Union of Myanmar Economic Holdings Ltd
UN	United Nations
UNCITRAL	United Nations Commission on International Trade Law

UNCTAD	United Nations Conference on Trade and Development
UNP	United National Party (Sri Lanka)
US	United States
VCCR	Vienna Convention on Consular Relations
VCLT	Vienna Convention on the Law of Treaties
VCST	Vienna Convention on Succession of States
VIAC	Vietnam International Arbitration Centre
WTO	World Trade Organization

PART I

Introduction

1

Introduction

The Asian Turn in Foreign Investment

Mahdev Mohan and Chester Brown

For the most of the last 150 years, the substantive content of international investment law has largely been shaped by capital-exporting States in Western Europe and North America.[1] This is unsurprising given the dominant economic position held by those States during that period, which resulted in outflows of foreign direct investment largely into developing States which were less successful in influencing the process and outcomes of trade and investment treaty negotiations; and that did not have the institutional capacity to impartially settle complex investment disputes.[2] However, this dynamic has been gradually changing, with the significance of Asia coming increasingly to the fore. This is consistent with projections that Asia would 'regain the dominant economic position it held some 300 years ago, before the industrial revolution' by 2050.[3] Asia has indeed cemented its position as a global growth engine in recent years. It has for instance been estimated that by 2050, Asia could count for half of global production, trade and investment.[4] The economies of China and India are predicted to grow at a rate of 6.3 per cent in 2020, and the economies of the Association of Southeast Asian Nations (ASEAN) are expected to grow at a rate of 5.0 per cent in 2020, both well above the expected global average of 3.6 per cent.[5] China, as one of the top prospective FDI destinations, has become the second highest recipient of FDI inflows in the world (with USD 139 billion in 2018); when combined with Hong Kong, China receives the most FDI in the world, with USD 255 billion, compared with the United States, which received USD 252 billion in 2018.[6] The same picture also emerges with respect to FDI outflows: China is in second place in 2018, with USD 130 billion, and when combined with Hong Kong, accounts for USD 215 billion, which easily surpasses Japan, which was responsible for capital exports of USD 143 billion.[7] Further to this, ASEAN is now the third largest trading bloc in the world after the European Union (EU) and the North American Free Trade Area.[8] If the ten-member regional bloc were a single country, it would be the fifth largest economy in the

[1] Stephan W.Schill, 'Special Issue: Dawn of an Asian Century in International Investment Law?' (2015) 16 *Journal of World Investment and Trade* 765.

[2] See generally Stephan W. Schill, 'Whither Fragmentation? On the Literature and Sociology of International Investment Law' (2011) 22 *European Journal of International Law* 875.

[3] Asia Development Bank, 'Executive Summary' in *Asia 2050: Realizing the Asian Century* (2011), 3.

[4] See, e.g., ibid., xiii.

[5] ASEAN, *ASEAN Economic Integration Brief* (No. 5, June 2019), 2, available at https://asean.org/storage/2019/06/AEIB_5th_Issue_Released.pdf (last accessed 20 February 2020).

[6] United Nations Conference on Trade and Development ('UNCTAD'), *World Investment Report* 2019 (2020), available at https://unctad.org/en/PublicationsLibrary/wir2019_en.pdf (last accessed 14 February 2020), p. 4.

[7] Ibid., p. 7.

[8] ASEAN Briefing, 'Understanding ASEAN's Free Trade Agreements' (13 February 2014), available at: www.aseanbriefing.com/news/2014/02/13/understanding-aseans-free-trade-agreements.html (last accessed 20 February 2020).

world, with a combined economy of USD 2.8 trillion in 2018.[9] And Australia, being geographically proximate to Asia, is one of the world's top eight host economies, with USD 60 billion worth of FDI inflows into the country in 2018.[10]

It can therefore be said – as has been remarked by Stephan Schill – that recent years have witnessed a marked shift in the geography of international investment law from a 'transatlantic to a transpacific core', and that Asia is becoming a focal point 'in rule-making in international investment law'.[11] Indeed, Asia has been at the epicentre of negotiations for novel and exciting mega-regional investment agreements. The Comprehensive and Progressive Agreement for Trans-Pacific Partnership (CPTPP) is, despite the need for it to be renegotiated after the United States' decision to withdraw from its predecessor, the Trans-Pacific Partnership (TPP),[12] still a triumph for the Asia Pacific region as it promotes a new trend of multiregional trade and investment in the twenty-first century through economic connectivity, and creates global value chains. Notwithstanding the United States' withdrawal from the TPP, the ongoing negotiations of the US–China bilateral investment treaty (BIT) illustrates the importance that Washington, DC, places on investment flows with Asia.[13] Asia's prominent role is also evidenced by the recent successful conclusion of the Regional Comprehensive Economic Partnership Agreement (RCEP), which includes the ten ASEAN States and the five of the six States with which ASEAN has existing FTAs (namely, Australia, China, Japan, Korea and New Zealand; India has decided for the time being not to sign the RCEP.)[14] On 4 November 2019, these States announced that the negotiation of twenty substantive chapters of the RCEP had been completed, and that most market access commitments on goods, service and investment had been substantially agreed. The States agreed that they would work towards the rapid conclusion of the RCEP, and on 15 November 2020, it was signed by Ministers from 15 countries.[15] And outside the space of international investment law, the signing in August 2019 of the Singapore Convention on International Settlement Agreements Resulting from Mediation also saw Asia located at the centre of developments in international commercial law.[16]

In addition to the ambitious mega-regional agreements, individual ASEAN States have also been busy negotiating bilateral FTAs with the EU. As things stand, the European Union has signed an Economic Partnership Agreement with Japan in June 2016 (which entered into force in February 2019),[17] and it has also signed a bilateral free trade agreement (FTA) and

9 US – ASEAN Business Council, 'ASEAN's Economy' (22 July 2019), available at www.usasean.org/why-asean/asean-economy (last accessed 20 February 2020).

10 UNCTAD, *World Investment Report* 2019, above n 5, 4.

11 Schill, above n 1, 766.

12 See, e.g., David Smith, 'Trump Withdraws from Trans-Pacific Partnership amid Flurry of Orders', *The Guardian* (24 January 2017), available at www.theguardian.com/us-news/2017/jan/23/donald-trump-first-orders-trans-pacific-partnership-tpp (last accessed 14 February 2020).

13 Schill, above n 1, 766.

14 'India Decides to Opt Out of RCEP, Says Key Concerns not Addressed', The Economic Times (5 November 2019), available at https://economictimes.indiatimes.com/news/economy/foreign-trade/india-decides-to-opt-out-of-rcep-says-key-concerns-not-addressed/articleshow/71896848.cms?from=mdr (last accessed 20 February 2020).

15 For example, Government of Australia, Department of Foreign Affairs and Trade, 'Regional Comprehensive Economic Partnership', available at https://www.dfat.gov.au/trade/agreements/not-yet-in-force/rcep (last accessed 20 February 2021).

16 United Nations Convention on International Settlement Agreements Resulting from Mediation, opened for signature 7 August 2019, UN Doc No A/RES/73/198, available at https://uncitral.un.org/en/texts/mediation/conventions/international_settlement_agreements (not yet in force) ('Singapore Convention').

17 EU – Japan Economic Partnership Agreement, signed 30 October 2016 (entered into force 1 February 2019), available at https://ec.europa.eu/trade/policy/in-focus/eu-japan-economic-partnership-agreement/ (last accessed 20 February 2020).

separate investment protection agreement with Singapore in October 2018 and with Vietnam in June 2019 (neither of which is in force).[18] The EU has also commenced negotiations with Malaysia, Thailand, the Philippines, Indonesia, India, Myanmar, Australia and New Zealand.[19]

Elsewhere in Asia we have witnessed Sri Lanka's 'Look East' strategy to 'court ASEAN' manifesting itself.[20] Sri Lanka's most recently concluded IIA, the Sri Lanka–Singapore FTA, was signed in January 2018 and can be considered as being Sri Lanka's first modern and comprehensive FTA. Were Sri Lanka to join the RCEP, it would stand to gain the benefit of 'simultaneous access to an enormous regional market and dynamic Asian FDI'.[21]

Instinctively, one would anticipate that the perceived 'shift' in the geography of international investment law from West to East would result in an increase in Asian participation in investment arbitrations, being the predominant ISDS mechanism in IIAs. In general, the resort to investor–State dispute settlement (ISDS) continues to be popular: in 2018 alone, seventy-one new ISDS cases were launched, which continues a general upward trend in the annual number of new cases in recent years, and thirty-one new claims were started in the first seven months of 2019.[22] But the involvement of Asia remains comparatively limited, with the statistics instead indicating that the number of cases involving States from South Asia and the Asia Pacific remains relatively low.[23] Nonetheless, it has been suggested that a number of considerations suggest that there will be an increase of investor–State arbitration in the region.[24] In particular, several considerations feature prominently in this book; these include the modernization in ASEAN States, the trends that point towards increase in the number of investor–State disputes in future, and the bringing together of different stakeholders in the ASEAN region.

Another current issue in international investment law is the proposed reform of ISDS. In this respect, many States and other stakeholders have expressed dissatisfaction with the current regime, particularly as regards the perceived imbalance of rights and obligations of investors and States under IIAs, as well as the ISDS mechanism contained within these treaties.[25] Certain States, in particular the EU and its Member States, have in fact stepped

18 EU – Singapore FTA, signed 19 October 2018 (entered into force 21 November 2019); EU – Singapore Investment Protection Agreement, signed 19 October 2018 (not yet in force), both treaties available at https://ec.europa.eu/trade/policy/in-focus/eu-singapore-agreement/ (last accessed 20 February 2020). EU – Vietnam FTA, signed 30 June 2019 (entered into force 1 August 2020); EU – Vietnam Investment Protection Agreement, signed 30 June 2019 (not yet in force), both treaties available at https://ec.europa.eu/trade/policy/in-focus/eu-vietnam-agreement/ (last accessed 20 February 2020).

19 EU, 'Overview of FTA and other Trade Negotiations' (February 2020), available at https://trade.ec.europa.eu/doclib/docs/2006/december/tradoc_118238.pdf (last accessed 20 February 2020).

20 Lasanda Kurukulasuriya, 'Does Sri Lanka's "Look East" Strategy to Court ASEAN Make Sense?', *The Diplomat* (1 February 2018), available at https://thediplomat.com/2018/02/does-sri-lankas-look-east-strategy-to-court-asean-make-sense/ (last accessed 20 February 2020).

21 For example, Ganeshan Wignaraja, 'What Does RCEP Mean for Insiders and Outsiders? The Experiences of India and Sri Lanka', *Asia-Pacific Research and Training Network on Trade, Working Paper No. 181/2018*, p. 18, available at www.unescap.org/sites/default/files/AWP%2081_Formatted.pdf (last accessed 18 March 2020).

22 UNCTAD, *ISDS Navigator Update* (30 September 2019), available at https://investmentpolicy.unctad.org/news/hub/1625/20190930-isds-navigator-update-980-known-investment-treaty-cases-by-31-july-2019 (last accessed 20 February 2020).

23 See, e.g., cases such as *Vodafone International Holdings BV* v. *India* (PCA Case No. 2016-35); *Indian Metals & Ferro Alloys Ltd* v. *Indonesia* (PCA Case No. 2015-40) ; *Mohammad Reza Dayyani* v. *Korea* (PCA Case No. 2015-38); *Ansung Housing Co Ltd* v. *China* (ICSID Case No ARB/14/25, Award of 9 March 2017).

24 Loretta Malintoppi and Charis Tan, 'Introduction', in Loretta Malintoppi and Charis Tan (eds.), *Investment Protection in Southeast Asia* (2016), 1–3.

25 UNCTAD, 'Reform of the IIA Regime: Four Paths of Action and a Way Forward' (IIA Issues Note No. 3, June 2014), available at http://unctad.org/en/PublicationsLibrary/webdiaepcb2014d6_en.pdf (last accessed 20 February 2020), p. 1.

away from negotiating traditional ISDS provisions in their IIAs, and have instead proposed the creation of a permanent tribunal for the resolution of investor–State disputes, with the addition of an appellate body. These efforts which were made in the context of bilateral negotiations (including with Canada, Singapore and Vietnam) have led to UNCITRAL's attention being turned to a possible multilateral reform agenda. In April 2017, the UNCITRAL Secretariat published a Note, 'Possible future work in the Field of Dispute Settlement: Reform of Investor-State Dispute Settlement (ISDS)', which identified certain concerns, such as a perceived lack of consistency and predictability in decisions and awards, and the lack of a code of conduct for arbitrators.[26] In July 2017, UNCITRAL charged Working Group III with 'a broad mandate to work on the possible reform of investor–State dispute settlement (ISDS)'.[27] In discharging its mandate, Working Group III was to ensure that its deliberations, 'while benefiting from the widest possible breadth of available expertise from all stakeholders, would be government-led with high-level input from all governments, consensus-based and fully transparent'.[28] The approach followed by Working Group III was that it would proceed in three stages: first, it would 'identify and consider concerns regarding ISDS'; secondly, it would 'consider whether reform was desirable in light of any identified concerns'; and thirdly, 'if the Working Group were to conclude that reform was desirable, develop any relevant solutions to be recommended to the Commission'.[29]

As of the time of writing, Working Group III has now reached the third of these phases, having already identified and considered concerns regarding ISDS, and having concluded that reform was desirable in light of those concerns. States remain divided on what the appropriate reforms should be, with States being loosely grouped into (a) those States which favour systemic reform (such as the creation of a permanent multilateral investment court (MIC) and/or an appellate mechanism; (b) those States which favour incremental reform, which would involve improvements to the existence *ad hoc* system of ISDS; (c) those States which are implacably opposed to any form of ISDS, whether before a permanent MIC or *ad hoc* tribunals;[30] and (d) those States which are yet to settle on a position.

The approach of many Asian States with respect to ISDS Reform largely remains to be seen. It is significant, however, that certain States have already declared their hand. For instance, China has come out in support of the development of an appellate mechanism for ISDS disputes.[31] Thailand, for its part, appears to favour incremental reform, and has expressed support for the drafting of new UNCITRAL Rules for ISDS disputes, the drafting of guidelines on dispute prevention, the establishment of an Advisory Centre on Investment Law, and the drafting of model substantive clauses for IIAs.[32] Japan also favours incremental

26 UNCITRAL Secretariat, Note on 'Possible Future Work in the Field of Dispute Settlement: Reforms of Investor-State Dispute Settlement (ISDS)', UN Doc. A/CN.9/917 (20 April 2017).

27 Report of Working Group III on the Work of its Thirty-fifth Session, UN Doc No A/CN.9/935 (14 May 2018), para. 2; see also *Official Records of the General Assembly, Seventy-second Session, Supplement No.* 17 (UN Doc No A/72/17), paras. 263–64.

28 Report of Working Group III on the Work of its Thirty-fifth Session, UN Doc No A/CN.9/935 (14 May 2018), para. 2.

29 Ibid.

30 For example, Anthea Roberts, 'Incremental, Systemic, and Paradigmatic Reform of Investor-State Arbitration' (2018) 112 *American Journal of International Law* 410.

31 Government of China, 'Possible Reform of Investor-State Dispute Settlement (ISDS)', UN Doc No A/CN.9/WGIII/WP.177 (19 July 2019), p. 4.

32 Government of Thailand, 'Possible Reform of Investor-State Dispute Settlement (ISDS)', UN Doc No A/CN.9/WGIII/WP.162 (8 March 2019).

reform, and it has also submitted joint papers with Chile and Israel,[33] as well as with Mexico and Peru,[34] in which they have proposed the negotiation of a multilateral instrument which would enable States to opt in with respect to a 'suite' of various reforms.[35] As they explain, this 'suite' approach aims to provide a solution which allows for 'maximum flexibility to develop a menu of relevant solutions, which may vary in form, and that member States can choose to adopt, based on their specific needs and interests, including those of developing countries'.[36]

The two proposed systemic reform options – namely the creation of a permanent MIC providing direct access to private parties and States parties alike for investment-related matters, and the creation of an appellate mechanism for investor–State arbitral awards – has long been championed by the EU, and successfully negotiated the inclusion of such provisions in the investment chapter of its FTA with Canada ('the Comprehensive Economic Trade Agreement'),[37] as well as in the EU–Vietnam Investment Protection Agreement,[38] and the EU–Singapore Investment Protection Agreement.[39]

Against this background, it is evident that the ISDS regime is at a crossroads. At this important juncture, arguably more than ever before, Asian States find themselves well positioned to assist in shaping the next phase of international investment law. Asia is the next bastion of economic activity, providing growth opportunities for States in Europe, the Americas, Africa and beyond.[40] Given Asia's newly found position of potential influence, this raises the question whether it can be said that there is an 'Asian' approach to international investment law? To locate an answer to this question, it is evident that the Asian response to international investment law is a variegated one, which goes beyond the various reform options which have been proposed by UNCTAD, States and other stakeholders. To use a culinary analogy, although all Asian States may be dining at the same table of international investment law, each State comes with different preferences, different experiences and a different way of conducting its affairs – bringing a different dish to the table. And just as the decision-making process of each guest at the Asian dinner table as to which dishes to select will depend on a range of factors, so the approach of each Asian State when it comes to negotiating terms in their IIAs will take into account the very unique preferences and circumstances of each State, shaped by history, culture and other contextual factors.

Over twenty-two chapters, this book strives to present a picture of what individual Asian States bring to the table and how as a region they are already, and will continue, to drive the IIA regime forward. It also brings together some of the pertinent issues that the Asian States have to grapple with as they move forward in their treaty negotiations. Readers are invited to

33 Governments of Chile, Israel and Japan, 'Possible Reform of Investor-State Dispute Settlement (ISDS)', UN Doc No A/CN.9/WGIII/WP.163 (15 March 2019).

34 Governments of Chile, Israel, Mexico, Japan and Peru, 'Possible Reform of Investor-State Dispute Settlement (ISDS)', UN Doc No A/CN.9/WGIII/WP.182 (2 October 2019).

35 Ibid., Annex.

36 Ibid.

37 EU–Canada Comprehensive Economic and Trade Agreement, signed 30 October 2016, (entered into force 21 September 2017), available at https://ec.europa.eu/trade/policy/in-focus/ceta/ (last accessed 20 February 2020).

38 EU–Vietnam Investment Protection Agreement, signed 30 June 2019 (not yet in force), both treaties available at https://ec.europa.eu/trade/policy/in-focus/eu-vietnam-agreement/ (last accessed 20 February 2020).

39 EU–Singapore Investment Protection Agreement, signed 19 October 2018 (not yet in force), available at https://ec.europa.eu/trade/policy/in-focus/eu-singapore-agreement/ (last accessed 20 February 2020).

40 See, e.g., Derrick Olsen, 'Asia Pacific key to future of metropolitan U.S. economic growth' *Brookings* (27 July 2015); ' Asia poised to play dominant role in Africa's future growth' *International Enterprise Singapore* (24 August 2016).

explore what the 'Asian approach' is, which may lead to a more layered understanding of whether Asian States are 'rule takers' or 'rule makers' and whether Asia as a region is well-poised to take the lead in ISDS reform.

This volume proceeds as follows. After this introduction, the collection starts by considering various national approaches within Asia to the regulation and protection of foreign investment (Part II). Mahdev Mohan begins by observing that at a time of global uncertainty in trade and investment regimes, Singapore's policymakers and legal advisers have been involved in negotiating 'next generation' amendments to the Singapore–Australia Free Trade Agreement, while also working to resurrect a familiar international economic law framework– that is, bifurcating EU–Singapore trade and investment commitments into two separate agreements. Singapore courts are now also prepared, as he notes, to review the scope of an arbitral tribunal's jurisdiction afresh by interpreting the underlying investment treaty.[41] Prabhash Ranjan then considers a particular issue facing India, which is the interface between intellectual property rights and international investment law; he discusses whether foreign investors, specifically pharmaceutical companies, are empowered to challenge regulatory measures that may be introduced by the Indian government and that impact the investor's patents under the investment chapters of India's BITs and FTAs.[42] Ei Ei Aung, Mahdev Mohan and Aziah Hussin then examine Myanmar's approach to international investment protection in the form of the Myanmar Investment Law, 2016.[43] Sheng Zhang then provides an examination of the different levels of development that have characterized China's BIT practice, and suggests this is a microcosm of China's growing participation in the international legal order.[44] In Jie (Jeanne) Huang's chapter, readers find a consideration of China's experience in upgrading its BITs; this chapter categorizes the modernization of Chinese BITs into five models, consistent with UNCTAD's recommendations for reform.[45]

In Part III, the contributions consider the tensions that are at play in the ISDS regime more generally, particularly as States are increasingly finding that they are having to defend investor–State claims, in striking the correct balance between regulatory space and investor protection. The Japanese approach to striking this balance is discussed by Shotaro Hamamoto. In comparing Japan's 'old generation' treaties against the 'new generation' ones, the author illustrates how Japan is shifting the balance in a way that will better preserve the regulatory space of the host State.[46] In the following chapter, Antony Crockett provides a thorough overview of the investment treaty regime in Indonesia, and provides insight into how the government is trying to preserve its regulatory space, whilst providing foreign investments better protection and fair treatment.[47] The next chapter, by Shreyas Jayasimha and Abhimanyu George Jain, sheds light on India's experience in responding to the increased use of ISDS against it, and its development of the Model BIT of 2015.[48] Naazima Kamardeen and Dinush Panditaratne then bring readers through the Sri Lankan experience of FDI, especially in light of its 'first modern and comprehensive' FTA with Singapore in January 2018.[49]

41 See Chapter 2.
42 See Chapter 3.
43 See Chapter 4.
44 See Chapter 5.
45 See Chapter 6.
46 See Chapter 7.
47 See Chapter 8.
48 See Chapter 9.
49 See Chapter 10.

The contributions in Part IV of this volume take a step back for a broader survey of multilateral rule-making in Asia on trade and investment, that is, how Asian States and the ASEAN bloc as a whole are building, strengthening or revising relationships with other regional blocs. This is done through examining the recent mega-regional agreements that have been at the centre of talks of IIA for the past few years, in particular, the CPTPP, TPP and the RCEP, amongst others. Chester Brown and Henry Winter begin with an analysis of ASEAN's legal framework for free trade and the promotion and protection of foreign investment.[50] In the next chapter, Nguyen Manh Dzung and Dang Vu Minh Ha examine Vietnam's role as a 'rule-taker' in having accepted the EU's proposed ISDS mechanism in the EU–Vietnam Free Trade Agreement.[51] Julien Chaisse and Xu Jian's chapter on investment rule-making in Asia–European Union relations provides a macro-analysis of Asian rule-making and then delves into the evolving international regime for investment in Asia, coming at a crucial time for the EU when it is increasing the number of treaty negotiations with Asian members.[52] Lastly, Chin Leng Lim discusses the rebalancing of investor and investment protection in light of the regulatory concerns of the original twelve signatory countries to TPP's investment chapter.[53]

Part V then turns to consider emerging trends and seeks to situate Asia in relation to these novel developments. Thus, Aloysius Llamzon and Jessica Beess und Chrostin discuss the leading cases on investor wrongdoing in international investment arbitration, including a focus on the obligations of foreign investors to exercise diligence when making foreign investment decisions.[54] Robert McCorquodale and Mark Mangan then discuss the responses by ASEAN Member States to transboundary haze pollution, and analyse whether the responsibility of States to prevent transboundary pollution and to protect the human rights of those within their jurisdiction as well as those residing in neighbouring States can be enforced under investment treaties.[55] The next chapter, by N Jansen Calamita and Ewa Zelazna, outlines the drivers of change regarding transparency in investor–State arbitration and asks critically about the role of Asian States in this process, particularly in light of the considerable doubts expressed by Asian States in the UNCITRAL negotiations about both the need for the Rules on Transparency and the Mauritius Convention.[56] Next, Ingrid Coinquet and Siraj Shaik Aziz write about how third party funding has gained a foothold in Asia through Hong Kong and Singapore.[57] Following from this, Jaemin Lee reviews recent initiatives which embrace the use of mediation for the resolution of ISDS cases, and reflects further on the significance of the recent conclusion of the Singapore Convention in this respect.[58] In the last chapter of this part, Nadja Alexander and Shouyu Chong consider the origins of the Singapore Convention on Mediation and how it may impact upon ISDS, going forward.[59]

Finally, the contributions in Part VI discuss future trajectory for investment law in the region. In Surya P Subedi QC's chapter, 'Reconciling Public Interests with Private Interests in ISDS:

[50] See Chapter 11.
[51] See Chapter 12.
[52] See Chapter 13.
[53] See Chapter 14.
[54] See Chapter 15.
[55] See Chapter 16.
[56] See Chapter 17.
[57] See Chapter 18.
[58] See Chapter 19.
[59] See Chapter 20.

Securing Effective Remedy for Investment-Related Human Rights Violations', he considers the particular issue of 'land grabbing' in the region and highlights the practice of certain developing countries in responding to the position of the developed countries with which they enter into IIAs.[60] And Luke Nottage's chapter provides a holistic assessment of Asian practices and trends for future agreements.[61]

The contents of this volume amply demonstrate that Asian States have learned that flexibility and being able to adapt to the international geopolitics is essential to continued cooperation, continued foreign investment flows and economic growth. This is also appreciated by investors, non-governmental organizations, members of civil society and other stakeholders in the Asian region. We hope that readers will find this book a buffet of information that tantalises and delights the mind.

60 See Chapter 21.
61 See Chapter 22.

PART II

National Approaches within Asia to the Regulation and Protection of Foreign Investment

2

Investment Agreements and Dispute Settlement in Singapore

Setting Standards

Mahdev Mohan

2.1 INTRODUCTION

While international investment agreements (IIAs) have been part of the international law landscape for a long time, with the first bilateral investment treaty (BIT) being signed more than sixty years ago,[1] there has been a recent proliferation of investor–State arbitrations as private actors seek to enforce their treaty obligations under international law.[2] The Chief Justice of Singapore, Sundaresh Menon, has referred to this phenomenon as indicating the 'privatisation of public international law', which brings into sharp focus the importance of public international law in advancing the commercial interests for both investors and States. Chief Justice Menon has noted that 'as Asian commerce becomes more influential in the global economy ... Asian commercial lawyers should become more influential in shaping the rules and practices of the global commercial arena'.[3]

Indeed, since 2014 Singapore has positioned itself to be a hub for international dispute resolution in a series of moves towards providing a full suite of dispute resolution services (viz. litigation, arbitration, mediation) to cater to the varied needs of commercial users. These include the Singapore International Mediation Centre (SIMC), the Singapore International Mediation Institute and the establishment of the Singapore International Commercial Court (SICC). In addition, the Singapore International Arbitration Centre (SIAC) and the SIMC have collaborated to develop the SIAC–SIMC arb-med-arb protocol, which allows a party to commence arbitration under the auspices of the SIAC and then proceed to mediation under the SIMC.

The promulgation of the SIAC Investment Rules in 2017 to specifically govern investment arbitrations – unprecedented for a private arbitral institution at the time – and the provisions of the investment chapter of the European Union–Singapore Free Trade Agreement (EUSFTA) (as originally negotiated), which subsequently took shape as the European Union–Singapore Investment Protection Agreement (EUSIPA), represent steps Singapore has taken towards emerging as a 'rule-maker' in connection with investor–State dispute settlement (ISDS). Among other things, the EUSIPA 'offers investors a new investment

1 Treaty for the Promotion and Protection of Investments, Germany–Pakistan (25 November 1959) 457 UNTS 6575.

2 The interpretation and enforcement of IIAs, bilateral investment treaties (BITs) and investment chapters of free trade agreements (FTAs) are governed by the corpus of *public* international law rules that apply to all treaties. However, unlike typical treaties, most investment treaties also have a private dimension. *See* Zachary Douglas, 'The Hybrid Foundations of Investment Treaty Arbitration' (2003) 74 *British Yearbook of International Law* 151–55.

3 Sundaresh Menon, 'The Impact of Public International Law in the Commercial Sphere and Its Significance to Asia' (2015) 16 *Journal of World Investment & Trade* 772, 798.

dispute resolution mechanism under which the EU and Singapore will set up a standing international and independent investor-State dispute settlement dispute system'. This ISDS system aims to ensure that 'investment protection rules are adhered to, and strike a balance between protecting investors in a transparent manner and safeguarding a state's right to regulate to pursue public policy objectives'.[4]

Recent developments indicate that Singapore's investment treaty policy and reception of investment law in its local courts, when taken together, portray it as a 'first mover' State willing to pursue modern and systematic reforms that aim to address the ISDS regime's current challenges.[5]

Section 2.2 of this chapter will examine the United Nations Conference on Trade and Development's (UNCTAD) various proposals for investment law reform. Section 2.3 will flesh out central aspects of 'next generation' IIAs to which Singapore is a party, such as the EUSIPA and the latest amendments to the investment chapter of the Singapore–Australia Free Trade Agreement (SAFTA), which provide parties to an investor–State dispute with greater party autonomy. In the context of *Swissbourgh Diamond Mines (Pty) Ltd* v. *The Kingdom of Lesotho*, which arose out of mining investments made by the claimants in Lesotho in the 1990s and their allegation that their ability to bring an investment treaty claim was frustrated, Section 2.4 will discuss the potential for continued curial intervention in ISDS where a court finds that the arbitral tribunal did not have jurisdiction over the claim and adopted a balanced interpretation of the underlying treaty provisions. Section 2.5 concludes the chapter.

2.2 INTERNATIONAL INVESTMENT LAW: UNCTAD'S REFORM OPTIONS

It is trite to say that international investment law is primarily shaped by a central tension between the economic interests pursued by investors and the policy space of the host State.[6] An increasing number of disputes have been brought against States to challenge measures taken in the public interest and in good faith, such as anti-tobacco legislation,[7] a phase-out of nuclear power,[8] environmental regulations,[9] restrictions on development of hazardous waste facilities,[10] domestic decisions regarding the scope of intellectual property rights[11] and efforts to regulate tariffs for electricity[12] and water[13] in concessions operated by foreign investors. It is the comparatively strong protection enjoyed by investors that underscores the need to hold

[4] See press release issued by the Ministry of Trade and Industry of Singapore (19 October 2018), at p. 5, www.mti.gov.sg/-/media/MTI/Microsites/EUSFTA/Press-Release-on-Signing-of-EUSFTA–EUSIPA-on-19-Oct-18–v2.pdf (last accessed 25 February 2020).

[5] UNCTAD, 'Reform of the IIA Regime: Four Paths of Action and a Way Forward', IIA Issues Note, November 2015, pp. 1 and 3.

[6] S. Hindelang and M. Krajewski (eds.), *Shifting Paradigms in International Investment Law: More Balanced, Less Isolated, Increasingly Diversified* (Oxford: Oxford University Press, 2016).

[7] *Philip Morris Asia* v. *The Commonwealth of Australia* (UNCITRAL, PCA Case No. 2012–12, Award on Jurisdiction and Admissibility, 17 December 2015).

[8] *Vattenfall AB and others* v. *Federal Republic of Germany* (ICSID Case No. ARB/12/12, Decision Pursuant to ICSID Arbitration Rule 41(5) of 2 July 2013).

[9] *Adel A Hamadi Al Tamimi* v. *Sultanate of Oman* (ICSID Case No. ARB/11/33, Award of 3 November 2015).

[10] *Metalclad Corporation* v. *United Mexican States* (ICSID Case No. ARB(AF)/97/1, Award of 30 August 2000).

[11] *Eli Lilly and Company* v. *Canada* (UNCITRAL, ICSID Case No. UNCT/14/2, Final Award of 16 March 2017).

[12] *National Grid plc* v. *Argentine Republic* (UNCITRAL, Award of 3 November 2008).

[13] *Compañía de Aguas del Aconquija S.A. and Vivendi Universal SA* v. *Argentine Republic* (ICSID Case No. ARB/97/3, Award of 20 August 2007).

these investors accountable, as well as the corresponding obligation on States to regulate in the public interest.[14]

In 2016, UNCTAD had noted that there was '[i]ncreasing dissatisfaction with the functioning of the current system that governs the protection of international investment'[15] and that there was 'an urgent need for reform'.[16] The proposal focused on reforms in safeguarding the right to regulate, while providing protection; reforming investment dispute settlement; promoting and facilitating investment; ensuring responsible investment; and enhancing systemic consistency.[17] UNCTAD has reviewed the progress of reform and examined the costs and benefits of a menu of different policy options for the current phase of IIA reform: (i) jointly interpreting treaty provisions; (ii) amending treaty provisions; (iii) replacing 'outdated' treaties; (iv) consolidating the IIA network; (v) managing relationships between co-existing treaties; (vi) referencing global standards; (vii) engaging multilaterally; (viii) abandoning unratified old treaties; (ix) terminating existing old treaties; and (x) withdrawing from multilateral treaties.[18]

In recent years, States have adopted various combinations of these measures to advance their trade and investment policies. The EUSIPA, which shall be examined in detail later, stands as an example of this. For example, the agreement provides for a joint tribunal comprising representatives from both parties. This joint tribunal can issue binding interpretations of the provisions in the agreement and is a reflection of UNCTAD's action option of 'jointly interpreting treaty provisions'. Moreover, the EUSIPA's provisions on dispute resolution established a mechanism that is enforceable on multiple States, reflecting the option of 'engaging multilaterally'. Examination of the code of conduct of arbitrators under the EUSIPA reveals the parties' desire to reference global standards, another 'action option' in UNCTAD's overview.

2.3 EUSIPA AND SAFTA: TOWARDS 'NEXT GENERATION' IIAs

Singapore has twelve bilateral FTAs in force (with Australia, China, Jordan, India, Japan, the Republic of Korea, New Zealand, Panama, Peru, Turkey, Sri Lanka and the United States).[19] FTAs listed as being under negotiation include those with Canada, Mexico, Pakistan and Ukraine, while those signed are with Costa Rica and the Cooperation Council for the Arab States of the Gulf Cooperation Council.[20] Singapore has also entered into about forty-seven BITs.[21] As a member of the Association of Southeast Asian Nations (ASEAN), Singapore is

[14] K. Nowrot, 'How to Include Environmental Protection, Human Rights and Sustainability in International Investment Law?' (2014) 15 *Journal of World Investment & Trade* 612, 619.

[15] UNCTAD, *UNCTAD's Roadmap for IIA Reform of Investment Dispute Settlement* (10 October 2016), available at http://investmentpolicyhub.unctad.org/Upload/Documents/Joerg%20Weber%20Cath%20Titi%20article_with%20copyright.pdf (last accessed 30 December 2019).

[16] Ibid.

[17] Ibid. See also UNCTAD, *IIA Issues Note: Phase 2 of IIA Reform* (June 2017), p. 1, available at https://unctad.org/en/PublicationsLibrary/diaepcb2017d3_en.pdf (last accessed 18 March 2020).

[18] UNCTAD, *UNCTAD's Roadmap for IIA Reform*, p. 1.

[19] For a list of ASEAN FTAs with trade partners and other regional FTAs, see International Enterprise Singapore, 'Singapore Free Trade Agreements', available at www.iesingapore.gov.sg/Trade-From-Singapore/International-Agreements/free-trade-agreements/Singapore-FTA (last accessed 2 February 2017).

[20] Ibid.

[21] 'Investment Treaty Arbitration 2016 – Singapore', in *Global Arbitration Review*, available at http://globalarbitrationreview.com/jurisdiction/2000152/singapore (last accessed 2 February 2017).

part of the ASEAN Economic Community established in December 2015, and is party to the ASEAN Comprehensive Investment Agreement, and ASEAN+ FTAs.[22]

To buttress its position as a forum of choice for investment arbitration, Singapore has given much deference to party autonomy. This section will discuss the provisions in EUSIPA and the 2016 Agreement to Amend the SAFTA[23] (SAFTA Amendment Agreement) as cases in point. The latter in particular is testament to the influence that new-generation IIA provisions can have in the retrofitting of key provisions into old bilateral FTAs. Although first signed by Australia in 2003 and entering into force in July of the same year, SAFTA has been subsequently amended several times. Constituting the most recent amendment, which entered into force in December 2017, the SAFTA Amendment Agreement reflects the outcomes of the third review conference of SAFTA in connection with the Australia–Singapore Comprehensive Strategic Partnership (CSP) and, inter alia, adopts EUSIPA-style provisions on transparency, a code of conduct for arbitrators and the filtering of unmeritorious claims.

Under the EUSIPA, parties to an investment arbitration can avail themselves of a few options. First, they can engage a joint committee, comprising representatives from both States to an investment agreement, to issue decisions on interpretation which would bind arbitral tribunals.[24] Secondly, if they choose to go to arbitration, parties can submit their disputes to a Tribunal of First Instance, consisting of six members (and which sits in chambers of three).[25] Finally, parties can hold the members of the Tribunal accountable for conduct during and even after the arbitration through a published Code of Conduct for Arbitrators.[26]

The Court of Justice of the European Union (CJEU) was asked for an opinion (Opinion 2/15) 'to determine whether the EU has exclusive competence enabling it to sign and conclude the envisaged agreement by itself'.[27] While the CJEU found that the EU had the 'exclusive competence' to enter into most of the commitments, the EU had only 'shared competence' in two areas – non-direct foreign investment and 'the regime governing dispute settlement between investors and States'.[28] Notably, the request from the Commission related specifically to the EU's agreement with Singapore and acknowledged that '[i]n case of the EU-US trade talks, for instance, there will most likely be a number of elements that will require ratification by national parliaments'.[29] Opinion 2/15 shows that while Singapore may have largely entertained ISA as it stands, EU Member States are wary of the ISA regime removing disputes from the jurisdiction of national courts. It followed that all EU Member States had to ratify the areas of the agreement that fell within their competence.[30]

22 Ibid.

23 *Agreement to Amend the Singapore–Australia Free Trade Agreement*, signed 13 October 2016, [2017] ATS 26 (entered into force 1 December 2017).

24 EUSIPA, Art. 4.1(4).

25 Ibid., Art. 3.9.

26 Ibid., Art. 3.11.

27 CJEU, Press Release No. 52/17, 16 May 2017 http://curia.europa.eu/juris/document/document_print.jsf?doclang=EN&text=&pageIndex=0&part=1&mode=req&docid=190727&occ=first&dir=&cid=441679 (last accessed 25 February 2020).

28 CJEU, n 46.

29 Matthew Weiniger and V Naish, 'European Commission Requests European Court of Justice Opinion on Competence to Enter into EU-Singapore FTA' (6 November 2014), available at https://hsfnotes.com/publicinternationallaw/2014/11/06/european-commission-requests-european-court-of-justice-opinion-on-competence-to-enter-into-eu-singapore-fta/ (last accessed 25 February 2020).

30 See also Mahdev Mohan, 'The European Union's Free Trade Agreement with Singapore – One Step Forward, 28 Steps Back?' in Julien Chaisse and Luke Nottage (eds.), *International Investment Treaties and Arbitration Across Asia* (Leiden: Brill Nijhoff, 2017), p. 180.

In response to Opinion 2/15, the EUSFTA's trade and investment protection components were bifurcated. On 19 October 2018, the EUSFTA was signed together with the EU–Singapore Investment Protection Agreement (EUSIPA). EU Member States approved the EUSFTA on 8 November 2019, and it entered into force on 21 November 2019. As for the EUSIPA, it is a 'mixed agreement' and also has to be sent to the thirty-seven regional and national parliaments of the EU Member States for approval, before it enters into force.[31] The EUSIPA replaces the twelve previous bilateral investment agreements between Singapore and various EU Member States.

Even though the final status of the EUSIPA itself remains uncertain due to the approval needed from the EU and the EU Member States' national parliaments, it is highly likely that modern provisions of the EUSIPA may still serve as model clauses for future investment agreements within and beyond Europe, as they have done for the retrofitting of SAFTA's Investment Chapter. The relevant provisions of these treaties will now be examined in detail.

2.3.1 *Joint Committee*

Article 4.1 of the EUSIPA establishes a Committee consisting of representatives from both parties. Essentially the Committee is tasked with overseeing the smooth implementation of the EUSIPA, considering amendments and issuing binding decisions on interpretation. The decisions of the Committee then become binding on the Parties and all bodies established under the FTA.[32] Importantly, interpretations adopted by the Committee are also binding on the Tribunal deciding a dispute on the interpretation and application of the EUSIPA.[33] Such a provision is not novel globally and to Singapore; an early and relatively well-known example of such a provision in an investment treaty is in the North American Free Trade Agreement (NAFTA). The treaty established a Free Trade Commission (FTC) made up of cabinet-level representatives of the NAFTA parties or their designees, and Article 1131(2) states that any 'interpretation by the [Free Trade Commission] shall be binding' on investor–State tribunals. Under the Singapore–United States FTA, an identical provision is made under Article 15.21. The adoption of such a provision in the EUSIPA continues this trend and comes on the heels of joint interpretation mechanisms being vogue in recent agreements entered into by many of the States which negotiated the Comprehensive and Progressive Agreement on Trans-Pacific Partnership (CPTPP). For example, under the ASEAN–Australia–New Zealand Free Trade Agreement (AANZFTA), Article 27(2) of the investment chapter authorizes a tribunal to request a joint interpretation by the Parties of any provision of the agreement, and Article 27(3) establishes the binding nature of joint interpretations. Similarly, Article 22.2 of the United States–Korea Free Trade Agreement (KORUS) authorizes a Joint Committee made up of party representatives, to issue interpretations of any provision of the agreement, and Article 11.22, like Article 27(3) of the AANZFTA investment chapter, establishes the binding nature of joint interpretations.

This renewed enthusiasm for a Committee adopting interpretations of the EUSIPA is perhaps a response to concerns that ISDS cases have caused. Without treaty-created interpretive boards, arbitral tribunals have been able to decide on the bargain between the States

[31] See press release issued by the Ministry of Trade and Industry of Singapore (19 October 2018), at www.mti.gov.sg/-/media/MTI/Microsites/EUSFTA/Press-Release-on-Signing-of-EUSFTA–EUSIPA-on-19-Oct-18–v2.pdf (last accessed 25 February 2020).

[32] EUSIPA, Art. 4.1(4)(f).

[33] Ibid.

parties with only limited restrictions. These tribunals have been criticized as having little to no accountability to the States parties.[34] Hence, the arbitral jurisprudence has been described as having 'little consideration of the views and practices of states in general or the treaty parties in particular'.[35] This resulted in a high likelihood of a gap between the expectation of the States parties and the tribunals which interpreted the treaty.[36] The developments in introducing the concept of a Committee in the EUSIPA with the ability to deliver binding decisions entirely close this gap on issues of interpretation. Other countries and agreements have also reflected this development. It has been suggested that the ability of such 'Joint Committees' to issue an interpretation of any obligation in the Agreement that is binding on an arbitral tribunal can be considered a key procedural protection.[37]

In the case a party believes that particular provisions in the Agreement have been interpreted in an overly broad way by the tribunal, which the party had not anticipated, the Committee may intervene, at the request of the States parties, to issue an interpretation that is binding on the tribunal. In this way, the States parties' exposure to a relatively high degree of uncertainty that may flow from the tribunal's wide interpretation can be decreased considerably. A committee may also provide a better guarantee of appropriate interpretation of the terms of the investment agreement between countries. This is because it can convey more accurately the present parties' intention to the tribunals, the fast-changing global investment environment and be betterable to consider other similar situations pending between the States concerned, and the policy dimension of the measure at issue in a comprehensive manner. While investment tribunals can undertake a legal enquiry, it will not be as well-placed to consider the practical and policy paradigms to the matter at hand.[38]

2.3.2 *Tribunal of First Instance*

Like its Canadian[39] and Vietnamese[40] counterparts, the EUSIPA provides for the establishment of a standing Tribunal of First Instance (Tribunal), which is to consist of six members: two to be nominated by the EU, two to be nominated by Singapore, and two to be nominated jointly by the EU and Singapore, and who shall not be nationals of any Member State of the EU or of Singapore.[41]

It might be said that the establishment of the Tribunal should give rise to greater consistency and coherence in the interpretation of legal issues in ISDS proceedings. However this is by no means certain; the bilateral nature of standing tribunals such as those created under the EUSIPA, the EU–Canada Comprehensive Economic Trade Agreement (CETA), and the

34 Sundaresh Menon, 'Public International Law – A Requirement for Every Private Lawyer', Keynote Speech at the Pacific Rim Advisory Council Conference (17 October 2011, Singapore), p. 6.

35 Anthea Roberts, 'Power and Persuasion in Investment Treaty Interpretation: The Dual Role of States' (2010) 104 *American Journal of International Law* 179.

36 Menon, 'Public International Law – A Requirement for Every Private Lawyer', above n 15.

37 The Parliament of the Commonwealth of Australia, 'Report 142: Treaty Tabled on 13 May 2014 – Free Trade Agreement between the Government of Australia and the Government of the Republic of Korea (Commonwealth of Australia, September 2014) 27.

38 J. Chaisse and T-Y. Lin (eds.), *International Economic Law and Governance: Essays in Honour of Mitsuo Matsushita* (Oxford: Oxford University Press, 2016) at p. 147.

39 EU – Canada Comprehensive Economic and Trade Agreement, signed 30 October 2016, (entered into force 21 September 2017), available at https://ec.europa.eu/trade/policy/in-focus/ceta/ (last accessed 20 February 2020).

40 EU–Vietnam Investment Protection Agreement, signed 30 June 2019 (not yet in force), both treaties available at https://ec.europa.eu/trade/policy/in-focus/eu-vietnam-agreement/ (last accessed 20 February 2020). See also chapter 12 of this book by Nguyen and Dzang, and chapter 13 by Chaise and Xu.

41 EUISPA, Art. 3.9.

EU–Vietnam Investment Protection Agreement provides no greater certainty towards how issues would be adjudicated when compared with current ISDS mechanisms. As noted earlier, the FTAs and investment agreements that the EU has concluded with Canada and Vietnam each have provisions for a standing tribunal whose members are to be appointed by the EU and Canada, and the EU and Vietnam, respectively.

2.3.3 *Code of Conduct for Arbitrators*

Unlike CETA or even the CPTPP, which are comparatively less detailed and focus more on the qualifications of the arbitrator,[42] Art. 3.11 of the EUSIPA introduces a binding code of conduct for Members of the Tribunal, Members of the Appeal Tribunal and mediators (the Code).[43] This Code was subsequently inserted into the CETA text during its legal scrubbing, and thus the latter may have influenced the former.[44] The Code, found at Annex 7 of the EUSIPA, arguably imposes a higher standard of conflict and disclosure obligations on Members of the Tribunal than in any other rules or guidelines, including the UNCITRAL Model Law, UNCITRAL Arbitration Rules and the IBA Guidelines on Conflicts of Interest in International Arbitration. Going beyond the requirements for independence and impartiality, as found in the IBA Guidelines for example, Members must also 'avoid impropriety and the appearance of impropriety' and 'avoid direct and indirect conflicts of interest'.[45] Furthermore, they must, on an on-going basis, 'avoid creating appearance of bias or impropriety' and 'not be influenced by self-interest, outside pressure, political considerations, public clamour, loyalty to a disputing party or a non-disputing Party or fear of criticism'.[46] Prior to confirmation of his or her appointment, an arbitrator must disclose 'any past or present interest, relationship or matter that is likely to affect his or her independence or impartiality or that might reasonably create an appearance of impropriety or bias in the proceeding'.[47]

The Code also clarifies that even former Members of a Tribunal are not free from obligations after their term of office.[48] Furthermore, the Code contains provisions which stipulate that Members may not, after the conclusion of their term of office, become involved in proceedings which were pending before the Tribunal during their term of office, or act as a representative of parties before the Tribunal for a three-year period.[49] Former Members also have ongoing confidentiality obligations, according to which Members shall not disclose or use any non-public information.[50] There is no list of safe harbours, as in the IBA Rules' 'Green' List. The Code also establishes a 'Consultative Committee' for each of the Tribunal and the Appeal Tribunal, which consists of the President and Vice-President, and next most senior member of the Tribunal or the Appeal Tribunal, to ensure the proper application of the Code.[51] A similarly worded Code of Conduct has since been transposed onto the SAFTA. Notably, unlike the EUSIPA, it also stipulates consequences that flow from violations of the

42 Trans-Pacific Partnership (signed 4 February 2016, not in force) ch 28.
43 EUSIPA, Art. 3.11(1).
44 This conclusion can be reached when the 2015 report prepared for the European Parliament by its Policy Department at p. 64 is juxtaposed with the consolidated CETA text at p. 536, available at http://trade.ec.europa.eu/doclib/docs/2014/september/tradoc_152806.pdf (last accessed 25 February 2020).
45 EUSIPA, Annex 7, para. 2.
46 Ibid., Annex 7, para. 10.
47 Ibid., Annex 7, para. 3.
48 Ibid., Annex 7, para. 15.
49 Ibid., Annex 7, paras. 16–18.
50 Ibid., Annex 7, paras. 19–21.
51 Ibid., Annex 7, para. 24.

Code. Specifically, Annex 7–22 of the SAFTA Amendment Agreement empowers parties to remove the arbitrator, waive the violation, or request the arbitrator to take steps within a specified time period to cease or ameliorate the violation. Furthermore, if the parties agree to waive the violation or determine that, after taking steps, the violation in question has ceased, the arbitrator may continue to serve on the tribunal.

2.3.4 *Transparency*

The EUSIPA adopts full transparency in ISDS disputes. All documents, including submissions by the parties, decisions of the tribunal, and expert reports, will be publicly available on a website administered by the UN and financed by the EU.[52] All hearings will also be open to the public, which calls to mind the UN Convention on Transparency in Treaty-based Investor-State Arbitration,[53] also known as the Mauritius Convention on Transparency ('Mauritius Convention').[54] Article 29 of Chapter 8 of the SAFTA Amendment Agreement now likewise requires that the above-mentioned documents are made available to the public. Article 28(4) of the same also commits parties to strive to ensure that any appellate mechanism they consider adopting provides for transparency of proceedings similar to the transparency provisions established in Article 29. These suggest that Singapore's investment policy regarding transparency now keeps pace with global developments.[55]

2.3.5 *Filtering unmeritorious claims*

Article 3.14 of the EUSIPA, inspired by Rule 41(5) of the ICSID Rules of Procedure for Arbitration Proceedings,[56] establishes a fast-track system for rejecting unfounded or frivolous claims, by providing for the summary dismissal of claims which are 'manifestly without legal merit'.[57] While the EUSIPA does not clarify the term 'manifestly without legal merit', guidance can be sought from awards rendered in pursuance of Rule 41(5) of the ICSID Arbitration Rules. The rule has been used, for example, to bring arbitrations where there was obviously no investment within the meaning of Article 25 of the ICSID Convention, or where the respondent wanted to re-open a case already decided elsewhere to an early end.[58] This safety valve against frivolous claims has since been adopted in the SAFTA Amendment Agreement. Article 28(4) of Chapter 8 of the SAFTA in the Amendment Agreement empowers a tribunal to address and decide, as a preliminary question, whether a claim is 'manifestly without legal merit'.

[52] EUSIPA, Art. 3.16, Annex 8.

[53] UNGA Resolution 69/116 (10 December 2014) www.uncitral.org/pdf/english/texts/arbitration/transparency-convention/Transparency-Convention-e.pdf (last accessed 25 February 2020).

[54] Stephan Schill, 'The Mauritius Convention on Transparency: A Model for Investment Law Reform?', *EJIL: Talk! Blog* (8 April 2015) www.ejiltalk.org/the-mauritius-convention-on-transparency-a-model-for-investment-law-reform/ (last accessed 25 February 2020).

[55] João Ribeiro and Michael Douglas, 'Transparency in Investor – State Arbitration: the Way Forward' (2015) 11 *Asian International Arbitration Journal* 1, 49–67.

[56] John Crook, 'Four Tribunals Apply ICSID Rule for Early Ouster of Unmeritorious Claims', *ASIL insights* (2011), available at www.asil.org/insights/volume/15/issue/10/four-tribunals-apply-icsid-rule-early-ouster-unmeritoriousclaims#_edn20 (last accessed 25 February 2020), see also Chester Brown and Sergio Puig, 'The Power of ICSID Tribunals to Dismiss Proceedings Summarily: An Analysis of Rule 41(5) of the ICSID Arbitration Rules' (2011) 10 *Law and Practice of International Courts and Tribunals* 227.

[57] EUSIPA, Art. 3.14(1).

[58] See, e.g., Brown and Puig, above n 56.

2.3.6 *Most-Favoured Nation Clause*

The most-favoured nation (MFN) clause, which guarantees that the host State will not subject investors from the other contracting party to treatment less favourable than that afforded to investors from a third State, has been considered a central pillar of trade policy[59] and has also been dubbed one of the 'most important standards of treatment for investors and their investments'.[60] The absence of an MFN clause from the EUSIPA and the original SAFTA text is conspicuous. This omission is striking in the case of EUSIPA, a new generation IIA. In Article 15 of the original SAFTA, rather than guaranteeing the same treatment accorded to third parties, the parties agreed to a 'best endeavours' approach requiring that a party 'give positive consideration to a request by the other Party for the incorporation herein' of treatment no less favourable than that provided to a third party or resulting from unilateral liberalization.[61] These omissions are likely motivated by the legal uncertainty of whether MFN clauses can serve as titles of jurisdiction for claimant investors independent of the treaty's dispute settlement provision. This is exemplified in the decision of *Maffezini* v. *Spain*,[62] where the tribunal permitted the claimant to get around a clause in the Argentine–Spain BIT which required it to litigate before the local courts of the host State for eighteen months by relying on an MFN clause in the same to import the dispute settlement clause in the Chile–Spain BIT, which did not contain such a requirement.

One might argue that the EUSIPA drafters could have resorted to interpretative footnotes to limit the effects of the MFN clause which they perceived as undesirable; particularly when interpretative footnotes are ubiquitous elsewhere in the EUSIPA, as well as in the EUSFTA. These footnotes serve as explanatory statements which clarify the wording of the treaty so as to preclude disputes on interpretation. For instance, the final draft text of the US–Dominican Republic–Central America FTA included an interpretative footnote to Article 10.4 making clear that it 'could not reasonably lead to a conclusion similar to that of the *Maffezini* case'.[63] Fortunately, the SAFTA Amendment Agreement now includes an MFN clause which expressly provides, in Article 4(2) of Chapter 8 of the SAFTA Amendment Agreement, that the most favoured nation treatment 'does not encompass international dispute resolution procedures or mechanisms'. This inclusion of the MFN Clause is consistent with the treatment of traditional investment provisions by sophisticated treaty parties, and seems to take into account the fact that SAFTA is a central pillar of the economic relationship with Singapore, Australia's largest trade and investment partner in South-East Asia.

2.3.7 *Exclusion of Tobacco Control Measures from ISDS*

Article 22 of Chapter 8 of the SAFTA Amendment Agreement states that 'no claim may be brought under this Section in respect of a tobacco control measure'. A tobacco control measure is defined as 'a measure of a Party related to tobacco products (including products made or derived from tobacco), such as for their production, consumption, distribution,

[59] OECD, 'Most-Favoured-Nation Treatment in International Investment Law' (2004) OECD Working Papers on International Investment 2004/02, 3 www.oecd.org/daf/inv/investment-policy/WP-2004_2.pdf (last accessed 2 February 2017).

[60] Ibid., 16.

[61] SAFTA, Art. 15.

[62] *Emilio Agustin Maffezini* v. *Kingdom of Spain* (ICSID Case No ARB/97/7, Decision on Jurisdiction of 25 January 2000).

[63] Free Trade Area of the Americas Draft Agreement (Derestricted 21 November 2003) www.ftaa-alca.org /FTAADraft03/ChapterXVII_e.asp#note13 (accessed 18 September 2016).

labelling, packaging, advertising, marketing, promotion, sale, purchase, or use, as well as fiscal measures such as internal taxes and excise taxes, and enforcement measures, such as inspection, recordkeeping, and reporting requirements'. This is one of the first international agreements in force in which a particular industry will be singled out and excluded from the scope of ISDS, and may appear controversial for several reasons. First, the provisions contained in the original SAFTA text already permit governments to take appropriate public health measures. For instance, Article 18(b) of the SAFTA states 'nothing in this Chapter shall be construed to prevent the adoption or enforcement by a Party of measures necessary to protect human, animal or plant life or health'.

However, it appears that the pro-State outcomes in *Philip Morris v. Australia*[64] and *Philip Morris v. Uruguay*[65] cases did not persuade the SAFTA Amendment Agreement drafters. In these cases, the tribunals weighed in favour of governmental regulations taken for public welfare, demonstrating that contemporary ISDS tribunals can construe older treaty provisions to reach decisions that give due deference to host state regulatory space for genuine and proportionate public health measures. While the arbitral award in *Philip Morris v. Australia* turned on a jurisdictional objection, namely that Philip Morris had re-arranged its corporate structure to facilitate its Hong Kong subsidiary interests in the Australian tobacco market *after* Australia had announced its plain packaging policy, the tribunal in *Philip Morris v. Uruguay* expressly upheld Uruguay's sovereign power to regulate public health over Philip Morris's investment claims, and further found that the tobacco control measures adopted by Uruguay did not amount to an indirect expropriation of the tobacco company's investment nor to a denial of the company's right to fair and equitable treatment under the Switzerland–Uruguay BIT.

One might argue that SAFTA Article 22 seems unnecessary as there is little to no evidence that the mere threat of investment arbitration leads to a 'regulatory chill'. To illustrate, from the date of Philip Morris issuing its notice of intent to pursue ISDS against Australia for its plain packaging regulations until the date of the Award on Jurisdiction and Admissibility,[66] more than thirty countries tightened tobacco control laws in a host of ways, ranging from banning retail displays to plain packaging and raising the minimum legal age for smoking.[67] Several other countries, including Ireland, New Zealand, the United Kingdom, and Singapore, have also now adopted plain packaging regulations.

This measure also sets a precedent of excluding specific industries from the ISDS provisions in bilateral free trade and investment agreements which may be invoked by other states that incorporate similar provisions into their own 'next generation' IIAs.

2.4 THE SINGAPORE COURTS AND ISDS: *LESOTHO*

With a judiciary that has been known for its efficiency, competence, and integrity,[68] Singapore has been highly regarded as a neutral venue for dispute resolution between parties from different jurisdictions. This bodes well for parties to an IIA who may prefer curial intervention. The Singapore Court of Appeal's judgment in *Sanum Investments Ltd*

64 *Philip Morris Asia Limited* v. *The Commonwealth of Australia*, UNCITRAL, PCA Case No. 2012–12.
65 *Philip Morris Brand Sàrl (Switzerland), Philip Morris Products S.A. (Switzerland)* v. *Oriental Republic of Uruguay*, ARB/10/7.
66 *Philip Morris Asia Limited* v. *The Commonwealth of Australia*, UNCITRAL, PCA Case No. 2012–12.
67 Professor Bryan Mercurio, *Public Consultation Submission 4*, p. 8.
68 Klaus Schwab, 'The Global Competitiveness Report 2011–2012' (World Economic Forum 2011).

v. Government of the Lao People's Democratic Republic reflects the viability of curial intervention through the Singapore court system given the ability and willingness of the judiciary to examine complex issues that ISDS would entail.[69] In *Sanum*, the Singapore Court of Appeal (SGCA), which ultimately reinstated the arbitral tribunal's reasoning but seemingly departed from the Asian States' (belated) expression of what they understood the relevant treaty provisions to mean. The SGCA did not set out to construe the underlying BIT against the intention of the contracting States, nor did it defer to the views of the arbitral tribunal. On the contrary, from the outset, the CA seems to have been animated by a desire to consider the proper scope of the PRC–Lao BIT in light of all the evidence before it, examining 'the question of admissibility and weight within the framework of any other applicable principles of international law, such as the critical date doctrine'.[70]

In another seminal decision, the SGCA upheld the Singapore High Court's first instance decision to set aside an investor–State arbitral award on the basis that the tribunal exceeded its jurisdiction. In particular, in *Kingdom of Lesotho v. Swissbourgh Diamond Mines (Pty) Limited*,[71] the Singapore High Court set aside a Permanent Court of Arbitration (PCA) award in its entirety, after finding in favour of the Kingdom of Lesotho in respect of five out of the six jurisdictional objections. *Lesotho* is a rare instance of a successful application to set aside an award in Singapore. Of note is the extent of divergence between the High Court's conclusions and that of an award made by arbitrators distinguished in the field of investor–State arbitration.

The dispute arose out of Lesotho's alleged uncompensated expropriation of certain diamond mining leases issued to Swissbourgh Diamond Mines Pty. Ltd., Van Zyl and other claimants through measures the Kingdom of Lesotho took between 1991 and 1995. In 2009, Swissbourgh Diamond Mines commenced arbitral proceedings under the 1993 Treaty of the Southern African Development Community[72] ('SADC Treaty') against the Kingdom, before the SADC tribunal which ensures adherence to and interprets the Treaty with the jurisdiction to adjudicate disputes and issue advisory opinions.[73] This action was undertaken on the basis that the said expropriation was in breach of Lesotho's obligations under the SADC Treaty. In 2010, the SADC tribunal was suspended as a result of a series of resolutions adopted by the SADC Summit which included the Kingdom of Lesotho. Consequently, the SADC tribunal was prevented from determining the cases pending before it, which included the SADC Claim. The SADC tribunal was never able to reach a decision as the expropriation claim predated the Tribunal Protocol establishing the said tribunal and the dissolution left the investors without a forum to resolve the dispute. Therefore, in 2012, they commenced an international arbitration against Lesotho under Article 28(1) of Annex 1 of the 2010 Protocol on Finance and Investment to the 1993 SADC Treaty ('Annex 1'). By a majority, the PCA tribunal in the *ad hoc* proceedings ('PCA tribunal') issued an award which dismissed various jurisdictional objections made by the Kingdom and found in favour of the defendants in respect of the Shuttering Dispute. By way of relief, the PCA tribunal found that the parties should establish a new tribunal to hear and determine the SADC Claim.

69 [2016] SGCA 57 ('*Sanum*').
70 *Sanum Investments* at [103].
71 [2017] SGHC 195 ('*Lesotho*').
72 Treaty of the Southern African Development Community (17 August 1992) 32 ILM 116 (entered into force 30 September 1993).
73 On 7 August 2007, the Protocol on Tribunal in the Southern African Development Community ('Tribunal Protocol') was signed. The Tribunal Protocol clarified the operation of the SADC Tribunal, including its composition, powers, functions, jurisdictions and procedures. It entered into force on 14 August 2001.

The Kingdom of Lesotho sought to have the PCA Award set aside on the basis that the PCA Tribunal lacked jurisdiction and that the Award exceeded the scope of the submission to arbitration. The Kingdom of Lesotho's challenge to the jurisdiction of the PCA Tribunal was based on several grounds which were analysed and found to be successful in relation to each ground.

Much of the decision rested on the Court's reading of Annex 1 of the SADC Protocol. Notably, Article 28(1) of Annex 1 provided that disputes 'between an investor and a State Party concerning an obligation of the latter in relation to an admitted investment of the former, which have not been amicably settled, and after exhausting local remedies shall … be submitted to international arbitration'. Applying a *de novo* standard of review in assessing the Kingdom's jurisdictional objections, the High Court disagreed with all of the PCA Tribunal's key jurisdictional holdings, including whether or not (a) the claimants had exhausted all available and effective remedies; (b) the claimants had an investment eligible for arbitration; and (c) the SADC Finance and Investment Protocol extends its protections to domestic investors.

The Singapore High Court first dealt with the objections raised by the investors to its own jurisdiction. It held that it was seized of jurisdiction under Article 34(2)(a)(iii) of the Model Law to set aside the award as the award 'deals with a dispute not contemplated by or not falling within the terms of the *submission to arbitration*, or contains decisions on matters beyond the scope of the submission to arbitration' (emphasis added). Taking a broad approach to the words 'submission to arbitration', the High Court concluded that the Model Law permitted setting aside, where a tribunal decides a matter which is beyond the scope of the arbitration agreement. In reaching this decision, the High Court undertook a review of jurisprudence and legal commentary on the nature and purpose of Article 34(2)(a)(iii), ultimately deciding that 'as a matter of policy, to hold that Art 34(2) (a)(iii) does not apply, where no other limb under Art 34(2) would be engaged, would allow an arbitral tribunal to immunize its awards against judicial scrutiny by delivering its conclusions on both jurisdiction and merits in a single award', which would have been an 'unsatisfactory result'.[74]

The judgment also deals with the court's residual discretion not to set aside an award even where grounds under Article 34(2) of the Model Law are made out; it states that this discretion should only be exercised 'if no prejudice has been sustained by the aggrieved party'. The prejudice in this case was the fact that jurisdiction had been wrongly assumed by the PCA tribunal and the award was set aside in its entirety.[75] The court cited the Singapore Court of Appeal decision in *CRW Joint Operation v. PT Perusahaan Gas Negara (Persero) TBK* as authority for the proposition that the court's residual discretion should only be exercised 'if no prejudice has been sustained by the aggrieved party'. Interestingly, *CRW* did not offer any direct case authority for this proposition, but relied on paragraph 20.140 of Halsbury's Laws of Singapore Volume 2, the context for which is enforcement rather than setting aside of arbitral awards and the footnote to which refers to an earlier Singapore case on the issue of enforcement as opposed to set aside.[76]

Having established its own jurisdiction, the High Court proceeded to undertake a *de novo* review of Lesotho's suite of jurisdictional defences in relation to the arbitral award. It found

74 *Lesotho* at [85].

75 *Lesotho* at [341].

76 Roger Milburn, 'Singapore court sets aside investment treaty award on merits for the first time', Practical Law Arbitration Blog, 23 October 2017.

the Tribunal correct in finding jurisdiction *ratione temporis*, but incorrect in finding jurisdiction *ratione materiae* and incorrect in its reasons for lacking jurisdiction *ratione personae*.

The determination of jurisdiction *ratione temporis* turned on whether the true dispute before the PCA Tribunal was the shuttering of the SADC Tribunal or the alleged expropriation of the mining leases. After analysing a series of awards cited by the parties in support of their respective positions on the distinctiveness of the shuttering dispute from the expropriation dispute, the High Court accepted the defendants' position that the true dispute before the PCA Tribunal was the shuttering dispute; a distinct dispute that arose after the Investment Protocol came into force and so the tribunal had not exceeded its temporal jurisdiction. In reaching this conclusion, the court relied on the metric set out in *ATA v. Jordan*[77] and *Chevron v. Ecuador*[78] in setting out three considerations to separate a pre-existing dispute from the actual dispute submitted to arbitration; whether the disputes (a) were the same; (b) stemmed from the same cause; and (c) related to the same conduct. It ruled in the negative on all three counts in the present case.

In relation to jurisdiction *ratione materiae*, the High Court considered whether there was an 'investment', whether such investment had been 'admitted' and whether the dispute in question concerned an 'obligation in relation to' the admitted investment. After analysing the ordinary meaning, textual context and various legal commentaries on the definition of investments, the High Court interpreted the definition under the SADC Treaty to encompass only 'rights or property acquired in the host State arising under its domestic laws'. The High Court then considered whether the secondary right to bring a claim before the SADC Tribunal nonetheless could be construed as part of the 'bundle of rights' created by the underlying investment in the mining leases in 1988; an argument favoured by the majority in the PCA Tribunal.

Ultimately, the High Court found that the right to bring such a claim did not derive from the leases themselves, but from the 1993 SADC Treaty and a 2001 Investment Protocol to the same. It considered the PCA tribunal's attempts to link the treaty obligations to the secondary right to be 'contrived and unnatural' and accordingly rejected them.[79] Although academic in light of the above findings, the High Court assessed Lesotho's objection to jurisdiction *ratione personae*. The PCA tribunal had determined that all nine claimants were capable of being 'investors' under the SADC Treaty which it held extended to both domestic and foreign investors; though the PCA tribunal had only granted relief to three of the investors in the partial final award on account of the other investors having assigned their claims. The High Court found that Swissbourgh and the fifth to ninth defendants were not 'investors' for the purposes of Article 28(1) of the Annex 1. Having regard to the context, object and purpose of Annex 1, the High Court also rejected the argument that 'investors' in Article 28(1) was intended to extend to domestic investors. The court reasoned that applying the definition of 'investor' to Lesotho nationals would invariably include 'every national who had ever purchased property, acquired company shares, or acquired licenses to exploit natural resources',[80] which would constitute a significant intrusion into State sovereignty. This

77 *ATA Construction, Industrial and Trading Company* v. *The Hashemite Kingdom of Jordan*, ICSID Case No ARB/08/2, Award, 18 May 2010.

78 *Chevron Corporation (USA) and Texaco Petroleum Company (USA)* v. *The Republic of Ecuador*, PCA Case No. 2007–02, Interim Award, 1 December 2008.

79 *Lesotho* at [269].

80 *Lesotho* at [333].

precluded personal jurisdiction over the Lesotho defendants, leading to the same outcome on jurisdiction *ratione personae* as the Tribunal.[81]

As a question of admissibility, the High Court considered whether the investors had exhausted local remedies as required by the Investment Protocol. It concluded that the investors had not done so, because the earlier litigation was related to the separate dispute involving expropriation. Furthermore, Lesotho's domestic courts recognized a special 'Aquilian action' to seek compensation for economic loss. The High Court rejected the investors' argument that an Aquilian action would be futile, noting Lesotho court precedents favour of investors. The High Court also dispelled the notion, suggested by the investors, that a local court judgment's unenforceability meant that the test for no effective remedy had been met. It held that a local remedy need not be capable of yielding the exact same relief as that the international tribunal could give. In making this finding, the High Court also disagreed with the PCA Tribunal which held that an Aquilian action would not have provided effective redress since the primary remedy for the shuttering claim was to provide the investors with an opportunity to have their expropriation claim heard and the domestic courts simply did not have the power to order such a remedy. The High Court disagreed with what it deemed as a conflation of the shuttering and expropriation disputes, holding that the shuttering of the SADC Tribunal amounted to a loss of opportunity, which could be addressed by any remedy that compensates for the loss of that opportunity.

This analysis regarding exhaustion of local remedies may attract some debate, since the law on this issue is far from settled and the High Court was willing to accept the possibility of an Aquilian action, while acknowledging that there was no direct authority confirming its availability in the Lesotho courts and that it would require 'a significant extension' of the existing case law for Lesotho's courts to recognize an Aquilian claim by the Investors.[82] Notably, the High Court held, as a matter of principle that, 'the mere absence of judicial authority showing that the remedy would be available does not justify concluding that it is unavailable'.[83] The investors bore the burden of establishing that they had exhausted local remedies.

To discharge this burden, the investors had to, in the words of the Court, adduce 'evidence positively demonstrating' that an Aquilian action is unavailable or ineffective with reference to the shuttering dispute.[84] With the Court recording that the investors had acknowledged that no steps had been taken in Lesotho's legal system regarding the shuttering dispute, this would have been a tall order.[85]

The Court of Appeal, in a unanimous judgment delivered by Chief Justice Sundaresh Menon, upheld the High Court's decision that the PCA Tribunal did not have jurisdiction and that the award had to be set aside.[86] It is noteworthy that although the Court relied on the 'generally accepted principle in international investment law' of territoriality, that jurisdictional limitation is usually invoked to ensure that the underlying investment has the necessary economic link with the host state to justify the treaty's investment protections.[87] The Court of

81 Rachel Tan and Lucy Reed, 'Developing Singaporean Jurisprudence on Reviewing Investor-State Arbitral Award' (9 October 2017).
82 *Lesotho* at [309].
83 *Lesotho* at [303].
84 *Lesotho* at [309].
85 Darius Chan, 'Lesotho sets aside award before the Singapore High Court', Kluwer Arbitration Blog, 18 September 2017.
86 *Swissbourgh Diamond Mines (Pty) Ltd* v. *Kingdom of Lesotho* [2018] SGCA 81 (*Lesotho* (SGCA)).
87 See, for example, the decision of the majority in *Abaclat* v. *Argentina* (ICSID Case No ARB/07/5, Decision on Jurisdiction and Admissibility of 4 August 2011), para. 374.

Appeal held that Lesotho was not estopped by statements its officials had made which were not directed at the *jurisdiction* of the PCA Tribunal, but were directed instead at the *merits* question of whether the claimants should have an alternative forum available, and in this case was expressly conditional on the PCA Tribunal having jurisdiction in the first place. The Court of Appeal made clear that since 'an investment treaty reflects the balance that has been struck between investor protection and the State's interests (generally following a considered period of negotiations between two or more States), *neither an unequivocally pro-investor nor pro-State approach should be adopted in interpreting the provisions* of an investment treaty'(emphasis added).[88]

While most of the Court's findings were arguably specific to the particular facts of the dispute and the wording of the SADC Treaty, this judgment nevertheless provides useful guidance, together with *Sanum*, as to the Singapore apex court's fair and balanced approach to the interpretation of international treaties in the context of investor–State arbitrations. Both the *Sanum* and *Lesotho* cases show that parties to investor–State arbitrations which may have subsequent recourse to Singapore courts for curial assistance can expect a robust, *de novo* analysis of the underlying treaty in light of international investment law jurisprudence, even if that analysis departs from the position taken by the treaty parties or arbitral tribunals. These judicial developments, coupled with the promulgation of the SIAC Investment Arbitration Rules and the recent establishment of regional offices for both the PCA and ICC in Singapore, demonstrate that Singapore is well placed to become a regional hub for investment arbitration.

2.5 CONCLUSION

Courts in Singapore are perceived to have given due recognition to international arbitration, party autonomy and the finality of the arbitral process. The Singapore government has been equal to the task by ensuring that domestic UNCITRAL Model Law-based arbitration legislation keeps apace with international jurisprudence. Singapore 'has adopted a very supportive environment for enforcement of international arbitration agreements and arbitral awards in line with its pro-arbitration philosophy'.[89] That is not to say, however, that the regulation of investment disputes should always be left to arbitrators alone. There is an increased desire among Asian States – some of which have become large-scale capital exporters – to preserve the *flexibility* to set legislative and regulatory priorities in striking a balance between safeguarding public welfare objectives and protecting the legal rights and interests of investors.[90]

As Asian States such as Singapore seek to be 'rule-makers', there is also a call to reform the ISDS process to ensure consistency, accountability, and transparency. We see this manifest in the provisions of new generation treaties such as the EUSIPA, which *inter alia*, establishes a two-tier investment adjudication system aimed at ensuring impartial, swift and transparent dispute resolution.

Singapore has also established the Singapore International Commercial Court (SICC), an internationalised court within the jurisdiction and as a division of the Singapore High Court,

88 *Lesotho(SGCA)* at [63].

89 Loretta Malintoppi and Charis Tan, 'Singapore', in Loretta Malintoppi and Charis Tan (eds.), *Investment Protection in Southeast Asia* (2016), p. 301; see generally *India v Vedanta Resources plc* [2020] SGHC 208.

90 M. Sornarajah, *Resistance and Change in the International Law on Foreign Investment* (Cambridge: Cambridge University Press, 2015), p. 214.

with a mix of local and foreign judges. The SICC has been touted to be an avenue to alleviate the limitations of investor-State arbitration, particularly in the realm of a state's regulatory protection.[91] Much like the European Commission's vision of a multilateral international investment court with tenured judges to replace *ad hoc* bilateral mechanisms, the SICC is a standing court. Notably, the SICC offers litigants, including those in ISDS-type cases, the option of having their disputes adjudicated by a 'panel of experienced judges comprising specialist commercial judges from Singapore and international judges from both civil law and common law traditions', and all appeals will be heard by the Court of Appeal of Singapore .[92] The country's Senior Minister of State for Law and Finance (as she then was) has noted as follows:[93]

> International economic trends point towards continued demand for international commercial dispute resolution in Asia. These include continued ASEAN economic integration and cross border infrastructure projects, including the Belt and Road Initiative. *The economic centre of gravity is slowly but surely shifting to Asia. Demand for dispute resolution will grow.* The SICC is well positioned to meet the growth of international litigation (emphasis added).

Viewed in this light, Singapore is poised to set further standards in the gravitational shift towards Asia as an early adopter of the next phase of significant IIA and ISDS reforms.

91 Juanito James Losari, 'Innovation in international arbitration: does the Emperor need new clothes? A Domestic Solution to an International Concern: Potential Appellate Solutions for Investor-State Dispute Settlement', CIArb Singapore Branch International Essay Competition (2015).

92 'About the SICC' (*SICC website*, 2014) www.sicc.gov.sg/About.aspx?id=21.

93 Indranee Rajah, 'The Supreme Court of Judicature (Amendment) Bill and the Singapore International Commercial Court' (*A Note from Indranee Rajah, Senior Minister of State for Law and Finance, 16 January 2018*).

3

Pharmaceutical Patents and Expropriation in Indian Bilateral Investment Treaties

Prabhash Ranjan[1]

3.1 INTRODUCTION

In the last few years, foreign investors have start using investor–State dispute settlement (ISDS) to challenge a host State's regulatory measures pertaining to intellectual property rights (IPR).[2] To give some examples, foreign investors have used ISDS to challenge the following regulatory measures: invalidation of a pharmaceutical patent by a domestic court on the ground of 'inutility';[3] adoption of legislation mandating plain packaging of tobacco products;[4] and adoption of regulations that prohibit tobacco companies from selling different variants for each family brand combined with the regulation that images of the health warning on cigarette packets should increase from taking up 50 per cent to 80 per cent of the cigarette packets.[5] Although the analysis of the interface between IPR and international investment law began before investors started using ISDS to challenge IPR-related host State regulatory measures,[6] the topic has started to attract much more attention after these arbitral

1 Assistant Professor, Faculty of Law, South Asian University. The author is extremely grateful to Souvik Mukherjee, LLM Candidate at the South Asian University, for his very proficient research assistance for this paper.

2 *Eli Lilly and Company* v. *Canada*, ICSID Case No. UNCT/14/2, Notice of Intent to Submit a Claim to Arbitration under NAFTA Chapter 11, 7 November 2012; *Philip Morris Asia Limited* v. *Australia*, PCA Case No. 2012–12, Award on Jurisdiction and Admissibility, 17 December 2015; *Philip Morris* v. *Uruguay*, ICSID Case No. ARB/10/7, Award, 8 July 2016.

3 Eli Lilly, a US pharma company, has challenged the invalidation of its patent by a Canadian federal court – *Eli Lilly* v. *Canada*, above n 2; *See also* Valentia Vadi, 'Towards a New Dialectics: Pharmaceutical Patents, Public Health and Foreign Direct Investments' (2015) 5 *New York University Journal of Intellectual Property and Entertainment Law* 113 at 117; Henning Grosse Ruse-Khan, 'Challenging Compliance with International Intellectual Property Norms in Investor-state Dispute Settlement' (2016) 19 *Journal of International Economic Law* 241–77 at 246–48; Kathleen Liddell and Michael Waibel, 'Fair and Equitable Treatment and Judicial Patent Decisions' (2016) 19 *Journal of International Economic Law* 145–74 at 155–56.

4 Philip Morris challenged Australia's legislation requiring tobacco products to be sold in plain packets of a specified colour without graphic logos and with health warnings on the front and back side of the pack covering 75 percent and 90 percent of the space – *see* Tania Voon et al., 'Intellectual Property Rights in International Investment Agreements: Striving for Coherence in National and International Law' in CL Lim and Bryan Mercurio (eds.), *International Economic Law after the Crisis: A Tale of Fragmented Disciplines* (Cambridge: Cambridge University Press, 2015), p. 380.

5 *Philip Morris* v. *Uruguay*, above n 2.

6 Carlos Correa, 'Bilateral Investment Agreements: Agents of New Global Standards for the Protection of Intellectual Property Rights' (2004), available at www.grain.org/article/entries/125-bilateral-investment-agreements-agents-of-new-global-standards-for-the-protection-of-intellectual-property-rights (last accessed 8 July 2019); Carlos Correa, 'Investment Protection in Bilateral and Free Trade Agreements: Implications for the Granting of Compulsory Licenses' (2004) 26 *Michigan Journal of International Law* 331; Lahra Liberti, 'Intellectual Property Rights in International Investment Agreements: An Overview' (2010) *OECD Working Paper on International Investment*, available at www.oecd.org/daf/inv/investment-policy/WP-2010_1.pdf (last accessed 8 July 2019); Rachel A Lavery, 'Coverage of Intellectual Property Rights in International Investment Agreements: An Empirical Analysis of Definitions in a Sample of Bilateral Investment Agreements and Free Trade Agreements' (2009) 6 *Transnational*

notices were issued.[7] Notwithstanding the growing literature, there is a dearth of country-specific studies examining the interface between IPR and international investment law. This chapter is a modest attempt to partially fill the dearth of such country-specific studies by discussing whether foreign investors, specifically pharmaceutical companies, are empowered to challenge regulatory measures that may be introduced by the Indian government and that impact the investor's patents under the investment chapters of India's bilateral investment treaties (BITs)[8] and free trade agreements (FTAs).[9] Specifically, this chapter focuses on whether regulatory measures, in particular the compulsory licensing of pharmaceutical patents, amount to indirect expropriation under India's BITs.[10] The focus of this chapter is on compulsory licenses (CL) issued on patented medicines. Compulsory licensing is defined generally as the granting of a license by a government to a third party to use the patent without the consent of the patent holder.[11] The Indian Patents Act of 1970[12] provides that three years after the grant of a patent, a CL may be granted on certain grounds[13] and under certain terms and conditions.[14] One such condition given in Section 90(1)(i) is that reasonable royalty and other remuneration should be paid to the patent holder. CLs provide important flexibility and are expressly included in the

Dispute Management Journal 1; Prabhash Ranjan, 'Medical Patents and Expropriation in International Investment Law' (2008) 5(3) *Manchester Journal of International Economic Law* 72; Christopher Gibson, 'A Look at the Compulsory License in Investment Arbitration: The Case of Indirect Expropriation' (2010) 25(3) *American University International Law Review* 368.

7 Bryan Mercurio, 'Awakening the Sleeping Giant: Intellectual Property Rights in International Investment Agreements' (2012) 15 *Journal of International Economic Law* 871; Lukas Vanhonnaeker, *Intellectual Property Rights as Foreign Direct Investments: From Collision to Collaboration* (Cheltenham: Edward Elgar, 2015), pp. 9–27.

8 India has signed 83 BITs – *see* Investment Policy Hub, UNCTAD, India, BITs available at https://investmentpolicy.unctad.org/international-investment-agreements/countries/96/india?type=bits (last accessed 8 July 2019). The Indian government recently stated that it has terminated 58 of these BITs – *see* Government of India, Ministry of Commerce & Industry, Department of Industrial Policy & Promotion, Lok Sabha Unstarred Question No. 1290 (25 July 2016). Generally most BITs continue to remain effective for a period of 10 to 15 years (depending on treaty language) for the investments made before the termination of the BIT. For example, Article 15(3) of the India-Indonesia BIT states: 'Notwithstanding termination of this Agreement . . . .the Agreement shall continue to be effective for a further period of fifteen years from the date of its termination in respect of investments made or acquired before the date of termination of this Agreement'. For the evolution of India's BITs, *see* Prabhash Ranjan, 'India and Bilateral Investment Treaties – A Changing Landscape' (2014) 29 *ICSID Review – Foreign Investment Law Journal* 419.

9 India has signed five free trade agreements (FTAs) containing investment chapters – Investment Policy Hub, UNCTAD, India, Treaties with Investment Provisions, available at https://investmentpolicy.unctad.org/international-investment-agreements/countries/96/india?type=bits (last accessed 8 July 2019);. For the evolution of India's BITs, *see* Prabhash Ranjan, 'India and Bilateral Investment Treaties – A Changing Landscape' (2014) 29 *ICSID Review – Foreign Investment Law Journal* 419.

10 It is important to bear in mind that regulatory measures related to pharmaceutical patents such as the invalidation of patents or the issuance of compulsory licenses could also be challenged under other substantive BIT provisions such as fair and equitable treatment. Liddell and Waibel discuss the tensions between the interpretation of national patent laws by domestic courts and how fair and equitable treatment (FET) obligations under BITs could be challenged – *see* Liddell and Waibel, above n 3. *See also* Mercurio, who discusses the various substantive BIT grounds such as national treatment, most favoured nation and FET under which foreign investors can challenge regulatory measures pertaining to IPRs – Mercurio, 'Awakening the Sleeping Giant', above n 7, at 882–901. However, given the constraints of space, this paper only focuses on expropriation.

11 WTO, Compulsory Licensing of Pharmaceuticals and TRIPS, available at www.wto.org/english/tratop_e/trips_e/public_health_faq_e.htm (September 2006) (last accessed 8 July 2019); *see also* Sara M Ford, 'Compulsory Licensing Provisions under TRIPS Agreement: Balancing Pills and Patents' (2000) 15 *American University Law Review* 941; Theresa Beeby Lewis, 'Patent Protection for the Pharmaceutical Industry: A Survey of Patent Laws of Various Countries' (1996) 30 *International Lawyer* 835 at 845.

12 Intellectual Property India, The Patents Act, 1970, available at www.wipo.int/edocs/lexdocs/laws/en/in/in065en.pdf (last accessed 8 July 2019).

13 *See* Section 84, Indian Patents Act, 1970.

14 *See* Section 90, Indian Patents Act, 1970.

Agreement on Trade-Related Aspects of Intellectual Property Rights (TRIPS Agreement) provisions to enable countries to achieve the objective of public health by increasing accessibility to affordable medicines.[15]

While the significance of CL in India for public health purposes has been adequately highlighted,[16] its interface with Indian BITs has rarely been discussed.[17] Exploring this interface is important for three reasons. First, globally, in addition to foreign investors suing host States under BITs for regulatory measures pertaining to IPRs in general, there are specific examples of pharmaceutical companies challenging various regulatory measures pertaining to patents under BITs.[18]

Second, in recent years, concerns have been expressed in India about the possibility of foreign investors challenging regulatory measures pertaining to pharmaceutical patents as unlawful expropriation under India's BITs. For instance, the Ministry of Commerce and Industry of India first articulated this concern in a 2011 discussion paper on BITs. The paper, in addition to highlighting other concerns pertaining to the exercise of regulatory power vis-à-vis BITs, highlighted that the issuance of CLs by the Indian government on a drug patented by a foreign pharmaceutical company could trigger claims of indirect expropriation.[19] This concern was expressed again[20] when India issued its first CL in March 2012 in favour of a domestic generic pharmaceutical company called 'Natco Pharma', for a patent granted on a drug to treat kidney and liver cancer to Bayer.[21] This CL was issued under Section 84 of the Indian Patent Act on the following grounds: unreasonable prices, reasonable requirements of public not being met and lack of local manufacturing.[22] The issuance of the CL was upheld by the Supreme Court of India.[23]

15 *See* Article 5(b), Declaration on the TRIPS Agreement and Public Health, WT/MIN(01)/DEC/2, 20 December 2001, available at www.wto.org/english/thewto_e/minist_e/min01_e/mindecl_trips_e.htm (last accessed 8 July 2019), that clearly recognises the importance of CLs as a flexible measure within the TRIPS Agreement to help countries achieve the objective of public health.

16 K. M. Gopakumar and Tahir Amin, 'Patents Amendment Bill 2005: A Critique' (2005) 40(15) *Economic and Political Weekly* 1503; Jodie Liu, 'Compulsory Licensing and Anti-Evergreening: Interpreting the TRIPS Flexibilities in Section 84 and 3(d) of the Indian Patents Act' (2015) 56(1) *Harvard International Law Journal* 207 at 212; Yogesh Pai, 'The Growing Irrelevance of a TRIPS Challenge to India's Patent Law' in Won-Mog Choi (eds.) *International Economic Law: The Asia-Pacific Perspectives* (Cambridge Scholars Publishing, 2015), p. 286; V. K. Unni, 'Compulsory Licensing of Pharmaceutical Patents in India: Whether the Natco Decision will meet the Global Benchmarks?' (2015) 37 *European Intellectual Property Review* 296; Feroz Ali, *The Access Regime: Patent Law Reforms for Affordable Medicines* (New Delhi: Oxford University Press, 2016).

17 The concern regarding the issuance of compulsory licensing being challenged by foreign investors under Indian BITs as indirect expropriation was first flagged by this author in 2008. *See* Ranjan, above n 6.

18 These include: *Eli Lilly* v. *Canada*, above n 3; *Apotex Holdings Inc* v. *United States (Apotex III)*, ICSID Case No ARB(AF)/12/1, Award, 25 August 2014; *Les Laboratoires Servier, SAS., Biofarma, SAS., Arts et Techniques du Progres* v. *Republic of Poland*, Award, 14 February 2012.

19 Ministry of Commerce, 'International Investment Agreements Between India and Other Countries' (2011) (document on file with author).

20 Biswajit Dhar et al., 'India's Bilateral Investment Agreements: Time to Review' (2012) 47(52) *Economic and Political Weekly* 113 at 117; Nandan Nelivigi et al., 'Indian Patent Office Grants Compulsory License for Bayer's Nexavar: Implications for Multinational Drug Companies' available at www.whitecase.com/publications/alert/indian-patent-office-grants-compulsory-license-bayers-nexavar-implications (2 April 2012) (last accessed 8 July 2019).

21 *Bayer Corp.* v. *Natco Pharma. Ltd.*, Order No. 45/2013 (Intellectual Property Appellate Board, Chennai, 2013); Shamnad Basheer, 'Breaking News: India's first Compulsory License Granted' available at https://spicyip.com/2012/03/breaking-news-indias-first-compulsory.html (12 March 2012) (last accessed 8 July 2019); Unni, above n 16, at 296.

22 For more details on this case, *see* Unni, above n 16; Pai, above n 16; Yogesh Pai, 'Promoting Diversity in Pharmaceutical Innovation and Access: India's Experience in the Post-TRIPS World' in Irene Calboli and Srividhya Ragavan (eds.), *Diversity in Intellectual Property: Identities, Interests and Intersections* (Cambridge: Cambridge University Press, 2015), p. 76; Enrico Bonadio, 'India Grants a Compulsory License of Bayer's Patented Cancer Drug: The Issue of Local Working Requirement' (2012) 2 *European Journal of Risk Regulation* 247.

23 *Bayer Corporation* v. *Union of India*, Petition for Special Leave to Appeal (C) NO (S). 30145/2014 (12 December 2014).

Third, and more generally, a large number of foreign investors have sued India in recent years, under different BITs, for a range of regulatory measures. Towards the end of 2011, a tribunal in *White Industries v. India*[24] found that India had violated its obligations under the India–Australia BIT.[25] This award is significant because it is the first known adverse ISDS award against India. It was followed by a number of foreign corporations slapping investment treaty arbitration (ITA) notices against India: Vodafone has issued an arbitral notice to India under the India–Netherlands BIT for an allegedly retrospective taxation measure;[26] Cairn Energy has also dragged India into arbitration under the India–UK BIT for an alleged retrospective taxation measure;[27] Germany's Deutsche Telekom has issued a notice of arbitration to India under the India–Germany BIT over a cancelled satellite venture;[28] France's Louis Dreyfus Armateurs (LDA) has brought a case against India under the India–France BIT, challenging a series of measures adopted by the Indian government that allegedly prevented the implementation of a joint venture project to modernize the Haldia port in Kolkata, India;[29] and Tenoch Holdings, another foreign investor, has issued an arbitral notice against India under the India–Russia and India–Cyprus BITs for its withdrawal of approval to grant telecom licenses.[30] Recently, the Permanent Court of Arbitration (PCA), in a dispute between Devas Multimedia's Mauritian investors and India,[31] concluded that India had violated the India–Mauritius BIT.[32] These cases demonstrate India's increased vulnerability to BIT claims, including claims from foreign pharmaceutical companies, which underscores the need to examine the regulatory space accorded to patent-related regulatory measures.

In order to address the core question posed, Section II of this chapter first determines whether pharmaceutical patents qualify as 'foreign investment' under Indian BITs. This examination will be done at two levels – by considering, first, whether pharmaceutical patents fall under the definition of 'investment' under the BIT, and second, whether pharmaceutical patents satisfy the economic characteristics of 'investment'. This approach has been adopted by many arbitral tribunals in determining whether they have jurisdiction over the dispute. In Section III, the chapter asks specifically whether the issuance of CLs on medicines amounts to unlawful expropriation under Indian BITs, with special reference to the 2016 Model BIT.[33]

24 *White Industries Australia Limited* v. *Republic of India*, UNCITRAL, Final Award, 30 November 2011.

25 *White Industries Australia Limited* v. *Republic of India*, above n 24, para. 16.1.1 (a).

26 *Vodafone International Holdings BV* v. *Government of India [I]*, UNCTIRAL, PCA Case No. 2016–35, Notice of Arbitration (not public), 17 April 2014.

27 *Cairn Energy PLC and Carin UK Holdings Limited* v. *The Republic of India*: PCA Case No. 2016–7. In this case, the arbitration tribunal has been constituted.

28 *Deutsche Telekom* v. *India*, PCA Case No. 2014–10, Interim Award of 17 December 2010.

29 *Louis Dreyfus Armateurs SAS* v. *The Republic of India*, PCA Case No. 2014–26. On this also *see* Bhushan Satish and Shreyas Jayasimha, Indian Courts First Brush with Investment Treaty Arbitration: Taking Some Lessons from the Calcutta High Court, available at http://kluwerarbitrationblog.com/2015/03/16/indian-courts-first-brush-with-investment-treaty-arbitration-taking-some-lessons-from-the-calcutta-high-court (20 February 2017) (last accessed 8 July 2019). In this case, an arbitration tribunal has also been constituted.

30 *Tenoch Holdings Limited, Mr Maxim Naumchenko and Mr Andre Poluektov* v. *The Republic of India*, PCA Case No. 2013–23.

31 *CC/Devas (Mauritius) Ltd., Devas Employees Mauritius Private Limited, and Telcom Devas Mauritius Limited* v. *Republic of India*, PCA Case No. 2013–09, UNCITRAL, 30 September 2013.

32 'Antrix-Devas Deal: Permanent Court of Arbitration rules against Indian government', The Indian Express, Bengaluru, 27 July 2016 available at http://indianexpress.com/article/business/business-others/antrix-devas-deal-hague-international-tribunal-rules-against-indian-govt/ (25 September 2016) (last accessed 8 July 2019).

33 Model Text of the Indian Bilateral Investment Treaty 2016, www.mygov.in/sites/default/files/master_image/Model%20Text%20for%20the%20Indian%20Bilateral%20Investment%20Treaty.pdf (last accessed 8 July 2019) [hereinafter '2016 Indian Model BIT']. It is important to keep in mind that the Indian Model BIT contains two dates: 28 December 2015, given in the letter accompanying the text, and 14 January 2016, provided on the website of the Ministry of Finance, Government of India (www.finmin.nic.in/ (last accessed 8 July 2019) as the date of

In this context, the chapter also discusses the draft Indian Model BIT of 2015.[34] This question will be answered by dividing the discussion into two parts – first by looking at the investment chapters in BITs or FTAs that specifically exempt issuance of CL from the ambit of expropriation; and then by considering the position under the BITs or FTAs with no such exemption. This part of the chapter also examines whether payment of royalty or remuneration to patent holders for issuing a CL, as mandated by Section 90 of the Indian Patents Act, disqualifies the issuance of the CL being pronounced an act of expropriation. Section IV offers the conclusion that pharmaceutical patents would easily qualify as foreign investments under Indian BITs, and some final thoughts.

3.2 PHARMACEUTICAL PATENTS AS FOREIGN INVESTMENTS: THE JURISDICTIONAL QUESTION

Host States only owe obligations under a BIT to 'investments that fall within the treaty's scope of applications or treaty definitions'.[35] Therefore, it is pertinent to examine whether pharmaceutical patents are considered 'investments' under Indian BITs.[36] We will follow what is known as the two-tier examination[37] or the 'double-keyhole approach'.[38] At the first level, also called the 'subjective' or 'variable' criteria for defining 'investment', we will determine whether pharmaceutical patents fall under the definition of 'investment' based on the wording of the specific BIT in question.[39] The second level is called the 'fixed' or 'objective' criteria to define investment whereby for an asset to qualify as an 'investment', it should satisfy certain economic requirements such as a commitment of capital, the expectation of gain or profit, assumption of risks, and so on.[40] Under the second level, we will find out whether pharmaceutical patents qualify as 'investment' under the jurisdictional terms of arbitral rules authorized by the concerned BIT (such as Article 25 of the ICSID Convention under which a tribunal's jurisdiction extends 'to any legal dispute arising directly out of an investment'). The origin of this two-tier examination lies in the manner in which ICSID arbitral tribunals, deciding on the issue of jurisdiction, have approached the question of what constitutes

adoption of the Model BIT. In this paper, we use the date of 14 January 2016, and thus refer to the Model BIT as the 2016 Indian Model BIT and *not* the 2015 Indian Model BIT. For a detailed discussion on the 2016 Indian Model BIT, *see* Prabhash Ranjan et al., 'The 2016 Model Indian Bilateral Investment Treaty: A Critical Deconstruction' (2017) 38(1) *Northwestern Journal of International Law and Business* 1–53.

34 Draft Model Text of the Indian Bilateral Investment Treaty, available at www.mygov.in/sites/default/files/master_image/Model%20Text%20for%20the%20Indian%20Bilateral%20Investment%20Treaty.pdf (last accessed 8 July 2019).

35 Jeswald Salacuse, *The Law of Investment Treaties* (Oxford: Oxford University Press, 2015), p. 174.

36 On IPRs as investment *see* Correa, 'Bilateral Investment Agreements' (2004), above n 6; Liberti, 'Intellectual Property Rights in International Investment Agreements' (2010), above n 6; Lavery, 'Coverage of Intellectual Property Rights in International Investment Agreements' (2009), above n 6; Vanhonnaeker, *Intellectual Property Rights as Foreign Direct Investments*, above n 7, pp. 9–27.

37 This two-tier examination of IPRs as investments has been done by James David Mortenson, 'Intellectual Property as Transnational Investment: Some Preliminary Observations' (2009) 2 *Transnational Dispute Management Journal* 1 at 6–7. *See also* Christopher Gibson, 'Latent Grounds in Investor-State Arbitration: Do International Investment Agreements Provide New Means to Enforce Intellectual Property Rights? in K. Sauvant (eds.) *Yearbook on International Investment Law and Policy* (Oxford: Oxford University Press, 2009–10), pp. 431–32; Voon et al., 'Intellectual Property Rights in International Investment Agreements' (2015), above n 4, pp. 384–86; Vanhonnaeker, *Intellectual Property Rights as Foreign Direct Investments* (2015), above n 7, pp. 9–27.

38 R. Dolzer and C. Schreuer, *Principles of International Investment Law* (Oxford: Oxford University Press, 2008).

39 Voon et al. (2015), above n 4, p. 384.

40 Voon et al. (2015), above n 4, p. 384; *see also* C. Schreuer with L. Malintoppi, A. Reinisch and A. Sinclair, *The ICSID Convention: A Commentary* (Cambridge: Cambridge University Press, 2nd edition, 2009); Katia Yannaca-Small, 'Definition of Investment: An Open-ended Search For a Balanced Approach' in Katia Yannaca-Small (ed.) *Arbitration Under International Investment Agreements* (Oxford: Oxford University Press, 2010), p. 254.

foreign investment. Many ICSID tribunals have held that for them to have jurisdiction over a dispute between a foreign investor and the host State, an asset must be an 'investment' under Article 25 of the ICSID Convention and also under the definition of 'investment' given in the BIT.[41] An important case in this regard is *Salini v. Morocco*, which laid down certain characteristics an asset has to satisfy to be an investment under Article 25 of the ICSID Convention.[42] This tribunal laid down the following criteria (also known as '*Salini* criteria') that need to be satisfied for an asset to be an 'investment' under Article 25 of the ICSID Convention – an investment should make a contribution, be of a certain duration, involve a certain element of risk, and contribute to the economic development of the country.[43] However, is this two-tier examination relevant in the case of pharmaceutical patents in Indian BITs since India is not a member of the ICSID Convention? We will examine this issue when we discuss the 'fixed' or 'objective' criteria.

3.2.1 *Subjective or Variable Criteria*

Patents are part of the definition of 'investment' in all Indian BITs, though the exact formulation differs from one BIT to another. For instance, many Indian BITs broadly provide for IPRs under the definition of 'investment' without specifically listing patents. One example is Article 1(b) of the India–Iceland BIT, which provides: 'investment means every kind of asset established or acquired, including changes in the form of such investment . . . though not exclusively includes intellectual property rights'.[44] This BIT neither lists patents nor any other IPR such as copyrights or trademarks as a covered investment.[45] However, reference to IPRs is sufficient to bring patents within the ambit of a covered investment. On the other hand, some Indian BITs specifically list patents as a covered investment. For instance, Article 1(2)(d) of the India–Austria BIT provides: 'the term investment shall mean every kind of asset established or acquired by an investor . . . though not exclusively: intellectual property rights such as copyrights, trademarks, patents, industrial designs'.[46] Although the 2016 Model BIT has moved away from a broad asset-based definition of 'investment' and provides for an enterprise-based definition of 'investment',[47] 'investment' includes assets of the enterprise, where one group of assets are IPRs with specific inclusion of patents.[48]

Despite this difference in formulation, the common aspect of IPR, within the definition of 'investment' in all Indian BITs, is the reference to the words 'in accordance with the relevant

[41] *Salini* v. *Morocco*, ICSID Case No ARB/00/4, Decision on Jurisdiction, 23 July 2001; *CSOB* v. *Slovakia*, ICSID Case No. ARB/97/4, Decision on Jurisdiction, May 24, 1999, para. 251.

[42] *Salini* v. *Morocco*, above n 41, paras. 51–58.

[43] Ibid., para. 52.

[44] *Agreement for The Promotion and Protection of Investments (India-Iceland)* (signed 26 June 2007, entered into force 2008).

[45] Similar language also exists in the following instruments: India-Armenia BIT, Art. 1(2); India-Bahrain BIT, Art. 1 (b); India-Bangladesh BIT, Art. 1(b); India-Belarus BIT, Art. 1(1); India-BLEU BIT, Art. 1(b); India-Bulgaria BIT, Art. 1(2); India-China BIT, Art. 1(b); India-Cyprus BIT, Art. 1(b); India-Egypt BIT, Art. 1(b); India-Jordan BIT, Art. 1(a); India-Latvia BIT, Art. 1(a); India-Mongolia BIT, Art. 1(b); India-Morocco BIT, Art. 1(1); India-Vietnam BIT, Art. 1(b) ; India-Mozambique BIT, Art. 1(b); India-Oman BIT, Art. 1(b); India-Philippines BIT, Art. 1(1); India-Portugal BIT, Art. 1(1); India-Romania BIT, Art. 1(b).

[46] India-Austria BIT, Art. 1(2)(d); similar or related formulation specifically including 'patents' as a covered investment also exist in the following treaties: India-Saudi Arabia BIT, Art. 1(1)(d); India-Slovakia BIT, Art. 1(1)(d); India-Spain BIT, Art. 1(2)(d); India-Finland BIT, Art. 1(1)(e); India-Germany BIT, Art. 1(b)(iv); India-Hungary BIT, Art. 1(1)(d); India-Czech BIT Republic, Art. 1(b)(iv); India-Denmark BIT, Art. 1(1)(iv); India-Italy BIT, Art. 1(1)(d); India-Senegal BIT, Art. 1(a)(iv); India-Kuwait BIT, Art. 1(2)(d); India-UAE BIT, Art. 1(1)(iv); India-Switzerland BIT, Art. 1(2)(d).

[47] *See* 2016 Indian Model BIT, above n 33, Art. 1.4, which gives the definition of 'investment'.

[48] Ibid., Art. 1.4 (f).

laws of the respective contracting party'.[49] For example, Article 1(1)(d) of the India–Philippines BIT states that 'investment means every kind of asset established or acquired . . . though not exclusively includes intellectual property rights in accordance with the relevant laws of the respective contracting party'.[50] The 2016 Model BIT also includes IPR within the definition of 'investment' 'to the extent they are recognized under the law of a Party'.[51] In other words, for an asset to be recognized as an IPR, and thus an 'investment' under Indian BITs, it must be a valid IPR as per Indian laws.[52] The significance of something like this can be gauged from the pre-2005 era in India when Indian law did not recognize product patents on pharmaceuticals.[53] Although all Indian BITs signed between 1994 to 2004 include IPR in the definition of investment without any exceptions, since product patents on pharmaceuticals was not a valid IPR in India, it would not have been part of the definition of 'investment' under the IPR category.[54]

However, the asset held by the foreign investor could still qualify as an 'investment' under some other category of 'investment' given in the BIT such as 'know-how',[55] provided the asset was legally valid under the domestic law.[56] Indeed, some Indian BITs specifically recognize 'know-how' as a separate category of 'foreign investment'.[57] Voon, Mitchell and Munro also argue that given the fact that tribunals have broadly interpreted the term 'asset' to mean any kind of property and everything of economic value, even if IPR are not part of the definition of 'investment', it would fall under the definition of 'investment' as 'an asset of any kind'.[58] In the case of India, this debate is only of academic significance now because from 1 January 2005, the Indian patent law was amended[59] to introduce product patents on pharmaceuticals owing to India's obligations

49 India-Austria BIT, Art. 1(2)(d); India-Italy BIT, Art. 1(1)(d); India-Germany BIT, Art. 1(b)(iv); India-Denmark BIT, Art. 1(1)(iv).

50 India-Philippines BIT, Art. 1(1)(d). *See also* India-Armenia BIT, Art. 1(2)(iv); India-Bangladesh BIT, Art. 1(b)(iv); India-Belarus BIT, Art. 1(1)(iv); India-Cyprus BIT, Art. 1(b)(iv); India-Portugal BIT, Art. 1(1)(d); India-China BIT, Art. 1(b)(iv); India-Iceland BIT, Art. 1(b)(iv); India-Jordan BIT, Art. 1(a)(iv); India-Latvia BIT, Art. 1(a)(iv); India-Qatar BIT, Art. 1(2)(iv); India-Romania BIT, Art. 1(b)(iv).

51 2016 Indian Model BIT, above n 33, Art. 1.4(f).

52 Correa and Vinaules describe this as the reliance model, whereby which investments enjoy treaty protection is delegated to domestic laws defining IPRs – *see* Carlos Correa and Jorge E Vinalues, 'Intellectual Property Rights as Protected Investments: How Open are the Gates?' (2016) 19 *Journal of International Economic Law* 91 at 95. *See also* Dolzer and Schreuer (2012), above n 38, p. 64.

53 Shamnad Basheer, 'India's Tryst with TRIPS: The Patents (Amendment) Act 2005' (2005) 1 *The Indian Journal of Law and Technology* 15.

54 *Salini* v. *Morocco*, above n 41, para. 46, which held that the words 'in accordance with the laws and regulations of the aforementioned party', occurring in Article 1 of the Italy-Jordan BIT, 'refers to the validity of the investment'. *See also Tokio Tokeles* v. *Ukraine*, ICSID Case No, ARB/02/18, Decision on Jurisdiction, 29 April 2004; *Alasdair Ross Anderson et al.* v. *Republic of Costa Rica*, ICSID Case No. ARB(AF)/07/31, Award, May 29, 2010; Salacuse (2010) above n 35, pp. 185–88. *See also* Ranjan (2008) above n 6; Voon et al. (2015) above n 4, p. 391; Marie Louise Seelig, 'Can Patent Revocation or Invalidation Constitute a Form of Expropriation?' (2009) 6(2) *Transnational Dispute Management* 1; Vanhonnaeker (2015), above n 7, pp. 15–16.

55 Correa and Vinuales (2016), above n 52, at 98.

56 The phrase 'in accordance with domestic laws' governs the legality of the investment and not its definition, which continues to be guided by the definition given in the BIT and, depending on certain factors, on the applicable arbitration rules such as the ICSID convention – *See Salini* v. *Morocco*, above n 41, para. 46.

57 India-UK BIT, Art. 1(b)(iv); India-Austria BIT, Art. 1(2)(d); India-Finland BIT, Art. 1(e); India-Spain BIT, Art. 1(2)(d); India-Germany BIT, Art. 1(b)(iv).

58 Voon et al. (2015), above n 4, pp. 391–92; *Romak SA* v. *Uzbekistan*, Permanent Court of Arbitration, Case No. AA280, Award, (26 November 2009), paras. 177–80; *Mytilineos Holdings SA* v. *Serbia and Montenegro and Serbia*, UNCITRAL, Partial Award on Jurisdiction, 8 September 2006, para. 106. Correa also argues that even if an IPR is not recognised as such in a host country, it could still be a covered investment falling under the category of 'intangible property' – *See* Correa (2004), above n 6.

59 Patents (Amendment) Act 2005, available at www.wipo.int/edocs/lexdocs/laws/en/in/in018en.pdf (last accessed 8 July 2019).

under WTO's TRIPS Agreement.[60] In other words, under India's extant legal system, product patents on pharmaceutical products are legally recognized IPR and thus will satisfy the subjective or variable criteria of the definition of 'investment' under the IPR category in all Indian BITs.

The treaty practice regarding specific reference to host States' domestic laws to determine the legality or validity of IPRs for the purpose of foreign investment is diverse in India's FTAs' investment chapters or investment agreements signed as part of an FTA. On one hand, under the India–Malaysia FTA investment chapter and India–ASEAN investment agreement, 'investment' includes IPRs but only those 'recognised pursuant to the laws and regulations of each party'.[61] On the other hand, India's other FTAs with Korea and Singapore do not make any specific reference to domestic laws of the host State to determine the validity or legality of the IPR so as to qualify as 'investment'.[62] A slightly different formulation exists in the India–Japan FTA, where the meaning of IPR for the purposes of definition of 'foreign investment' is to be taken from the TRIPS Agreement and not from India's domestic laws.[63] As far as pharmaceutical patents are concerned, this will not create any difference because India's patent laws are consistent with India's obligations under the TRIPS Agreement.[64]

3.2.2 *Fixed or Objective Criteria*

As mentioned before, for pharmaceutical patents to qualify as an 'investment', they may also need to satisfy the 'fixed' or 'objective' economic criteria, such as a commitment of capital, the expectation of gain or profit, or assumption of risks. In order to better understand this, we divide the discussion into two parts: BITs that contain the 'economic characteristics' test; and BITs that do not contain the 'economic characteristics' test.

3.2.2.1 BITs Containing the 'Economic Characteristics' Test

At times, these criteria are mentioned in the definition of 'investment' of the BIT but only with very few Indian BITs. For instance, Article 2.3 of the India–Colombia BIT states that minimum characteristics of investment shall be 'the commitment of capital or other resources', 'the expectation of gain or profit', and 'the assumption of risk for the investor'. These three criteria are also mentioned in the India–Mexico BIT[65] and in all Indian FTA investment chapters.[66] In other words, for a pharmaceutical patent to pass the jurisdictional obstacle, it will have to satisfy these economic characteristics. These economic characteristics could play an important role in situations where a pharmaceutical patent is granted, but the patent is not locally exploited (i.e. the drug is not domestically manufactured but imported). This has been found to be the case in India, where many foreign pharmaceutical companies merely import patented drugs and do not manufacture locally.[67] In situations such as this, it could be argued that by not manufacturing the patented drug in India, there is neither an

60 Basheer, 'India's Tryst with TRIPS' (2005), above n 53; Unni (2015), above n 16, at 298.

61 India-Malaysia FTA, Art. 10.2(d)(vi); India-ASEAN BIT, Art. 2(e)(iv).

62 India-Korea FTA, Art. 10.1.

63 India-Japan FTA, Arts. 3(i) and 102(2).

64 Pai, 'The Growing Irrelevance of a TRIPS Challenge' (2015), above n 16, 286.

65 *Agreement for The Promotion and Protection of Investments (India-Mexico)* (signed 21 May 2007, entered into force 23 February 2008), Art. 1(7).

66 India's FTA investment chapters with Korea, Singapore, Japan, Malaysia and ASEAN.

67 S. Basheer, 'The non-working of Patent working norms' (7 April 2011), available at https://spicyip.com/2011/04/non-working-of-patent-working-norms.html (last accessed 8 July 2019); G. B. Reddy and H. A. Kadri, 'Local Working of Patents – Law and Implementation in India' (2013) 18 *Journal of Intellectual Property Rights* 15.

assumption of risk nor a commitment of capital. Consequently, such pharmaceutical patents are not a 'covered investment' under the BIT.

The enterprise-based definition of 'investment' in the 2016 Model BIT[68] not only lists the three economic characteristics mentioned above (commitment of capital, assumption of risk and expectation of profit), but also two more characteristics – 'duration' (the period is not specified) and 'significance of the development for the country where the investment is made'.[69] However, it is not amply clear whether these characteristics have to be satisfied by the assets of the enterprise or by the enterprise[70] itself. This confusion arises because there is a comma after the words 'taken together with the assets of the enterprise' in Article 1.4. After the comma, the following words appear: 'has the characteristics of an investment such as . . . '. If the assets owned by the enterprise have to satisfy the 'characteristics test', then in place of the comma, the word 'that' should have been inserted. Thus, the text would have read: 'taken together with the assets of the enterprise that has the characteristics of an investment . . . '.[71] In the absence of the word 'that', it seems that an enterprise alone has to satisfy the 'characteristics test'.

The language of Article 1.4(h) also seems to suggest the same. Article 1.4(h) states 'any other interests of the enterprise which involve substantial economic activity and out of which the enterprise derives significant financial value'. In other words, 'any other interests of the enterprise' seems to have its own 'characteristics tests', which has two components: first, the 'interest' of the enterprise should involve substantial economic activity; second, the enterprise should derive significant financial value from this substantial economic activity. This indicates that the remaining assets, as they are identified as not having such a requirement, do not in fact need to pass the 'characteristics test'.

This might have implications at the practical level. For example, let us assume that a foreign pharmaceutical enterprise, legally constituted in India for last 10 years, gets a patent on a drug. After six months of granting the patent, the Indian government revokes the patent in public interest,[72] which the enterprise wishes to challenge before an arbitral tribunal. Here, will the 'characteristics test' of investment be required to be satisfied by the asset (patent) or by the enterprise? If it is the patent, then it will be difficult to satisfy the 'characteristics test' due to the short duration for which the asset has been in existence. If, on the other hand, the 'characteristics test' has to be satisfied by the enterprise, it will be relatively easier to fall under the definition of 'investment' and the short duration for which the patent right has been in existence will not matter.

Another related development that merits attention is that in early 2016, India initiated the process of endeavouring to issue a joint interpretative statement regarding the interpretation of India's BITs[73] with twenty-five countries.[74] On the question of the definition of 'investment,' the

68 2016 Indian Model BIT, above n 33.

69 Dolzer and Schreuer argue that this is a controversial criterion because any such examination will depend on the subjective assessment of the host State – *see* Dolzer and Schreuer (2012), above n 38, p. 75.

70 Enterprise is defined in Article 1.3 as '(i) any legal entity constituted, organised and operated in compliance with the law of a Party, including any company, corporation, limited liability partnership or a joint venture; and (ii) a branch of any such entity established in the territory of a Party in accordance with its law and carrying out business activities there'.

71 2012 US Model BIT, Art. 1.

72 Section 66 of the Indian Patent Act allows the central government of India to revoke a patent for public interest.

73 Government of India, Issuing Joint Interpretative Statement for Indian Bilateral Investment Treaty (8 February 2016); see discussion in Sarthak Malhotra, 'India's Joint Interpretative Statement for BITs: An Attempt to Slay the Ghosts of the Past', *Investment Treaty News* (12 December 2016), available at www.iisd.org/itn/2016/12/12/indias-joint-interpretive-statement-for-bits-an-attempt-to-slay-the-ghosts-of-the-past-sarthak-malhotra/#_edn3 (last accessed 17 July 2019).

74 So far only Bangladesh has accepted India's interpretative statement – *see* Jarrod Hepburn, 'Unable to Unilaterally Terminate a 2011 BIT, The Government of India Persuades Counter-Party to Agree Joint Interpretive Note to Clarify BIT's Implications', Investment Arbitration Reporter, 17 July 2017, available at www

statement provides that the 'minimum characteristics of an investment are (a) the lasting contribution of capital or other resources; (b) the expectation of gain or profit; (c) the assumption of risk by the investor; and (d) significance for development of the Contracting Party receiving the investment'.[75] This statement has no legal value until India's treaty partner countries accept it.

3.2.2.2 BITs That Do Not Contain the 'Economic Characteristics' Test

Barring the BITs and FTA investment chapters discussed before, Indian BITs do not mention these economic characteristics of investment in the definition of 'investment'. So, are the economic criteria mentioned above relevant in determining whether pharmaceutical patents are investments in these BITs? The answer to this question would depend on the approach adopted by an arbitral tribunal.[76] For instance, the approach of a large number of ICSID tribunals has been to consider these economic characteristics of investment 'as a threshold requirement for the exercise of jurisdiction'[77] though the number of economic criteria has fluctuated from three to six.[78] In this regard, the most controversial characteristic has been investment contributing to the host State's economic development due to the inherent subjectivity involved in making such determinations.[79] There are also some ICSID tribunals that have emphasized party autonomy, thus emphasizing that the definition of 'investment' in the BIT is key to determining jurisdiction and not random economic characteristics that are not mentioned in the ICSID Convention.[80]

This issue is particularly important in the case of India because India is not a member of ICSID, and thus only a non-ICSID tribunal will hear a dispute against her. Therefore, the question is to what extent these economic characteristics, when absent in the treaty, will be taken into account by non-ICSID tribunals in deciding the jurisdictional question. Again, there is no single answer. Some non-ICSID arbitral tribunals have used these economic characteristics.[81] For example, the tribunal in *Romak v. Uzbekistan* said that the term 'investments' under the BIT has an 'inherent meaning', irrespective of whether the dispute arises under the ICSID or UNCITRAL Rules.[82] According to the tribunal, this 'inherent meaning' of investment entails 'a contribution that extends over a certain period of time and that involves some risk'.[83]

On the other hand, some non-ICSID tribunals like *Flemingo* v. *Poland*,[84] while interpreting the definition of 'investment' in the India–Poland BIT, held that 'jurisdictional restrictions deriving

.iareporter.com/articles/unable-to-unilaterally-terminate-a-2011-bit-the-government-of-india-persuades-counter-party-to-agree-joint-interpretive-note-to-clarify-bits-implications/ (last accessed 8 July 2019).

75 Article 4(3) of Draft Joint Interpretative Statement, above n 73.

76 Ruth L. Okediji, 'Is Intellectual Property 'Investment'? *Eli Lilly* v. *Canada* and the International Intellectual Property System' (2014) 35 *University of Pennsylvania Journal of International Law* 1121 at 1126.

77 Voon et al., (2015), above n 4; *Salini* v. *Morocco*, above n 41; *Joy Mining Machinery Ltd.* v. *Arab Republic of Egypt*, ICSID Case No. ARB/03/11, Award on Jurisdiction, 6 August 2004, para. 63.

78 Dolzer and Schreuer (2012), above n 38, p. 75.

79 *See Phoenix Action, Ltd.* v. *Czech Republic*, ICSID Case No. ARB/06/5, Award, 15 April 2009, para. 85. For a more recent award, *see Philip Morris* v. *Uruguay*, above n 2.

80 *Malaysian Historical Salvors SDN BHD* v. *Malaysia*, ICSID Case No. ARB/05/10, Decision on Application for Annulment, 16 April 2009.

81 *Romak SA* v. *Uzbekistan*, Permanent Court of Arbitration, Case No. AA280, Award, 26 November 2009, paras. 115–20.

82 Ibid., para. 207.

83 Ibid. *See also Alps Finance and Trade AG* v. *Slovak Republic*, UNCITRAL, Award, 5 March 2011, paras. 230–47.

84 *Flemingo Duty Free Shop Private Limited* v. *Republic of Poland*, UNCITRAL, Award, 12 August 2016. This was the first instance of an Indian investor successfully suing a host State for a BIT violation.

from the notion of "investment" in Article 25 of the ICSID Convention, as emphasised by various ICSID tribunals such as the *Salini* panel, do not apply to the present arbitration'.[85] Thus, the tribunal clearly rejected the need for an asset to satisfy the different economic characteristics. Another case pertaining to India in this matter is *White Industries* v. *India*, where a non-ICSID arbitral tribunal, while first stating that the test developed by ICSID tribunals (where an asset also has to satisfy economic characteristics to qualify as an investment) was not applicable since the dispute was under a non-ICSID tribunal,[86] nonetheless went on to examine later, curiously, whether the four characteristics given by the *Salini* tribunal were satisfied or not.[87]

This will have implications in deciding questions such as whether pharmaceutical patents not utilized in India, as discussed previously, would qualify as 'covered investments' or not. If a tribunal were to adopt an approach similar to the one adopted in *Flemingo v. Poland*, the fact that a pharmaceutical patent is non-working might not be a bar in deciding whether it is a covered investment. Also, if economic characteristics are not taken into account, then arguably a patent application could fall under the definition of 'investment' as an 'intangible property'[88] or under headings such as 'activities associated with investments, such as the organisation and operation of business facilities, the acquisition, exercise and disposition of property rights including intellectual property rights' given in the India–Australia BIT.[89]

To summarize this discussion, whether pharmaceutical patents and activities associated with or related to the acquisition of the patent qualify as 'investment' requires a case-by-case examination. In the case of Indian BITs, pharmaceutical patents would easily satisfy the variable or subjective criteria. However, to what extent pharmaceutical patents would meet the requirements of fixed or objective criteria (or the so-called 'economic characteristics' test) would, to a great extent, depend on the language of the BIT and the approach adopted by the arbitral tribunal deciding this question. We now turn to the question of whether the issuance of CLs on a patented drug would amount to expropriation of the pharmaceutical patent under Indian BITs, including the 2016 Indian Model BIT.

3.3 EXPROPRIATION OF PHARMACEUTICAL PATENTS

We now consider whether an issuance of CLs on a patented drug would amount to expropriation under Indian BITs. We will first look at the how expropriation is understood in international investment law. Protection from expropriation – 'taking' of privately owned property by the government, except when expropriation is for public purpose, following due process and against due compensation – is one of the core guarantees given by host States to foreign investors under BITs.[90] If a state expropriates foreign investment satisfying the above stated requirements, the expropriation is lawful and not a breach of the BIT. If the host State

85 Ibid., para. 298.

86 *White Industries* v. *India*, above n 24, para. 7.4.9.

87 Ibid., paras. 7.4.10 to 7.4.19.

88 Liberti, 'Intellectual Property Rights in International Investment Agreements' (2010), above n 6; Gibson, 'Latent Grounds in Investor-State Arbitration' (2010), above n 37, at 433. *See also* Mercurio, 'Awakening the Sleeping Giant' (2012), above n 7, at 878; Vadi, 'Towards a New Dialectics' (2015), above n 3, at 150–52. An arbitral tribunal in *Apotex Holdings Inc* v. *United States (Apotex III)*, ICSID Case No ARB(AF)/12/1, Award, 28 December 2012, based on the facts of that case, held that patent applications were not investments within NAFTA (*see* para. 7.62). However, one arbitrator dissented and viewed the patent applications as property rights (*see* paras. 7.64 to 7.66).

89 *Agreement for The Promotion and Protection of Investments (India-Australia)* (signed 26 February 1999, entered into force 4 May 2000), Art. 1(c)(v).

90 Christopher F. Dugan et al., *Investor-State Arbitration* (New York: Oxford University Press, 2008), p. 429.

expropriates foreign investment without satisfying all these conditions, however, the expropriation would be unlawful and thus a breach of the BIT. Expropriation, in its classical sense, refers to direct or formal expropriation, which means that the host State takes away the legal title of the investment.[91] This can be achieved either by nationalization, which is referred to as expropriation of entire industry or sector,[92] confiscation, requisition or acquisition.[93]

Direct expropriations, which are easily identifiable, have become rare.[94] As modern States increasingly regulate various spheres of life, instances of indirect interference with investor's property rights have become more prominent. However, the difficulty is in determining when such indirect interference constitutes expropriation.[95] Indirect expropriation refers to the deprivation of the substantial benefits flowing from the investment without any formal 'taking' of the property.[96] The Iran–US Claims Tribunal in *Starrett Housing Corporation* v. *Iran* and *Tippetts* said the following on indirect expropriation:

> [I]t is recognized in international law that measures taken by a state can interfere with property rights to such an extent that these rights are rendered so useless that they must be deemed to have been expropriated, even though the state does not purport to have expropriated them and the legal title to the property formally remains with the original owner.[97]

Thus, the question is whether the issuance of CLs amounts to indirect expropriation by interfering with the exclusivity rights that a patent bestows on the patentee. We will answer this question for Indian BITs by dividing the treaties into two categories: first, those treaties that specifically provide that the issuance of CLs do not amount to expropriation; and second, BITs that do not contain any such provision.

3.3.1 *FTA Investment Chapters Exempting Certain Regulatory Measures from the Ambit of Expropriation*

India's FTA investment chapters provide that the expropriation provisions shall not apply to the issuance of CLs. For instance, Article 92.5 of the India–Japan FTA states that the expropriation provision shall not apply with respect to the granting of CLs concerning intellectual property in accordance with the TRIPS Agreement.[98] Similarly, Article 8(7) of the India–ASEAN investment agreement provides that 'this article does not apply to the

91 Salacuse (2010), above n 35, p. 294; M. Sornarajah, *The International Law on Foreign Investment* (New York: Cambridge University Press, 2010), p. 363; A. Newcombe and L. Paradell, *Law and Practice of Investment Treaties: Standards of Treatment* (Alphen aan den Rijn, The Netherlands: Wolters Kluwer Law and Business, 2009), p. 323.

92 Newcombe and Paradell (2009) above n 91, p. 323.

93 *See above* n 91.

94 *Feldman* v. *Mexico*, ICSID Case No ARB(AF)/99/1, Award, 16 December 2002, para. 100.

95 The *Feldman* tribunal recognised the difficulty by saying, at para. 100, that direct expropriation was relatively easy, whereas '*it is much less clear when the governmental action that interferes with broadly-defined property rights . . . crosses the line from valid regulation to compensable taking*'.

96 Dolzer and Schreuer (2008), above n 38, p. 92; Salacuse (2010), above n 35, p. 297.

97 *Starrett Housing Corporation* v. *Islamic Republic of Iran* (1983) 4 Iran-US CTR 122, 154. *See also Tippetts, Abbett, McCarthy, Stratton and TAMS-AFFA Consulting Engineers of Iran* v. *Islamic Republic of Iran* (1984) 6 Iran-US CTR 219, 225.

98 Article 92.5 of the India-Japan FTA states, 'This Article shall not apply with respect to the grant of compulsory licenses concerning intellectual property in accordance with the TRIPS Agreement'. *See also* India-Malaysia FTA, Art. 10.7(6); India-Korea FTA, Art. 10.12(6); India-Singapore FTA, Art. 6.5(6).

issuance of compulsory licenses granted in relation to intellectual property rights, in accordance with the TRIPS Agreement'.[99]

Article 6.5(6) of the India–Singapore FTA provides that:

> This Article does not apply to the issuance of compulsory licenses granted in relation to intellectual property rights, or to the revocation, limitation or creation of intellectual property rights to the extent that such issuance, revocation, limitation or creation is consistent with the WTO Agreement on Trade Related Aspects of Intellectual Property Rights.[100]

While the India–Malaysia and India–Japan FTAs discuss only the non-applicability of the expropriation provision in the situation of an issuance of CLs, the India–Korea FTA goes beyond this and also exempts the application of expropriation provisions to the revocation, limitation or creation of intellectual property provided that such revocation, limitation or creation is consistent with the TRIPS agreement.

Three points need to be made here. First, investment treaties that exempt the issuance of CLs from expropriation, but not the revocation or limitation of pharmaceutical patents, imply that foreign investors can still challenge the revocation or limitation of patents as indirect expropriation under these investment chapters. Second, even in India's investment chapters, notwithstanding the specific exemption of CLs from expropriation, foreign investors can still challenge the issuance of CLs as expropriation, arguing that CLs have not been issued in accordance with the TRIPS Agreement.[101] In other words, an ISDS tribunal, which may not have expertise in WTO law,[102] would then have to make a substantive determination as to whether the issuance of CLs is consistent with the TRIPS Agreement – if not, then the expropriation provision would continue to apply.[103] This also means that for all practical purposes wherever exemption of CLs from expropriation is made contingent on the consistency of CLs with the TRIPS Agreement, it does not exclude the jurisdiction of an ISDS tribunal from examining issuance of CLs as violations of the BIT. From the perspective of reconciling investment protection with a host State's right to regulate, allowing an ISDS tribunal to review issuance of CLs for its consistency with the TRIPS Agreement will minimize the possibility of host States misusing their right to issue CLs. Third, since these FTA investment chapters exempt issuance of CLs and other regulatory measures like revocation of patents only from the ambit of expropriation, these measures could still be challenged for violating other substantive obligations such as fair and equitable treatment (FET). This might be useful from the point of view of reconciling investment protection with the State's right to regulate.

99 *See also* Article 10.7(6) of the India-Malaysia FTA, which provides, 'This Article does not apply to the issuance of compulsory licenses granted in relation to intellectual property rights in accordance with the WTO Agreement on Trade Related Aspects of Intellectual Property Rights.'

100 Article 10.12(6) of the India-Korea FTA contains language exactly similar to Article 6.5(6) of the India-Singapore FTA – 'This Article does not apply to the issuance of compulsory licences granted in relation to intellectual property rights, or to the revocation, limitation or creation of intellectual property rights, to the extent that such issuance, revocation, limitation or creation is consistent with the TRIPS Agreement.'

101 *See* Gibson, 'Latent Grounds in Investor-State Arbitration' (2010), above n 37, at 421; Mercurio (2012), above n 7, at 905–06.

102 Mercurio (2012), above n 7, at 905.

103 Ibid.

3.3.2 *2016 Indian Model BIT*

The 2016 Model BIT, unlike India's FTA investment chapters, has a slightly different formulation as regards issuance of CLs and other regulatory measures like revocation or limitation of IPRs. Article 2.4(iii) provides that the treaty shall not apply to:

> the issuance of compulsory licenses granted in relation to intellectual property rights, or to the revocation, limitation or creation of intellectual property rights, to the extent that such issuance, revocation, limitation or creation is consistent with the international obligations of Parties under the WTO Agreement.

The major difference from India's FTA investment chapters is that the Model BIT makes the entire treaty inapplicable to the issuance of CLs and is not restricted merely to expropriation. The similarity is with respect to the Model BIT also making a reference to the WTO Agreement. As a result, the foreign investor can always challenge the issuance of CLs or revocation of a patent before an ITA tribunal arguing that the regulatory measure in question is not consistent with the WTO Agreement. As discussed before, this would give an ISDS tribunal the jurisdiction to decide consistency of the domestic regulatory measure with India's WTO obligations.

It is important to recall the different formulation given in the draft 2015 Model BIT. Article 2.6(v) of the draft model provided that the treaty shall not apply to:

> the issuance of compulsory licenses granted in relation to intellectual property rights, or to the revocation, limitation or creation of intellectual property rights, to the extent that such issuance, revocation, limitation or creation is consistent with the Law of the Host State.

The draft, unlike the final version, did not make any reference to the WTO Agreement, but made reference instead to domestic laws. This would better serve the host country's regulatory power. We can better understand this with the help of a practical example. Assume that the Indian government issues a CL on a patented drug, which is upheld by the Indian Supreme Court, as happened in the case of *Natco* v. *Bayer* discussed earlier. If the foreign investor challenges this before an ISDS tribunal, under the 2016 Model, she or he would have to show that the issuance of CL is inconsistent with the WTO Agreement. On the other hand, the foreign investor, under the draft 2015 Model, would have to show the CL has been issued inconsistently with Indian law. It is expected that the arbitral tribunal will more deferential to the Indian court's assessment as to whether CL has been issued in accordance with Indian law, whereas it will be less deferential when it comes to consistency with the WTO Agreement because here compliance with international law and not India's domestic law will be in question.

3.3.3 *Indian BITs that Do Not Make Any Reference to Issuance of CL*

Large numbers of Indian BITs do not specify the non-applicability of the expropriation to issuance of CLs. Thus, in all these BITs, foreign investors can challenge the issuance of CLs as indirect expropriation, irrespective of whether such issuance is consistent with the TRIPS Agreement. Since issuance of CLs would not involve any formal transfer of the title, foreign investors would challenge it as indirect expropriation. Determination of indirect expropriation, also known as regulatory expropriation, is difficult.

ISDS tribunals have developed three tests to determine whether indirect or regulatory expropriation has occurred. First, the 'sole effects' test, whereby the crucial factor in determining whether an indirect expropriation has occurred, is solely the effect of the governmental measure on the property, the purpose of the regulatory measure being irrelevant.[104] Focus on 'effect' of the regulatory measure to determine indirect expropriation raises the question of how severe the 'effect' must be to come to the conclusion that indirect expropriation has taken place. Tribunals have answered this question by saying that 'under international law, expropriation requires a 'substantial deprivation'.[105] In other words, tribunals have said that the effect should be such that it substantially deprives the investment and hence the test is of 'substantial deprivation' to determine indirect expropriation.[106] The effect can certainly be more than substantial such as in cases where the deprivation is complete or total. For example, the tribunal in *Total SA v. Argentina*[107] held that under international law, those measures that do not constitute direct expropriation may nevertheless result in indirect expropriation 'if an effective deprivation of the investment is thereby caused'.[108]

Second is the 'police powers' test whereby the purpose and context of the regulatory measure assumes significance in the determination of expropriation.[109] This doctrine basically means that if a State adopts a measure in the exercise of that State's police powers, there is no liability for any claim of expropriation due to that measure.[110] The best illustration of the police powers doctrine in international investment law is in *Methanex* v. *United States*[111] where the tribunal stated:

> As a matter of general international law, a non-discriminatory regulation for a public purpose, which is enacted in accordance with due process and, which affects, inter alios, a foreign investor or investment is not deemed expropriatory and compensable unless specific commitments had been given by the regulating government to the then putative foreign investor contemplating investment that the government would refrain from such regulation.[112]

Third is the proportionality test, which is defined by Kingsbury and Schill as 'a method of legal interpretation and decision making in situations of collisions or conflict of different principles and legitimate public policy objectives'.[113] The proportionality test will have three

104 R. Dolzer and F. Bloch, 'Indirect Expropriation: Conceptual Realignments?' (2003) 5 *International Law Forum du droit International* 155.

105 *Pope and Talbot* v. *Canada*, Ad hoc Tribunal (UNCITRAL), Interim Award, 26 June 2000, para. 96.

106 *PSEG* v. *Turkey*, ICSID Case No. ARB/02/5, Award, 19 January 2007, paras. 278–80; *CMS Gas Transmission Company* v. *Argentine Republic*, ICSID Case No ARB/01/8, Award, 12 May 2005, para. 262. *See also* other Argentina cases that have endorsed the 'substantial deprivation' test to determine indirect expropriation – *LG&E* v. *Argentine Republic*, ICSID Case No ARB/02/1, Decision on Liability, 3 October 2006, para. 194; *Sempra Energy International* v. *Argentine Republic*, ICSID Case No ARB/02/16, Award, 28 September 2007, paras. 284–85; *BG Group plc* v. *Argentine Republic*, UNCITRAL, Award, 24 December 2007, paras. 258–66; *Enron Corporation and Ponderosa Assets LP* v. *Argentine Republic*, ICSID Case No ARB/01/3, Award, 22 May 2007), para. 245.

107 *Total SA* v. *Argentina*, ICSID Case No. ARB/04/01, Decision on Liability, 27 December 2010.

108 *Total SA* v. *Argentina*, above n 107, para. 195.

109 M. Brunetti, 'Indirect Expropriation in International Law' (2003) 5 *International Law Forum du droit International* 150 at 151.

110 Ben Mostafa, 'The Sole Effects Doctrine, Police Powers and Indirect Expropriation under International Law' (2008) 15 *Australian International Law Journal* 267 at 272–73.

111 *Methanex Corporation* v. *United States of America*, UNCITRAL, Final Award on Jurisdiction and Merits, 3 August 2005.

112 Ibid., Part IV, Ch D, p. 4, para. 7; *Saluka Investments BV* v. *The Czech Republic*, UNCITRAL, Partial Award, 17 March 2006; *El Paso* v. *Argentina*, ICSID Case No. ARB/03/15, Award, 31 October 2011, para. 240.

113 Benedict Kingsbury and Stephan Schill, 'Public Law Concepts to Balance Investors' Rights with State Regulatory Actions in the Public Interest – The Concept of Proportionality', in Stephan Schill (ed.), *International Investment Law and Comparative Public Law* (Oxford: Oxford University Press, 2010), p. 79.

steps,[114] which must be assessed cumulatively.[115] First, whether the measure is suitable for the legitimate public purpose – this will require a causal link between the measure and its object.[116] If the measure satisfies the first step, then, the second step would be to find out whether the measure is necessary, that is, whether there is a less restrictive alternative measure that would achieve the same objective.[117] If indeed the measure is 'necessary', then the third step (also known as proportionality *stricto sensu*) will involve balancing the effects of the measure on the right that has been affected with the public benefit sought to be achieved by the measure.[118]

One of the first ISDS disputes which made a somewhat elaborate reference to the principle of proportionality is *Tecmed v. Mexico*.[119] The tribunal cited the European Court of Human Rights (ECtHR) jurisprudence[120] to support the proportionality test in its determination of indirect expropriation.[121] The tribunal held that 'there must be a reasonable relationship of proportionality between the charge or weight imposed to the foreign investor and the aim sought to be realized by any expropriatory measure'.[122]

Whether issuance of CLs amounts to indirect expropriation would depend on the approach adopted by the arbitral tribunal. If a tribunal were to adopt the police powers doctrine, then issuance of CLs for a non-discriminatory public health objective, in a manner consistent with the TRIPS Agreement and with Indian laws, will not amount to indirect expropriation.[123] The argument for application of the police powers doctrine will be stronger in the cases of those Indian BITs where the BIT provides a textual basis.

For instance, the India–Jordan BIT states:

> Except in rare circumstances, non-discriminatory regulatory actions by a Party that are designed and applied to protect legitimate public welfare objectives including health, safety and the environment concerns do not constitute expropriation or nationalisation.[124]

In view of a provision such as this, it could be argued that issuance of CLs for public health purposes does not amount to expropriation barring certain rare circumstances. Save for the India–Brunei BIT[125] and India–Korea FTA investment chapter,[126] these treaties do not define the meaning of 'except in rare circumstances'. The India–Brunei BIT states that 'except in rare

114 Ibid., 85–88; Andreas Kulick, *Global Public Interest in International Investment Law* (Cambridge: Cambridge University Press, 2012), pp. 186–89.

115 E Leonhardsen, 'Looking for Legitimacy: Exploring Proportionality Analysis in Investment Treaty Arbitration' (2011) 1 *Journal of International Dispute Settlement* 1; Jan H Jans, 'Proportionality Revisited' (2000) 27 *Legal Issues of Economic Integration* 239, at 240–41.

116 Hans (2000) above n 115, at 240.

117 Ibid.; Kingsbury and Schill (2010) above n 113, pp. 86–87.

118 Hans (2000) above n 115, at 241; Kingsbury and Schill (2010) above n 113, pp. 87–88.

119 ICSID Case No. ARB(AF)/00/2, Award, 29 May 2003.

120 *Mellacher and Others* v. *Austria* (App no. 10522/83, 11011/84, 11070/84) (1989) Series A no. 169, 24; *Pressos Compañía Naviera and Others* v. *Belgium* (App. no. 17849/91) (1995) Series A no. 332, 19; *James and Others* (App. nos. 8793/79) (1986), 19–20.

121 *Técnicas Medioambientes Tecmed S.A.* v. *United Mexican States*, ICSID Case No. ARB(AF)/00/2, Award, 29 May 2013, para. 115.

122 Ibid., para. 122. *See also LG&E* v. *Argentina*, ICSID Case No. ARB/02/1, Decision on Liability, 3 October 2006, para. 195; *Azurix* v. *Argentina*, ICSID Case No. ARB/01/12, Award, 14 July 2006, para. 312.

123 Mercurio (2012), above n 7, at 912.

124 India-Jordan BIT, Art. 3, Annex A. Similar provisions exist in India-Iceland BIT, Art. 3, Annex; India-Syria BIT, Art. 3, Annex; India-Senegal BIT, Art. 3, Annex 5.1; India-Latvia BIT, Art. 5(4)(c), Protocol; India-Singapore FTA, Art. 6.11; India-Korea BIT, Art. 10.18; and India-Brunei BIT, Protocol II(d).

125 India-Brunei BIT, Art. 5(d), Annex.

126 India-Korea FTA, Annex 10A(3)(b).

circumstances' refers to 'measures [that] are so severe in light of their purpose that they cannot be reasonably viewed as having been adopted and applied in good faith'. Thus, issuance of CLs will have to be assessed against the purpose for which it has been adopted and if the adverse effect of the measure (on foreign investment) outweighs the purpose (public health benefits of the measure), only then will such issuance of CLs be viewed as unreasonable and not adopted in good faith. Similarly, Annex 10A(3)(b) of the India–Korea FTA investment chapter states that 'except in rare circumstances' refers to 'when measures are extremely severe or disproportionate in light of its purpose and effect'. Thus, whether issuance of CLs amounts to expropriation or not will depend on whether the public health benefits of the measure are severely disproportionate to the effect of the measure on foreign investment (such as determining how severe is the curtailment of the exclusivity right of the patent holder).

There are also some Indian BITs that simply exempt all kinds of non-discriminatory regulatory measures adopted for public benefit such as health, safety and environment, from the purview of expropriation without the phrase 'except in rare circumstances' prefacing the provision.[127] As a result, in these Indian BITs, in no situation shall non-discriminatory issuance of a CL for public health purpose amount to expropriation.

Many Indian BITs do not contain the kind of provisions discussed earlier. Most Indian BITs provide that 'investments shall not be nationalised, expropriated or subject to measures having effect equivalent to nationalisation or expropriation'. Thus, under these BITs, India is prohibited not only from nationalizing and expropriating foreign investment but also from adopting a regulatory measure that has an effect equivalent to nationalization or expropriation.[128] The only criterion mentioned in these BITs to determine indirect expropriation is the effect of the regulatory measure on foreign investment. This is a clear reference to the 'sole effect test', where indirect expropriation would occur if the regulatory measure results in substantial deprivation of foreign investment. The purpose behind the regulatory measure does not matter in this analysis. Thus, if issuance of a CL results in substantial deprivation (depending on the degree of interference)[129] either because the CL is issued for a longer duration, or if the remuneration provided to the patent holder is inadequate, then it could potentially amount to indirect expropriation.[130] One critical factor here could be the role that Article 31 of the TRIPS Agreement could play in determination of indirect expropriation; provided that the TRIPS Agreement is 'an applicable rule in the relation between the parties' under Article 31(3)(c) of the Vienna Convention on the Law of Treaties.

An important case in this regard that paid close attention to the language of the BIT in determining indirect expropriation is *Servier* v. *Poland*. In this case, the tribunal held that Poland indirectly expropriated foreign investment by denying marketing authorizations to drugs.[131] The tribunal looked closely at the language of the France–Poland BIT that provided that 'any divestment' would give rise to prompt and adequate compensation.[132]

On the other hand, it is quite possible that an arbitral tribunal may adopt the 'police powers' approach in determining expropriation even if the language of the expropriation

127 India-Trinidad Tobago BIT, Art. 5(3); India-Saudi Arabia BIT, Art. 5(3); India-Malaysia BIT, Annex 3.

128 *See* India-Netherlands BIT, Art. 5(1); India-Denmark BIT, Art. 5(1); India-Germany BIT, Art. 5(1); India-UK BIT, Art. 5(1); India-Sri Lanka BIT, Art. 5(1); India-Vietnam BIT, Art. 5(1); India-Oman BIT, Art. 5(1); India-Indonesia BIT, Art. 5(1); and India-Myanmar BIT, Art. 5(1).

129 Gibson, 'Latent Grounds in Investor-State Arbitration,' (2010) above n 37, at 456.

130 Mercurio, (2013) above n 7, at 914–15.

131 *Servier* v. *Poland*, UNCITRAL, Final Award, 14 February 2012, para. 576.

132 Ibid., para. 643; Vadi, 'Towards a New Dialectics' (2015), above n 3, at 158–60.

provision does not specifically provide for adopting a 'police powers' approach.[133] If such an approach is adopted, then even if issuance of CLs amounts to a severe degree of interference with the rights of the investor, it will not amount to expropriation if the CL has been issued for public health purposes.[134]

If a tribunal were to use the test of proportionality, then whether issuance of the CL would amount to expropriation would depend on whether issuance of the CL is suitable for the public health purpose; whether the CL is necessary to achieve the public health objective, that is, there is no other less restrictive regulatory measure that would achieve the same objective; and whether the benefits of issuing the CL outweigh the costs imposed on foreign investors.

Given the fact that ISDS tribunals may use any of the three tests mentioned earlier, whether the issuance of the CL would amount to indirect expropriation or not would, to a considerable extent, depend on the test applied.

The final argument that needs to be dealt with is that since Section 90 of the Indian Patent Act requires payment of royalties and other remuneration to the patent holder, the question is then whether the issuance of a CL in India amounts to expropriation. Section 90(1) of the Indian Patent Act provides that:

> In settling the terms and conditions of a [compulsory] licence under section 84, the Controller shall endeavour to secure— that the royalty and other remuneration, if any, reserved to the patentee or other person beneficially entitled to the patent, is reasonable, having regard to the nature of the invention, the expenditure incurred by the patentee in making the invention or in developing it and obtaining a patent and keeping it in force and other relevant factors.

This is an important point because BITs do not prohibit States from expropriating foreign investment. Host States can adopt regulatory measures that are tantamount to expropriation if the objective is to achieve some public purpose, provided the regulatory measure is non-discriminatory and due compensation is paid to the foreign investor in accordance with what the BIT provides.

Although Section 90(1) provides for payment of royalties or remuneration to the patent holder, the critical difference between this remuneration requirement and the requirement to pay compensation for expropriation in Indian BITs is the quantum of compensation to be paid. For instance, Article 5(1) of the India–Germany BIT states that for expropriation, compensation has to be paid:

> which shall be equivalent to the value of the expropriated or nationalised investment immediately before the date on which such expropriation or nationalisation became publicly known. Such compensation shall be effectively realisable without undue delay and shall be freely convertible and transferable. Interest shall be paid in a fair and equitable manner for the period between the date of expropriation or nationalisation and the date of actual payment of compensation.

The BIT imposes a more onerous obligation on India in terms of paying compensation that must be equal to the value of investment, which is not the case with Section 90(1). For instance, in *Natco v. Bayer*, under Section 90(1), was awarded a royalty of seven percent of

[133] For example, in *Saluka* v. *Czech Republic*, the tribunal adopted the police powers approach in determining expropriation, though Article 5 of the Czech-Netherlands BIT, that provided for expropriation, does not contain any specific language (of the kind given in some of the Indian BITs discussed above), concerning the police powers approach in determining expropriation.

[134] Gibson, 'Latent Grounds in Investor-State Arbitration' (2010), above n 37, at 458–59.

total sales,[135] which is not the same as the compensation requirement given in the India–Germany BIT, that is, had Bayer challenged the issuance of a CL under the India–Germany BIT. In other words, the fact that the issuance of a CL in India is accompanied by remuneration does not mean that it satisfies an important requirement of expropriation in BITs, that is, paying due compensation due to onerous compensation requirements in BITs. Consequently, the issuance of CLs in India on medicines could still be challenged as expropriation in Indian BITs.

3.4 CONCLUSION

The discussion in the chapter shows that pharmaceutical patents would easily qualify as foreign investments under Indian BITs, especially when the 'economic characteristics' test is not satisfied. Whether the issuance of CLs on these foreign investments under Indian BITs amounts to unlawful expropriation, the outcome depends on two factors – first, the language of the treaty such as whether it exempts issuance of CLs from the ambit of what is considered to be expropriation (in which case the Indian government is free to issue CLs, as long as these are consistent with the TRIPS Agreement) or whether the BIT makes a reference to the police powers test (in which case an issuance of a CL will not amount to expropriation if the CL had been issued for public health purposes); and second, the approach of the arbitral tribunal, such as whether the tribunal uses the 'sole effect' test or the 'police powers' test to determine indirect expropriation.

The draft 2015 Model BIT empowered the Indian government to regulate its internal affairs through the use of CLs. By providing that the treaty did not apply at all to the issuance of CLs granted in relation to IPRs, or to the 'revocation, limitation or creation of IPRs, to the extent that such issuance, revocation, limitation or creation is consistent with the Law of the Host State', the Indian government would have been able to reduce risks it would have faced in investor–State arbitration, while ensuring reasonable protection for foreign investors. If the formulation on the draft 2015 Model BIT had made no reference to the WTO Agreement, it would have better served the host country's regulatory power. The 2016 Model BIT, on the other hand, required that issuance of CLs be consistent with the TRIPS Agreement, so as to be outside the ambit of the BIT. That formulation empowers an ISDS tribunal, which may not have expertise in WTO law, to substantively judge the consistency of the actions of the Indian government with WTO law. From the perspective of reconciling investment protection with the host State's right to regulate, allowing an ISDS tribunal to review the issuance of a CL for its consistency with the TRIPS Agreement will minimize the possibility of host States misusing their right to issue CLs. This might present a better balance between States' right to regulate and investment protection.

[135] Mansi Sood, 'Natco Pharma Limited v Bayer Corporation and the Compulsory Licensing Regime in India' (2013) 6 *NUJS Law Review* 99 at 110.

4

Out with the Old, In with the New?

Unpacking Myanmar's Consolidated Investment Law

Ei Ei Aung, Mahdev Mohan and Aziah Hussin

4.1 INTRODUCTION

The Myanmar Investment Law (MIL) was enacted in October 2016 and took effect in 2017, along with the detailed Myanmar Investment Rules (MI Rules).[1] Its enactment followed the publication of a draft MIL which was subject to three rounds of public consultations, and that sought, *inter alia*, to address foreign investors' complaints that the previous investment approval process was complex and lengthy.[2]

The MIL, as adopted, consolidates and replaces the 2012 Myanmar Foreign Investment Law (MFIL)[3] and the 2013 Myanmar Citizens Investment Law (MCIL).[4] Unlike its predecessors,[5] the MIL applies to both local and foreign investments, and treats them equally in terms of expansion and management. Unless prohibited under Section 41, investment activities are either (a) restricted in a negative list clearly set out in MIL Section 36, and therefore require an 'investment permit'; or (b) deemed to be open for investment and eligible for an 'endorsement application' that expedites the approval process for investments. Notwithstanding its reforms, the MIL affirms Myanmar's established investment objectives of 'promotion and expansion of export, exploitation of high technology, supporting and involving large capital, opening up of more employment, development of works which would save energy consumption and aid regional development'.[6]

The MIL seeks to bolster the favourable investment environment first created by the 2012 MFIL and further guarantee the rights of both domestic and foreign investors in accordance with international law and standards. For example, the MIL contains investor-friendly provisions, such as Article 48, which aims to guarantee 'regulatory transparency and fair and equitable treatment'. This chapter examines the MIL's stated goal of protecting investors in accordance with the law and, at the same time, preserve the Union Government of

1 The Myanmar Investment Law (Pyidaungsu Hluttaw Law No. 40/2016, 18 October 2016) ('MIL') and the Myanmar Investment Rules (Notification No. 35 / 2017, 30 March 2017) ('MI Rules') are available at www.dica.gov.mm/sites/dica.gov.mm/files/document-files/myanmar_investment_law_official_translation_3-1-2017.pdf and www.dica.gov.mm/sites/dica.gov.mm/files/document-files/myanmar_investment_rules_official_translation.pdf respectively (last accessed 7 February 2020).

2 See, e.g., Jonathan Bonnitcha, 'International Investment Arbitration in Myanmar: 'Bounded Rationality', But Not As We Know It', in Julien Chaisse and Luke Nottage (eds.), *International Investment Treaties and Arbitration Across Asia* (2017), 335, 343–45.

3 2012 Myanmar Foreign Investment Law (Pyidaunghu Hluttaw Law No. 21/2012) ('MFIL 2012').

4 2013 Myanmar Citizens Investment Law (Pyidaunghu Hluttaw Law No. 18/2013) ('MCIL 2013').

5 MFIL 2012 and MCIL 2013.

6 See also Dr Tun Shin, *Why Invest in Myanmar? and other Notable Legal Articles* (2013), p. 20.

Myanmar's (the 'Government') regulatory authority to pursue legitimate objectives that are consistent with well-established principles of international investment law, and are also in keeping with Section 41 that sets out categories of prohibited investments contrary to the public interest.

The MIL and related reforms (such as the autonomous Myanmar Investment Commission [MIC] and investment bodies it creates) seek to provide a level-playing field for local and foreign investors; ensure adequate investor protections that promote investor confidence; and provide a nascent mechanism for the settlement of any investor–State dispute. This chapter examines this modern framework that the MIL seeks to advance to protect investors; and at the same time, to preserve Myanmar's regulatory authority to pursue legitimate objectives that are consistent with international investment law, such as to prohibit investments that are contrary to the public interest. It is also crucial that the military's approach to investment protection aligns with the country's treaty and legal commitments.

This chapter is organized in accordance with the following structure. After this introduction, the purpose of the MIL is explained (Part II). The substantive provisions of the MIL concerning the treatment of foreign investors are then elucidated (Part III), and the next section sets forth and explains the MIL's provisions on the settlement of investment disputes (Part IV). Then follows a discussion of the general exceptions under the MIL (Part V), and a review of Myanmar's experience in investor–State disputes (Part VI). It is concluded the MIL is to be welcomed. Although some ambiguities and uncertainty remain, it is anticipated that sound investment law and policy will come to underpin the robust institutional framework and governance structure the MIL seeks to advance, and facilitate the achievement of the MIC's stated policy objectives.

4.2 THE PURPOSE OF THE MIL

The MIL is tailored to capitalize on the wave of foreign investment catalysed by ASEAN's economic integration and the termination of sanctions by the United States in 2016. Its objectives (as stated in Article 3) include the protection of 'investors and their investment businesses in accordance with the law', the 'creation of job opportunities for the people', the development of 'human resources', the development of 'high functioning production, service and trading sectors', the development of the 'technology, agriculture, livestock and industrial sectors', the development of 'various professional fields', the facilitation of citizens 'working alongside the international community', and the creation of 'businesses and investment business that meet international standards'.[7] The MIL's objectives call to mind the ASEAN Comprehensive Investment Agreement (ACIA), which provides for applicable investment protections in line with international agreements, enhancing the attractiveness of ASEAN as a single investment destination.[8] Indeed, the Preamble of the Draft MIL of 2015 made express reference to Myanmar's place within the ASEAN Economic Community.[9]

7 MIL, Art. 3(b)-(i).

8 ASEAN Comprehensive Investment Agreement, opened for signature 26 February 2009, available at http://investasean.asean.org/files/upload/Doc%2005%20-%20ACIA.pdf (entered into force 24 February 2012) ('ACIA'). The ACIA covers almost all forms of investment (excluding only the reservations made by members in the ACIA schedule of reservations), with liberalization provisions covering the four main sectors of manufacturing, agriculture, fishery, mining and quarrying, as well as services incidental to these sectors.

9 Draft Myanmar Investment Law of 2015 ('Draft MIL of 2015'), available at www.burmalibrary.org/docs21/2015-Myanmar-Investment-Bill-V2-24–02-2015.pdf (last accessed 8 February 2020).

The Government's restructuring of the MIC as an autonomous body (which is located in Yangon, the commercial capital, rather than Napyidaw, the country's political capital and seat of government) is a welcome move. Chapters IV–VII of the MIL set out the MIC's legal framework and its legal relationship with the Government; for example, the President of Myanmar has the authority to decide the composition and membership of the MIC.[10] The MIC plays an advisory role in relation to the government's investment policies,[11] including setting the requirements for, or expectations of, responsible business conduct by investors. Such a structure has the potential to strengthen the legitimacy and reliability of the legal framework. Under Article 36, the MIC has the discretion whether or not to grant permits to potential investors. Significantly, the MIC also has the duty to establish a grievance mechanism to prevent or resolve disputes concerning the effective implementation of the MIL.[12] Articles 21 and 22 contain provisions on conflicts of interest, and Article 16 expressly gives the government the right to dismiss an MIC member on various grounds, including the failure to properly perform their duties. These are significant initiatives to elevate and entrench the role of the MIC whilst increasing transparency and accountability within the MIC.

Recent reform indicates that Myanmar has advanced clear efforts to align its domestic legislation with regional plans for economic integration. This is significant given that, collectively, ASEAN represents a market in excess of 649 million people, with a combined GDP of about US$2.986 trillion and upwards of US$2.8 trillion in international trade.[13] From the time the MFIL was first adopted in 1988,[14] Myanmar saw a rush of investment from countries such as Australia, Canada, China, France, Hong Kong, Korea, Malaysia, Singapore, Thailand, the United Kingdom and the United States. A mere seven years later, investment figures in Myanmar (as of 30 September 1995) were estimated to have risen significantly.[15] Foreign direct investment (FDI) in Myanmar has continued to increase steadily, averaging US$556.19 million from 2012 to 2016.[16] According to available current data, the total FDI in Myanmar is projected to reach US$450 million by 2020.[17] Increased urbanization has channelled more ASEAN households into the consumer class.[18] This growth will demand more than $7 trillion of investment in core infrastructure, housing and commercial real estate across ASEAN through 2030.[19] There are potential benefits to be reaped by not just Myanmar but the entire region. The increased connectivity of the ASEAN region could 'significantly increase intra-regional trade'.[20] In this regard, ASEAN States will need to 'tackle restrictions on foreign investment and build a more competitive manufacturing sector as well as critical foundations such as infrastructure, logistics, and workforce skills'.[21] This brings Southeast Asia's bilateral investment treaties (BITs) and the investment

[10] MIL, Chapters IV and V.

[11] E.g., MIL, Art. 24(d).

[12] MIL, Art. 82.

[13] HKTDC Research, 'ASEAN: Market Profile' (27 November 2019), available at http://emerging-markets-research.hktdc.com/business-news/article/Asia/ASEAN-Market-Profile/mp/en/1/1X000000/1X09WKZD.htm (last accessed 8 February 2020).

[14] Myanmar Foreign Investment Law of 30 November 1988.

[15] Shin, above n 6, 77.

[16] Trading Economics, 'Myanmar Foreign Direct Investment', available at: https://tradingeconomics.com/myanmar/foreign-direct-investment (last accessed 7 February 2020).

[17] Ibid. FDI dropped to US$94.79 million in March 2020, likely due to the global impact of the COVID-19 pandemic.

[18] ASEAN Economic Community Blueprint, p. 5, available at https://asean.org/wp-content/uploads/archive/5187–10.pdf (last accessed 7 February 2020).

[19] Ibid.

[20] McKinsey Institute, 'Southeast Asia at the crossroads: Three Paths to Prosperity' (November 2014), pp. 21–22.

[21] Ibid.

chapters of its free trade agreements (FTAs) into sharp relief, as with domestic regulatory frameworks such as the MIL.

The MIL is timely, particularly as well with the implementation of the ASEAN Economic Community,[22] and the Asian Infrastructure Investment Bank and China's 'One Belt, One Road' initiative. The MIL's statutory and institutional reforms reflect Myanmar's commitment to becoming more investor-friendly, and are compatible with the economic cohesion that ASEAN aims to achieve to allow the free flow of investments within the region. In addition to the ACIA and regional BITs and FTAs, certain provisions of the MIL are consistent with, or draw inspiration from, international agreements outside the region, such as the North Atlantic Free Trade Agreement (NAFTA).

These investor-friendly provisions are aligned with provisions in the Japan–Myanmar BIT (2013), Republic of Korea–Myanmar BIT (2014) and the Republic of Singapore–Myanmar BIT (2020), and will be elaborated on in this chapter.

Other than the MIL, there is also evidence of other investor-friendly domestic legislative reform, such as the passing of the new Myanmar Companies Law in December 2017, which support the new investment regime,[23] and the new Arbitration Law 2016,[24] following Myanmar's accession to the New York Convention on the Recognition and Enforcement of Foreign Arbitral Awards ('New York Convention') in 2013.

4.3 TREATMENT OF INVESTORS

4.3.1 *Non-discrimination*

Where the provisions of international treaties provide a more favourable treatment to investors than the treatment provided by the domestic legislation of Myanmar, the treaty provisions will prevail.[25] Previously, when investments by foreign investors and domestic investors were governed separately by the 2012 MFIL and the MCIL respectively, the different laws gave rise to different standards of treatment of foreign investors *apropos* domestic investors; for example, foreign investors were prohibited from taking part in certain types of businesses.[26] Today, the MIL has helped to standardize the treatment of foreign and domestic investors.

4.3.1.1 'National Treatment' Clause

Article 47(a) of the MIL states that the government shall provide to 'foreign investors and their direct investments' treatment that is not less favourable than that which it accords to Myanmar investors. Commonly known as a 'national treatment' clause, the objective of this provision is to prevent discrimination on the basis of nationality.[27] The national treatment clause in Article 47(a) of the MIL is consistent with that found in other international

[22] Ibid.
[23] Pyidaungsu Hluttaw Law No. 29, 2017; see, for example, the definition of 'foreign company' in s. 1(xiv).
[24] Pyidaungsu Hluttaw Law No. 5, 2016, available at www.myanmar-law-library.org/law-library/laws-and-regulations/laws/myanmar-laws-1988-until-now/union-solidarity-and-development-party-laws-2012–2016/myanmar-laws-2016/pyidaungsu-hluttaw-law-no-5–2016-law-on-arbitration-decisions-burmese.html (last accessed 7 February 2020).
[25] MIL, Article 91.
[26] MFIL, Article 3.
[27] Surya P Subedi QC, *International Investment Law – Reconciling Policy and Principle* (2012), p. 70.

agreements of a similar nature, such as Article 2.3 of the EU–Singapore Investment Protection Agreement.[28]

4.3.1.2 'Most Favoured Nation' Clause

Article 47(b) of the MIL states that the government shall, in like circumstances, accord all foreign investors and their direct investments treatment that is no less favourable than that of the investors of third countries. Foreign investors seek such most-favoured-nation (MFN) protection to avoid any discrimination which would put them at a disadvantage compared to other investors from third countries. Article 47(b) sets out restrictions on the MFN clause, which mirror those found in many other international investment agreements; they essentially provide that the MFN obligation does not require the States parties to the BIT to accord the benefit of any 'treatment, preferences or privileges' arising from membership of any customs union, free trade area, or economic union, or any double taxation agreement or other agreement regarding matters of taxation.[29]

4.3.2 *Regulatory Transparency and Fair and Equitable Treatment*

Article 48 of the MIL purports to guarantee the Government's fair and equitable treatment (FET) of the investor in respect of two defined matters: (a) 'the right to obtain the relevant information on any measures or decision which has a significant impact for an investor and their direct investment', and (b) 'the right to due process of law and the right to appeal on similar measure, including any change to the terms and conditions under any license or permit and endorsement granted by the Government to the investor and their direct investment'.[30] This is a revised version of the previous Draft MIL of 2015, Article 11 of which sets out a list of non-exhaustive examples of what could constitute FET, as follows:

(a) The obligation on the Government to not deny justice in criminal, civil or administrative adjudicatory proceedings in accordance with the principle of due process (section 11(1));
(b) The investor's right to obtain information on any action or decision which has an effect on any Investor and Direct Investment (section 11(2)(a));
(c) The investor's right to due process and right to appeal including, but not limited to, any changes to the terms of approval, permission or license granted to by the Government to the investors and their direct investments (section 11(2)(b));
(d) The obligation of due compliance incumbent on the Government and Government Entities with contracts, if any, that may have entered into with any investor (section 1 1(2)(c)); and
(e) The Government's obligation to ensure that all laws, regulations, procedures, administrative rulings of general application and adjudicatory decisions respecting any matter covered by the MIL are to be promptly published or otherwise made publicly available (section 11(2)(d)).[31]

28 EU – Singapore Investment Protection Agreement, signed 19 October 2018, Art. 2.3 (not yet in force).
29 MIL, Art. 47(b).
30 MIL, Art. 48.
31 Draft MIL (2015), available at: www.burmalibrary.org/docs21/2015-Myanmar-Investment-Bill-V2-24-02-2015.pdf (last accessed 7 February 2020).

Some criticisms might be made of the MIL's FET clause. This is because such provisions may on the one hand refer to the customary international law minimum standard for the treatment of aliens.[32] Where that is the case, the protection afforded by the customary international law minimum standard of treatment arguably addresses a wider range of considerations than the terms of Article 48 of the MIL, such as due process and lack of arbitrariness, which ultimately turn on the facts of each case.[33] Alternatively, the FET clause in a BIT or domestic investment law may refer to an autonomous standard, much like Article 11 of the Draft MIL of 2015. Provisions that are autonomous do not expressly refer to customary international law. Instead, they only state that the host State is obliged to offer the investor 'fair and equitable treatment'. Absent reference to contemporary international law or standards, such provisions have been subject to criticism.[34] One commentator notes that a draft text of an Indian Model BIT departs from the 'fair and equitable treatment standard in favour of a standard – egregious or outrageous behaviour – that hearkens back to legal touchstones of an earlier era'.[35] The People's Republic of China's Foreign Investment Law (China FIL) has no dedicated FET clause that may be used as a starting point.[36]

Article 48 of the MIL makes no express reference to the application of customary international law or to a minimum standard. Nonetheless, given that the MIL refers to certain standards which are recognized as being part of the corpus of customary international law, such as the observance of due process, it is arguable that the MIL may be considered to be consistent with relevant international agreements. Certainly, the FET clause in Article 11 of the Draft MIL of 2015 would have readily permitted this argument to be made. And in applying the MIL, any tribunal 'is bound to find the meaning of these terms under international law bearing in mind their ordinary meaning, the evolution of international law and the specific context in which they were used'.[37] In the circumstances, further inspiration could have been drawn from provisions such as that in Article 2.4(2) of the EU–Singapore Investment Protection Agreement which sets out four instances that constitute a breach of a State party's obligations, namely: (a) denial of justice; (b) fundamental breach of due

[32] E.g., NAFTA, Art. 1105; and US Model BIT, Art. 5(1) The Free Trade Commission states that 'Article 1105(1) prescribes the customary international law minimum standard of treatment of aliens as the minimum standard of treatment to be afforded to investments of investors of another Party': see Free Trade Commission, *Notes of Interpretation* (31 July 2001), available at: www.sice.oas.org/tpd/nafta/Commission/CH11understanding_e.asp (last accessed 26 September 2019).

[33] The scope of what constitutes FET has been expanded by arbitral case-law. In *Waste Management, Inc v The United Mexican States* (ICSID Case No. ARB(AF)/00/3, Award of 30 April 2004), the Tribunal held that the fair and equitable standard in NAFTA Article 1105 comprises conduct which guards against *idiosyncratic* and discriminatory practices, and a manifest failure of natural justice: '[T]he minimum standard of fair and equitable treatment is infringed by conduct attributable to the State and harmful to the claimant if the conduct is arbitrary, grossly unfair, unjust or idiosyncratic, is discriminatory and exposes the claimant to sectional or racial prejudice, or involves a lack of due process leading to an outcome which offends judicial propriety – as might be the case with a manifest failure of natural justice in judicial proceedings or a complete lack of transparency and candour in an administrative process'.

[34] Krista Nadakavukaren Shafer, *International Investment Law (Text, Cases and Materials)* (Edward Elgar, 2013), p. 339.

[35] Luke Eric Peterson, 'India invites comments on draft model investment treaty; text offers radical departure, and calls to mind Norway's past efforts at revision', *IA Reporter* (24 March 2015).

[36] The Foreign Investment Law of the People's Republic of China was adopted by the National People's Congress on 15 March 2019, and was implemented on 1 January 2020: see Zhong Nan, Chen Jia, 'Draft foreign investment law advances', *China Daily* (31 January 2019), available at www.chinadaily.com.cn/a/201901/31/WS5c5203dca3106c65c34e767a.html (last accessed 7 February 2020), see also the Foreign Investment Law of the People's Republic of China, available at www.fdi.gov.cn/1800000121_39_4872_0_7.html (last accessed 7 February 2020).

[37] *Siemens AG v. Argentine Republic* (ICSID Case No ARB/02/8, Decision on Jurisdiction of 3 August 2004).

process; (c) manifestly arbitrary conduct; and (d) harassment, coercion, abuse of power or similar bad faith conduct.[38] Article 2.4(3) of the EU–Singapore Investment Protection Agreement further provides that:

> In determining whether the fair and equitable treatment obligation, as set out in paragraph 2, has been breached, a Tribunal may take into account, where applicable, whether a Party made specific or unambiguous representations to an investor so as to induce the investment, that created legitimate expectations of a covered investor and which were reasonably relied upon by the covered investor, but that the Party subsequently frustrated.[39]

Each of the standards listed in Article 2.4(2) of the EU–Singapore Investment Protection Agreement arguably reflects customary international law but the provision itself does not make express reference to custom. In this regard, Article 11(1) of the Draft MIL of 2015 mirrored Article 11(2)(a) of the ACIA. Article 11(2) of the ACIA is generally worded, compared to Article 2.4(2) of the EU–Singapore Investment Protection Agreement, which sets out specific instances of the standard of treatment that is to be afforded to an investor. While Article 11(2) of the Draft MIL of 2015 sets out specific instances of what can be included under the FET standard, a more stringent application of what constitutes a breach of an FET obligation, such as that which are found in Article 2.4(2) of the EU–Singapore Investment Protection Agreement, should have been taken for the benefit of Myanmar's interests. For example, while Article 11(1) of the Draft MIL of 2015 obliged Myanmar to comply with FET standards, which is understood to include the obligation to act in accordance with 'principles of due process', Article 2.4(2)(b) of the EU–Singapore Investment Protection Agreement applies a higher standard. It obliges a State party to act only such that there is no '*fundamental* breach of due process'.

The final version of Article 48 still retains broad reference to 'the right to due process', which might still lead to FET obligations. But the definition of FET under the Article 48 has been criticized as being 'much narrower than the way FET provisions in investment treaties have been interpreted and applied by tribunals. It appears to address issues of process, without making the state liable for regulatory changes that adversely affect investors'.[40] This is significant, especially given that other investment protection provisions demonstrate a similar trend. For example, Article 54, which appears to be modelled after paragraph 4 of Annex 2 of ACIA, clarifies that non-discriminatory regulatory measures of general application do not amount to indirect expropriation. Article 53 provides that compensation for the indirect expropriation would normally be equal to an investment's fair market value, but that other factors should also be taken into account. And Article 56 contains a carefully qualified guarantee of free transfer of funds. Given that FET is one of the most powerful investor rights granted by investment treaties, the application of Article 48 should be monitored closely.

4.3.3 *Access to Land*

Article 50 guarantees an investor the 'right to obtain a long-term lease of land or building from the owner if it is private land or building, or from the relevant government departments or

[38] EU – Singapore Investment Protection Agreement, signed 15 October 2018 (not yet in force), Art. 2.4(2) (footnotes omitted).

[39] Ibid., Art. 2.4(3) (footnotes omitted).

[40] Jonathan Bonnitcha, *Investment Laws of ASEAN Countries: A Comparative Review* (International Institute for Sustainable Development, December 2017), p. 16, available at www.iisd.org/sites/default/files/publications/investment-laws-asean-countries.pdf (last accessed 8 February 2020).

government organization if it is land managed by the government'. Under the same provision, foreign investors have the right to lease land up to a maximum initial period of fifty years, and after that 'a consecutive period of (10) years and a further consecutive period of (10) years extension to such period of lease of land or building may be obtained with the approval of the Commission'.[41]

It bears noting that section 5 of the Transfer of Immovable Property Restrictions Act 1987 (TIPRA) states that:

> 5. No person shall grant a lease of immovable property, for a term exceeding one year:
>
> (a) To a foreigner or foreigner owned company.
> (b) No foreigner or foreigner owned company shall receive a lease of immovable property, for a term exceeding one year.[42]

Section 13(2) of the Draft MIL of 2015 stated that in the event of any conflict under the MIL and the TIPRA, the provisions under the MIL would prevail. This provision is however absent in the final text of the MIL, as adopted. Despite the absence of an express provision, the time frame (which allows the right to lease land for an initial period of fifty years, and to extend the lease for ten years, and for a further ten years thereafter) afforded to foreign investors mirrors the existing Articles 31 and 32 of the 2012 MFIL. It is encouraging to note that the MIL affords foreign investors increased protection over land rights by allowing them to lease land in Myanmar for a significantly longer time than that which was previously allowed by the TIPRA. In this respect, Article 50 assures foreign investors that they have 'the right to lease land for a maximum initial period of 50 years' with further extensions of up to twenty years thereafter.

Article 50(e) states that '[t]he Government may grant more favourable terms and conditions for the lease of land and the use of land by Myanmar citizen investors'. In comparison, as Article 13(3) of the Draft MIL, the clause stated that '[t]he Union Government may provide better terms and conditions of land use or lease terms to Domestic Investors'. Article 50(e) of the MIL must be read together with Article 52(b) which provides that for any government measure that results in a nationalization, expropriation, or termination of an investment to be deemed lawful, it must, *inter alia*, be conducted in a 'non-discriminatory manner'.

When a similar provision was contained in Article 10(1) of the Draft MIL, it provided that:

> Subject to the other specific provision of this Law the Union Government is committed to providing non-discriminatory treatment to all Investors and their Investments, in particular ... shall accord to Foreign Investors and their Investments treatment no less favourable than that it accords, in like circumstances, to Domestic Investors and their Direct Investments.

It is noteworthy, as this chapter will highlight, that the government made the final decision to have 'non-discrimination' as a stand-alone clause in Article 52. Non-discrimination in the draft clause had to be shown in a comparison between 'Foreign Investors and their Investments treatment' and 'Domestic Investors and their Direct Investments'. This would likely have compromised the government's ability to 'provide better terms and conditions of land use or lease terms to Domestic Investors'. Although the wording of Draft Article 13(3) was

[41] MIL, Art. 50.
[42] Transfer of Immovable Property Restrictions Act 1987, Art. 5.

amended to provide more clarity on the definition of 'Domestic Investors', separating the 'non-discrimination' clause in such a manner allows the government the regulatory space to provide 'more favourable terms and conditions' for its citizen investors, without running afoul of the non-discrimination clause.

4.3.4 *Protection against Expropriation*

4.3.4.1 Standards of Prohibition of Expropriation

Pursuant to Article 52, the government shall not expropriate (directly or indirectly) unless it is: (a) actually necessary for the interest of the Union or its citizen; (b) in a non-discriminatory manner; (c) measured in accordance with the applicable Laws; and (d) against prompt, fair and adequate payment of compensation.

The term 'expropriation' refers to a State's taking of property – something of value – away from its owner. As international investment law protects both an investor's legal title to its investment and the investor's rights to use and profit from its investment, government actions that take away any of these may constitute unlawful expropriation.[43] While the State has the right under customary international law to expropriate alien property, such rights are not absolute, and certain conditions must be complied with, such as those identified in Article 52 of the MIL.[44] Nonetheless, customary international law also recognizes an exception to the requirement to satisfy these conditions, which is known as the 'police powers' exception. As the *Methanex* tribunal put it:

> As a matter of general international law, a non-discriminatory regulation for a public purpose, which is enacted in accordance with due process and, which affects, inter alios, a foreign investor or investment is not deemed expropriatory and compensable unless specific commitments had been given by the regulating government to the then putative foreign investor contemplating investment that the government would refrain from such regulation.[45]

Significantly, Article 54 of the MIL contains a caveat that permits the government to take non-compensatory regulatory measures 'for the purposes of regulating economic or supporting social interest', which would appear to be consistent with the police powers doctrine.

4.3.4.2 Compensable Expropriation

For the average investor, the right to compensation is the most critical element in the event of an expropriation. Evidently, what constitutes 'prompt, fair, adequate and effective' compensation will be the subject of much scrutiny and debate, should a dispute relating to Article 52 (d) arise between an investor and the government. The form of compensation to the investor has been subject of many investor–State arbitral cases. International agreements have provided some clarity on acceptable standards of compensation.

By way of example, Article 14(2) of the ACIA, Articles 1110(2) and 1110(3) of NAFTA, and Article 2.6(2) of the EU–Singapore Investment Protection Agreement provide details on the compensation to be paid to the investor in the case of expropriation. Three key points are

43 *Grand River Enterprises Six Nations Ltd v United States of America* (Award of 12 January 2011). paras. 146–55.

44 E.g., *Tecnicas Medioambientales Tecmed S.A. v Mexico* (ICSID Case No ARB(AF)/00/2, Final Award of 29 May 2003).

45 *Methanex Corporation v United States* (Final Award of 3 August 2005), 44 ILM 1345, 1410–12, para. 7.

raised in these provisions, namely that the compensation shall be: (a) paid without delay; (b) be equivalent to the fair market value before or at the time the expropriation was announced or occurred; and (c) be fully realisable.

The provisions of Article 53 explain what amounts to 'prompt, fair, adequate and effective' compensation, and states as follows:

> A fair and adequate compensation shall be designated as an equivalent to the market value prevailing at the time of expropriation of the investment. However, that designation shall be based on a fair consideration of public interest as well as the interests of the private investor, and shall take into account the present and past conditions of investment, the reason for expropriation of the business or property, the fair market value of the investment, the purpose of expropriating the business or property, the profits acquired by the investor during the term of investment, and also the duration of the investment.

Article 13 of the Japan–Myanmar BIT (2013) sets out terms upon which compensation is to be made for expropriated or nationalized investments: (a) equivalent to fair market value at the time the expropriation was publicly announced or when it occurred, whichever earlier; (b) without delay and including interest; and (c) right to seek prompt review (of the affected investor's case) and amount of compensation, from courts of justice, administrative tribunals or agencies of the Contracting Parties.[46]

4.4 DISPUTE PREVENTION AND RESOLUTION

Article 82 of the MIL provides that the MIC 'shall establish and manage a grievance mechanism to resolve, prevent the occurrence of disputes, and carry out the relevant inquiries for the investment issues before reaching at the stage of legal dispute'.[47] For its part, under Rule 165 of the MI Rules, an Investment Assistance Committee is tasked to provide 'assistance to the establishment and administration of a grievance or dispute mechanism according to subsection (n) of sections 25, 82 and 83' of the MIL. The MIC and IAC are responsible for the mechanism, which appears to be a novel idea, although the specifications of that mechanism appear unclear.

These provisions must be read together with Article 27 of the MIL, which empowers the MIC to form committees as required. The Investor Assistance Committee (IAC) may accept formal grievance notices from investors if the investor believes that (a) a decision of a government department or governmental organization was incorrectly made; (b) an application for a permit, licence, registration or approval was incorrectly refused; or (c) any right or protection benefiting them under the MIL has been frustrated. The IAC has the authority to consult with other government departments and organizations on the investor's behalf, request relevant officials to meet with the investor, obtain advice from the Attorney General or other professional advisor, or request the Chairman of the MIC to consult with the Minister responsible for the relevant authority. Viewed in this light, the IAC has a potentially powerful role in protecting the rights of investors and on maintaining a robust the regulatory framework in Myanmar.

Article 83 mandates that 'all disputing parties shall use due attempts to settle the disputes amicably' before any dispute can be taken to court or any arbitral tribunal. If the dispute

46 Japan – Myanmar BIT (2013), Art. 13, available at https://investmentpolicy.unctad.org/international-investment-agreements/treaty-files/3113/download (last accessed 9 February 2020).

47 MIL, Art. 82.

cannot be settled amicably, then parties would turn to the contract to see if there is a dispute settlement mechanism. If a dispute settlement mechanism was not stipulated, in accordance with Article 84(a), the dispute 'shall be settled in the competent court or the arbitral tribunal in accord with the applicable laws' (although there is no guidance as to how, or on what basis that arbitral tribunal is to be constituted, which contrasts with the Draft MIL of 2015). If a mechanism was stipulated, then in accordance with Article 84(b), the agreed upon provision between parties 'shall be complied with and carried out in accord with the mechanism'.

In contrast to the (as yet unspecified) grievance mechanism provided for in Article 82 of the MIL, the dispute settlement provisions in the draft MIL (which were ultimately not adopted) had gone into more detail. Thus, Article 21 of the Draft MIL of 2015 provided that disputes were to be resolved through 'alternative dispute resolution mechanisms including mediation, consultation and negotiation'. Thereafter, the foreign investor could submit its claim to: (a) domestic courts and administrative tribunals; or (b) Arbitration under relevant Myanmar law; or (c) Arbitration under the Rules of the UNCITRAL Arbitration Rules; or (d) Arbitration under the ICSID. Article 82 is a welcome revision from the Draft MIL, which needed to be strengthened. These provisions were not included in the MIL as adopted nor is there any mention in the MIL (or the MI Rules) of receiving complaints from local communities allegedly affected by permitted investments. In the present authors' view, this is a missed opportunity; especially since Section 25(n) of the MIL empowers the MIC to establish and manage a comprehensive 'system that is able to carry out activities such as systematically scrutinizing disputes, identifying the causes for disputes, responding, inquiring and settling losses before the stage of dispute resolution'.

By way of example of dispute resolution mechanisms in BITs already in force, in the Republic of Korea–Myanmar BIT 2014, Articles 10 and 11 set out provisions relating to the resolution of disputes between the contracting parties, and between a contracting party and an investor of the other contracting party.[48] In Article 10, between the contracting parties, disputes are to be settled through consultations or other diplomatic channels, failing which, they are to be submitted to an ad hoc tribunal.[49] In Article 11, between a contracting party and an investor of the other contracting party, disputes are to be settled by negotiations or consultations, failing which, to courts or arbitration under the ICSID Convention, the ICSID Additional Facility Rules, UNCITRAL Rules or any other arbitration rules, on agreement.[50]

The Republic of Singapore–Myanmar BIT, in force as of October 2020, similarly grants access to international arbitration to resolve investment disputes and grants rights to investors to submit dispute claims on behalf of their locally established enterprises in the host State.[51]

48 Republic of Korea – Myanmar BIT (2014), Arts. 10–11, available at https://investmentpolicy.unctad.org/international-investment-agreements/treaty-files/5183/download (last accessed 9 February 2020).

49 Ibid., Art. 10.

50 Ibid., Art. 11.

51 Singapore – Myanmar BIT (2019), see Singapore Ministry of Trade and Industry, 'Singapore and Myanmar Sign Bilateral Investment Treaty at the 7th Singapore – Myanmar Joint Ministerial Working Committee Meeting' (24 September 2019), available at www.mti.gov.sg/-/media/MTI/Newsroom/Press-Releases/2019/09/SINGAPORE-AND-MYANMAR-SIGN-BILATERAL-INVESTMENT-TREATY-AT-THE-7TH-SINGAPOREMYANMAR-JOINT-MINISTERIAL.pdf (last accessed 7 February 2020).

4.5 GENERAL EXCEPTIONS

Article 22 of the Draft MIL of 2015 stated that the government could: adopt or maintain reasonable non-discriminatory measures for prudential reasons relating to Myanmar's financial sector (Article 22(1)); or take any actions that it considered necessary for the protection of its essential security interests (i) relating to the traffic in arms, ammunition and implements of war and to such traffic and transactions in other goods, materials, services and technology undertaken directly and indirectly for the purpose of supplying a military or other security establishment; and (ii) taken in time of war or other emergency in international relations (Article 22(2)).

This mirrored Article 1410 of NAFTA, which sets out exceptions relating to a Party's financial security. These measures were likely taken to protect Myanmar's financial security. However, under a heading of 'general exceptions', the provisions listed should not only consist of exceptions relating to financial security. The Draft MIL had adopted the words of Section 18 of the ACIA with regard to 'security exceptions'. Section 17 of the ACIA, which is titled 'general exceptions', lists the measures that Member States can undertake to protect, among other things, the imposition of direct taxes, the protection of its national treasures and the conservation of exhaustible natural resources.

As adopted, the MIL has followed the structure of the ACIA in separating the 'General Exceptions' from the 'Security Exceptions'. Article 89 of the MIL provide that:

> 89. Nothing in this Law shall be construed to prohibit the following fair measures adopted or maintained prudently by the Government:
>
> (a) lifespan or health of human, animals, or plants;
>
> the protection of investors, depositors, financial market participants, policyholders, policy-claimants, or persons to whom a fiduciary duty is owed by a financial institution;
>
> (b) ensuring the safety, standing, soundness and stability of financial institutions;
> (c) ensuring the integrity and stability of the financial system of the Union;
> (d) aiming to ensure fair and effective assessment of tax or direct taxation relating to investors;
> (e) carrying out the protection of artistic, historical or archaeological valued national treasures and heritage;
> (f) preservation of natural resources not to be damaged, where effect is caused by domestic production or consumption.

And Article 90 provides that:

> 90(a). Nothing in this Law shall be construed to prohibit the Government from adopting or enforcing necessary measures for the protection of its essential security interests.
>
> (b) The provisions under this Law shall not prevent any of the following actions necessary for the Government to protect essential security interests, including but not limited to:
>
> (i) action relating to the traffic in arms, ammunition and to such traffic in other goods and materials as is carried on directly or indirectly for the purpose of supplying military or other security forces;
> (ii) action taken, as required, in time of war or other emergency in international relations.

4.6 INVESTOR–STATE DISPUTES

At the time of writing, the only known investor–State arbitration commenced pursuant to an investment treaty and involving the Government of Myanmar is the case of *Yaung Chi Oo v. Myanmar*.[52] The dispute in question arose from a joint venture between a Singapore company[53] and Myanmar Foodstuff Industries – a state-owned enterprise that is described as an 'agency' of the Ministry of Industry in the award and that did not appear to have a separate legal personality from the Ministry as a matter of Myanmar law.[54] The joint venture concerned the construction and operation of a brewery in Mandalay and had been approved by the Myanmar Foreign Investment Commission,[55] as was required under the Myanmar Foreign Investment Law. The claimant alleged that, in the period December 1997 to January 1998, armed agents of the Myanmar government seized the brewery. Myanmarese bank accounts belonging to the claimant and the claimant's majority shareholder were subsequently frozen. In 1999, the Myanmar courts issued orders that the joint venture company be wound up.

The claimant brought the dispute to arbitration under the 1987 ASEAN Agreement on the Promotion and Protection of Investments, which contained standard investment treaty provisions guaranteeing fair and equitable treatment and compensation for expropriation. Myanmar was not a party to this treaty when it first entered into force, but became party to it on accession to ASEAN in 1997.

The Tribunal's decision turned on the interpretation of an unusual provision requiring that foreign investment be approved in writing in order to be eligible for the protection of the Agreement. In particular, Article II(3) provided that:

> This Agreement shall also apply to investments made prior to its entry into force, provided such investments are specifically approved in writing and registered by the host country and upon such-conditions as it deems fit for purpose of this Agreement subsequent in its entry into force.

The Tribunal held that this provision applied to the claimant's investment because the investment had been made in 1994, prior to the treaty's entry into force in Myanmar in 1997.

The claimant argued that its investment had been approved at the time it was made, and that the Myanmar government had not established any additional processes or requirements for approval of investments for the purposes of Article II(3).[56] The respondent admitted that it had not established any process for the approval of investments for the purposes of Article II(3) but argued that it was incumbent on the claimant to seek an 'express subsequent act amounting at least to a written approval' from the host State in order to satisfy the requirements of Article II(3).[57] In the crucial passage cited below, the Tribunal accepted the Respondent's argument:

[52] *Yaung Chi Oo Trading Pte. Ltd. v. Government of the Union of Myanmar*, ASEAN ID Case No ARB/01/1, Award (31 March 2003) (*Yaung Chi Oo v Myanmar* Award). See: www.italaw.com/sites/default/files/case-documents/ita0909.pdf

[53] From the award, it appears that the Win Win Nu – the majority shareholder in the Singapore company – was a Myanmar citizen. However, her nationality is never expressly clarified.

[54] *Yaung Chi Oo Trading Pte. Ltd. v. Government of the Union of Myanmar*, ASEAN ID Case No ARB/01/1, Award (31 March 2003), para. 3. This is typical of many Myanmar SOEs.

[55] The award does not specify the date at which the investment permit was granted, although from the context it is clear that the date was between November 1993 and September 1994: *Yaung Chi Oo Trading Pte. Ltd. v. Government of the Union of Myanmar*, ASEAN ID Case No ARB/01/1, Award (31 March 2003), para. 5.

[56] Ibid., para. 56.

[57] Ibid., para. 55.

> It follows from the actual language of Article II(3) that investments made before that date are not automatically covered, even if they were approved in writing and registered under the law of the host State when they were made. It is not uncommon for investment protection treaties to apply to pre-existing investments, but the extent to which the 1987 ASEAN Agreement does so is expressly stated in Article II(3). It is true that the procedure for giving approval under Article II(3) is not spelled out, and there appear to be no indications to be drawn from ASEAN practice on this point. But *effect must be given to the actual language of Article II(3), which requires an express subsequent act amounting at least to a written approval and eventually to registration of the investment.* The mere fact that an approval and registration earlier given by the host State continued to be operative after the entry into force of the 1987 ASEAN Agreement for that State is not sufficient(emphasis added).[58]

The decision in this case is primarily of historical interest as ACIA, which replaced the 1987 ASEAN Agreement when it entered into force in 2012,[59] does not contain a general requirement of approval in writing.[60] However, a similar question did arise in *Walter Bau v. Thailand*, an arbitration under the Germany–Thailand BIT. That treaty also contained a provision providing that only 'approved investments' made prior to the treaty's entry into force are eligible for the treaty's protection. Although the award on jurisdiction is not public, it appears from a subsequent US Court decision relating to the enforcement of the award that Thailand argued that the investment was not eligible for the protection of the BIT because it had never obtained a 'Certificate of Admission' from Thailand's Ministry of Foreign Affairs.[61] The Tribunal rejected that argument, and concluded that it did have jurisdiction over the dispute. The issue is now central to Thailand's efforts to resist the enforcement of the award in German court proceedings.

In the realm of commercial arbitration, Myanmar entities are beginning to use international arbitration to resolve disputes. In 2014, Myanmar military-linked Union of Myanmar Economic Holdings Ltd (UMEHL) commenced arbitral proceedings against Singaporean company Fraser & Neave (F&N) pursuant to the joint venture agreement concerning Myanmar Brewery Ltd (MBL). UMEHL successfully argued that F&N breached a term in the agreement (related to the change of shareholding structure of F&N after a takeover), conferring on UMEHL the right to acquire F&N's stake in MBL at market value.[62] In a statement issued by UMEHL's deputy managing director, it stated '[t]he conduct of this arbitration shows our commitment to the rule of law and that we will always adhere to due process'.[63]

4.7 CONCLUSION

Myanmar's adoption of the MIL follows an extensive law reform process. The Draft MIL of 2015 went through three rounds of consultations with the public and extensive amendments

58 Ibid., para. 60.

59 Article 47 of ACIA establishes a three-year transitional period during which investors may elect to bring claims under either the 1987 ASEAN Agreement or ACIA, but this three year transitional period has now also expired.

60 Article 4(a) of ACIA allows State parties to specifically require investments to be approved in writing by a designated authority in order to be covered by that treaty. Only Thailand has made written approval a requirement for an investment to fall within ACIA's coverage.

61 For detailed discussion of the case, see Luke Nottage and Sakda Thanitcul, 'The Past, Present and Future of International Investment Arbitration in Thailand', Sydney Law School Research Paper No. 16/31. https://papers.ssrn.com/sol3/papers.cfm?abstract_id=2770889 (accessed 17 October 2016).

62 Bonnitcha, 'International Investment Arbitration in Myanmar', above n 2, 342.

63 Reuters, 'Update 2 – Military-linked Myanmar group wins brewery spat with Singapore F&N' (31 October 2014), available at www.reuters.com/article/mehl-fn-myanmarbrewery/update-2-military-linked-myanmar-group-wins-brewery-spat-with-singapores-fn-idUSL4N0SQ5XZ20141031, (last accessed 9 February 2020).

before it was enacted. This clearly shows a contemplative attempt at creating robust legislation that would bolster Myanmar's participation in international investment. Some might posit that the Myanmar government's mindful and careful drafting exercise is a result of challenging experiences in investor–State disputes and multilateral and bilateral efforts at systemic reform.[64] Recent data from UNCTAD's World Investment Report 2019 revealed that seventy-one new ISDS cases were initiated in 2018, bringing the total number of known cases to 942.[65] The growth of ISDS claims has prompted 'a desire to recalibrate the importance of economic goals, as many states seek to curb some of the advantages and roles previously accorded to private actors'.[66]

However, Myanmar's background does not neatly fit into the narrative of a State that fears an impending ISDS claim. Myanmar did not sign any BITs providing for investor–State arbitration prior to the early 2000s. The only investment treaty allowing for investor–State arbitration that it did enter into prior to the 2000s was the multilateral ASEAN Agreement on the Promotion and Protection of Investments, to which Myanmar acceded in 1997. Yaung Chi Oo, the claimant in the aforementioned arbitration *Yaung v. Myanmar*, initiated its claim under this treaty in June 2000 and the arbitral tribunal held its first hearing in September 2001. The BITs providing for investor–State arbitration that Myanmar signed before 2002 are with the Philippines, China and Vietnam, though the last never entered into force.[67] Most of Myanmar's investment treaties currently in force – both multilateral investment treaties through ASEAN and BITs – were signed *after* Myanmar's first experience of investment treaty arbitration.

Although Myanmar only had limited interaction with the investment treaty regime before 2008, it has been suggested that Myanmar's period of military rule before the 1990s, and having been subject to Western economic sanctions in the 1990s and 2000s, has driven the Government's desire to re-engage with the international economy.[68]

Developments since 2013 such as the BITs with Japan, Korea and Singapore, and arbitrations of international commercial disputes, such as the aforementioned *UMEL v. F&N* dispute, signal this desire and the demand from foreign investors and international financial institutions. At the time of writing, there is increased political instability between Myanmar's military and civilian government.

Against this backdrop, the consolidated MIL is much welcomed. While there remain some ambiguities and uncertainty, sound investment law and policy should inform appropriate investment strategies, consistent with the MIC's stated policy objectives to promote investor confidence by enabling legal recourse.

64 See for example Lauge Poulsen, *Bounded Rationality and Economic Diplomacy* (2015).

65 United Nations Conference on Trade and Development, 'Fact Sheet on Investor-State Dispute Settlement Cases in 2018', *IIA Issues Note: International Investment Agreements* (May 2019), 1, available at https://unctad.org/en/PublicationsLibrary/diaepcbinf2019d4_en.pdf (last accessed 26 September 2019).

66 Anthea Roberts, 'Incremental, Systemic, and Paradigmatic Reform of Investor-State Arbitration' (2018) 112 *American Journal of International Law* 410, 432.

67 www.dica.gov.mm/files/uploads/pdf/agreement_vietnam_en.pdf. The UNCTAD website also lists a 2001 Myanmar-Laos BIT, which was quickly superseded by 2003 Myanmar-Laos BIT http://investmentpolicyhub.unctad.org/IIA/CountryBits/144 accessed 15 September 2016. The UNCTAD website does not provide a link to the text of this agreement. Aside from the UNCTAD website, the author has not been able to find any other record that such an agreement existed, and the 2003 treaty makes no reference to any earlier treaty. It is possible that UNCTAD's listing of the 2001 Myanmar-Laos BIT is the result of a clerical error.

68 Bonnitcha, 'International Investment Arbitration in Myanmar', above n 2, 335.

5

China and the Investment Treaty Regime

Rule Taker or Rule Maker?

Sheng Zhang

5.1 INTRODUCTION

The year 2018 marks the fortieth anniversary of China's opening-up policy, which presents a great opportunity to review China's developments and contributions in the area of international investment treaties. Since its first bilateral investment treaty (BIT) with Sweden in 1982, China has signed BITs with more than 130 countries. China's changing practice in the arena of international investment law is a microcosm of its growing participation in the international legal order. When signing BITs, China largely follows the template or style set by Western countries, and this regularly features in the BITs they sign. However, with China's recent rapid economic growth, which inevitably translates to greater political and negotiating power, China is more motivated to establish its own approach in the investment treaties it signs. The Belt and Road Initiative (BRI), and the BITs that China has been separately negotiating with the United States and the EU, reveals China's new proactive approach to not merely participating, but playing an influential role, in global economic governance. China's experience in dealing with cases filed by foreign investors against China also enables China to review its BIT policy. In a time of anti-globalization, China's more open and liberal attitude towards foreign investment helps not only to restore foreign investors' confidence in its economy but also to maintain the stability of the international investment law regime.

Against this background, this chapter takes stock of China's practice in international investment law. This chapter is broken down into five parts: Section 5.2 describes the development of China's foreign direct investment (FDI) policy and BITs practice; Section 5.3 focuses on China's practice of international investment arbitration by delving into the reasons for why there have been only a few cases against China; Section 5.4 compares China's BITs practice with those of the EU and the United States, identifying how China is situated in relation to certain basic positions; and Section 5.5 discusses China's proactive approach, in particular with the implementation of the BRI. Following from these discussions, this chapter, in its conclusion, hopes to reveal the approach of utilitarianism and flexibility that underpins China's BITs negotiations, and illustrates how this approach will produce templates that can be taken into account for the reform of investor–State dispute settlement (ISDS). Importantly, China is not simply copying or adopting in a wholesale manner the treaty texts presented by the EU or the United States, but is making the necessary adjustments to craft agreements that take into account its own political system and economic realities. China also maintains some basic positions to incorporate the concept of sovereignty and the identity of a developing country.

5.2 THE EVOLVING APPROACH OF CHINA'S FDI POLICY AND ITS BITS PRACTICE

In 1978, when China decided to commence economic reform, it decided to open up several special economic zones as 'windows' to attract foreign investment and as 'experimental fields' in order that China might have some practice in operating a market economy.[1] As part of this 'opening up' policy, the BIT programme was launched in 1982, with China's first BIT signed with Sweden, and was intended to attract FDI to fuel economic growth. Earlier Chinese BITs mainly targeted developed countries.

By 1986, China had already signed BITs with many European States. Yet, the initial BITs were very conservative, and reflected China's traditional scepticism towards international law.[2] Most of the BITs then either did not grant foreign investors national treatment or only provided them with a limited national treatment subject to domestic laws. Meanwhile, China insisted that only disputes about the amount of compensation could be submitted to international arbitration.

The 1990s witnessed a surge of foreign investment into China. To better accommodate the benefits of FDI and further stimulate the flow of FDI, China started to make adjustments to its economic system, abandoning the planned economy and accepting the 'market economy' in the form of the 'socialist market economy'. The constitutional status of these changes was established in 1993 through amendments to the Constitution.[3] At the international level, in line with further economic reform and the 'opening up' policy, China signed the ICSID Convention on 9 February 1990 and ratified it on 7 January 1993.[4]

China has applied a more liberal approach to foreign investment since 1998. The unprecedented amount of FDI and the intensified competition with Latin American and Eastern European States for FDI caused China to update its BIT programme. At the same time, China's rapid economic growth, particularly in relation to the increase in its foreign exchange reserves, created the need for an outward direct investment strategy.[5] In 1998, the 'going abroad' strategy was introduced in order to explore international markets and take advantage of foreign resources to strengthen the development and potential of the Chinese economy. This strategy was officially revealed in the Outline of the Tenth Five-Year Plan (FYP) for the National Economy and Social Development in 2001.[6] Another step in this direction was China's accession to the World Trade Organisation (WTO) in 2001. Unlike the first stage of BITs, which was characterized by the need to attract FDI and therefore emphasized capital importation, the investment policy post-1998 has been based on both the importation and exportation of capital, with an emphasis on the protection of outward direct investment.

[1] Wenhau Shan and Hongrui Chen, 'China-US BIT Negotiation and the Emerging Chinese BIT 4.0, in C. Lim (ed.), *Alternative Visions of the International Law on Foreign Investment: Essays in Honour of Muthucumaraswamy Sornarajah* (Cambridge: Cambridge University Press, 2016), pp. 223–52.

[2] Stephan Schill, 'Tearing Down the Great Wall: the New Generation Investment Treaties of the People's Republic of China' (2007) 15 *Cardozo Journal of International and Comparative Law* 73 at 82. See also Jiangyu Wang, 'China and the Universal Human Rights Standards' (2001–2002) 29 *Syracuse Journal of International Law and Commerce* 135–58 at 146.

[3] Norah Gallagher and Wenhua Shan, *Chinese Investment Treaties: Policies and Practice* (Oxford: Oxford University Press, 2009), pp.7–8.

[4] Ibid., p. 38.

[5] Wenhua Shan, Norah Gallagher and Sheng Zhang, 'National Treatment for Foreign Investment in China: A Changing Landscape' (2012) 27(1) *ICSID Review* 120–44 at 123.

[6] Zhu Rongji, 'Report on the Outline of the Tenth Five-Year Plan for National Economic and Social Development' (2001), 5 March 2001, available at www.gov.cn/english/official/2005–07/29/content_18334.htm (last accessed 12 July 2019).

Since the 1998 China–Barbados BIT, the first treaty to accommodate these policy changes, most Chinese BITs have included clauses for full national treatment and access of all investor–State disputes to international arbitration.

Notably, most of China's liberal BITs remain focused solely on investment protection and are silent on sustainable development issues. Three factors influence these focus areas within the BITs. First, since 1998, apart from renegotiating BITs with European States, China has mainly signed BITs with developing countries from Asia, Africa, and Latin America. These BITs, like other BITs between developing countries, show few deviations from the European-style BITs.[7] Indeed, the traditional European-style BITs still play a dominant role in world BITs.[8] Secondly, China's BIT strategy has continued to be based on economic considerations, particularly the need for inbound FDI to power rapid economic growth.[9] At the same time, the implementation of 'going abroad' policies has meant that China needs to facilitate and protect the interests of China's overseas enterprises. Thirdly, from a theoretical perspective, the restrictions implied in the clause 'in accordance with the domestic laws and regulations', which was common in Chinese BITs, have entitled the host State to impose regulatory measures.

This approach has changed in recent years, in particular since 2008, when China adopted a more balanced type of investment treaty, with a recalibration of the substantive provisions.[10] A notable development is the introduction of the concept of sustainable development. In fact, it was developments in China's internal policies that had led China's investment treaties to embrace the concept of sustainable development. Since 2006, China shifted its emphasis from the quantity of FDI to the quality of FDI. This change was clearly demonstrated in the 11th FYP on Foreign Capital Utilisation, where China asserted that it would propel the fundamental conversion from 'being quantity-oriented' to 'being quality-oriented' and focus more on sustainable development, which was further supported by the introduction of a 'scientific outlook on development'.[11] By pursuing a 'people-oriented, comprehensive, co-ordinated and sustainable

7 UNCTAD, *South-South Cooperation in International Investment Arrangements*, UNCTAD Series on International Investment Policies and Development (New York and Geneva: United Nations Publications, 2005), p. 31. It is also observed that the dynamic of BITs between more developed Southern countries versus the lesser-developed Southern countries mirrors that of the BITs between developed countries and developing countries, and, therefore the North-South European template is used. Furthermore, such a template could allow the Southern countries to negotiate specialist legal instruments given that they have traditionally have had limited capacity and knowledge. See Mahnaz Malik, 'South-South Bilateral Investment Treaties: The same old story?', IV Annual Forum for Developing Country Investment Negotiators Background Paper, New Delhi, October 27–29, 2010, available at www.iisd.org/pdf/2011/dci_2010_south_bits.pdf (last accessed 12 July 2019).

8 For instance, an observation of the examples of BITs concluded in 2010 and 2011 reveals that several countries continued to adopt such a traditional approach. See Stephan Schill and Marc Jacob, 'Trends in International Investment Agreements, 2011–2012: The Increasing Complexity of International Investment Law' in Karl Sauvant (ed.), *Yearbook on International Investment Law & Policy 2011–2012* (Oxford: Oxford University Press, 2013), p. 155.

9 Indeed, despite the high rate of growth, there was a severe environmental degradation. However, among the leadership and the public, development was primarily regarded as economic growth, while damage to the environment or natural resources was perceived as 'growing pain' and unavoidable costs for economic development. See Hanqin Xue, *Chinese Contemporary Perspectives on International Law: History, Culture and International Law*, Hague Academy of International Law (Leiden: Brill, 2012), p. 172.

10 Axel Berger, 'Hesitant Embrace: China's Recent Approach to International Investment Rule-Making' (2015) 16(3) *Journal of World Investment and Trade* 843–68 at 843.

11 The 11th Five-Year Plan on the Utilization of Foreign Capital Investments, published by the State Development and Reform Commission ('SDRC') on 6 November 2006. The English version is available at www.fdi.gov.cn/1800000121_39_3819_0_7.html (last accessed 12 July 2019). In line with this new FDI policy, China also made steady efforts to reform the domestic laws to eliminate the preferential treatment enjoyed by foreign investment. For details, please *see* Shan, Gallagher, and Zhang, above n 6, 129–38.

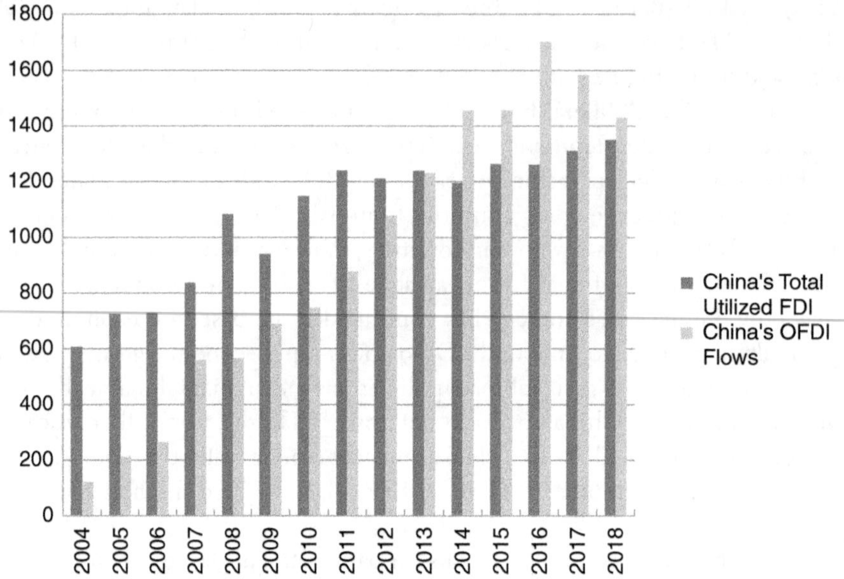

FIGURE 5.1 China's FDI and OFDI from 2004–2016 (unit: 100 million USD)
Source: MOFCOM

development', the 'scientific outlook on development' is similar to or even broader than the concept of sustainable development.[12]

China's BIT entered into a new phase in 2013 when China and the United States agreed to negotiate an investment treaty based on the pre-establishment of national treatment with a negative list,[13] which promises to accord national treatment during the pre-investment phase by limiting national treatment to particular economic sectors or activities. This approach offers full rights of entry and establishment based on the better national treatment, subject only to reserved 'negative' lists of industries to which such rights do not apply.[14] Such a move by China was regarded as the beginning of an emerging Chinese BIT 4.0,[15] and is the result of a combination of economic and political factors. Economically, as revealed in Figure 5.1, with the steady increase of outward direct investment, China has been a net capital-exporting country since 2014. It is unsurprising that China would play a more proactive role to provide sufficient support of the outward FDI. Politically, when domestic reform enters a deep-water zone, a push from external forces would be necessary to ensure that internal reform proceeds smoothly. As opening up and reform have been launched as integral parts of the same initiative, a breakthrough in investment treaty practice would lead to deeper reform. This round of reform is now referred to as 'China's Reform 2.0', and covers a wide range of areas,

12 Xue, Chinese Contemporary Perspectives on International Law, above n 10, pp. 192–93.

13 MOFCOM, 'MOFCOM spokesman Shen Danyang comments on China and US to promote energetically negotiations on bilateral investment agreement', 16 July 2013, available at http://english.mofcom.gov.cn/article/newsrelease/policyreleasing/201307/20130700200566.shtml (last accessed 12 July 2019).

14 The 'Pre-establishment with a negative list approach' is one of the five major categories or models regarding approaches to entry and establishment concluded by UNCTAD. See U.N. Conference on Trade & Dev., Admission and Establishment, at 3–4, U.N. Doc. UNCTAD/ITE/IIT/10 (Vol. II), UN Sales No. E.99.II.D.10 (1999).

15 Wenhua Shan and Hongrui Chen, 'China-US BIT Negotiation and the Emerging Chinese BIT 4.0?' in Chin Leng Lim (ed.), *Alternative Visions of the International Law on Foreign Investment* (Cambridge: Cambridge University Press, 2016), pp. 223–54.

including economic, political, cultural, societal and ecological systems.[16] The negative list approach, in particular, requires a reform of state governance, the streamlining of the administration and of all administrative approval procedures for economic activities under the effective regulation of the market mechanism.[17] In 2019, the approach of pre-establishment national treatment plus negative list was written into China's new Foreign Investment Law, demonstrating China's endeavour to provide a level playing field for foreign investors.

Alongside with BITs, China is also proactive in FTA negotiations. Currently, China has concluded fifteen FTAs covering twenty-three countries or regions.[18] FTAs are deemed by China to be a new platform for further opening up and speeding up domestic growth, as well as an effective approach to integrating into the global economy. FTAs also help to strengthen China's economic cooperation with other economies. China's early FTAs were confined to trade affairs,[19] but its more recent ones provide wider coverage in goods, services, investment, and most of them explicitly consider the concept of sustainable development. For example, China's FTA with Singapore refers to the Sino-Singapore Tianjin Eco-city project, which is the first inter-governmental eco-city in the world and is aimed at becoming a model for environmental cooperation and sustainable cities. China's most recent FTAs with Switzerland (2014) and Korea (2015) went one step further by including dedicated chapters on the environment. In the Sino–Swiss FTA, the two parties agree to 'facilitate and promote investment and dissemination of goods, services, and technologies beneficial to the environment,' and to provide 'the necessary resources for the implementation of environmental cooperation.' The Sino–Korean FTA includes a provision on conducting an environmental impact assessment of the FTA. It also addresses the enforcement problem by requiring parties not to 'fail to effectively enforce its environmental measures including laws and regulations, through a sustained or recurring course of action or inaction, in a manner affecting trade or investment between the Parties.'[20] Furthermore, and as can be gleaned from the earlier illustrations, FTAs normally include a broader understanding of environmental protection than BITs.[21]

5.3 CHINA'S PRACTICE IN INTERNATIONAL INVESTMENT DISPUTE SETTLEMENT

Although China has signed a great number of investment treaties, its exposure to international investment arbitration remains low. This may seem surprising as China continues to be a source of increasing FDI, but can be explained through the lens of law and culture.

16 Shan and Chen, above n 2.

17 CPC, Decision of the CCCPC on Some Major Issues Concerning Comprehensively Deepening the Reform, China.org.cn, 17 January 2014, available at www.china.org.cn/chinese/2014–01/17/content_31226494_4.htm (last accessed 12 July 2019).

18 China FTA Network, http://fta.mofcom.gov.cn/english/index.shtml (last accessed 12 July 2019).

19 Such as the Closer Economic Partnership Agreements concluded in 2001 with Hong Kong and Macau and the FTA with Chile in 2005.

20 See Henry Gao, 'China's evolving approach to environmental and labour provisions in regional trade agreements', International Centre for Trade and Sustainable Development, 25 August 2017, available at www.ictsd.org/opinion/china-3. Also see International Enterprise Singapore, 'Overview of the Sino-Singapore Tianjin Eco-city project', available at www.iesingapore.gov.sg/Content-Store/Industrial-Parks-and-Projects/Overview-of-the-Sino-Singapore-Tianjin-Eco-City-project (both last accessed 12 July 2019).

21 Jarrod Hepburn, et al., 'Sustainable Development in Regional Trade and Investment Agreements: Policy Innovations in Asia?', Legal Working Paper, Centre for International Sustainable Development Law (2007), p. 40.

First, as mentioned earlier, almost all the Chinese BITs signed before 1998 only allow disputes concerning or involving the amount of compensation for expropriation to be submitted to international investment arbitration. This limited offer of consent to arbitration suggests that China would not get sued frequently in investment arbitration. However, such a position may not be as solid as it seems. The tribunals that decided both the cases of *Tza Yap Shum v. Peru* and *Sanum v. Laos* held that the word 'involving' in the phase 'involving the amount of compensation for expropriation' in the 1994 China–Peru BIT and the 1993 China–Laos BIT was broad enough to cover claims of expropriation.[22] However, while the wording allegedly supports claims of expropriation, it would not cover other claims, such as those regarding fair and equitable treatment or full protection and security, as held by the tribunal in *Tza Yap Shum v. Peru*.[23] Further, uncertainty still exists in case law. A Swedish appeal court, for instance, rejected a broad interpretation when interpreting a similarly narrowly worded treaty provision in the Spain–Russia BIT. Article 10 of the Spain–Russia BIT only allows arbitration for disputes relating to the amount or method of payment of the compensation for expropriation. The Court of Appeal concluded that the arbitral tribunal's jurisdiction under the treaty did not cover a review as to whether expropriation occurred or not.[24]

Secondly, most of the Chinese BITs oblige foreign investors to go through the appropriate domestic administrative review process before seeking international arbitration. Even in the BITs where China has agreed to grant investors full access to international investment arbitration, China has continued to insist on this as a pre-requisite. For instance, the Protocol of the 2003 China–Germany BIT (which is often cited as an example of a Chinese third-generation BIT)[25] adds the following to Article 9 which provides for investor–State dispute settlement:[26]

With respect to investments in the People's Republic of China an investor of the Federal Republic of Germany may submit a dispute for arbitration under the following conditions only if:

(a) the investor has referred the issue to an administrative review procedure according to Chinese law,
(b) the dispute still exists three months after he or she has brought the issue to the review procedure, and
(c) the issue has been brought to a Chinese court, it can be withdrawn by the investor according to Chinese law.

[22] *Señor Tza Yap Shum* v. *The Republic of Peru*, ICSID Case No. ARB/07/6, Decision on Jurisdiction and Competence, 19 June 2009, para. 188. *Sanum Investments Limited* v. *Lao People's Democratic Republic*, UNCITRAL, PCA Case No. 2013–13, Award on Jurisdiction, 13 December 2013, para. 342. Some may also argue that the Most Favoured Nation (MFN) clause in the BITs would be applied to broaden the scope of consent of arbitration, as held by the tribunal of *RosInvest* v. *Russia*. By referring to the MFN provision of the UK–Russia BIT and relying on a more extensive dispute settlement provision in the Denmark–UK BIT, the tribunal held that the investors from UK could submit a claim over expropriation to arbitration, while the basic treaty only allowed for arbitration over claims involving the amount of compensation for expropriation. *See RosInvest Co UK Ltd.* v. *The Russian Federation*, SCC Case No. V079/2005, Award on Jurisdiction, October 2007, para. 139.

[23] *Tza Yap Shum* v. *The Republic of Peru*, ICSID Case No. ARB/07/6, Decision on Jurisdiction and Competence, 19 June 2009, para. 216.

[24] SVEA Court of Appeal, Judgment, 18 January 2016, available at www.italaw.com/sites/default/files/case-documents/italaw7714_8.pdf (last accessed 12 July 2019).

[25] Shan and Chen, above n 2.

[26] 2003 China–Germany BIT, available at https://investmentpolicy.unctad.org/international-investment-agreements/treaty-files/736/download (last accessed 12 July 2019).

Under such an obligation, foreign investors cannot immediately commence investment arbitration. Indeed, there have been cases between foreign investors and Chinese local governments that were settled through administrative remedies.[27]

Thirdly, the legal regime relating to the recognition and enforcement of investment arbitral awards also discourages foreign investors from seeking international investment arbitration. When acceding to the New York Convention on the Recognition and Enforcement of Foreign Arbitral Awards ('New York Convention'), the Chinese government made a commercial reservation that China would apply the New York Convention only to differences arising out of legal relationships which are considered as commercial under Chinese national law.[28] Subsequently, the People's Republic of China issued the Notice on the Implementation of the New York Convention, which clearly excluded arbitral awards in relation to international investment disputes from the list of awards that could be recognized and enforced in China.[29] Such a commercial reservation does not apply to an arbitral award rendered by an ICSID arbitral tribunal in accordance with the ICSID Convention, as Article 54 of the ICSID Convention creates a system of self-execution. However, China has not enacted any specific legislation to comply with the recognition and enforcement obligations under the ICSID Convention, creating uncertainty regarding China's compliance with these obligations.[30] Meanwhile, given that Article 54(3) of the ICSID Convention provides that the 'execution of the award shall be governed by the laws concerning the execution of judgment in force in the State in whose territories such execution is sought', the execution against the property of a State would be a problem in China, particularly since China continues to insist on the principle of absolute sovereign immunity. This would also prevent the local courts from attaching the assets of a State to execute an ICSID award.[31]

Finally, in a country where the traditional culture prefers an amicable settlement of disputes, arbitration or litigation could be perceived to be serious challenges to harmony and good relationships.[32] In most Asian countries, law and contracts are subordinated to evolving circumstances and relational values. Contracts are seen more as the beginning of a good relationship than as a conclusion of a deal.[33] Particularly in China, there has been a longstanding traditional dislike for litigation. As of now, Confucianism, which attaches much significance to harmony, still maintains a great degree of cultural influence over Chinese society.[34] In light of this cultural context, commencing investment arbitration proceedings may be considered to be jeopardizing the good relationship between foreign investors and host governments, which may eventually lead to a phasing out of foreign investment in China.

27 For details, please see Gallagher and Shan, above n 4, pp. 371–76.

28 New York Arbitration Convention, Contracting States, www.newyorkconvention.org/countries (last accessed 12 July 2019).

29 People's Supreme Court of China, Notice of the Supreme People's Court on Implementing the Convention on the Recognition and Enforcement of Foreign Arbitral Awards Acceded to by China, No. 5 (1987) of the Supreme People's Court, 4 October 1987.

30 Julian Ku, 'The Enforcement of ICSID Awards in the People's Republic of China' (2013) 6(1) *Contemporary Asian Arbitraiton Journal* 31–48.

31 Guiguo Wang, 'Chinese Mechanisms for Resolving Investor-State Disputes' (2011) 1(1) *Jindal Journal of International Affairs* 204–33 at 228.

32 Ibid., at 222.

33 Michael Hwang, 'Why Is There Still Resistance to Arbitration in Asia' in Gerald Aksen and Robert Briner (eds.), Global Reflections on International Law, Commerce and Dispute Resolution: liber amicorum in honour of Robert Briner, International Chamber of Commerce, 2005, pp. 410–11.

34 Wang, 'Resolving Investor-State Disputes', 222–24.

As of July 2019, China is registered as having been involved in only three ICSID cases, one filed by a Malaysian investor in 2011, one filed by a South Korean investor in 2014, and the third one filed by a German investor in 2017. These three cases will be analysed further.

5.3.1 *Ekran v. China*

This was the first ICSID case against China.[35] This case, which was filed by a Malaysian investor in 2011, arose out of a dispute concerning the rights under a lease over 900 hectares of land in one Chinese local province held by Ekran Berhad's (Ekran's) local subsidiary. Ekran claimed that the local government had revoked its subsidiary's rights to the leasehold land due to a failure to develop the land as required under local regulations. This case was settled even before the tribunal was constituted.[36] While further details remain unknown to the public, one thing is for sure: China normally takes a cautious approach towards international disputes. This may explain why the first ICSID case against China ended up in a settlement rather than arbitration.

5.3.2 *Ansung Housing v. China*

Ansung Housing ('Ansung') is a South Korean investor that invested in a golf course and condominium development project in the Jiangsu province. By alleging that the various arbitrary and illegal actions and omissions of the local government had deprived it of use and enjoyment of its investment, Ansung brought an ICSID claim against China on 4 November 2014.[37]

China's representatives filed the respondent's objection pursuant to Rule 41(5) of the ICSID Arbitration Rules, asserting that Ansung's claim was 'manifestly without legal merit' and should be dismissed, on the basis that Ansung's claim was time-barred, pursuant to Article 9(7) of the 2007 China–South Korea BIT, which provides that '[a]n investor may not make a claim pursuant to paragraph 3 of this article if more than three years have elapsed from the date on which the investor first acquired, or should have first acquired, the knowledge that the investor had incurred losses or damage.' According to the respondent, Ansung instituted the ICSID arbitration more than three years after the date on which it first acquired knowledge it had incurred loss or damage and the MFN clause in the BIT could not save Ansung's untimely claim.[38] China argued that Article 9(7), providing the temporal requirement, referred to knowledge of the *fact* that there had been a loss, but not knowledge of the *quantum* lost, and Ansung necessarily knew of the fact that it had incurred loss on some date prior to the disposal of its investment in October 2011. Given that the case was registered by ICSID only on 4 November 2014, China asserted that Ansung did not comply with the temporal requirement under Article 9(7), which rendered the claim time-barred.[39] The tribunal agreed that the facts revealed that Ansung first acquired or should have first acquired knowledge that it had incurred loss or damage before October 2011.[40] In the tribunal's view, 'Ansung's actual sale of its shares on December 17, 2011 marked the date on which it could

35 *Ekran Berhad* v. *People's Republic of China*, ICSID Case No. ARB/11/15.

36 Tong Qi, 'How Exactly Does China Consent to Investor-State Arbitration: on the First ICSID Case against China' (2012) 5(2) *Contemporary Asia Arbitration Journal* 265–91.

37 *Ansung Housing Co., Ltd.* v. *People's Republic of China*, ICSID Case No. ARB/14/25.

38 Ibid., para. 56.

39 Ibid., para. 85.

40 Ibid., para. 114.

finalize or *liquidate* its damage, not the *first* date on which it had to know it was incurring damage'.[41] With respect to the *dies ad quem* for the applicable temporal limitation period, the tribunal argued that the plain language in Article 9(7) of the 2007 China–South Korea BIT pointed to the date on which the investor deposited its request for ICSID arbitration, which was the date of 7 October 2014 electronically and the date of 8 October 2014 physically. As either date would reflect more than three years after the *dies a quo*,[42] the tribunal concluded that the three-year limitation period had elapsed and the claim was time-barred.[43]

The tribunal further considered whether the MFN clause found in Article 3 of the BIT could save Ansung's claim from being time-barred. Article 3(3) provides:

> Each Contracting Party shall in its territory accord to investors of the other Contracting Party and to their investments and activities associated with such investments by the investors of the other Contracting Party *treatment no less favourable* than that accorded in like circumstances to the investors and *investments and associated activities* by the investors of any third State (hereinafter referred to as 'most-favoured-nation treatment') with respect to investments and business activities, including the admission of investment (emphasis added).

Ansung argued that the terms 'treatment' and 'investment activities' in Article 3(3) should be interpreted to cover dispute settlement procedures because investor–State arbitration is critical to protect investment activities. China, on the other hand, contested that a contextual interpretation of Article 3(5), which provides MFN treatment with respect to 'access to courts of justice and administrative tribunals and authorities', demonstrated that Article 3(3) is unrelated to dispute settlement.[44] By referring to Article 3(5), the tribunal concluded that a plain reading of Article 3 does not extend to MFN treatment for a State's consent to arbitrate with investors and, in particular, not to the three-year period in Article 9(7) of the treaty.[45] Article 3(5) only offers MFN protection in relation to an investor's remedies through domestic avenues, while such express reference to international dispute resolution is conspicuously absent in Article 3(3).[46]

As a result, the tribunal determined that China established its Rule 41(5) objection 'clearly and obviously, with relative ease and despatch'.[47] The tribunal therefore found Ansung's claim to be manifestly without legal merit.[48]

5.3.3 *Hela Schwarz v. China*

On 21 June 2017, ICSID registered its third case against China.[49] It was brought by a German investor in accordance with the 2003 China–Germany BIT. The tribunal was constituted on 8 January 2018. The claimant, Hela Schwarz GmbH ('Hela Schwarz'), was a German-owned spice and food additive manufacturer, and it had invested in the city of Jinan since 1996.[50] In

41 Ibid., para. 110.
42 Ibid., para. 115.
43 Ibid., para. 122.
44 Ibid., paras. 127–28.
45 Ibid., para. 138.
46 Ibid., para. 139.
47 Ibid., para. 142.
48 Ibid., para. 143.
49 *Hela Schwarz GmbH* v. *People's Republic of China*, ICSID Case No. No. ARB/17/19.
50 Luke Eric Peterson and Zoe Williams, 'Asia round-up: China and Vietnam face new BIT claims – by Hela Schwarz GmbH and Trinh Vinh Binh, respectively – as proceedings against Korea and Indonesia move forward', *Investment Arbitration Reporter*, 22 June 2017.

2014, the Jinan government adopted a Decision to expropriate some State-owned lands in a local district. Being unsatisfied with the compensation, Hela Schwarz launched an administrative review of this Decision, and then it went into a negotiation of settlement with the local government. At the same time, some local citizens filed an administrative litigation, challenging the legality of the Decision. The local court of first instance rendered the judgment on 30 April 2015 that the Decision was made on the basis of conclusive evidence, a correct legal basis and due legal procedures, thus dismissing the claim.[51] A claim of appeal was soon filed, yet a settlement was reached during the appeal. The court of appeal finally allowed the appellants to withdraw their claim.[52]

Failing to reach a settlement with the local government, Hela Schwarz filed for an administrative litigation on 3 May 2016, seeking to revoke the Decision. By referring to an 'Interpretation of the Supreme People's Court on Several Issues concerning the Application of the Administrative Litigation Law', the Court of First Instance held that the Decision challenged by Hela Schwarz was already bound by an effective judgment, which was the appeal judgment mentioned earlier. In this case, the claim was dismissed. The judgment of the Court of First Instance was upheld by the appeal court.[53] However, Hela Schwarz claimed that it had launched the administrative review process before the administrative litigation filed by the local citizens, while the review process was delayed because the local government wanted to settle the dispute. For the litigations between the local citizens and the government, Hela Schwarz claimed that it was not invited to attend the proceedings as a stakeholder. Further, Hela Schwarz pointed out that local citizens' settlement with the government did not mean that they accepted the legality of the Decision. Hence it should not be bound by such judgments and should not be deprived of its rights to challenge the Decision.[54]

Considering that China has taken a proactive stance in the development of the international investment treaty regime, and with foreign investors becoming increasingly aware of their rights and protections under the BITs, it is not unlikely that more cases will be brought against China in the future. It was reported recently that Asiaphos Ltd, a phosphate mining company registered in Singapore, has threatened to file for arbitration against China, after a central province rejected its application to renew its mining rights.[55] Moreover, China's participation in the ICSID cases illustrates that China's attitude towards international investment arbitration is evolving towards greater acceptance and engagement.[56] More cases can be expected, particularly if the China–US BIT and the China–EU BIT are successfully concluded.

51 First Instance Judgment of Intermediate People's Court of Jinan on Administrative Expropriation between Chen Yunjuan et al. and the People's Government of Jinan Municipality, (2015) Ji Xing Chu Zi No.72, www.lawsdata.com/detail?id=58101f502f12c63192756c80&key= (in Chinese) (last accessed 12 July 2019).

52 Appeal Judgment of Higher People's Court of Shandong Province on Administrative Expropriation between Kang Xiaomei et al. and the People's Government of Jinan Municipality, (2015) Lu Xing Zhong Zi No.444, www.lawsdata.com/detail?id=57a66247c2265c04d1db9816&key= (in Chinese) (last accessed 12 July 2019).

53 Appeal Judgment of Higher People's Court of Shandong Province on Administrative Expropriation between Hela Schwarz and the People's Government of Jinan Municipality, (2016) Lu Xing Zhong Zi No.1491, www.lawsdata.com/detail?id=5865ee9c8a860383c4289e61&key= (in Chinese) (last accessed 12 July 2019).

54 Ibid.

55 Jarrod Hepburn and Luke Eric Peterson, 'China Warned of Possible Investment Treaty Arbitration', Investment Arbitration Reporter, 6 March 2018.

56 Harriet Moynihan, 'China's Evolving Approach to International Dispute Settlement', Chatham House, March 2017, available at www.chathamhouse.org/sites/files/chathamhouse/publications/research/2017-03-29-chinas-evolving-approach-international-dispute-settlement-moynihan-final.pdf (last accessed 12 July 2019).

5.4 RULE-TAKER OR RULE-MAKER?

In contrast to the uncompromising position taken by the United States, China maintains great flexibility in its BITs negotiations.[57] Such an approach, termed 'utilitarianism' or 'pragmatism',[58] offers an explanation as to why China mainly follows the prototype of the States it is negotiating with. As observed by Axel Berger, China normally chooses the partner country's BIT template as the starting point, and only when such a BIT template does not exist or the partner country fails to put forward a template will China propose its own model to facilitate the negotiations.[59] Since most of the Chinese BITs signed in the 1980s were between China and the European States, it is understandable that most of the BITs signed by China have adopted the European style, focusing mainly on investment protection.[60] All three versions of Chinese model BITs also resemble European-style BITs. Given that the European-style BIT is simple and short, it is more manageable and makes it much easier to push negotiations forward, in particular when there is a tight agenda and the negotiators lack sufficient expertise in the earlier stages.[61] However, the European-style BITs may fall short in addressing non-economic concerns, such as the environment, labour, and national security. Hence, there is an increasing Americanization of investment treaties, as the American BITs, represented by the NAFTA, are much more comprehensive, featuring broad coverage and a balanced regime.[62]

With the fast development of its economy, in particular the development of outward FDI flows, China has grown from being a mere capital-importing country to a country with a mixed status of being a top capital-importing and capital-exporting country. Meanwhile, the featured debate of international investment law-making seems to have shifted from a 'north-south divide' to a 'private-public divide'.[63] Against this background, China has considered pursuing a partially 'NAFTA'-inspired investment policy, and seems to have shifted from the European investment treaty model to the American one in its recent IAAs, in particular since the 2008 China–New Zealand FTA.

Yet, in its BIT practice, China does not mechanically imitate the European States or the United States. A closer look at the treaty texts reveals that China still maintains a degree of flexibility to accommodate its political system and economic reality.

First, China attaches a large significance to the concept of sovereignty. The principle of sovereignty was the foundation of China's relationship with the international community, and it was the source of China's other principles, such as the principle of non-interference.[64]

57 *See* Qingjiang Kong, 'Bilateral Investment Treaties: the Chinese Approach and Practice' (1998) 8 *Asian Yearbook of International Law*, 105–36 at 110 and Berger, above n 11, at 866.

58 As pointed out by Professor Kenneth Vandevelde, the United States mainly proposed to negotiate the BITs largely based on its model BIT, and it was extremely reluctant from the beginning to compromise on any but a few of the BIT provisions. If such a proposal was not accepted, there would be no BIT with that state. See Kenneth Vandevelde, *US International Investment Agreements* (Oxford: Oxford University Press, 2009), p. 32.

59 Berger, above n 11, at 865–66.

60 Yongjie Li, 'Factors to be Considered for China's Future Investment Treaties' in Wenhua Shan and Jinyuan Su (eds.), *China and International Investment Law: Twenty Years of ICSID Membership* (Leiden: Brill, 2014), p. 174.

61 Manjiao Chi, 'From Europeanization toward Americanization: the Shift of China's Dichotomic Investment Treaty-making Strategy' (2017) 23(2) *Canadian Foreign Policy Journal* 158–70 at 164.

62 Wolfgang Alschner, 'Americanization of the BIT Universe: The Influence of Friendship, Commerce and Navigation (FCN) Treaties on Modern Investment Treaty Law' (2013) 5(2) *Goettingen Journal of International Law* 455–86.

63 Wenhua Shan, 'From "North-South Divide" to Private-Public Debate: Revival of the Calvo Doctrine and the Changing Landscape in International Investment Law' (2007) 27(3) *Northwestern Journal of International Law and Business* 631–64 at 664.

64 Xue, above n 10, pp. 68–94.

China's persistent stand has its roots in the miserable and humiliating experience of foreign oppression and invasion since the Opium War in the 1840s.[65] This position also affects China's attitude towards international investment disputes, namely featuring a hesitant embrace of international investment arbitration. Given that the jurisdiction of domestic courts is one manifestation of the exertion of sovereignty, some of China's BITs, such as the BIT with Sri Lanka, also requires the legality of any measure of expropriation to be reviewed by the competent domestic court in the manner prescribed by domestic law.[66]

Based on the principle of sovereignty and the 'Five Principles of Peaceful Co-existence', China further developed 'three guiding principles' of international economic co-operation and exchange: the principle of sovereignty; equality and mutual benefit; and reference to international practice.[67] These guiding principles have been expressly referenced in China's BIT practice. Most of the BITs concluded by China between 1988 and 1993 include a reference to the principles of mutual respect for sovereignty and equality and mutual benefit in their preambles. These BITs have mainly been signed with Asian countries and former Soviet Union countries. Some of the BITs with developed countries also have such preambular wordings, such as the 1988 China–Australia BIT and the 1992 China–Spain BIT. While a direct reference to the principle of mutual respect for sovereignty is omitted in most of the BITs concluded after 1993, this does not render the concept of sovereignty unimportant. The principle of equality and mutual benefit remains to be seen, and the recent China–Tanzania BIT witnessed a return of this novel concept, as it emphasizes the principle of respecting economic sovereignty in the preamble. This reveals that China mainly considers the BIT to be an instrument of economics and it should hence bear the essence of depoliticization. This could also explain why China refused to put the issue of human rights on the table during the negotiations, such as during the FTA talk with Australia.[68]

Secondly, BITs negotiations should reflect the political system and economic reality.[69] As mentioned by Li Shishi, China maintains that BITs should be based on the political independence and economic self-determination of Contracting States.[70] Before China's Constitution was revised to make the development of a socialist market economy one of its fundamental policy goals in 1993, China maintained a planned economy, in which state ownership, collective ownership and individual ownership co-existed. Given that the Chinese economy was quite different from the market economy, it was impossible for China to grant foreign investors national treatment.[71] It was only once the role of the market was changed from being at the edge to being central to economic development that national treatment became a common reference in Chinese BITs.

In spite of its rapid economic growth, China still sees itself as a developing country. This perspective enables China to adhere to different approaches from the developed countries. For instance, China used to stand firmly with other developing countries in fighting against

65 Indeed, Judge Wang Tieya described China as having been 'a most enthusiastic champion' for the principle of sovereignty. See Tieya Wang, 'International Law in China: Historical and Contemporary Perspective' (1990) 221 *Recueil des Cours II (Collected Courses)* 203 at 252–53.

66 China–Sri Lanka BIT (1986), Art. 6(2).

67 Kong, above n 58, at 109.

68 Jadranka Petrovic and Benjamin Grunberg, 'Intersecting Trade, Politics and Human Rights: The Negotiation Phase of the Australia-China Free Trade Agreement' (2017) 51(1) *Journal of World Trade* 67–104.

69 Shan and Chen, above n 2, pp. 248–50.

70 Shishi Li, 'Bilateral Investment Promotion and Protection Agreements: Practice of the People's Republic of China' in Paul J. I. M. de Waart, Paul Peter, and Eric M. G. Denters (eds.), *International Law and Development* (London: Martinus Nijhoff Publisher, 1988), p. 164.

71 Ibid., p. 167.

the 'Hull Formula' of 'adequate, effective and prompt compensation' with respect to the standard of expropriation. While changes have been made in the recent BITs to gradually conform to the practice of the United States, China is still hesitant to refer directly to the 'Hull Formula'. Meanwhile, China does not accept that the 'Hull Formula' reflects a customary international law obligation of States with respect to expropriation.[72] Under international law, the general approach of States has been that expropriation should be made against compensation, yet there is no uniform standard of compensation. Indeed, the standard of compensation is a subject to be discussed during the BITs negotiations.[73] It should also be noted that the 'Hull Formula' is not adopted by the International Law Commission in the 'Responsibility of States for Internationally Wrongful Acts' (2001), which only provides that 'the compensation shall cover any financially assessable damage including loss of profits insofar as it is established'.

China's identity as a developing country also makes it better placed to consider the different levels of development of the Contracting States in its investment treaty negotiations, such as in the Regional Comprehensive Economic Partnership (RCEP) negotiations, which directly refers to special and different treatment. Under such a principle, the RCEP negotiations should take into consideration the different levels of development of the participating countries, and the RCEP will include appropriate forms of flexibility in drafting specific provisions.[74] This principle has already been incorporated in the preamble of the China-Association of Southeast Asian Nations (ASEAN) Agreement on Investment.[75]

Political system and economic realities also affect China's position on State-owned enterprises (SOEs). Although the share of SOEs in China's outward foreign direct investment (OFDI) has decreased in recent years, SOEs still play a dominant role in China's OFDI. By the end of 2015, SOEs represented a share of 50.4 per cent in China's non-financial outward FDI stock.[76] It would be impossible for Chinese BITs not to offer protection to SOEs.[77] When defining 'enterprise' as a covered investor, Article 1(2) of the 2013 China–Tanzania BIT provides that it means:

> any entity, including companies, firms, associations, partnerships and other organizations, incorporated or constituted under the law and regulations of either Contracting Party and that have their seat and substantial business activities in that Contracting Party, irrespective of whether it is owned or controlled by a private person or the government.

Similar wording can also be found in the recent FTAs, such as in Article 1(f) of the 2009 FTA between China and the ASEAN. In practice, as held by the tribunal in the case of *Beijing Urban v. Yemen*, China's publicly funded and wholly state-owned enterprises could file for investment arbitration with ICSID.[78] There is no doubt that Chinese SOEs should follow the rules of the host States, but they should also be entitled to the same protection as private

72 See Annex B of the 2012 US Model BIT.

73 Muthucumaraswamy Sornarajah, *The International Law on Foreign Investment* (3rd edition) (Cambridge: Cambridge University Press, 2010), p. 209.

74 Guiding Principles and Objectives for negotiating the Regional Comprehensive Economic Partnership, available at https://asean.org/storage/2012/05/RCEP-Guiding-Principles-public-copy.pdf (last accessed 12 July 2019).

75 China FTA Network, Agreement on Investment of the Framework Agreement on Comprehensive Economic Co-operation between China and ASEAN, http://fta.mofcom.gov.cn/dongmeng_phase2/annex/touzixieyi_en.pdf (last accessed 12 July 2019).

76 MOFCOM, 2015 Statistical Bulletin of China's Outward Foreign Direct Investment, China Statistics Press, 2016, p.110.

77 Shan and Chen, above n 2, pp. 249–50.

78 *Beijing Urban Construction Group Co. Ltd.* v. *Republic of Yemen*, ICSID Case No. ARB/14/30, Decision on Jurisdiction, 31 May 2017, paras. 40–41.

investors as long as they are not acting as an agent for the government or performing government functions.

Thirdly, China's BIT practice is also shaped by the reflection on investment treaties by the international society, and in such a process China is seeking a different approach. As discussed in Section 5.2 of this chapter, China is only involved in a handful of investment arbitration disputes as a respondent. But as mentioned by Ms Li Yongjie, the Deputy Director-General of the Treaty and Law of MOFCOM, China needs to take into account global and domestic factors when considering a new generation of investment treaties, and the global context lies in the recent practice to improve BITs by drawing on lessons from ISDS practice.[79] The 2012 China–Canada BIT illustrates that parties are increasingly having greater control over ISDS. Under Article 20(2) of the China–Canada BIT, when a dispute arises out of a prudential measure, the investor–State tribunal must decide whether and to what extent the defence of prudential measures is a valid defence, and it shall first seek the joint decision of the financial services authorities of the Contracting States. If such a joint decision is unattainable, a state-to-state arbitral tribunal should be established, and the holdings of the state-to-state arbitral tribunal shall be binding on the investor–State tribunal. In this respect, it seems that China is exploring a different approach from the United States or Canada, as according to the Canadian or American model BITs, if the financial service authorities fail to reach a joint decision, the investor–State tribunal established could still proceed to reach a decision.[80] China's position, in actual fact, demonstrates the re-emergence of state-to-state dispute settlement, which represents a development towards a new 'third era' of the investment treaty regime, featuring a co-existence of state-to-state arbitration and investor–State arbitration.[81] In recent treaty practice, such as the 2012 China–Canada BIT, 2015 China–South Korea FTA, and 2015 China–Australia FTA, China has already considered exploring the consensus-building approach between the Contracting States to interpret the meaning and scope of the treaty, and limiting the scope of disputes subject to the ISDS.

5.5 CHINA'S ROLE IN FUTURE INTERNATIONAL INVESTMENT LAW

The international investment treaty regime has manifested, to some extent, China's growing confidence in adopting international rules and making its contribution. As an emerging power in international law, China is still discovering the optimal approach to establishing its soft power. Some have argued that China has failed to 'provide the world with an ideological contribution that fundamentally challenges the triumph of liberal ideology in the wake of the end of the Cold War'.[82] However, recent years have already shown a more proactive China with regard to IIA developments.

The BRI, which was first proposed by Chinese president Xi Jinping in 2013, has gone beyond Asia to cover countries from all continents. While still in the early stages of its implementation, it has been greeted with excitement globally and has been incorporated

[79] Li, above n 71, p. 173.

[80] 2004 Canadian Model BIT, Art. 17 and 2012 US Model BIT, Art. 20.

[81] Anthea Roberts, 'State-to-State Investment Treaty Arbitration: A Hybrid Theory of Interdependent Rights and Shared Interpretive Authority' (2014) 55(1) *Harvard International Law Journal* 1–70.

[82] David P. Fidler, 'The Asian Century: Implications for International Law' (2005) 9 *Singapore YearBook of International Law* 19–35.

by the United Nations in its resolution entitled 'The Situation in Afghanistan', urging further efforts to strengthen the process of regional economic cooperation through BITs and other regional development efforts.[83]

As the BRI mainly covers emerging countries, the political, social, and economic climate of these countries will have essential bearings on the success of the investment under the BRI, including infrastructure investment that needs a higher volume of capital. However, the current dispute settlement mechanism is not well positioned to solve the investment disputes. A closer look at the investment agreements between China and the countries of the BRI reveals that these treaties do not accord sufficient investment protection, nor do they sufficiently address the States' right to regulate.[84] In particular, there exists a large degree of divergence in the provisions of the ISDS in these investment agreements. No consistent approach can be found in areas of arbitral institutions and rules, the pre-conditions for submitting a claim, and the enforcement of arbitral awards.[85] Hence, a well-set out dispute resolution mechanism would be imperative to minimize the potential risks. China could voice its contributions to build a consistent, predictable, and balanced system to effectively solve investment disputes.[86] Steps have been taken by China to facilitate dispute settlement in the context of the BRI. On 16 June 2015, China's Supreme People's Court issued the 'Several Opinions of the Supreme People's Court Concerning Judicial Services and Safeguards Provided by the People's Courts for the "Belt and Road" Construction'[87] to provide effective services and to guarantee the smooth construction of the BRI. It was pointed out, in particular, that 'Chinese courts should further expand the channels for international judicial exchange, closely watch the progress of the Asian Investment Bank and the construction of the Silk Road Fund, study in-depth the development trends of international law especially in finance, trade, investments, and maritime issues, and actively take part in and promote the formulation of relevant international rules'.[88] In 2018, China's International Commercial Courts were established by the Supreme People's Court to solve the international commercial disputes in a fair, professional and effective manner.[89] In September 2017, the China International Economic and Trade Arbitration Commission (CIETAC) adopted the CIETAC Investment Arbitration Rules.[90] This is the first time that a Chinese arbitral

83 United Nations, General Assembly Adopts Resolution Supporting Afghanistan's Efforts, as Speakers Vow to Help Conflict-affected Nation Achieve Untapped Potential, 17 November 2016, available at www.un.org/press/en/2016/ga11858.doc.htm (last accessed 12 July 2019).

84 *See* Anna Chuwen Dai, 'The International Investment Agreement Network under the "One Belt One Road" Initiative' (2017) 14(3) *Transnational Dispute Management*, available at www.transnational-dispute-management.com/article.asp?key=2474 (last accessed 12 July 2019).

85 Zhang Shu, 'China's Approach in Drafting the Investor-State Arbitration Clause: A Review from the "Belt and Road" Regions' Perspective' (2017) 5(1) *Chinese Journal of Comparative Law* 79–109 at 98. As mentioned by the UNCTAD, it is time to move to a new phase of the reform of international investment agreements by modernizing the existing stock of old-generation treaties. See UNCTAD, Phase 2 of IIA Reform: Modernizing the Existing Stock of Old-Generation Treaties, IIA Issue Note, Issue 2 (New York and Geneva: United Nations Publications), June 2017, p. 1.

86 Shu, 'China's Approach in Drafting the Investor-State Arbitration Clause: A Review from the "Belt and Road" Regions' Perspective', ibid., at 106.

87 The People's Supreme Court of The People's Republic of China, Opinions of the Supreme People's Court on people's courts providing judicial services and guarantees for the construction of the Belt and Road Initiative (in Chinese), 7 July 2015, available at www.court.gov.cn/zixun-xiangqing-14900.html (last accessed 12 July 2019).

88 Ibid., para. 15.

89 Sheng Zhang, 'China's International Commercial Court: Background, Obstacles and the Road Ahead' (2020) 11 (1) *Journal of International Dispute Settlement* 150–74.

90 CIETAC, CIETAC Investment Arbitration Rules (for Trial Use) (in Chinese), 26 September 2017, available at www.cietac.org/Uploads/201709/59c8d60367bb5.pdf (last accessed 12 July 2019).

institution has adopted a set of rules specially designed for the settlement of international investment disputes. By referring to the practice in international investment arbitration, the CIETAC Investment Arbitration Rules include provisions on transparency[91] and third-party funding.[92] This set of rules also incorporates some culture specific features, including the principle of good faith (*chengshi xinyong*)[93] and the combination of conciliation and arbitration.[94] In January 2018, the Leading Group for Deepening Overall Reform headed by President Xi Jinping approved a guideline to establish a procedure and organization to handle the resolution of investment and trade disputes arising from issues related to the BRI.[95]

Meanwhile, under the active promotion of China, the Group of Twenty (G20) has reached a multilateral consensus on investment matters. The G20 Guiding Principles for Global Investment Policymaking, which was endorsed by the G20 leaders at the Hangzhou Summit in September 2016, lays out the first global framework of multilateral rules governing international investment. These guiding principles feature the concrete efforts of G20 countries to push forward the development of international investment treaty regime towards multilateralism. Although these guiding principles are non-binding, they could serve as a guiding instrument for updating domestic FDI policies and negotiating BITs.[96]

In addition, the ongoing negotiations of the China–US BIT and the China–EU BIT have great implications on the global investment regime. BITs between the world's largest developing country, the world's largest developed country and the world's largest economy would not only incorporate the reflections by these countries on ISDS, but also set up a model for other countries to refer to when considering improving their BITs. It should also be noted that during these negotiations, China will not purely imitate the text proposed by the EU and the United States. Instead, with its experience in negotiating BITs, China will naturally bring its interests to the table.[97] For instance, reports of the China–EU BIT negotiations demonstrate that China did not follow the proposal by the European Commission and there are divided opinions in some areas.[98] With respect to ISDS, it seems that China is trying to maintain a balanced position between two ends separately held by the EU and the United States. While the EU is vigorously pursuing the establishment of the international investment court system to reform the current ISDS system, the United States still considers arbitration to be the priority method of solving investment disputes.[99] A leaked text of China's proposal of the draft investment chapter of the RCEP revealed that China would choose to accept the appeal mechanism but would allow foreign investors to choose the arbitrator in the first instance

91 See, e.g., Article 44, 'Third Party Written Submission' and Article 55, 'Publication', of the CIETAC Investment Arbitration Rules.

92 Article 27, 'Third Party Funding', of the CIETAC Investment Arbitration Rules.

93 Article 6, 'Good Faith', of the CIETAC Investment Arbitration Rules.

94 Article 43, 'Combination of Conciliation with Arbitration' of the CIETAC Arbitration Rules.

95 Zhang Yubin, 'Process Eyed to Solve Belt, Road Disputes', *China Daily*, 24 January 2018.

96 UNCTAD, *World Investment Report 2017: Investment and the Digital Economy* (New York and Geneva: United Nations Publications), pp. 118–19.

97 Sheng Zhang, 'The China-United States BIT Negotiations: A Chinese Perspective', Columbia FDI Perspectives, No. 112, 6 January 2014.

98 European Commission, EU-China Investment Agreement: Report of the 13th Round, 15 June 2017, available at http://trade.ec.europa.eu/doclib/docs/2017/june/tradoc_155625.pdf (last accessed 12 July 2019).

99 According to Michael Froman, the US Trade Representative in the Transatlantic Trade and Investment Partnership (TTIP) negotiations, the United States is wary of the investment court system. He said, 'It's not obvious to me why you would want to give companies a second bite of the apple.' See Krista Hughes and Philip Blenkinsop, US Wary of EU Proposal for Investment Court in Trade Pact, Reuters, 30 October 2015, available at www.reuters.com/article/us-trade-ttip/u-s-wary-of-eu-proposal-for-investment-court-in-trade-pact-idUSKCN0SN2LH20151029 (last accessed 12 July 2019).

arbitration.[100] On the contrary, the EU's investment court system would deprive foreign investors of the right to appoint arbitrators.

With the steady increase of China's OFDI, China may not be averse to international investment arbitration, which would also be essential to solving international investment disputes during the implementation of the BRI. Yet, this does not mean China would be loyal to traditional mechanisms. Recent treaty practice has revealed that China would like to maintain a more restrictive scope of application for arbitration and maintain greater control over investment arbitration, such as through the establishment of carve-out provisions, the use of alternative dispute resolution, the introduction of joint interpretations by the Contracting States, the increasing use of state-to-state dispute settlement,[101] and the appeal mechanism.[102]

These observations are confirmed by China's proposal on possible reform of ISDS submitted by her to UNCITRAL in July 2019. In her submission, China recommends, to improve the ISDS system, establishing a permanent appellate mechanism, reserving the rights of the parties to appoint arbitrators, exploring alternative dispute resolutions, and enhancing transparency.[103]

5.6 CONCLUSION

Within its forty years of development since the implementation of its opening-up policy, China's practice in international investment law has developed from just being peripheral to being the centre of its focus. It has also helped to promote the transformation of related domestic law. Indeed, such a development is just a microcosm of China's active role in the international law-making process in all fields. In its process to integrate into the global system, China is also trying to find an approach that does not blindly follow the path of developed countries, but incorporates its identity as a developing country and its political economy. Against a backdrop of rising protectionism and anti-globalization, China's implementation of the BRI could help to continue building a more liberal and open world. Ongoing negotiations on the RCEP, the China–US BIT and the China–EU BIT could help the global investment treaty regime to grow in a more balanced direction and serve as the template for ISDS reform, in particular since the United Nations Commission on International Trade Law is considering reforms to this dispute settlement mechanism.[104]

100 RCEP Draft Investment Text: China, Bilaterals.org, 16 August 2016, available at www.bilaterals.org/IMG/pdf/rcep-draft-investment-text-china.pdf (last accessed 12 July 2019).

101 See, e.g., 2012 China-Canada BIT, section 3.

102 See, e.g., 2015 China-Australia FTA, Chapter 9, Art. 23.

103 UNCITRAL, Possible Reform of Investor-State Dispute Settlement (ISDS): Submission from the Government of China, UN Doc. A/CN.9/WG.III/WP.177(New York: United Nations Publications), 19 July 2019, available at, https://undocs.org/en/A/CN.9/WG.III/WP.177 (last accessed 16 May 2020).

104 For details, please *see* UNCITRAL, Possible future work in the field of dispute settlement: Reforms of investor–State dispute settlement (ISDS), UN Doc. A/CN.9/917, 2017, available at, https://documents-dds-ny.un.org/doc/UNDOC/GEN/V17/023/69/PDF/V1702369.pdf?OpenElement (last accessed 12 July 2019).

6

Procedural Models to Upgrade BITs

China's Experience

Jie (Jeanne) Huang[1]

6.1 INTRODUCTION

Modernizing or 'upgrading' existing bilateral investment treaties (BITs) appears to be critically important to States[2] mindful of the rise of a new generation of investment policies.[3] Treaty-making power is shifting from the bilateral to the regional level.[4] For example, the European Commission (EC) can negotiate investment treaties on behalf of their member States, and the European Union (EU) can conclude investment agreements on behalf of their member States in most aspects.[5] The rise of new investment policies is also embodied in the shift from BITs to free trade agreements (FTAs) and investment regulations becoming increasingly intertwined with other areas of law.[6]

Aware that there is no 'one-size-fits-all' solution, the United Nations Conference on Trade and Development (UNCTAD) has identified ten options 'available for countries that wish to change existing treaties to bring them into conformity with new policy objectives and priorities and to address the challenges arising from the fragmentation of the IIA regime'.[7] For the People's Republic of China (China), the new investment policies are driven by the

1 This article is made possible partly through the China National Social Science Fund Project (16BFX202). The author is very grateful for Professor Mahdev Mohan's comments. All errors remain mine.

2 Eighty-six countries were involved in BIT renegotiation, *see* T. Broude, Y. Z. Haftel, and A. Thompson, 'Legitimation Through Renegotiation: Do States Seek More Regulatory Space in Their BITs?' (2016) Hebrew University of Jerusalem Legal Research Paper 6, available at https://ssrn.com/abstract=2845297 (last accessed 8 July 2019).

3 UNCTAD, 'World Investment Report 2017: Investment and the Digital Economy', available at http://unctad.org/en/PublicationsLibrary/wir2017_en.pdf; and UNCTAD, 'IIA Issues Note' (June 2017), available at http://unctad.org/en/PublicationsLibrary/diaepcb2017d3_en.pdf (both last accessed 8 July 2019).

4 UNCTAD, 'World Investment Report 2012: Towards a New Generation of Investment Policies', p. 84, http://unctad.org/en/PublicationsLibrary/wir2012_embargoed_en.pdf (last accessed 8 July 2019).

5 W. Shan and L. Wang, 'The China–EU BIT and the Emerging "Global BIT 2.0"' (2015) 30 *ICSID Review: Foreign Investment Law Journal* 260 at 260–67; European Court of Justice ('ECJ') Opinion 2/15, available at http://curia.europa.eu/juris/document/document.jsf?text&docid=190727&pageIndex=0&doclang=en&mode=req&dir&occ=first&part=1&cid=373854 (last accessed 8 July 2019). (On 16 May 2017 the ECJ rendered its Opinion on the competence of the EU to conclude the FTA with Singapore. The Opinion recognizes exclusive EU competence over most of the agreement and largely settles a long-standing dispute between the Commission and the Member States on the division of competences under the Lisbon Treaty. ISDS remains the individual States prerogative.)

6 M. Chi, 'The "Greenization" of Chinese Bits: An Empirical Study of the Environmental Provisions in Chinese Bits and its Implications for China's Future Bit-Making' (2015) 18 *Journal of International Economic Law* 511–42 at 511; Q. J. Kong, 'The "State-Led-Economy" Issue in the BIT Negotiations and Its Policy Implications for China' (2016) 5 *China-EU Law Journal* 13–29 at 13.

7 UNCTAD, 'IIA Issues Note', p. 7, available at http://unctad.org/en/PublicationsLibrary/diaepcb2017d3_en.pdf (last accessed 8 July 2019).

significant economic changes experienced by States in recent decades that have resulted in multiple generations of different investment agreements, the first of which now seems outdated.[8]

Like many countries, China[9] is also impacted by these new investment policies, especially in the context of its pioneering 'One Belt and One Road' initiative.[10] In the past decades, China has upgraded thirty-two BITs, making up 28 per cent of its investment treaties.[11] China has attempted a whole range of different methods of upgrade, including concluding FTAs or regional investment agreements, replacing old BITs with new ones, enacting amendments and making diplomatic announcements regarding BITs.[12] Recently, two investment arbitration tribunals and one apex court at the seat of arbitration have rendered decisions favouring the application of old-generation Chinese BITs over the upgraded ones.[13] China's experience with upgrading BITs may provide general policy discourse and direction for other countries that plan to upgrade their BITs.

This chapter categorizes the modernization of Chinese BITs into five models, consistent with the framework of what the UNCTAD has termed 'Phase 2 of IIA Reform'[14]: (1) the Co-existence Model (parties to an old BIT join existing or new FTAs or a regional investment agreement), (2) the Replacement Model (replace an old BIT with a new one), (3) the Amendment Model (amend an old BIT by a protocol), and (4) the Joint Interpretation Model (issue a diplomatic announcement to interpret a BIT). Denunciation of a BIT is excluded and is thus considered an alternative strategy to upgrading.[15] The author adopts an empirical approach to examine the benefits and challenges of each Model and provide directions for future BIT upgrading.

[8] K. Rooney, 'ICSID and BIT Arbitrations and China' (2007) 24 *Journal of International Arbitration* 689 at 701–03; G. G. Wang, 'Trade, Investment and Dispute Settlement: China's Practice in International Investment Law: From Participation to Leadership in the World Economy' (2009) 34 *Yale Journal of International Law* 575 at 577; WH. Shan and N. Gallagher, 'Chinese Model BIT: A Commentary' in Chester Brown (ed.),*Commentaries on Selected Model International Investment Agreements* (Oxford University Press, 2013), pp. 131–33. N. Gallagher, 'China's BIT's and Arbitration Practice: Progress and Problems' in WH. Shan and JY. Su (eds.), *China and International Investment Law: Twenty Years of ICSID Membership* (Brill, 2014), pp. 183–88.

[9] For the purposes of this Paper, China refers to Mainland China, excluding the Hong Kong Special Administrative Region ('SAR'), the Macau SAR and Taiwan.

[10] C. Y. Cai, 'China-Us BIT Negotiations and the Future of Investment Treaty Regime: A Grand Bilateral Bargain with Multilateral Implications' (2009) 12 *Journal of International Economic Law* 457 at 461.

[11] As of July 2019, China has signed 145 BITs and a trilateral investment treaty (109 in force) and 16 FTAs (14 in force) containing investment chapters. For China's BIT list, *see* http://tfs.mofcom.gov.cn/article/Nocategory/201111/20111107819474.shtml and https://investmentpolicy.unctad.org/international-investment-agreements/countries/42/china?type=bits. For China's FTA list, *see* http://fta.mofcom.gov.cn/english/fta_qianshu.shtml and https://investmentpolicy.unctad.org/international-investment-agreements/countries/42/china (all last accessed 8 July 2019).

[12] The thirty-two upgraded BITs are: (1) the China–Pakistan BIT; (2) the China–Australia BIT; (3) the China–New Zealand BIT; (4) the China–Chile BIT; (5) the China–Peru BIT; (6) the China–Iceland BIT; (7) the China–Japan BIT; (8) the China–South Korea BIT; (9) the China–Switzerland BIT; (10) the China–Thailand BIT; (11) the China–Singapore BIT; (12) the China–Malaysia BIT; (13) the China–Philippines BIT; (14) the China–Viet Nam BIT; (15) the China–Laos BIT; (16) the China–Indonesia BIT; (17) the China–Cambodia BIT; (18) the China–Myanmar BIT; (19) the China–Sweden BIT; (20) the China–Germany BIT; (21) the China–France BIT; (22) the China–Belgium and Luxembourg BIT; (23) the China–Finland BIT; (24) the China–the Netherlands BIT; (25) the China–Portugal BIT; (26) the China–Spain BIT; (27) the China–Uzbekistan BIT; (28) the China–Nigeria BIT; (29) the China–Romania BIT; (30) the China–Cuba BIT; (31); the China–Bulgaria BIT; (32) the China–Czechoslovakia BIT.

[13] *Ping An Life Insurance Company of China, Limited and et al.* v. *Belgium* ('*Ping An* v. *Belgium*'), ICSID Case No. ARB/12/29, Decision on Jurisdiction, 30 April 2015; *Sanum Investments Ltd* v. *Government of the Lao People's Democratic Republic* (*Sanum* v. *Laos*), Award on Jurisdiction, PCA Case No. 2013–13, 13 December 2013; *Government of the Lao People's Democratic Republic* v. *Sanum Investments Ltd* [2015] SGHC 15; *Sanum Investments Limited* v. *The Government of the Lao People's Democratic Republic* [2016] SGCA 57.

[14] UNCTAD, 'IIA Issues Note', above n 7.

[15] For termination of treaties, *see* T. Voon, A. Mitchell and J. Munro, 'Parting Ways: The Impact of Investor Rights on Mutual Termination of Investment Treaties' (2014) 29 *ICSID Review: Foreign Investment Law Journal* 451 at 463.

This chapter has five parts, each considering one aspect of the aforementioned typology. Part I focuses on the most popular model, the Co-existence Model, which has been adopted by eighteen Chinese BITs. However, this Model creates vertical 'overlaps and fragmentation in treaty relationships and poses interaction challenges'[16] in China's investment treaty regime and may lead to treaty shopping in dispute resolution. Part II analyses the Replacement Model. China has used new BITs to replace twelve BITs. Although vertical treaty overlap is avoided, most of China's BITs adopting this Model suffer from vague transition clauses. As *Ping An v. Belgium*[17] demonstrates, these clauses may create gaps of jurisdiction *ratione temporis* and cause unpredictability in investment protection. Part III examines the Amendment Model, which has been adopted by four Chinese BITs. Amendments to the jurisdiction of a BIT, and amendments to the substantive rights and obligations of contracting States may have different jurisdiction *ratione temporis*. Part IV outlines the Joint Interpretation Model, which is used only in the China–Laos BIT. *Sanum v. Laos*[18] demonstrates that China should clarify the application of its BITs to its special administrative regions (SAR). Part V proposes a direction for upgrading BITs, going forward: in the future, States may begin to move away from the Co-existence Model to the Replacement Model, and more States may adopt multiple Models to upgrade their BITs consecutively.

6.2 CO-EXISTENCE MODEL

In the Co-existence Model, States under an old BIT join an existing or new FTA or a regional investment agreement. This 'allows for a holistic approach to reform' as parties are able to take into consideration evolving policy objectives.[19] The commencement of the new FTA or regional investment agreement does not affect the validity of the old BIT, and in fact, they co-exist. China has frequently adopted the Co-existence Model in recent years. Currently, China has eighteen BITs that co-exist with FTAs or regional investment agreements, concluded between the same States.[20] When an FTA contains a substantial investment chapter, the Co-existence Model creates complex issues of vertical treaty overlap and the potential for treaty shopping.[21]

6.2.1 *Disputes Crystallize after the Commencement of a Later Agreement*

China and Pakistan concluded a BIT in 1989[22] and an FTA in 2006.[23] The FTA contains an investment chapter that provides a higher level of protection to investors and investments than the 1989 BIT. Article 3 of the China–Pakistan FTA provides that the contracting parties

16 UNCTAD, 'IIA Issues Note' (June 2017), above n 7.
17 *Ping An* v. *Belgium*, above n 13.
18 *Sanum* v. *Laos*, above n 13.
19 UNCTAD, 'IIA Issues Note', (June 2017), above n 7, p. 11.
20 The BITs that use the Co-existence Model are: (1) the China–Pakistan BIT; (2) the China–Australia BIT; (3) the China–New Zealand BIT; (4) the China–Chile BIT; (5) the China–Peru BIT; (6) the China–Iceland BIT; (7) the China–Japan BIT; (8) the China–South Korea BIT; (9) the China–Switzerland BIT; (10) the China–Thailand BIT; (11) the China–Singapore BIT; (12) the China–Malaysia BIT; (13) the China–Philippines BIT; (14) the China–Viet Nam BIT; (15) the China–Laos BIT; (16) the China–Indonesia BIT; (17) the China–Cambodia BIT; (18) the China–Myanmar BIT.
21 W. Alschner, 'Regionalism and Overlap in Investment Treaty Law: Towards Consolidation or Contradiction' (2014) 17 *Journal of International Economic Law* 271, at 271–98; R. Adlung and M. Molinuevo, 'Bilateralism in Services Trade: Is There Fire Behind the (BIT-) Smoke?' (2008) 11 *Journal of International Economic Law* 365 at 370.
22 The China–Pakistan 1989 BIT, signed on 12 February 1989 and effective on 30 September 1990.
23 The China–Pakistan FTA, signed in November 2006 and effective in July 2007.

affirm the existing rights and obligations under the World Trade Organisation (WTO) Agreement and other agreements to which both parties are members. There are two possible interpretations of Article 3. The first view is that either the FTA is subject to the BIT or the FTA is simply not considered to be incompatible with the BIT.[24] The basis for this view is that, under Article 30.2 of the Vienna Convention on the Law of Treaties (VCLT),[25] the BIT takes precedence over the FTA. The second view is that, because Article 55 of the China–Pakistan FTA provides that the FTA will not affect more favourable treatment to investors in existing or future agreements, the FTA only confirms the existing rights and obligations under the other agreements which are more favourable to investors and investments than the FTA. In this view, the BIT takes precedence over the FTA only if the BIT gives more favourable treatment to investors and investments. The second view should be preferred because, according to Articles 30 and 31 of the VCLT generally, Articles 3 and 55 of the FTA must be construed together in light of the object and purpose of the FTA, parties' subsequent practice and special intention. The preamble of the FTA indicates that the FTA builds on existing treaties between parties and resolves to promote reciprocal trade, raise the standard of living and lower unemployment. After concluding the FTA, both States implemented the high standard of protection required under the FTA rather than staying with the low-standard BIT.[26] Since 2015, China and Pakistan have negotiated to expand their FTA and further liberalize bilateral trade and investment.[27] It was not the parties' intention, despite Article 3, that the 1989 BIT should prevail over the FTA so that the investment regime between the two States remains as the 1989 version.

Moreover, the first interpretation prioritizes the BIT over the FTA, which is a result manifestly absurd or unreasonable[28] under Article 32 of the VCLT. Article 73, paragraph 1 of the Vienna Convention on Consular Relations (VCCR) is a classic example of a Convention conceding priority to other treaties.[29] However, it is improper to conclude that simply because Article 3 of the China–Pakistan FTA is similarly worded to Article 73 paragraph 1 of 'VCCR', the *lex prior*-rule should be applied to the FTA without qualification. Article 30.2 of the VCLT 'concerns solely … the conflict clause in a treaty which aims at granting priority to another treaty.'[30] Article 3 of the China–Pakistan FTA does not aim to give priority to less favourable investment treatments, as this would be against parties' intention.[31]

[24] 'Incompatible' means 'two treaties are not capable of being applied at the same time', as per Art. 59.1 of the VCLT: J. Pauwelyn, *Conflict of Norms in Public International Law: How WTO Law Relates to Other Rules of International Law* (Cambridge: Cambridge University Press, reprinted, 2004), p. 283.

[25] *Vienna Convention on the Law of Treaties*, opened for signature 23 May 1969, 1155 UNTS 331 (entered into force 27 January 1980).

[26] For the subsequent practice of the parties as a means of interpretation, *see Legality of the Threat or Use of Nuclear Weapons* [1996] ICJ Reports p. 226, paras. 19, 22 and 76.

[27] For news reports regarding parties' implementation and further expansion of the FTA, *see* http://fta.mofcom.gov.cn/pakistan/pakistan_special.shtml (last accessed 8 July 2019). For interpreting of subsequent practice, *see* H. Fox, 'Article 31 (3) (A) and (B) of the Vienna Convention and the Kasikili/Sedudu Island Case' in M. Fitzmaurice, et al. (eds.), *Treaty Interpretation and the Vienna Convention on the Law of Treaties: 30 Years on* (Martinus Nijhoff, 2010), p. 69.

[28] M. E. Villiger, *Commentary on the 1969 Vienna Convention on the Law of Treaties* (Martinus Nijhoff, 2009), p. 447 (indicting that recourse may be had to Article 32 in the unlikely event that Article 31 leads to a result which is manifestly absurd or unreasonable).

[29] Article 73 para. 1 of Vienna Convention on Consular Relations provides that '[t]he provisions of the present Convention shall not affect other international agreements in force as between States Parties to them': O. Dörr and K. Schmalenbach, *Vienna Convention on the Law of Treaties: A Commentary* (Springer, 2011), p. 512.

[30] *See* Villiger, above n 28, p. 405.

[31] Art. 31.4 of the VCLT provides that a special meaning shall be given to a term if it is established that the parties so intended.

Therefore, the Co-existence Model causes a 'patchy' treaty network, overlaps between treaties and creates divergence or inconsistencies in treaty clauses when disputes arise.

Significant vertical treaty overlap also exists between China and South Korea. The China–South Korea FTA was concluded in 2015, the China–Japan–South Korea Investment Agreement in 2012 and the China–South Korea BIT in 2007.[32] Article 25 of the China–Japan–South Korea Investment Agreement and Article 1.3 of the China–South Korea FTA are similar to Articles 3 and 55 of the China–Pakistan FTA. The earlier arguments apply here as well. These articles should not be construed so earlier treaties, which are less favourable to investment, should prevail over later treaties.[33] One issue with this interpretation is, if all three treaties are applicable to an investment dispute, can investors select favourable clauses from each treaty and combine them for the most effective protection? This is possible. *Ioannis Kardassopoulos v. Georgia* demonstrates that an investor can combine favourable substantive and jurisdictional clauses from different treaties concluded by the same States in investment arbitration. Both Greece and Georgia are members of the Energy Charter Treaty (ECT) and a BIT. Mr. Kardassopoulos was a Greek national who invested in Georgia. His claim utilized both the ECT and the Greece–Georgia BIT. The tribunal, after deciding it had jurisdiction *ratione materiae* under both the ECT and the BIT,[34] held that it also had jurisdiction *ratione temporis* under the ECT.[35] However, since the tribunal eventually found that Georgia had violated the ECT by expropriating Mr. Kardassopoulos' investment, determining the question of jurisdiction *ratione temporis* under the Georgia–Greece BIT was unnecessary.[36]

If contracting States' purpose for the upgrade is to improve investment protection, an FTA easily achieves this goal without the need to maintain the old one. In domestic law, old laws are repealed when a new law applicable to the same subject matter is enacted. The underlying policy to this approach is to consolidate laws, facilitate their implementation and assist lawyers and judicial bodies with application of the law. In sharp contrast, the international investment regime norm is that new FTAs neither replace old BITs nor contain clear application clause; yet States complain that investment arbitration tribunals have too much discretion in interpreting and applying treaties.[37] Good practice would be to terminate an old BIT when signing a new FTA with a comprehensive investment protection regime. For example, Australia has now terminated its BITs with Mexico, Peru and Vietnam after what was then the Trans-Pacific Partnership Agreement – now the Comprehensive and Progressive

32 The China–South Korea FTA Investment Chapter, the China–Japan–South Korea Investment Agreement and the China–South Korea BIT (2007) differ in definitions of investment, fair and equitable treatment clauses, MFN clauses, transparency and prohibition of performance requirements clauses, clauses for entry of personnel and the protection of intellectual property, expropriation and compensation clauses, temporary safeguard measures, clauses for prudential measures relating to financial services, and tax clauses. Therefore, three different investment protection regimes exist between China and South Korea.

33 Note of Article 3 of the China–Japan–South Korea Investment Agreement indicates that Article 3.2 (national treatment) should not be inconsistent with Articles 3.2 and 3.3 of the China–Japan BIT (1988). Therefore, Articles 3.2 and 3.3 of the China–Japan BIT (1988) prevail against Article 3.2 of the China–Japan–South Korea Investment Agreement. This is because parties especially indicate so.

34 *Ioannis Kardassopoulos* v. *Georgia*, ICSID Case Nos. ARB/05/18, Decision on Jurisdiction, 6 July 2007, para. 107.

35 Ibid., para. 66.

36 *Ioannis Kardassopoulos and Ron Fuchs* v. *Georgia*, ICSID Case Nos. ARB/05/18 and ARB/07/15, Award, 3 March 2010, para. 241.

37 C. Henckels, 'Balancing Investment Protection and the Public Interest: The Role of the Standard of Review and the Importance of Deference in Investor–State Arbitration' (2013) 4 *Journal of International Dispute Settlement* 197 at 201–03.

Agreement for Trans-Pacific Partnership, after the withdrawal of the United States, that was signed in Chile in March 2018[38] – entered into force.[39] Although the US withdrawal made the future of the TPP uncertain, trade ministers from the eleven remaining States have reached agreement on what is now called the Comprehensive and Progressive Agreement for Trans-Pacific Partnership.[40] The Australian plan should be applauded because it avoids the uncertainty in applicable law.

6.2.2 *Disputes Crystallize before the Commencement of a Later Agreement*

The China–ASEAN Investment Agreement,[41] the China–New Zealand FTA,[42] the China–Australia FTA[43] and the China–Peru FTA[44] contain application clauses for jurisdiction over disputes that crystallized before the commencement of the Agreements. Of the four, the China–ASEAN Investment Agreement has the most comprehensive application clause.

China and the ASEAN members (Laos, Cambodia, Indonesia, Malaysia, Thailand, Myanmar, the Philippines, Singapore, and Viet Nam) all concluded BITs. Afterwards, in 2009, China and the ASEAN signed an Investment Agreement. According to Article 3.2 of the China–ASEAN Investment Agreement, although the Agreement applies to all investments made by investors of a party in the territory of the other party before or after the Agreement entered into force, it does not bind any party in relation to any act or fact that took place or any situation that did not exist before the date of its entry into force.[45] Article 14.2 provides that the investor–State dispute resolution mechanism does not apply to investment disputes arising out of events that occurred and investment disputes that were settled or already under judicial or arbitral process, prior to the entry into force of this agreement.[46] Article 23 outlines the Agreement's relationship with other agreements in that it shall not derogate from the existing rights and obligations of a member State under any other international agreements to which it is a party.[47] The three articles complement one another: Article 3.2 regulates the scope of application to investment, Article 14.2 specifies when the investor–State dispute resolution

38 'CPTPP: 11 countries sign Pacific Trade Deal in Chile', The Santiago Times, 9 March 2018, available at https://santiagotimes.cl/2018/03/09/cptpp-11-countries-sign-pacific-trade-deal-in-chile/ (last accessed 9 July 2019).

39 Exchange of letters between Steven Ciobo, Minister for Trade, Tourism and Investment (Australia) and Ildefonso Guajardo Villarreal, Minister of Economy (Mexico) (8 March 2018); Exchange of letters between Steven Ciobo, Minister for Trade, Tourism and Investment (Australia) and Ana Maria Sánchez De Ríos, Minister of Foreign Affairs (Peru) (8 March 2018), referring to exchange of letters between Andrew Robb, Minster for Trade and Investment (Australia) and Ana Maria Sanchez De Rios, Minister of Foreign Affairs (Peru) (4 February 2016); Exchange of letters between Steven Ciobo, Minister for Trade, Tourism and Investment (Australia) and Tran Tuan Anh, Minister of Industry and Trade (Vietnam) (8 March 2018) referring to Exchange of Letters between Andrew Robb, Minister for Trade and Investment (Australia) and Vu Huy Hoang, Minister of Trade and Industry (Vietnam) (6 November 2015).

40 Comprehensive and Progressive Agreement for Trans-Pacific Partnership, opened for signature 8 March 2018, (entered into force on 30 December 2018), available at https://dfat.gov.au/trade/agreements/in-force/cptpp/official-documents/Pages/official-documents.aspx (last accessed 8 July 2019).

41 'ASEAN' refers to the Association of Southeast Asian Nations. Agreement on Investment of the Framework Agreement on Comprehensive Economic Cooperation between China and the ASEAN (China–ASEAN Investment Agreement) signed on 15 August 2009 and effective on 1 January 2010.

42 The China–New Zealand FTA, signed in April 2008 and effective on 1 October 2008.

43 The China–Australia FTA, signed in 17 June 2015 and effective on 20 December 2015.

44 The Agreement between the Government of the PRC and the Government of Peru on the Reciprocal Encouragement and Protection of Investments ('the China–Peru BIT (1994)'), signed on 9 June 1994 and effective on 1 February 1995.

45 China–ASEAN Investment Agreement, Art. 3.2. *See also* Art. 23.

46 Ibid., Art. 14.2.

47 Ibid., Art. 23.

mechanism cannot be applied and Article 23 provides that the China–ASEAN Investment Agreement co-exists with the BITs that China concluded with individual ASEAN members.

The application clauses in the China–New Zealand FTA are different from those in the China–ASEAN Investment Agreement. The BIT between China and New Zealand came into force in 1989 and the FTA in 2008. Article 137 of the China–New Zealand FTA provides the scope of its investment chapter. Article 137.4 indicates that *the provisions of the investment chapter* do not bind either party in relation to any act or fact that took place or any situation that did not exist before the date of its entry into force.[48] Article 137.6 replicates Article 3.2 of the China–ASEAN Investment Agreement but adds that the investor–State dispute resolution regime does not apply to any investment dispute or claim already under judicial or arbitral process before the entry into force of the Agreement.[49] The second half of Article 137.6 is broader than Article 14.2 of the China–ASEAN Investment Agreement. Article 3 provides that the China–New Zealand FTA co-exists with other agreements to which China and New Zealand are parties and in the event of inconsistency, the parties shall immediately negotiate to find a mutually satisfactory solution.[50] Different from Article 23 of the China–ASEAN Investment, Article 3 of the China–New Zealand FTA provides a procedure in the event of inconsistency.

Suppose a Chinese investor made an investment in Laos in 2006 and the expropriation dispute between this investor and the Laos government crystallized in 2007. In terms of jurisdiction *ratione temporis*, the investment is covered by the China–ASEAN Investment Agreement according to its Article 3.2. However, the investor cannot invoke the investor–State dispute resolution mechanism in the Agreement because of Article 14.2. The dispute must then be solved under the China–Laos BIT (1993).[51]

Suppose the same events transpired in New Zealand. In terms of jurisdiction *ratione temporis*, the investment is covered by Article 137.6 of the China–New Zealand FTA. However, Article 137.4 excludes the expropriation dispute because it is an act or fact that took place before the commencement of the China–New Zealand FTA. The China–New Zealand BIT (1988)[52] should be applied to this dispute.

Therefore, although the same result may be reached under the two FTAs, the reasoning is different. Article 3.2 of the China–ASEAN Investment Agreement and Article 137 of the China–New Zealand FTA are phrased similarly; however, the former applies to investment only while the latter applies to the whole investment chapter. The latter is applicable to expropriation measures but the former is not.

The application clauses in an FTA can generally resolve jurisdiction for disputes that crystallized before its came entry into force. However, overlap between the FTA and an old BIT between the same parties still exists for disputes that crystallize after the commencement of the FTA. Investors may bring arbitration under the International Centre for Settlement of Investment Disputes (ICSID) mechanism of the FTA, and if it fails, they can bring *ad hoc* arbitration by invoking the old BIT on the same facts, or vice versa. Thus, the Co-existence

48 China–New Zealand FTA, Art. 137.4.

49 Ibid., Art. 137.6.

50 Ibid., art. 3.

51 Agreement Between the Government of the People's Republic of China and the Government of the Lao People's Democratic Republic Concerning the Encouragement and Reciprocal Protection of Investments ('the China–Laos BIT (1993)'), signed on 31 January 1993 and effective on 1 June 1993.

52 The Agreement between the Government of the PRC and the Government of New Zealand on the Reciprocal Encouragement and Protection of Investments ('the China–New Zealand BIT (1998)'), signed on 22 November 1988 and effective on 25 March 1989.

Model allows the investor to bite the same apple twice, creates uncertainty in treaty application and the possibility of undesirable treaty shopping.

6.2.3 *Incorporation*

Incorporating the BIT into the FTA can avoid vertical treaty overlaps, and 'ensures that countries are not subject to simultaneously applicable obligations found in overlapping treaties'[53] For example, China concluded a BIT with Iceland in 1994 and an FTA in 2013. The latter incorporated the former into its investment chapter.[54] Thus, although the China–Iceland FTA and the China–Iceland BIT are both valid, there are no treaty applicability issues. Nevertheless, incorporation is like pouring old wine (BIT) into a new bottle (FTA). The level of investment protection and promotion between China and Iceland remains as it was in 1994.

The relationship between the China–Singapore BIT (1985), the China–Singapore FTA (2008), and the China–ASEAN Investment Agreement is a more complicated case. The China–Singapore FTA was signed before the conclusion of the China–ASEAN Investment Agreement. Taking into consideration that Singapore would be party to the, at the time, soon to be concluded China–ASEAN Investment Agreement, Article 84 of the China–Singapore FTA incorporated the China–ASEAN Investment Agreement into its investment chapter, with the latter prevailing in event of conflict. This clause resolves the applicability issue between the China–Singapore FTA and the China–ASEAN Investment Agreement. However, the China–Singapore FTA did not replace the China–Singapore BIT (1985), because Article 112 of the FTA provides that it does not derogate existing obligations and rights under existing bilateral and multilateral agreements between the parties.[55] In case of inconsistency the parties shall immediately consult with each other,[56] but the FTA does not provide which treaty prevails. As Article 14.2 of the China–ASEAN Investment Agreement was incorporated into the FTA,[57] the China–Singapore FTA does not apply to investment disputes arising out of events that occurred and investment disputes that had been settled or were already under judicial or arbitral process, prior to the entry into force of this agreement. However, this Article does not help to resolve the treaty overlap between the China–Singapore FTA (2008) and the China–Singapore BIT (1985) if the event crystallizes after the FTA came into force.

6.3 REPLACEMENT MODEL

Under the Replacement Model, States replace an old BIT with a new BIT. China has used this model to upgrade twelve old BITs, making it the second most frequently adopted model.[58] China's frequent use of the Replacement Model is also consistent with the global trend that, since the early 2000s, the BIT negotiations have placed more emphasis on

53 UNCTAD, 'IIA Issues Note' (June 2017), above n 7, p. 13.

54 China–Iceland FTA, Art. 92. *See also* Art. 4.

55 China–Singapore FTA, Art. 112.

56 Ibid.

57 *See* Section 1.3 above.

58 The BITs that use the Replacement Model are: (1) the China–Germany BIT; (2) the China–France BIT; (3) the China–Belgium and Luxembourg BIT; (4) the China–Finland BIT; (5) the China–the Netherlands BIT; (6) the China–Switzerland BIT; (7) the China–Portugal BIT; (8) the China–Spain BIT; (9) the China–Uzbekistan BIT; (10) the China–Nigeria BIT; (11) the China–South Korea BIT.

replacing older BITs than creating new BITs with countries with which no previous treaty relation existed.[59] For the Replacement Model to function properly, a new BIT must clarify its jurisdiction *ratione temporis*.

China's BITs adopting the Replacement Model can be divided into two categories.[60] Firstly, BITs with a transition clause for jurisdiction *ratione temporis* over investment and secondly, BITs with transition clauses that demarcate jurisdiction *ratione temporis* over investment and investment disputes.

6.3.1 *Jurisdiction* Ratione Temporis *over Investment*

China and Nigeria concluded a BIT in 2001 to replace the BIT signed in 1997. Article 11 of the 2001 BIT states: '[t]his Agreement shall apply to investments, which are made prior to or after its entry into force by investors of either Contracting Party .... ' The 2001 BIT is silent on jurisdiction *ratione temporis* over investment disputes. Jurisdiction *ratione temporis* over investment made before the commencement of the new BIT does not necessarily connote jurisdiction *ratione temporis* for arbitral tribunals to hear disputes which occurred before the commencement date of the BIT. For example, *Walter Bau AG v. Thailand* involved two successive BITs which adopted the Replacement Model. Germany and Thailand concluded a BIT in 1961. Later in 2002, they signed a new BIT, which took effect in 2004 and terminated the 1961 BIT. The 1961 BIT did not permit investor–State claims and provided only for State-to-State claims. The 2002 BIT does not expressly restrict claims that arose before its commencement. The survival clause in the 1961 BIT provided that it continues to apply for ten years after termination over investment made prior to its termination. This case concerns the 2002 BIT, which provides for ICSID arbitration. The *Walter Bau* tribunal held that, although the 2002 BIT could apply to investment made before its entry into force, the dispute resolution clause in the 2002 BIT did not provide the tribunal jurisdiction *ratione temporis* to consider disputes that had arisen before the commencement of the 2002 BIT.[61] Essentially, this award demonstrates that if a later BIT allows for investor–State arbitration when the earlier BIT does not, the dispute resolution settlement provision of the former will not displace the presumption against retroactivity under Article 28 of the VCLT.[62]

6.3.2 *Jurisdiction* Ratione Temporis *over Investment and Investment Disputes*

Ten of China's BITs contain transition clauses that provide jurisdiction *ratione temporis* over investment and investment disputes.[63] A typical example is Article 10 of the China–Belgium BIT, which was signed in 2005 and entered into force in 2009 ('the China–Belgium BIT (2009)'). Article 10 has two paragraphs. The first paragraph provides that the China-Belgium BIT (2009) substitutes and replaces the old BIT that came into force in 1986 (the China–Belgium BIT (1986)). The second paragraph indicates that the China–Belgium BIT (2009):

59 K. Gordon and J. Pohl, 'Investment Treaties over Time – Treaty Practice and Interpretation in a Changing World', available at www.oecd.org/investment/investment-policy/WP-2015–02.pdf (last accessed 8 July 2019).

60 The exception is the China–Switzerland BIT (2009), which replaced the China–Switzerland BIT (1986), has no provision for jurisdiction *ratione temporis*.

61 *Walter Bau* AG v. *Thailand* (UNCITRAL), Award, IIC 429, July 1, 2009 at paras. 9.67–9.68, 9.72–9.73.

62 Art. 28 of the VCLT will be further discussed in Section 6.4.1. For cases, *see Blečić* v. *Croatia*, App. No. 59532/00 (ECtHR, 29 July 2004), para. 397.

63 The list of Chinese BITs is in file with the author.

> shall apply to all investments made by investors of either Contracting Party in the territory of the other Contracting Party, whether made before or after the entry into force of this Agreement, but *shall not apply to any dispute or any claim concerning an investment which was already under judicial or arbitral process before its entry into force*. Such disputes and claims shall continue to be settled according to the provisions of the Agreement of 1984 mentioned in paragraph 1 of this Article.[64]

Similar articles have been adopted by many of China's BITs, such as Article 16 of the China–Germany BIT (2003) (replacing the China–Germany BIT(1983)), Article 11 of the China–France BIT (2005) (replacing the China–France BIT(1984)), Article 10 of the China–Finland BIT (2004) (replacing the China–Finland BIT (1984)), Article 10 of China–Holland BIT (2001) (replacing the China–Holland BIT (1985)), and Article 12 of the China–Spain BIT (2005) (replacing the China–Spain BIT (1992)).

Ping An v. Belgium shows that this widely adopted article may create controversies in jurisdiction *ratione temporis* over investment disputes.[65] In *Ping An*, the dispute arose under the 1986 BIT, before the 2009 BIT came into force. The claimants relied on the 1986 BIT for the substance of their claim and on the 2009 BIT for jurisdiction to utilize the ICSID tribunal, rather than resolve the dispute by *ad hoc* arbitration as prescribed by the 1986 BIT. The claimants argued that the dispute was not under judicial or arbitral process before the commencement of the 2009 BIT, so the 2009 BIT should be applied. The tribunal held that Article 10.2 does not necessarily imply this.[66] First, the tribunal considered the wording of the notification procedure under the 2009 BIT, which states: '[w]hen a legal *dispute arises* between an investor of one Contracting Party and the other Contracting Party, either party to the dispute shall notify the other party to the dispute in writing.'[67] The tribunal held that use of 'arises' and 'notify', instead of 'arises or has arisen' and 'notify or shall have notified', means that the notification procedure of the 2009 BIT is not applicable to disputes that have arisen and been notified of before its entry into force.[68] Article 10.2 should be read together with the notification procedure to refer to disputes arising after the 2009 BIT came into force. Secondly, it cannot be inferred from the preamble and Article 10 of the 2009 BIT that it applies to pre-2009 disputes notified under the earlier BIT but not under judicial or arbitral process. Thirdly, an expansive interpretation of the 2009 BIT would apply its wider dispute resolution clause to a dispute already notified under the 1986 BIT, which has a more restrictive dispute resolution clause. The tribunal holds that if this were the contracting States' true intention, it would have been expressly stated in the treaty.

The tribunal concluded that neither express nor implied language in the 2009 BIT can justify the application of more extensive remedies from the 2009 BIT to pre-existing disputes that were notified under the 1986 BIT but not yet subject to arbitral or judicial process.[69] Such disputes should be resolved under the 1986 BIT.[70]

[64] China–Belgium BIT (2009), Art. 10 (emphasis added).

[65] For criticism and comment of the *Ping An* case, *see* Q. Ren, 'Ping An v Belgium Temporal Jurisdiction of Successive BITs' (2016) 31 *ICSID Review: Foreign Investment Law Journal* 129 at 130; G. Andriotis, 'Ping An Life Insurance Company of China, Limited and Ping An Insurance (Group) Company of China, Limited v. Kingdom of Belgium (Ping An v. Belgium)' (2016) 15 *World Trade Review* 532 at 532–34.

[66] *Ping An*, above n 13, para. 207, where the tribunal indicates that '… there is a real risk that disputes arising prior to the 2009 BIT but not the subject of judicial or arbitral process might fall into some "black hole" or "arbitration gap" between the two BITs.'

[67] China–Belgium BIT (2009), Art. 8.1 (emphasis added).

[68] Ibid.

[69] *Ping An* v. *Belgium*, above n 13, para. 231.

[70] Even if the 2009 BIT terminates the 1986 BIT, the survival clause in the 1986 BIT can cover such disputes for ten years after the termination, *see* T. Voon and A. D. Mitchell, 'Denunciation, Termination and Survival: The

If contracting States intend to apply the expansive investor–State dispute resolution under a new BIT to disputes not yet under judicial or arbitral process before its commencement, it must be explicitly stated in the transition clause or preamble of the new BIT. For example, transition clauses in the China–Portugal BIT (2005) (replacing the China–Portugal BIT (1992)) and the China–South Korea BIT (2007) (replacing the China–South Korea BIT (1992)) provide that if an investment dispute arose before the new BIT comes into effect, this dispute shall be bound by the old BIT regardless of whether it was already under judicial or arbitral process.[71]

6.4 AMENDMENT MODEL

Article 39 of the VCLT provides that '[a] treaty may be amended by agreement between the parties ... ' Under the Amendment Model, States conclude protocols or other agreements to amend their BIT, these agreements become part of the BIT, and except what has been removed by protocols, the BIT continues to be effective. China has used the Amendment Model to upgrade four BITs, which can be divided into two categories: amendment to the substantive rights and obligations of contracting States, and amendment to jurisdiction of a BIT.[72]

6.4.1 *Amendment to the Substantive Rights and Obligations of Contracting States*

China concluded protocols to amend the China–Bulgaria BIT (1989), the China–Czechoslovakia BIT (1991) and the China–Romania BIT (1994).[73] The amendments cover the national treatment clause and the transfer clause of the old BITs.[74] National treatment and transfer concerns substantive rights and obligations of the States to protect investment and investors, for example substantive rights and obligations in investor–State arbitration, as opposed to determining jurisdiction. Article 28 of VCLT provides that:

> Unless a different intention appears from the treaty or is otherwise established, its provisions do not bind a party in relation to any act or fact which took place or any situation which ceased to exist before the date of the entry into force of the treaty with respect to that party.

An amendment to the substantive rights and obligations of a BIT cannot be applied retroactively. For example, in *Liechtenstein v. Germany*, the European Court of Human Rights declined to hear a dispute on expropriation that took place prior to the entry into force of the European Convention on Human Rights.[75]

Interplay of Treaty Law and International Investment Law' (2016) 31 *ICSID Review: Foreign Investment Law Journal* 413 at 429.

71 China–Portugal BIT (2005), Art. 11 and China–South Korea BIT (2007), Art. 12.

72 The BITs that use the Amendment Model are: (1) the China–Romania BIT; (2) the China–Cuba BIT; (3) the China–Bulgaria BIT; (4) the China–Czechoslovakia BIT.

73 Additional Protocol Between the Government of the People's Republic of China and the Government of the People's Republic of Bulgaria Concerning the Reciprocal Encouragement and Protection of Investments (the China–Bulgaria Protocol), signed on 26 June 2007 and effective on 10 November 2007. Additional Protocol between the Government of the People's Republic of China and the Government of the Slovak Republic to the BIT signed in 2005 and Additional Protocol to the Agreement between the Government of the People's Republic of China and the Government of Romania on the Mutual Promotion and Protection of Investments signed in 2010. Every protocol provides that it becomes an integral part of the old BIT: *see, e.g.*, China–Bulgaria Protocol, Art. 3.

74 Ibid.

75 *Prince Hans-Adam II of Liechtenstein* v. *Germany* (*Liechtenstein* v. *Germany*) App no. 42527/98 (ECtHR, 12 July 2001) paras. H8-9.

The three Chinese protocols mentioned earlier do not substantially amend old BITs. Consequently, the investment regimes between China and Bulgaria, Czechoslovakia and Romania have not improved significantly. If China and its contracting States believe an old BIT has failed to serve their economic needs and they have the political will to significantly upgrade it, they should either follow the Modification concluded by China and Cuba to dramatically amend the old BIT ('the Modification of the China-Cuba BIT', which will be discussed later),[76] or they should adopt the Replacement Model using a new BIT to replace the old one.

6.4.2 *Amendment to Jurisdiction of a BIT*

China and Cuba concluded a BIT in 1995 and signed the Modification of the China–Cuba BIT in 2007. The Modification not only amends the substantive rights and obligations of the parties but also expands the jurisdiction of investor–State arbitration.[77] Prior to the amendment, investor–State arbitration only applied to disputes over the amount of compensation paid for expropriation.[78] After the amendment, arbitration could be applied to all disputes.[79] Like the protocols between China and Bulgaria, Czechoslovakia and Romania, respectively, the Modification of the China–Cuba BIT only indicates the date of its entry into force:

> [t]hese modifications shall enter into force the first day of the month following the date on which both Contracting parties have notified each other in writing that their respective internal legal procedures have been concluded.[80]

It does not contain a transition or application clause to determine whether it is applicable to disputes that crystallized before its commencement. Unlike an amendment to substantive rights and obligations, the amendment to the jurisdiction of the BIT can be applied to disputes that crystallized before it came into effect. This was the conclusion reached in *Nordzucker AG v. Poland*.[81] Germany and Poland signed a BIT in 1991 containing an investor–State arbitration clause limited to expropriation and capital transfer. The two countries then concluded a Protocol in 2005 ('the Germany–Poland Protocol (2005)') to amend the 1991 BIT, expanding the investor–State arbitration clause to all investment disputes. The Germany–Poland Protocol (2005) does not contain a transition clause to help determine whether it applies to disputes crystallizing before its commencement. The Germany–Poland Protocol came into force on 28 October 2005. In *Nordzucker*, the disputes crystallized before the commencement of the Germany–Poland Protocol (2005) but the claimant submitted the disputes to investor–State arbitration. The claimant argued that the extensive investor–State arbitration clause in the Germany–Poland Protocol (2005) should be applied. The tribunal distinguished the substantive obligation (to protect investments) that must have been in force at the time of the alleged breach of that obligation, and the procedural obligation to arbitrate that only needed to be in force at the time of filing the

[76] The Modification of the Agreement on the promotion and Mutual Protection of Investments between China and Cuba signed on 20 April 2007 and effective on 1 December 2008.

[77] Ibid., Arts. 1–10. Seven aspects of the 1995 BIT are amended: the definitions of investor and investment, MFN treatment, transfer, subrogation, State-to-State dispute resolution, and investor–State dispute resolution.

[78] China–Cuba BIT (1995), Art. 9.3.

[79] Modification of the China–Cuba BIT, Art. 10.1 and 10.3.

[80] Modification of the China–Cuba BIT.

[81] *Nordzucker* AG v. *Poland* (UNCITRAL), Partial Award, 10 December 2008, Section 6.2.

dispute,[82] and came to the conclusion that the distinction was important when substantive and procedural rights and obligations were not created simultaneously. The tribunal held that, unless a different intention appears from the BIT, Protocol or otherwise, the investor–State arbitration clause in the Protocol governed, not only future breaches, but also past breaches as long as they were not time-barred or had otherwise become inadmissible when the Protocol became effective.[83] This is not a retroactive application of the investor–State arbitration clause, but a correct application of Article 28 of VCLT.[84] As Article 28 does not specify that it applies only to substantive rights and obligations, it may apply to jurisdiction as well. The tribunal, quoting Article 28, held that the term "'any act of [*sic*] fact which took place before the date of entry into force of the Treaty' may have a different meaning, depending on the substantive or procedural nature of the provision or obligation which is at stake."[85] After analysing the context, object, and purposes of the BIT and its Protocol as well as the wording of other Polish BITs, the tribunal concluded that no alternative intention existed in the BIT and Protocol.[86] Therefore, the 2005 Protocol applies to 'old' disputes, provided they constitute a breach of the 1991 BIT.[87] Another example is *Tradex v. Albania*.[88] The dispute crystallized before Albanian investment law providing for ICSID arbitration entered into force.[89] The *Tradex* tribunal found that the arbitration provision in the new law could be invoked for the 'old' dispute.[90]

In the Amendment Model, modification of jurisdiction can govern disputes that arose before it came into force, unless parties indicate otherwise. However, in the Replacement Model, a new BIT may not be applied to disputes crystallizing prior to its commencement. The reason is that in the Amendment Model, States generally do not put a transition clause in the amendment to carve out disputes existing before the commencement of the amended jurisdiction clause. With the Replacement Model, transition clauses are included to restrict jurisdiction *ratione temporis* over investment and/or investment disputes. Moreover, in the Amendment Model, unamended substantive rights and obligations become effective earlier than the amended jurisdiction clause, whereas they become effective simultaneously with the jurisdiction clause in the Replacement Model when the new BIT replaces the old one. As the *Nordzucker* tribunal indicates, the immediate applicability of a jurisdictional clause of an amendment implies that it can also be applied to pre-exit events, provided that those events breached the BIT at the time they occurred and arbitration was brought after the commencement of the amendment.[91]

If an amendment removes rather than bestows on investors the right to investment arbitration, could this procedural amendment govern disputes that have already crystallized? The answer is yes if the investor commences arbitration after the commencement of the amendment, the amendment has no transition clause, the amendment to jurisdiction is applicable immediately and State parties do not intend to carve out pre-existing disputes. This amendment will have a negative effect on investors who have pre-existing disputes. A BIT is a triangular treaty which is signed by States but gives rights to a third party

[82] Ibid., paras. 103–07.
[83] Ibid., para. 108.
[84] Ibid., paras. 105 (iv), 107, and 109.
[85] Ibid., para. 107 (iv).
[86] Ibid., paras. 113–14.
[87] Ibid., para. 110.
[88] *Tradex Hellas SA (Greece)* v. *Republic of Albania*, ICSID Case No. ARB/94/2, Decision on Jurisdiction 24 December 1996.
[89] Ibid., Section B.
[90] Ibid., Section D7.
[91] *Nordzucker* AG v. *Poland* (UNCITRAL), Partial Award, paras. 105, 110–12.

(investors).[92] However, for two reasons it is difficult for the investor to argue that an amendment does not apply. First, the Amendment Model will not trigger the survival clause of a BIT. Survival clauses in China's BITs generally provide for a treaty to remain effective for ten years and continue in force if not terminated. After the initial ten-year period, *either contracting State* may, with one year's written notice, terminate the BIT, after which the BIT will continue to apply to investments made prior to the date of termination for a further period of ten years from the date of termination.[93] The wording 'either contracting State' means the survival clause is relevant only to *unilateral termination* and not amendments *jointly* made by two States. Secondly, Article 70 of the VCLT provides that, unless otherwise agreed, termination of a treaty shall not affect any existing right, obligation or legal situation of the parties. 'Parties' refers to contracting States to a treaty, not investor beneficiaries of a BIT. To be a responsible host State, China should avoid using the Amendment Model to restrict the jurisdiction of a BIT. For example, when the United States and Morocco signed an FTA and jointly terminated the US–Morocco BIT, they permitted investor–State and State-to-State claims with respect to existing investments and investment disputes arising under the BIT to continue for another ten years from the date of replacement.[94] This demonstrated their policy objectives to protect and promote foreign investment.

6.5 JOINT INTERPRETATION MODEL

The Joint Interpretation Model contains two scenarios. First is that member States jointly interpret a BIT by using devices such as side agreements, protocols, and understanding; and the second means that a State publishes a diplomatic announcement about an existing BIT with the other contracting State's understanding or to answer its inquiry.[95] The second scenario is used to resolve issues specific to one State but with potential impact on the interests of the other State. The Joint Interpretation Model distinguishes from the Amendment Model when States consider their interpretation is not an amendment to the existing BIT but reflects its original meaning. The Joint Interpretation Model is relevant to 'upgrading' a BIT because it helps to clarify the meaning of the BIT so may enhance its implementation.

China has only used this Model once.[96] In *Sanum v. Laos*, the Laotian government made diplomatic announcements (*Notes Verbales*) stating that the China–Laos BIT did not extend to Macau and requesting China's response.[97] China announced in return that, according to the Macau Basic Law,[98] Macau is not bound by the BITs concluded by the Central Government, unless the Central Government seeks Macau government's opinion and makes separate arrangements with its contracting State.[99] These announcements were

92 A. Roberts, 'Triangular Treaties: The Extent and Limits of Investment Treaty Rights' (2015) 56 *Harvard International Law Journal* 353 at 368.

93 E.g., China–Laos BIT, Art. 12.

94 US–Morocco FTA, Arts. 1.2.3 and 1.2.4.

95 If a member State makes a diplomatic announcement about an existing BIT to answer the other member State's inquiry, the announcement may be also in the form of exchanges of letters.

96 The only BIT that uses the Diplomatic Announcement Model is the China–Laos BIT.

97 3rd affidavit of Outakeo Keodouangsinh dated 19 February 2014, pp. 8, 10–12; *Sanum* v. *Laos*, [2015] SGHC 15, above n 13, paras. 39–40.

98 The Macao Basic Law (adopted at the First Session of the Eighth National People's Congress on 31 March 1993, effective 20 December 1999), www.umac.mo/basiclaw/english/ch1.html (last accessed 8 July 2019).

99 *Sanum* v. *Laos* [2015] SGHC 15, above n 13, paras. 39–40. The first diplomatic announcement was made by the Chinese Embassy in Laos in 2014 and the second was made by the China Ministry of Foreign Affairs in 2015.

made when Laos lost an investment arbitration case against Sanum and tried to set aside the award in courts at the seat of arbitration, Singapore. The issue was whether China's diplomatic announcements should be applied to the dispute that had been submitted to arbitration before they were made. China, Laos and the Singapore High Court[100] considered the announcements to be interpretations of the BIT so they could be applied retroactively, while the Singapore Court of Appeal held that they were amendments to the BIT without retroactive effect.[101]

6.5.1 *Sanum v. Laos*

In 1987, China and Portugal signed a Joint Declaration on the Question of Macau, as Macau was at the time a Portuguese colony, which specified the procedure and requirements under which Macau would be transferred to Chinese sovereignty in 1999.[102] The China–Laos BIT was concluded and became effective in 1993. It does not explicitly indicate its applicability to Macau. When Macau was returned to China, it became a SAR[103] under China's 'One Country, Two System' regime in 1999.[104] Both China and Laos were silent on whether the BIT extended to Macau after the handover. The silence was maintained even after the China–Laos BIT was renewed in 2003.

The Singapore Court of Appeal held that China's diplomatic announcements were inadmissible, and even if admitted, they did not change the applicability of the China–Laos BIT to Macau.[105] First, the court held that the 'moving treaty frontier' rule (MTF Rule) under Article 15 of the Vienna Convention on Succession of States (VCST) and Article 29 of VCLT constituted customary international law and should be applied. According to the MTF Rule, after China took sovereignty of Macau, Chinese treaties (including the China–Laos BIT) presumably applied to Macau from the date of the succession, unless an intention 'appears' from the BIT or 'otherwise established' evidence shows that it does not. The text, objects and purposes of the China–Laos BIT, as well as the circumstances of its conclusion show no intention to displace the MTF rule. The silence of China and Laos favours the conclusion that the default MTF Rule was not displaced when the dispute crystallized.

Secondly, even assuming that evidence prior to the date when the dispute crystallized ('the critical date') is inconclusive on whether the China–Laos BIT applies to Macau so diplomatic announcements are admissible, the announcements should not constitute a retroactive amendment of the BIT. This is because the MTF Rule is customary international law that can be derogated only if the parties to a treaty expressly agree or share an understanding that it will be excluded. Even if China had intended to exclude the MTF Rule in relation to Macau by way of the China–Portugal Joint Declaration in 1987, Laos did not express its agreement before the dispute with Sanum crystallized. The diplomatic announcements do not prove that China and Laos shared a common understanding over the applicability of the BIT to

[100] Ibid.

[101] *Sanum* v. *Laos* [2016] SGCA 57, above n 13, para. 116.

[102] For discussion of SAR in constitutional law, *see* A Gonçalves, 'A Paradigm of Autonomy: The Hong Kong and Macau Sars' (1996) 18 *Contemporary Southeast Asia* 36–60.

[103] PRC Constitution [Xian Fa] (adopted at the Fifth Session of the Fifth National People's Congress on 4 December 1982, amended 14 March 2004), Art. 31.

[104] For discussion of the policy of One Country, Two Systems, *see* G. G. Wang and P. M. F. Leung, 'One Country, Two Systems: Theory into Practice' (1998) 7 *Pacific Rim Law & Policy Journal* 279–321.

[105] *Sanum* v. *Laos* [2016] SGCA 57, above n 13, para. 116. The Court held that, because the 2014 diplomatic announcement were not admissible, it was unnecessary to consider the 2015 one.

Macau prior to the crystallization of the dispute. The diplomatic announcements are not interpretations of the BIT, rather they are 'based on an understanding of how the rules of international law would apply to the two States in light of the domestic constitutional arrangements in [China].'[106] China's domestic arrangements should not affect the applicability of international law, namely the MTF Rule. Therefore, the BIT should be applied to Macau.

The reasoning of the Singapore Court of Appeal contrasts with that of *Tza Yap Shum v. Peru*, which is the first investment arbitration involving an investor from China's SAR who would like to apply a BIT concluded by China.[107] The tribunal held that whether the China–Peru BIT (1994) should be applied to Tza depends on his nationality and whether he is a Chinese national is a Chinese domestic law issue. The Chinese Nationality Law confers Chinese nationality to natural persons of Chinese descent born in China.[108] The Hong Kong Basic Law provides that Chinese Nationality Law applies to Hong Kong, so Hong Kong residents of Chinese descent and born in the Chinese territories (including Hong Kong) are Chinese nationals.[109] Because the definition of 'investor' in the China–Peru BIT rests on nationality, the tribunal held that Tza had standing to bring arbitration under this BIT. Following this logic, Sanum would not be able to invoke the China–Laos BIT.[110] Sanum is a corporate established according the Macau law. Article 1.2(b) of the China–Laos BIT provides that it applies to economic entities established in accordance with the laws and regulations of each contracting State. The Macau Basic Law does not indicate that Chinese Corporate Law applies to Macau.[111] Therefore, Sanum is not a qualified investor under the China–Laos BIT.[112]

It is unsurprising that soon after the Singapore Court of Appeal rendered its judgment, China's Foreign Ministry Spokesperson stated that this judgment was incorrect.[113] As a principle, the BITs that China concluded do not apply to SARs, unless otherwise decided by the Central Government after seeking the views of the SAR governments and consulting with the other contracting party of a BIT.[114]

6.5.2 *Applicability of China's BITs to Its SARs*

China has five thousand years of ancient history, but Hong Kong and Macau remind it of its modern history of semi-colonization. China disagrees that the handover of Macau and Hong Kong from Portugal and the UK respectively is State succession. During negotiations with the UK and Portugal, China repeatedly emphasized its historical sovereignty over Hong Kong and Macau and how resumption of that sovereignty is unrelated to State

106 *Sanum* v. *Laos* [2016] SGCA 57, above n 13, para. 116.
107 *Tza Yap Shum* v. *The Republic of Peru*, ICSID Case No. ARB/07/6, Decision on Jurisdiction and Competence, 19 June 2009.
108 Ibid., paras, 58, 61.
109 Ibid., paras, 54, 60.
110 *See* W. Shen, 'The Good, the Bad or the Ugly? A Critique of the Decision on Jurisdiction and Competence in Tza Yap Shum v. The Republic of Peru' (2011) 10 *Chinese Journal of International Law* 55 at 61–63.
111 Annex III of the Macao Basic Law.
112 N. Hart and S. Srikumar, 'Investor-State Arbitration before the High Court of Singapore: Territoriality, Nationality and Arbitrability Case Note' (2015) 4 *Cambridge Journal of International and Comparative Law* 191 at 195.
113 Foreign Ministry Spokesperson Hua Chunying's Regular Press Conference on 21 October 2016, www.italaw.com/sites/default/files/case-documents/italaw7687.pdf (last accessed 8 July 2019).
114 Ibid.

succession.[115] For China, the MTF Rule should not be applied because it is a rule for State succession.[116]

The Singapore Court of Appeal does not discuss whether the turnover of Macau from Portugal to China constitutes State succession. This is because both Sanum and Laos did not dispute this point.[117] Under public international law, whether the turnover of a territory to a State is a State succession is not only based upon the view of the international community but also on the self-perception of the States involved.[118] *Sanum* is not only concerned with the interests of Sanum and Laos, but also has great implications on China. China is a third party who has a direct interest in the outcome of the case. Sanum's acceptance of VCST alone cannot represent China's position. Although the court has no obligation to do so, it could have considered China's opinion at least via an amicus brief. Even if the court holds that it is unnecessary to consider China's opinion because it only decides the jurisdiction of the particular dispute between Sanum and Laos, the court should have refrained from making a sweeping conclusion that the China–Laos BIT applies to *Macau* generally before the critical date:[119]

> We therefore do not find the evidence relating to the period between the handover of Macau and the Critical Date relevant, persuasive or sufficient to 'otherwise establish' that contrary to the operation of the MTF Rule, the PRC-Laos BIT was not intended to apply to Macau.[120]
>
> ... We are therefore satisfied that there is insufficient evidence to prove that it has been otherwise established that the PRC-Laos BIT was not to apply to Macau ...[121]
>
> We therefore find that that the PRC-Laos BIT does apply to Macau and reverse the Judge's ruling in this regard and restore the decision of the Tribunal on this point.[122]

With respect, properly examined, one might conclude that the China–Laos BIT applies to *Sanum and its investment* before the critical date. Such a position is not unprecedented. In the *Tza* award, for example, the tribunal explicitly indicated that it would deal with Tza's investment only insofar as 'determining the applicability of the Peru-China BIT to Hong Kong is unnecessary.'[123]

Although Article 27 of the VCLT provides that a party may not invoke its internal law to justify its failure to perform a treaty, Article 27 is without prejudice to Article 46.[124] Article 46

115 H. Xu, 'The Practice of Applying International Treaties to Hong Kong and Macau Special Administrative Regions', *Legal Daily*, http://news.xinhuanet.com/legal/2016–10/22/c_129333036.htm (last accessed 8 July 2019). The author is the Head of Treaty and Law Department, China Ministry of Foreign Affairs.

116 A similar view can be found in C. J. Tams, 'State Succession to Investment Treaties: Mapping the Issues' (2016) 31 *ICSID Review: Foreign Investment Law Journal* 314, at 340 (indicating that the handovers of China's SARs are unusual cases of successions and the MTF Rule needs to be qualified).

117 Sanum and Laos agree that Article 15 of the VCST should be considered customary international law and applied to this case: *Sanum* v. *Laos* [2016] SGCA 57, above n 13, para. 17. The Singapore High Court also bases its judgment on parties' agreement on succession: *Sanum* v. *Laos* [2015] SGHC 15, above n 13, para. 60. For criticism of the High Court judgment, *see* M. Hwang and A. Chang, 'Government of the Lao People's Democratic Republic v Sanum Investments Ltd' (2015) 30 *ICSID Review: Foreign Investment Law Journal* 506 at 517–18.

118 A. Zimmermann and J. G. Devaney, 'Succession to Treaties and the Inherent Limits of International Law' in C. J. Tams, A. Tzanakopoulos and A. Zimmermann (eds.), *Research Handbook on the Law of Treaties* (Edward Edgar Publishing, 2014), p. 515.

119 *Sanum* v. *Laos* [2016] SGCA 57, above n 13.

120 Ibid., at para. 99.

121 Ibid., at para. 12.

122 Ibid., at para. 122.

123 *Tza Yap Shum* v. *The Republic of Peru*, ICSID Case No. ARB/07/6, Decision on Jurisdiction and Competence, 19 June 2009, para. 68.

124 VCLT, above n 25, Art. 27.

provides that if a State's violation of its internal law regarding its competence to conclude a treaty is manifest and concerned a fundamental rule of domestic law, the State can withdraw its consent to the treaty. 'A violation is manifest if it would be objectively evident to any State conducting itself in the matter in accordance with normal practice and in good faith.'[125] If China concludes a BIT and applies it to Macau without consulting the Macau government, China manifestly violates the Macau Basic Law.[126] Article 2 of the Macau Basic Law provides that Macau has a high degree of autonomy and enjoys executive, legislative and independent judicial power.[127] This high degree of autonomy is derived from the China–Portugal Joint Declaration. Article 136 of the Macau Basic Law authorizes the SAR government to conclude treaties with a foreign State in appropriate fields including the economic, trade, financial and monetary, shipping, communications, tourism, cultural, science and technology and sports fields.[128] Accordingly, after reuniting with China, Hong Kong and Macau have concluded many treaties with foreign States.[129] Article 138 provides that the application to the SAR of international agreements to which China is a member or becomes a party shall be decided by the Central Government after seeking the views of the SAR government.[130] Considering the fundamental importance of 'One Country, Two Systems' to China and as an international commitment to Portugal, the Singapore Court of Appeal should have exhibited more caution in rejecting China's diplomatic announcements.

Article 31.3(a) of the VCLT requires that any subsequent agreement between member States regarding the interpretation of a treaty shall be taken into account. If the subsequent agreement is an interpretation of the treaty, it should be applied both retroactively and proactively. However, member States to a BIT have dual roles: 'treaty parties (with an interest in interpretation) and actual or potential respondents in investor–State disputes (with an interest in avoiding liability).'[131] Therefore, courts and arbitration tribunals are with caution when member States made a joint interpretation detrimental to an investor's interests after an investment dispute crystalizes.[132] In *Sanum*, China's diplomatic announcements were made at a very late stage – after the tribunal had rendered the award. China and Laos are improperly silent regarding whether the BIT shall be applied to China's SARs even after it has been renewed. In this scenario, the tension between Laos' role as a treaty party and respondent becomes stark. The Singapore Court of Appeal does not find convincing evidence to support that China and Laos had agreed upon the territorial application of the BIT before the investment dispute crystallized. From this aspect, the Singapore Court of Appeal's decision that China's diplomatic announcements shall not be applied to Sanum is supported by the general presumption of international law against retroactivity.

125 Ibid., Art. 46.

126 For a discussion about the similar scenarios in Hong Kong, *see* A. Chen, 'Queries to the Recent ICSID Decision on Jurisdiction upon the Case of Tza Yap Shum v. Republic of Peru: Should China-Peru BIT 1994 Be Applied to Hong Kong SAR under the One Country Two Systems Policy' (2009) 10 *Journal of World Investment and Trade* 829, at 839–45.

127 Macau Basic Law, Art. 2.

128 Macau Basic Law, Art. 136; Hong Kong Basic Law, Art. 150.

129 For BITs concluded by Macau, https://investmentpolicy.unctad.org/country-navigator/126/macao-sar-china. For BITs concluded by Hong Kong, https://investmentpolicy.unctad.org/country-navigator/95/hong-kong-sar-china (both last accessed 8 July 2019).

130 Macau Basic Law, Art. 138; Hong Kong Basic Law, Art. 153.

131 A. Roberts, 'Power and Persuasion in Investment Treaty Interpretation: The Dual Role of States' (2010) 104 *The American Journal of International Law* 179 at 180.

132 Ibid., at 212–13.

To avoid doubt and controversy,[133] China should review its BITs and work with its contracting States to clarify whether its BITs apply to SARs.[134] China's FTAs generally contain a territorial application provision providing that the FTAs apply to the customs territory of China.[135] This excludes SARs because they are separate customs territories. In contrast, China's BITs, except the China–Russia BIT,[136] do not include such a provision. It is unclear whether this omission was deliberate because China has not completed consultation procedures with its SARs governments or whether China and its contracting States improperly ignore the applicability of the BITs to China's SARs. Nevertheless, non-application of China's BITs to its SARs is a double-edged sword. SARs are of special significance in China's investment regime, because China's SARs have served as a critical springboard for China's outbound investment.[137] China needs to carefully review all of its BITs and issue diplomatic announcements to expressly clarify their applicability to SARs. This may best balance China's twin desires – a need to comport with domestic constitutional requirements (and historical and political pride, more generally) on the one hand; and to preserve, protect and promote foreign direct investment, on the other.

6.6 DIRECTION OF BIT UPGRADING

In the final analysis, China's experience demonstrates that the direction of BIT upgrading is two-fold. First, the Co-existence Model and the Replacement Model are the most frequently adopted Models because they can comprehensively improve investment regulation regimes. They are States' favourite strategies in BIT upgrading. However, States may begin to move away from the Co-existence Model to the Replacement Model. This is mainly because the vertical treaty overlap arising from the Co-existence Model and the consequent controversial treaty application may result in an older BIT prevailing over the investment chapter of a new FTA, which may contradict States' intentions.

Realizing these issues, the EU has attempted to use EU-wide investment treaties to replace all BITs between an EU treaty partner and individual EU members. Mexico appears to prefer the Replacement Model as well. The Mexico–Central America FTA (2011) replaces the Mexico–Costa Rica FTA (1994), Mexico–Nicaragua FTA (1997) and the Mexico–El Salvador–Guatemala–Honduras FTA (2000). For the economic benefits from streamlining

133 The applicability of China's BITs to its SARs have been much debated in literature, *see* Hwang and Chang, above n 118, at 509 and 516; N. Gallagher, 'Role of China in Investment: BITs, SOEs, Private Enterprises, and Evolution of Policy' (2016) 31 *ICSID Review: Foreign Investment Law Journal* 88 at 98; O. G. Repousis, 'On Territoriality and International Investment Law: Applying China's Investment Treaties to Hong Kong and Macao' (2015) 37 *Michigan Journal of International Law* 113 at 115.

134 A comparable example is the EU. In order to avoid international court or arbitral tribunal from interpreting or applying EU law in investment arbitration, in 2009, the European Court of Justice rendered three important judgments on the relationship between pre-accession BITs of EU member States with third State and the EU law. Case C-205/06, *Commission* v. *Austria* [2009] ECR I-1301; Case C-249/06, *Commission* v. *Sweden* [2009] ECR I-1335; Case C-118/07, *Commission* v. *Finland* [2009] ECR I-10889. For comments, N. Lavranos, 'Bilateral Investment Treaty (BITs) and EU Law', p. 3, available at www.researchgate.net/publication/228148786 (last accessed 8 July 2019).

135 E.g., Art, 1.5, China–South Korea FTA.

136 Art. 1 of the Protocol of the China–Russia BIT excludes Hong Kong and Macau SARs from its application. The Protocol was concluded the same date as the BIT.

137 'China Outbound Investment Deals from Hong Kong Rise 66.6 Per Cent', South China Morning Post, 12 October 2013, available at www.scmp.com/business/china-business/article/1329807/china-outbound-investment-deals-hong-kong-rise-666-cent (arguing the 66.6 per cent rise highlights Hong Kong's importance as a hub for overseas investments from China) (last accessed 8 July 2019).

investment legal regimes, China should follow these examples to work with its contracting States to terminate old BITs that co-exist with new FTAs.

However, despite the United States withdrawal from the TPP, the CPTPP was nonetheless concluded and Chinese-led and ASEAN-centred Regional Cooperative Economic Partnership (RCEP) negotiations have continued.[138] Some have hopes that the RCEP could be a reality in the near future.[139] The fact that mega-FTAs are still actively being negotiated might encourage China to maintain the Co-existence Model. One might even suggest that mega-regionals are a Model unto themselves. This is because China concludes mega-regional FTAs not only for economic benefits but also due to political and cultural considerations.[140]

Second, more States will possibly adopt multiple Models consecutively to upgrade their BITs. The China–South Korea BIT, the China–Japan BIT, the China–Switzerland BIT, and the China–Laos BIT were upgraded by more than one Model. Adoption of multiple Models depends on States' economic needs and negotiation agendas. For example, China and Switzerland concluded a BIT in 2009 replacing the China–Switzerland BIT (1986), and they also signed an FTA with an investment chapter in 2003.[141] Although the China–Switzerland FTA and the China–Switzerland BIT (2009) co-exist, there is no *de facto* vertical treaty overlap between them. This is because the investment chapter of the China–Switzerland FTA is so brief and contains no contradictory provisions when compared to the China–Switzerland BIT (2009).[142] When China and Switzerland concluded the FTA, they may have already envisioned that they would soon replace their old BIT with a new one and thus deliberately chose to leave the investment chapter of the FTA almost blank.

This chapter suggests if States plan to conclude an FTA with a comprehensive investment chapter, they should consider terminating their old BIT to avoid vertical treaty overlap. In replacing a BIT, a clear transition clause should be included in the new BIT. If the Amendment Model is chosen, States should bear in mind that jurisdiction *ratione temporis* of the amendments to jurisdiction of a BIT differs from the amendments to the substantive rights and obligations of contracting States. Regarding the Joint Interpretation Model, China should work with its contracting States to clarify whether its BITs apply to its SARs as soon as possible.

138 'RCEP Negotiators Conclude Nineteenth Round, Push for "Accelerated" Progress', *International Centre for Trade and Sustainable Development*, 3 August 2017, www.ictsd.org/bridges-news/bridges/news/rcep-negotiators-conclude-nineteenth-round-push-for-accelerated-progress (last accessed 8 July 2019).

139 Shefali Rekhi, 'Will RCEP be a reality by the end of 2017?', The Straits Times, 23 April 2017, available at www.straitstimes.com/asia/se-asia/will-rcep-be-a-reality-by-the-end-of-2017 (last accessed 8 July 2019).

140 *See* Christian Riffel, 'Mega-Regionals', Max Planck Encyclopedia of Public International Law, para. 86, available at http://opil.ouplaw.com/view/10.1093/law:epil/9780199231690/law-9780199231690-e2177 (last accessed 8 July 2019).

141 Chapter 9, China-Switzerland FTA.

142 Ibid., Arts. 9.1 and 9.2.

PART III

The Rebalancing of Regulatory Space and Investor Protection in Asia

7

Regulatory Power and Investors' Interests

Striking a Balance in Investment Treaties Concluded by Japan

Shotaro Hamamoto

7.1 INTRODUCTION

Japan has concluded thirty-two bilateral investment treaties (BITs),[1] one trilateral investment treaty with China and the Republic of Korea (ROK),[2] twelve economic partnership agreements (EPAs)[3] that contain a chapter on investment[4] and is a party to the Energy Charter Treaty. Currently, it is negotiating almost twenty BITs and EPAs with an investment chapter, including a multilateral Regional Comprehensive Economic Partnership (RCEP). Together with ten other countries,[5] Japan has also signed the recently concluded Comprehensive and Progressive Agreement for Trans-Pacific Partnership (CPTPP).[6]

The author has had several opportunities to analyse these treaties and Japan's international investment law policy.[7] As explained in those studies, Japan concluded only a small number

[1] This number does not include the investment treaty concluded with Mongolia in 2002, which was terminated in 2016 in accordance with Art. 10.19 of the Japan–Mongolia EPA, which entered into force in 2016, and which includes a chapter on investment. It includes three BITs which have been signed but which are not yet in force: the Argentina–Japan BIT (signed on 1 December 2018); the Japan–Jordan BIT (signed on 27 November 2018); and the Japan–United Arab Emirates BIT (signed on 30 April 2018): Ministry of Foreign Affairs of Japan, available at www.mofa.go.jp/ecm/ep/index.htmll (last accessed 22 October 2019).

[2] Japan concluded a BIT with China in 1988 and with the ROK in 2002. These two treaties are still in force and the 2012 trilateral treaty explicitly provides that the investor may rely on either the new trilateral treaty or the old bilateral treaty (Art. 25).

[3] These are essentially identical to free trade agreements (FTAs). *See* Shotaro Hamamoto, 'Economic Partnership Agreements Concluded by Japan' (2015) 6 *European Yearbook of International Economic Law* 191.

[4] This does not include three EPAs concluded with Peru, Vietnam and ASEAN. The Japan–Peru EPA and the Japan–Vietnam EPA simply incorporate the BITs already existing between respective parties. The Japan–ASEAN EPA has a chapter on investment, containing a single article, which provides that the parties shall continue to discuss and negotiate provisions for investment.

[5] The signatories of this multilateral treaty that was formed in the wake of the withdrawal of the United States from its predecessor, the Trans-Pacific Partnership (TPP) by its new administration in 2017, are Australia, Brunei, Canada, Chile, Japan, Malaysia, Mexico, New Zealand, Peru, Singapore and Vietnam. Before that, Japan had already signed and ratified the original TPP: see Ministry of Economy, Trade and Industry (METI). (2016). 'EPA/FTA/Investment Agreements', available at www.meti.go.jp/policy/trade_policy/epa/ (last accessed 8 July 2019). For news of the United States withdrawal from the TPP, see Office of the United States Trade Representative, 'The United States Officially Withdraws from the Trans-Pacific Partnership' (30 January 2017), available at https://ustr.gov/about-us/policy-offices/press-office/press-releases/2017/january/US-Withdraws-From-TPP (last accessed 8 July 2019).

[6] The full treaty text of the CPTPP is available on the Government of New Zealand's website, www.mfat.govt.nz/en/trade/free-trade-agreements/free-trade-agreements-concluded-but-not-in-force/cptpp/comprehensive-and-progressive-agreement-for-trans-pacific-partnership-text/ (last accessed 8 July 2019).

[7] Shotaro Hamamoto, 'Passive Player in International Investment Law: Typically Japanese?' in Vivienne Bath and Luke Nottage (eds.), *Foreign Investment and Dispute Resolution Law and Practice in Asia* (London: Routledge, 2011), pp. 53–67; Shotaro Hamamoto and Luke Nottage, 'Foreign Investment In and Out of Japan: Economic

of simple, 'old-generation' BITs until 2001 due to its strong belief in multilateralism. However, what looked at the time like the complete collapse in negotiations for a Multilateral Agreement on Investment[8] and the stalemate in the Doha Round led it to negotiate an increasing number of far more detailed 'new-generation' BITs and EPAs with an investment chapter, starting from 2002. This chapter does not attempt to reproduce what has already been explained in the author's previous publications,[9] but analyses Japan's treaty practice from the perspective of the core theme of the present book, that is, the balancing exercise between regulatory power of States and investors' interests within the framework of what the United Nations Conference on Trade and Development (UNCTAD) has termed 'Phase 2 of IIA Reform'.[10]

As indicated earlier, Japan's 'old-generation' BITs, those concluded between 1977 (with Egypt) and 2001 (with Mongolia), are very simple ones. The small number and inconsistent content of these treaties suggest the absence of Japan's deliberated policy on investment treaties during this period.[11] Not surprisingly, the 'old-generation' BITs contain few wordings that would ensure the protection of the regulatory space of the host State. Japan started to conclude more detailed 'new-generation' treaties in 2002, many of which contain provisions on the protection of regulatory space of the host State. For these reasons, the present chapter excludes the 'old-generation' BITs from the scope of its analysis.

Japan's 'new-generation' treaties include detailed provisions intended to guarantee the regulatory space of the host space. This is evidently because Japan takes into account, as do many States, the evolution of arbitral jurisprudence. Japan's Minister for Foreign Affairs thus stated in the Diet:

> As the honourable member points out, there have been examples of abusive claims. That led States to stipulate exceptions and reservations in investment treaties. We will discuss these issues in the TPP negotiations.[12]

The present chapter consists of two parts. Section 7.2 summarizes Japan's treaty practice concerning the protection of the regulatory space of the host State, revealing that it is not always consistent. Section 7.3 analyses the rationale underlying this apparent inconsistency.

Backdrop, Domestic Law, and International Treaty-Based Investor-State Dispute Resolution' (2011) 8 *Transnational Dispute Management* 1–59 at 5; Shotaro Hamamoto, 'Japan' in Wenhua Shan (ed.), *The Legal Protection of Foreign Investment* (Oxford: Hart Publishing, 2012), pp. 445–518; Shotaro Hamamoto and Luke Nottage, 'Japan' in Chester Brown (ed.), *Commentaries on Selected Model Investment Treaties* (Oxford: Oxford University Press, 2013), pp. 347–91; Shotaro Hamamoto, 'Debates in Japan over Investor-State Arbitration with Developed States' (2016) *CIGI Investor-State Arbitration Series* 5.

8 See, e.g., 'Okay, the Trans-Pacific Partnership is dead. What was it?', The Washington Post, 20 March 2018, available at www.washingtonpost.com/news/monkey-cage/wp/2017/01/23/okay-the-trans-pacific-partnership-is-dead-what-was-it/?utm_term=.0adfcd74c315 (last accessed 8 July 2019).

9 See Jonathan T. Stoel, Tomoko Ishikawa and Michael Jacobson, 'Japan's Ambitious International Investment Agreement Policy' (2014) 12 *Transnational Dispute Management* 1–27; METI, '2015 Report on Compliance by Major Trading Trade Partners with Trade Agreements', available at www.meti.go.jp/english/report/index_report.html (last accessed 8 July 2019); Luke Nottage, 'The TPP Investment Chapter and Investor-State Arbitration in Asia and Oceania' (2016) 17 *Melbourne Journal of International Law* 1–36.

10 UNCTAD, 'IIA Issues Note' (June 2017), available at http://unctad.org/en/PublicationsLibrary/diaepcb2017d3_en.pdf (last accessed 8 July 2019).

11 See Ministry of Economy, Trade and Industry (METI), 'EPA/FTA/Investment Agreements' (2016), available at www.meti.go.jp/policy/trade_policy/epa/ (last accessed 8 July 2019).

12 Mr Koichiro Gemba (Minister for Foreign Affairs), Committee on Budget, House of Representatives, 1 February 2012, available at http://kokkai.ndl.go.jp/ (last accessed 8 July 2019) [translated by Hamamoto].

7.2 SUMMARY OF JAPAN'S TREATY PRACTICE CONCERNING THE REGULATORY SPACE OF THE HOST STATE

Investment treaties may set forth a wide variety of provisions with a view to securing the regulatory space of the host State.[13] Japan's treaties often contain provisions declaring the general policy, detailed substantive provisions, exceptions and limited remedies. These provisions are examined in turn within this section.

7.2.1 *Provisions Declaring the General Policy*

Almost all 'new-generation' treaties contain a provision stating that parties 'should not waive or otherwise derogate from such environmental measures as an encouragement for the establishment, acquisition or expansion in its territory of investments by investors of the other Contracting Party'.[14] More recent treaties – those concluded in and after 2011 – also refer to labour standards in this context.[15] Strictly speaking, it is not a provision that 'protects' the regulatory space of the host State, since it uses soft wording ('should') and does no more than discourage State Parties from engaging in a 'race to the bottom'.[16] Therefore, positive measures taken by the host State to protect the environment or to promote labour standards are beyond the scope of this provision.

On the other hand, some treaties explicitly recognize the host State's power to take measures to protect the environment, or more generally, to achieve regulatory objectives. They allow the host State to take action 'provided that such [a] measure is consistent with this Agreement' (Article 21(2), Japan–Columbia BIT (2011)) or 'otherwise consistent with this Chapter' (Article 9.16, CPTPP (2018)). These provisos, apparently modelled after the North American Free Trade Agreement (NAFTA) (Article 1114(1)), are reasonable in that investment treaties need not tolerate environmental or regulatory measures if they are adopted or enforced, for example, in an unfair or inequitable manner. They are nevertheless often criticized for 'negat[ing] any protection otherwise purported to be given under this article'.[17] From a logical point of view, it is true that a circular provision that 'you can do X, provided that you respect this agreement' in no way modifies the content of the agreement.[18] However, it would be an overstatement to say that '[c]onsequently, [...] good faith measures taken in the public interest can still be successfully challenged under the agreement [such as the CPTPP] as violating [its] investor protections',[19] because 'good faith' measures will not violate the fair and equitable treatment (FET) clause or

[13] See generally Walid Ben Hamida, 'La prise en compte de l'intérêt général et des impératifs de développement dans le droit des investissements' (2008) 4 *Journal du droit international* 999–1033.

[14] For example, Art. 21, Japan–ROK BIT (2002). The only exception is the Japan-Singapore EPA (2002), which is the very first of the 'new-generation' treaties.

[15] For example, Art. 26, Japan–Peru BIT (2011).

[16] Article 74 of the Japan–Mexico EPA (2004) further provides that '[i]f a Party considers that the other Party has offered such an encouragement, it may request consultations with the other Party and the Parties shall consult with a view to avoiding any such encouragement'.

[17] Lise Johnson and Lisa Sachs, 'The TPP's Investment Chapter: Entrenching, Rather than Reforming, a Flawed System', *CCSI Policy Paper* (November 2015), pp. 1–2, available at http://ccsi.columbia.edu/files/2015/11/TPP-entrenching-flaws-21-Nov-FINAL.pdf (last accessed 8 July 2019).

[18] Amokura Kawharu, 'TPPA: Chapter 9 on Investment' (2015) *Trans-Pacific Partnership Agreement New Zealand Expert Paper Series*, Expert Paper #2, p. 9, available at https://tpplegal.files.wordpress.com/2015/12/ep2-amokura-kawharu.pdf (last accessed 8 July 2019).

[19] Johnson and Sachs, above n 17.

constitute indirect expropriation.[20] Therefore, although the *raison d'être* of such provisions is doubtful from a strictly legal point of view, these provisos will not be harmful at all to the regulatory power of the host State.[21]

7.2.2 *Detailed Substantive Provisions*

Since the clauses on the FET and indirect expropriation are most frequently discussed and applied in treaty-based investor–State arbitration, a number of recent investment treaties try to qualify them in order to secure the regulatory space of the host State. Likewise, Japan's treaties also often try to restrict the scope of these clauses.

7.2.2.1 Fair and Equitable Treatment

It is frequently argued that an expansive interpretation of the highly ambiguous term 'fair and equitable treatment' undermines the legitimate regulatory powers of the host State.[22] An early attempt to restrict or prevent an 'expansive' interpretation is the well-known notes of interpretation issued by the NAFTA Free Trade Commission in 2001, which linked FET to the minimum standard of treatment of foreigners under customary international law.[23] Although it is not certain that such a link will produce desired effects,[24] the NAFTA example is followed by a number of recent treaties,[25] including those of Japan.

Japan's first FET clause linked to customary international law is Article 60 of the Japan–Mexico EPA (2004). This was most probably proposed by Mexico, which already had a rich experience in treaty-based investment arbitration and had participated in the NAFTA Free Trade Commission

[20] Shotaro Hamamoto, 'Requiem for Indirect Expropriation: On the Theoretical and Practical Uselessness of a Contested Concept', PILAGG e-series/IA/1, École de Droit, Sciences Po de Paris, 2013, 1–28; Arnaud de Nanteuil, *L'expropriation indirecte en droit international de l'investissement* (Paris: Pedone, 2014), p. 164.

[21] It is often pointed out that the *Al Tamimi* tribunal found a similarly worded provision in the US–Oman BIT indicating that the treaty 'places a high premium on environmental protection' (*Al Tamimi* v. *Oman*, ICSID Case No. ARB/11/33, Award, 3 November 2015, para. 387). See Nottage, above n 9, p. 22, n 97. However, this statement, though reasonable, should not be overestimated because the tribunal would have certainly arrived at the same conclusion even if the applicable treaty had not contained that provision. See *Al Tamimi* v. *Oman*, paras. 430–31, 435, 449. See also Hamamoto, above n 20. See also *Philip Morris* v. *Uruguay*, ICSID Case No. ARB/10/7, Award, 8 July 2016, paras. 398–401.

[22] See, e.g., Alfred de Zayas, *Report of the Independent Expert on the promotion of a democratic and equitable international order*, UN Doc. A/HRC/33/40 (11 July 2016), para. 44. On this and other relevant reports of the Independent Expert appointed by the UN Human Rights Council, see Shotaro Hamamoto, 'Traité d'investissement et arbitrage investisseur-Etat vus par un expert des droits de l'homme: exemen critique des rapports de l'Expert indépendant pour la promotion d'un ordre international démocratique et équitable', Catherine Titi, sous la direction de, *Droit de l'homme et droit international économique*, Bruxelles, Bruylant, 2019, pp. 205–22.

[23] Notes of Interpretation of Certain Chapter 11 Provisions (NAFTA Free Trade Commission, 31 July 2001), available at www.international.gc.ca/trade-agreements-accords-commerciaux/topics-domaines/disp-diff/NAFTA-Interpr.aspx?lang=eng (last accessed 8 July 2019).

[24] Carlo Santulli convincingly argues that in certain situations, an FET clause linked to customary international law could be more protective of investments and investors than an autonomous FET clause. Carlo Santulli, 'Le traitement juste et équitable: stipulation particulière ou principe général de bonne conduite ?' (2015) *Revue générale de droit international public* 69 at 81. In any case, a number of tribunals found little difference between an autonomous FET clause and the one linked to customary international law since customary international law on the minimum standard of the protection of foreigners evolves in line with the development of other relevant rules of international law, particularly those relating to human rights. Even the *Glamis Gold* tribunal, which found that the FET standard was that articulated in *Neer* v. *Mexico* (15 October 1926, *Reports of International Arbitral Awards*, vol. VI, pp. 60–62) considered the *Neer* standard itself would evolve. *Glamis Gold* v. *USA*, Award, 8 June, 2009, para. 613.

[25] See UNCTAD, *Fair and Equitable Treatment*, 2012, UN Doc. UNCTAD/DIAE/IA/2011/5, 22–29.

which issued the 2001 note.[26] Since then, Japan has concluded thirty-three investment treaties. A little more than half (eighteen) of them contain an FET clause explicitly linked to customary international law.[27] The most detailed provision is found, quite unsurprisingly, in the CPTPP (retained from the original text of the TPP). Article 9.6(2)(a) provides that the FET includes the obligation not to deny justice 'in accordance with the principle of due process embodied in the principal legal systems of the world', suggesting that what is protected here is the very bottom line or the absolute minimum of due process guaranteed in the world. In addition, the protection of an investor's legitimate expectations is excluded from the scope of the FET (Article 9.6(4)).

Quite interestingly, fifteen out of the thirty-three investment treaties post-Japan–Mexico EPA do not explicitly link the FET clause to customary international law. However, an entirely autonomous FET clause is found only in six of them,[28] as the FET is more frequently included in 'treatment in accordance with international law'[29] or 'minimum standard of treatment of aliens in accordance with international law'.[30]

7.2.2.2 Indirect Expropriation

The clause on indirect expropriation is another frequent target of criticism by those who consider that investment treaties unduly constrain the regulatory space of the host State.[31] It is true that, under an investment treaty containing such a clause, the host State cannot take any measures for whatever purpose without paying compensation if they constitute those 'equivalent to expropriation'[32] or 'tantamount to expropriation'.[33] Recent investment treaties thus try to make clear circumstances under which measures taken by the host State are considered to be 'equivalent' or 'tantamount' to expropriation.[34]

Some of Japan's treaties concluded in and after 2007 also contain more or less detailed provisions on the conditions for indirect expropriation. The first of such treaties is the Japan–Chile EPA (2007), Annex 9 of which provides:

> [t]he determination of whether an action or a series of actions by a Party, in a specific fact situation, constitutes an indirect expropriation requires a case-by-case, fact-based inquiry that considers, among other factors:
>
> [. . .]

26 NAFTA Free Trade Commission, 'Notes of Interpretation of Certain Chapter 11 Provisions' (31 July 2001), available at www.international.gc.ca/trade-agreements-accords-commerciaux/topics-domaines/disp-diff/NAFTA-Interpr.aspx?lang=eng (last accessed 12 September 2019).

27 Japan–Mexico EPA (2004), Art. 60; Japan–Philippines EPA (2006), Art. 91; Japan–Brunei EPA (2007), Art. 59; Japan–Chile EPA (2007), Art. 75; Japan–Thailand EPA (2007), Art. 95; Japan–Laos BIT (2008), Art. 5(1); Japan–Peru BIT (2008), Art. 5(1), (2); Japan–Columbia BIT (2011), Art. 4(1), (2); Japan–India EPA (2011), Art. 87(1); Japan–China–ROK investment treaty (2012), Art. 5(1); Japan–Australia EPA (2014), Art. 14.5; Japan–Mongolia EPA (2015), Art. 10.5(1); Japan–Uruguay BIT (2015), Art. 5(1), (2); Japan–Iran BIT (2016), Art. 5; Japan–Kenya BIT (2016), Art. 5(1); TPP (2016), Art. 9.6(1), (2); Japan–UAE BIT (2018), Art. 5(1); Japan–Jordan BIT (2018), Art. 5; Japan–Argentina BIT (2018), Art. 4(1).

28 Japan–Malaysia EPA (2005), Art. 77; Japan–Indonesia EPA (2007), Art. 61; Japan–Uzbekistan BIT (2008), Art. 3(1); Japan–Switzerland EPA (2008), Art. 86(1); Japan–Iraq BIT (2012), Art. 5(1); Japan–Kazakhstan BIT (2014), Art. 5(1).

29 Japan–Cambodia BIT (2007), Art. 4; Japan–Papua New Guinea BIT (2011), Art. 4(1); Japan–Kuwait BIT (2012), Art. 4(1); Japan–Mozambique BIT (2013), Art. 4(1); Japan–Myanmar BIT (2013), Art. 4(1); Japan–Saudi Arabia BIT (2013), Art. 4; Japan–Oman BIT (2015), Art. 5(1); Japan–Ukraine BIT (2015), Art. 5(1).

30 Japan–Armenia BIT (2018), Art. 4.

31 See de Zayas, above n 22.

32 For example, Japan–Israel BIT (2017), Art. 11(1).

33 For example, Japan–Mexico EPA (2004), Art. 61(1).

34 See UNCTAD, *Expropriation*, 2012, UN Doc. UNCTAD/DIAE/IA/2011/7, pp. 57–78.

(iv) the objectives of the government action, including whether such action is taken for legitimate public objectives.

The Japan–India EPA (2011) includes a similar provision in its Annex 10.

The Japan–Peru BIT (2008) is slightly more specific, as its Annex IV provides:

(c) Non-discriminatory measures of a Contracting Party that are designed and applied to protect legitimate public welfare objectives stated in paragraph 1 of Article 19 [on general exceptions] do not constitute indirect expropriation.

Note: It is understood that paragraph 1 of Article 19 includes measures to protect the environment.

The Japan–Colombia BIT (2011) contains a similar provision in its Annex III.

The Japan–China–ROK treaty (2012) adopts another formulation of the rule protecting the regulatory space of the host State in the context of indirect expropriation. Article 2 of the protocol to the trilateral treaty provides:

(c) Except in rare circumstances, such as when an action or a series of actions by a Contracting Party is extremely severe or disproportionate in light of its purpose, non-discriminatory regulatory actions adopted by the Contracting Party for the purpose of legitimate public welfare do not constitute indirect expropriation.

The Japan–Australia EPA (2014, Annex 12), the Japan–Mongolia EPA (2015, Annex 10) and the Japan–Uruguay BIT (2015, Annex III) include essentially identical provisions.

The TPP (Annex 9-B) adds that '[for] greater certainty and without limiting the scope of this subparagraph, regulatory actions to protect public health include, among others, such measures with respect to the regulation, pricing and supply of, and reimbursement for, pharmaceuticals (including biological products), diagnostics, vaccines, medical devices, gene therapies and technologies, health-related aids and appliances and blood and blood-related products.'

However, here again, Japan's practice is not consistent. In fact, a majority of 'new-generation' treaties provide for no specific conditions for indirect expropriation at all.[35]

7.2.3 *General and Security Exceptions*

Most of Japan's 'new-generation' treaties contain a clause on general and security exceptions modelled after the General Agreement on Tariffs and Trade (GATT) Articles XX and XXI and GATS Articles XIV and XIV bis,[36] which allow the host State to adopt or enforce measures, for example, 'necessary to protect human, animal or plant life or health'. However, this once-consistent policy slightly changed in 2012: while roughly half of the treaties concluded in and after 2012 stand on tradition,[37] many of the other half include

35 Japan–Singapore EPA (2002), Art. 77; Japan–ROK BIT (2002), Art. 10; Japan–Mexico EPA (2004), Art. 61; Japan–Malaysia EPA (2005), Art. 81; Japan–Philippines EPA (2006), Art. 95; Japan–Brunei EPA (2007), Art. 63; Japan–Cambodia BIT (2007), Art. 12; Japan–Indonesia EPA (2007), Art. 65; Japan–Thailand EPA (2007), Art. 102; Japan–Laos BIT (2008), Art. 12; Japan–Uzbekistan BIT (2008), Art. 11; Japan–Switzerland EPA (2009), Art. 91; Japan–Papua New Guinea BIT (2011), Art. 11; Japan–Iraq BIT (2012), Art. 11; Japan–Kuwait BIT (2012), Art. 11; Japan–Mozambique BIT (2013), Art. 12; Japan–Myanmar BIT (2013), Art. 13; Japan–Saudi Arabia BIT (2013), Art. 9; Japan–Kazakhstan BIT (2014), Art. 12; Japan–Oman BIT (2015), Art. 10; Japan–Ukraine BIT (2015), Art. 13; Japan–Iran BIT (2016), Art. 8; Japan–Kenya BIT (2016), Art. 10; Japan–Israel BIT (2017), Art. 11; Japan–Armenia BIT (2018), Art. 12; Japan–Jordan BIT (2018), Art. 11; Japan–UAE BIT (2018), Art. 12; Japan–Argentina BIT (2018), Art. 11.

36 For example, Japan–Singapore EPA (2002), Art. 83; Japan–Israel BIT (2017), Art. 17.

37 Japan–Kuwait BIT (2012), Art. 17; Japan–Mozambique BIT (2013), Art. 18; Japan–Myanmar BIT (2013), Art. 19; Japan–Australia BIT (2014), Arts. 1.9, 1.10; Japan–Mongolia EPA (2015), Art. 1.10; Japan–Iran BIT (2016), Art. 13;

only the security exceptions clause modelled after GATT Article XXI and GATS Article XIV bis[38] and there are two treaties without any exceptions clause.[39]

7.2.4 *Remedies*

If the arbitral tribunal is given a power to order specific performance and/or judicial restitution, the host State may be obliged to revoke a judgment of its domestic court or to amend its legislation, even if such judgment or legislation is perfectly lawful or constitutional under its domestic law. In this respect, most of Japan's 'new-generation' treaties allow the arbitral tribunal to grant one or both of the following remedies: (i) payment of monetary damages and applicable interest; and (ii) restitution of property, in which case the award shall provide that the disputing Party may pay monetary damages and any applicable interest in lieu of restitution.[40] The Japanese government often points out these provisions to explain that the arbitral tribunal has no power to order specific performance and/or judicial restitution.[41]

On the other hand, the Japan–Iraq BIT (2012) includes the following provision (Article 17(12)):

> The award rendered by the arbitral tribunal shall be final and binding upon the disputing parties. This award shall be executed by the applicable laws and regulations concerning the execution of award in force in the country where such execution is sought.

There exist several other treaties containing a similar provision.[42] It is not clear whether this kind of provision allows the tribunal to order specific performance and/or juridical restitution. Although the first sentence, which talks simply of 'the award', could cover specific performance and/or juridical restitution, the second sentence suggests that 'this award', meaning 'the award' in the first sentence, is supposed to be the one that can be executed 'by the applicable laws and regulations concerning the execution of award in force in the country where such execution is sought'. It is therefore possible to interpret this provision also as excluding specific performance and judicial restitution, to the extent that they cannot be executed by such laws and regulations. If this interpretation is adopted, there will be little practical difference between this provision and ones such as Article 92(1) of the Japan–Mexico EPA mentioned earlier.

Japan–Israel BIT (2017), Art. 15; Japan–Armenia BIT (2018), Art. 16; Japan–Jordan BIT (2018), Art. 15; Japan–Argentina BIT (2018), Art. 15.

38 Japan–China–ROK Treaty (2012), Art. 18; Japan–Kazakhstan BIT (2014), Art. 18; Japan–Oman BIT (2015), Art. 16; Japan–Ukraine BIT (2015), Art. 19; TPP (2016), Art. 29.2; Japan–Kenya BIT (2016), Art. 16; Japan–UAE BIT (2018), Art. 18.

39 Japan–Iraq BIT (2012); Japan–Saudi Arabia BIT (2013).

40 Japan–Mexico EPA (2004), Art. 92(1); Japan–Malaysia EPA (2005), Art. 85(14)(b); Japan–Brunei EPA (2007), Art. 67(20)(b); Japan–Cambodia BIT (2007), Art. 17(18)(b); Japan–Chile EPA (2007), Art. 103(1); Japan–Indonesia EPA (2007), Art. 69(18)(b); Japan–Thailand EPA (2007), Art. 106(12)(b); Japan–Laos BIT (2008), Art. 17(18)(b); Japan–Peru BIT (2008), Art. 18(19)(b); Japan–Colombia BIT (2011), Art. 39(1)(b); Japan–India EPA (2011), Art. 96(18)(b); Japan–China–ROK treaty (2012), Art. 15(9)(b); Japan–Mozambique BIT (2013), Art. 17(11)(b); Japan–Myanmar BIT (2013), Art. 18(11)(b); Japan–Saudi Arabia BIT (2013), Art. 14(18)(b);, Japan–Kazakhstan BIT (2014), Art. 17(19)(b); Japan–Mongolia EPA, Art. 10.13(18)(b); Japan–Oman BIT (2015), Art. 15(11); Japan–Uruguay BIT, Art. 21(17)(b); TPP (2016), Art. 9.29(1)); Japan–Kenya BIT (2016), Art. 15(12)(b); Japan–Israel BIT (2017), Art. 24(13)(b); Japan–Armenia BIT, Art. 24(15)(b); Japan–Argentina BIT (2018), Art. 25(15)(b); Japan–UAE BIT (2018), Art. 17(19)(b); Japan–Jordan BIT (2018), Art. 23(15)(b).

41 For example, Mr. Yasushi Masaki (Assistant Vice-Minister, Ministry of Foreign Affairs), Committee on Finance and Financial Services, House of Councilors, (22 March 2013), available at http://kokkai.ndl.go.jp/ (last accessed 8 July 2019).

42 Japan–Vietnam BIT (2003), Art. 14(5); Japan–Uzbekistan BIT (2008), Art. 16(5); Japan–Papua New Guinea BIT (2011), Art. 16(12); Japan–Kuwait BIT (2012), Art. 16(12); Japan–Ukraine BIT (2015), Art. 18(10).

However, there exists a third type of provision on the scope of the award. The Japan–Iran BIT (2016) simply provides that '[t]he arbitral award shall be final and binding upon the parties to the dispute' (Article 18(5)). This clearly allows the tribunal to order specific performance and/or juridical restitution. Another example is Article 94(13) of the Japan–Switzerland EPA (2009), which provides that '[t]he decision of arbitration shall be final and binding upon the disputing parties and shall be executed without delay in accordance with the law of the disputing Party'.[43] Since a revocation of a court judgment or an amendment of legislation can be carried out 'in accordance with the law of the disputing Party', this provision also allows the tribunal to order specific performance and/or judicial restitution.

7.3 WHEN TO PROTECT THE REGULATORY SPACE OF THE HOST STATE?

The previous section reveals that Japan's recent treaty practice is somewhat inconsistent, except for remedies.[44] Although Japan often tries to 'modernize' the treaty language in response to the evolution of arbitral jurisprudence, it does not always do so. Where does this inconsistency come from?

One may speculate that Japan adapts its position in accordance with the evolution of arbitral jurisprudence as well as that of treaty practice of other States. Another possibility is that Japan changes its position according to its counterpart. In order to verify these hypotheses, we draw up Table 7.1.

7.3.1 *Chronological Development*

Is it possible to see any chronological development in Japan's treaty practice? With respect to the FET, indirect expropriation and remedies, it is difficult to see a clear trend. On the other hand, one can see some chronological development as regards general exceptions. Until 2011, all treaties contained general exceptions. However, since 2012, a majority of the treaties do not.

Why was the clause included in all 'new-generation' treaties until 2011? The first of the 'new-generation' treaties is the Japan–Singapore EPA (2002). Like many other FTAs, it contains a general exception clause applicable to the entire treaty,[45] and some of its chapters also include a general exception clause specifically designed for each of them.[46] Japan and Singapore might have simply included an exception clause in the investment chapter as they did with respect to the other chapters.[47] This first 'new-generation' treaty set a precedent, which was followed by subsequent treaties supposedly through inertia.

43 A similar provision is found in the Japan–ROK BIT (2002), Art. 15(6).

44 As indicated in Table 7.1, Japan's treaty practice on remedies is not perfectly consistent. However, the sporadic character of exceptions (treaties with Switzerland and Iran) and the lack of publicly available information concerning the possible reasons for the two exceptions do not allow any meaningful discussion.

45 Art. 4.

46 Art. 19 (Chapter 2: trade in goods), Art. 54 (Chapter 6: mutual recognition), Art. 69 (Chapter 7: trade in services), Art. 83 (Chapter 8: investment), Art. 95 (Chapter 9: movement of natural persons); Art. 101 (Chapter 11: government procurement).

47 No exception clause is not included in the following chapters, where such a clause is apparently unnecessary due to the nature of the subject (Chapter 3 (rules of origin), Chapter 4 (customs procedures), Chapter 13 (financial services co-operation), Chapter 14 (information and communication technology), Chapter 15 (science and technology), Chapter 16 (human resource development), Chapter 17 (trade and investment promotion)) or to the simplicity of the rules provided for (Chapter 5 (paperless trading), Chapter 10 (intellectual property), Chapter 12 (competition), Chapter 18 (small and medium enterprises), Chapter 19 (broadcasting), Chapter 20 (tourism)).

TABLE 7.1 *Relevant provisions of Japan's 'new-generation' treaties*

		FET		Indirect expropriation		General exceptions		Remedies	
		Pro-State	Pro-investor	Pro-State	Pro-investor	Pro-State	Pro-investor	Pro-State	Pro-investor
Year of signature	Counter-party	Linked to customary int'l law	Autonomous	Detailed conditions	No conditions	General exceptions	No exceptions	No specific performance	No limitation
2002	Singapore		x		x	x		x	
2002	ROK		x		x	x		x	
2003	Vietnam		x		x	x		x*	
2004	Mexico	x			x	x		x	
2005	Malaysia		x		x	x		x	
2006	Philippines	x			x	x		x	
2007	Chile	x		x		x		x	
2007	Thailand	x			x	x		x	
2007	Brunei	x			x	x		x	
2007	Cambodia		(x)		x	x		x	
2007	Indonesia		x		x	x		x	
2008	Laos	x			x	x		x	
2008	Uzbekistan		x		x	x		x[a]	
2008	Peru	x		x		x		x	
2009	Switzerland		x		x	x			x
2011	India	x		x		x		x	
2011	Papua New Guinea		(x)		x	x		x[a]	
2011	Colombia	x		x		x		X	
2012	Kuwait		(x)		x	x		x[a]	

(*continued*)

TABLE 7.1 *(continued)*

		FET		Indirect expropriation		General exceptions		Remedies	
		Pro-State	Pro-investor	Pro-State	Pro-investor	Pro-State	Pro-investor	Pro-State	Pro-investor
Year of signature	Counter-party	Linked to customary int'l law	Autonomous	Detailed conditions	No conditions	General exceptions	No exceptions	No specific performance	No limitation
2012	China–ROK	x		x			x	x	
2012	Iraq		x		x		x	x[a]	
2013	Saudi Arabia		(x)		x		x	x	
2013	Mozambique		(x)		x	x		x	
2013	Myanmar		(x)		x	x		x	
2014	Australia	x		x		x		x	
2014	Kazakhstan		x		x		x	x	
2015	Uruguay	x		x			x	X	
2015	Ukraine		(x)		x		x	x[a]	
2015	Mongolia	x		x		x		x	
2015	Oman		(x)		x		x	x	
2016	TPP	x		x			x	x	
2016	Iran	x			x	x			x
2016	Kenya	x			x		x	x	
2017	Israel		x		x	x		x	
2018	Armenia		(x)		x	x		x	
2018	UAE	x			x		x	x	
2018	Jordan	x			x	x		x	
2018	Argentina	x			x	x		x	

[a] The relevant clause may be interpreted as not excluding specific performance and/or judicial restitution. Refer to section I(D) earlier.

The reason why a majority of post-2012 treaties do not include a general exception clause is not clear. The parliamentary records or other publicly available official documents do not reveal any reasons for this sudden change. One can therefore only speculate, and it is submitted that there are two interrelated factors that may have prompted the change in Japan's policy in this respect. The first is the lack of arbitral precedents where a general exception clause was applied. In contrast with the security exception clause, which has been frequently invoked in cases relating to the Argentine financial crisis,[48] the general exception clause has been rarely invoked. Secondly, taking into account the lack of precedent, two reports dealing with the role of general exception clauses in investment treaties were submitted to institutions affiliated to the METI of Japan in 2011 and 2014.[49] Neither paper considers that a general exception clause will play a meaningful role in practice. For example, a measure taken by the host State genuinely for the purpose of protecting health would not constitute a breach of the FET clause or an indirect expropriation. It is certainly difficult to conceive an 'unfair and/or inequitable measure taken genuinely for purposes of public interest'. In cases where such a measure is found to be unfair and/or inequitable, for example being discriminatory, it is difficult to consider that such a measure was taken genuinely for public purposes.[50] The Japanese government may thus have come to understand the practical uselessness of general exceptions in investment treaties. On the other hand, a general exception clause is not particularly harmful for the investor or for the host State. It is probably for this reason that Japan continues to include it, possibly where the counterpart insists that it be included in the investment treaty.

7.3.2 *The Policy of the Counterpart*

As observed in the preceding subsection, it is difficult to see any chronological development with respect to the FET or indirect expropriation. However, Table 7.1 reveals an interesting tendency. The following countries are States with which Japan concluded a treaty containing pro-State FET and indirect expropriation provisions: Chile, Peru, India, Colombia, China–ROK, Australia, Uruguay and Mongolia. The CPTPP is another example of such a treaty.

The list includes Latin American States, which are frequent respondents in treaty-based investor–State arbitration. It is also well known that investor–State arbitration has been much criticized in India, Australia, and the ROK. It is therefore no wonder that these countries wish to include pro-State provisions in their treaties. In fact, investment treaties concluded by most of these States during the corresponding period include an FET clause linked to customary international law and detailed provisions on the conditions for indirect expropriation.[51]

48 See, e.g., *Continental Casualty* v. *Argentina*, ICSID Case No. ARB/03/9, Award, 5 September 2008, paras. 196ff.

49 Shotaro Hamamoto, 'Reigai to Saikeikokutaigu Joko [Exceptions and the Most-Favoured-Nations Clause]', Toshi Kyotei Tyuusai Kenkyukai Hokokusho [Report of the Study Group on Investment Treaty Arbitration] (2011), available at www.meti.go.jp/policy/trade_policy/epa/investment/materials.html; Tadashi Mori & Akira Kotera, 'Kokusai Toshi Kyotei niokeru Ippanteki Reigai Kitei ni tsuite [General Exception Clauses in International Investment Agreements Concluded by Japan]', RIETI Discussion Paper Series 14-J-007, available at www.rieti.go.jp/en/publications/summary/14010017.html (both last accessed 8 July 2019).

50 See, e.g., *S.D. Myers* v. *Canada*, Partial Award, 13 November 2000, paras. 194, 255–56, 266.

51 See, e.g., Peru–Colombia BIT (2007), Art. 4 and Annex C; Chile–Uruguay BIT (2010), Art. 5 and Annex A; Australia–ROK FTA (2014), Art. 11.5 and Annex 11-B; Mongolia–Canada BIT (2016), Art. 6 and Annex B.10. India's

With Mexico, the Philippines, Thailand, Brunei, Laos, Iran and Kenya, Japan concluded treaties containing an FET clause linked to customary international law but no detailed conditions for indirect expropriation. This is basically in line with the treaty practice that these States adopted during the corresponding period.[52]

With Singapore, ROK (2002), Vietnam, Malaysia, Cambodia, Indonesia, Uzbekistan, Switzerland, Papua New Guinea, Kuwait, Iraq, Saudi Arabia, Mozambique, Myanmar, Kazakhstan, Ukraine, Oman and Israel, Japan concluded treaties containing an autonomous FET and no detailed conditions for indirect expropriation. This, again, is in conformity with the treaty practice that these States have adopted during the corresponding period.[53]

The aforementioned classification indicates that Japan has been flexible with respect to the FET and indirect expropriation, usually accepting the formulation of these provisions as adopted by its counterpart. It follows that Japan does not consider that the FET clause needs to be linked to customary international law or that the treaty needs to set forth precise conditions for indirect expropriation.

Does that mean that Japan is not interested in securing the regulatory space of the host State or always sees investment treaties from the perspective of a capital-exporting State? Such a conclusion is not tenable, given the government's position as explained in the Diet. As explained elsewhere, the Japanese government consistently argues that investment treaties do not constitute a threat to Japan's sovereignty or its regulatory space.[54] It thus follows that Japan considers that investment treaties with an autonomous FET clause and without detailed conditions for indirect expropriation can and do sufficiently secure the regulatory space of the State.

7.4 CURRENT STATE OF MULTILATERAL NEGOTIATIONS

7.4.1 *RCEP*

In 2012, the ten ASEAN Member States and six others (Australia, China, India, Japan, New Zealand and the ROK) launched negotiations for the RCEP.[55] The Guiding Principles and Objectives for Negotiating the Regional Comprehensive Economic Partnership, adopted in

treaties concluded during this period continue to include an autonomous FET but its 2015 Model BIT replaced it with a customary international law standard. Art. 3.1, Model Text for the Indian Bilateral Investment Treaty (2015). See also Grant Hanessian and Kabir Duggal, 'The 2015 Indian Model BIT: Is This Change the World Wishes to See?' (2015) 30(3) *ICSID Review* 729.

52 Mexico–Iceland BIT (2005), Art. 3(1) and Protocol, Art. 3, Paragraph (1); Iran–Slovakia BIT (2016), Art. 3; ASEAN-ROK BIT (2006), Art. 5(1), (2). Kenya's practice is inconsistent. See Kenya–Slovakia BIT with an autonomous FET (Art. 2(2)) and no detailed conditions for indirect expropriation and Kenya–ROK BIT with an FET linked to customary international law (Art. 2(2), (3)) and detailed conditions for indirect expropriation (Protocol, Art. 4). The same applies to the Philippines' practice: *see* Philippines–Austria BIT (2002) (Art. 2(1)).

53 Singapore–Uzbekistan BIT (2003), Art. 3(2); ROK–Vietnam BIT (2003), Art. 2(2); Malaysia–Slovakia BIT (2007), Art. 2(2); Cambodia–Czech Republic BIT (2008), Art. 2(2); Indonesia–Finland BIT (2006), Art. 2(2); Switzerland–China BIT (2009), Art. 4(1); Kuwait–Turkey BIT (2010), Art. 2(2); Saudi Arabia–Czech Republic BIT (2009), Art. 2(1); Mozambique–India BIT (2009), Art. 3(2); Myanmar–Israel BIT (2014), Art. 2(2); Kazakhstan–Macedonia FYR (2012), Art. 2(2); Ukraine–Singapore BIT (2006), Art. 3(2); Oman–Netherlands BIT (2009), Art. 2(2). Iraq's treaty practice is difficult to identify due to the lack of publicly available information. Papua New Guinea concluded no treaties during the period when it concluded one with Japan.

54 Shotaro Hamamoto, 'Recent Anti-ISDS Discourse in the Japanese Diet: A Dressed-Up but Glaring Hypocrisy' (2016) 16 *Journal of World Investment and Trade* 931–51.

55 Hamamoto, above n 3, at 197–98.

2012,[56] set forth principles of the negotiations. The most notable among them is the emphasis on flexibility in consideration of developing States. Principle 4 thus provides that '[t]aking into consideration the different levels of development of the participating countries, the RCEP will include appropriate forms of flexibility including provision for special and differential treatment, plus additional flexibility to the least-developed ASEAN Member States'.[57] Likewise, Principle 7 states that '[p]rovisions for technical assistance and capacity building may be made available ... to the developing and least-developed countries participating in the RCEP to enable all parties to fully participate in the negotiations, implement obligations under the RCEP and enjoy the benefits from the RCEP'.[58]

The Guiding Principles and Objectives also sets forth areas of negotiations: trade in goods, trade in services, investment, economic and technical cooperation, intellectual property, competition and dispute settlement. The scope of negotiations is thus narrower than the CPTPP, which also includes chapters on State-owned enterprises, labour and environment.[59]

Although the Guiding Principles and Objectives states that the negotiations aim to complete by end of 2015, the negotiations are ongoing and the possibility of completion, especially in the wake of the US withdrawal from the TPP, seems to be dim.[60] Negotiations are still ongoing at the time of writing this chapter with no clear prospects.[61]

7.4.2 *EU–Japan Economic Partnership Agreement*

Currently, the EU has concluded FTAs with Canada, Vietnam, Singapore and Mexico. It is in negotiations with other States, such as India, Myanmar, the Philippines and Thailand.[62] In July 2018, the EU and Japan signed the EU–Japan Economic Partnership Agreement.[63] EU companies already export over 58 billion Euros in goods, and 28 billion Euros in services to Japan annually.[64] The EU has stated that the trade agreement with Japan is negotiated with hopes to remove trade barriers that make it difficult for European companies to remain competitive, to help 'shape global trade rules in line with [their] high standards and shared

[56] Guiding Principles and Objectives for Negotiating the Regional Comprehensive Economic Partnership (30 August 2012), available at https://asean.org/storage/2012/05/RCEP-Guiding-Principles-public-copy.pdf (last accessed 12 September 2019).

[57] Guiding Principles and Objectives for Negotiating the Regional Comprehensive Economic Partnership, available at http://asean.org/storage/2012/05/RCEP-Guiding-Principles-public-copy.pdf (last accessed 8 July 2019).

[58] Ibid.

[59] Although government procurement is not mentioned in the Guiding Principles and Objectives, a working group on government procurement was established in the negotiating committee in 2017. Nineteenth Round of Negotiations – 18 to 28 July 2017, Hyderabad, India, available at https://dfat.gov.au/trade/agreements/negotiations/rcep/news/Pages/nineteenth-round-of-negotiations-18-to-28-july-2017-hyderabad-india.aspx (last accessed 8 July 2019).

[60] 'Countries grapple with perplexing RCEP puzzle', Nikkei Asian Review, 12 September 2017, available at https://asia.nikkei.com/Politics-Economy/International-Relations/Countries-grapple-with-perplexing-RCEP-puzzle (last accessed 8 July 2019).

[61] For the negotiation process, see Ministry of Foreign Affairs of Japan, 'Regional Comprehensive Economic Partnership (RCEP)', available at www.mofa.go.jp/policy/economy/page2e_000001.html (last visited on 22 October 2019).

[62] For a full list of ongoing negotiations, see European Commission, 'Negotiations and Agreements', available at http://ec.europa.eu/trade/policy/countries-and-regions/negotiations-and-agreements/#_being-negotiated (last accessed 8 July 2019).

[63] European Commission, 'EU and Japan sign Economic Partnership Agreement', 17 July 2018, available at http://trade.ec.europa.eu/doclib/press/index.cfm?id=1891 (last accessed 8 July 2019).

[64] European Commission, 'In focus: EU-Japan Economic Partnership Agreement', available at http://ec.europa.eu/trade/policy/in-focus/eu-japan-economic-partnership-agreement/ (last accessed 8 July 2019).

values', and to 'send a powerful signal that two of the world's biggest economies reject protectionism'.[65]

This agreement is hailed as 'the most important bilateral trade agreement ever concluded by the EU'.[66] It will remove 'the vast majority of the €1 billion of duties paid annually by EU companies exporting to Japan', including the long-standing barriers on cars in the Japanese automobile industry.[67] On the other hand, 99 per cent of EU's tariffs on Japanese goods will be removed, including the 10 per cent tariff on Japanese car exports that will be lowered to zero within eight years.[68] In addition, the agreement outlines the 'highest standards of labour, safety, environmental and consumer protection, fully safeguards public services and has a dedicated chapter on sustainable development'.[69] Furthermore, it maintains high standards of data protection.[70]

The agreement entered into force on 1 February 2019.[71] The EU and Japan are also continuing negotiations on investment protection issues, so as to work towards 'a stable and secure investment environment in Europe and Japan'.[72] As with FTAs concluded with Canada, Vietnam, Singapore and Mexico, the EU will also be proposing the set-up of a Multilateral Investment Court.[73]

7.5 CONCLUSION

The inconsistency in Japan's treaty practice with respect to general exception, FET and indirect expropriation indicates that Japan does not consider a general exception clause necessary, that the FET clause needs to be linked to customary international law, or that detailed conditions for indirect expropriation need to be provided for, in order to secure the regulatory space of the host State.

As the author has argued elsewhere, despite often strongly worded criticisms addressed at investment treaties and treaty-based investment arbitration, the arbitral tribunals have been prudent enough to ensure that the regulatory space of the host State is not adversely affected by the application of an FET clause, whether autonomous or linked to customary international law, or the clause on indirect expropriation.[74] Such restriction of the FET clause or

65 Ibid.

66 European Commission – Press Release, 'EU and Japan reach agreement in principle on Economic Partnership Agreement', 6 July 2017, available at http://europa.eu/rapid/press-release_IP-17-1902_en.htm (last accessed 8 July 2019).

67 European Commission, 'EU and Japan sign Economic Partnership Agreement', above n 63.

68 'EU, Japan sign major trade deal in 'message against protectionism'', SBS News, 17 July 2018, available at www.sbs.com.au/news/eu-japan-sign-trade-deal-in-message-against-protectionism (last accessed 8 July 2019).

69 European Commission – Press Release, 'EU and Japan reach agreement in principle on Economic Partnership Agreement', above n 64.

70 Ibid.

71 See Ministry of Foreign Affairs of Japan, 'Exchange of Diplomatic Notes Concerning Entry into Force of the Agreement between the European Union and Japan for an Economic Partnership', available at www.eu-japan.eu/epa-helpdesk (last accessed 12 September 2019).

72 Ibid.

73 European Commission – Press Release, 'EU and Japan reach agreement in principle on Economic Partnership Agreement', above n 66.

74 Hamamoto, above n 20; Shotaro Hamamoto, 'Protection of the Investor's Legitimate Expectations: Intersection of a Treaty Obligation and a General Principle of Law' in Wenhua Shan (ed.), *China and International Investment Law* (Leiden: Brill, 2014), pp. 141–69; Shotaro Hamamoto, 'L'État situé dans le droit international de l'investissement' in Shotaro Hamamoto, Akiho Shibata and Hironobu Sakai (eds.), *'L'être situé, Effectiveness and Purposes of International Law: Essays in honour of Professor Ryuichi Ida* (Leiden: Brill/Nijhoff, 2015), pp. 3–22; Miharu Hirano and Shotaro Hamamoto, 'Is Investment Arbitration Inimical to the Human Right to Water?' in Julien Chaisse (ed.), *Charting the Water Regulatory Future* (Cheltenham: Edward Elgar, 2017), pp. 145–66.

the indirect expropriation clause may be politically necessary,[75] but Japan's practice suggests that it is not necessary from a strictly legal point of view.

Notwithstanding this, it is quite understandable that States wish to qualify these clauses, considering that 'tribunal deference may be accorded by one tribunal and denied by another, in other words it is a matter for the tribunal's discretion, and so it may not be safely relied upon by states'.[76] Japan's treaty practice suggests its confidence in the evolution of the arbitral jurisprudence. Could this be because Japan has not been a respondent in an investment arbitration? Would its position radically change if it is (eventually) brought to arbitration, and is ordered to pay a hefty sum in damages to a foreign investor? These questions, of course, remain unanswered.

[75] 'In addition to legal certainty and predictability, the political acceptability to contracting states is another quality factored into in considering substantive reform of investment treaties. This is due to the fact that substantive reform of investment treaties needs a political decision of each sovereign state': Taejoon Ahn, 'The Utility of Carve-Out Clauses in Addressing Regulatory Concerns in Investment Treaty Arbitration' (2016) 12 *Asian International Arbitration Journal* 65 at 71.

[76] Aikaterini Titi, *The Right to Regulate in International Investment Law* (Baden-Bade: Nomos, 2014), p. 294.

8

Investment Agreements and Regulatory Space in Indonesia

*Antony Crockett**

8.1 INTRODUCTION

Indonesia has a population of more than 260 million[1] and is the largest economy in the Association of Southeast Asian Nations (ASEAN).[2] In 2016, Indonesia attracted net inward foreign direct investment (FDI) of 397 trillion rupiah (close to US$30 billion),[3] making it the second largest recipient (in absolute terms) of FDI in ASEAN, just behind Singapore.[4] Alongside its pursuit of economic reforms, the current Government of Indonesia (GOI) has aimed to further increase inbound FDI, in particular to encourage infrastructure investment.[5] At the same time, President Joko Widodo has had to fend off accusations of protectionism, in light of the GOI's recent moves to terminate its bilateral investment treaties (BITs) and controversies over the forced renegotiation of contracts in the mining sector.[6]

Since the late 1960s, Indonesia has signed sixty-seven BITs.[7] In addition to these BITs, Indonesia has more recently entered into a number of multilateral and bilateral agreements containing investment provisions similar to those found in BITs, including the ASEAN Comprehensive Investment Agreement (ACIA) and the so-called 'ASEAN Plus' free trade agreements (FTAs) with Australia, China, India, Japan, Korea and New Zealand.

* Views expressed in this paper are the personal opinions of the author.

1 United Nations Data, 'Indonesia', available at http://data.un.org/en/iso/id.html (last accessed 8 July 2019).

2 ASEANup, '4 ASEAN infographics: population, market, economy', available at https://aseanup.com/asean-infographics-population-market-economy (last accessed 8 July 2019).

3 Indonesia Investment Coordinating Board, 'Domestic and Foreign Direct Investment Realisation in Quarter IV and January – December 2016' (2017), available at www.bkpm.go.id/images/uploads/file_siaran_pers/Bahan_Paparan_-_Eng_-_TW_IV_2016-250117_FINAL.pdf (last accessed 8 July 2019).

4 ASEAN, 'Foreign direct investment net inflows, intra- and extra-ASEAN' (2016), available at http://asean.org/storage/2015/09/Table-25_oct2016.pdf (last accessed 8 July 2019). Singapore acts as an investment hub for the region and it is likely that a significant proportion of FDI inflows into Singapore were ultimately invested in other ASEAN States, including Indonesia.

5 'Jokowi-Kalla administration: Three years of moving forward', The Jakarta Post, 14 November 2017, available at www.thejakartapost.com/adv/2017/11/14/jokowi-kalla-administration-three-years-of-moving-forward.html (last accessed 8 July 2019).

6 Rieka Rahadiana, Thomas Kutty Abraham & Rosalind Mathieson, 'Indonesia Hunts for Investors for Projects Worth Hundreds of Billions', Bloomberg, 17 October 2017, available at www.bloomberg.com/news/articles/2017-10-16/jokowi-roots-for-private-investment-as-freeport-dispute-lingers (last accessed 8 July 2019).

7 *See* United Nations Conference on Trade and Investment ('UNCTAD'), Investment Policy Hub, 'Indonesia: Bilateral Investment Treaties', available at https://investmentpolicy.unctad.org/international-investment-agreements/countries/97/indonesia?type=bits (last accessed 8 July 2019). In total, Indonesia has signed seventy-two BITs since 1968. Earlier BITs were replaced by new treaties in the case of Denmark (1968 and 2007), the Netherlands (1968 and 1994), Germany (1968 and 2003), and Singapore (1990, 2005 and 2018).

In early 2014, Indonesia announced the termination of the Indonesia–Netherlands BIT. Since then, Indonesia has terminated a further twenty-four BITs[8] and is expected to progressively terminate those which remain in force. Indonesia remains bound, however, by the investment chapters of the ACIA and various other agreements. It has also commenced negotiations for a new FTA with the EU,[9] and has signed a number of new FTAs containing investment provisions including, most recently, the Indonesia–Australia Comprehensive Economic Partnership (IA-CEPA).[10]

In late 2014, Indonesia had also indicated interest in joining the Trans-Pacific Partnership (TPP), and despite the withdrawal of the United States from the trade deal in 2017, maintains an interest in the Comprehensive and Progressive Agreement for Trade-Pacific Partnership (CPTPP) that the eleven remaining members signed in March 2018.[11] Indonesia has stated that it ultimately intends to replace its older BITs with agreements based on a new, modern, template.[12] In this context, there is evidence that Indonesia intends to preserve foreign investors' rights to refer disputes with the State to international arbitration.[13] However, because Indonesia has not published a new model BIT, it is more difficult to predict the ways in which Indonesia might seek to protect its regulatory space, or to identify Indonesia's particular priorities in this respect.

This chapter therefore investigates potential areas for reform and innovation based on a review of Indonesia's extant BITs and other treaties containing investment provisions (TIPs). In particular, it considers the extent to which Indonesia has sought to incorporate provisions insulating certain areas of regulation from investor claims and to improve and reform Investor–State Dispute Settlement (ISDS) procedures.

8.2 PROMOTING FOREIGN INVESTMENT BUT DETERRING PUBLIC INTEREST REGULATION?

BITs and the investment protection provisions commonly found in other types of international investment agreements (IIAs)[14] are generally designed to attract foreign investment by offering foreign investors certain protections which provide some comfort as to the predictability and stability of the legal framework covering their investment.[15] This goal is reflected, for example, in the preamble of Indonesia's first BIT, signed with Denmark in 1968, which records the desire of the contracting parties 'to create favourable conditions for capital

[8] Ibid.

[9] Ayomi Amindoni, 'Indonesia-EU CEPA set for 2019', The Jakarta Post, 26 April 2016, available at www.thejakartapost.com/news/2016/04/26/indonesia-eu-cepa-set-for-2019.html (last accessed 8 July 2019).

[10] Indonesia–Australia Comprehensive Economic Partnership, signed 4 March 2019 (not yet in force), available at https://dfat.gov.au/trade/agreements/not-yet-in-force/iacepa/iacepa-text/Pages/default.aspx (last accessed 12 September 2019).

[11] *See* the final text of the CPTPP, released by the New Zealand government on their website, available at www.mfat.govt.nz/assets/CPTPP/Comprehensive-and-Progressive-Agreement-for-Trans-Pacific-Partnership-CPTPP-English.pdf (last accessed 28 February 2018), signed on 8 March 2018 in Santiago, Chile.

[12] *See* Michael Ewing-Chow and Junianto James Losari, 'Indonesia is letting its bilateral treaties lapse so as to renegotiate better ones', Financial Times, 14 April 2014, available at https://cil.nus.edu.sg/wp-content/uploads/2010/12/Ewing-Chow+Losari-FT-Article-Indonesia-is-letting-its-bilateral-treaties-lapse-15Apr2014.pdf (last accessed 8 July 2019).

[13] *See* Antony Crockett, 'The Termination of Indonesia's BITs: Changing the Bathwater, but Keeping the Baby?' (2017) 18(5–6) *Journal of World Investment and Trade* 836 at 843–44.

[14] The acronym IIA as used by UNCTAD encompasses both BITs and TIPs.

[15] *See, e.g.*, Rudolph Dolzer and Christoph Schreuer (eds.), *Principles of International Investment Law* (United Kingdom: Oxford University Press, 2012), p. 13.

investments in both States and to intensify the co-operation between private enterprises in both States with a view to stimulating the productive use of resources'.[16]

The goal of creating a favourable investment environment in order to attract foreign investment has not changed over the decades. For example, the first paragraph of the preamble to the ACIA explains that an objective of the agreement is 'to increase intra-ASEAN investments and to enhance ASEAN's competitiveness in attracting inward investments into ASEAN'.[17] Similarly, the negotiating objectives for the investment chapter of the Regional Comprehensive Economic Partnership (RCEP), a mega-regional agreement involving the ASEAN member States, Australia, China, India, Japan, Korea and New Zealand, states that the agreement 'will aim at creating a liberal, facilitative, and competitive investment environment in the region [and that the agreement] will cover the four pillars of promotion, protection, facilitation and liberalisation'.[18]

IIAs necessarily constrain the sovereign powers of the State parties, including the State's legislative and regulatory powers. IIAs have come to be seen as particularly powerful in this respect, because they give private investors a right to refer disputes with the host State to international arbitration.[19] The private investor can allege that the host State has violated the provisions of the treaty and may seek compensation for any losses suffered as a result. As of September 2019, there have been at least 942 treaty-based investor–State arbitrations[20] and tribunals have awarded billions of dollars to investors for breaches of IIAs.

In recent years, critics of IIAs have argued that investors' ability to challenge legislative, regulatory and other measures by threatening or bringing claims against the State has led to a 'chilling effect' whereby States are deterred from pursuing the implementation of measures in the public interest, for example, to protect public health or the environment.[21] It is beyond the scope of this chapter to consider in detail whether the supposed 'chilling effect' has been experienced in Indonesia as a result of the country signing dozens of IIAs since the 1960s. However, some brief observations may be made.

It has been alleged[22] that a specific threat of BIT arbitration from Newcrest Mining resulted in the GOI deciding to exempt Newcrest from the operation of Law Number 41 of 1999 Concerning Forestry Affairs (the 'Forestry Law') which, among other things, sought to impose a ban on open pit mining in protected forest areas.[23] In these accounts, the threat of arbitration from foreign companies and '[t]he resulting fear of huge compensation payouts'

[16] Denmark and Indonesia: Agreement concerning the encouragement and the reciprocal protection of investments (with protocol), Djakarta, 30 January 1968, in force 11 March 1970, No. 10352, available at https://investmentpolicy.unctad.org/international-investment-agreements/treaty-files/2977/download (last accessed 8 July 2019).

[17] ACIA, available at www.asean.org/storage/images/2013/economic/aia/ACIA_Final_Text_26%20Feb%202009.pdf (last accessed 8 July 2019).

[18] Department of Foreign Affairs and Trade, 'Guiding Principles and Objectives for Negotiating the Regional Comprehensive Economic Partnership', available at https://asean.org/storage/2012/05/RCEP-Guiding-Principles-public-copy.pdf (last accessed 8 July 2019).

[19] Private investors are arguably more likely to refer disputes to arbitration relative to Governments, who may prefer to seek diplomatic solutions.

[20] UNCTAD Investment Dispute Settlement Navigator, available at http://investmentpolicyhub.unctad.org/investment-dispute-settlement (last accessed 8 July 2019).

[21] See Kyla Tienhaara, 'Regulatory Chill and the Threat of Arbitration: A View from Political Science', in Chester Brown and Kate Miles (eds.), *Evolution in Investment Treaty Law and Arbitration* (Cambridge University Press, 2011), pp. 606–28.

[22] Chris Hamby, 'The Billion Dollar Ultimatum', available at www.buzzfeed.com/chrishamby/the-billion-dollar-ultimatum (last accessed 8 July 2019).

[23] Article 38(4) of the Forestry Law.

were key reasons for the GOI's decision.[24] This conclusion appears to overlook two important issues.

First, the ban on open pit mining also affected domestic mining companies. Of the thirteen companies ultimately granted exemptions, seven are domestically owned and two of these are majority State-owned.[25] Moreover, the relevant decree states that the exemption was granted to allow companies which held pre-existing contracts to continue mining activities until the expiration of those contracts.[26] Apart from these exempted operations, the ban on open pit mining in protected forest areas remains in force.

Second, it is unclear if the affected investors had threatened to bring *treaty* claims. Newcrest Mining and the other affected mining companies are party to so-called 'Contracts of Work' which contain clauses providing for disputes to be referred to international arbitration. In this respect, it has been suggested that affected investors 'best recourse would have been to claim breach of contract, based on the argument that [Contracts of Work] are stabilised', whereas treaty claims would have had little prospect of success.[27]

Regardless of the question as to whether it was provoked by the threat of treaty claims (or other threats of arbitration), the about turn on the Forestry Law also illustrates a problem which remains a major challenge for the GOI, namely, how to coordinate policy and government actions across the various ministries and agencies with responsibilities pertaining to, for example, mining, forestry, environmental protection and investment promotion. This remains a serious problem today, twenty years after the Forestry Law controversy.

This problem arises in large part due to the massive decentralization of government power in Indonesia that was effected through political reforms following the resignation of President Suharto in 1998. One of the consequences of decentralization has been extraordinary growth of legislation and regulation, described by Simon Butt as follows:[28]

> In 1998 – the year before the first batch of decentralisation laws, discussed below, was passed – Indonesia had approximately 292 local governments outside Jakarta. The number has since grown as provinces, districts and cities have split into two or more. In 2003 – the year before a second batch of decentralisation laws was enacted – there were around 440 districts and cities. By 2009 there were 33 provinces and 484 districts and cities. At the time of writing then, over 1000 bodies and individuals had lawmaking powers – at least 50 per cent more than in 1999 when regional autonomy was designed and put into place. This number is likely to increase further as provinces, districts, cities and other tiers of government are carved out from existing regions.
>
> These new lawmakers have, through the laws they have passed, added great bulk and complexity to the Indonesian legal system – a system which, well before 1999, had been described as a 'vast and extensive jungle of law'. Yet, it is impossible to estimate with certainty how many local laws have been produced because there is no central repository of them. As discussed below, local lawmakers are required to send all the laws they pass to the central government. By 2006, at least 12,000 had been sent. Yet, given the abundance of lawmakers

24 See also Alan Khee-Jin Tan, 'Environmental Laws and Institutions in Southeast Asia: A Review of Recent Developments' (2004) *Singapore Yearbook of International Law* 177 at 178.

25 *See* Annex to Presidential Decree No. 41 of 2004 concerning Licences or Agreements for Mines in the Forests.

26 *See* the first paragraph of Presidential Decree No. 41 of 2004.

27 Kyla Tienhaara, 'Unilateral Commitments to Investment Protection: Does the Promise of Stability Restrict Environmental Policy Development?' in Ole Kristian Fauchald and David Hunter (eds.), *Yearbook of International Environmental Law Volume 17 (2006)* (Oxford: Oxford University Press 2008), p. 151.

28 Simon Butt, 'Regional Autonomy and Legal Disorder: The Proliferation of Local Laws in Indonesia' (2010) 32(2) *Sydney Law Review* 177 at 178.

and that many local governments do not send their local laws to the central government as required, the true number is likely to be much higher.

Consistent with patterns elsewhere in the world, the majority of Indonesia's BITs were signed in the late 1990s.[29] It does not appear that these treaties have retarded, even to the slightest degree, the extraordinary proliferation of laws and regulations on the books in Indonesia in the post-Suharto era, notwithstanding the challenges and costs that Indonesia's legal jungle has posed for foreign and domestic investors alike.[30]

In its (limited) public statements regarding the termination of Indonesia's BITs, the GOI has not raised the 'chilling effect' argument as justifying its decision. Some commentators have, however, linked the policy to concerns regarding the pending case of *Churchill Mining and Planet Mining* v. *Indonesia*, which involves a claim in damages exceeding US$1 billion.[31] The investors' claims in this case were dismissed in December 2016, on grounds of abuse of process, and the investors ordered to pay Indonesia's costs.[32] A subsequent application for annulment of the award was dismissed in early 2019.[33]

The *Churchill* case continues to be identified by critics of BITs as an example of the risks they pose to the State's right to regulate.[34] (Early in the case, Indonesia itself argued that the Claimant's statements in the case jeopardized Indonesia's 'rights to regulate and promote investments in its natural resources, and to enforce regulations on investments' in these resources.)[35] It should be noted, however, that the dispute in *Churchill* arises in relation to the cancellation of specific mining licences following allegations of forgery,[36] and does not involve a challenge to legislative or regulatory measures of more general application. There are, therefore, reasons to doubt that this particular case has had a chilling effect on regulation in Indonesia.

According to the database of IIA claims maintained by the United Nations Conference on Trade and Development (UNCTAD), Indonesia has faced only seven BIT claims.[37]

29 *See* Crockett, above n 13.

30 The OECD concluded in 2012 that 'the advent of democracy and "big bang" decentralisation has not been sufficient to deliver a competitive market and trade-friendly regulatory regime. The extensive institutional transformation within the Indonesian administration over the past decade is also resulting in a complex if not disorderly policy-making process. Likewise, rapid decentralisation results in much regulatory overlap and inconsistencies across the national economy. Potentially more worrying, decentralisation may also create more opportunities for corruption by increasing the number of decision makers across the Indonesian archipelago with the power to exploit the policy-making process for personal gain.' *See* OECD, *OECD Review of Regulatory Reform: Indonesia: Government Capacity to Assure High Quality Regulation*, September 2012, available at www.oecd.org/gov/regulatory-policy/chap%202.%20Capacity%20for%20High%20Quality%20Regulation%20in%20Indonesia.pdf (last accessed 8 July 2019).

31 *Churchill Mining PLC and Planet Mining Pty. Ltd.* v. *Republic of Indonesia*, ICSID Case No. ARB/12/14 and 12/40.

32 *Churchill Mining* v. *Indonesia*, Award, 6 December 2016.

33 *Churchill Mining* v. *Indonesia*, Decision on Annulment, 18 March 2019.

34 *See, e.g.*, 'The case of *Newmont Mining vs Indonesia*', accessible at www.tni.org/en/briefing/netherlands-indonesia-bit-rolls-back-implementation-new-indonesian-mining-law (last accessed 8 July 2019).

35 *See Churchill Mining* v. *Indonesia*, Procedural Order No. 3 (Provisional Measures), accessible www.italaw.com/sites/default/files/case-documents/italaw1312.pdf (last accessed 8 July 2019), para. 49.

36 The Tribunal concluded that the licences in question were forged, with the connivance of Indonesian public officials. *See Churchill Mining* v. *Indonesia*, Award, para. 459.

37 The claim in *Indian Metals & Ferro Alloys Ltd (India)* v. *Indonesia* was successfully defended by Indonesia (PCA Case No. 2015-40, Award of 29 March 2019 (confidential)): see Indian Metals & Ferro Alloys Ltd, 'Intimation under Regulation 30 of SEBI (Listing Obligations and Disclosure Requirements) Regulations, 2015' (29 March 2019), available at www.thehindubusinessline.com/companies/announcements/others/indian-metals-ferro-alloys-ltd-intimation-under-regulation-30-of-sebi-listing-obligations-and-disclosure-requirements-regulations2015/article26679205.ece (last accessed 14 October 2019); see also https://investmentpolicy.unctad.org/investment-dispute-settlement/country/97/indonesia (last accessed 14 October 2019).

Indonesia has a very good track record; in particular, it bears emphasizing that Indonesia has never been ordered to pay compensation to an investor for breaches of a BIT.[38]

Of the seven BIT claims against Indonesia, the only case known to have involved a challenge to a legislative measure was *Nusa Tenggara* v. *Indonesia*.[39] In this case, Nusa Tenggara Partnership B.V. (a Dutch company owned by Newmont Mining Corporation and Sumitomo Corporation) and PT Newmont Nusa Tenggara (the Indonesian subsidiary of Nusa Tenggara Partnership B.V.), challenged the introduction of a rule banning the export of unprocessed mineral ores that caused a production halt at the Batu Hijau mine.[40] The *Nusa Tenggara* proceedings were, however, discontinued within two months of the request for arbitration, after talks between the investor and the GOI.[41] Time-limited exemptions from the export ban were subsequently granted to PT Newmont Nusa Tengarra and a number of other investors in return for undertakings that the investors will construct smelters or other processing facilities in Indonesia.[42]

The earlier observations do not prove that Indonesia's BITs have not had a 'chilling effect'. There is, however, scant evidence that BITs have posed a significant obstacle to the introduction of new laws and regulations in Indonesia. Nevertheless, Indonesia's decision to terminate its BITs suggests that the GOI is sensitive to the risk of claims. Of course, the risk of claims also depends on the conduct of the GOI, as well as regional and local arms of government. As a result, treaty reform alone will not be sufficient to avoid claims in the future.[43]

8.3 OUT WITH THE OLD, IN WITH THE NEW

In a comprehensive study of Indonesia's earlier IIAs, Jan Knörich and Axel Berger suggest that these 'can roughly be divided into three generations'.[44] The first generation includes a small number of treaties signed in the late 1960s and early 1970s. The authors note that 'these BITs followed the typical brief format of most BITs concluded at that time – in line with the protection approach – and included provisions such as [fair and equitable treatment], [most-favoured nation treatment], expropriation, transfer of funds and in some cases national

38 Indonesia was ordered to pay compensation of US$2.7 million in *Amco Asia Corporation and others* v. *Republic of Indonesia*, ICSID Case No. ARB/81/1, but the claim in that case was not brought under a BIT. *See* C. Karina Aritonang, '*Amco* v. *Republic of Indonesia*: Resubmitted Case Decision on Jurisdiction' (1988) 3(1) *ICSID Review —Foreign Investment Law Journal* 166.

39 *Nusa Tenggara Partnership B.V. and PT Newmont Nusa Tenggara* v. *Republic of Indonesia*, ICSID Case No. ARB/14/15, Award.

40 The rule is encapsulated in Law No. 4/2009 on Mineral and Coal (Mining Law) – Article; details of the disputing parties are available at https://investmentpolicy.unctad.org/investment-dispute-settlement/country/97/indonesia (last accessed 8 July 2019).

41 *Nusa Tenggara Partnership B.V. and PT Newmont Nusa Tenggara* v. *Republic of Indonesia*, ICSID Case No. ARB/14/15, Order of the Secretary-General Taking Note of the Discontinuance of the Proceeding, 29 August 2014.

42 *See* Press Release by PT Newmont Nusa Tenggara, 'PTNNT Discontinues and Withdraws Arbitration Claim in Anticipation of Formal MoU Negotiations with Indonesian Government', 26 August 2014, available at https://lbrcdn.net/cdn/files/gar/articles/NNT_News_Release_26_August_2014_PTNNT_Discontinues_and_Withdraws_Arb.pdf (last accessed 8 July 2019).

43 See also Junianto James Losari and Michael Ewing-Chow, 'Reflective or Reactionary? Indonesia's Approaches to International Investment Agreements and Recommendations for the Future' (2015) 12(1) *Transnational Dispute Management*.

44 Jan Knörich and Axel Berger, *Friends or Foes? Interactions between Indonesia's International Investment Agreements and National Investment Law* (German Development Institute, 2015), pp. 47–54, available at http://edoc.vifapol.de/opus/volltexte/2015/5614/pdf/Studies_82.pdf (last accessed 8 July 2019).

treatment'.[45] Indonesia then negotiated a second generation of BITs in the 1990s guided by a model text, which remains available on the UNCTAD database.[46]

Knörich and Berger concluded that these second-generation BITs also largely followed the protection approach, with the exception that most did not guarantee national treatment to foreign investors.[47] During the '*reformasi*' era following the fall of President Suharto in 1998, Indonesia then began to focus on negotiating broader and more ambitious FTAs and regional or multilateral agreements, which include liberalization commitments in addition to investment protection. In this third generation of agreements, Indonesia has often agreed to national treatment including in the pre-establishment phase.[48]

As noted in the introduction to this chapter, Indonesia has said that it intends to replace its older BITs with new treaties based on a more modern template. Indonesia signed a new BIT with Singapore on 11 October 2018,[49] replacing an older BIT, first signed in 2005 and which was terminated in June 2016.[50] To date, the text of the new BIT has not been made public.

Previously, the most recent BIT signed by Indonesia had been the Indonesia–Serbia BIT (on 6 September 2011) and the last Indonesian BIT to enter into force was the Indonesia–Russia Agreement (on 15 October 2009). Although it signed no new BITs between 2011 to 2018, Indonesia continued to negotiate bilateral and multilateral FTAs containing investment chapters.

The coverage of Indonesia's existing and prospective FTAs would appear to make it unlikely that Indonesia will ultimately need to enter into any new BITs to replace those it has terminated.[51] Nevertheless, following the announcement that the Indonesia–Netherlands BIT was to be terminated, it was reported that the GOI was preparing a new model BIT which it would use as the basis for negotiating new agreements.[52] As noted earlier, Indonesia has also signed a new BIT with Singapore notwithstanding that the ACIA includes an investment chapter.

At the time of writing, no new model BIT has been published. However, in UNCTAD's 2015 World Investment Report (which observed that an increasing number of States were in the process of reviewing their IIAs)[53] it is suggested that the new Indonesian model BIT:[54]

> will consider the exclusion of portfolio investment from the definition of investment and will add a contribution to economic development requirement in its definition clauses. National treatment will be subject to exceptions related to special treatment in favour of domestic small and medium enterprises and investments and measures affecting natural resources. The new model will also clarify in greater detail the scope of the FET standard and will

45 Ibid., p. 52.

46 Indonesian Model BIT, available at https://investmentpolicy.unctad.org/international-investment-agreements/treaty-files/2844/download (last accessed 27 February 2018).

47 Knörich and Berger, above n 44, p. 53.

48 Ibid., p. 54.

49 Ministry of Trade and Industry (Singapore), 'Singapore and Indonesia Sign Bilateral Investment Treaty to Promote Stronger Economic Ties' (11 October 2018), available at www.mti.gov.sg/-/media/MTI/Newsroom/Press-Releases/2018/10/Singapore-and-Indonesia-sign-Bilateral-Investment-Treaty-to-promote-stronger-economic-ties-11Oct2018/press-release-on-signing-of-indonesia-singapore-bit-on-11-oct-2018.pdf (last accessed 14 October 2019).

50 See UNCTAD database at https://investmentpolicy.unctad.org/country-navigator/99/indonesia (last accessed 14 October 2019).

51 Crockett, above n 29, at 841–42.

52 *See, e.g.*, David Price, 'Indonesia's Bold Strategy on Bilateral Investment Treaties: Seeking an Equitable Climate for Investment?' (2017) 7 *Asian Journal of International Law* 124 at 143.

53 UNCTAD, *World Investment Report 2015: Reforming International Investment Governance* (Geneva: United Nations, 2015) ('World Investment Report'), p. 106, available at http://unctad.org/en/PublicationsLibrary/wir2015_en.pdf (last accessed 8 July 2019).

54 Ibid., p. 110.

provide a list of State obligations including a prohibition against denial of justice in criminal, civil or administrative proceedings and assurance of police protection from any physical harm. Finally, investor-State arbitration will be subject to host country consent. An investor may submit a case to international arbitration if the host country provides a specific consent letter.

In the absence of an official model text or other official statements regarding the GOIs position on treaty reform, the remainder of this chapter considers potential areas for reform, based on agreements previously signed by Indonesia, which the author understands will remain in force, and by reference to Indonesia's recent treaty practice.

To the extent that the GOI does consider that the 'outdated' provisions of its BITs pose a threat to regulatory space, it should also bear in mind that most of these treaties contain 'sunset' clauses, which typically provide that investments will continue to be protected following termination for periods of up to fifteen years. In theory, Indonesia can seek to persuade its BIT counterparts to agree to immediate or earlier termination of these sunset clauses.[55] Whether such efforts will be successful may depend on the extent to which Indonesia also seeks to narrow the protections offered to investors in any future agreements.

It has been reported, for example, that Indonesia and Argentina agreed in 2015 to 'kill' the sunset clause in the 1995 Indonesia–Argentina BIT.[56] This is, however, not of great significance given that very little FDI into Indonesia originates in Argentina.[57] By contrast, Australian investors have played a more significant role in Indonesia, particularly in the natural resources sector, and it is worth noting that the IA-CEPA does not provide for the termination of the 1992 Indonesia–Australia BIT.[58]

Notwithstanding the challenges that may be associated with negotiating the earlier termination of sunset provisions,[59] it is arguable that this should be a priority for the GOI.[60] Having these older agreements remain in place alongside various new generation agreements may cause real headaches for Indonesia, in particular by complicating disputes where investors have access to two or more overlapping agreements. It is for similar reasons that UNCTAD has argued for the progressive harmonization of investment rules, including by phasing out BITs and replacing them with multilateral agreements, such as the RCEP.[61]

55 *See* Tania Voon, Andrew Mitchell and James Munro, 'Parting Ways: The Impact of Mutual Termination of Investment Treaties on Investor Rights' (2014) 29(2) *ICSID Review—Foreign Investment Law Journal* 467.

56 'Indonesia ramps up termination of BITS – and kills survival clause in one such treaty – but faces new $600 million claim from Indian mining investor', Investment Arbitration Reporter (2015), available at www.iareporter.com/articles/indonesia-ramps-up-termination-of-bits-and-kills-survival-clause-in-one-such-treaty-but-faces-new-600-mil-claim-from-indian-mining-investor/ (last accessed 8 July 2019).

57 In 2016, total Argentine investment in Indonesia was only US$400,000, that is, 0.000014 per cent of total inbound FDI. *See* www.bkpm.go.id/images/uploads/file_siaran_pers/Bahan_Paparan_-_Eng_-_TW_IV_2016-250117_FINAL.pdf (last accessed 8 July 2019), p. 20.

58 Absent mutual termination, the Indonesia–Australia BIT will remain in force until 29 July 2023. *See* https://investmentpolicy.unctad.org/international-investment-agreements/treaty-files/155/download (last accessed 8 July 2019).

59 *See* UNCTAD, 'Phase 2 of IIA Reform: Modernizing the Existing Stock of Old-Generation Treaties', available at http://unctad.org/en/PublicationsLibrary/diaepcb2017d3_en.pdf (last accessed 8 July 2019).

60 Tania Voon and Andrew Mitchell, 'Old Agreements Must be Terminated to Bring Life to Investment', in East Asia Forum (18 May 2019), available at www.eastasiaforum.org/2019/05/18/old-agreements-must-be-terminated-to-bring-life-to-investment/ (last accessed 18 October 2019).

61 There are sixteen members of RCEP – 10 ASEAN Member States and 6 ASEAN Free Trade Area (FTA) Partners: Australia, People's Republic of China, India, Japan, Republic of Korea and New Zealand. The RCEP focuses on trade and investment related activities and economic development among the sixteen members. *See* http://asean.org/?static_post=rcep-regional-comprehensive-economic-partnership (last accessed 8 July 2019).

8.4 MOVING FORWARD: PROTECTING THE RIGHT TO REGULATE IN NEW TREATIES

UNCTAD has further described a range of options for States seeking to protect the right to regulate, and more generally to modernize investment treaties including:[62]

i. incorporation of new treaty provisions to safeguard the right to regulation including through circumscribing key standards of protection;
ii. carve-outs from treaty protection, including by limiting the scope of protected investments or the situations to which ISDS applies;
iii. making protection contingent upon a host State's level of development or establishing differentiated responsibilities for less developed treaty partners;
iv. creating mechanisms such as appellate institutions of standing investment courts; and
v. referring to other bodies of law, including in the area of corporate social responsibility.

A number of the features reflected earlier are already included in Indonesia's IIAs and the following part considers, in particular, how Indonesia has or might seek to reformulate key standards of protection, the potential for Indonesia to introduce carve-outs in new agreements and possible future reforms to ISDS mechanisms and procedure which might serve the goal of protecting Indonesia's policy space.

8.4.1 *Fair and Equitable Treatment: Double Standards, Double Trouble*

The vast majority of IIAs impose an obligation on States to accord fair and equitable treatment (FET) to foreign investors.[63] However, as UNCTAD has noted, the 'vague and broad wording of the obligation carries a risk of an overreach in its application' and that '[a]s interpreted by arbitral tribunals, the FET standard raises highly complex and contentious issues as to the types of administrative and governmental action that can be reviewed under the standard and the degree of seriousness of breach that is required to activate a compensable claim'.[64] It is beyond the scope of this chapter to attempt to resolve the debate as to whether the FET standard has had a serious adverse impact on States' right to regulate. However, it is certainly true that the obligation to accord FET has traditionally been worded in very broad terms.

For example, Article II of Indonesia's model BIT[65] (which is undated but appears to have been in use since around the 1990s) provides that:

> Investments of investors of either Contracting Party shall at all times be accorded fair and equitable treatment and shall enjoy adequate protection and security in the territory of the other Contracting Party.

Curiously, FET is mentioned again in Article III (1) of the Indonesian model, which provides that:[66]

[62] UNCTAD, World Investment Report, above n 53, pp. 133–35.
[63] See Ioana Tudor, *The Fair and Equitable Treatment Standard in the International Law of Foreign Investment* (Oxford: Oxford University Press, 2008), p. 23.
[64] UNCTAD, 'Fair and Equitable Treatment' (UNCTAD Series on Issues in International Investment Agreements II 2011), pp. 1–2, available at http://unctad.org/en/Docs/unctaddiaeia2011d5_en.pdf (last accessed 8 July 2019).
[65] Above n 48.
[66] The language used in this article appears to be based on Article 5(1) of the 1968 Indonesia–Netherlands BIT which provides that 'Each Contracting Party shall ensure fair and equitable treatment to the investments, goods,

> Each Contracting Party shall ensure fair and equitable treatment of the investments of investors of the other Contracting Party and shall not impair, by unreasonable or discriminatory measures, the operation, management, maintenance, use, enjoyment or disposal thereof by those investors. Each Contracting Party shall accord to such investment adequate physical security and protection.

In a number of instances, other States have agreed to this two-fold articulation of the FET standard. For example, in the 1994 Indonesia–Malaysia BIT, Article II (2) provides that '[i] nvestments of investors of each Contracting Party shall at all time [*sic*] be accorded equitable treatment' and Article III (1) provides that '[i]nvestments made by investors of either Contracting Party in the territory of the other Contracting Party and/or returns accrued, shall receive treatment which is fair and equitable'.[67] Similar formulations (i.e. where the obligation to accord FET is stated twice) appear in the Indonesia–Laos[68] and Indonesia–Cambodia[69] BITs, but not in Indonesia's BITs with South Korea[70] or Vietnam.[71]

In some of the more recent IIAs signed by Indonesia, there is only one reference to FET. Further, there has been a trend away from the very broad language used in the model BIT. For example, Article 11 of ACIA provides as follows:

Treatment of Investment

1. Each Member State shall accord to covered investments of investors or any other Member State, fair and equitable treatment and full protection and security.
2. For greater certainty:
   a. fair and equitable treatment requires each Member State not to deny justice in any legal or administrative proceedings in accordance with the principle of due process; and
   b. full protection and security requires each Member State to take such measures as may be reasonable necessary to ensure the protection and security of the covered investments.

The FET standard has proved controversial because it has been interpreted broadly so as to encompass not only denial of justice, but also lack of transparency, arbitrary, unreasonable or discriminatory conduct and failure to provide a stable and predictable regulatory framework

rights and interests of nationals of the other Contracting Party and shall not impair, by unjustified or discriminatory measures, the management, maintenance, use, enjoyment or disposal thereof by those nationals.'

[67] Agreement between the Government of Malaysia and the Government of the Republic of Indonesia for the promotion and protection of investments, available at https://investmentpolicy.unctad.org/international-investment-agreements/treaty-files/1625/download (last accessed 8 July 2019).

[68] Agreement between the Government of the Republic of Indonesia and Government of the Lao People's Democratic Republic concerning the promotion and protection of investments, available at https://investmentpolicy.unctad.org/international-investment-agreements/treaty-files/1624/download (last accessed 8 July 2019).

[69] Agreement between the Government of the Republic of Indonesia and the Government of the Kingdom of Cambodia concerning the promotion and protection of investments, available at https://investmentpolicy.unctad.org/international-investment-agreements/treaty-files/578/download (last accessed 8 July 2019).

[70] Agreement between the Government of the Republic of Korea and the Government of the Republic of Indonesia concerning the promotion and protection of investment, Jakarta, 16 February 1991, in force 10 March 1994, available at https://investmentpolicy.unctad.org/international-investment-agreements/treaty-files/1622/download (last accessed 8 July 2019).

[71] Agreement between the Government of the Republic of Indonesia and the Government of the Socialist Republic of Vietnam for the Promotion and Protection of Investments, available at https://investmentpolicy.unctad.org/international-investment-agreements/treaty-files/1648/download (last accessed 8 July 2019).

that protects the legitimate expectations of the investor.[72] In this regard, it is debatable as to whether ACIA Article 11(2) narrows the scope of FET with the result that it encompasses *only* the obligation not to deny justice in legal or administrative proceedings.

In contrast to ACIA Article 11, Article 7 of the ASEAN–China investment agreement provides as follows:

Treatment of Investment

1. Each Party shall accord to investments of investors of another Party, fair and equitable treatment and full protection and security.
2. For greater certainty:
   a. fair and equitable treatment *refers* to the obligation of each Party not to deny justice in any legal or administrative proceedings; and
   b. full protection and security requires each Party to take such measures as may be reasonably necessary to ensure the protection and security of the covered investments.

In the earlier clause, the use of the word 'refers' arguably limits the FET obligation to the obligation not to deny justice whereas the use of the word 'requires' in the ACIA arguably leaves scope for an argument that the FET obligation in that agreement has broader import.

A slightly different approach is taken in the FTA signed between the ASEAN States, Australia and New Zealand (AANZFTA), which contains a further proviso that 'the concepts of "fair and equitable treatment" and "full protection and security" do not require treatment in addition to or beyond that which is required under customary international law, and do not create additional substantive rights'.[73] To further complicate matters, however, there is a footnote to Article 6 which states that this proviso shall not apply where Indonesia is the party according treatment. As such, it would appear that Australian and New Zealand investors invoking this article of AANZFTA vis-à-vis Indonesia may be able to argue (as would also appear to be arguable under ACIA) that the FET standard includes but is not limited to the obligation not to deny justice.

States have sought to link the FET standard to customary international law, and to the concept of denial of justice, in an attempt to reduce the risk of liability. This seems to have led to significant conceptual confusion, with the result that language intended to further clarify the FET standard (such as that discussed earlier) may ultimately confuse matters further. In particular, while it is arguable that the FET standard as it has appeared in most BITs is broader than the so-called 'international minimum standard' under customary international law,[74] the scope of the latter standard is also a subject of significant debate.[75] Moreover, the 'international minimum standard' will, in any event, evolve as State practice evolves over time.

A further alternative to the traditional formulation of the FET standard is the approach taken in the EU–Canada Comprehensive Economic and Trade Agreement (CETA).[76]

[72] *See, e.g.*, Dolzer and Schreuer, *Principles of International Investment Law*, above n 15, pp. 142–60.

[73] Article 6(2)(c), available at https://investmentpolicy.unctad.org/international-investment-agreements/treaty-files/2590/download (last accessed 8 July 2019). A similar proviso is included at Article 7(2) of the ASEAN–India agreement, available at https://investmentpolicy.unctad.org/international-investment-agreements/treaty-files/3337/download (last accessed 8 July 2019).

[74] *See, e.g.*, Hussein Haeri, 'A Tale of Two Standards: "Fair and Equitable Treatment" and the Minimum Standard in International Law' (2011) 27(1) *Arbitration International* 27.

[75] Andrew Mitchell, Elizabeth Sheargold and Tania Voon, 'Good Governance Obligations in International Economic Law' (2016) 17 *Journal of World Investment and Trade* 7.

[76] Comprehensive Trade and Economic Agreement between Canada and the European Union, available at https://investmentpolicy.unctad.org/international-investment-agreements/treaty-files/3593/download (last accessed 8 July 2019).

CETA imposes an obligation to accord FET and then goes on to define a list of circumstances in which the obligation may be breached, as follows:

2. A Party breaches the obligation of fair and equitable treatment referenced in paragraph 1 where a measure or series of measures constitutes:
   a. Denial of justice in criminal, civil or administrative proceedings;
   b. Fundamental breach of due process, including a fundamental breach of transparency, in judicial and administrative proceedings;
   c. Manifest arbitrariness;
   d. Targeted discrimination on manifestly wrongful grounds, such as gender, race or religious belief;
   e. Abusive treatment of investors, such as coercion, duress and harassment; or
   f. A breach of any further elements of the fair and equitable treatment obligation adopted by the Parties in accordance with paragraph 3 of this Article.
3. The Parties shall regularly, or upon request of a Party, review the content of the obligation to provide fair and equitable treatment.
4. When applying the above fair and equitable treatment obligation, a tribunal may take into account whether a Party made a specific representation to an investor to induce a covered investment, that created a legitimate expectation, and upon which the investor relied in deciding to make or maintain the covered investment, but that the Party subsequently frustrated.

It has been suggested that the closed list approach makes the FET standard easier and more predictable to apply[77] (albeit the inclusion of a reference to legitimate expectations has been criticized as likely to lead to legal uncertainty).[78]

The CETA provisions quoted earlier are particularly relevant for Indonesia given the ongoing negotiations for the EU–Indonesia CEPA.[79] Based on discussions with persons involved in the negotiations, it is understood that a FET provision similar to that contained in CETA and the EU–Singapore Investment Protection Agreement[80] has been proposed for the EU–Indonesia Agreement.

8.4.2 *Clarifying and Limiting the Circumstances in Which a Regulatory Measure will Constitute Indirect Expropriation*

Indonesia's early BITs were negotiated in the wake of widespread expropriations of foreign-owned properties and businesses by the government of President Sukarno, who ruled the country from independence in 1945 until 1967. In a period of less than three years (from 1963 to 1965), at least ninety enterprises were taken over, including plantations, factories and oil companies.[81] The only

77 UNCTAD, 'Fair and Equitable Treatment' (UNCTAD Series on Issues in International Investment Agreements II 2011), p. 29.

78 Nathalie Bernasconi-Osterwalder and Howard Mann, 'A Response to the European Commission's December 2013 Document "Investment Provisions in the EU–Canada Free Trade Agreement" (CETA)' (International Institute of Sustainable Development, 2014), p. 7.

79 European Union, 'EU and Indonesia start the New Year with a comprehensive second round of FTA negotiations', accessible at https://eeas.europa.eu/delegations/indonesia/18883/node/18883_en (last accessed 8 July 2019).

80 *See* EU–Singapore Investment Protection Agreement, Art. 2.4.

81 *See* William Redfern (2010), 'Sukarno's Guided Democracy and the Takeovers of Foreign Companies in Indonesia in the 1960s, A dissertation submitted in partial fulfillment of the requirements for the degree of Doctor of Philosophy (History), the University of Michigan, accessible at https://datapdf.nyc3.digitaloceanspaces.com/guided-democracy-in-indonesia/wredfern_1.pdf%3Fsequence%3D1 (last accessed 8 July 2019).

known case where Indonesia has been ordered to compensate a foreign investor for measures taken in violation of international law, *Amco v Indonesia*, also involved an expropriation. In that case, a hotel had been seized by Indonesian military and police personnel and the investor's licence was subsequently cancelled and various contracts relating to the operation of the hotel annulled by the Indonesian courts.[82]

That compensation should be paid where property is physically seized or ownership title forcibly transferred has not generally been seen as controversial (although there are ongoing debates about the approach to calculating compensation in some cases). However, in more recent cases, investors have brought claims alleging indirect expropriation in relation to regulatory measures affecting their economic rights and interests but falling short of the outright taking of property.[83] In response, various States have sought to clarify or limit the circumstances in which a regulatory measure will constitute indirect expropriation.[84]

According to UNCTAD's IIA Mapping Tool, all of Indonesia's BITs and IIAs (including those which have been terminated) contain provisions regarding expropriation. The expropriation provision in Indonesia's model BIT is in the following terms:

> Each Contracting Party shall not take any measures of expropriation, nationalisation or any other dispossession, having effect equivalent to nationalisation or expropriation against the investments of an investor of the other Contracting Party except under the following conditions:
>
> (a) the measures are taken for a lawful purpose or public purpose and under process of law;
> (b) the measures are non-discriminatory;
> (c) the measures are accompanied by provisions for the payment of prompt, adequate and effective compensation. Such compensation shall amount to the fair market value without delay before the measure of dispossession became public knowledge. Such market value shall be determined in accordance with internationally acknowledged practices and methods or, where such fair market value cannot be determined, it shall be such reasonable amount as may be mutually agreed between the Contracting Parties hereto, and it shall be freely transferable in freely usable currencies from the Contracting Party.

While many BITs and IIAs continue to refer to both direct and indirect expropriation, it is now common for States to include clarifications to expropriation provisions in a separate annex. For example, in the ACIA, Annex 2 provides that:

1. An action or a series of related actions by a Member State cannot constitute an expropriation unless it interferes with a tangible or intangible property right or property interest in a covered investment.
2. Article 14(1), the expropriation provision, addresses two situations:
   a. the first situation is where an investment is nationalized or otherwise directly expropriated through formal transfer of title or outright seizure; and

82 Aritonang, '*Amco* v. *Indonesia*', above n 38, at 167.

83 *See, e.g.*, Ursula Kriebaum, 'Regulatory Takings: Balancing the Interests of the Investor and the State' (2007) 8(5) *Journal of World Investment and Trade* 717.

84 *See, e.g.*, Yvette Anthony, 'The Evolution of Indirect Expropriation Clauses: Lessons from Singapore's BITs/FTAs' (2016) *Asian Journal of International Law* 1.

   b. the second situation is where an action or series of related actions by a Member State has an effect equivalent to direct expropriation without formal transfer of title or outright seizure.
3. The determination of whether an action or series of actions by a Member State, in a specific fact situation, constitutes an expropriation of the type referred to in sub-paragraph 2(b), requires a case-by-case, fact-based inquiry that considers, among other factors:
   a. the economic impact of the government action, although the fact that an action or series of actions by a Member State has an adverse effect on the economic value of an investment, standing alone, does not establish that such an expropriation has occurred;
   b. whether the government action breaches the government's prior binding written commitment to the investor whether by contract, licence or other legal document; and
   c. the character of the government action, including, its objective and whether the action is disproportionate to the public purpose referred to in Article 14(1).
4. Non-discriminatory measures of a Member State that are designed and applied to protect legitimate public welfare objectives, such as public health, safety and the environment, do not constitute an expropriation of the type referred to in sub-paragraph 2(b).

These provisions provide guidance in determining whether a regulatory measure might constitute an indirect expropriation (and in this regard the provisions guide not only tribunals but also governments).[85] It should be noted, however, that even ACIA gives substantial discretion to tribunals, whereas the 'closed list' of measures which might breach the FET standard in CETA (discussed earlier) may be seen as better protecting regulatory discretion.

The AANZFTA includes a similar annex to ACIA and equivalent provisions are included in Article 8 of the ASEAN–India agreement. By contrast, the ASEAN–China Investment Agreement[86] and the ASEAN–Korea Economic Agreement[87] do not contain such provisions. Nor does the Indonesia–Japan Economic Partnership Agreement[88] (negotiated prior to the ACIA) contain provisions seeking to limit the measures which may be found to constitute indirect expropriation. It is likely, however, that the RCEP will adopt the approach of including an annex on expropriation similar to the ACIA, given the use of similar provisions in the AANZFTA and the IA-CEPA.[89]

85 *See* Manjiao Chi, *Integrating Sustainable Development in International Investment Law: Normative Incompatibility, System Integration and Governance Implications* (Routledge, 2017).

86 Agreement on Investment of the Framework Agreement on Comprehensive Economic Co-operation Between The Association of Southeast Asian Nations and the People's Republic of China, Cambodia, 4 November 2002, in force 1 January 2010; Article 8(1) of the ASEAN–China Economic Agreement covers expropriation and nationalization subject to: '. . .*(a) for public purpose, (b) in accordance with applicable domestic laws, including legal procedures, (c) carried out in a non-discriminatory manner and (d) on payment of compensation in accordance with paragraph 2*'.

87 Agreement of Investment Under The Framework Agreement on Comprehensive Economic Cooperation Among the Governments of the Member Countries of the Association of Southeast Asian Nations and the Republic of Korea, Kuala Lumpur, 13 December 2005, in force 1 July 2006; Article 12 (1) of the ASEAN–Korea Economic Agreement prohibits both direct and indirect expropriation except when the measure is done: '. . . *(a) for public purpose, (b) in accordance with due process of law, (c) on a non-discriminatory basis, (d) upon payment of prompt, adequate and effective compensation*'.

88 Indonesia–Japan Economic Partnership Agreement, Indonesia, 20 August 2007 in force 1 July 2008.

89 *See* IA-CEPA, above n 10, Annex 14B.

8.4.3 *Carve-outs: One Country's Policy Space is another Country's Market*

The ACIA seeks to provide further protection for the right to regulate via the device of a general exceptions provision based on Articles XX and XIV, respectively, of the General Agreement on Tariffs and Trade (GATT) and the General Agreement on Trade in Services (GATS).[90] A similar approach has been taken in each of the ASEAN Plus FTAs and in the CPTPP. These provisions provide, in summary, that measures 'necessary to protect public morals, human, animal or plant life and health' shall not be prohibited unless they are applied in an arbitrary or discriminatory manner.

Given that the same parties are involved, it is assumed that a similar approach will be taken in RCEP. A leaked draft of the investment chapter published in April 2016[91] included no general exceptions provision, which suggests that there will be a separate exceptions chapter. This has been the approach taken in the CPTPP, which incorporates, *mutatis mutandis*, Article XX of the GATT and Article XIV of the GATS. In addition, there are additional and specific carve-outs in the CPTPP exceptions chapter for security, temporary safeguard measures (in relation to restrictions on payments and transfers), taxation measures, tobacco control measures, and measures adopted by New Zealand in pursuit of its obligations under the Treaty of Waitangi.[92]

The tobacco control carve-out (at Article 29.5 of the CPTPP allows a Party to elect to deny the benefits of that investment chapter with respect to claims challenging tobacco control measures (at the time, Australia was facing a claim from Philip Morris under the Australia–Hong Kong BIT concerning the *Tobacco Plain Packaging Act 2011*).[93] In the IA-CEPA, the States did not include an express carve-out in relation to tobacco control measures; although Chapter 17 (General Provisions and Exceptions) includes an exception in relation to 'measures necessary to protect human, animal, or plant life or health'.[94] It is perhaps unsurprising that the Agreement does not include such a provision, given the GOI's support for the Indonesian tobacco industry[95] and in light of the complaint Indonesia is pursuing at the World Trade Organisation regarding Australia's plain packaging regulations.[96]

On the other hand, according to what UNCTAD has reported regarding Indonesia's rumoured new model BIT, the GOI may be seeking to introduce further carve-outs of its own, including for measures affecting the natural resources sector. This particular exception might prove very difficult to negotiate in, for example, RCEP given the significant presence of Australian, Chinese and Japanese investors in Indonesia's natural resource sector. It is, however, obvious why this carve-out might be an objective for the GOI given its efforts to push through a number of contentious reform packages affecting that sector, including to

90 General Agreement on Tariffs and Trade, Geneva 15 April 1994, in force 1 January 1995; General Agreement on Trade in Services, 15 April 1994, in force 1 January 1995.

91 'RCEP- draft chapter on investment: temporary safeguard measures' (2016), available at www.bilaterals.org/?rcep-draft-investment-chapter (last accessed 8 July 2019).

92 New Zealand Foreign Affairs and Trade, 'Exceptions and General Provisions', available at www.mfat.govt.nz/assets/Trans-Pacific-Partnership/Text/29.-Exceptions-and-General-Provisions.pdf (last accessed 8 July 2019).

93 For an overview of the case, *see* Jarrod Hepburn and Luke Nottage, 'Case Note: *Philip Morris Asia* v. *Australia*' (2017) 18(2) *The Journal of World Investment and Trade* 307.

94 IA-CEPA, above n 10, Article 17.2(3)(b).

95 'Indonesia on track to world's highest smoking rates', The Jakarta Post, 1 June 2016, available at www.thejakartapost.com/news/2016/06/01/indonesia-on-track-to-worlds-highest-smoking-rates.html (last accessed 8 July 2019).

96 'Australia – Certain Measures Concerning Trademarks, Geographical Indications and Other Plain Packaging Requirements Applicable to Tobacco Products and Packaging', World Trade Organization, available at www.wto.org/english/tratop_e/dispu_e/cases_e/ds467_e.htm (last accessed 8 July 2019).

implement a ban on export of unprocessed mineral ores, to require further divestment by foreign owned mining companies and to force the conversion of so-called 'Contracts of Work' into mining business licences.

8.4.4 *Reforming Investor–State Dispute Settlement*

Perhaps a more promising and obvious area for reform in the Indonesia context is the ISDS system. This is particularly the case given that Indonesia has faced more ISDS claims than other States in ASEAN, but also in light of pending negotiations where the potential adoption of new ISDS procedures is a real possibility including in the mooted Indonesia–EU CEPA (discussed further) and the ASEAN–Hong Kong Investment Agreement signed in November 2017 and which provides that the parties will enter into further negotiations regarding the mechanism for the settlement of investor–State disputes.[97]

UNCTAD has identified various options for ISDS reform, including improving transparency in relation to ISDS, limiting investor's ability to initiate claims, enhancing party control and introducing local litigation requirements. UNCTAD has also suggested 'building in effective alternative methods of dispute resolution' and the establishment of an appeals mechanism or creation of a standing international investment court.[98] The EU has subsequently taken the lead in efforts to establish an international investment court, particularly in order to ensure fairness and independence with respect to decisions implicating States' right to regulate.[99]

Indonesia's past treaty practice provides limited guidance on the position the GOI may take in relation to these matters. The EU has proposed an investment court system (ICS) (modelled on the investment court provisions of the EU–Vietnam FTA) to be included in the Indonesia–EU CEPA and it is understood that this proposal is under active consideration by Indonesia. If the proposal is accepted, this will also entail the acceptance by Indonesia of provisions anticipating the eventual establishment of a multilateral investment court.[100]

If Indonesia does decide to accept the ICS option for the Indonesia–EU CEPA, this leads to the question of who Indonesia might appoint to the new investment court. One of the more controversial criticisms of BITs and ISDS has been that tribunals are biased against developing States by virtue of the fact that the majority of arbitrators in ISDS cases are commercial practitioners from developed States.[101] Assuming that this criticism has some validity, it points to some practical steps that developing States, such as Indonesia, could pursue in the interests of balance, namely to promote initiatives to increase the size and diversity of the pool of arbitrators both in terms of subject-matter expertise and professional background and, of course, nationality.[102]

97 Agreement on Investment among the Governments of the Hong Kong Special Administrative Region of the People's Republic of China and the Member States of the Association of Southeast Asian Nations, available at www.tid.gov.hk/english/ita/fta/hkasean/files/IPPAASEAN.pdf (last accessed 8 July 2019).

98 UNCTAD, World Investment Report, above n 53, p. 133.

99 Piero Bernardini, 'Reforming Investor–State Dispute Settlement: The Need to Balance Both Parties' Interests' (2017) 32(1) *ICSID Review—Foreign Investment Law Journal* 38.

100 European Commission, 'Establishment of a Multilateral Investment Court for investment dispute resolution', available at http://ec.europa.eu/smart-regulation/roadmaps/docs/2016_trade_024_court_on_investment_en.pdf (last accessed 8 July 2019).

101 M. Sornarajah (ed.), *Resistance and Change in the International Law on Foreign Investments* (Cambridge: Cambridge University Press, 2015).

102 In this respect, it is remarkable that Indonesia has not designated any new arbitrators to the ICSID panel since the terms of Prof. Priyatna Abdurrasyid (now deceased), Mr Harianto Sunidja & Mr Husseyn Umar expired on

In relation to transparency, Indonesia is yet to sign the United Nations Convention on Transparency in Treaty-Based Investor-State Arbitration.[103] Indonesia's BITs do not contain provisions on transparency in relation to ISDS proceedings; and the ACIA and ASEAN Plus agreements only provide for transparency with the consent of the respondent State.[104] Indonesia has also not favoured transparency in practice. In *Al Warraq* v. *Indonesia*, the GOI objected to transparency[105] although in the more recent *Churchill Mining* case, Indonesia appears to have consented to the publication of procedural orders, decisions and awards (but not submissions or evidence).[106] No transparency orders appear to have been made in the pending cases *Indian Metals & Ferro Alloys* v. *Indonesia* (which is being heard under UNCITRAL Rules) or *Oleovest* v. *Indonesia* (proceeding under ICSID Rules).

It was suggested in 2015 that Indonesia might seek to limit access to ISDS in future BITs or TIPs by including a specific consent requirement.[107] This would in fact seem unlikely given the publication in mid-2016 of a draft regulation on ISDS, the terms of which appear to clarify not only that Indonesia would give standing consent to arbitration in BITs and TIPs but also that Indonesia would consent to arbitration for claims arising under its domestic investment law.[108] The draft regulation was also accompanied by an announcement that the Investment Coordinating Board of Indonesia was considering the establishment of a mediation facility to deal with investment disputes.[109]

Indonesia has historically pressed for ISDS provisions in its BITs to allow for both conciliation and arbitration. For example, Indonesia requested that conciliation be included in the 1976 Indonesia–United Kingdom BIT, and this was agreed notwithstanding the United Kingdom's preference to provide only for arbitration.[110] Twenty of Indonesia's BITs (and its Model BIT) provide for conciliation[111] in addition to arbitration, including its BITs with Cambodia, Laos, Malaysia, Singapore and Thailand. The ACIA also provides for conciliation, but without prejudice to the rights of the parties to also commence arbitration proceedings.[112]

In a notable development, Article 14.23 of the more recent IA-CEPA provides for mandatory conciliation at the option of the Respondent State, with arbitration to follow if the conciliation is unsuccessful. It is almost certainly the case that this provision was included at the request of the Indonesian side, given the GOI's previous indications that it would seek to encourage the resolution of investment disputes through non-adversarial means.[113] To the

5 July 2010, available at https://icsid.worldbank.org/en/Pages/about/MembershipStateDetails.aspx?state=ST65 (last accessed 8 July 2019).

103 United Nations Convention on Transparency in Treaty-based Investor-State Arbitration, Mauritius, 10 December 2014, in force 17 March 2015.

104 ACIA, Art. 39; ASEAN-India Free Trade Area, Art. 14; AANZFTA, Art. 26.

105 Andrew Newcombe and Jean-Michel Marcoux, '*Hesham Talaat M. Al-Warraq* v. *Republic of Indonesia*: Imposing International Obligations on Foreign Investors' (2015) 30(3) *ICSID Review—Foreign Investment Law Journal* 525.

106 *Churchill Mining* v. *Indonesia*, Procedural Order No. 1, 6 December 2012.

107 *See* UNCTAD, World Investment Report, above n 53.

108 Crockett, above n 13, 844–45.

109 Ibid., 846.

110 The negotiating history of the Indonesia–United Kingdom BIT is discussed in *Churchill* v. *Indonesia*, Decision on Jurisdiction, 24 February 2014, para. 220.

111 Based on the UNCTAD database. This includes Indonesia's BITs with Cambodia, Croatia, Cuba, Finland (1996), India, Jordan, Kyrgyzstan, Laos, Malaysia, Mongolia, Mozambique, the Netherlands (1994), Singapore, Sudan, Thailand, Ukraine, the United Kingdom, Uzbekistan, Yemen and Zimbabwe.

112 ASEAN Comprehensive Investment Agreement, Cha-Am, 26 February 2009, in force 29 March 2012, Art. 30.

113 *See* Crockett, above n 13.

best of the author's knowledge, this is the first agreement signed by any country which makes conciliation (or any other ADR process) mandatory before a claim may be referred to arbitration.

8.5 CONCLUSION

Indonesia's economy is the eighth largest in the world (on a purchasing power parity basis) and some forecasts suggest it will be the fourth largest by 2050 (behind China, India and the United States).[114] While Indonesia is presently a net capital importer, this may change in time. Given the relatively long life-span of IIAs and as Indonesian investors increasingly seek opportunities outside the archipelago, the GOI will, in its approach to IIA policy, need to strike a balance between protecting domestic policy space and protecting Indonesian investors' interests abroad.[115] The same challenge is faced by Indonesia's partners, who will need to take into account the interests of their nationals investing in Indonesia and not only their particular domestic interests.

While it is not clear that Indonesia's BITs have acted as a deterrent to the introduction of regulations in Indonesia (whether in the public interest, or otherwise), it is evident that the GOI is sensitive to the risk of claims and the need to modernize its treaties, including the need to protect domestic policy space. In this respect, changes in future agreements are likely to be incremental and, because Indonesia is increasingly negotiating mega-regional agreements, will be constrained, one assumes, by the need to preserve at least a degree of uniformity with the provisions contained in the more recent treaties it has signed, including the ASEAN FTAs and the IA-CEPA.

114 PriceWaterhouseCoopers, 'The Long View: How will the global economic order change by 2050', available at www.pwc.com/gx/en/world-2050/assets/pwc-the-world-in-2050-full-report-feb-2017.pdf (last accessed 8 July 2019).

115 Claudia T Salomon and Sandra Friedrich, 'Investment Arbitration in East Asia and the Pacific: A Statistical Analysis of Bilateral Investment Treaties, Other International Investment Agreements and Investment Arbitrations in the Region' (2015) 16 *Journal of World Investment and Trade* 800 at 823–24.

9

Regulation of Foreign Investments in India

Analysing India's 2015 Model BIT

Shreyas Jayasimha and Abhimanyu George Jain[*]

9.1 INTRODUCTION

Reconciling the regulatory freedom of States with the legal protection of foreign investors has long been a contentious issue in international investment law. In this century, as the use of investment arbitration has increased, States have perceived a real and significant threat to their regulatory freedom. In response, States have sought to mould the terms of investment treaties to maintain space for regulatory manoeuvre while preserving protections (and thereby incentives) for in-bound foreign investment and also for the outbound investments of their own nationals.

In 2015, India released the final text of a model bilateral investment treaty (BIT) which sought to optimize the balance between these two goals, and which was to form the basis for negotiations of BITs with other countries ('the 2015 Model BIT'). The text was perceived as a particularly radical departure from the existing status quo, and has been the subject of significant commentary and discussion.[1]

This contribution seeks to situate the 2015 Model BIT in the historico-legal context of India's engagement with investment arbitration. Section I sets out a brief history of India's engagement with investment treaties and investment arbitration in an attempt to place the 2015 Model BIT in the historical context of India's engagement with investment treaties and investment arbitration. Sections II to IV undertake a detailed analysis of scope and jurisdictional issues (Section II), substantive provisions (Section III) and the dispute resolution mechanism (Section IV) in the new Model BIT, in an effort to provide a legal context to the model. By analysing the text of the Model BIT and comparing it against previous model and negotiated texts, these sections hope to provide an insight into the genesis and rationale for the major innovations introduced by the 2015 Model BIT. In comparing it with existing

* The authors are grateful for the excellent research assistance provided by Medha Rao. This analysis is current as of March 2018

[1] See, e.g., Grant Hanessian and Kabir Duggal, 'The Final 2015 Indian Model BIT: Is This the Change the World Wishes to See?' (2017) 32(1) *ICSID Review* 216 (hereafter 'Hanessian and Duggal'); Prabhash Ranjan and Pushkar Anand, 'The 2016 Indian Model Bilateral Investment Treaty: A Critical Deconstruction' (2017) 38 *Northwestern Journal of International Law and Business* 1 (hereafter '*Ranjan and Anand*'). A recent issue of the *Jindal Global Law Review* (7(2)) convened a symposium on the model text. A recent issue of *Transnational Dispute Management* ((2018), vol 15(2)) on international commercial and investment disputes in and with India also features a number of papers analysing the new model text and contextualizing it within the broader context of international investment law and the specific context of India's engagement with foreign investment: the papers from that issue are available at www.transnational-dispute-management.com/journal-browse-issues-toc.asp?key=77 (last accessed 4 November 2019).

Indian BITs, reference is made to a subset of India's BITs which have been invoked in investment arbitration cases, whether against India or by Indian nationals.[2]

9.2 INDIA'S ENGAGEMENT WITH INVESTMENT TREATIES AND INVESTMENT ARBITRATION

India signed its first BIT with the United Kingdom in 1994,[3] in the aftermath of the privatization and liberalization of its economy in 1991.[4] Over the next two decades India proceeded to sign BITs with eighty-three other countries.[5] These were initially based on a 1993 Model BIT which was based on the OECD Draft Convention for the Protection of Foreign Property of 1967,[6] and then negotiated on the basis of a 2003 Model BIT (the '2003 Model BIT').[7]

Inevitably this proliferation in investment treaties spawned the initiation of investment arbitration claims by foreign investors. The first wave of cases resulted from the termination of a power purchase agreement with a consortium of foreign investors led by Enron in relation to the Dabhol power plant in Maharashtra.[8] These claims were settled and did not seem to leave any lasting impact on the Indian attitude towards investor–State arbitration.

The turning point came with an adverse decision in the *White Industries* case in 2011.[9] The claim was based on the India–Australia BIT and the award impugned the Indian judicial system for its failure to provide effective means of asserting claims and enforcing rights.[10] Though the India–Australia BIT lacked any such obligation, it did contain a most-favoured nation (MFN) clause, which the tribunal interpreted as allowing it to import this 'effective means' obligation from the BIT in force between India and Kuwait.[11]

The outcome of this case triggered a re-evaluation of India's approach to international investment agreements (IIAs), as the Indian government was confronted with the scope and

2 These comparator BITs include: the India–UK BIT 1994; the India–Mauritius BIT 1998; the India–Netherlands BIT 1995; the India–France BIT 1997; the India–Germany BIT 1995; the India–UAE BIT 2013; the India–Indonesia BIT 1999; the India–Poland BIT 1996; the India–Russia BIT 1994; the India–Switzerland BIT 1997; the India–Australia BIT 1999; the India–Austria BIT 1999; and the India–Cyprus BIT 2002.

3 Bilateral investment treaties entered into by India are by and large referred to as 'bilateral investment promotion agreements'. For consistency with international practice in this chapter bilateral Indian treaties dealing with investment protection and promotion are referred to as BITs.

4 Law Commission of India, *Report No. 260: Analysis of the 2015 Draft Model Indian Bilateral Investment Treaty*, 27 August 2015, p. 1, available at http://lawcommissionofindia.nic.in/reports/Report260.pdf (last accessed 9 July 2019) (hereafter 'LCI Report').

5 Ibid. A full list of the BITs entered into by India and the text of the treaties is available on the website of the Ministry of Finance of the Government of India, at http://dea.gov.in/bipa (last accessed 9 July 2019).

6 Department of Economic Affairs, Ministry of Finance, Government of India, 'Statement by India at the World Investment Forum 2014, UNCTAD – Transforming the International Investment Agreement Regime: The Indian Experience', p. 3, available at http://worldinvestmentforum.unctad.org//wp-content/uploads/2015/03/India_side-event-Wednesday_model-agreements.pdf (last accessed 9 July 2019).

7 LCI Report, above n 4, 1. The text of the 2003 Model BIT is available at www.italaw.com/sites/default/files/archive/ita1026.pdf (last accessed 9 July 2019) (hereafter '2003 Model BIT').

8 Ronald J Bettauer, 'India and International Arbitration: The Dabhol Experience' (2009) 41 *George Washington International Law Review* 381; Preeti Kundra, 'Looking Beyond the Dabhol Debacle: Examining its Causes and Understanding its Lessons' (2009) 41 *Vanderbilt Journal of Transnational Law* 907.

9 *White Industries Australia Limited* v. *Republic of India*, UNCITRAL Final Award, 30 November 2011 (hereafter '*White Industries*').

10 Ibid., section 11.4.

11 Ibid., section 11.2.

extent of its potential liability through its network of BITs.[12] The perception of this threat was accentuated by a series of investor challenges arising from changes in taxation laws and Supreme Court nullifications of allocations of spectrum and coal-mining rights on account of corruption.[13]

Anxious as the Indian government was to protect its space for regulatory manoeuvre, the promotion of foreign investment and the protection of the rights of Indian investors in foreign countries was also a key concern. For instance, the Arbitration and Conciliation Act of 1996 has recently been revised in an effort to promote foreign investment.[14]

It is in this context that the government undertook a review of the 2003 Model BIT. Its explicit goal in doing so was 'to provide appropriate protection to foreign investors in India and Indian investors in the foreign country, in the light of the relevant international precedents and practices, while maintaining a balance between the investor's rights and the Government obligations'.[15] In fact, in a statement in 2014, the Government of India said that there was no evidence that investment agreements promoted foreign investment, and that the goal of India's engagement with investment agreements would be to balance investor and regulatory rights.[16] The result of the review was a draft model BIT text released in 2015 (the '2015 Draft Model').[17] The 2015 Draft Model was widely considered to be a significant departure from existing notions of investment protection,[18] and the comments received on the draft by and large indicated a need to shift the balance towards investor rights. This conclusion was endorsed by the Law Commission of India in a report on the 2015 Draft Model (the 'LCI Report').[19] The result of these comments was a watered-down model BIT text released in December 2015 (i.e. the 2015 Model BIT),[20] which, while less radical than the draft, is still a significant deviation from conventional investment treaties. Following the release of the 2015 Model BIT India has sought to terminate fifty-seven BITs whose initial duration had expired or was nearing expiry, and sought to enter into 'joint

[12] See, e.g., DEA Statement, above n 6, p. 4; LCI Report, above n 4, p. 3; Prabhash Ranjan, 'Most favoured nation provision in Indian bilateral investment treaties: A case for reform' (2015) 55(1) *Indian Journal of International Law* 39.

[13] At least six of the thirteen pending investment arbitration cases in which the Republic of India is the respondent State stem from these policy decisions. See https://investmentpolicy.unctad.org/investment-dispute-settlement/country/96/india (last accessed 9 July 2019).

[14] 'Amendments to the Arbitration and Conciliation Bill, 2015', *Press Release Issued by the Government of India*, 26 August 2015, available at http://pib.nic.in/newsite/PrintRelease.aspx?relid=126356 (last accessed 9 July 2019); 'Lok Sabha Passes Arbitration and Reconciliation Amendment Bill, 2015', *Press Release Issued by the Government of India*, 17 December 2015, available at http://pib.nic.in/newsite/PrintRelease.aspx?relid=133513 (last accessed 9 July 2019).

[15] LCI Report, above n 4, pp. 3–4; 'Statement by HE Mr. Saurabh Garg, Joint Secretary, Department of Economic Affairs, Ministry of Finance, Republic of India at the World Investment Forum 2016', 19 July 2016, available at http://worldinvestmentforum.unctad.org//wp-content/uploads/2016/07/WIF-2016-Statement-India-.pdf (last accessed 9 July 2019) (hereafter *DEA Statement* 2).

[16] DEA Statement, above n 6, p. 7.

[17] The 2015 Draft Model is available at: www.mygov.in/sites/default/files/master_image/Model%20Text%20for%20the%20Indian%20Bilateral%20Investment%20Treaty.pdf (last accessed 9 July 2019) (hereafter '2015 Draft Model').

[18] See, e.g., Luke Eric Peterson, 'India Invites Comments on Draft Model Investment Treaty; Text Offers Radical Departure, and Calls to Mind Norway's Past Efforts at Revision', Investment Arbitration Reporter, 24 March 2015, available at www.iareporter.com/articles/analysis-india-invites-comments-on-draft-model-investment-treaty-text-offers-radical-departure-and-calls-to-mind-norways-past-efforts-at-revision/ (last accessed 9 July 2019).

[19] LCI Report, above n 4, pp. 3–4.

[20] The 2015 Model is available at: www.finmin.nic.in/sites/default/files/ModelTextIndia_BIT%20%281%29.pdf?download=1 (last accessed 9 July 2019) (hereafter '2015 Model BIT').

interpretive statements' (JIS)[21] in line with the 2015 Model BIT in relation to other existing BITs.[22]

This brief overview of the historical context for the 2015 Model BIT demonstrates a policy dilemma between regulatory freedom and investment protection that is far from unique to India. Increasingly, this concern is being articulated by many countries. It may even be gaining urgency in light of evolving rules on preventing base erosion and profit shifting by transnational corporations.[23] While the context for the 2015 Model BIT may not be particularly unique, the Indian response is definitely far more radical than many others. Understanding and evaluating the merits of the 2015 Model BIT may provide insights and suggestions of broader relevance on how these issues should be addressed.

9.3 ISSUES OF SCOPE AND JURISDICTION IN THE 2015 MODEL

This section discusses the preamble of the 2015 Model BIT (Section 9.3.1), the scope of the 2015 Model (Section 9.3.2) and the definition of 'investor' and 'investment' in the 2015 Model (Section 9.3.3).

9.3.1 *Preamble*

Preambular paragraphs of BITs routinely include references to the desirability of foreign investment and the desire to incentivize and increase such foreign investment. However, the preamble of the 2015 Model BIT is rather different.

Preambular paragraph 2 refers to the desire 'to promote bilateral cooperation between the Parties with respect to foreign investment'. Preambular paragraph 3 recognizes 'that the promotion and the protection of investments of investors of one Party in the territory of the other Party will be conducive to the stimulation of mutually beneficial business activity, to the development of economic cooperation between them and to the promotion of sustainable development'. Preambular paragraph 4 reaffirms 'the right of Parties to regulate investments in their territory in accordance with their law and policy objectives'.

There are three interesting features here. First, the first and second preambular paragraphs link the promotion and protection of foreign investment to cooperation, mutually beneficial business activity and economic cooperation between the Parties to the BIT. Secondly, the second preambular paragraph explicitly refers to 'sustainable development' as a justification for the protection and promotion of foreign investment. Thirdly, there is an explicit reference to the regulatory objectives and autonomy of the Parties in the third preambular paragraph.

Traditionally, investment treaties, including the 2003 Model BIT,[24] usually placed the importance and incentivizing of foreign investment front and centre in their preambles and treated foreign investment as an independent and uncontested good.

21 The text of the JIS is available at http://indiainbusiness.nic.in/newdesign/upload/Consolidated_Interpretive-Statement.pdf (last accessed 9 July 2019) (hereafter *JIS*). The preamble of the JIS takes into account *'the power of the Contracting Parties to provide clarification on the object and purposes of the Agreement'* and presents the JIS as 'subsequent practice' to be taken into account in the interpretation of the relevant BITs as per the customary and treaty-based rules of treaty interpretation.

22 DEA Statement 2, above n 15.

23 This topic has featured prominently on the agenda of the OECD. See www.oecd.org/ctp/beps/ (last accessed 9 July 2019).

24 See, e.g., the preamble of the 2003 Model BIT, above n 7.

Increasingly, there is a trend towards the inclusion of the concept of sustainable development in BITs and model texts, and towards carve-outs of enumerated policy priorities and goals from the scope of the BITs.[25] The 2015 Model BIT is an example, and arguably an extension, of this trend. It qualifies the desirability of investment promotion by reference to the mutual interests of the parties, the achievement of sustainable development, and the regulatory autonomy of the parties. In fact, the Government of India has explicitly stated that the 2015 Model BIT is not intended to be an instrument for investment promotion, as there is little evidence linking IIA to an increase in foreign direct investment.[26]

This is not simply a change in economic and political policy or philosophy. It may affect the interpretation of BITs based on the 2015 Model BIT.

Under the customary rules of treaty interpretation set out in Articles 31 and 32 of the Vienna Convention on the Law of Treaties (VCLT),[27] treaty terms are to be interpreted in their 'context', and that context includes the preamble to the treaty.[28] Tribunals in investment arbitration cases have frequently referred to preambular provisions in interpreting the provisions of BITs.[29] Consequently, it is possible that arbitral tribunals tasked with interpreting BITs based on the 2015 Model BIT will have occasion to consider these explicit and deliberate policy inclinations in their interpretation.

For instance, the tribunal in the *Salini* case,[30] in defining the concept of 'investment' for the purposes of Article 25 of the ICSID Convention, referred to the preamble of the ICSID Convention in including a contribution to the economic development of the host country as an element of an 'investment'.[31] Similarly, the decisions on jurisdiction in *Churchill Mining plc and Planet Mining Pty Ltd v. Indonesia* found that references to both the private interests of investors and the public interests of the State neutralized each other and did not support the interpretation of the relevant BITs as advancing the interests of either side.[32] Given that the preambular text of the 2015 Model BIT clearly prioritizes public over private interests, this may create a strong interpretive inference. It is worth emphasizing that the language that the tribunal construed as representing the public interests of the State in the *Churchill* and *Planet* decisions closely resembled the language used in the preamble of the 2015 Model BIT.[33]

Thus, it is very plausible that the particular and unusual phrasing of the preamble of the 2015 Model BIT may indicate an interpretive preference for the 'public interests of the State' over the 'private interests of investors'. This conclusion is reinforced by Article 23.1 of the 2015

25 Ibid.

26 DEA Statement, above n 6, p. 7.

27 See, e.g., *Case Concerning Maritime Dispute (Peru* v. *Chile)*, International Court of Justice, 27 January 2014, p. 28, para. 57; *Salini Costruttori S.p.A. and Italstrade S.p.A.* v. *Hashemite Kingdom of Jordan*, ICSID Case No. ARB/02/13, Decision on Jurisdiction, 29 November 2004, para. 75.

28 2015 Model BIT, above n 20, Art. 23.3 confirms the role of public international law principles of treaty interpretation in the interpretation of any BITs based on the 2015 Model BIT by investment tribunals.

29 See, e.g., *SGS Société Générale de Surveillance S.A.* v. *Republic of the Philippines*, ICSID Case No. ARB/02/6, Decision on Jurisdiction, 29 January 2004, para. 116; *Saluka Investments B.V.* v. *Czech Republic*, UNCITRAL, Partial Award, 17 March 2006, para. 299; *Ioan Micula and others* v. *Romania*, ICSID Case No. ARB/05/20, Award, 11 December 2013, para. 322–323.

30 *Salini Costruttori S.P.A. and Italstrade S.P.A.* v. *Kingdom of Morocco*, ICSID Case No. ARB/00/4, Decision on Jurisdiction, 16 July 2001, para. 52 (hereafter '*Salini*').

31 In this regard, see also, *Abaclat and others (formerly Giovanna a Beccara and others)* v. *Argentine Republic*, ICSID Case No. ARB/07/5, Dissenting Opinion, Georges Abi-Saab, 28 October 2011, paras. 49–50.

32 *Planet Mining Pty Ltd* v. *Republic of Indonesia*, ICSID Case No. ARB/12/14 and 12/40, Decision on Jurisdiction, 24 February 2014, para. 172; *Churchill Mining Plc* v. *Republic of Indonesia*, ICSID Case No. ARB/12/14 and 12/40), Decision on Jurisdiction, 24 February 2014, para. 178.

33 Ibid.

Model BIT which provides that it should be interpreted in the 'context of the high level of deference that international law accords to States with regard to their development and implementation of domestic policies'.

The importance of the foregoing analysis should not be overstated. The use or application of the preambular text by a tribunal cannot be predicted with certainty, and it is unlikely that preambular text will be invoked to water down investment protection standards. Nonetheless, it is useful to recognize the significance, even if tentative and limited, of this choice of words. This recognition also provides a context within which to understand the intention behind and the drafting of the substantive provisions of the 2015 Model BIT.

The intention behind the phrasing of the preambular text is further emphasized by the language used in the JIS. Article 1(3) of the JIS provides that the 'interpretation of this Agreement shall be done in accordance with the high level of deference international law accords to States with regard to their development and implementation of domestic policies. Interpretation and application of the Agreement shall also reflect the strong presumption of legitimacy and regularity international law provides to domestic legislative, administrative and judicial determinations made by the Contracting Parties.' Clearly, there is an expectation of deference to the regulatory jurisdiction of the contracting States parties.[34]

The 2015 Draft Model set out an even stronger version of the text used in the 2015 Model BIT. The preamble of the 2015 Draft Model excluded the text currently in the third preambular paragraph which acknowledges the importance of foreign investment, and referred only to the promotion of bilateral cooperation,[35] the regulatory rights and interests of the parties,[36] and the alignment of investment objectives with sustainable development and inclusive growth.[37] The tempering of the preambular language between the 2015 Draft Model and the 2015 Model BIT seems to be attributable to the LCI Report which noted the importance of assuring certainty and transparency to Indian investors abroad as well as foreign investors in India.[38]

9.3.2 *Scope*

The scope of the 2003 Model BIT was very broad. It included all investments whether made before or after the coming into force of the agreement.[39] In contrast, the 2015 Draft Model and the 2015 Model BIT have a much narrower scope. The 2015 Model BIT is substantially similar to the 2015 Draft Model in terms of scope, and so the 2015 Draft Model has not been separately addressed here. The 2015 Model BIT is narrower in the following ways. First, it does not apply to measures enacted before entry into force of the treaty or to amendments of such measures,[40] or to events or claims from before the entry into force of the treaty.[41] Secondly, it does not apply to pre-investment activity.[42] Thirdly, it does not apply to government procurement,

34 It is worth emphasizing that it is not suggested that the text of the JIS will be invoked as an aid in the interpretation of any BITs based on the 2015 Model.
35 2015 Draft Model, above n 17, preambular para. 1.
36 Ibid., preambular para. 2.
37 Ibid., preambular para. 3.
38 LCI Report, above n 4, pp. 6–8.
39 2003 Model BIT, above n 7, Art. 2.
40 2015 Model BIT, above n 20, Art. 2.1. See also 2015 Draft Model, above n 17, Art. 2.1.
41 2015 Model BIT, above n 20, Art. 2.3. See also 2015 Draft Model, above n 17, Art. 2.5.
42 2015 Model BIT, above n 20, Art. 2.2. See also 2015 Draft Model, above n 17, Art. 2.2.

subsidies or grants, services supplied in exercise of governmental authority, taxation measures or the issuance of compulsory licenses.[43] Fourthly, it expressly excludes measures in furtherance of defined policy objectives (subject to being non-discriminatory) and national security imperatives from its scope.[44] And fifthly, it does not apply to any measures taken by local governments (defined as all governmental authorities other than the central and State governments in the case of India).[45]

9.3.3 *Definition of 'Investor' and 'Investment'*

The 2003 Model BIT[46] and the Comparator BITs[47] adopted an asset-based definition of 'investment' which covered all assets provided that they had been established or acquired in accordance with the laws of the host State. They adopted a similarly broad definition of 'investor' which extended to all nationals and companies of the parties.[48]

The 2015 Draft Model BIT, however, adopted a radically different and very restricted enterprise-based definition of 'investment'. Thus, the term 'investment' was defined to mean an enterprise which was: (a) legally established and operated in the host State; (b) owned and controlled in good faith by an investor in accordance with the BIT; and (c) in compliance with obligations relating to corruption, disclosures, taxation and host State laws.[49] The definition of 'enterprise' (being a constituent element of the definition of 'investment') further introduced a requirement of having 'management and real and substantial business operations' in the host State.[50] 'Real and substantial business operations' was defined as requiring substantial and long-term capital commitments, employment of a substantial number of persons, assumption of entrepreneurial risk and a substantial contribution to the development of the host State.[51] Tax avoidance strategies, passive investments and property investments were explicitly carved out of this definition.[52] The term 'ownership' was defined as meaning direct or indirect, legal or beneficial ownership of over 50 per cent of the enterprise, and 'control' was defined in terms of rights to appoint a majority of the directors or to control the management and policy decisions of the enterprise.[53]

43 2015 Model BIT, above n 20, Art. 2.4. See also 2015 Draft Model, above n 17, Art. 2.6.

44 2015 Model BIT, above n 20, Arts. 32, 33 and Annex 1. See also 2015 Draft Model, above n 17, Arts. 16, 17.

45 2015 Model BIT, above n 20, Art. 2.4(i). See also, 2015 Draft Model, above n 17, Arts. 16.3, 1.3.

46 2003 Model BIT, above n 7, Art. 1(b).

47 India–UK BIT 1994, Art. 1(b); India–Mauritius BIT 1998, Art. 1(a); India–Netherlands BIT 1995, Art. 1(a); India–France BIT 1997, Art. 1(1); India–Germany BIT 1995, Art. 1(b); India–UAE BIT 2013, Art. 1(1); India–Indonesia BIT 1999, Art. 1(1); India–Poland BIT 1996, Art. 1(1); India–Russia BIT 1994, Art. 1(1); India–Switzerland BIT 1997, Art. 1(2); India–Australia BIT 1999, Art. 1(c); India–Austria BIT 1999, Art. 1(2); India–Cyprus BIT 2002, Art. 1(b).

48 2003 Model BIT, above n 7, Art. 1(c); India–UK BIT 1994, Art. 1(c); India–Mauritius BIT 1998, Art. 1(b); India–Netherlands BIT 1995, Art. 1(d); India–France BIT 1997, Art. 1(4); India–Germany BIT 1995, Art. 1(c); India–UAE BIT 2013, Art. 1(2); India–Indonesia BIT 1999, Art. 1(2); India–Poland BIT 1996, Art. 1(2); India–Russia BIT 1994, Art. 1(2); India–Austria BIT 1999, Art. 1(1); India–Cyprus BIT 2002, Art. 1(c). Two exceptions in this regard are the BITs entered into with Switzerland and Australia, which included third-State companies in the definition of 'investor' provided that those companies were controlled or majority-owned by nationals of the parties to the BITs. See India–Switzerland BIT 1997, Art. 1(1); India–Austria BIT 1999, Art. 1(1).

49 2015 Draft Model, above note 17, Art. 1.6.

50 Ibid., Art. 1.2.

51 Ibid., Art. 1.2.1.

52 Ibid., Art. 1.2.2.

53 Ibid., Art. 1.6.1.

The 2015 Draft Model BIT defined the term 'investor' as including a legal entity established in the home State which conducted 'real and substantial business operations' in the home State, and which has made an investment in the host State.[54]

It is important to note that there was also a list of 'assets' which were explicitly excluded from the definition of 'investment'.[55] These include interests in public debt security interests, pre-operational expenditure, portfolio investments, contractual rights to money arising from sales of goods or services, goodwill and similar intangible rights along with related claims to money, judgment rights and holding or investment companies. The Government of India justified the shift from an asset-based definition of 'investment' to an enterprise-based model on the grounds that the asset-based definition contradicts the long-term nature and goal of foreign investment.[56] The LCI Report, while endorsing the shift to the enterprise-based definition of 'investment', criticized the restrictive definitions of 'ownership' and 'control', the exclusion of goodwill from the definition of 'investment' and suggested an exhaustive asset-based definition of 'investment' as an alternative.[57]

The 2015 Model BIT thus adopts a hybrid enterprise-based definition of 'investment' with an exhaustive list of eligible investments. The term 'investment' is defined as an 'enterprise' (being a legal entity established and operated in either the host or home States in compliance with the law, and a legally-established branch of any such entity carrying out business activities there),[58] along with defined eligible assets, which must be established and operated by an investor in good faith and in compliance with the laws of the host State; and which must possess the characteristics of an investment, such as capital commitment, duration, expectation of profit or gain, assumption of risk and a significance for the development of the host State.[59]

The exhaustive list of eligible assets includes equity instruments, debt instruments of other enterprises, loans to affiliates, loans of terms greater than three years, licenses and similar rights, contractual rights of a long-term nature, intellectual property rights recognized in the host State, movable and immovable property and related rights and other interests involving substantial economic activity and significant financial value.[60] Eligible assets expressly exclude portfolio investments, public debt securities, loans to government owned or controlled enterprises, pre-operational expenditure,[61] claims to money arising from sales of goods or services from an enterprise in the territory of one party to enterprises in the territory of the other party, goodwill and similar intangible rights, claims to money arising solely from the extension of credit, judgment creditor rights and any other claims to money that do not involve the kind of interests of operations set out in the definition of 'investment'.[62]

The definition of 'investor' includes natural and juridical persons of either of the parties.[63] For natural persons, in the case of dual nationality, ordinary or permanent residence controls nationality.[64] For juridical persons there is a requirement of substantial business activities in the territory of the party of establishment.[65]

54 Ibid., Art. 1.9.
55 Ibid., Arts. 1.7 and 1.8.
56 DEA Statement, above n 6, p. 8.
57 LCI Report, above n 4, pp. 9–11.
58 2015 Model BIT, above n 20, Art. 1.3.
59 Ibid., Art. 1.4.
60 Ibid.
61 This is defined further in 2015 Model, above n 20, Art. 1.11.
62 2015 Model BIT, above n 20, Art. 1.4.
63 Ibid., Art. 1.5.
64 Ibid., Art. 1.9.
65 Ibid., Art. 1.5.

The definitions of 'investor' and 'investment' in the 2015 Model BIT present several interesting features.

First, most of the recommendations from the LCI Report were incorporated, with the exception of the recommendation that goodwill be included in the list of eligible assets. Goodwill has almost universally considered to be included in the definition of 'investment' in the decisions of investment tribunals.[66] However, none of those decisions related to treaties which expressly excluded goodwill from the scope of 'investment' as the 2015 Model BIT does.

Secondly, an 'enterprise' which qualifies as an 'investment' must be established and operated in 'good faith'. In the context of Article 25 of the ICSID Convention investment tribunals have disagreed as to whether investments must be made in good faith to qualify as investments.[67] The 2015 Model BIT, however, expressly posits this as a requirement.

Thirdly, both the good faith requirement and the requirement of juridical persons conducting substantial business activities in the territory of the home State seem to represent attempts to prevent treaty shopping.[68] This has expressly been flagged as a concern of the government,[69] particularly in the context of taxation avoidance agreements with Mauritius.[70] This is also reflected in the JIS.[71]

Fourthly, the definition of 'investment' includes the requirement that the enterprise and its assets together have 'the characteristics of an investment such as the commitment of capital or other resources, certain duration, the expectation of gain or profit, the assumption of risk and a significance for the development of the Party'.[72] This is also reflected in the JIS.[73] These criteria closely track those set out in the *Salini* case.[74] However, the *Salini* criteria, and particularly the requirement of contribution to development have proved to be controversial with a number of investment tribunals expressing degrees of disagreement.[75] Interestingly, one of these disagreeing tribunals was the tribunal in the *White Industries* case (though the

66 See, e.g., *Achmea B.V. (formerly Eureko B.V.)* v. *Slovak Republic [I]*, PCA Case No. 2008-13, Final Award, 7 December 2012, para. 161; *Tidewater Investment SRL and Tidewater Caribe, C.A.* v. *Bolivarian Republic of Venezuela*, ICSID Case No. ARB/10/5, Award, 13 March 2015, para. 118. See also, however, *Patrick Mitchell* v. *Democratic Republic of the Congo*, ICSID Case No. ARB/99/7, Excerpts of Dissenting Opinion of Mr. Yawovi Agboyibo, 9 February 2004, para. 18, referring to the fact that Congolese law and the law of countries following the French tradition do not include goodwill amongst the elements of 'investment'.

67 Such a requirement was found in *Phoenix Action, Ltd.* v. *Czech Republic*, ICSID Case No. ARB/06/5, Award, 15 April 2009, para. 114. However, this finding was expressly disagreed with in *Saba Fakes* v. *Republic of Turkey*, ICSID Case No. ARB/07/20, Award, 14 July 2010, para. 112; *Metal-Tech Ltd.* v. *Republic of Uzbekistan*, ICSID Case No. ARB/10/3, Award, 4 October 2013, para. 127.

68 2015 Model BIT, above n 20, Art. 1.5.

69 DEA Statement, above n 6, pp. 8–9; LCI Report, above n 4, pp. 10–11.

70 See, e.g., 'Revised Indo-Mauritius Tax Treaty to Curb Tax Evasion', The Economic Times, 29 August 2016, available at https://economictimes.indiatimes.com/news/economy/policy/revised-indo-mauritius-tax-treaty-to-curb-tax-evasion-finance-ministry/articleshow/53912921.cms (last accessed 9 July 2019); Shaji Vikraman, 'In Fact: The Good and Not-So-Good in the Mauritius Tax Treaty', *Indian Express*, 5 April 2017, available at http://indianexpress.com/article/explained/india-mauritius-tax-treaty-indian-economy-2805967/ (last accessed 9 July 2019); Gireesh Chandra Prasad, 'India, Mauritius Set to Hold Fresh Talks on DTAA Amendments', *LiveMint*, 28 August 2017, available at www.livemint.com/Money/HalsryNEuYb6su8CaxJLII/India-Mauritius-set-to-hold-fresh-talks-on-DTAA-amendments.html (last accessed 9 July 2019); Vanessa Houlder, 'Tax Change Threatens Close Ties Between India and Mauritius', *Financial Times*, 29 September 2016, available at www.ft.com/content/c4f2b8c6-75b1-11e6-bf48-b372cdb1043a (last accessed 9 July 2019).

71 JIS, above n 21, Art. 2.

72 2015 Model BIT, above n 20, Art. 1.4.

73 JIS, above n 21, Art. 4(3).

74 *Salini*, above n 30, para. 52.

75 For an overview of the debate, see Rudolf Dolzer and Christoph Schreuer, *Principles of International Investment Law* (Oxford: Oxford University Press, 2nd edition, 2012), pp. 65–76. For a criticism of the *Salini* test in the context of the 2015 Model BIT, see Bhagirath Ashiya, 'The Shift Towards an Enterprise Based Definition of

tribunal went on to apply the *Salini* test in the alternative anyway);[76] the inclusion of the *Salini* test in the text of the 2015 Model BIT may be a reaction to the *White Industries* decision.

9.4 SUBSTANTIVE PROTECTIONS

This section discusses the provisions of the 2015 Model BIT relating to standards of protection (Section 9.4.1), expropriation (Section 9.4.2) and investor obligations (Section 9.4.3). The 2015 Model BIT also guarantees investor rights such as free movement of funds[77] and personnel,[78] non-discrimination in compensation,[79] subrogation[80] and transparency in administration,[81] but these have not been discussed here owing to limitations of space.

9.4.1 *Standards of Protection*

The 2003 Model BIT and the Comparator BITs guaranteed fair and equitable treatment (FET),[82] national treatment (NT)[83] and MFN treatment[84] to investors. Additionally, though the 2003 Model did not refer to the full protection and security standard (FPS), a number of the Comparator BITs also provide the FPS guarantee.[85]

The 2015 Draft Model did not provide for FET, FPS or MFN. A government statement has explained that FET was excluded because of the inherent vagueness and unpredictability of the FET standard,[86] while MFN was excluded because the ability to claim benefits under third-country treaties defeats the purpose of bilateral negotiations and treaties.[87]

Investment: The Quagmire of the *Salini* Test and India's Model BIT' (2016) 7(2) *Jindal Global Law Review* 263 (hereafter *Ashiya*).

76 *White Industries Australia Limited* v. *Republic of India*, UNCITRAL, Final Award, 30 November 2011, paras. 7.4.9–7.4.19.

77 2015 Model BIT, above n 20, Art. 6.

78 Ibid., Art. 9.

79 Ibid., Art. 7.

80 Ibid., Art. 8.

81 Ibid., Art. 10.

82 2003 Model BIT, above n 7, Art. 3(2); India–UK BIT 1994, Art. 3(2); India–Mauritius BIT 1998, Art. 4(1); India–Netherlands BIT 1995, Art. 4(1); India–France BIT 1997, Art. 4(2); India–Germany BIT 1995, Art. 3(2); India–UAE BIT 2013, Art. 5(1); India–Indonesia BIT 1999, Art. 3(2); India–Poland BIT 1996, Art. 3(2); India–Russia BIT 1994, Art. 3(2); India–Switzerland BIT 1997, Art. 3(2); India–Austria BIT 1999, Art. 2(1); India–Australia BIT 1999, Art. 3(2); India–Cyprus BIT 2002, Art. 3(2).

83 2003 Model BIT, above n 7, Art. 4(1); India–UK BIT 1994, Arts. 4, 6(1); India–Mauritius BIT 1998, Arts. 4, 5; India–Netherlands BIT 1994, Art. 4; India–France BIT 1997, Arts. 5, 6(4); India–Germany BIT 1995, Arts. 4, 6; India–UAE BIT 2013, Art. 5; India–Indonesia BIT 1999, Arts. 4, 6; India–Poland BIT 1996, Arts. 4, 6; India–Switzerland BIT 1997, Arts. 4, 6; India–Australia BIT 1999, Arts. 4, 8; India–Austria BIT 2002, Art. 3; India–Cyprus BIT 2002, Arts. 4, 6(1).

84 2003 Model BIT, above n 7, Art. 4(2); India–UK BIT 1994, Arts. 4, 6(1); India–Mauritius BIT 1998, Arts. 4, 5; India–Netherlands BIT 1994, Art. 4; India–France BIT 1997, Arts. 5, 6(4); India–Germany BIT 1995, Arts. 4, 6; India–UAE BIT 2013, Art. 5; India–Indonesia BIT 1999, Arts. 4, 6; India–Poland BIT 1996, Arts. 4, 6; India–Switzerland BIT 1997, Arts. 4, 6; India–Australia BIT 1999, Arts. 4, 8; India–Austria BIT 2002, Art. 3; India–Cyprus BIT 2002, Arts. 4, 6(1).

85 India–UK BIT 1994, Art. 3(2); India–Netherlands BIT 1995, Art. 4(1); India–France BIT 1997, Art. 4(1); India–Germany BIT 1995, Art. 3(2); India–UAE BIT 2013, Art. 4(1); India–Russia BIT 1994, Art. 3(2); India–Switzerland BIT 1997, Art. 3(2); India–Australia BIT 1999, Art. 3(3).

86 DEA Statement, above n 6, p. 12.

87 Ibid., p. 13.

In place of these standards, Article 3.1 of the 2015 Draft Model provided guarantees against denial of justice under customary international law,[88] un-remedied and egregious violations of due process,[89] and manifestly abusive treatment involving continuous, unjustified and outrageous coercion or harassment.[90] The text also provided that breaches of other provisions of the 2015 Draft Model or other international agreements would not establish a violation of this standard.[91]

The 2015 Draft Model did provide for NT,[92] but this was qualified in a number of ways. First, the NT obligation could only be breached if the challenged measure constituted intentional and unlawful discrimination based on nationality.[93] Secondly, the NT obligation did not apply to laws or measures of regional or local governments. Thus, effectively the NT obligation only applied to measures or laws of the national government.[94] Thirdly, exercises of discretion, including discretion as to enforcement of laws, pursuant to national law would not constitute violations of the NT obligation.[95] Fourthly, extensions of financial assistance or measures favouring national investors in pursuit of public purposes including health, safety and environment would not constitute violations of the NT obligation.[96] Fifthly, a footnote to the text elaborates upon the meaning of 'like circumstances' for the purposes of determining breaches of the NT requirement.[97] The footnote provides that there may be legitimate reasons for differentiating between investments, including (but not limited to) '(a) the goods or services consumed or produced by the investment; (b) the actual and potential impact of the investment on third persons, the local community, or the environment; (c) whether the investment is public, private, or State-owned or controlled; and (d) the practical challenges of regulating the investment'. The footnote further goes on to state that 'the factors and determinations used by the Host State to distinguish between Investors and Investments are to be given substantial deference by any tribunal'.

The LCI Report endorsed the exclusion of the FET standard.[98] However, it criticized the overly restrictive language of Article 3.1,[99] and while acknowledging the government's concerns in relation to MFN clauses, suggested the introduction of a restricted MFN clause preventing discrimination amongst foreign investors of different States in the application of domestic measures.[100] It did not discuss the exclusion of the FPS guarantee or the phrasing of the NT guarantee.

The 2015 Model BIT retains the 2015 Draft Model's exclusion of the MFN standard, but unlike the 2015 Draft Model and the 2003 Model, includes an FPS guarantee. However, this is restricted to physical security only.[101]

The standard of treatment provided for in Article 3.1 of the 2015 Draft Model is different from that included in Article 3.1 of the 2015 Model BIT in a number of ways. First, the 2015

88 2015 Draft Model, above n 17, Art. 3.1(i).
89 Ibid., Art. 3.1(ii).
90 Ibid., Art. 3.1(iii).
91 Ibid., Art. 3.2.
92 Ibid., Art. 4.1.
93 Ibid., Art. 4.2.
94 Ibid., Art. 4.3.
95 Ibid., Art. 4.4.
96 Ibid., Art. 4.5.
97 Ibid., footnote 2.
98 LCI Report, above n 4, pp. 15–16.
99 Ibid., p. 16.
100 Ibid., pp. 22–24.
101 2015 Model BIT, above n 20, Art. 3.2.

Draft Model referred to customary international law as the standard for the determination of denial of justice alone.[102] The 2015 Model BIT includes customary international law in the chapeau as the standard for all the standards of treatment guaranteed.[103] Secondly, the standards guaranteed in the respective Articles 3.1 of the 2015 Draft Model and 2015 Model BIT are different. The 2015 Draft Model provided for guarantees against denial of justice, violations of due process and manifestly abusive treatment.[104] The 2015 Model BIT: (a) restricts the denial of justice standard to judicial and administrative proceedings;[105] (b) reduces the threshold for due process violations from the 'un-remedied and egregious' threshold of the 2015 Draft Model to 'fundamental breach';[106] (c) removes the qualification of 'involving continuous, unjustified and outrageous coercion or harassment' from the manifestly abusive treatment standard and replaces it with a reference to 'coercion, duress or harassment' examples of manifestly abusive treatment;[107] and, (d) adds a fourth standard – that of targeted discrimination on manifestly unjustified grounds.[108] Thus, for the most part, Article 3.1 of the 2015 Model BIT seems to be less restrictive than Article 3.1 of the 2015 Draft Model. This may reflect the recommendations of the LCI Report.[109]

The 2015 Model BIT follows the 2015 Draft Model in providing that breaches of other provisions of the treaty or of other international agreements will not constitute a breach of the guaranteed standards of treatment. However, it goes further than the 2015 Draft Model in providing that tribunals are required to consider pursuit of local remedies in considering alleged breaches of the guaranteed standards.[110] Arguably, this reference to 'pursuit' of local remedies is qualified by the explanation of 'exhaustion' of remedies in Article 15.1 of the 2015 Model BIT which provides that the exhaustion requirement is not applicable if there are no available domestic remedies which are capable of reasonably providing the same relief.[111]

The substance of the NT obligation is similar in both the 2015 Draft Model and the 2015 Model BIT, including the footnoted explanation of 'like circumstances'. However, the restrictions of the scope of the NT obligation included in the 2015 Draft Model are excluded from the 2015 Model BIT.[112] Furthermore, while the 2015 Draft Model restricted the scope of the NT obligation to the national government, the 2015 Model BIT extends it to sub-national governments but clarifies that in such cases the comparison would be with treatment of other investors by the same sub-national government.[113]

The JIS seeks to align the protections offered to investors under existing BITs with those proposed under the 2015 Model. Thus, it clarifies the FET standard as equivalent to the customary international law minimum standard of treatment of aliens and defines that standard as comprised of the standards guaranteed in the 2015 Model.[114] It also excludes

102 2015 Draft Model, above n 17, Art. 3.1.(i).
103 2015 Model BIT, above n 20, Art. 3.1.
104 2015 Draft Model, above n 17, Art. 3.1.
105 2015 Model above n 20, Art. 3.1(i).
106 *Compare* 2015 Draft Model, above n 17, Art. 3.1(ii), with 2015 Model BIT, above n 20, Art. 3.1(ii).
107 *Compare* 2015 Draft Model, above n 17, Art. 3.1(iii), with 2015 Model BIT, above n 20, Art. 3.1(iv).
108 2015 Model BIT, above n 20, Art. 3.1(iii).
109 Above n 99 and accompanying text.
110 2015 Model BIT, above n 20, Art. 3.4.
111 The explanation of the requirements of exhaustion of remedies set out in 2015 Model, above n 20, Art. 15.1 are in the context of claims of breaches of Chapter II of the 2015 Model BIT, which includes the standards of treatment in Art. 3. Thus, it is suggested that notwithstanding the fact that Art. 3.4 refers to pursuit of remedies and Art. 15.1 refers to exhaustion of remedies, Art. 3.4 should be interpreted in light of Art. 15.1.
112 Above nn 93–96 and accompanying text.
113 *Compare* 2015 Draft Model, above n 17, Art. 4.3, with 2015 Model BIT, above n 20, Art. 4.2.
114 JIS, above n 21, Art. 6(1).

other breaches of the BIT and other treaties,[115] public policy-oriented measures[116] and contractual breaches[117] from the FET guarantee. Further, it explains that the FPS guarantee is restricted to physical security.[118]

In addition, the JIS restricts the scope of the MFN obligation to prevent incorporation of obligations, especially dispute settlement mechanisms, from other treaties.[119] It also clarifies the definition of 'like circumstances' in line with the footnotes in the 2015 Draft Model and 2015 Model BIT,[120] and retains the exclusion of discretionary application of law from the scope of the NT obligation in line with the 2015 Draft Model (though this exclusion was omitted from the 2015 Model).[121]

There are a number of other interesting features in the 2015 Model BIT which should be noted. The first of these is that the standards currently articulated in Article 3.1 of the 2015 Model BIT constitute specific 'elements' of the FET standard.[122] Thus, the 2015 Model BIT significantly narrows the broad spectrum of obligations available under the 2003 Model BIT. As discussed, the 2015 Model BIT seems to be less restrictive in the abuses it encompasses than the 2015 Draft Model,[123] and the exclusion of breaches of other treaty obligations also provides useful clarification. Secondly, investment tribunals have found that the FPS guarantee extends beyond physical security to legal and other forms of security.[124] The 2015 Model BIT's restriction of the FPS guarantee to physical security may, thus, be seen as a response to this possibility. The third additional feature to note is that the consideration of exhaustion of local remedies (particularly in relation to denial of justice claims) is well established in the case law of investment tribunals.[125] However, the threshold for exhaustion of remedies (absence of remedies) is significantly higher than the futility exception to exhaustion requirements (futility or lack of reasonableness of local remedies) recognized in the jurisprudence of investment tribunals.[126] And fourthly, the enumeration of circumstances negating 'like circumstances' seems superfluous. Investment tribunals have frequently recognized that the determination of 'like circumstances' must be fact-specific and have included some of the non-exhaustive factors listed in the 2015 Model.[127] Perhaps this clarification is best understood as an attempt to freeze a desirable trend in investment arbitration case law.

115 Ibid., Art. 6(2).
116 Ibid., Art. 6(3).
117 Ibid., Art. 6(5).
118 Ibid., Art. 6(6).
119 Ibid., Arts. 9(1), 9(2).
120 Ibid., Art. 9(3).
121 Ibid., Art. 9(4).
122 See, e.g., *Rumeli Telekom A.S. and Telsim Mobil Telekomunikasyon Hizmetleri A.S.* v. *Republic of Kazakhstan*, ICSID Case No. ARB/05/16, Award, 29 July 2008, para. 651 (including denial of justice under FET); *Ronald S. Lauder* v. *Czech Republic*, UNCITRAL, Final Award, 3 September 2001, paras. 292–93 (including arbitrariness under FET); *PSEG Global Inc. and Konya Ilgin Elektrik Üretim ve Ticaret Limited Sirketi* v. *Republic of Turkey*, ICSID Case No. ARB/02/5, Award, 19 January 2007, paras. 248–49 (including inconsistent administrative actions under FET); *Bayindir Insaat Turizm Ticaret Ve Sanayi A.S.* v. *Islamic Republic of Pakistan*, ICSID Case No. ARB/03/29, Award, 27 August 2009, para. 178 (including discrimination under FET).
123 Above nn 104–109 and accompanying text.
124 See, e.g., *CME Czech Republic B.V.* v. *Czech Republic*, UNCITRAL, Partial Award, 13 September 2001, para. 613; *Azurix Corp.* v. *Argentine Republic*, ICSID Case No. ARB/01/12, Award, 14 July 2006, para. 408.
125 See, e.g., *Jan de Nul N.V. and Dredging International N.V.* v. *Arab Republic of Egypt*, ICSID Case No. ARB/04/13, Award, 6 November 2008, paras. 195, 256–59; *Duke Energy Electroquil Partners and Electroquil S.A.* v. *Republic of Ecuador*, ICSID Case No. ARB/04/19, Award, 18 August 2008, paras. 399–400.
126 Hanessian and Duggal, above n 1, at 222.
127 *Cargill, Incorporated* v. *Republic of Poland*, ICSID Case No. ARB(AF)/04/2, Award, 5 March 2008, paras. 310–12, 339; *Total S.A.* v. *Argentine Republic*, ICSID Case No. ARB/04/01, Decision on Liability, 27 December 2010, paras. 211–12.

9.4.2 *Expropriation*

The 2003 Model BIT and India's 'comparator' BITs set out a relatively simple and short position on expropriation.[128] By and large, they provided for guarantees against expropriation or measures having an effect equivalent to expropriation, unless the expropriation was for a public purpose, in accordance with law, on a non-discriminatory basis and against fair and equitable compensation. The compensation was to be calculated on the basis of the fair/market/real/genuine value of the expropriated investment, and as of the earlier of the dates immediately before the expropriation and when the impending expropriation became public knowledge. By and large no valuation criteria were specified. In addition, the compensation included interest until the date of payment, was to be made without delay and was required to be effectively realisable and freely transferable. Affected investors were guaranteed rights of judicial review.

The 2015 Draft Model provided significantly more detail on the guarantee against expropriation. Thus, expropriation or measures having an effect equivalent to expropriation were only allowed if taken for reasons of public purpose, in accordance with the procedure established by law and on payment of adequate compensation.[129] The determination of whether a measure amounted to expropriation in effect required the satisfaction of three cumulative and onerous criteria: permanent and complete or near complete deprivation of the value of the investment, permanent and complete or near complete deprivation of the investor's right of management and control over the investment, and transfer of the value of the investment to the expropriating State or one of its agencies or instrumentalities.[130] A footnote explained that restrictions on management implemented through financial or insolvency laws or national laws relating to the nationality of senior management in sensitive industries would not constitute expropriation.[131] The defined scope of expropriation explicitly excluded commercial actions of the expropriating State as well as non-discriminatory regulatory measures designed to protect legitimate public welfare objectives.[132] Investment tribunals were barred from considering whether an expropriating measure was taken for a public purpose or whether it was in compliance with domestic law.[133] Presumably the assessment of the host State in this regard would be dispositive. An explanatory footnote added that expropriation of land by India and related questions of public purpose would be assessed in accordance with Indian laws on land acquisition.[134]

The 2015 Draft Model provided for relatively detailed valuation criteria: (a) it specified that compliance with the requirements of Article 5.1[135] would not affect the value of the compensation;[136] (b) it provided an illustrative list of mitigating factors to be taken into consideration

[128] 2003 Model BIT, above n 7, Art. 5; India–UK BIT 1994, Art. 5; India–Mauritius BIT 1998, Art. 6; India–Netherlands BIT 1995, Art. 5; India–France BIT 1997, Art. 6; India–Germany BIT 1995, Art. 5; India–UAE BIT 2013, Art. 7; India–Indonesia BIT 1999, Art. 5; India–Poland BIT 1996, Art. 5; India–Russia BIT 1994, Art. 5; India–Switzerland BIT 1997, Art. 5; India–Austria BIT 1999, Art. 4; India–Australia BIT 1999, Art. 7; India–Cyprus BIT 2002, Art. 5.

[129] 2015 Draft Model, above n 17, Art. 5.1.

[130] Ibid., Art. 5.2.

[131] Ibid., footnote 4.

[132] Ibid., Art. 5.3, 5.4.

[133] Ibid., Art. 5.5.

[134] Ibid., footnote 3.

[135] Art. 5.1 sets out the restriction on expropriation unless it is for a public purpose, in accordance with the procedure established by law and upon payment of adequate compensation.

[136] 2015 Draft Model, above n 17, Art. 5.6.

for valuation purposes;[137] (c) it explained that compensation would exclude 'consequential or exemplary losses or speculative or windfall profits ... including those related to moral damages or loss of goodwill';[138] and (d) it set the date for calculation of compensation as the date immediate before the expropriation takes place.[139]

The LCI Report concentrated its comments on Article 5.2 of the 2015 Draft Model (discussing whether a measure had an effect equivalent to expropriation).[140] It recommended that the requirements of deprivation of the value and management of the investment (economic and legal expropriation respectively under Articles 5.2(i) and 5.2(ii)) be made disjunctive rather than conjunctive requirements, and that the requirement that the expropriation result in transfer of value to the expropriating State (Article 5.2(iii)) be removed.[141]

Like the 2015 Draft Model, the 2015 Model BIT excludes commercial actions and public welfare-oriented policy changes from the scope of expropriation.[142] It also retains the same valuation date (the date before the expropriation takes place), though it makes explicit what was left unsaid in the 2015 Model BIT: that any changes in valuation resulting from the expropriation being made known earlier will not be considered.

But the 2015 Model BIT differs from the 2015 Draft Model in a number of ways. For instance, the core prohibition of expropriation (unless it is for a public purpose, in accordance with law and on payment of compensation) is retained; but where the 2015 Draft Model referred to 'procedure established by law', the 2015 Model BIT refers to 'due process'.[143] In another example, the definition of 'indirect' expropriation is very different.[144] Instead of the three cumulative requirements of permanent economic deprivation, permanent legal deprivation and transfer to the expropriating State, the 2015 Model BIT defines indirect expropriation as one which '*substantially or permanently deprives the investor of the fundamental attributes of property in its investment, including the right to use, enjoy and dispose of its investment, without formal transfer of title or outright seizure*'.[145] Furthermore, the 2015 Model BIT notes that the determination of indirect expropriation is a fact-specific inquiry and lists factors which should be taken into account in this assessment.[146] These factors include

137 2015 Draft Model, above n 17, Art. 5.7: 'Mitigating Factors under Article 5.6 include: (a) current and past use of the Investment, including the history of its acquisition and purpose; (b) the duration of the Investment and previous profits made by the Investment; (c) compensation or insurance payouts received by the Investor or Investment from other sources; (d) the value of property that remains subject to the Investor or Investment's disposition or control; (e) options available to the Investor or Investment to mitigate its losses, including reasonable efforts made by the Investor or Investor towards such mitigation, if any; (f) conduct of the Investor that contributed to its damage; (g) any obligation the Investor or its Investment is relieved of due to the expropriation; (h) liabilities owed in the Host State to the government as a result of the Investment's activities; (i) any harm or damage that the Investor or its Investment has caused to the environment or local community that have not been remedied by the Investor or the Investment; and (j) any other relevant considerations regarding the need to balance the public interest and the interests of the Investment'.

138 2015 Draft Model, above n 17, Art. 5.7, explanation I.

139 Ibid., Art. 5.7, explanation II.

140 The LCI Report also suggested that it was not clear from the phrasing of Art. 5 of the 2015 Draft Model whether the expropriation obligation referred to the investment as a whole or to distinct assets. LCI Report, above n 4, p. 18. However, in light of the clear enterprise-based definition of investment, the validity of this comment is questionable.

141 LCI Report, above n 4, pp. 17–19.

142 2015 Model BIT, above n 20, Art. 5.5.

143 *Compare* 2015 Draft Model, above n 17, Art. 5.1, with 2015 Model BIT, above n 20, Art. 5.1.

144 *Compare* 2015 Draft Model, above n 17, Arts. 5.1, 5.2 with 2015 Model BIT, above n 20, Arts. 5.1, 5.3.

145 2015 Model BIT, above n 20, Art. 5.3(a)(ii).

146 2015 Model BIT, above n 20, Art. 5.3(b).

economic impact, duration, character of the measures and breach of prior commitments by the expropriating State.

Furthermore, the 2015 Model BIT abandons the detailed valuation criteria adopted by the 2015 Draft Model, and refers, instead, to an illustrative list of factors including going concern value, asset value (including declared tax value of tangible property) and other criteria as appropriate.[147] The 2015 Model BIT omits the 2015 Draft Model's exclusion of consequential or exemplary losses and speculative losses or windfall profits (including moral damages or loss of goodwill). And the 2015 Model BIT adds a requirement that investment tribunals considering claims based on expropriation consider pursuit of local remedies. This requirement has also been incorporated in relation to the standards of treatment guaranteed in Art. 3 of the 2015 Model BIT, and the comments made in that context are equally applicable here.[148] The provisions of the JIS relating to expropriation introduce a definition of indirect expropriation[149] and carve out public policy measures from the scope of expropriation.[150] However, while the scope of the public policy measure exception is similar to that in the 2015 Model BIT (which, in turn, was similar to that in the 2015 Draft Model), the definition of indirect expropriation follows that set out in the 2015 Draft Model rather than the definition set out in the 2015 Model BIT.[151] The JIS refers to the three cumulative criteria of permanent economic deprivation, permanent legal deprivation and transfer to the expropriating State. Thus, there will potentially be a mismatch between the provisions on expropriation across various Indian BITs.

The revised provisions on expropriation present a few interesting features. First, several features of Article 5 are consistent with the practice of investment tribunals, including the definition of indirect expropriation on the basis of substantial or permanent deprivation, the fact-specific nature of the determination of indirect expropriation, the reference to economic impact and duration of measures in determining indirect expropriation, and the exclusion of acts taken in commercial capacity and public policy measures from the scope of expropriation. Secondly, the practice of investment tribunals demonstrates different positions on the relevance of character or intent of the measure in establishing indirect expropriation; at best, however, they have considered it as one criterion.[152] In this context, the reference to character of the measure as a factor for assessing indirect expropriation ensures that it will at least be considered as a factor, but it is not clear how much importance it will be given in relation to other factors. Thirdly, Article 5.3(b)(iv) includes, as a criterion for assessing indirect expropriation, whether the measure in question breached a prior commitment. It is not clear what

[147] *Compare* 2015 Draft Model, above n 17, Arts. 5.6, 5.7 with 2015 Model BIT, above n 20, Art. 5.1.

[148] Above nn 125–126 and accompanying text.

[149] JIS, above n 21, Art. 10.2.

[150] Ibid., Art. 10.3.

[151] As was noted above in n 121 and accompanying text, this is also true of certain aspects of the JIS's treatment of the NT obligation.

[152] Cases which consider intent or character as relevant include: *Rumeli Telekom A.S. and Telsim Mobil Telekomunikasyon Hizmetleri A.S. v. Republic of Kazakhstan*, ICSID Case No. ARB/05/16, Award, 29 July 2008, para. 700; *Spyridon Roussalis* v. *Romania*, ICSID Case No. ARB/06/1, Award, 1 December 2011, para. 330. Cases which exclude character or intent, or treat it as a purely secondary consideration include: *Siemens* A.G. v. *Argentine Republic*, ICSID Case No. ARB/02/8, Award, 6 February 2007, para. 270; *Compañía de Aguas del Aconquija S.A. and Vivendi Universal S.A.* v. *Argentine Republic*, ICSID Case No. ARB/97/3, Award, 20 August 2007, para. 7.5.20; *Inmaris Perestroika Sailing Maritime Services GmbH and others* v. *Ukraine*, ICSID Case No. ARB/08/8, Excerpts of Award, 1 March 2012, para. 304.

purpose is served by this criterion, or what it adds to the exclusion of actions *jure gestionis* in Article 5.4. Fourthly, the 2015 Model is remarkably ambiguous on the valuation methodology to be adopted. Given the contentious and technical nature of this subject, and the details included in the 2015 Draft Model, the phrasing of Article 5.1 of the 2015 Model is puzzling. And fifthly, in setting out the circumstances under which expropriation is permissible, the change from 'procedure established by law' in the 2015 Draft Model to 'due process' in the 2015 Model BIT is a significant change.[153]

9.4.3 *Investor Obligations*

An interesting innovation introduced by the 2015 Draft Model, and absent from the 2003 Model, is that of explicitly articulated investor obligations. Articles 8–12 of the 2015 Draft Model specified investor obligations including those related to corruption,[154] disclosure,[155] taxation[156] and compliance with host State law generally.[157] Importantly, the 2015 Draft Model also provided for jurisdiction of the investment tribunal over breaches of these obligations,[158] and provided for home State obligations to ensure the availability of judicial processes for violations of these obligations through conduct taking place within the jurisdiction of the home State.[159]

The LCI Report noted that the inclusion of explicit investor obligations was increasingly a trend in investment treaties.[160] It also recommended diluting the investor obligations in order to better attract foreign investment in India, and also to protect the interests of Indian investors abroad.[161]

It was subsequently decided to scale down the 2015 Model BIT's provisions on investor obligations. Each of the obligations included in Articles 9–12 of the 2015 Draft Model are included in the 2015 Model BIT, but they are compressed to individual sub-clauses of Article 11. Additionally, an obligation to 'endeavour to voluntarily incorporate internationally recognized standards of corporate social responsibility' is included in Article 12.

Crucially, however, the 2015 Model BIT includes no equivalent of Article 8.4 of the 2015 Draft Model which allowed for breaches of investor obligations to trigger the jurisdiction of the investment tribunal. Nor does it include any equivalent of Article 13 of the 2015 Draft Model which required the home State of the investor to ensure judicial processes for prosecuting breaches of investor obligations in relation to the investment in the home State. Moreover, the 2015 Model BIT does not allow for counterclaims.[162] All that the 2015 Model BIT provides on this front is Article 13.4, which bars the jurisdiction of investment

153 While this change is significant in terms of its interpretation by an investment tribunal, its genesis is more innocent than it might seem, and is probably a function of the Indian legal lexicon. Art. 21 of the Indian Constitution guarantees life and liberty as a fundamental right, save where deprived by 'procedure established by law'. In case law this requirement of legal procedural propriety has been interpreted as a requirement closer to that of due process. Thus, in Indian legal practice these phrases are actually rather similar, and the amendment possibly reflects an attempt to harmonise the wording with that usually seen in investment treaties, rather than an attempt to broaden the scope of the provision.

154 2015 Draft Model, above n 17, Art. 9.

155 Ibid., Art. 10.

156 Ibid., Art. 11.

157 Ibid., Art. 12.

158 Ibid., Art. 8.4.

159 Ibid., Art. 13.

160 LCI Report, above n 4, pp. 26–28.

161 Ibid., pp. 29–36.

162 Below nn 197-198 and accompanying text.

tribunals in respect of claims relating to investments made through 'fraudulent misrepresentation, concealment, corruption, money laundering or conduct amounting to an abuse of process or similar illegal mechanisms'.[163]

The purpose served by the insertion of Articles 11, 12 and 13.4 in the 2015 Model BIT is not entirely clear. The requirement for compliance with local law is already hard-wired into the definitions of 'investor',[164] 'investment'[165] and 'enterprise',[166] and these provisions do not create any additional hurdles beyond those already present in the 2015 Model BIT. Arguably, this is an indication of the intent of the parties to the treaty, but in the absence of any consequences being attached to these specific requirements (especially the corporate social responsibility obligations) it is unlikely that these obligations will exercise any real influence on the deliberations of investment tribunals.

9.5 DISPUTE RESOLUTION

The dispute resolution clause in the 2003 Model BIT was very broad. Any dispute between an investor and the host State in relation to an investment under the BIT was covered under the dispute resolution mechanism.[167] The tribunal was required to decide the dispute in accordance with the provisions of the BIT,[168] and to deliver a reasoned decision.[169] The tribunal's award would bind the parties.[170] The procedure for triggering the jurisdiction of the investment tribunal required six months of negotiation,[171] following which the parties to the dispute were required to attempt resolution through domestic law mechanisms or conciliation under the UNCITRAL Rules.[172] If the dispute could not be so resolved or conciliated, arbitration could be initiated.[173] Arguably, the 2003 Model BIT allowed for counterclaims, given that the dispute resolution provision provided for jurisdiction over 'any dispute … in relation to an investment'.[174]

The dispute resolution clauses in India's comparator BITs differed slightly in terms of the procedure for triggering the jurisdiction of the investment tribunal, but they all have a similarly broad scope.[175] Only in one case is the scope restricted to measures taken by central and State governments alone.[176]

163 On the treatment of investor obligations and counterclaims in the 2015 Model BIT, see also Eric Leikin, Stuti Gadodia and Charles Loudon, 'The State Doesn't Strike Back After All: India's Final Model BIT Takes the Bite out of Investor Obligations and Eliminates State Counterclaims' (2018) 15(2) *Transnational Dispute Management*.

164 2015 Model BIT, above n 20, Art. 1.5.

165 Ibid., Art. 1.4.

166 Ibid., Art. 1.3.

167 2003 Model BIT, above n 7, Art. 9(1).

168 Ibid., Art. 9(3)(c)(iii).

169 Ibid., Art. 9(3)(c)(iv).

170 Ibid., Art. 9(3)(c)(iii).

171 Ibid., Art. 9(1).

172 Ibid., Art. 9(2).

173 Ibid., Art. 9(3).

174 In determining consent for counterclaims, tribunals have focused on whether the dispute resolution clause in the treaty refers to obligations of the host State alone, or all obligations arising from the investment. In the former case tribunals have held that there is no consent for counterclaims, because the scope of consent for arbitration does not extend to investor obligations. In the latter case tribunals have found consent for counterclaims. See Abhimanyu George Jain, 'Consent to Counterclaims in Investor-State Arbitration: A Post-Roussalis Analysis' (2013) 5 *International Arbitration Law Review* 135 at 140.

175 India–UK BIT 1994, Art. 9; India–Mauritius BIT 1998, Art. 8; India–Netherlands BIT 1995, Art. 9; India–France BIT 1997, Art. 9; India–Germany BIT 1995, Art. 9; India–Indonesia BIT 1999, Art. 9; India–Poland BIT 1996, Art. 9; India–Russia BIT 1994, Art. 9; India–Switzerland BIT 1997, Art. 9; India–Austria BIT 1999, Art. 9; India–Australia BIT 1999, Art. 12; India–Cyprus BIT 2002, Art. 9.

176 India–UAE BIT 2013, Art. 10.

The 2015 Draft Model and the 2015 Model BIT, on the other hand, have very detailed clauses relating to dispute settlement mechanisms. The provision on investor–State dispute settlement (ISDS) is the single longest in the 2015 Draft Model and the chapter on ISDS in the 2015 Model BIT contains eighteen provisions (out of a total of thirty-eight in the 2015 Model BIT). This section draws out some of the innovations introduced in this regard in the 2015 Draft Model and the 2015 Model BIT, focusing on scope of investment arbitration (Section 9.5.1), powers and jurisdiction of the arbitral tribunal (Section 9.5.2), and exhaustion of remedies and procedure for initiating arbitration (Section 9.5.3).

The key features of note here are the reduced scope of investment arbitration (in terms of exclusion of contractual breaches), enhanced checks on the powers and jurisdiction of the tribunal, strengthened exhaustion of remedies requirements, and the removal of jurisdiction over counterclaims (which were available under the 2003 Model BIT and the 2015 Draft Model).

The 2015 Draft Model and the 2015 Model BIT also deal in some detail with a number of procedural questions including the appointment of arbitrators,[177] conflicts of interest and challenges to the appointment of arbitrators,[178] conduct of arbitral proceedings,[179] the award,[180] costs,[181] diplomatic exchanges between the parties,[182] disputes between the parties,[183] an appeals facility,[184] finality and enforcement of awards[185] and expert reports.[186] Owing to limitations of space these aspects have not been considered further here.

9.5.1 *Scope of Investment Arbitration*

Beginning with the 2015 Draft Model, Article 14.1 provided that 'an investor shall not use or threaten to use this Article in order to obtain money, property, or any other thing of value from the Host State'. The scope was restricted to breaches of Chapter II obligations by the host State, that is, breaches of the standard of treatment, NT, expropriation and transfers of funds and personnel.[187] Counterclaims were expressly permitted.[188] The scope of counterclaims was restricted to breaches of the investor obligations set out in Chapter III of the 2015 Draft Model (compliance obligations relating to corruption, disclosures, taxation and host State laws generally). Article 14.11 provided that a successful counterclaim would be taken into account in determining damages due to the investor,[189] that the decision of the investment tribunal would not operate as *res judicata* for any other proceedings arising out of the same cause of action in the host State, and that the filing of a counterclaim would not constitute submission to the tribunal's jurisdiction.

177 2015 Draft Model, above n 17, Art. 14.5; 2015 Model BIT, above n 20, Art. 18.
178 2015 Draft Model, above n 17, Art. 14.6; 2015 Model BIT, above n 20, Art. 19.
179 2015 Draft Model, above n 17, Art. 14.7; 2015 Model BIT, above n 20, Art. 20.
180 2015 Draft Model, above n 17, Art. 14.10; 2015 Model BIT, above n 20, Art. 26.
181 2015 Draft Model, above n 17, Art. 14.12; 2015 Model BIT, above n 20, Art. 28.
182 2015 Draft Model, above n 17, Art. 14.13; 2015 Model BIT, above n 20, Art. 30.
183 2015 Draft Model, above n 17, Art. 15; 2015 Model BIT, above n 20, Art. 31.
184 2015 Model BIT, above n 20, Art. 29. The 2015 Draft Model does not contain any comparable provision.
185 2015 Model BIT, above n 20, Art. 27. The 2015 Draft Model does not contain any comparable provision.
186 2015 Model BIT, above n 20, Art. 25. The 2015 Draft Model does not contain any comparable provision.
187 2015 Draft Model, above note 17, Art. 14.2(i)(a).
188 Ibid., Arts. 14.2(i)(b), 14.11.
189 In this regard, see also 2015 Draft Model, above n 17, Art. 14.10(ii).

Subject to applicable law relating to protection of confidential information, the arbitration proceedings and antecedent events would be made public.[190] The arbitral tribunal was required to interpret the treaty in the context of 'the high level of deference that international law accords to States with regard to their development and implementation of domestic policies'.[191] The governing law for interpreting the treaty was the treaty itself, public international law rules relating to treaty interpretation, the law of the host State (in relation to questions of its domestic law), joint interpretive statements issued by the parties to the treaty, and subsequent practice relating to the interpretation of the treaty, as recognized under the VCLT.[192] The burden of proof for establishing jurisdiction, existence of an obligation, breach of that obligation, suffering of actual and non-speculative losses, and requirements of foreseeability and causality were placed upon the investor.[193]

The LCI Report recommended the removal of Article 14.1.[194] The 2015 Model BIT accepted this recommendation of the LCI Report, and introduced two further changes to the 2015 Draft Model. The first was that in restricting the jurisdiction of the investment tribunal to breaches of Chapter II, breaches of Articles 9 and 10 (entry and sojourn of personnel, and transparency, respectively) were excluded from the jurisdiction of the tribunal.[195] Additionally, the 2015 Model BIT specifically removed contractual disputes from the scope of investment arbitration.[196] The second was that the possibility of counterclaims was removed. As discussed earlier,[197] the requirement of compliance with local law in the definitions of 'investment', 'investor' and 'enterprise', and the text of the new Article 13.4[198] effectively ensure that failure to comply with local law bars investors from raising claims against the host State, but the possibility of counterclaims, and the accounting for the substance of those counterclaims in decisions on alleged breaches by the tribunal, has been removed.

The other innovations introduced by the 2015 Draft Model have been retained in the 2015 Model BIT. For its part, the JIS clarifies that disputes falling within the jurisdiction of the tribunal relate to breaches of the terms of the treaty, that the burden of proof lies upon the investor (though the JIS also requires the investor to establish the ripeness of claims), and confirms the binding nature of subsequent interpretations and practice of the parties upon investment tribunals.[199]

9.5.2 *Powers and Jurisdiction of the Arbitral Tribunals*

In the 2015 Draft Model the jurisdiction and powers of the arbitral tribunal were curtailed in several ways: it could not re-examine any legal issue relevant to the dispute that had

[190] 2015 Draft Model, above n 17, Art. 14.8.
[191] Ibid., Art. 14.9(i).
[192] Ibid., Arts. 14.9(iii), 14.9(iv), 14.9(v).
[193] Ibid., Art. 14.9(ii).
[194] LCI Report, above n 4, p. 40.
[195] 2015 Model BIT, above n 20, Art. 13.2.
[196] Ibid., Art. 13.3.
[197] Above nn 164–166 and accompanying text.
[198] Art. 13.4 bars the jurisdiction of investment tribunals in respect of claims relating to investments made through 'fraudulent misrepresentation, concealment, corruption, money laundering or conduct amounting to an abuse of process or similar illegal mechanisms'.
[199] JIS, above n 21, Art. 12.

been finally settled by the host State courts;[200] it was barred from reviewing the merits of a decision made by a judicial authority of the host State;[201] it could not accept jurisdiction over any claims which had been the subject of inter-State arbitration under Art. 15;[202] it could not review the applicability of exceptions relating to financial regulation, foreign exchange regulation and national security;[203] it could not compel production of documents which the host State claimed were protected from disclosure by the rules of confidentiality or privilege under its domestic law;[204] it could only order monetary compensation (punitive or moral damages and injunctive relief was excluded);[205] and the tribunal was required to state in the award that the award was binding only in relation to that particular dispute.[206]The LCI Report recommended the removal of the bar on re-examination of legal issues decided by domestic courts (on the grounds that this would make investment arbitration unworkable),[207] and inclusion of financial regulation and foreign exchange exceptions in the scope of investment arbitration.[208]

In terms of powers and jurisdiction of the arbitral tribunal, the 2015 Model BIT differed significantly from the 2015 Draft Model. Thus, the bars on tribunals re-examining legal issues decided by domestic courts, and on review of the applicability of exceptions, were removed,[209] as was the specification that the award of a tribunal was only binding in relation to that particular dispute;[210] and the tribunal is now required to take account of a wide range of issues in calculating monetary damages (such as any restitution of property, repeal or modification of the impugned measure, or other mitigating factors including current and past use, history of acquisition and purpose, other sources of compensation, un-remedied harms caused by the investor, and considerations of public interest).[211] The 2015 Model BIT also requires tribunals to take account of proceedings brought pursuant to other agreements by staying their proceedings or taking account of the related proceedings in their awards (which may be a response to India's recent experience in arbitration of related claims before investment tribunals).[212] Finally, the tribunal is empowered to seek a joint interpretation of any provision of the treaty from the parties.[213]

9.5.3 *Exhaustion of Remedies and Procedure for Initiating Arbitration*

Finally, the 2015 Model BIT has a specific procedure for initiating arbitration. The procedure proposed under the 2015 Draft Model was that, within a year of acquiring knowledge of any actionable loss or damage, the investor had to initiate legal proceedings before the domestic

200 2015 Draft Model, above n 17, Art. 14.2(ii)(a).
201 Ibid., Art. 14.2(ii)(b).
202 Ibid., Art. 14.2(ii)(c).
203 Ibid., Art. 14.2(ii)(d).
204 Ibid., Art. 14.7(vii).
205 Ibid., Art. 14.10(ii)-(iii).
206 Ibid., Art. 14.10(iv).
207 LCI Report, above n 4, p. 41.
208 Ibid., p. 42.
209 Above nn 200 and 203 and accompanying text.
210 Above n 207 and accompanying text.
211 2015 Model BIT, above n 20, Art. 26.3.
212 Ibid., Art. 14.
213 Ibid., Art. 24.3.

courts of the host State.[214] If all domestic remedies had been exhausted, or if domestic relief was futile because there were no reasonably available domestic remedies capable of providing relief, or the procedure for obtaining such relief provides no reasonable possibility of relief in a reasonable period of time, a notice of dispute may be issued.[215] Following the receipt of the notice, the investor and host State had to engage in meaningful negotiations to resolve the dispute amicably.[216] The requirements of exhaustion of local remedies and best-efforts negotiation were mandatory and conditions precedent to initiation of arbitration.[217] If good faith negotiations proved unsuccessful, a claim for arbitration may be initiated, but a strict timeline is specified for this. The claim must be initiated before the later of three years from the investor learning of any actionable loss or damage, and eighteen months from the conclusion or abandonment of domestic judicial proceedings.[218] Additionally, ninety days before submission of the claim to arbitration, the investor must provide a notice of arbitration to the host State.[219] The notice is required to specify the claims being made, the amount and basis of calculation of damages, and waive any rights to continuation of domestic legal proceedings.[220]

The LCI Report only recommended certain clarificatory drafting changes, with the result that the procedure for initiating arbitration under the 2015 Model BIT is not significantly different from the procedure under the 2015 Draft Model.[221] Thus, as was the case under the 2015 Draft Model, local judicial remedies must be sought within a year of the investor learning of the breach of obligation.[222] As for the requirement to exhaust local remedies, while the 2015 Draft Model defined the futility exception in terms of the absence of a reasonable remedy *or* the absence of a remedy in a reasonable period of time, the 2015 Model BIT only refers to the absence of reasonable remedy.[223] In relation to unreasonable judicial delay, it posits a five year waiting period for exhaustion of domestic judicial process.[224] Once the exhaustion requirement has been satisfied, a notice of dispute may be sent to the host State.[225] There is then a six month good faith negotiation requirement.[226]

Unlike the 2015 Draft Model, the 2015 Model BIT does not posit the exhaustion and negotiation requirements as conditions precedent to the initiation of arbitration, but the position is not materially different. Following failure of good faith negotiations, a claim of arbitration may be submitted, provided certain additional conditions are satisfied. These include: no more than six years having elapsed from the date of first knowledge of the alleged breach; no more than a year having elapsed from the conclusion of domestic proceedings; waiver of rights to initiate or continue domestic proceedings; and filing of a notice of arbitration with the host State ninety days before initiating the claim.[227]

214 Ibid., Art. 14.3(i).
215 2015 Draft Model, above n 17, Art. 14.3(ii), see the requirements for such a notice in Art. 14.3(iii).
216 Ibid., Art. 14.3(iv).
217 Ibid., Art. 14.4(v).
218 Ibid., Art. 14.4(i)(A).
219 Ibid., Art. 14.4(i)(B).
220 Ibid., Art. 14.4(i)(B).
221 LCI Report, above n 4, pp. 42–45.
222 2015 Model BIT, above n 20, Art. 15.1.
223 Ibid., Art. 15.1.
224 Ibid., Art. 15.2.
225 Ibid., Art. 15.3.
226 Ibid., Art. 15.4.
227 Ibid., Art. 15.5.

9.6 CONCLUSION

The events leading up to and following on from the release of the 2015 Model BIT were explicitly motivated by a desire to recalibrate the balance between investment promotion and regulatory autonomy. In its reconciliation of these interests the 2015 Model BIT is very clearly very different from the 2003 Model BIT and existing Indian BITs. The foregoing sections have sought to draw out and contextualize these differences.

The 2015 Model BIT has been the subject of much criticism – for being too friendly to the interests of the host State,[228] on technical aspects of the legal devices employed,[229] for compromising the interests of Indian investors abroad,[230] for overly restricting the scope of the dispute settlement mechanism,[231] and for innovations not pursued.[232] But the balance that has been struck between State and investor interests has been the key theme running through analyses of the 2015 Model.[233]

It is too early to say whether this is the optimal balance between these competing interests, or whether the Indian position on this issue will ultimately prevail. To begin with, it is hard to identify an optimal balance between the interests of States and investors, given the flexibility and speed of adaptation of foreign investors and transnational corporations.

More importantly, the 2015 Model BIT is merely that – a model text that will form the basis of further negotiation. The contents of the next generation of Indian BITs and IIAs will be the products of negotiations with other countries. For instance, media reports indicate that the Indian government is considering relaxing its position in ongoing negotiations with Canada;[234] at the same time India and Bangladesh have already signed a joint interpretive statement in relation to the 2009 India–Bangladesh BIT,[235] and India has recently concluded new BITs with Brazil and Cambodia.[236]

What can be said with some certainty is that there is a clearly discernible global shift towards carving out and protecting regulatory interests from the purview of international law

228 See, e.g., Ranjan and Anand, above n 1.

229 See, e.g., Deepak Raju, 'General Exceptions in the Indian Model BIT: Is the "Necessity" Test Workable?' (2016) 7(2) *Jindal Global Law Review* 227 (discussing the necessity exception included in Chapter VI of the 2015 Model); Ashiya, above n 75 (discussing the Salini-influenced characteristics of investment which have been incorporated in the definition of investment in the 2015 Model).

230 Epaminontas E. Triantafilou and Jagdish Menezes, 'The Other Side of the Coin: India's 2015 Model BIT and Indian Investors Abroad' (2018) 15(2) *Transnational Dispute Management*.

231 Arthad Kurlekar and Leah Thomas, 'Reflections on Dispute Resolution Provisions of the Indian 2015 Model Bit – Demonstrating a Protectionist Approach' (2018) 15(2) *Transnational Dispute Management*.

232 See, e.g., Sanhita Ambast, 'Human Rights Protections in India's Model BIT: A Bit Left to Go' (2017) 57(1/2) *Indian Journal of International Law*, available at https://link.springer.com/article/10.1007/s40901-018-0073-z (last accessed 9 July 2019); Prabhash Ranjan, 'ISDS Transparency Provisions in the Indian Model BIT: A Half-Hearted Attempt?' (2018) 15(2) *Transnational Dispute Management*.

233 For an argument that the 2015 Model successfully achieves this balance, see Rohini Singh Sisodia and Ramya Raman, 'Evolution of the Indian Model Bilateral Investment Treaty Vis-à-vis Investor-State Dispute Settlement Mechanism – A Balancing Act' (2018) 15(2) *Transnational Dispute Management*.

234 See, e.g., Amiti Sen and Surabhi, 'India may deviate from model BIT to meet Canada's Demands', *The Hindu*, 4 August 2017, available at www.thehindubusinessline.com/economy/policy/india-may-deviate-from-model-bit-to-meet-canadas-demands/article9803014.ece (last accessed 9 July 2019).

235 The press release announcing the signing of the joint interpretive statement is available at http://pib.nic.in/newsite/PrintRelease.aspx?relid=167345 (last accessed 9 July 2019). The joint interpretive statement itself is available at https://dea.gov.in/sites/default/files/Signed%20Copy%20of%20JIN.pdf (last accessed 9 July 2019).

236 The texts of these agreements are not yet available. Confirmation of their signing is available at www.iisd.org/itn/2016/12/12/brazil-and-india-initial-bilateral-investment-treaty-bit-text-yet-to-be-published/ (last accessed 9 July 2019) and http://pib.nic.in/newsite/PrintRelease.aspx?relid=147849 (last accessed 9 July 2019).

rules for the promotion of foreign interest. This shift recognizes the value of foreign investment – indeed India, too, is actively courting foreign investment;[237] but it also recognizes the imperative to protect regulatory interests and sovereignty.

[237] This is reflected both in policy pronouncements and priorities of the government, and in legal reforms such as the amendment of laws on international commercial arbitration.

10

The Regulation of Foreign Investments in Sri Lanka

A Policy-Based Perspective

Naazima Kamardeen and Dinusha Panditaratne[*]

10.1 INTRODUCTION

This chapter provides a policy-driven analysis of the regulation of Sri Lanka's foreign investment, proceeding in two parts. Part 1 outlines the political and legal history of Sri Lanka's experience with foreign investment. It considers Sri Lanka's regulatory framework for foreign investment, including its international investment treaties and analyses international cases in which Sri Lanka has been a party.

It is a premise of this chapter, however, that investment treaties and international cases have played a limited role in facilitating foreign investment in Sri Lanka. There is only a weak correlation between Sri Lanka's investment treaties and the inflow of investment to the country. Part 2 of this chapter therefore focuses on the political challenges – both national and geopolitical – and broader legal impediments (including rule of law indicators) to growing Sri Lanka's foreign investment. These challenges and impediments are analysed through a comparative study of the successful experiences of other countries in the Asia-Pacific, particularly Singapore and New Zealand, in attracting consistently high foreign investment.

It is concluded that Sri Lanka is currently in a difficult grey zone between a 'leader-driven' model of foreign direct investment (FDI), in which FDI depends on strong political leaders and their own networks, and a 'rules-based' model that prevails in developed countries, in which investors rely on clear and efficient frameworks without the complications of frequent policy changes, cronyism and graft. It is suggested that Sri Lanka needs to move resolutely and quickly to the latter model with a multi-step program, which will help to attract consistently better levels of FDI than competitor host States in Asia.

10.2 RECENT HISTORY OF FOREIGN INVESTMENT (1970s TO PRESENT)

10.2.1 *Political Background*

10.2.1.1 Reaction to Colonial Era Practices in Ceylon

In the colonial era, foreign investment in the region was characterized by unequal powers and extractive practices by foreign entities. This was apparent in colonial Ceylon, for example, in

* The authors wish to thank Adam Collins, Pabasara Kannangara and Daniella Kern of LKI for their assistance in preparing this chapter, as well as Dr Ganeshan Wignaraja of LKI and Professor Mahdev Mohan and the team at Singapore Management University for their advice and guidance. This chapter also benefited from comments by academics and practitioners on a prior version of this chapter, presented at the University of Colombo's Annual Research Symposium on 15 November 2017. All errors and omissions remain the authors' own.

the tea and other plantation industries. As one commentator noted, the 'tea industry was dominated by sterling companies based in London and managed by British-controlled agency houses in Colombo'.[1]

Spurred by local resentment of these colonial-era practices, Sri Lanka moved to nationalize foreign-owned property after its independence in 1948. This development culminated in large-scale nationalization of industry in 1971–1972 under the government of Prime Minister Sirimavo Bandaranaike, the then leader of the left-leaning Sri Lanka Freedom Party (SLFP) which was founded by her husband S. W. R. D. Bandaranaike in 1951. Mrs Bandaranaike's government pursued a closed economy in keeping with socialist policies, which stymied the inflow of foreign investment.[2]

10.2.1.2 1977 as a Turning Point in Sri Lanka

Mrs. Bandaranaike's government was swept out of power by the resounding electoral victory of the pro-market United National Party (UNP) in 1977, led by J. R. Jayawardene. The assumption of power by the UNP in 1977 has been described as a paradigm shift in Sri Lanka's economic history.[3] The government of Prime Minster Jayawardene, who later became Sri Lanka's first President in 1978 after a major constitutional change that replaced a Westminster-style system with an executive Presidency, reopened Sri Lanka's economy to international trade and foreign investment, via several measures.

These measures, more fully described in Section 10.2.2, included establishing free trade zones, and creating a Greater Colombo Economic Commission in 1978 to facilitate foreign investment and drive economic development. Beginning in 1980, the Sri Lankan government also began entering into successive bilateral investment treaties (BITs) and other treaties with investment provisions (TIPs) with partner countries.

Sri Lanka's BITs and TIPs (collectively, 'international investment agreements' or IIAs) now number thirty-four in total,[4] the last of which was part of the Sri Lanka–Singapore Free Trade Agreement that was signed in January 2018 and according to the Ministry of Trade and Industry of Singapore is Sri Lanka's 'first and modern comprehensive free trade agreement'.[5] As indicated in Figure 10.1, however, Sri Lanka's BITs with major partner countries have not shown a correlative effect on Sri Lanka's foreign investment, which has grown haphazardly since the liberalization of the economy in the late 1970s.

10.2.1.3 1983–2009: The Years of Civil War

The modern political history of Sri Lanka helps to explain the uneven growth in FDI. The UNP government, for all its economic reforms, did little to address the ethnic tensions in Sri

[1] 'Shift of Fortunes of Sri Lanka's Tea Enterprise', History of Ceylon Tea, available at www.historyofceylontea.com/ceylon-publications/maxwell-fernando-archive/shift-of-fortunes-of-sri-lankas-tea-enterprise.html (last accessed 9 July 2019).

[2] Ibid.

[3] Ibid.

[4] UNCTAD Investment Policy Hub, 'International Investment Agreements Navigator', available at https://investmentpolicy.unctad.org/international-investment-agreements/countries/198/sri-lanka?type=bits (last accessed 9 July 2019).

[5] Ministry of Trade and Industry, 'Singapore and Sri Lanka sign comprehensive free trade agreement', 23 January 2018, available at www.mti.gov.sg/-/media/MTI/Newsroom/Press-Releases/2018/04/Sri-Lanka-Singapore-Free-Trade-Agreement-enters-into-force-on-1-May-2018/sri-lanka-singapore-free-trade-agreement-enters-into-force-on-1-may-2018.pdf (last accessed 9 July 2019).

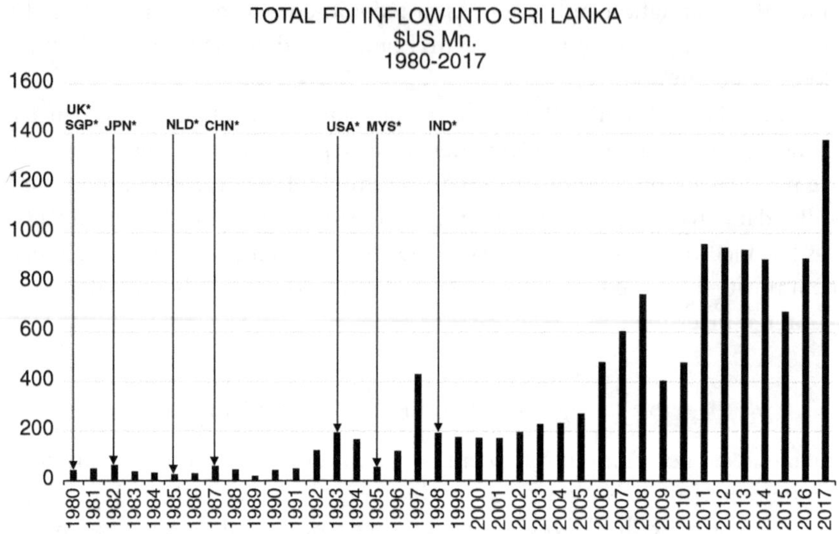

FIGURE 10.1 Sri Lanka's FDI growth, showing BITs with major partners

Lanka that had been building for decades; and in particular, since the introduction of the 'Sinhala Only' Act in 1956 by the SLFP government of S. W. R. D. Bandaranaike.[6] The 1956 legislation replaced English as the official language with Sinhala, the language spoken by the Sinhalese majority who comprised approximately 70 per cent of Sri Lanka's population at the time.[7] The complacency, and even complicity, by the UNP on the issue of ethnic relations eventually had calamitous political and economic effects.

Specifically, festering nationalist sentiments and minority grievances led to the outbreak of civil war in July 1983, which resulted in a (conservatively) estimated 80,000 deaths.[8] In the midst of the war, there was also a shift back towards a more protectionist economy, consistent with the centre-left policies of President Chandrika Kumaratanga (the daughter of S. W. R. D. Bandaranaike and Sirimavo Bandaranaike), who served as President of Sri Lanka from 1994 to 2005. It has been noted that 'protectionist pressure began to build in 2001, and from 2004, the relatively open trade policies of the past were explicitly and systematically reversed through the proliferation of a variety of para-tariffs'.[9]

Counter-intuitively, however, the bitter years of civil war in Sri Lanka did not stem the inflow of foreign investment. As has been observed, FDI increased from US$47 million in 1979 to US$752 million in 2008.[10] The civil war continued until a 'no-holds-barred military assault' ended it in 2009, under the government of then President Mahinda Rajapaksa.[11]

[6] The Official Language Act No. 33 (7 July 1956).

[7] United States Institute of Peace, 'Simulation on Sri Lanka: Setting the Agenda for Peace' (Report, 2001), available at www.usip.org/sites/default/files/srilanka.pdf (last accessed 9 July 2019).

[8] Ibid.

[9] Ravi Ratnasabapathy, 'Reviving Sri Lanka's exports and attracting FDI to the export sector', Echelon.lk, 25 July 2017, available at http://echelon.lk/home/reviving-sri-lankas-exports-and-attracting-fdi-to-the-export-sector/ (last accessed 9 July 2019).

[10] B. Thilakaweera, 'Economic Impact of Foreign Direct Investment in Sri Lanka' (2012) 41(1) *Staff Studies* 89–115 at 91, available at https://ss.sljol.info/article/download/4684/3784/ (last accessed 9 July 2019).

[11] Kadira Pethiyagoda, 'Sri Lanka: A small state response to a multipolar world', Lowy Institute, 24 February 2017, available at www.lowyinstitute.org/the-interpreter/sri-lanka-small-state-response-multipolar-asia (last accessed 9 July 2019).

President Rajapaksa's victory over the Liberation Tiger of Tamil Eelam (LTTE) rebels gave him the public support to remain in power until 2015, despite the increasing authoritarianism of his government, widespread allegations of corruption, and concern over a new foreign policy that strongly favoured China over India, Europe, and the United States.

10.2.1.4 Coalition Governance since 2015

After decisively winning the 2010 presidential election, President Rajapaksa lost the next election held in January 2015 to a candidate from his own party and his former Health Minister, Maithripala Sirisena. President Sirisena, who was elected on a manifesto promising '*yahapalanaya*' (good governance) has since governed in a coalition arrangement with the pro-market UNP, led by Ranil Wickremesinghe as prime minister, whose party won the national parliamentary elections held in August 2015.

The economic policy of the coalition government has been largely driven by Prime Minister Wickremesinghe, who is concurrently the Minister of National Policies and Economic Affairs. Key leadership positions in economic policy, including the Chairman of the Board of Investment of Sri Lanka and the Minister of Development Strategies and International Trade, have also been filled or appointed by the UNP.

Foreign investment initially declined from US$0.9 billion in 2014 to US$0.7 billion in 2015, a decrease that was attributed to policy uncertainty around the new coalition government,[12] which is an unprecedented alliance between members of the left-leaning SLFP and the pro-market UNP. As shown in Figure 10.2, however, foreign investment rebounded in 2016, and in 2017, rose to its highest-ever figure of US$1.4 billion (US$1.9 billion when including loans to the Board of Investment of Sri Lanka).

As observed in Part 2 of this chapter, a substantial portion of foreign investment in 2017 came from China.[13] Before discussing the challenges to diversifying FDI and steadily increasing it to the government's current target of US$5 billion in annual FDI by 2020,[14] it is worth understanding how foreign investment has been regulated in Sri Lanka and the perceived 'losses' to Sri Lanka of that regulation due to arbitral decisions in favour of foreign investors.

10.2.2 *Regulatory Developments*

10.2.2.1 International Context

The treaties of Friendship, Commerce and Navigation (FCN), which have been operational since the eighteenth century,[15] are regarded as precursors to modern BITs. These treaties were more concerned with trade than investment, and also contained provisions relating to peaceful navigation. However, their rules on the treatment of foreign nationals, and concepts such as the most-favoured-nation (MFN) treatment, were transposed from FCN treaties to

[12] 'World Development Indicators Database', World Bank, available at http://databank.worldbank.org/data/reports.aspx?source=World-Development-Indicators (last accessed 9 July 2019; 'FDI in 2016 dips 54% to $ 450 m as policy inconsistency weighs', Daily FT, 30 January 2017, available at www.ft.lk/article/594657/FDI-in-2016-dips-54–to–450-m-as-policy-inconsisten (last accessed 9 July 2019).

[13] Information provided to authors by the Board of Investment of Sri Lanka (BOI).

[14] Government of Sri Lanka, 'Vision 2025: A Country Enriched', Prime Minister's Office, p. 13, available at www.pmoffice.gov.lk/download/press/D00000000061_EN.pdf (last accessed 9 July 2019).

[15] Ibid., p. 180.

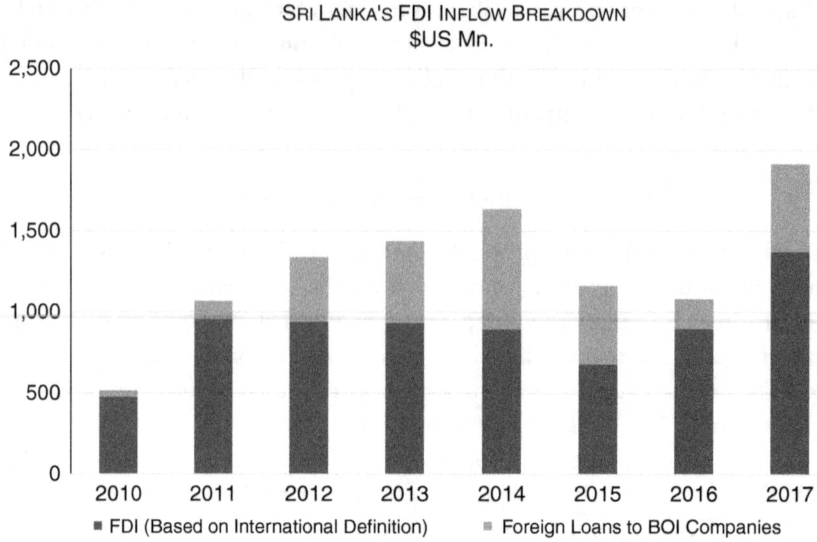

FIGURE 10.2 Sri Lanka's FDI breakdown

modern BITs. One feature of FCN treaties that is particularly relevant to the Sri Lankan context is that they envisaged contracting parties who were quite evenly balanced in bargaining power.

The post–Second World War era brought a different investment framework to that of FCN treaties. Newly independent States were poor and required financial assistance, yet there was no State capable of providing such assistance, since even relatively affluent nations had been weakened by the war. International financial institutions were established and were tasked with promoting foreign investment in newly independent States, hoping that the influx of capital would help spearhead economic growth. Such States began to invite foreign investment, and as the law of international trade and investment became more formalized, the legislative framework evolved as well.

The creation of the World Trade Organisation (WTO) in 1995 brought in new standards to regulate global trade.[16] However, its signature investment agreement – the Agreement on Trade-Related Investment Measures (TRIMs) – remains surprisingly threadbare. The proliferation of BITs, in comparison to the TRIMs, exposes an underlying truth: States do not want to give up the bargaining power they possess vis-à-vis another State in a bilateral context by agreeing to common standards in a multilateral context.

10.2.2.2 Sri Lankan Framework

From a local perspective, as described earlier, Sri Lanka underwent a wave of nationalization after gaining independence. After a closed-market system failed to generate economic growth, the government instituted an open economic model from 1977 and developed a legal regime to support this endeavour. The first step in this process was the creation of the Greater Colombo Economic Commission in 1978,[17] which was renamed the Board of Investment of Sri Lanka

[16] World Trade Organization, 'Understanding the WTO – what is the world trade organization?' (2017), available at www.wto.org/english/thewto_e/whatis_e/tif_e/fact1_e.htm (last accessed 9 July 2019).

[17] The Commission was created through the Greater Colombo Economic Commission Law No. 4 of 1978.

(BOI) in 1992.[18] The BOI aims to be a 'one stop shop' for the facilitation of foreign investment. It has the authority to grant approval for projects[19] under section 17 of the BOI Act,[20] and for projects under the Strategic Development Projects Act No 14 of 2008.[21]

Sri Lanka permits foreign investment to take place through a company incorporated under company registration laws,[22] or with the additional protection of a contract between the investor and the government, which may take place under the broader framework of a BIT. Currently, there are BITs in force between Sri Lanka and the following jurisdictions (stated in the order in which they came into force): South Korea, Singapore, United Kingdom, Switzerland, France, Sweden, Romania, Japan, Belgium–Luxembourg Economic Union, Netherlands, Denmark, Norway, China, Finland, Italy, United States, Malaysia, Thailand, Indonesia, India, Egypt, Pakistan, Germany, Australia and the Czech Republic.

While not mandatory, investors may find it more advantageous to invest through a BIT, for additional protection to the investment. However, it is unclear whether Sri Lanka's BITs have had a positive impact on its foreign investment. As noted by Professor Sornarajah:

> Many smaller developing states have signed a large number of treaties without witnessing significant inward investment flows. ... Institutions which have assiduously promoted investment treaties, have expressed scepticism of the proposition that there is a correlation between investment treaties and flows of investment. They now seem to take the view that other factors such as *political stability and economic circumstances* play a greater role in promoting investments.[23]

In addition to the standards in its BITs, Sri Lanka's membership of the WTO has mandated that certain standards – like MFN treatment and National Treatment Standard – be maintained in the treatment of investors and investments.[24]

[18] The Commission was renamed as the Board of Investment of Sri Lanka (Act No. 4 of 1978].

[19] Board of Investment Law (No. 4 of 1978), as amended (hereinafter, the 'BOI Act'), Section 16. This section permits entry of foreign investment without any fiscal concessions; the minimum required investment is US$ 250,000. Trading is not permitted for those entering under this section. For more information, see Board of Investment of Sri Lanka, 'Setting up', available at http://investsrilanka.com/invetor/how/ (last accessed 19 September 2019).

[20] Ibid., Section 17. Projects entering under section 17 require a higher investment commitment and are exempt from the application of several laws such as the Inland Revenue Act, Exchange Control Act and Customs Ordinance, provided the specified requirements are fulfilled.

[21] Ibid. Projects deemed to be of strategic importance to the country are granted approval in terms of this law, which provides the greatest possible fiscal exemptions, including the following laws:

1 The Inland Revenue Act, No. 10 of 2006;
2 The Value Added Tax Act, No. 14 of 2002;
3 The Value Added Tax Act, No. 14 of 2002;
4 The Excise (Special Provision) Act, No. 13 of 1989;
5 The Economic Service Charge Act, No. 13 of 2006;
6 Nation Building Tax Act No. 09 of 2009;
7 Port & Airports Development Levy Act No. 18 of 2011;
8 Customs Ordinance (Chapter 235);
9 The Sri Lanka Export Development Act No. 40 of 1979; and
10 The Betting and Gaming Levy Act No. 40 of 1988.

[22] Majula Sirimane, 'Doing business in Sri Lanka: overview', Thomson Reuters, 1 March 2017, available at https://uk.practicallaw.thomsonreuters.com/w-007-2092?transitionType=Default&contextData=(sc.Default)&firstPage=true&bhcp=1 (last accessed 9 July 2019).

[23] M. Sornarajah, *The International Law on Foreign Investment* (Cambridge: Cambridge University Press, 4th edition, 2017), p. 222 (emphasis added).

[24] Board of Investment of Sri Lanka, 'Setting up', available at http://investsrilanka.com/invetor/how/ (last accessed 20 September 2019).

10.2.3 *Case Law*

Given the political challenges to foreign investment in Sri Lanka – including civil strife and continued policy uncertainty, and the resulting likelihood of disputes – the means of dispute resolution in Sri Lanka, as well as how the government responds to legal action against it, are crucial factors for potential foreign investors in the country.

As in other countries, the primary method of resolving a legal dispute is the court system. The law relating to commercial disputes was developed almost exclusively by domestic courts.[25] In disputes involving foreign investment, however, international arbitration tribunals generally hear cases between investors and States.

At present, there are several options for arbitration. Almost every nation, including Sri Lanka, has its own arbitration centre.[26] Sri Lanka is also a Contracting State of the New York Convention[27] governing international arbitrations, and a Contracting State of the Convention on the Settlement of Investment Disputes between States and Nationals of Other States (ICSID Convention).[28] Though Sri Lanka's record as a host State for foreign investment is not impressive, its record in international dispute resolution is remarkable, as is evident from the three decisions explained below.

10.2.3.1 Asian Agricultural Products Ltd. v. Democratic Republic of Sri Lanka (1990)

Sri Lanka was a party to the second ICSID arbitration involving an Asian host State, known as the 'AAPL case',[29] which involved the destruction of a shrimp farm in an area of Sri Lanka where hostilities took place. The investor was a Hong Kong company, which alleged that rebel fighters took refuge in the shrimp farm, and that security forces retaliated by destroying the farm and killing many people.

The claimant company asserted the liability of the government, under the BIT that existed between the United Kingdom and Sri Lanka. It invoked Article 2 of the BIT, which guaranteed full protection and security to the investment, and Article 4(2), which required the government to pay adequate compensation for losses suffered by investors due to war or any other civil disturbances. The tribunal rejected the claimant's contention that Article 2 of the BIT imposed a strict liability on the government and was also unwilling to proceed against the government on the basis of Article 4(2), as it was not clear from the evidence whether the government forces were solely to blame for the attacks.

The tribunal proceeded, however, to hold the Sri Lankan government liable under general principles of international law, stating that it failed to take reasonable measures to prevent the destruction and loss of life. That an ICSID tribunal chose to use general principles of international law (instead of specific treaty provisions) to solve a question of international investment law was controversial, causing considerable debate in legal circles and in

[25] David Sloss and Michael Van Alstine, 'International Law in Domestic Courts' (2015) 9 *Santa Clara Law*, available at http://digitalcommons.law.scu.edu/cgi/viewcontent.cgi?article=1891&context=facpubs (last accessed 9 July 2019).

[26] The Arbitration Centre of the Institute for the Development of Commercial Law and Practice (ICLP), situated in Colombo, had ambitious plans to become the arbitration hub for South Asia but unfortunately, the ethnic conflict prevented this from happening. The ICLP facilitates many domestic arbitrations. Since Sri Lanka is a signatory to the New York Convention, the awards given by the ICLP can be enforced in many other jurisdictions.

[27] Convention on the Recognition and Enforcement of Foreign Arbitral Awards 1958.

[28] ICSID Convention, Regulations and Rules 2006.

[29] *Asian Agricultural Products Ltd (AAPL) v. Republic of Sri Lanka*, ICSID Case No. ARB/87/3.

academic writing.[30] Though the government thereby had grounds to challenge the award or refrain from paying compensation, it chose to honour the award. This was probably because several other investors would have been keeping a watchful eye on the proceedings, with a view to making decisions on investing in Sri Lanka.

10.2.3.2 *Mihaly International Corporation v. Democratic Republic of Sri Lanka* (2002)

A later case, which Sri Lanka won but which spawned a range of literature on the definition of 'investment', and what types of pre-contractual undertakings can be included as 'investment', is that of *Mihaly v. Sri Lanka*.[31]

Mihaly International Corporation was a Canadian power company, which wanted to build a power generation facility in Sri Lanka. During negotiations between its subsidiary, Mihaly (Canada) and the Government of Sri Lanka, several documents including letters of intent were exchanged between the parties, which expressly denied the existence of any legal obligations until signing of the final contract relating to the investment. This planned final contract never transpired. All that remained from the abandoned negotiations were some initial costs borne by Mihaly (Canada) for preparatory work associated with the project.

Mihaly (Canada) was sufficiently frustrated about the waste of time and money that it wanted to take action against the government. As Canada was not a party to the ICSID Convention and therefore could not invoke its jurisdiction, Mihaly (Canada) assigned all its interests and claims to a related company, Mihaly (the United States), which initiated the ICSID claim and invoked provisions of the US–Sri Lanka BIT. Mihaly (the United States) requested reimbursement of pre-investment and development expenses, including lost profits.[32] Sri Lanka raised objections on two grounds. First, it contested the jurisdiction of the centre and tribunal, by questioning the purported relationship between Mihaly (Canada) and Mihaly (the United States). Second, it contested the existence of an 'investment' under Article 25 of the ICSID Convention.

While the tribunal held that Mihaly (the United States) had capacity to file the claim, it agreed with the State's second objection, and found that the company's pre-investment expenditures did not amount to 'investment' under Article 25 of the ICSID Convention.[33]

[30] Ibid. See Sornarajah, above n 23, p. 97, who notes that 'the competence of the tribunal to deal with such issues must be raised. It was never intended by the creators of ICSID that ICSID tribunals should have jurisdiction to deal with general areas of state responsibility.' Cf. Amerasinghe, who also wrote a critique of the award, in 'Prawn Farm Arbitration' (1992) *Sri Lanka Journal of International Law* 98, in which he questions the composition of the tribunal and its competence to decide on matters of international law.

[31] *Mihaly International Corp. v. Democratic Socialist Republic of Sri Lanka*, ICSID Case No. ARB/00/2 (hereinafter 'the award'). See comments on the award as well as the classification of pre-investment expenses as investment in Dugan et al., *Investor-State Arbitration* (Oxford University Press, 2008), pp. 288–89. The award was also analysed in Robert N. Hornick, 'The Mihaly Arbitration: Pre-Investment Expenditure as a Basis for ICSID Jurisdiction' (2003) 20(2) *Journal of International Arbitration* 189–197. See also Devashish Krishnan, 'A Notion of ICSID Investment' (2009) *Transnational Dispute Management* 1, available at www.transnational-dispute-management.com/article.asp?key=1348 (last accessed 9 July 2019); and Dilini Pathirana, who analyses the cases from a Sri Lankan perspective in relation to BITs and investor-state arbitration in 'An Overview of Sri Lanka's Bilateral Investment Treaties: Status Quo and Some Insights into Future Modifications' (2017) 7(2) *Asian Journal of International Law* 287–318.

[32] Hornick, above n 31, at 190.

[33] Though the concurring opinion of Arbitrator Suratgar suggested that pre-investment expenses should be considered under the definition of investment, and this view was supported by Robinson, nevertheless, such a position is not favoured by Hornick, above n 31, who points out at p. 192 that 'the potential benefit of providing an international forum in which to arbitrate pre-investment disputes must be carefully weighed against the potential burden to states. This burden is likely to be much greater in the case of pre-investment disputes than in the case of investment disputes.'

The tribunal therefore found itself unable to consider the substantive matters of the case and dismissed it. Although Sri Lanka proposed that the claimant pay costs, the final award required each party to bear its own costs.

10.2.3.3 *Deutsche Bank AG v. Democratic Republic of Sri Lanka* (2012)

The third and final concluded international case, known as the 'Deutsche Bank case'[34] is actually one of four related cases that arose from oil hedging activity by the Ceylon Petroleum Corporation (CPC), a governmental entity. In early 2007, CPC entered into hedging agreements with five banks – namely, Standard Chartered Bank (SCB or Standard Chartered), Citibank, Deutsche Bank (Deutsche), People's Bank of Sri Lanka and the Commercial Bank of Ceylon. These hedging agreements between CPC and the banks proposed to limit CPC's liability if the price of oil rose further, by fixing a ceiling price of US$130 per barrel (pb) and a floor price of US$100 pb for what CPC would purchase through the banks.

Unfortunately for CPC, the price of oil dropped drastically from US$130 pb at the end of 2006 to around US$60 pb after the 2008 global financial crisis. The agreement therefore became onerous for the CPC and by extension, for the Sri Lankan government. It eventually suspended the transaction on the basis that the hedging agreement was 'substantially tainted'.[35]

This resulted in CPC defaulting on its payments, which led to SCB and Citibank filing action against CPC, and Deutsche filing action against the State. Standard Chartered filed action in the High Court of London, which held in favour of the bank, for a sum of US$ 180 million. Citibank took its claim to the London Court of International Arbitration (LCIA), in April 2011, with the seat of arbitration in Singapore.[36] Its claim, made against CPC rather than against the State, was in a sum of US$192 million plus interest. CPC succeeded because it could prove that it was the speculative nature of the contract that was at issue, and not the hedging derivative contract. The speculative contract was beyond CPC's capacity and therefore the contract was void.

By contrast, Deutsche initiated arbitral proceedings against the State of Sri Lanka, at ICSID in Washington, DC. The tribunal had to consider whether the hedging agreement between Deutsche and CPC was an 'investment'. This was done by testing the facts against the terms of both the Germany–Sri Lanka BIT and Article 25 of the ICSID Convention. The tribunal relied somewhat loosely on Deutsche's negotiations and correspondence with the CPC and Central Bank of Sri Lanka to hold that the hedging contract was indeed an 'investment' and awarded Deutsche US$ 60 million.[37]

10.2.3.4 *Raymond Eyre and Montrose Developments v Sri Lanka*

More recently, a British investor filed an action against the Sri Lankan government at ICSID under the UK – Sri Lanka BIT[38] over the re-acquisition of land close to the Parliament

34 *Deutsche Bank AG v. Democratic Socialist Republic of Sri Lanka*, ICSID Case No. ARB/09/02.

35 Jung-Yeop Woo and Uk Heo, 'Corruption and Foreign Direct Investment Attractiveness in Asia' (2009) 1(2) *Wiley Online Library*, available at http://onlinelibrary.wiley.com/doi/10.1111/j.1943–0787.2009.01113.x/abstract (last accessed 9 July 2019).

36 J. Hepburn, *Domestic Law in International Investment Arbitration* (Oxford University Press, 2017), p. 159.

37 UNCTAD Investment Policy Hub, 'Deutsche Bank v Sri Lanka', available at http://investmentpolicyhub.unctad.org/ISDS/Details/337 (last accessed 8 July 2019).

38 *Raymond Charles Eyre and Montrose Developments (Private) Limited v. Democratic Socialist Republic of Sri Lanka*, ICSID Case No. ARB/16/25. See also 'Re-acquisition of Kotte land: British investor takes Lanka to ICSID', The Sunday Times, 22 October 2017, available at www.sundaytimes.lk/171022/news/re-acquisition-of-kotte-land-british-investor-takes-lanka-to-icsid-265337.html (last accessed 8 July 2019).

complex in Kotte (near Colombo), which had earlier been given to construct a hotel. The case was filed by the investor, Raymond Eyre and his company Montrose Developments. On 5 March 2020, the ICSID tribunal issued an award in which it found that it lacked jurisdiction over the dispute, and ordered the claimant to pay one-third of the Sri Lankan government's legal costs.[39]

10.2.3.5 *Policy Implications of the Cases*

A point of concern from several of the above concluded cases is the manner in which arbitral tribunals interpret treaty provisions. In the *Deutsche Bank* case, the tribunal broadly interpreted the term 'investment', but did not justify why it did so by referring to valid sources of law. Even though tribunals are not bound by the same standards as courts of law, their awards can later be persuasively cited by judges and become concretized into judicial standards.

A related point of concern is the extent to which arbitral tribunals tend to repeat the decisions of previous tribunals, in a similar manner to the rules of judicial precedent. Arbitral tribunals are not expected to follow precedent, but there seems to be a growing trend to do so.[40] This may be influenced by the fact that the same set of arbitrators repeatedly sit on tribunals, or that arbitrators follow the same line of thinking.

Therefore, if a previous tribunal has adopted an extremely liberal interpretation of a particular term there is a danger of that term becoming the standard definition after being adopted a few times.[41] This is a cause for concern for Sri Lanka, which has lost two out of three ICSID cases, on points that could have been challenged.[42] Such experiences may induce developing States like Sri Lanka to reconsider its recourse to ICSID arbitration and instead look to other options.

10.3 CURRENT CONTEXT AND POLICY PRIORITIES

The analysis in Part 1 earlier of Sri Lanka's political history and its experience of regulating foreign investment reveals Sri Lanka's challenges to steadily increasing its FDI. Despite establishing its BOI and other relevant national institutions, having over two dozen BITs and complying with international legal decisions even when they could have been challenged in law, Sri Lanka is yet to see a sustained upward trend in its FDI, a factor which has in turn constrained its economic growth.

Sri Lanka's relatively unimpressive record in attracting FDI can be seen in Figure 10.3 and is amplified when comparing Sri Lanka to neighbouring economies. This disparity does not simply reflect economic fluctuations and it is necessary to also examine the underlying domestic factors in Sri Lanka.

39 *Raymond Charles Eyre and Montrose Developments (Private) Limited v. Democratic Socialist Republic of Sri Lanka*, ICSID Case No. ARB/16/25, Award of 5 March 2020, para. 316.

40 Gabrielle Kaufmann-Kohler, 'Arbitral Precedent: Dream, Necessity or Excuse?' (2007) 23(3) *Arbitration International* 357–78.

41 Sornarajah has raised the issue of the legitimacy of arbitral tribunals making 'soft law': see Sornarajah, above n 23, p. 423.

42 In the Deutsche case, for example, the tribunal did not consider that the state was a client of the bank, and that the bank owed an ethical duty to inform the client of any unfavourable conditions that might arise from the contract. It is also contended that the complexities of the hedging agreement were beyond the comprehension of the CPC officials, but were very well understood by the banks. Clearly, the CPC entered into the hedging agreement without fully understanding the implications of a crash in oil prices. The dissenting opinion in the Deutsche award refers to all these factors, which the majority opinion glossed over.

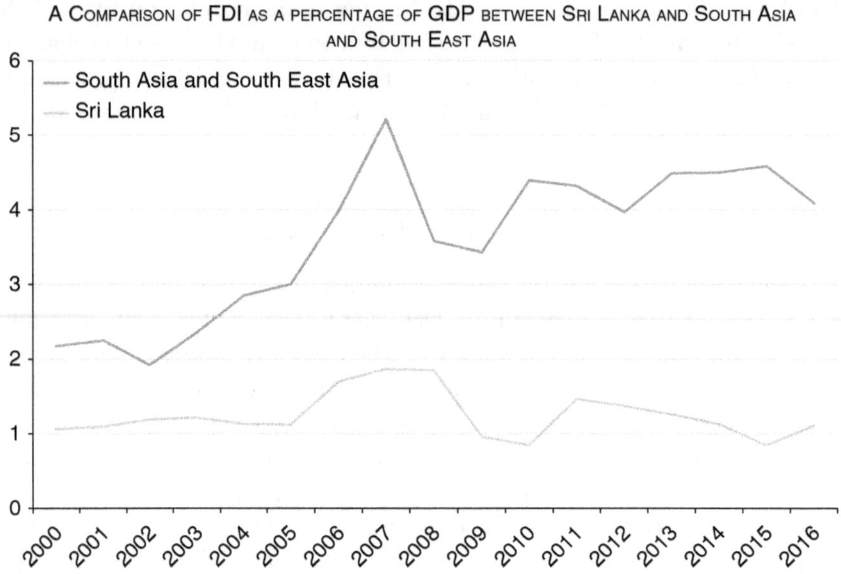

FIGURE 10.3 FDI as share of GDP in South and South East Asia versus Sri Lanka, 2000–2016

10.3.1 *Political Challenges*

The lack of steady growth in Sri Lanka's FDI can be attributed to multiple intersecting factors, which can be broadly categorized as *political* and *legal* factors. Among the political factors, explained in this section, the key challenge has been a lack of policy consensus and consistency – both at the national level and with respect to Sri Lanka's foreign policy. In particular, there has not been a sufficient and cross-partisan will to move quickly to a user-friendly and rules-based framework of FDI, which can attract diverse sources of foreign investment for reasons other than infrastructure projects. These challenges are detailed further.

10.3.1.1 Partisan Policymaking and 'Leader-Driven' Investment

Sri Lanka's national political system remains highly partisan, with a civil service and civil actors (e.g. think tanks) that are relatively weak[43] and therefore unable to support consistent policies on foreign investment. As described in Section 10.2.1, governments have swung between socialist, open-market, and social market systems since the 1970s. Although a return to a closed-market system is no longer likely, the governments of the day nevertheless continue to pursue different investment policies and institutional structures without a multi-party, democratic consensus on basic policy tenets that can survive a change in government.

In the absence of such a cross-partisan consensus, FDI in Sri Lanka has depended on individual leaders and their networks, rather than on the BOI and more broadly, a national institutional and policy framework. The clearest recent example of this is the authoritarian Rajapaksa government and its personally driven procurement of large

[43] S. Aliff and A. Sarjoon, 'The Role of Civil Society in Democratic Governance: State-Civil Society Relations in Democratization – Special Focus on Contemporary Sri Lanka' (2010) IV *South Eastern University of Sri Lanka Kalam Journal* 26–34, available at http://ir.lib.seu.ac.lk/bitstream/handle/123456789/424/KALAM%20iv-26.pdf?sequence=1 (last accessed 9 July 2019).

infrastructure projects, particularly those funded by China. These included highways, port development projects in Colombo and Hambantota, and major hotel development projects with foreign chains.[44]

10.3.1.2 Drawbacks of 'Leader-driven' Investment

This 'leader-driven' model of foreign investment has at least two drawbacks, compared to the 'rules-based' model in developed countries, in which investors rely on a clear and efficient legal framework that operates irrespective of the leader or party in power. The first drawback is that a 'leader-driven' model is, almost by definition, more prone to economic leakages via corruption than a rules-based model. There remains an unfortunate tolerance for corruption in Sri Lanka, among segments of the public who consider it a trade-off for efficiency.[45] Repeated studies make clear, however, that corruption is not conducive to economic development and specifically, does not increase FDI.[46]

The second drawback of a 'leader-driven' model of foreign investment is that it is dependent on the personality and proclivities of the leaders in power. A relatively uncharismatic leader, for example, may be less successful in securing FDI than his or her more persuasive predecessor. Moreover, investors may need to devote considerable time to ingratiating themselves with incumbent leaders, to enter and remain in the market. Even if they do this, they could still be driven out of the market for spurious or otherwise unpredictable reasons, as happened in 2008 in Sri Lanka when the Rajapaksa government took actions that induced Emirates Airlines to end its management contract with Sri Lankan Airlines.

10.3.1.3 Foreign Policy Challenges: Non-Alignment in Name

As a related issue to the absence of a clear *national* framework that encourages foreign investment, there has been inconsistency in Sri Lanka's *foreign* policy. In principle, Sri Lanka has had a 'non-aligned' foreign policy since the Cold War,[47] which maintains neutrality between the great powers. In practice, however, its foreign relations with the US, Europe, China and India, have significantly changed course with successive elections and governments.[48] Each government in Sri Lanka has sought to 'rebalance' the (perceived and actual) foreign tilts of its predecessor – a practice that has unfortunately resulted in a swaying foreign policy, rather than a 'balanced' one that would be expected from a non-aligned stance.[49]

Recent experience illustrates this problem. In the aftermath of the civil war that ended in 2009, Sri Lanka faced international criticism (largely, but not solely, by Western

[44] Ministry of Highways, Ports & Shipping, 'Annual Performance Report' (Parliament of Sri Lanka Report, 2014), available at www.parliament.lk/uploads/documents/paperspresented/performance-report-ministry-of-highways-ports-and-shipping-2014.pdf (last accessed 9 July 2019).

[45] Ranga Jayasuriya, 'Was corruption under the Rajapaksa regime "Efficient"?', Daily Mirror, 26 May 2015, available at www.dailymirror.lk/73697/was-corruption-under-the-rajapaksa-regime-efficient (last accessed 9 July 2019).

[46] Woo and Heo, above n 35.

[47] Leelananda De Silva, 'Non Aligned Summit in Colombo, 1976', *The Island*, 11 February 2012, available at www.island.lk/index.php?page_cat=article-details&page=article-details&code_title=45077 (last accessed 9 July 2019).

[48] N. De Mel, et al, 'Remarks at the Sri Lanka Foreign Policy Forum' (*Lakshman Kadirgamar Institute*, audio recording, 2017), available at https://soundcloud.com/lk_institute/day-1-session-1-foundations-of-sri-lankan-foreign-policy (last accessed 9 July 2019).

[49] Ibid.

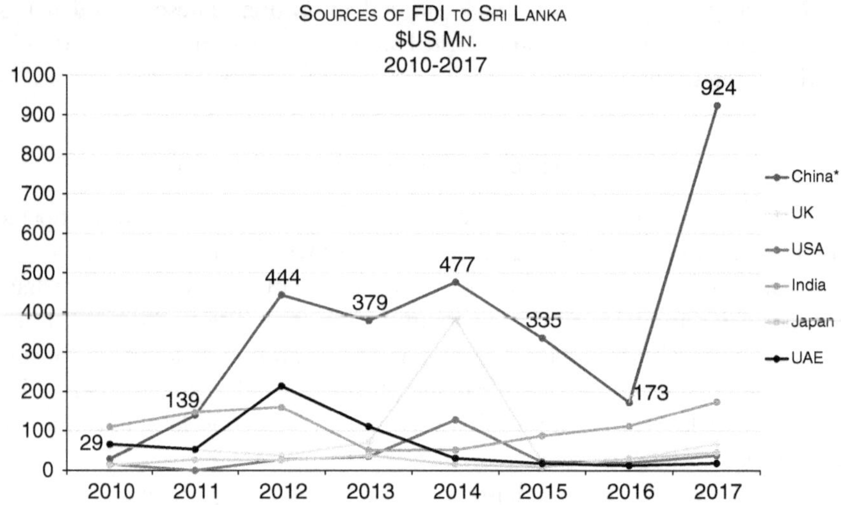

FIGURE 10.4 Sources of FDI to Sri Lanka, 2010–2017

governments and non-governmental actors), including at the UN Human Rights Council in Geneva.[50] The Rajapaksa government responded by engaging less with the United States and India (who supported resolutions in the UN Human Rights Council on human rights and transitional justice issues in Sri Lanka)[51] and engaging significantly more with a small array of governments who expressed little or no interest in issues of human rights and justice, especially with China.[52]

Unsurprisingly, therefore, the greatest growth in FDI in the final years of the Rajapaksa government (2012–2014) came from China, with China becoming the top source of FDI in 2013.[53] Equally, FDI declined in these years from India, Japan and the UAE, with a modest increase in FDI from the United States.[54] After the government changed in 2015 and reviewed the Colombo Port City project (now known as the Colombo International Financial City or CIFC), Chinese investment declined markedly in the years 2015 and 2016 – as shown in Figure 10.4.

As Figure 10.4 also shows, however, Chinese investment surged again in 2017. This appears to reflect the government's decisions in 2016 to allow the CIFC to resume (albeit under a long lease, rather than the freehold arrangement envisioned by the Rajapaksa government) and to accept major new Chinese investments; decisions that appear to be driven by concern over the low levels of foreign investment in 2015 and 2016 and about servicing accumulated

50 T. Ramakrishnan, 'U.N. body asks Sri Lanka to probe "rights abuses"', *The Hindu*, 1 October 2015, available at www.thehindu.com/news/international/unhrc-adopts-consensus-resolution-on-sri-lanka/article7712259.ece (last accessed 9 July 2019).

51 N. Sathiya Moorthy, 'UNHRC Bug Now Bites India, But Sri Lanka Is Where the Action Is Still . . . ', *The Sunday Leader*, 25 September 2016, available at www.thesundayleader.lk/2016/09/19/unhrc-bug-now-bites-india-but-sri-lanka-is-where-the-action-is-still/ (last accessed 9 July 2019).

52 Ministry of Foreign Affairs, 'China – Sri Lanka Relations an All Weather Partnership – Vice President of China' (Press Release, 2013), available at www.mfa.gov.lk/index.php/en/media/media-releases/4419-china-sri-lanka-relations-an-all-weather-partnership-vice-president-of-china (last accessed 9 July 2019).

53 R. Deyshappriya, 'China is Sri Lanka's biggest source of FDI, but there's room for more', LSE South Asia Centre, 12 September 2017, available at http://blogs.lse.ac.uk/southasia/2017/09/12/china-is-sri-lankas-biggest-source-of-fdi-but-there-is-room-for-more/ (last accessed 9 July 2019).

54 Ibid.

external debt.[55] Most notably, the government agreed to a US$1.1 billion investment by China Merchants Port Holdings in the Hambantota port, the first instalment of which it received in 2017.[56]

The swings in the sources of foreign (and especially Chinese) investment underscore the recurring challenge of Sri Lanka's foreign policy. That challenge is to maintain consistently good relations with all major powers, in a manner that does not interrupt the potential flow of investments from any bloc or country, and which maintains the confidence of even politically 'unconnected' investors.

10.3.1.4 Limits of Playing the 'China Card' to Increase FDI

The strategic concern of India and other countries, about China's rise in stature and its presence in Sri Lanka, has prompted some to argue that Sri Lanka should play the 'China card' against these countries, to secure more investment from them.[57] This, however, would be at best a limited approach, and at worst a risky strategy, for Sri Lanka. In particular, it will be difficult for Sri Lanka to secure substantial investments from India and other countries in the short to medium term, given their relative lack of investment funds, compared to the US$50 billion that China has already spent worldwide to support its expansive and long-term Belt & Road Initiative.[58]

Moreover, to the extent that investment can be sourced from India, Japan and similarly concerned countries, playing to their fears is unlikely to incentivize the type of FDI that Sri Lanka most needs – including FDI to stimulate exports and tap into global supply chains.[59] Instead, playing the 'China card' is more likely to induce additional 'strategic' investments that mitigate other countries' anxieties about Chinese investments. Indeed, among the investments that India and Japan appear to be considering at the time of writing are investments in an airport close to Hambantota port[60] and in the port of Trincomalee on Sri Lanka's east coast.[61]

To increase and diversify FDI for its own varied needs, it is therefore important that Sri Lanka move beyond simply playing into India's fears or China's interests and that it focuses on developing a broader, investor-friendly framework via the multi-step plan detailed in Section 10.3.3.

[55] Nimal Sanderatne, '2018 crucial for strengthening foreign reserves to meet massive debt repayment in 2019', *The Sunday Times*, 21 January 2018, available at www.sundaytimes.lk/180121/columns/2018-crucial-for-strengthening-foreign-reserves-to-meet-massive-debt-repayment-in-2019–278032.html (last accessed 9 July 2019).

[56] 'China-owned port in Sri Lanka could alter trade routes', *Financial Times*, 25 September 2017, available at www.ft.com/content/f0d88070-9f99-11e7-9a86-4d5a475ba4c5 (last accessed 9 July 2019); MAREX, 'India and China Face Off at Sri Lankan Port', *The Maritime Executive*, 16 November 2017, available at https://maritime-executive.com/article/india-and-china-face-off-at-sri-lankan-port (last accessed 9 July 2019).

[57] M. Srinivasan. 'Sri Lanka a pearl in the Indian Ocean', The Hindu, 16 September 2014, available at www.thehindu.com/news/international/south-asia/xi-jinping-to-launch-port-city-in-sri-lanka/article6415994.ece (last accessed 9 July 2019).

[58] J. Perlez and Y. Huang, 'Behind China's $1 Trillion Plan to Shake Up the Economic Order', *New York Times*, 13 May 2017, available at www.nytimes.com/2017/05/13/business/china-railway-one-belt-one-road-1-trillion-plan.html (last accessed 9 July 2019). The exact amounts are unclear: W. Shepard, 'Why the Ambiguity Of China's Belt And Road Initiative Is Perhaps Its Biggest Strength', *Forbes*, 19 October 2017, available at www.forbes.com/sites/wadeshepard/2017/10/19/what-chinas-belt-and-road-initiative-is-really-all-about/#5138ab9de4de (last accessed 9 July 2019).

[59] Ganeshan Wignaraja, 'Sri Lanka's Future Lies in Emulating Factory Asia – The Lakshman Kadirgamar Institute', Lakshman Kadirgamar Institute, 19 July 2017, available at www.lki.lk/blog/sri-lankas-future-lies-in-emulating-factory-asia/ (last accessed 9 July 2019).

[60] Meera Srinivasan, 'India keen to run Sri Lanka airport', *The Hindu*, 12 August 2017, available at www.thehindu.com/todays-paper/tp-international/india-keen-to-run-sri-lanka-airport/article19477500.ece (last accessed 9 July 2019).

[61] Sri Lanka Ports Authority, 'Trincomalee Port', available at www.slpa.lk/port-colombo/trincomalee (last accessed 9 July 2019).

10.3.1.5 Comparative Analysis

Competitor host States in the region offer instructive examples of how to build an effective and *consistent* policy on foreign investment and it is especially worth examining the successful examples of democracies, given that it is easier to achieve a consistent policy in a one-party State like Vietnam or China. In the region, two useful examples are New Zealand (a liberal democracy) and Singapore (which might be described as a directed democracy, governed in practice by a single party, albeit with elections).[62]

Importantly, New Zealand and Singapore are also multicultural nations that have long prized *ethnic harmony* as a bedrock of their stable political environments. New Zealand has pursued this since at least 1840, the date on which the British Crown signed the Treaty of Waitangi with indigenous Maori chiefs.[63] More recently, New Zealand has facilitated the peaceful relations of its peoples by enacting the New Zealand Human Rights Act of 1993, and by a Human Rights Commission which implements a pro-diversity cultural programme.[64] While, in Singapore, ethnic harmony has been facilitated by use of English as the country's main working language, notwithstanding recognition of three other official languages (Malay, Mandarin and Tamil).[65] A common language has enabled easy interaction among the Malay, Chinese and Tamil communities – Singapore's three main ethnic groups. Singapore's language policy is complemented by other measures to ensure interracial harmony, including an electoral system that guarantees significant minority representation in Parliament and ethnic quotas in public housing schemes.[66]

As a result of these policies, those considering whether to invest in New Zealand and Singapore can remain confident that a peaceful multiculturalism will prevail in those countries, and thereby not adversely affect their investments.

Both countries also have *strong national brands*, to underscore their drive for foreign investment. New Zealand has maintained its '100% Pure New Zealand' brand since 1999, despite a change of the party in government in 2008 and another in 2017.[67] Singapore has periodically changed its national brand (it was previously known as the 'Garden City' and most recently, the government adopted a 'Passion Made Possible' brand that shows a mindset of enterprise and determination).[68] However, it has pursued a consistent objective in rebranding, namely to highlight different positive aspects of Singapore and 'adaptability to customer needs'.[69] It has also been noted that Lee Kuan Yew's almost daily pronouncements on

62 'Treaty Of Waitangi', New Zealand History, available at https://nzhistory.govt.nz/politics/treaty-of-waitangi (last accessed 9 July 2019).

63 Human Rights Act 1993 No. 82.

64 NZ Human Rights Commission, 'The NZ Diversity Action Programme', available at www.hrc.co.nz/our-work/race-relations-and-diversity/race-relations/our-work/nz-diversity-action-programme-te-ngira/ (last accessed 9 July 2019).

65 Republic of Singapore Independence Act 1965 (Act 9 of 1965), section 7.

66 For two different perspectives on these policies, see Chan Sek Keong, 'Multiculturalism in Singapore: A Way to a Harmonious Society' (2013) 25 *Singapore Academy of Law Journal* 84–109 at 84, available at http://journalsonline.academypublishing.org.sg/Journals/Singapore-Academy-of-Law-Journal/e-Archive/ctl/eFirstSALPDFJournalView/mid/495/ArticleId/500/Citation/JournalsOnlinePDF (last accessed 9 July 2019); 'Singapore expands its paternalistic policy on race', *The Economist*, 15 December 2016, available at www.economist.com/news/asia/21711939-president-will-now-be-chosen-partly-racial-criteria-singapore-expands-its-paternalistic (last accessed 9 July 2019).

67 'Buy Pure', available at http://buypurenewzealand.com/ (last accessed 9 July 2019).

68 Koh Xing Hui, 'Singapore's new international brand by STB and EDB: Passion Made Possible', *The Straits Times*, 24 August 2017, available at www.straitstimes.com/singapore/singapores-new-international-brand-by-stb-and-edb-passion-made-possible (last accessed 9 July 2019).

69 Koh Buck Song, *Brand Singapore: Nation Branding After Lee Kuan Yew in A Divisive World* (Singapore: Marshall Cavendish Business, 2nd edition, 2017).

Singapore's governance and foreign relations provided a 'sub-text [that] was really nation branding, even if no one overtly mentioned the term'.[70] This helped investors to trust Singapore to maintain a strong governance framework, with stability in its foreign relations.

Lastly, New Zealand and Singapore have demonstrated a consistent commitment to enhancing three key factors in attracting FDI: (i) plentiful and high-quality *human resources*, which enable businesses to scale rapidly; (ii) *infrastructure and connectivity*, both physical and digital;[71] and (iii) a *corruption-free* society. Both countries have consistently ranked among the best in the world on all three of these aspects.

10.3.2 *Legal Issues and Needs*

10.3.2.1 Overlapping Laws and Institutions

Sri Lanka also has to streamline its legal regime that governs foreign investment, which includes the following laws:[72] the BOI Act,[73] the Companies Act,[74] the Exchange Control Act,[75] the Strategic Development Projects Act,[76] and the Finance Act.[77] In addition, there are many governmental agencies whose approval may be required to commence operations, and administrative delays at their end can be disastrous for an investment.

To speed up the process, the BOI has developed an online one stop shop (OSS), i.e. a 'single window' virtual platform that can receive an application for investment and forward it to the various institutions whose approval is required. The OSS is known as 'SWIFT', the 'Single Window Investment Facilitation Taskforce', which is intended to be 'the effective and efficient single point of contact for investors and to provide a total solution in realizing in investment in Sri Lanka'.[78] Its mission is to provide smooth and quick investor facilitation, making the investment landscape easier to navigate, through efficiency and transparency; this will fuel Sri Lanka's transformation into a leading investment destination of choice.[79]

While the BOI prides itself on being efficient and facilitative and should be commended for recent strides in increasing FDI, there remains work to do towards a user-friendly and uniform legal framework. This was highlighted in the 2015 and 2017 US Investment Climate Statements on Sri Lanka, which described Sri Lanka as a 'challenging place to do business, with high transaction costs related to an unpredictable economic policy environment'.[80]

70 Ibid.

71 On the importance of infrastructure for attracting FDI to Sri Lanka, see K. Ravinthirakumaran et al., 'Determinants of Foreign Direct Investment in Sri Lanka' (2015) 16(2) *South Asia Economic Journal* 1–22, available at https://editorialexpress.com/cgi-bin/conference/download.cgi?db_name=ACE2015&paper_id=104 (last accessed 9 July 2019), who correspondingly note that with regard to human resources, maintaining low wages is *not* important.

72 Board of Investment of Sri Lanka, 'Invest in Sri Lanka: Legal Aspects', available at http://investsrilanka.com/wp-content/uploads/2019/03/legal_brochure_new.pdf (last accessed 9 July 2019).

73 Board of Investment Law (No. 4 of 1978) as amended and its Regulations.

74 Companies Act (No. 7 of 2007).

75 Exchange Control Act (No. 24 of 1953) and its Regulations.

76 Strategic Development Projects Act (No. 14 of 2008) as amended.

77 Finance Act (No. 12 of 2012) Part (iv) as amended (Hub Operation Regulations).

78 Single Window Investment Facilitation Taskforce, available at http://swiftinvest.lk/investor/#sop_list (last accessed 20 September 2019).

79 Ibid.

80 U.S. Department of State's Investment Climate Statements, 'Investment Climate Statements', available at www.state.gov/investment-climate-statements/ (last accessed 9 July 2019).

10.3.2.2 Transparency, Governance and Land Issues

The 2017 US Investment Climate Statement specified several drawbacks, including that the government's 'overall provision of services is impeded by inefficiency', 'economic growth is stymied by lingering opaque government procurement practices', and 'foreigners are prohibited from purchasing land and real estate except for apartments above the 3rd floor'.[81] It notes that the Underutilized Assets Act of 2011, which resulted in the seizure of thirty-seven companies, would be of concern to investors. It also observes that, 'local investors cite the risks of contract repudiation, cronyism, damage to reputation, and de facto or de jure expropriation as concerns, although the [new government] has started to address these issues'.

10.3.2.3 Comparative Analysis

Singapore is a highly instructive example of a transparent, rules-based system. Its FDI has grown consistently in the past twenty years, and Singapore is now a global leader in attracting and optimizing investment for economic growth.[82] In addition to having over forty international investment agreements,[83] it has a remarkable twenty-two free trade agreements (FTAs), including one with Sri Lanka signed in January 2018 – thereby offering investors a much greater market size beyond its small population.[84] By contrast, besides its recently concluded FTA with Singapore, Sri Lanka has only five agreements (bilateral FTAs in goods with India and Pakistan and three regional FTAs).

Investors in Singapore are generally subject to the same laws as local companies (with the exception that foreigners are restricted in buying freehold land), and there is no law that compels foreign investors to transfer ownership to local interests.[85] There is also no share capital requirement, and no restrictions on reinvestment or repatriation of profits. The government agencies that regulate investment are listed on one website and are accessible remotely to investors.[86] Furthermore, laws that regulate investment are clearly accessible and help investors learn about the legal system prior to deciding to invest and setting up operations. Singapore has recently set up a new OSS named 'Enterprise Singapore', which resulted from the merger of two pre-existing government agencies, 'International Enterprise Singapore' and 'SPRING'.[87]

Singapore is also a standard-bearer in commercial dispute resolution, allowing for maximum party autonomy in arbitral proceedings. It takes an estimated 164 days to enforce a contract in Singapore.[88] New Zealand is almost as efficient (216 days), whereas enforcing

81 Ibid.

82 World Bank, 'Foreign direct investment, new inflows', available at https://data.worldbank.org/indicator/BX.KLT.DINV.CD.WD?year_high_desc=false (last accessed 9 July 2019).

83 UNCTAD, 'International Investment Agreements Navigator: Singapore', available at https://investmentpolicy.unctad.org/international-investment-agreements/countries/190/singapore (last accessed 20 September 2019). Newer generation FTAs contain investment chapters that generally go beyond the scope of standard investment agreements, covering elements such as investment liberalisation and investment facilitation.

84 Ibid.

85 There are, however, a few restrictions in the financial services, professional services and media sectors.

86 This is extremely useful to investors, who otherwise do not know what to expect until they have physically visited the authority in question. See Contact Singapore, 'Government Assistance', available at www.contactsingapore.sg/en/investors-business-owners/invest-in-singapore/government-assistance (last accessed 9 July 2019).

87 Enterprise Singapore, 'About Enterprise Singapore', www.enterprisesg.gov.sg/about-us/overview (last accessed 20 September 2019).

88 World Bank, 'Time required to enforce a contract', available at https://data.worldbank.org/indicator/IC.LGL.DURS?year_high_desc=false (last accessed 9 July 2019).

a contract in Sri Lanka takes a protracted 1318 days.[89] Singapore's leading role in dispute resolution is supported by the presence of several major international law firms in the city state.[90] This helps to position Singapore as a welcoming place for foreign investment as there is an ample supply of legal practitioners whose firms are already familiar to foreign investors, who are aware of legal developments in both Singapore and competitor markets, and who can propel local lawyers and policymakers to meet or exceed the best international standards.

10.3.3 A *Multi-Step Plan*

10.3.3.1 Political Measures

The analysis in Sections 10.3.1 and 10.3.2 indicates that a crucial challenge to attracting to FDI to Sri Lanka has been the policy inconsistency associated with successive changes of government. Sri Lanka needs a cross-partisan policy on foreign investment, which should start with the specific and achievable task of formulating a clear and politically sustainable *national brand*. This is especially important because studies have shown a correlation between a strong national brand and inward FDI.[91] In this regard, the government can learn from and emulate the national branding experience of New Zealand as outlined in Section 10.3.1.

As a related matter, Sri Lanka can learn from New Zealand's and Singapore's emphasis on building *social cohesion*, especially among its ethnic communities. Due to improvements in its human rights record, Sri Lanka recently regained GSP+, a preferential tariff arrangement with the EU that it lost in 2010 under the Rajapaksa government.[92] This is a clear example of how non-economic improvements yield economic benefits. Sri Lanka must similarly prioritize building an enduring respect among its different communities. This is a good thing in and of itself but will also help to address any lingering doubts of potential foreign investors as to whether the country is committed to, and can ensure, a sustainable peace.

Implementing a transparent and comprehensive policy of environmental, labour and other *governance standards* for foreign investment and loans will help to address investor concerns discussed in Section 10.3.1, about inconsistencies in Sri Lanka's foreign policy and possible reversals of agreed projects. The standards should be robust enough to ensure (i) sustainable and shared economic benefits of infrastructure development projects, and (ii) confidence of the general public and any new government in Sri Lanka that predecessor governments have agreed to foreign loans with due process and on terms that are in Sri Lanka's long-term interests. Developing this policy will take time but as a minimum, Sri Lanka and China can

89 Ibid.

90 Singapore International Dispute Resolution Academy, 'The Singapore Dispute Resolution Institutions – What and Why (Part 1 of 4)', available at www.sidra.academy/blog/singapore-dispute-resolution-institutions-part-1/ (last accessed 9 July 2019).

91 See, e.g., M. Kalamovayand and K. Konrad, 'Nation Brands and Foreign Direct Investment' (Max-Planck-Institute for Intellectual Property Rights, Competition and Tax Law, Research Paper, 28 September 2009), available at www.tax.mpg.de/fileadmin/templatesnew/pdf/nation-brands-09–09-28_with_figure.pdf (last accessed 9 July 2019). After considering branding examples such as Britain's 'Cool Britannia', the authors state at p. 27, 'We show that FDI flows into a host country rise as its nation image, the value of its intangibles, improves. We also show that this effect is not driven by "fundamental" or "economic" variables … We found that the Anholt Nation Brands Index, our measure for intangibles in the host country, has a large positive effect on FDI: a one-point increase in the index is associated with a 27% increase in the inflow of inward FDI.'

92 See European External Action Service, 'The EU grants enhanced market access for Sri Lanka as a reform incentive' (Press Release, 16 May 2017), available at https://eeas.europa.eu/delegations/sri-lanka/26153/eu-grants-enhanced-market-access-sri-lanka-reform-incentive_en (last accessed 9 July 2019).

begin by adhering to the Environmental and Social Framework that has already been adopted by the China-initiated Asian Infrastructure Investment Bank (AIIB).[93]

Finally, Sri Lanka must address two longstanding deficiencies in its attractiveness as a host State for foreign investment: *corruption*, and limited *human resources* to attract large-scale investments. While the current government's manifesto of good governance has led to many improvements, including the resumption of judicial independence[94] and media freedom,[95] there has been little progress in addressing the country's record of corruption, and especially with regard to allegations made against the previous government.

Part of the problem may lie in the sheer volume and scale of those allegations. If so, Sri Lanka may benefit from adopting the approach that Hong Kong took decades ago, to transcend its sordid history of corruption until the mid-1970s. Hong Kong took the first step to ending this history when it established its Independent Commission Against Corruption (ICAC) in 1974.[96] Faced with an apparent mountain of cases, involving many who were still working in the public sector, the government later took the bold decision of granting a partial amnesty, whereby only the most serious cases of the past would be pursued.[97]

The announcement of a partial amnesty in 1977 provided a new lease of life to the police and others (who had been previously been implicated) to pursue the few most egregious cases.[98] Their eventual success in doing so assuaged the public's sense of injustice about the *past*, while also establishing ICAC's status as a serious bulwark against corruption in the *future*. Likewise, the current government in Sri Lanka should adopt a vigorous but practical focus (whether by a partial amnesty or otherwise) in pursuing the allegations of corruption in the past decade. Without this focus, the most serious allegations – and thereby also the lack of confidence in 'clean' governance among the general public and potential investors – will remain unaddressed.

The long-term challenge of improving Sri Lanka's human resources can be alleviated somewhat by harnessing Sri Lanka's large diaspora, who comprise over 8 per cent of all Sri Lankans.[99] The current government laudably introduced a system for obtaining dual citizenship in 2015, pursuant to which several thousand members of the diaspora have re-engaged

93 See Asian Infrastructure Investment Bank, 'Environmental and Social Framework' (February 2016), available at www.aiib.org/en/policies-strategies/framework-agreements/environmental-social-framework.html (last accessed 9 July 2019). China appears willing and interested to set some other regulatory standards, as indicated here: China Council for International Cooperation on Environment and Development, 'Environmental Protection Strategy for the 'One Belt One Road' Initiative', available at www.jica.go.jp/english/our_work/social_environmental/index.html (last accessed 9 July 2019).

94 Asanga Welikala, 'What is Happening in the Sri Lankan Supreme Court?', *Ground Views*, 16 November 2017, available at http://groundviews.org/2017/11/16/what-is-happening-in-the-sri-lankan-supreme-court/ (last accessed 9 July 2019).

95 See the references to Sri Lanka in Freedom House, *Press Freedom's Dark Horizon* (Report, 2017), available at https://freedomhouse.org/report/freedom-press/freedom-press-2017 (last accessed 9 July 2019).

96 See Hong Kong Independent Commission Against Corruption, 'Brief History', (available at www.icac.org.hk/en/about/history/index.html (last accessed 9 July 2019).

97 L. Lam, 'Forty years since its creation, how the ICAC cleaned up corruption in Hong Kong', South China Morning Post, 15 February 2014, available at www.scmp.com/news/hong-kong/article/1428093/forty-years-its-creation-how-icac-cleaned-corruption-hong-kong (last accessed 9 July 2019).

98 Ibid.

99 R. Hausmann, 'Prof Ricardo Hausmann Presentation Part 2' (YouTube, 20 January 2017), available at www.youtube.com/watch?v=_kn_3imLWqw (last accessed 9 July 2019); LBO, 'Sri Lanka should rethink immigration, diaspora policies: Hausmann', Lanka Business Online, 10 January 2017, available at www.lankabusinessonline.com/sri-lanka-should-rethink-immigration-diaspora-policies-hausmann/ (last accessed 9 July 2019); Deshal de Mel, 'Opinion: Economic Priorities in Sri Lanka's Foreign Policy', Lanka Business Online, 31 January 2017, available at www.lankabusinessonline.com/opinion-economic-priorities-in-sri-lankas-foreign-policy/ (last accessed 9 July 2019).

with their country of birth. However, more can be done, including allowing those holding an 'Ex-Sri Lankan' visa (available to non-Sri Lankan citizens of Sri Lankan origin) to undertake employment in the country.[100]

10.3.3.2 Legal Measures

Several of the recommended political measures above have a strong legal dimension. In addition, while the legal regime in Sri Lanka is relatively stable as far as investment is concerned, a few more specific and carefully considered initiatives could help to bolster this regime to become a selling point for investors. Among these, completing the setting up of *an effective OSS platform* would go a long way in promoting Sri Lanka among potential investors.

Allowing *foreign law firms* to operate in Sri Lanka would also help to develop the local expertise to handle legal issues relating to foreign investments, and strengthen local capacity to engage in desired forms of dispute resolution, particularly in arbitration. Moreover, foreign law firms in Sri Lanka would offer potential investors internationally recognized points of contact and information 'on the ground' about local investment opportunities and procedures. In time, they may also add pressure to accelerate the currently lengthy and economically punishing time to enforce contracts in domestic courts.

Another promising possibility is for Sri Lanka to join the *Information Technology Agreement of the WTO*, which has a membership that controls more than 97 per cent of world trade in information technology (IT) products.[101] This would help Sri Lanka to attract more FDI in fields related to IT,[102] and enable Sri Lanka to improve and upgrade its technological infrastructure to attract a wide range of FDI.[103]

Sri Lanka's recent major investments have been concentrated in infrastructure development. While this is useful, the authors are of the view that Sri Lanka also needs export-related FDI, which in turn will fuel export-driven growth. Given Sri Lanka's small population, the government is rightly now pursuing a *network of FTAs* in the region, including with Thailand and Malaysia. Concluding its planned FTAs with India and China remains vital, as these agreements would help position Sri Lanka a gateway to a multi-billion consumer population and thereby attract more export-oriented FDI.

10.4 CONCLUSION

During the decades of civil strife and war, it was easy (and perhaps understandable) to blame Sri Lanka's lacklustre performance in attracting foreign investment on security concerns. However, even after the war ended in 2009, Sri Lanka has struggled to consistently grow its FDI and it lags behind the performance of regional peers in South and South-East Asia,

100 For other valuable suggestions on expanding the size and skills of Sri Lanka's human resources, see Ganeshan Wignaraja, 'Fixing Sri Lanka's Labour Market: Comparative Lessons', Lakshman Kadirgamar Institute, 13 July 2018, available at www.ft.lk/columns/Fixing-Sri-Lanka-s-labour-market–Comparative-lessons/4–658844 (last accessed 9 July 2019).

101 See World Trade Organization, 'Information Technology Agreement', available at www.wto.org/english/tratop_e/inftec_e/inftec_e.htm (last accessed 9 July 2019); A. De Zylva et al., 'Is Sri Lanka Sitting on the Bench of Asia's Booming Digital Economy', Lakshman Kadirgamar Institute, 14 May 2018, available at www.lki.lk/publication/is-sri-lanka-sitting-on-the-bench-of-asias-booming-digital-economy/ (last accessed 9 July 2019).

102 Ratnasabapathy, above n 9.

103 S. Mayes, 'Opinion: FDI in Sri Lanka, a real estate perspective', *Lanka Business Online*, 8 May 2017, available at www.lankabusinessonline.com/opinion-fdi-in-sri-lanka-a-real-estate-perspective/ (last accessed 9 July 2019).

which has in turn constrained the country's economic growth. This underwhelming record is despite the existence of a number of national institutions to encourage foreign investment, numerous IIAs with other countries, and complying with international legal decisions on cases related to foreign investments even when they could have been legitimately challenged.

The authors have argued that this mediocre performance largely reflects a combination of *political weaknesses*, including a 'leader driven' model for attracting foreign investment and an inconsistent foreign policy, as well as *legal issues*, such as overlapping laws and a poor record for transparency. To address these issues and attract greater foreign investment, they suggest moving swiftly and resolutely to a rules-based approach that goes beyond signing investment treaties. Based on the successful experience of other countries in the Asia-Pacific, the authors have presented a multi-step plan of requisite political and legal measures.

The government has laudably begun some of these measures but it needs to quickly complete and appropriately introduce others, during its possibly short-lived time to pursue them on a bipartisan basis in the current coalition. This would go a long way to ensuring the sustainability of these measures and helping to secure Sri Lanka's future prosperity.

PART IV

Multilateral Rule-Making in Asia on Trade and Investment: From ASEAN to the Comprehensive and Progressive Agreement for Trans-Pacific Partnership

11

The ASEAN Legal Framework for Free Trade and the Promotion and Protection of Foreign Investment

Chester Brown and Henry Winter

11.1 INTRODUCTION

The focus of this collection is the recent pivot to Asia in the field of international investment law, which has seen the emergence of many innovations in the design of international investment agreements (IIAs). This marks a change from the origins of modern IIAs, which were decidedly Euro-centric.[1] This is not to say that Asian States have not played any role in the development of international investment law; the first bilateral investment treaty (BIT) was, after all, concluded by Germany with Pakistan in 1959, and the first claim under a BIT was initiated by a Hong Kong company against Sri Lanka (albeit under the United Kingdom–Sri Lanka BIT).[2] There are of course various analyses and critiques of the policies, which led Asian States (as well as other developing States) to enter into BITs with capital-exporting States in the early years of the nascent IIA regime.[3] But the focus of this chapter is on the activities of Member States of the Association of South-East Asian Nations (ASEAN), in particular their regional cooperation on trade and investment, their legal framework for free trade, and their efforts toward the promotion and protection of foreign investment.

Since the creation of ASEAN in 1967,[4] ASEAN's Member States have taken progressive steps to liberalize their economic and investment policies through the ASEAN

[1] See, e.g., Chester Brown, 'The Evolution of the Regime of International Investment Agreements: History, Economics and Politics' in Marc Bungenberg, Joern Griebel, Stephan Hobe, and August Reinisch (eds.), *International Investment Law: A Handbook* (CH Beck, Hart, Nomos, 2015), pp. 153, 161–75; see also Chester Brown, 'Introduction: The Development and Importance of the Modern Bilateral Investment Treaty', in Chester Brown (ed.), *Commentaries on Selected Model Investment Treaties* (OUP, 2013), pp. 1–13.

[2] *Asian Agricultural Products Ltd v. Sri Lanka*, ICSID Case No ARB/87/3, Award, 27 June 1990.

[3] For example, Jonathan Bonnitcha, Lauge Poulsen, and Michael Waibel, *The Political Economy of the Investment Treaty Regime* (Cambridge University Press, 2017), pp. 207–32; see also Lauge Poulsen, *Bounded Rationality and Economic Diplomacy: The Politics of Investment Treaties in Developing Countries* (Cambridge University Press, 2015).

[4] Bangkok Declaration, signed on 8 August 1967. The original Member States were Malaysia, Indonesia, the Philippines, Singapore and Thailand: available at http://asean.org/the-asean-declaration-bangkok-declaration-bangkok-8-august-1967/ (last accessed 3 June 2018). The original Member States were later joined by Brunei Darussalam (1984), Viet Nam (1995), Laos (1997), Myanmar (1997) and Cambodia (1999). The Agreement on the Establishment of the ASEAN Secretariat was signed on 24 February 1976, 1331 UNTS 243. In addition, there is now a Charter of the Association of Southeast Asian States, signed 20 November 2007 (entered into force on 15 December 2008), available at www.asean.org/storage/images/archive/21069.pdf (last accessed 11 July 2019). See further Simon Chesterman, 'Does ASEAN Exist? The Association of Southeast Asian Nations as an International Legal Person' (2008) 12 *Singapore Yearbook of International Law* 199; and Pieter Jan Kuiper, James Mathis and Natalie Morris-Sharma, *From Treaty-Making to Treaty-Breaking: Models for ASEAN External Trade Agreements* (Cambridge University Press, 2015), pp. 3–7.

framework.[5] After the conclusion of the Treaty of Amity and Cooperation in Southeast Asia of 1976 between the governments of Singapore, Indonesia, Malaysia, Thailand and the Philippines, in which the founding States of ASEAN set out guiding principles for the conduct of their mutual relations,[6] the first steps towards regional economic integration came with the signing of the Agreement on ASEAN Preferential Trading Arrangements (APTA) on 24 February 1977.[7] This was an early attempt at regional integration through the introduction of a system of preferential tariffs as well as the liberalization of non-tariff measures.[8] These policies were further developed, and culminated with the conclusion of the Framework Agreements on Enhancing Economic Cooperation (Framework Agreements) on 28 January 1992, in which the ASEAN Member States agreed to establish an ASEAN Free Trade Area (AFTA) within fifteen years.[9] The Framework Agreements introduced a comprehensive regime for the economic liberalization of the region; primarily through the elimination of both tariff and non-tariff barriers to trade, and the mechanism for achieving this was the Common Effective Preferential Tariff (CEPT) Scheme.[10] ASEAN Member States have also concluded other international agreements which seek to further liberalize trade, such as the ASEAN Framework Agreement on Services (AFAS), which was signed on 15 December 1995;[11] the ASEAN Trade in Goods Agreement, which was signed on 26 February 2009;[12] the ASEAN Agreement on the Movement of Natural Persons, which was

5 See generally Ashique Rahman and Chester Brown, 'Regional Economic Integration in Southeast Asia' (2013) 4 *European Yearbook of International Economic Law* at 353–54; Vivienne Bath and Luke Nottage, 'The ASEAN Comprehensive Investment Agreement and 'ASEAN Plus' – the Australia – New Zealand Free Trade Area (AANZFTA) and the PRC – ASEAN Investment Agreement' in Marc Bungenberg, Joern Griebel, Stephan Hobe, and August Reinisch (eds.), *International Investment Law: A Handbook* (CH Beck, Hart, Nomos, 2015), pp. 283, 283–87.

6 Treaty of Amity and Cooperation in Southeast Asia, signed 24 February 1976, available at http://asean.org/treaty-amity-cooperation-southeast-asia-indonesia-24-february-1976/ (last accessed 11 July 2019). The guiding principles, as set out in Article 2 of the Treaty, are: 'a. Mutual respect for the independence, sovereignty, equality, territorial integrity and national identity of all nations; b. The right of every State to lead its national existence free from external interference, subversion or coercion; c. Non-interference in the internal affairs of one another; d. Settlement of differences or disputes by peaceful means; e. Renunciation of the threat or use of force; f. Effective cooperation among themselves'. See also Rahman and Brown, above n 5, at 354.

7 Agreement on ASEAN Preferential Trading Arrangements, signed 24 February 1977 (entered into force 25 August 1977), available at https://cil.nus.edu.sg/wp-content/uploads/formidable/18/1977-Agreement-on-ASEAN-Preferential-Trading-Arrangements.pdf (last accessed 11 July 2019).

8 See, e.g., Article 3 of the APTA; see also Rahman and Brown, above n 5, at 354.

9 Framework Agreements on Enhancing Economic Cooperation, signed 28 January 1992 (entered into force 28 January 1992), Art. 2(1), available at www.asean.org/storage/images/2012/Economic/AFTA/Common_Effective_Preferential_Tariff/Framework%20Agreements%20on%20Enhancing%20ASEAN%20Economic%20Cooperation%20.pdf (last accessed 11 July 2019); see also Rahman and Brown, above n 5, 354.

10 Ibid., Art. 2(2). The modalities for the CEPT were set out in the Agreement on the Common Effective Preferential Tariff Scheme for the ASEAN Free Trade Area, which was signed and entered into force on the same date as the Framework Agreements: Agreement on the Common Effective Preferential Tariff Scheme for the ASEAN Free Trade Area, signed 28 January 1992 (entered into force 28 January 1992), available at www.asean.org/storage/images/2012/Economic/AFTA/Common_Effective_Preferential_Tariff/Agreement%20on%20the%20Common%20Effective%20Preferential%20Tariff%20Scheme%20for%20the%20ASEAN%20Free%20Trade%20Area.pdf (last accessed 11 July 2019). See also Rahman and Brown, above n 5, at 354–355.

11 ASEAN Framework Agreement on Services, signed on 15 December 1995, available at http://investasean.asean.org/index.php/page/view/asean-free-trade-area-agreements/view/757/newsid/870/asean-framework-agreement-on-services.html (last accessed 11 July 2019); see also the Protocol to Amend the ASEAN Framework Agreement on Services, signed on 2 September 2003 (entered into force on 31 December 2004), available at http://investasean.asean.org/index.php/page/view/asean-free-trade-area-agreements/view/757/newsid/870/asean-framework-agreement-on-services.html (last accessed 11 July 2019).

12 ASEAN Trade in Goods Agreement, signed 26 February 2009, available at http://investasean.asean.org/index.php/page/view/asean-free-trade-area-agreements/view/757/newsid/872/asean-trade-in-goods-agreement.html (last accessed 11 July 2019).

signed on 19 November 2012;[13] and the various ASEAN Mutual Recognition Arrangements, which were concluded to facilitate trade in services.[14]

In addition to the removal of trade barriers, the Member States of ASEAN have made significant progress towards the liberalization of its investment climate.[15] This was initially done through the ASEAN Agreement for the Promotion and Protection of Investment of 1987, and the Framework Agreement on the ASEAN Investment Area of 1998.[16] These two agreements on investment were consolidated into the ASEAN Comprehensive Investment Agreement (ACIA), which was signed on 26 February 2009, and entered into force on 1 March 2012.[17]

Against this backdrop, this chapter considers the early steps towards achieving economic integration in Southeast Asia, namely progress made in achieving the ASEAN FTA, the conclusion and entry into force of the ACIA, the conclusion of ASEAN+1 free trade agreements (FTAs) (with Australia and New Zealand, China, India, Japan, South Korea, and Hong Kong), and the unilateral negotiation of FTAs and BITs by ASEAN Member States (Part I). It then turns to various recent and ongoing developments in regional economic integration, including the negotiation of the Trans-Pacific Partnership Agreement (TPP Agreement) and its revival as the Comprehensive and Progressive Agreement on Trans-Pacific Partnership (CPTPP), the creation of the ASEAN Economic Community (AEC) and the conclusion of the Regional Comprehensive Partnership Agreement (RCEP) (Part II). It concludes with the observation that many innovations in the negotiation of IIAs are emerging from the practice of ASEAN and other Asian States which are having broader implications on the field of international investment law.

11.2 THE BEGINNINGS OF ASEAN AND THE NEGOTIATION OF ECONOMIC INTEGRATION AGREEMENTS IN SOUTHEAST ASIA

As is evident from the earlier introduction, the signing of the Bangkok Declaration on 8 August 1967 ushered in an era of the liberalization of trade and investment for ASEAN Member States. This has been achieved both through multilateral efforts using the ASEAN platform, as well as through the Member States' efforts in negotiating a number of bilateral

13 ASEAN Agreement on the Movement of Natural Persons, signed on 19 November 2012, available at http://investasean.asean.org/index.php/page/view/asean-free-trade-area-agreements/view/757/newsid/869/asean-agreement-on-the-movement-of-natural-persons.html (last accessed 11 July 2019).

14 ASEAN Mutual Recognition Arrangements (which deal with various professions, including engineering services, nursing services, architectural services, surveyors, dental and medical practitioners, accountancy services and tourism professionals), available at http://investasean.asean.org/index.php/page/view/asean-free-trade-area-agreements/view/757/newsid/868/asean-mutual-recognition-arrangements.html (last accessed 11 July 2019).

15 Rahman and Brown, above n 5, at 355–56.

16 Agreement among the Government of Brunei Darussalam, the Republic of Indonesia, Malaysia, the Republic of the Philippines, the Republic of Singapore and the Kingdom of Thailand for the Promotion and Protection of Investments, signed 15 December 1987 (entered into force 2 August 1988), available at https://investmentpolicy.unctad.org/international-investment-agreements/treaty-files/5679/download (last accessed 11 July 2019); Framework Agreement on the ASEAN Investment Area, signed 7 October 1998 (entered into force 25 May 1999), available at http://asean.org/?static_post=framework-agreement-on-the-asean-investment-area-2 (last accessed 11 July 2019).

17 ASEAN Comprehensive Investment Agreement, signed 26 February 2009 (entered into force 1 March 2012), available at www.asean.org/storage/images/2013/economic/aia/ACIA_Final_Text_26%20Feb%202009.pdf (last accessed 11 July 2019); Rahman and Brown, above n 5, at 355.

FTAs and bilateral IIAs.[18] This part reviews the creation and content of the AFTA, the ACIA, and the ACIA+1 Agreements, and ASEAN Member States' unilateral FTAs and IIAs.

11.2.1 *The ASEAN Free Trade Area*

Beginning with the AFTA, this marked a concerted joint effort to achieve free trade among ASEAN Member States. The AFTA's purpose was to create a free trade area primarily through the elimination of tariff and non-tariff barriers to trade through the CEPT scheme.[19] The AFTA establishes comprehensive coverage through a 'negative list' approach, whereby the CEPT applies to all goods originating in ASEAN Member States unless a particular good is expressly excluded by a Member State.[20] Thus, it was reported that the CEPT scheme would cover 'nearly 98 per cent of all tariff lines in ASEAN by the year 2003', after which 'the only products not included in the CEPT Scheme will be those in the General Exceptions category and sensitive agricultural products'.[21] ASEAN States also agreed to enact zero tariff rates on 'virtually all imports by 2010 for the original signatories, and 2015 for the four newer ASEAN members'.[22]

The CEPT's impact on tariff reduction has largely been successful. The average tariff rate of 11.44 per cent among the original ASEAN-6 at the time the AFTA was negotiated was reduced in the subsequent decade to an average tariff rate of 3.33 per cent for the ASEAN-10.[23] And as Somkiat Tangkitvanich and Saowaruj Rattanakhamfu noted in an otherwise critical commentary in 2017:

> The only clear success ASEAN can claim is the reduction of tariffs among member countries. Since the implementation of the Common Effective Preferential Tariff agreement in 1990s, about 99 per cent of tariff lines between member countries have been reduced to zero.[24]

Trade liberalization under the AFTA has been complemented through the conclusion of the AFAS on 15 December 1995.[25] This was a logical next step in ASEAN's trade liberalization, as the services sector accounts for approximately 37 per cent to 74 per cent of GDP in ASEAN countries.[26] The AFAS is designed to eliminate barriers to trade in services, such as market access limitations.[27] The AFAS framework even goes so far as to require ASEAN Member States to adopt specific commitments which go beyond the schedule of specific commitments which they have assumed under the General Agreement on Trade in Services (GATS).[28]

18 Rahman and Brown, above n 5, at 356.

19 Ibid.

20 Ibid.

21 US–ASEAN Business Council, 'Common Effective Preferential Tariff' (17 September 2016), available at www.usasean.org/regions/asean/afta/common-effective-preferential-tariff (last accessed 11 July 2019).

22 Ibid.

23 Myrnia Austria, 'The Pattern of Intra-ASEAN Trade in the Priority Goods Area' (August 2004) at 10, available at http://aadcp2.org/file/03-006e-ExecutiveSummary.pdf (last accessed 11 July 2019).

24 Somkiat Tangkitvanich and Saowaruj Rattanakhamfu, 'Assessing the ASEAN Economic Community' (21 March 2017), available at www.eastasiaforum.org/2017/03/21/assessing-the-asean-economic-community/ (last accessed 11 July 2019).

25 ASEAN Framework Agreement on Services, signed 15 December 1995 (entered into force 30 December 1998) ('AFAS'), available at http://asean.org/?static_post=asean-framework-agreement-on-services (last accessed 11 July 2019).

26 'Trade in Services in ASEAN', available at http://asean.org/asean-economic-community/sectoral-bodies-under-the-purview-of-aem/services/ (last accessed 11 July 2019).

27 AFAS, Article 3; Rahman and Brown, above n 5, at 357.

28 AFAS, Articles 1(c), 4; Rahman and Brown, above n 5, at 357.

Although a comprehensive framework for trade liberalization in the ASEAN region has been established, there have been challenges in implementing relevant trade liberalization measures which has diminished its effectiveness. For example, despite the relative success in overall tariff reduction, it has been observed that 'the free flow of goods among ASEAN member countries continues to be hindered by the use of non-tariff measures ('NTMs')'.[29] Furthermore, although ASEAN has placed importance on the minimization of non-tariff barriers, Tangkitvanich and Rattanakhamfu note that:

> ASEAN has relied on a voluntary approach to reduce them – with very limited success. Under the voluntary approach, member countries can have an adverse incentive to under-report the barriers they are using. What's more, there is no effective monitoring system to keep track of the changes of NTMs among member countries.[30]

In the context of the liberalization of services, the ASEAN Framework Agreement on Services also has its limitations, including that it does not require member States 'to address behind-the-border issues, such as interconnection for telecom services or access to ATMs for banking, which are crucial to the creation of competitive markets'.[31] Thus, as Tangkitvanich and Rattanakhamfu argue, '[s]ervice liberalisation under ASEAN in its current form would fail to create a single service market'.[32]

It therefore appears that although some progress has been made in the field of trade liberalization within ASEAN, further benefits could be realized by ensuring the comprehensive nature of existing agreements, as well as better implementation at the national level.[33]

11.2.2 *The ASEAN Comprehensive Investment Agreement*

In addition to seeking to liberalize trade in goods and services throughout ASEAN, the Member States of ASEAN have used the regional organization as a platform for the liberalization of foreign direct investment within ASEAN. This was initially achieved through negotiation of the ASEAN Agreement for the Promotion and Protection of Investment (1987) and the Framework Agreement on the ASEAN Investment Area (1998).[34] These two intra-ASEAN investment agreements were consolidated by the negotiation of the ACIA on 26 February 2009, and were terminated upon the ACIA's entry into force on 1 March 2012.[35]

As Bath and Nottage have explained, '[t]he purpose of ACIA is not only to consolidate and replace the terms of existing investment agreements but also to establish new principles to facilitate the free flow of investment in (and into) the ASEAN region'.[36] The ACIA is

29 Tangkitvanich and Rattanakhamfu, above n 24.

30 Ibid.

31 Ibid.

32 Ibid.

33 Rahman and Brown, above n 5, at 358.

34 Agreement among the Government of Brunei Darussalam, the Republic of Indonesia, Malaysia, the Republic of the Philippines, the Republic of Singapore and the Kingdom of Thailand for the Promotion and Protection of Investments, signed 15 December 1987 (entered into force 2 August 1988), available at https://investmentpolicy.unctad.org/international-investment-agreements/treaty-files/5679/download (last accessed 11 July 2019); Framework Agreement on the ASEAN Investment Area, signed 7 October 1998 (entered into force 25 May 1999), available at http://asean.org/?static_post=framework-agreement-on-the-asean-investment-area-2 (last accessed 11 July 2019).

35 ASEAN Comprehensive Investment Agreement (full text), 26 February 2009, Art. 47(1), available at www.asean.org/storage/images/2013/economic/aia/ACIA_Final_Text_26%20Feb%202009.pdf (last accessed 11 July 2019); Rahman and Brown, above n 5, at 358.

36 Bath and Nottage, above n 5, p. 287.

therefore designed to achieve the progressive liberalization of the investment regimes of Member States, the joint promotion of the ASEAN region as an 'integrated investment area', the provision of substantive protections to ASEAN investors and the promotion of the facilitation of investment.[37] The formula adopted under the ACIA to promote investment liberalization is to focus on the liberalization of specific sectors, and the relevant policies, if successful, are then implemented across to the entire market. For instance, the ACIA identifies the manufacturing, agricultural, fisheries, forestry, and the mining and quarrying sectors as being the focus of investment liberalization.[38]

The ACIA provides intra-ASEAN investors with the same type of investment protections that are typically found in other IIAs.[39] These protections include, among others, the obligation to provide national treatment to covered investments,[40] the obligation to provide most-favoured-nation (MFN) treatment to covered investments,[41] the obligation to accord fair and equitable treatment to protected investments,[42] the obligation to provide full protection and security to such investments[43] and compensation for the expropriation of investments.[44] The ACIA also contains provisions to protect senior management and the board of directors from discriminatory treatment,[45] and to provide compensation to investors who suffer losses due to armed conflict or other civil strife.[46]

In addition to these substantive protections, Article 25 of the ACIA contains certain obligations for the 'facilitation of investments'. Pursuant to their obligations under Article 25, Member States 'shall endeavour to cooperate in the facilitation of investments into and within ASEAN through', inter alia, 'creating the necessary environment for all forms of investments'.[47] This provision would appear to be (at least in part) designed to remove barriers to the establishment of investments within the ASEAN region.[48]

The dispute settlement provisions of the ACIA allow investors from Member States to initiate arbitration (after a compulsory consultation and negotiation period) against an ASEAN Member State which the investor considers to have breached its obligations under the ACIA.[49] The resulting arbitration may be conducted under the auspices of the International Centre for Settlement of Investment Disputes (ICSID), pursuant to the Arbitration Rules of the United Nations Commission on International Trade Law (UNCITRAL), or under the rules of a regional institution such as the Kuala Lumpur Regional Centre for Arbitration,[50] 'or any other regional centre for arbitration in ASEAN', which would (obviously) include the Singapore International Arbitration Centre.[51] In addition to the application of any institutional or ad hoc Rules selected by

[37] ACIA, Art. 1; Bath and Nottage, above n 5, p. 287.
[38] ACIA, Art. 3(3); Bath and Nottage, above n 5, p. 287; Rahman and Brown, above n 5, at 358–359.
[39] Bath and Nottage, above n 5, pp. 292–94.
[40] ACIA, Art. 5.
[41] Ibid., Art. 6.
[42] Ibid., Art. 11.
[43] Ibid., Art. 11.
[44] Ibid., Art. 14.
[45] Ibid., Art. 8.
[46] Ibid., Art. 12.
[47] Ibid., Art. 25.
[48] Rahman and Brown, above n 5, at 359.
[49] ACIA, Arts. 28 to 41.
[50] Ibid., Art. 33. The authors note that the KLRCA has now been renamed the Asian International Arbitration Centre: see www.aiac.world/ (last accessed 11 July 2019).
[51] ACIA, Art. 33(1)(f).

the Parties, the ACIA contains detailed rules for the arbitration, covering a number of procedural issues.[52]

There has only been one reported investor–State claim brought under one of the precursors to the ACIA, namely the ASEAN Agreement for the Promotion and Protection of Investment (1987). In that case, *Yaung Chi Oo Trading Pte Ltd v. Government of the Union of Myanmar*,[53] Myanmar successfully defended a claim brought by a Singaporean company on jurisdictional grounds, on the basis that the claimant was found to have made its investment before Myanmar had joined ASEAN and ratified the ASEAN Agreement for the Promotion and Protection of Investment (1987). As the claimant's investment preceded Myanmar becoming a State party to the ASEAN Agreement, the claimant was required under Article II(3) of the Agreement to obtain specific written approval for and the registration of its investment by Myanmar, which the claimant had failed to do. Consequently, the tribunal found that it did not have jurisdiction over the claimant's claim.[54] There have not been any reported cases that have been brought under the ACIA.

11.2.3 *ASEAN+1 Agreements*

In addition to entering into the ACIA, which promotes and protects intra-ASEAN investment, the ASEAN platform has also been used to negotiate a number of FTAs with external trade partners.

On 4 November 2002, a Framework Agreement on Comprehensive Economic Cooperation was signed by the Member States of ASEAN with China. The framework agreement led to the creation of the ASEAN–China Free Trade Area ('ASEAN-China FTA') which came into effect on 1 January 2010.[55] Following this, ASEAN and China entered into the Agreement on Investment of the Framework Agreement on Comprehensive Economic Cooperation between the People's Republic of China and ASEAN on 15 August 2009 ('ASEAN-China Investment Agreement').[56] Further FTAs have been concluded with key regional trading partners including Japan (however, this does not include a substantive investment chapter, but only an obligation to 'continue to discuss and negotiate provisions for investment'),[57] India,[58] South Korea,[59] Australia and

52 Ibid., Arts. 28–41.

53 *Yaung Chi Oo Trading Pte Ltd* v. *Government of the Union of Myanmar*, ASEAN ID Case No ARB/01/1, Award of 31 March 2003.

54 Ibid., paras. 53–63.

55 Framework Agreement on Comprehensive Economic Cooperation between the Governments of the Member States of ASEAN and the Government of the People's Republic of China, signed 4 November 2002 (entered into force on 1 January 2010).

56 Agreement on Investment of the Framework Agreement on Comprehensive Economic Cooperation between the People's Republic of China and ASEAN, signed on 15 August 2009, available at https://investmentpolicy.unctad.org/international-investment-agreements/treaty-files/2596/download (last accessed 11 July 2019) ('ASEAN-China Investment Agreement').

57 ASEAN–Japan Comprehensive Economic Partnership Agreement, signed on 28 March 2008 (entered into force 1 December 2008), Art. 51(2), available at https://investmentpolicy.unctad.org/international-investment-agreements/treaty-files/2570/download (last accessed 11 July 2019).

58 Agreement on Investment under the Framework Agreement on Comprehensive Economic Cooperation among the Governments of the Member Countries of ASEAN and India, signed on 12 November 2014 (not yet in force), available at https://investmentpolicy.unctad.org/international-investment-agreements/treaty-files/3337/download (last accessed 11 July 2019).

59 Agreement on Investment under the Framework Agreement on Comprehensive Economic Cooperation among the Governments of the Member Countries of ASEAN and the Republic of Korea, signed on 2 June 2009

New Zealand,[60] and Hong Kong.[61] Formal region-to-region talks on a framework setting out the parameters of a future FTA between ASEAN and the European Union (EU) have also been launched.[62] These 'ASEAN+1' FTAs all seek to liberalize trade in goods and services, and also promote and protect investments between ASEAN and its main trading partners.

11.2.4 *Unilateral Negotiation of FTAs and BITs*

In addition to the various multilateral agreements that are in place both within the ASEAN region and between the ASEAN+1 countries, a number of ASEAN States have separately negotiated FTAs and BITs with both regional trading partners and nations worldwide. Singapore has been particularly active in this practice, having separately negotiated FTAs and, in some cases, standalone Investment Protection Agreements (IPAs), with a number of nations and trading blocs including the European Free Trade Association (EFTA),[63] the United States,[64] Australia,[65] and the EU.[66] In addition, Vietnam has also signed an FTA (EUVFTA) and IPA with the EU.[67]

The EU–Singapore and EU–Vietnam Investment Protection Agreements contain some innovative mechanisms including a permanent 'Investment Tribunal System', the members of which are to be appointed in advance by the EU and by Singapore or Vietnam (as the case may be),[68] and will be subject to strict requirements of independence and integrity.[69] The EU–Singapore IPA and the EU–Vietnam IPA Agreement also provide for the creation of a permanent Appeal Tribunal,[70] which will aim to ensure legal certainty in the interpretation and application of the respective treaties. Enhanced transparency measures will apply to such proceedings, and interested third parties will be allowed to make *amicus curiae* submissions.[71]

In addition to the various agreements that are in place, there are many intra-ASEAN BITs, as well as BITs that have been negotiated with States which are traditional capital-exporting

(entered into force 1 September 2009), available at https://investmentpolicy.unctad.org/international-investment-agreements/treaty-files/3339/download (last accessed 11 July 2019).

60 Bath and Nottage, above n 5, pp. 285–86.

61 Agreement on Investment Among the Governments of the Hong Kong Special Administrative Region and the Member States of ASEAN, signed on 12 November 2017 (not in force), available at https://investmentpolicy.unctad.org/international-investment-agreements/treaty-files/5655/download (last accessed 11 July 2019).

62 ASEAN Economic Integration Brief (No. 01, June 2017), p. 4, available at http://asean.org/storage/2017/06/AEIB_No.01-June-2017_rev.pdf (last accessed 11 July 2019).

63 Singapore–EFTA FTA, signed 26 June 2002 (entered into force 1 January 2003), available at www.efta.int/free-trade/free-trade-agreements/singapore.aspx (last accessed 11 July 2019).

64 Singapore–United States FTA, signed 6 May 2003 (entered into force 1 January 2004), available at www.ustr.gov/trade-agreements/free-trade-agreements/singapore-fta (last accessed 11 July 2019).

65 Singapore–Australia FTA, signed 17 February 2003 (entered into force 28 July 2003), available at www.dfat.gov.au/fta/safta/index.html (last accessed 11 July 2019).

66 Singapore–European Union FTA, signed on 19 October 2018 (not yet in force); see also Singapore–EU Investment Protection Agreement, signed on 19 October 2018 (not yet in force), available at http://trade.ec.europa.eu/doclib/press/index.cfm?id=961 (last accessed 11 July 2019).

67 Vietnam–European Union FTA, signed on 30 June 2019 (not yet in force); Vietnam–EU Investment Protection Agreement, signed on 30 June 2019 (not yet in force), available at http://trade.ec.europa.eu/doclib/press/index.cfm?id=1437 (last accessed 11 July 2019).

68 EU–Singapore IPA, signed on 19 October 2018 (not yet in force), Art. 3.9; EU – Vietnam Investment Protection Agreement, Art. 3.38.

69 EU–Singapore IPA, Arts. 3.11, 3.44(4); EU – Vietnam IPA, Arts. 3.8, 3.23.

70 EU–Singapore IPA, Art. 3.10; EU – Vietnam IPA, Art. 3.39.

71 EU–Singapore IPA, Art. 3.16; EU – Vietnam IPA, Art. 3.46.

States.[72] For example, Indonesia has separately negotiated BITs with a number of ASEAN partners, including Vietnam, Malaysia, Thailand and Laos. Indonesia also has BITs with other Asian nations including India and China, and with traditional capital-exporting countries including the United Kingdom and Germany.[73] Another ASEAN member State, Malaysia, has entered into seventy-one BITs.[74] Singapore, for its part, has forty-nine BITs and thirty-five other investment agreements, including several FTAs.[75] These overlapping agreements create a 'spaghetti bowl' of rights and obligations which may bring about the potential risks of trade diversions and other market-distorting effects, as well as uncertainties regarding the potential application of multiple IIAs to the same claim.[76]

11.3 RECENT DEVELOPMENTS IN SOUTHEAST ASIA RELATING TO ECONOMIC INTEGRATION

The ASEAN Member States do not appear to be content with the progress that has been made in the furtherance of their economic integration, as they are pressing with bolder plans for even deeper regional integration and the creation of more extensive trade ties with non-Asian partners. These include in particular the CPTPP (which, although not an ASEAN initiative, involves a number of ASEAN Member States), the furtherance of the ASEAN Economic Community, and the negotiation of the RCEP.

11.3.1 *Negotiation of the Trans-Pacific Partnership Agreement, and Its Resurrection as the Comprehensive and Progressive Agreement for Trans-Pacific Partnership*

The original TPP Agreement was signed in Auckland, New Zealand, on 4 February 2016, after more than a decade of negotiations. The original twelve signatory States were Brunei Darussalam, Chile, New Zealand and Singapore (the original four from 2004), Australia, Malaysia, Peru, the United States and Vietnam (which joined the negotiations in 2008), plus

[72] Rahman and Brown, above n 5, at 361–62. For further commentary on the proliferation of BITs in Asia, see generally Luke Nottage and Romesh Weeramantry, 'Investment Arbitration in Asia: Five Perspectives on Law and Practice' (2012) 28 *Arbitration International* 19; Luke Nottage and Sakda Thanitcul, 'International Investment Arbitration in Southeast Asia: Guest Editorial' (2016) *Legal Studies Research Paper No.16/95*; Luke Nottage, 'The Investment Chapter and ISDS in the TPP: Lessons from Southeast Asia' (2017) *ISEAS Economics Working Paper No. 2017–2*.

[73] See, e.g., Simon Butt, 'Foreign Investment in Indonesia: The Problem of Legal Uncertainty' in Vivienne Bath and Luke Nottage (eds.), *Foreign Investment and Dispute Resolution Law and Practice in Asia* (Routledge, 2011), pp. 112, 117–18, 129–30. Indonesia has recently embarked on a programme of terminating its BITs: Luke Eric Peterson, 'Indonesia Ramps Up Termination of BITs – and Kills Survival Clause in One Such Treaty – But Faces New $600 Million Claim from Indian Mining Investor', Investment Arbitration Reporter, 20 November 2015, available at www.bilaterals.org/?indonesia-ramps-up-termination-of&lang=fr (last accessed 11 July 2019).

[74] Investment Policy Hub, Malaysia, available at https://investmentpolicy.unctad.org/international-investment-agreements/countries/127/malaysia (last accessed 11 July 2019). See also Salim Farrar, 'Foreign Investment Laws and the Role of FDI in Malaysia's 'New' Economic Model', in Bath and Nottage (eds.), above n 47, pp. 153, 164–66.

[75] Investment Policy Hub, Singapore, available at https://investmentpolicy.unctad.org/international-investment-agreements/countries/190/singapore (last accessed 11 July 2019). See also Jean Ho, 'Singapore' in Chester Brown (ed.), *Commentaries on Selected Model Investment Treaties* (Oxford University Press, 2013), p. 623.

[76] For example, Wojciech Paczyński and Michael Gasiorek (eds.), *Economic Integration in South East Asia and the Impact on the EU*, Centre for the Analysis of Regional Integration at Sussex (Final Report of 23 March 2011), p. 37, available at http://trade.ec.europa.eu/doclib/docs/2011/may/tradoc_147874.pdf (last accessed 11 July 2019); see also Vivienne Bath, 'ASEAN: The Liberalisation of Investment through Regional Agreements' in Leon Trakman and Nicola Ranieri (eds.), *Regionalism in International Investment Law* (Oxford University Press, 2013), p. 182.

Canada, Japan and Mexico (which joined in 2012–13). The TPP Agreement was described by its negotiating partners upon the adoption of the TPP text on 5 October 2015 as follows:

> After more than five years of intensive negotiations, we have come to an agreement that will support jobs, drive sustainable growth, foster inclusive development, and promote innovation across the Asia-Pacific region. Most importantly, the agreement achieves the goal we set forth of an ambitious, comprehensive, high standard and balanced agreement that will benefit our nation's citizens.[77]

The Ministers of the twelve signatory States went on to express the belief that:

> TPP brings higher standards to nearly 40 percent of the global economy. In addition to liberalizing trade and investment between us, the agreement addresses the challenges our stakeholders face in the 21st century, while taking into account the diversity of our levels of development. We expect this historic agreement to promote economic growth, support higher-paying jobs; enhance innovation, productivity and competitiveness; raise living standards; reduce poverty in our countries; and to promote transparency, good governance, and strong labor and environmental protections.[78]

Thus, the TPP Agreement sought to enhance market access through the elimination of tariffs and other barriers to goods and services trade and investment. As Rahman and Brown have explained, the TPP Agreement 'also sought to contain a number of innovative features which reflect the adoption of a holistic approach to regional economic liberalisation'.[79] In this regard, the TPP Agreement was to address 'the concerns of small and medium-sized enterprises regarding their understanding of the trade agreement so that small- to medium-sized businesses are better equipped to trade internationally through utilisation of the TPP Agreement'.[80]

The TPP Agreement made provision for capacity-building in developing States, and also included comprehensive chapters on e-commerce, the environment (including, potentially, rules on climate change, biodiversity and the conservation of marine life), financial services regulation (including commitments designed to allow regulators to better react to ensure the stability and integrity of financial markets in the event of a financial crisis), investment protection, commitments on labour rights protection, and a number of commitments which build upon the framework of the World Trade Organisation (WTO), including rules on Technical Barriers to Trade (TBT), Sanitary and Phytosanitary Standards (SPS) and Trade-Related Aspects of Intellectual Property (TRIPS).[81]

The TPP Agreement also included an investment chapter with the main protections usually found in other IIAs, such as non-discrimination compared to local investors (i.e. national treatment in 'like circumstances'),[82] non-discrimination compared to third-country investors (i.e. MFN treatment in 'like circumstances'),[83] fair and equitable treatment,[84] full

77 'TPP Ministers' Statement' (5 October 2015), available at http://dfat.gov.au/trade/agreements/not-yet-in-force/tpp/Pages/ministers-statement.aspx (last accessed 11 July 2019).

78 Ibid.

79 Rahman and Brown, above n 5, at 363.

80 Ibid.

81 Ibid.

82 Trans-Pacific Partnership Agreement, 4 February 2016, Art. 9.4, available at https://ustr.gov/trade-agreements/free-trade-agreements/trans-pacific-partnership/tpp-full-text (last accessed 11 July 2019).

83 TPP Agreement, Art. 9.5.

84 Ibid., Art. 9.6 and Annex 9-A.

protection and security,[85] and compensation for direct and indirect expropriation.[86] It also contained a 'denial of benefits' provision, which seeks to limit the scope of forum shopping in circumstances where an investor has 'no substantial business activities in the territory of any Party'.[87] The TPP Agreement also built in public welfare considerations for when foreign investors allege violations, such as Annex 9-B, which elaborated on what constituted an 'indirect expropriation'.[88] Article 9.16 also added that a host State may use measures that 'it considers appropriate to ensure that investment activity in its territory is undertaken in a manner sensitive to environmental, health or other regulatory objectives'.

The Investor–State Dispute Settlement (ISDS) procedure was set out at Section B of Chapter 9 of the TPP Agreement. Before any claim may be resolved by arbitration, a claimant investor must first attempt six months of consultation and negotiation, which may include 'the use of non-binding, third party procedures, such as good offices, conciliation or mediation'.[89] There was also a 'fork in the road' provision which required claimant investors to waive 'any right to initiate or continue before any court or administrative tribunal' of the host State.[90] A tribunal must also decide preliminary objections, such as those relating to a tribunal's jurisdiction or that a claimant's claim is 'manifestly without legal merit' as soon as possible after the tribunal is constituted.[91] The tribunal may also award a party's reasonable costs if such objection was 'frivolous'.[92]

The TPP Agreement also contained a provision dealing with the transparency of the arbitral proceedings,[93] pursuant to which certain documents would be made available to the public (such as the notice of arbitration, the pleadings and the final award), public hearings and written *amicus curiae* submissions.[94] The TPP Agreement, however, did not contain an appellate review mechanism. It merely states that in the event that 'an appellate mechanism for reviewing awards rendered by investor-State dispute settlement tribunals is developed in the future under other institutional arrangements, the Parties shall consider whether awards rendered under Article 9.29 (Awards) should be subject to that appellate mechanism'.[95]

However, the United States withdrew from the TPP Agreement on 30 January 2017, following the election of President Trump.[96] This left the ratification of the TPP Agreement, and its entry into force, in some doubt.[97] Nonetheless, discussions soon began

85 Ibid., Art. 9.6.
86 Ibid., Art. 9.8.
87 Ibid., Art. 9.15.
88 Ibid., Footnote 14 of Chapter 9; *see also* Luke Nottage, 'The Investment Chapter and ISDS in the TPP: Lessons from Southeast Asia' (2017) *ISEAS Economics Working Paper No. 2017–2*.
89 TPP Agreement, Arts. 9.18 and 9.19.
90 Ibid., Art. 9.21.
91 Ibid., Art. 9.23(4).
92 Ibid., Art. 9.23(6).
93 TPP Agreement, Art. 9.24.
94 Ibid., Art. 9.23(3).
95 Ibid., Art. 9.23(11).
96 Letter dated 30 January 2017 from Maria Pagan to the Trans-Pacific Partnership Depositary, available at https://ustr.gov/sites/default/files/files/Press/Releases/1–30-17%20USTR%20Letter%20to%20TPP%20Depositary.pdf (last accessed 11 July 2019).
97 See, e.g., Vanessa Lide, 'OK, the Trans-Pacific Partnership is Dead. What Was it?', The Washington Post, 23 January 2017, available at www.washingtonpost.com/news/monkey-cage/wp/2017/01/23/okay-the-trans-pacific-partnership-is-dead-what-was-it/?utm_term=.6dacc6ef8be9 (last accessed 11 July 2019); Karen Barlow, 'The TPP Is Not Dead, but It's Not Alive, Either', The Huffington Post, 24 January 2017, available at www.huffingtonpost.com.au/2017/01/23/the-tpp-is-not-dead-but-its-not-alive-either_a_21661133/ (last accessed 11 July 2019).

among other TPP signatory States on the question whether the TPP could be resurrected, even without the participation of the United States.[98] After months of negotiations, trade ministers from Australia, Brunei Darussalam, Canada, Chile, Japan, Malaysia, Mexico, New Zealand, Peru, Singapore and Vietnam (also known as the 'TPP-11') announced on November 2017 that they had reached an agreement on the core elements of the CPTPP.[99] The text of the CPTPP was signed on 8 March 2018.[100]

The investment chapter of the CPTPP is largely similar to that which was contained in the TPP. As Jarrod Hepburn explains:

> In relation to the TPP's investment chapter, the new agreement makes only two changes. First, investor-state arbitration will not be permitted for alleged breaches of investment agreements – that is, contracts concluded by CPTPP states with particular investors in the natural resources, utilities or infrastructure sectors – or investment authorisations. Investor claims remain available for alleged breaches of the protections in the CPTPP itself. . . .
>
> Second, the CPTPP excludes the possibility of claiming a breach of the minimum standard of treatment by investors in the financial services sector. Other claims – such as breaches of provisions on expropriation or free transfer of capital – remain available.[101]

A number of States have opted out of the ISDS provisions on a bilateral basis, namely Australia and New Zealand (which had concluded similar side letters in the context of the AANZFTA), New Zealand and Peru, and in the case of Brunei, Malaysia and Vietnam, 'New Zealand has agreed that a respondent host state must provide specific consent for an investor-state claim to proceed to arbitration under the CPTPP provisions'.[102]

The CPTPP entered into force on 30 December 2018 for Australia, Canada, Japan, Mexico, New Zealand and Singapore; and it entered into force on 14 January 2019 for Vietnam. The CPTPP will enter into force for Brunei Darussalam, Chile, Malaysia and Peru sixty days after they complete their respective ratification processes.[103]

11.3.2 *The ASEAN Economic Community*

At the Bali Summit in 2003, the ASEAN Member States declared that the formation of the AEC 'shall be the goal of regional economic integration'.[104] In January 2007, the ASEAN

98 See, e.g., Barlow, above n 97.

99 Australian Department of Foreign Affairs and Trade, Trans-Pacific Partnership Ministerial Statement, 11 November 2017, available at http://dfat.gov.au/trade/agreements/not-yet-in-force/tpp-11/news/Pages/trans-pacific-partnership-ministerial-statement.aspx (last accessed 11 July 2019).

100 Comprehensive and Progressive Agreement for Trans-Pacific Partnership, signed on 8 March 2018, available at www.mfat.govt.nz/en/trade/free-trade-agreements/free-trade-agreements-concluded-but-not-in-force/cptpp/comprehensive-and-progressive-agreement-for-trans-pacific-partnership-text/#chapters (last accessed 11 July 2019).

101 Jarrod Hepburn, 'Revived Trans-Pacific Partnership (TPP) Text is Released, With a Few Tweaks to the Previously-Negotiated Investment Chapter; Australia and New Zealand Continue to Disapply ISDS Between Them', Investment Arbitration Reporter, 21 February 2018, available at www.iareporter.com/articles/revived-trans-pacific-partnership-tpp-treaty-text-is-released-with-a-few-tweaks-to-the-previously-negotiated-investment-chapter-australia-and-new-zealand-continue-to-disapply-isds-between-them/ (last accessed 11 July 2019).

102 Jarrod Hepburn, 'Investor-State Arbitration Opt-Outs Proliferate in Newly-Disclosed Trans-Pacific Partnership Agreement Side Letters', Investment Arbitration Reporter, 8 March 2018, available at www.iareporter.com/articles/investor-state-arbitration-opt-outs-proliferate-in-newly-disclosed-trans-pacific-partnership-agreement-side-letters/ (last accessed 11 July 2019).

103 CPTPP, Art. 30.5.

104 ASEAN Economic Community Blueprint (20 November 2007), para. 2, available at http://asean.org/wp-content/uploads/archive/5187–10.pdf (last accessed 11 July 2019).

Member States decided to bring forward the agenda for the formation of the AEC, bringing its establishment forward from 2020 to 31 December 2015.[105] The AEC Blueprint (2008–2015), adopted by all ASEAN members in 2007, set out the key characteristics of the AEC:

> Based on the above and taking into consideration the importance of external trade to ASEAN and the need for the ASEAN Community as a whole to remain outward looking, the AEC envisages the following key characteristics: (a) a single market and production base, (b) a highly competitive economic region, (c) a region of equitable economic development, and (d) a region fully integrated into the global economy. These characteristics are interrelated and mutually reinforcing. Incorporating the required elements of each characteristic in one Blueprint shall ensure the consistency and coherence of these elements as well as their implementation and proper coordination among relevant stakeholders.[106]

The AEC Blueprint (2008–2015) identified a number of elements that would need to be implemented to achieve the AEC's economic liberalization goals. For instance, it was suggested that a single market and production base would be achieved by allowing the 'free' flow of goods, services, investments and skilled labour and the 'freer' flow of capital.[107] The free flow of goods was to be achieved through measures typically found in FTAs, such as the elimination of tariffs and non-tariff barriers, implementation of effective rules of origin, further trade facilitation between Member States, customs integration, and the elimination of technical barriers to trade.[108] It can be said that the AEC Blueprint recommended the adoption of a comprehensive approach towards economic liberalization.[109] This comprehensive vision for the AEC has been described as a 'hybrid FTA-plus arrangement' as it included characteristics of a common market but does not go so far as to create a common external tariff.[110]

The AEC Blueprint (2008–2015) culminated with the AEC being formally established on 31 December 2015, which marked an important milestone in ASEAN's journey towards deeper regional economic integration.[111] A new blueprint, the AEC Blueprint 2025, was also adopted by the ASEAN Leaders at the 27th ASEAN Summit on 22 November 2015 in Kuala Lumpur, Malaysia, which provides broad directions for the AEC from 2016 to 2025. Along with the ASEAN Community Vision 2025, and the ASEAN Political-Security Community (APSC) Blueprint 2025 and the ASEAN Socio-Cultural Community (ASCC) Blueprint 2025, the AEC Blueprint 2025 forms part of a suite of ASEAN blueprints collectively under the heading 'ASEAN 2025: Forging Ahead Together'.[112]

Similar to the AEC Blueprint (2008–2015), the AEC Blueprint 2025 consists of five interrelated and mutually reinforcing characteristics: (a) a highly integrated and cohesive economy; (b) a competitive, innovative and dynamic ASEAN; (c) enhanced connectivity and sectoral cooperation; (d) a resilient, inclusive, people-oriented and people-centred ASEAN;

[105] Cebu Declaration on the Acceleration of the Establishment of an ASEAN Community by 2015, 13 January 2007, available at http://asean.org/cebu-declaration-on-th-acceleration-of-the-establishment-of-an-asean-community-by-2015/ (last accessed 11 July 2019).

[106] ASEAN Economic Community Blueprint (20 November 2007), para. 8, available at http://asean.org/wp-content/uploads/archive/5187–10.pdf (last accessed 11 July 2019); Rahman and Brown, above n 5, at 364.

[107] Ibid.

[108] Ibid., paras. 14–17, 19.

[109] Rahman and Brown, above n 5, at 365.

[110] Ibid.

[111] 'ASEAN Economic Integration Brief', above n 62, p. 7, available at http://asean.org/storage/2017/06/AEIB_No.01-June-2017_rev.pdf (last accessed 11 July 2019).

[112] 'ASEAN Economic Community', available at http://asean.org/asean-economic-community/ (last accessed 11 July 2019).

and (e) a global ASEAN.[113] ASEAN has further noted that these five characteristics will be implemented through the work plans of various ASEAN sectoral bodies. To further aid implementation of the AEC Blueprint 2025, ASEAN will also seek partnership arrangements with the private sector, industry associations and the wider community at the regional and national levels to 'ensure an inclusive and participatory approach to the integration process'.[114]

ASEAN has further stated that the aim of the AEC Blueprint 2025 is to:

> lead towards an ASEAN that is more proactive, having had in place the structure and frameworks to operate as an economic community, cultivating its collective identity and strength to engage with the world, responding to new developments, and seizing new opportunities. The new Blueprint will not only ensure that the 10 ASEAN Member States are economically integrated, but are also sustainably and gainfully integrated in the global economy, thus contributing to the goal of shared prosperity.[115]

Since 2016, most sectoral work plans under the various AEC ministerial bodies have been adopted to operationalize the strategic measures outlined in the Blueprint, the most recent of which were the ASEAN Work Plan on Good Regulatory Practice and the Strategic Action Plan 2016–2025 for ASEAN Taxation Cooperation.[116] The effectiveness of the AEC Blueprint 2025 to respond to global and regional opportunities and challenges will largely depend on the extent to which its measures are adopted. The AEC 2025 Monitoring and Evaluation (M&E) Framework will therefore likely play a key role in assessing the implementation progress of the AEC Blueprint 2025.

11.3.3 *Regional Comprehensive Economic Partnership*

The Regional Comprehensive Economic Partnership (RCEP) is an FTA which was negotiated between the ASEAN Member States and ASEAN's six existing FTA partners – the People's Republic of China, the Republic of Korea, Japan, India, and Australia and New Zealand. The RCEP was built upon the existing ASEAN+1 FTAs with the intention of strengthening economic linkages, enhancing trade and investment related activities, and contributing to minimising the development gap among the parties.[117]

The RCEP was launched at the 21st ASEAN and Related Summit in Phnom Penh, Cambodia, in 2012, and the negotiations commenced early the following year. It sought to be an ASEAN-led process through which ASEAN would broaden and deepen its economic engagements with its FTA partners, with the purpose of leading to lead to greater economic integration, support equitable economic development and strengthening economic cooperation among the countries involved.[118] The RCEP covers trade in goods, trade in services,

[113] 'ASEAN Economic Community Blueprint 2025' (November 2015), para. 3, available at www.asean.org/wp-content/uploads/images/2015/November/aec-page/AEC-Blueprint-2025-FINAL.pdf (last accessed 11 July 2019).

[114] 'ASEAN Economic Community', available at http://asean.org/asean-economic-community/ (last accessed 11 July 2019).

[115] Ibid.

[116] 'ASEAN Economic Integration Brief', above n 62, p. 3, available at http://asean.org/storage/2017/06/AEIB_No.01-June-2017_rev.pdf (last accessed 11 July 2019).

[117] ASEAN, Regional Comprehensive Economic Partnership, available at http://asean.org/?static_post=rcep-regional-comprehensive-economic-partnership (last accessed 11 July 2019).

[118] Ministry of Trade and Industry: Singapore, Factsheet: What You Need to Know about Regional Comprehensive Economic Partnership (June 2014), available at www.mti.gov.sg/Resources/feature-articles/2014/FACTSHEET-WHAT-YOU-NEED-TO-KNOW-ABOUT (last accessed 11 July 2019).

investment, economic and technical cooperation, intellectual property, competition, dispute settlement and other issues.[119] One of the main aims of the RCEP is the progressive elimination of tariff and non-tariff barriers on substantially all trade in goods so as to establish a free trade area among the parties.[120] Priority is to be given to early tariff elimination on products of interest to the least developed ASEAN Member States.[121] Rules and obligations on trade in services under the RCEP are also to be consistent with the GATS and will be directed towards achieving liberalization commitments which build on the RCEP participants' commitments under the GATS and the ASEAN+1 FTAs.[122]

The RCEP has been subject to extensive negotiation. There were thirty-one rounds of negotiations, with the thirty-first round taking place (virtually) on 9 July 2020, and eight RCEP Ministerial Meetings, with the final one being held (virtually) on 27 August 2020, and an 'Inter-Sessional Virtual RCEP Ministerial Meeting' was held on 14 October 2020.[123] The RCEP negotiations took place behind closed doors and on 15 November 2020, the RCEP was signed by the ASEAN Member States, Australia, China, Japan, Korea, and New Zealand (i.e., all of the negotiating States with the exception of India.)[124]

In April 2016, the draft of the RCEP's investment chapter (dated October 2015) was leaked online.[125] While the authenticity of this document does not appear to have been verified (and the link to the draft has since been taken down from the website hosting it), the draft provided an insight into the proposed text of the investment chapter as well as into each negotiating party's initial positions.[126] For example, the draft investment chapter contained the following draft provision on 'Expropriation and Compensation':[127]

> [A, I: A Party shall not] [Au, C, J, K: No Party may] [NZ: No Party shall] expropriate or nationalise [NZ: or subject to measures equivalent to nationalisation or expropriation] [A, Au, C, J, K, NZ: a] covered investment/s [I: in its territory or adopt any other measures] [A, Au, C, J, K: either directly or through measures [I: having an effect] equivalent to expropriation [A, Au, C, J, K: or nationalisation ('expropriation')][A: 2], except:
>
> a. [A, Au, C, J, K, NZ: for a public purpose] [I: in the public interest];
> b. in/on a non-discriminatory [A, Au, C, J, K, NZ: manner] [I: basis];

119 Guiding Principles and Objectives for Negotiating the Regional Comprehensive Economic Partnership, available at https://asean.org/storage/2012/05/RCEP-Guiding-Principles-public-copy.pdf (last accessed 11 July 2019).

120 Ibid.

121 As determined by the criteria issued by ECOSOC's Committee for Development Policy.

122 As determined by the criteria issued by ECOSOC's Committee for Development Policy.

123 'Regional Comprehensive Economic Partnership: Latest News', available at https://dfat.gov.au/trade/agreements/negotiations/rcep/news/Pages/rcep-news.aspx (last accessed 27 October 2019).

124 Joint Leaders' Statement on the Regional Comprehensive Economic Partnership (15 November 2020), available at https://www.dfat.gov.au/trade/agreements/not-yet-in-force/rcep/news/joint-leaders-statement-regional-comprehensive-economic-partnership-rcep (last accessed 1 February 2021).

125 For an analysis of the leaked RCEP investment chapter, see Amokura Kawharu and Luke Nottage, 'Models for Investment Treaties in the Asian Region: An Underview' (2017) 34(3) *Arizona Journal of International and Comparative Law* 462–528, available at https://papers.ssrn.com/sol3/papers.cfm?abstract_id=2845088 (last accessed 11 July 2019).

126 Each party has an identifier next to a clause, phrase or word it supports. For instance 'A' for ASEAN, 'AU' for Australia, 'CH' for China, 'I' for India, 'JP' for Japan, 'KR' for South Korea, and 'NZ' for New Zealand.

127 All of the provisions in the draft are titled 'Article XX' and will therefore not be referenced.

c. On payment of [A, Au, I, J, K, NZ: prompt, adequate] [A, Au, J, K, NZ: and effective] compensation [Au, C, J, NZ: accordance with] [Au, J, NZ: paragraphs 2 through 4] [C: this Article] and
d. in accordance with [C: applicable legal procedure of that Party and] due process of law. [K: and Article X.5.1 through X.5.3.]

The final version of Article 10.13, as signed in November 2020, reveals the outcome of the negotiations, which evidently involved some compromise. The RCEP also contains the other usual standards of protection, including fair and equitable treatment, national treatment, MFN treatment, protections against the denial of justice, the free transfer of funds, and full protection and security. However, significantly, it does not contain ISDS provisions, with this being included in the Work Programme under Article 10.18.

The RCEP's conclusion has led to the creation of the world's largest trade bloc, covering nearly one third of the global economy. The combined output of the sixteen Participating Countries amounted to US$22.4 trillion or 30.6 per cent of world output in 2015. The total trade among the Participating Countries amounted to US$11.9 trillion in 2015, while total FDI inflows to Participating Countries reached US$329.6 billion.[128]

11.4 CONCLUSION

Although ASEAN was initially established as a quasi-political response to regional developments, it has over the years become a successful platform for the economic liberalization of the region, and the ASEAN Member States have become active participants in the development and negotiation of the international investment regime.

The ASEAN area is highly dependent on trade and investment originating from outside the region, and it therefore comes as no surprise that in recent years, a number of ASEAN+1 FTAs have been negotiated with regional powers. Through the negotiation of trade and investment agreements with global reach, Southeast Asia is now entering a new phase in economic liberalization. The successful negotiation of the CPTPP Agreement promises to be a landmark moment for the region, as is the long-awaited RCEP, even without India's participation (at this stage). What can be seen is that the IIAs which have been negotiated by ASEAN Member States – such as the EU–Vietnam IPA and the CPTPP – contain innovations that may have important implications for the further development of the field of international investment law.

128 'Joint Leaders' Statement on the Regional Comprehensive Economic Partnership' (8 September 2016), Vientiane, Lao PDR, available at http://asean.org/storage/2016/09/56-RCEP_Joint-Leaders-Statement_8-September-2016.pdf (last accessed 11 July 2019).

12

ISDS Reform and the EU–Vietnam Investment Protection Agreement

Challenge Accepted!

Nguyen Manh Dzung and Dang Vu Minh Ha

12.1 PAVING THE WAY FOR VIETNAM TOWARDS A NEW GENERATION OF FREE TRADE AGREEMENTS

Vietnam is now party to sixty-six bilateral investment treaties (BITs),[1] eleven concluded free trade agreements (FTAs) (ten of which are in effect) and in the process of negotiation for five others.[2] Recognizing early on that it would be one of the biggest potential beneficiaries of the mega-regional Trans-Pacific Partnership (TPP) – as it was then, before the withdrawal of the United States[3] – Vietnam had engaged in active economic reform to enjoy the benefits that would be offered by the TPP. In particular, the Government and the National Assembly had taken the initiative by introducing more than 100 pieces of new or reformed legislation to prepare the local framework for compliance with the international standards of the trade deal.[4]

The conclusion of the Comprehensive and Progressive Agreement for Trans-Pacific Partnership (CPTPP),[5] the revamped version of the TPP without the United States, signed in Chile in March 2018,[6] has been a testament to the commitment of the eleven signatories to the multilateral treaty to the collective goals of greater trade liberalization and regional economic integration. However, a number of provisions related to investment in general

[1] As of October 2019, according to UNCTAD's International Investment Agreements Navigator: see https://investmentpolicy.unctad.org/international-investment-agreements/countries/229/viet-nam (last accessed 14 October 2019). See also Tran Anh Tuan, '*The Mechanism on International Investment Dispute Resolution in Accordance with The Commitments under the Treaties on Encouragement and Protection of Investment in the Free Trade Areas and the Economic Partnership*' in Judicial Academy – Ministry of Justice, *Material for Training on the Knowledge of Law & International Dispute Resolution* (October 2016); and Nguyen Manh Dzung and Nguyen Thi Thu Trang, 'International Investment Dispute Resolution in Vietnam: Opportunities and Challenges' in Luke Nottage and Julien Chaisse (eds.), *International Investment Treaties and Arbitration Across Asia* (Brill Nijhoff, 2017), at pp. 280–302.

[2] As of December 2016, according to the Report of Minister of Trade & Industry to the Government dated 21 December 2016 regarding Resolution No. 1052/NQ-UBTVQH13 on guidelines, responsibilities and solutions to promote the process of economic integration.

[3] See, e.g., 'Vietnam vows full speed ahead with economic reforms, with or without TTP', South China Morning Post, 29 November 2016, available at www.scmp.com/news/asia/southeast-asia/article/2050035/vietnam-vows-full-speed-ahead-economic-reforms-or-without (last accessed 11 July 2019).

[4] Ibid.

[5] The CPTPP is an FTA between eleven countries: Australia, Brunei Darussalam, Canada, Chile, Japan, Malaysia, Mexico, New Zealand, Peru, Singapore and Vietnam. All eleven CPTPP countries are members of the Asia-Pacific Economic Cooperation (APEC).

[6] See, e.g., Tim McDonald, 'Asia-Pacific trade deal signed by 11 nations', BBC News, 8 March 2018, available at www.bbc.com/news/business-43326314 (last accessed 11 July 2019).

and the mechanism of ISDS in particular are listed as suspended provisions which will need further discussion and negotiation in the future.[7] This is coupled with the fact that New Zealand has signed separate agreements by way of side letters to exclude compulsory ISDS between them and five other CPTPP signatories, namely Australia, Brunei Darussalam, Malaysia, Peru and Vietnam,[8] thereby putting the effectiveness of the ISDS mechanism under this multilateral treaty into question.

On the other hand, the negotiations for the Regional Comprehensive Economic Partnership (RCEP), a separate agreement involving sixteen countries (including the 10 ASEAN members, as well as Japan, South Korea, Australia, New Zealand, India and China) intensified after the withdrawal of the United States from the TPP, which led many to believe that the TPP was 'dead'.[9] This agreement was expected to fill the perceived gap left by the TPP, as seven out of sixteen countries negotiating the RCEP, namely Australia, Brunei, Japan, Malaysia, New Zealand, Singapore and Vietnam, were signatories to the original TPP. However, the announcement by the eventual signatory countries of the CPTPP that negotiations for a modified CPTPP were underway, coupled with the recent signing of the CPTPP,[10] has slowed down the process of negotiation of the RCEP as predicted,[11] particularly given the differences in approach of the countries to the RCEP negotiations that do not have FTAs amongst them.[12] In any event, Vietnam has leveraged on the momentum for domestic reforms generated by the original TPP and CPTPP, taking strides to adapt and become a part of the global economic playground by welcoming opportunities that other trade deals would bring in aspiring towards greater international integration.

One such trade deal is the EVIPA, the subject of this chapter, which is expected to help Vietnam to expand its potential and benefit from the consequential growth of its trade opportunities. Notably, the EVIPA single-handedly addressed both options of ISDS reform considered by the Centre for International Dispute Settlement (CIDS),[13] as reported in the recent note of the Secretariat of the United Nations Commission on International Trade Law (UNCITRAL), namely (i) a permanent international dispute settlement body; and (ii) an appeal mechanism for investor–State arbitral awards.[14] Given its novelty, this chapter aims to

[7] The list of suspended provisions can be found at https://dfat.gov.au/trade/agreements/in-force/cptpp/outcomes-documents/Pages/cptpp-suspensions-explained.aspx (last accessed 14 October 2019).

[8] Hon. David Parker, 'New Zealand signs side letters curbing investor-state dispute settlement', New Zealand government website, 9 March 2018, available at www.beehive.govt.nz/release/new-zealand-signs-side-letters-curbing-investor-state-dispute-settlement. The side letters are available on the website of the New Zealand Ministry for Foreign Affairs & Trade, at www.mfat.govt.nz/en/trade/free-trade-agreements/free-trade-agreements-concluded-but-not-in-force/cptpp/comprehensive-and-progressive-agreement-for-trans-pacific-partnership-text/ (both last accessed 11 July 2019).

[9] See, e.g., Vanessa Lide, 'Okay, the Trans-Pacific Partnership Is Dead. What Was It?', *The Washington Post*, 23 January 2017, available at www.washingtonpost.com/news/monkey-cage/wp/2017/01/23/okay-the-trans-pacific-partnership-is-dead-what-was-it/?utm_term=.c1bb6ecddb14 (last accessed 11 July 2019).

[10] See, e.g., 'CPTPP: 11 Countries Sign Pacific Trade Deal in Chile', *The Santiago Times*, 9 March 2018, available at http://santiagotimes.cl/2018/03/09/cptpp-11-countries-sign-pacific-trade-deal-in-chile/ (last accessed 11 July 2019).

[11] Nhat Minh, 'RCEP Faces with Difficulties upon the Birth of the CPTPP', *Dantri News*, 16 November 2017, available at http://dantri.com.vn/the-gioi/hiep-dinh-rcep-doi-mat-nhieu-kho-khan-sau-khi-cptpp-ra-doi-20171116093104042.htm (in Vietnamese only; last accessed 11 July 2019).

[12] Cheryl Lim, 'Doubts Remain as RCEP Inches Closer to Conclusion', *The ASEAN Post*, 10 March 2018, available at https://theaseanpost.com/article/doubts-remain-rcep-inches-closer-conclusion (last accessed 11 July 2019).

[13] A joint research centre of the Graduate Institute of International and Development Studies and the University of Geneva Law School.

[14] UNCITRAL, 'Possible Future Work in the Field of Dispute Settlement: Reforms of Investor-State Dispute Settlement (ISDS)', *Report of the UNCITRAL Secretariat in the Fiftieth session (3–21 July 2017), UN Doc. A/CN.9/917*, available at https://documents-dds-ny.un.org/doc/UNDOC/GEN/V17/023/69/PDF/V1702369.pdf?OpenElement (last accessed 11 July 2019), p. 2.

provide an insight to the ISDS mechanism in the EVFTA that strikingly distinguishes it from other new generation FTAs and to analyse the effect of this mechanism on Vietnam.

12.2 OVERVIEW OF THE EVIPA

Negotiations for the EVIPA started in June 2012 and finally concluded in June 2019 with its signing, although the EVIPA was originally included as part of the broader EU–Vietnam Free Trade Agreement (EVFTA). After three years with fourteen official rounds and a number of unofficial rounds at the ministerial or lower level, on 2 December 2015, the prime minister of Vietnam and the president of the European Commission witnessed the minister of Trade and Industry of Vietnam and the European Commissioner for Trade sign the announcement on the conclusion of negotiations for the EVFTA, an event followed by the publication of the official text of the Agreement on 1 February 2016. However, further action with respect to the EVFTA was put on hold pending an opinion of the Court of Justice of the European Union, which concerned the EU's competence to conclude the EU–Singapore FTA (EUSFTA). The Court of Justice of the EU issued its opinion on 16 May 2017, in which it confirmed that the EU possessed the exclusive competence to conclude the EUSFTA, except for the provisions of Section A of the investment chapter on substantive investment protection, in so far as they concerned 'non-direct investment' between the EU and Singapore, and the provisions of Section B of the investment chapter, which concerned investor–State dispute settlement.[15] The EU and Singapore, and the EU and Vietnam, subsequently decided to negotiate separate investment protection agreements which were not included within the broader FTAs that they had negotiated.

The EVFTA is regarded as 'the most ambitious and comprehensive FTA that the European Union (EU) has ever concluded with a developing country' and is unquestionably a 'breakthrough of Vietnam-EU trade relations'.[16] In light of the evolution of the text of the EVFTA, it is unsurprising that it bears a resemblance to EUSFTA,[17] and it is also similar to the European Union–Canada Comprehensive Economic and Trade Agreement (CETA). It represents an important milestone in the strategic partnership of the EU and Vietnam. It also facilitates the EU's ability to foster a more comprehensive and ambitious inter-regional relationship with ASEAN, which is considered as an 'ultimate goal' of the EU.[18]

The EVFTA was subject to a process of legal review and translation into European languages and Vietnamese before it was granted the approval of the Council of Ministers and was ratified by the European Parliament. In addition, in accordance with the EU Court of Justice's Opinion No. 2/15, as noted earlier,[19] individual ratification by each EU country member was required in respect of a number of provisions of the EUSFTA, including the provisions on the investor–state arbitration (ISA) mechanism. As explained earlier, this Opinion, which affects all the FTAs of the EU including the EVFTA, showed that 'the EU

[15] Opinion No. 2/15 of the Court of Justice of the European Union, para. 305, available at http://curia.europa.eu/juris/document/document.jsf?text=&docid=190727&doclang=EN (last accessed 14 October 2019).

[16] Rouse, 'The EVFTA: A Breakthrough for Vietnam – EU Relations', *Lexology* (25 September 2015), available at www.lexology.com/library/detail.aspx?g=d3bb2a3a-8c92-409b-bd3e-ac3ee2f9c26c (last accessed 11 July 2019).

[17] For an overview and analysis of the EUSFTA, see Mahdev Mohan, 'The European Union's Free Trade Agreement with Singapore – One Step Forward, 28 Steps Back?' in Luke Nottage and Julien Chaisse (eds.), *International Investment Treaties and Arbitration Across Asia*, above n 1, pp. 180–214.

[18] 'Vietnam', European Commission, 1 August 2016, available at www.ec.europa.eu/trade/policy/countries-and-regions/countries/vietnam/ (last accessed 11 July 2019).

[19] European Court of Justice, Opinion 2/15 of the Court (Full Court), 16 May 2017. See also press release at https://curia.europa.eu/jcms/upload/docs/application/pdf/2017-05/cp170052en.pdf (both last accessed 11 July 2019).

itself is wary of the ISA regime potentially removing disputes from national courts'[20] and was responsible for delaying the signing of the EVFTA and the EVIPA.

12.3 FACTORS AFFECTING THE WORKABILITY AND EFFECTIVENESS OF THE ISDS MECHANISM UNDER THE EVFTA

12.3.1 *Vietnam's Attitude toward Investor–State Disputes*

As of August 2016, the Government of Vietnam has been identified as the respondent of eight investment arbitration cases,[21] of which, as far as open to public, Vietnam has successfully settled one case,[22] won three,[23] lost one,[24] and has three still pending.[25] Furthermore, the number of notices of intention to initiate arbitration that the Vietnamese government receives from foreign investors has been increasing over the years. In particular, in 2016, the Government of Vietnam received four notices, not to mention the claims at provincial level.[26] These figures indicate that Vietnam potentially faces a high risk of being involved in investor–State disputes. Therefore, the need for a sound legal framework to deal with these disputes is among the top priorities of the Government of Vietnam.

On 14 January 2014, the prime minister of Vietnam issued Decision No. 04/2014/QD-TTg on the Promulgation of the Regulation on Coordination in Resolution of International Investment Disputes ('2014 Regulation'). The 2014 Regulation clearly stipulates the tasks, powers and process of coordination among state agencies and relevant authorities in the resolution of international investment disputes before international arbitration or competent foreign tribunals, aiming at protecting the lawful rights and benefits of the Vietnamese government and Vietnamese state agencies. The 2014 Regulation splits the mechanism for cooperation and coordination with Vietnam in facing investor–State disputes into three stages, namely: (i) conflict management; (ii) dispute resolution; and (iii) award enforcement. The mechanism includes organization of process, information sharing and a regime for early

20 Mohan, above n 17, p. 214.

21 Tuan, above n 1.

22 *Trinh Vinh Binh and Binh Chau Joint Stock Company* v. *Socialist Republic of Viet Nam*, UNCITRAL, 2004, brief information of the case can be found at http://investmentpolicyhub.unctad.org/ISDS/Details/168 (last accessed 11 July 2019).

23 *Michael McKenzie* v. *Vietnam*, UNCITRAL, 2010 (a brief summary of the case can be found at http://investmentpolicyhub.unctad.org/ISDS/Details/382); *Dialasie SAS* v. *Vietnam*, PCA, 2011 (a brief summary of the case can be found at http://investmentpolicyhub.unctad.org/ISDS/Details/423); *Recofi* v. *Vietnam*, UNCITRAL, 2013 (a brief summary of the case can be found at http://investmentpolicyhub.unctad.org/ISDS/Details/554) (all last accessed 11 July 2019).

24 *Trinh Vinh Binh and Binh Chau Joint Stock Company* v. *Socialist Republic of Viet Nam*, UNCITRAL, 2014 (a brief summary of the case can be found at https://investmentpolicy.unctad.org/investment-dispute-settlement/cases/785/trinh-and-bin-chau-v-viet-nam-ii- (last accessed 14 October 2019).

25 *Baig* v. *Vietnam*, *ConocoPhillips and Perenco* v. *Vietnam*, and *Dangelas* v. *Vietnam*: see https://investmentpolicy.unctad.org/investment-dispute-settlement/country/229/viet-nam (last accessed 14 October 2019), and Sebastian Perry, 'Vietnam's Ex-Prime Minister Hit with Claim Over Power Project', *Global Arbitration Review* (9 September2019). See also Nguyen Manh Dzung and Nguyen Thi Thu Trang, 'Vietnam', Asia-Pacific Arbitration Review 2018, 23 May 2017; Luke Eric Peterson and Zoe Williams, 'Asia Round-up: China and Vietnam face new BIT Claims, as Proceedings against Korea and Indonesia Move Forward', *Investment Arbitration Reporter* (22 June 2017).

26 'Resolution of Investment Dispute: Prevention to Avoid the Risk', *Financial Journal* (Tap chi Tai chinh), 27 August 2017, available at http://tapchitaichinh.vn/tai-chinh-phap-luat/giai-quyet-tranh-chap-dau-tu-quoc-te-phong-ngua-de-tranh-rui-ro-120558.html (in Vietnamese only; last accessed 11 July 2019).

alert.[27] This proactive step taken by the Vietnamese government was calibrated to enable it to be well prepared and organized to be better able to respond to the investors' claims. The 2014 Regulation should also be regarded as a national effort to commence the second phase of IIA reform, namely reforming the investment dispute settlement mechanism in line with the Road Map for IIA Reform.[28]

The 2014 Regulation took effect from 3 March 2014 and seems to have proven effective in resolving investor–State disputes by successfully connecting the relevant agencies through coordination and cooperation. Before the promulgation of the 2014 Regulation, the preparation and participation of Vietnam in ISDS was passive and disorganized. The issuance of this Regulation has contributed to Vietnam's success in the *DialAsie* case at the end of 2014 and *Recofi* case in September 2015.

The *DialAsie case* stemmed from a commercial arbitration at the Vietnam International Arbitration Centre (VIAC) between a French investor, DialAsie, and Saigon Coop. In 2011, several years after the termination of the investment, DialAsie officially submitted their claims to the Permanent Court of Arbitration (PCA) under the UNCITRAL Arbitration Rules. DialAsie alleged that the actions of the Government of Vietnam (including the People's Committee of Ho Chi Minh city, the Enforcement Agency of Ho Chi Minh city, Ministry of Planning and Investment and Ministry of Health) amounted to the deprivation of the assets of the investor. On 17 November 2014, the PCA tribunal issued the final award dismissing DialAsie's claims and held that Vietnam had not violated the BIT between France and Vietnam. Accordingly, the Government of Vietnam had no obligation to compensate DialAsie. This case is significant as it was the first case Vietnam won on the merits, providing valuable lessons for the Government of Vietnam on the resolution of investment arbitrations brought against them.

The case of *Recofi* is another arbitration initiated based on the France–Vietnam BIT and conducted under the UNCITRAL Rules by the PCA. The claimant, Recofi, had participated in a state-run programme, which provided food and basic commodities to Vietnam when the country faced food shortages in the 1980s. In July 2013, the Claimant submitted its Notice of Arbitration claiming alleged outstanding payments by the Government of Vietnam related to the assistance programme.[29] The case was terminated on jurisdictional grounds in September 2015 when the arbitral tribunal ruled in favour of Vietnam. The jurisdictional award was challenged before the Federal Supreme Court of Switzerland, but was upheld in the Judgment of the Court dated 20 September 2016.[30]

At the commencement of these two cases, the Government of Vietnam was uncertain as to how to manage the disputes. As in the case of *DialAsie*, it might be the underestimation of the Vietnamese government that led a dispute of commercial nature to become an investment claim. However, the official guidance provided by the 2014 Regulation assisted the competent authorities to more actively cooperate to fulfil their assigned responsibilities. In the later stages of the arbitral proceedings, Vietnam was extremely diligent in complying with the

[27] Nguyen Thanh Tu and T. C. Q. Vu, 'Investor-State Dispute Settlement from the Perspective of Vietnam: Looking for a Post-Honeymoon' in J. E. Kalicki and Anna Joubin-Bret (eds.), *Reform of Investor-State Dispute Settlement: In Search of a Roadmap* (Brill Nijhoff, 2014).

[28] UNCTAD, 'IIA Issues Note' (June 2017), available at http://unctad.org/en/PublicationsLibrary/diaepcb2017d3_en.pdf (last accessed 11 July 2019), p. 2.

[29] Information on the case is available at http://investmentpolicyhub.unctad.org/ISDS/Details/554 (last accessed 11 July 2019).

[30] Judgment of the Federal Supreme Court of Switzerland (French), 20 September 2016, available at www.italaw.com/sites/default/files/case-documents/italaw7631.pdf (last accessed 11 July 2019).

arbitral procedures ordered by the Tribunal and cooperated with the counsels to defend the case. The success of Vietnam in three out of eight investment cases, with two on jurisdiction and one on the merits, has boosted the confidence of the Vietnamese government of its ability to deal with future investment claims from foreign investors.

The 2014 Regulation is just the first step taken by the Government of Vietnam to manage and resolve investment disputes in preparation for the trend of IIA reform. Through such efforts, the Government of Vietnam reveals its understanding of the drawbacks of traditional investment arbitration and the risk of claims by investors. Thus, Vietnam has sought a new regime of ISDS with the hope that the standing body under the EVFTA would remedy the problems present in the current model of ad hoc investment arbitration.

12.3.2 *Position of Vietnam Regarding the Tribunal in the Negotiation of the Trade Deal with the EU*

One of the innovations of the EVIPA is that it applies a new mechanism of ISDS, as proposed by the European Commission. Under this mechanism, disputes between a Vietnamese investor and the EU and/or its Member State or vice versa will be resolved through a two-tier tribunal system in which the decision of the Tribunal at first instance be subject to appeal before the Appellate Tribunal. This investment tribunal system (ITS – also known as the investment court system (ICS) is also reflected in the CETA,[31] and the EVIPA once again represents such new mechanism, but this time, with a developing country. The model is considered as a 'novel two-tier settlement mechanism for investment disputes, combining elements of traditional ISA with judicial features'.[32] Thus, following Canada, it can be said that Vietnam is one of the first partners accepting in full the ITS model proposed by the EU. There are several reasons behind such a deal.

First, at the negotiation table, next to the much larger EU, Vietnam is positioned as the 'rule-taker', with the EU being the 'rule-maker'. Having considered all the positive effects on trade, tariffs, and taxes a huge market like the EU could bring, Vietnam saw it reasonable to accept the proposed model of ISDS that the EU proposed for the FTA. Vietnam has seen the ITS, with all the potential challenges that will come with it, to be a fair price to pay for the benefits it will obtain as part of the EVFTA, including, *inter alia*, the cut off of tariffs and free movement of goods and services.

Second, Vietnam has little reason to prefer the traditional investment arbitration model over the ITS model, since the arbitration scene in Vietnam is still in the developmental phrase, lacking manpower, facilities and a robust legal framework.[33] Consequently, Vietnam is not in a position to follow a more conservative approach towards ISDS in the EVIPA. As such, Vietnam has become the test for the EU model of the permanent investment court for ISDS, which the EU had strongly argued for in the negotiation for the Transatlantic Trade and Investment Partnership (TTIP)[34] with the United States and its FTA with Japan.[35]

[31] The full text of the CETA can be accessed at http://ec.europa.eu/trade/policy/in-focus/ceta/ceta-chapter-by-chapter/ (last accessed 11 July 2019). The European Parliament voted in favour of the CETA on 15 February 2017. It entered into force provisionally on 21 September 2017.

[32] August Reinisch and Lukas Stifter, 'CETA's New Take on ISDS: Toward an International Investment Court', *CIGI Investor-State Arbitration Commentary Series No. 8* (2016), available at www.cigionline.org/publications/cetas-new-take-isds-toward-international-investment-court (last accessed 11 July 2019).

[33] Further analysed in Part E.

[34] The Transatlantic Trade and Investment Partnership ('TTIP'), available at http://ec.europa.eu/trade/policy/in-focus/ttip/ (last accessed 11 July 2019).

[35] See http://ec.europa.eu/trade/policy/countries-and-regions/countries/japan/ (last accessed 11 July 2019).

12.3.3 *The Effect of ECJ Opinion No. 2/15 and the Recent Ruling of CJEU in Achmea Case*

The ECJ Opinion No. 2/15 explicitly held that the ISDS regime under the EUSFTA 'cannot be established without the Member States' consent'.[36] This decision, while not directly ruling on the EVFTA, directly affected the conclusion of the EVFTA, as well as other new FTAs of the EU with other partners in general as it implied that the approvals of the Council of the EU, the European Parliament and thirty-eight national and regional parliaments of the EU Member States are required before treaties with the EU can be concluded.[37] Although the EU sought to accelerate the finalization of its negotiated agreements such as the EUSFTA and the EVFTA, it was inevitable that the conclusion and ratification of these agreements would be delayed, and indeed the investment chapters were extracted from the FTA texts and entered into as separate treaties.

Furthermore, previous experience has shown that the lack of a single Member State's approval and ratification can present a considerable obstacle to the conclusion of the treaties. For example, the EU–Korea FTA was almost blocked because of the Italian Parliament's concerns regarding the impact on its local car industry, or the rejection of the Association Agreement between the EU and Ukraine by the Netherlands, or the delays in the implementation of the CETA due to objection from the Belgian region of Wallonia.[38] In the case of Vietnam, the disagreement of EU Member States on some issues, such as human rights, though not directly relevant to the trade deal or ISDS, also may have contributed to delay in the conclusion of the entire agreement.

At the time of writing, Vietnam has concluded BITs with twenty-two of the twenty-eight EU Member States,[39] all of which only provides for the traditional investment arbitration model for ISDS. Meanwhile, the EVIPA would replace all the old-generation BITs, inclusive of their ISDS provisions, by adopting one of ten options in Phase 2 of IIA reform as proposed by the United Nations Conference on Trade and Development (UNCTAD).[40]

As the European Commission's request that culminated in ECJ Opinion No. 2/15 was limited to the question of the EU's competence in the conclusion of the FTA, the Opinion did not answer the question of 'whether the content of the agreement's provisions is compatible with EU law'.[41] Nevertheless, other potential risks are still present, as EU Member States like Belgium and Slovenia could request for an opinion of the ECJ on the compatibility of the ITS with EU Law, a question that the European Commission has tried to avoid being brought before the ECJ in the past few years.[42] An adverse answer to that question would significantly affect the ratification of the EVFTA, not only from the views of the individual EU Member States, but also from the perspective of the EU in general.

36 ECJ Opinion No. 2/15, para. 292.

37 Mohan, above n 17.

38 Sam Morgan, 'Singapore Trade Deal Cannot Be Concluded by EU Alone, ECJ Rules', *EURACTIV.com*, 16 May 2017, available at www.euractiv.com/section/economy-jobs/news/singapore-trade-deal-cannot-be-concluded-by-eu-alone-ecj-rules/ (last accessed 11 July 2019).

39 Including Austria, Bulgaria, Belgium–Luxembourg Economic Region, Czech Republic, Denmark, Estonia, Finland, France, Germany, Greece, Hungary, Iceland, Italy, Netherland, Latvia, Lithuania, Poland, Slovakia, Spain, Sweden and the United Kingdom: see https://investmentpolicy.unctad.org/international-investment-agreements/countries/229/viet-nam?type=bits (last accessed 11 July 2019).

40 UNCTAD, 'IIA Issues Note', above n 28, p. 7.

41 ECJ Opinion No. 2/15, above n 19, para. 30.

42 Laurens Ankersmit, 'Opinion 2/15 and the Future of Mixity and ISDS', European Law Blog, 18 May 2017, available at http://europeanlawblog.eu/2017/05/18/opinion-215-and-the-future-of-mixity-and-isds/ (last accessed 11 July 2019).

From the other side, the judgment of the Court of Justice of the EU in the case of *Slovak Republic* v. *Achmea B.V. (Case C-284–16)*[43] seems to pose another difficulty for the workability of the ITS. In particular, the judgment of CJEU held that the arbitration clause contained in Article 8 of the 1991 Netherlands–Slovakia BIT has an adverse effect on the autonomy of EU law and is accordingly incompatible with EU law. The CJEU found that the arbitral tribunal constituted under the arbitration clause in the BIT, which is usually called on to interpret and apply EU law, is not a court or tribunal of a Member State and not a part of the judicial system of any state member, with the result that it does not have the competence to interpret or apply EU law.

This decision seems to be a strong attack against the traditional arbitral tribunals established under the old-fashioned BITs. Furthermore, such a ruling by the CJEU also raises the question of whether the standing investment court as in the CETA and the EVIPA would be considered as a competent part of the judicial system of the EU to interpret and apply EU laws.[44] There would be a greater likelihood of a negative answer; it is possible that this may have also contributed to the delay in the conclusion of the EVFTA and EVIPA due to the concerns of EU member States regarding the compatibility of the ITS with the EU law; indeed, this question has been put to the Court of Justice of the EU by Belgium, and this request remains pending.[45]

12.4 THE EVIPA'S REGIME FOR SETTLEMENT OF INVESTOR–STATE DISPUTES

The regime for the settlement of investor–State disputes in the EVIPA is a two-tier standing panel based on the model of a permanent investment court, a model that has just been experimentally applied in the CETA,[46] which provisionally came into force on 21 September 2017. It is consistent with certain proposals for ISDS reform which are being discussed in UNCITRAL's Working Group III.[47] This model of a permanent standing body is believed to enhance impartiality, accountability, transparency and promotes greater quality and consistency across decisions.[48] Although untested, the ISDS regime under the EVIPA appears highly promising as the standing body can bring highly qualified and carefully appointed individuals to sit as 'arbitrators' on the Tribunal and Appeal Tribunal. These arbitrators would be bound by the Code of Conduct stipulated in Annex 8 of the EVIPA.

43 The judgment of 7 March 2018 can be found at: http://curia.europa.eu/juris/document/document.jsf?text=&docid=199968&pageIndex=0&doclang=EN&mode=req&dir=&occ=first&part=1&cid=367328 (last accessed 11 July 2019).

44 Dr. Szilárd Gáspár Szilágyi, 'The CJEU Strikes Again in Achmea: Is This the End of Investor-State Arbitration under intra-EU BITs?', *International Economic Law and Policy Blog*, 7 March 2018, available at http://worldtradelaw.typepad.com/ielpblog/2018/03/guest-post-the-cjeu-strikes-again-in-achmea-is-this-the-end-of-investor-state-arbitration-under-intr.html (last accessed 11 July 2019).

45 Request for an opinion submitted by the Kingdom of Belgium pursuant to Article 218(11) TFEU (Opinion 1/17) http://curia.europa.eu/juris/document/document.jsf?text=&docid=196185&pageIndex=0&doclang=en&mode=lst&dir=&occ=first&part=1&cid=1206213 (last accessed 14 October 2019).

46 General information of the CETA can be accessed at http://ec.europa.eu/trade/policy/in-focus/ceta/ (last accessed 11 July 2019).

47 UNCITRAL, 'Possible future work in the field of dispute settlement: Reforms of investor-State dispute settlement (ISDS)', above n 14.

48 Leon Trakman and David Musayelyan, 'Arguments For and Against Standing Panels of Arbitrators in Investor-State Arbitration: Evidence and Reality', University of Melbourne, 21 August 2014, available at http://law.unimelb.edu.au/__data/assets/pdf_file/0004/1954156/Trakman,-ARGUMENTS-FOR-AND-AGAINST-STANDING-PANELS-OF-ARBITRATORS-IN-INVESTOR-STATE-ARBITRATION-EVIDENCE-AND-REALITY.pdf (last accessed 11 July 2019).

However, the strict procedure relating to the appointment of the members of the Tribunal and Appeal Tribunal effectively eliminates party autonomy, which is a cornerstone of the traditional arbitration model, potentially presenting a significant disadvantage for investors.

This part shall provide an insight to the new mechanism of ISDS – the ITS, as stipulated by the EVIPA, which will be the basis for analysing the challenges that Vietnam may face in adopting such a brand-new model.

12.4.1 *Summary of the Amicable Dispute Resolution Methods under the EVFTA*

The EVIPA stipulates four methods for resolution of investor–State disputes, namely through (1) negotiation, (2) consultation, (3) mediation and (4) the ITS. These four methods must be utilized in turn, except for recourse to mediation. In particular, there must be an attempt to settle any dispute through negotiation before the submission of the request for consultation.[49]

Nevertheless, at any time in the dispute resolution process, either disputing party can refer the dispute to mediation.[50] The mediator is selected by mutual consent of the parties.[51] If parties cannot agree on the selection of mediator, the President of the Tribunal shall appoint a member of the Tribunal, who is neither a citizen of Vietnam nor the EU, to be the mediator. During the process of mediation, all the time limits on, inter alia, submission of a request for consultation or a notice of intent, are suspended until the termination of the mediation. The result of a successful mediation will be implemented by the parties without any compulsory enforcement mechanism or body. The mediation process including all the documents, opinions of the parties and the mutually agreed solution is to be kept confidential unless otherwise agreed by the parties.[52] Additionally, the person who acts as the mediator shall be bound by the Code of Conduct, which also applies to Members of the Tribunal and Appeal Tribunal.[53]

12.4.2 *The Procedure for Resolution of Investor-State Disputes through the ITS under the EVIPA*

Unlike traditional arbitral proceedings which reflect fundamental principles of arbitration such as party autonomy and finality of the arbitral awards, the dispute settlement procedure in the EVIPA is a two-tier settlement mechanism where the first instance Tribunal and Appeal Tribunal are constituted upon the appointment of a competent authority rather than the agreement of the parties. This particular procedure is further discussed subsequently.

12.4.2.1 Submission of Claim

Under the EVIPA, a claim will only be considered by the Tribunal if it has met the procedural pre-conditions to settling the dispute, namely that the other stipulated methods of dispute resolution like negotiation and consultation have taken place,[54] and that the Notice of Intent to submit a claim have been submitted.[55] Additionally, if the respondent is the EU or an EU Member State, the EVFTA requires the claimant to file a request for determination of the

49 EVIPA, Art. 3.29.
50 Ibid., Art. 3.31; Annex 10, Art. 2.
51 Ibid., Art. 3.31(4); Annex 10, Art. 3.
52 Ibid., Annex 10, Art. 6(3).
53 Ibid., Annex 8, para. 20.
54 Ibid., Arts. 3.32, 3.33, 3.35.
55 Ibid., Arts. 3.32 and 3.35.

respondent to the EU before officially submitting the claim to the Tribunal. The determination of the EU on that point is final and neither the EU nor the EU Member State, determined as the respondent, may oppose such a decision to assert the inadmissibility of the claim, lack of jurisdiction or to challenge the validity of the award on any ground based on such decision.

Though the claimant can choose the arbitral rules to be applied with clear intention made in its statement of claim, since Vietnam is not a member of the Convention on the Settlement of Investment Disputes between States and Nationals of other States ('ICSID Convention'), it appears that the cases in which Vietnam is the respondent would still be governed by the UNCITRAL Arbitration Rules.

12.4.2.2 First Instance Proceeding

Under the EVIPA, a specific case will be heard by a division of three members from the nine members of the Tribunal – one national of a Member State of the EU, a Vietnamese national and a Member who is a national of a third country.[56] The division is constituted upon the appointment of the President of the Tribunal on a rotation basis, ensuring that the composition of the divisions is random and unpredictable, while giving equal opportunity to all members to serve. Any party can challenge the appointment of any member of the division upon consideration of any conflict of interest. The final decision shall be made by the President of the Tribunal after considering the opinions and observations of the elected member and the parties.[57]

The division of the Tribunal will make every effort to decide the dispute based on consensus.[58] In the event that consensus cannot be reached, the matter at issue will be resolved by majority vote.[59] The decision made by the division of the Tribunal is regarded as a provisional award and can be subject to appeal.[60]

In special circumstances, upon the agreement of the disputing parties, the case may be heard by a sole member of the Tribunal who is a national of a third country. The respondent is required to give 'sympathetic consideration of such a request' made by a claimant, particularly if the claimant is a small- or medium-sized company where the compensation or damages claimed are relatively low. Such a request, however, must be made at the same time as the filing of the claim.[61]

The provisional award must be rendered within eighteen months from the date of submission of the claims.[62]

12.4.2.3 Appellate Proceeding

Either disputing party may appeal against the provisional award on one of the grounds set out in Article 3.54(1) of the EVIPA, namely: (a) that the Tribunal erred in the interpretation or application of the applicable law; (b) that the Tribunal manifestly erred in the appreciation of the facts, including the appreciation of relevant domestic law; or (c) those provided for in Article 52 of the ICSID Convention, insofar as they are not covered by (a) and (b). Similar to

[56] Ibid., Art. 3.38(6).
[57] Ibid., Art. 3.38(7).
[58] Ibid., Art. 3.38(12).
[59] Ibid.
[60] Ibid., Art. 3.53.
[61] Ibid., Art. 3.38(9).
[62] Ibid., Art. 3.53(6).

traditional investment dispute resolution, any domestic law of the disputing party will be considered as a matter of fact which will be taken into consideration by the Tribunal and the Appeal Tribunal in resolving the dispute.[63] Therefore, it is arguable that the grounds for appeal contained in the EVIPA, for example, error in interpretation of the domestic law, are overly broad and may lead to systematic abuse of the appeal process.[64]

The division of three members of the Appeal Tribunal will conduct the appellate proceedings similar to those of the first instance. Although it is stated that the composition of the division of the Appeal Tribunal hearing a case will be unpredictably and randomly established by the President of the Appeal Tribunal on a rotational basis,[65] the unpredictability of such division seems to be tempered by the limited number of members on the Appeal Tribunal.[66]

The Appeal Tribunal will decide to either (i) dismiss the appeal if they find that the appeal is unfounded; or (ii) if they find it is well founded, modify or reverse the findings and conclusions of the first instance Tribunal in the provisional award.[67] Under the appellate procedure, the Appeal Tribunal shall not re-consider the facts (including the interpretation of domestic law), which are established by the Tribunal, but only apply their own legal findings and conclusions to such facts in order to render the final award on relevant matters. If the Appeal Tribunal finds that the facts were wrongly established, they will refer the matter back to the Tribunal.[68] The award of the Appeal Tribunal shall be final and binding upon the disputing parties.[69]

12.4.2.4 Enforcement of the Final Award

The final award will be binding between the disputing parties with respect to the particular case and is not subject to any appeal, review, annulment or any other remedy in any jurisdiction.[70]

The final award will be recognized by the members of the agreement within its territory. Nonetheless, Vietnam will be granted a five-year transition period for the entry into force of the enhanced enforcement regime. Particularly, in the first five years after the entry into force of the EVIPA, the awards, in proceedings in which Vietnam is a respondent, must be recognized and enforced in Vietnam in compliance with the New York Convention. The period of five years may be extended upon the decision of the Trade Committee.[71]

12.4.2.5 Administered Secretariat of the Tribunal and Appeal Tribunal

The dispute resolution proceedings, in both first instance and appellate stages, will be assisted by the Secretariat of ICSID.[72]

63 Ibid., Art. 3.54(1)(b).
64 Athina Fouchard Papaefstratiou, 'The EU Proposal Regarding Investment Protection: The End of Investment Arbitration as We Know It?', Kluwer Arbitration Blog, 29 December 2015, published at http://kluwerarbitrationblog.com/2015/12/29/the-eu-proposal-regarding-investment-protection-the-end-of-investment-arbitration-as-we-know-it/ (last accessed 11 July 2019).
65 EVIPA, Art. 3.39(9).
66 Ibid., Art. 3.39(2).
67 Ibid., Art. 3.54.
68 Ibid., Art. 3.54(4).
69 Ibid., Art. 3.55.
70 Ibid., Art. 3.57(1).
71 Ibid., Art. 3.57(4).
72 Ibid., Art. 3.38(18).

12.4.2.6 Costs and Fees

The disputing parties have to pay the retainer fees of the members of the Tribunal and Appeal Tribunal handling the case.[73] If a party fails to pay the retainer fee, the other party may be elected to pay. The principle of 'costs follow the event' is applied.[74] In particular, the Tribunal in its award will order the costs of proceedings, including (i) the reasonable costs of expert advice and of other assistance required by the Tribunal; and (ii) the reasonable travel and other expenses of witnesses, to be borne by the unsuccessful party. In exceptional circumstances, the Tribunal may allocate costs between the disputing parties if they find that that method is more appropriate in the circumstances of the case.[75] Other reasonable costs, including reasonable costs of legal representation and assistance, will be borne by the unsuccessful disputing party, unless the Tribunal determines that such apportionment is unreasonable in the circumstances of the case. Where only some parts of the claims have been successful, the costs will be adjusted proportionately to the number or extent of the successful parts of the claims.[76]

***

The ISDS mechanism under the EVIPA is significantly different from the traditional investment arbitration model and it may take time for Vietnam to become fully acquainted with the operation of the standing bodies and the dispute settlement proceedings. Furthermore, a developing country like Vietnam will face a number of challenges in the interpretation and application of the relevant provisions of the agreement. The next part shall examine what Vietnam has to deal with in participating in such an ambitious IPA and how the country will tackle such challenges.

12.5 CHALLENGES THAT VIETNAM WILL FACE IN THE IMPLEMENTATION OF THE ITS UNDER THE EVIPA

12.5.1 *Transparency*

Unlike traditional treaty-based arbitral proceedings in which all the submissions and other documents are kept confidential, the ITS under the EVIPA will be fully transparent and a third party can seek to intervene in the proceedings.[77] Article 3.46(1) of the EVIPA makes direct reference to the UNCITRAL Rules on Transparency in Treaty-based Investor-State Arbitration ('UNCITRAL Transparency Rules'), and makes them applicable, subject to Article 3.46(2)–(8) of the EVIPA.[78] In particular, apart from the documents listed in Article 3(1) of the UNCITRAL Transparency Rules, the EVIPA also requires that the request for consultations, the notice of intent, the notice of determination of the respondent, the notice of challenge of the member of the Tribunal or Appeal Tribunal in a division and the decision on challenge shall also be made available to public,[79] save for the confidential or protected information as defined in Article 7(2) of the UNCITRAL Transparency Rules and classified

[73] Ibid., Art. 3.38(15).
[74] Ibid., Art. 3.53(4).
[75] Ibid., Art. 3.53(4).
[76] Ibid., Art. 3.53(4).
[77] Delegation of the European Union to Vietnam, *Guide to the EU–Vietnam Free Trade Agreement* (2016), p. 55.
[78] Ibid., Art. 3.46. The full text of the UNCITRAL Transparency Rules is available at www.uncitral.org/uncitral/en/uncitral_texts/arbitration/2014Transparency.html (last accessed 11 July 2019).
[79] EVIPA, Art. 3.46(2).

government information. The publication of other documents shall be made in compliance with the decision of the Tribunal upon its own initiative or request from any person after consultation with the disputing parties.

According to the UNCTAD's publicly available database on investor-State disputes, the investment arbitration cases involving Vietnam have, to date, always been kept confidential. As a characteristic of the more traditional treaty-based arbitration procedure, there is very little publicly available information. Though Vietnam is not a signatory to the 2014 United Nations Convention on Transparency in Treaty-based Investor-State Arbitration, in which member countries expressly agree to adopt the UNCITRAL Transparency Rules in any investor–State disputes they are involved in,[80] the UNCITRAL Transparency Rules have been clearly incorporated in the new 2013 UNCITRAL Arbitration Rules, and will therefore automatically apply to disputes arising out of treaties concluded on or after 1 April 2014 unless the parties agree otherwise. In addition, as mentioned earlier, a number of key provisions from the UNCITRAL Transparency Rules are adopted in the ITS of the EVIPA.

In light of the previous discussion, it is time for Vietnam to adapt to the transparency policies under the new generation of international investment treaties. Although the relevant treaties also provide for reservation of confidential and protected information, essential information on investment cases should be made available to the public along with any potential intervention from third parties. The Government of Vietnam should be prepared for such situations. Otherwise, Vietnam may need to enhance domestic policy to contain disputes from the pre-arbitration stages or try to settle the dispute through negotiation or mediation in order to ensure the confidentiality principle still applies.

12.5.2 *Qualifications of the Members of the Tribunal and Appeal Tribunal under the ISDS Mechanism of the EVIPA*

One of the most distinctive characteristics of the ISDS regime under the EVIPA is the ITS, which involves the appointment of a permanent standing body handling the resolution of disputes instead of deferring to party autonomy in the selection of arbitrators.

The process of selecting the adjudicators is one of the main elements in setting up the standing body as an ISDS reform, and should be 'transparent, rigorous, susceptible of being clearly monitored by all stakeholders in order ensure legitimacy and gain public confidence'.[81] Supporters of the ITS argued that standing arbitral panels would 'enhance transparency, expedite appointments and promote greater quality and consistency of decisions'.[82] On the other hand, opponents contend that the standing tribunal might not represent the interests and perspective of the investors as they have no role in the appointment of the tribunal members.[83] The debate is still on-going as the use of standing panels is exceedingly rare in the investor–State context.[84]

80 Under this Convention, Parties to investment treaties concluded before 1 April 2014 express their consent to apply the UNCITRAL Rules on Transparency in its Treaty-based Investor-State Arbitration. The Convention took effect from 18 October 2017 with only three members.

81 UNCITRAL, 'Possible future work in the field of dispute settlement: Reforms of investor-State dispute settlement (ISDS)', above n 14.

82 Trakman and Musayelyan, above n 49, Sections II(A) and (B).

83 Ruth Marie Mosch, 'Investment Arbitration in the EU-Vietnam Free Trade Agreement – The Times They Are a Changin'', Young ICCA Blog, 8 December 2016, available at www.youngicca-blog.com/investment-arbitration-in-the-eu-vietnam-free-trade-agreement-the-times-they-are-a-changin/ (last accessed 11 July 2019).

84 Trakman and Musayelyan, above n 49, Sections II(A) and (B).

Having departed from the traditional arbitration tribunal model, the EVIPA opts for a standing tribunal which operates similarly to a permanent investment court or the Dispute Settlement Body (DSB) of the WTO. The Tribunal is to comprise of nine standing members – three of them nationals of an EU Member State, three of them nationals of Vietnam and the remaining three nationals of third countries. Meanwhile, the Appeal Tribunal will comprise six appointees, two of whom will be nationals of Vietnam, two nationals of EU Member States and two nationals of third countries. The members of the Tribunal and Appeal Tribunal will be appointed by the decision of the 'Committee' which is established under Article 4.1 of the EVIPA, and which comprises representatives of the EU and Vietnam.[85] Furthermore, the Committee may decide to increase or decrease the number of members of the Tribunal and Appeal Tribunal by multiples of three.[86] Unlike the traditional investment arbitration model, in which party autonomy is vigorously upheld, under the ITS, the investor-claimant is deprived of its right to appoint and nominate an arbitrator, who may be better attuned to the perspectives of the investor as opposed to that of the State. This model has therefore created an impression that the new ITS would be disadvantageous for the investor in comparison to traditional arbitration.[87] Under the ITS reflected in the EVIPA, members of the Tribunal and Appeal Tribunal must be qualified for judicial office in their countries or jurists of recognized competence.[88] Both Tribunals require public international law expertise as a compulsory requirement while experience in international trade, investment law and resolution of dispute arising under international investment and international trade agreements are only considered desirable rather than compulsory.[89] The priority of public international law over international trade and investment law is also a point of controversy as it may be thought to reflect a perspective more favourable of the interests of the State than those of the investors.[90] Members of the Tribunal and the Appeal Tribunal shall be bound by the Code of Ethics, which is also applicable for the mediator resolving investor–State disputes.[91] Furthermore, these members must ensure their independence during the resolution of the dispute by not being affiliated or taking instructions from any government or organization with regard to the dispute. Last but not least, the ethical principles prevent the appointed members of the Tribunal or Appeal Tribunal from acting as counsel or as party-appointed expert or witness in any pending or new investment protection dispute under any international or domestic instrument.[92] From a practical point of view, this requirement excludes arbitration practitioners from appointment and hence may cause difficulties for the members of the EUVFTA in selecting candidates for the positions.[93] The high standards required in appointing members to the Tribunal and Appeal Tribunal are intended to address the critiques against the standing panel for the requisite qualifications of the persons seated in the roster.[94] There are challenges with this approach for Vietnam.

85 EVIPA, Art. 4.1.
86 Ibid., Art. 4.1(5); see also Art. 3.38(3), Art. 3.39(3).
87 Mosch, above n 84.
88 Ibid., Art. 3.38(4), Art. 3.39(7).
89 Ibid.
90 Mosch, above n 84.
91 Ibid., Art. 3.40; see also Annex 8.
92 Ibid.
93 Papaefstratiou, above n 65.
94 Trakman and Musayelyan, above n 49, Sections II(A) and (B).

As the investor-claimant has no voice in choosing the adjudicators, it is the right and responsibility of the contracting members to select the appointees who meet the dual conditions of being both qualified for appointment to judicial office in their home jurisdiction and demonstrating expertise in public international law, notwithstanding the desirable experience in investment, trade law, and resolution of investment disputes. Accordingly, the appointees should also (i) satisfy the qualifications as stipulated by the agreement; (ii) protect state interests; (iii) be pro-investor to ensure investors receive a fair hearing; and (iv) ensure the independence and impartiality as required by the Code of Conduct. It is argued that these multiple requirements overly restrict the pool of qualifying members.[95]

Hence, it would be a significant challenge for the Vietnamese government to select potential candidates who would meet all the requirements set out earlier. Additionally, it should also be noted that Vietnamese judges, who are qualified as jurists, may not have good knowledge in public international law, notwithstanding their ability to fluently use foreign languages in the proceedings. Meanwhile, persons who are experts on public international law may not meet the qualification of being appointed to judicial office or being of recognized competence. Having reviewed the background and expertise of the seventeen leading senior judges of the Supreme People's Court of Vietnam[96] who have just been appointed in accordance with the new Law on Organization of People's Court, it appears that there are very few senior judges who have expertise in economic and commercial issues, and even fewer who are familiar with international law or investment disputes. Thus, the selection of the appointees to the positions of the Tribunal and Appeal Tribunal under the regime of the EVIPA would not be easy for Vietnam.

On the other hand, from another practical point of view, before the 2015 Civil Procedure Code ('2015 CPC'),[97] Vietnamese laws had never provided for any regulations or guidance on proof of foreign law. Additionally, the 2015 CPC only has one provision concerning the proof of foreign law, requiring the litigating parties to bear the burden of proof. Vietnamese laws also do not distinguish whether the foreign law should be considered as a matter of law or matter of fact. Accordingly, Vietnamese judges would be unfamiliar with the application and interpretation of foreign law. This deficiency will be a serious difficulty for Vietnamese appointees to the Tribunal and Appeal Tribunal.

While it is true that Vietnam has the option of choosing a candidate of a third country nationality, this option is not in Vietnam's best interests politically as such candidates may be too neutral to protect the rights of Vietnam as a respondent. Taking all of these difficulties into consideration, the Vietnamese government should maximize their time and start seeking appropriate appointees before the EVFTA enters into force.

12.5.3 *Enforcement of the Final Award*

As mentioned earlier, under the EVIPA, Vietnam has five years of transition in enforcement of the final award of the ISDS, regardless of the extension that may be applied.[98] During such

95 L Woods, 'Fit for purpose? The EU's Investment Court System', Kluwer Arbitration Blog, 23 March 2016, available at www.kluwerarbitrationblog.com/2016/03/23/to-be-decided/ (last accessed 11 July 2019).

96 'Supreme People's Court Judges Appointed', *Nhan Dan Newspaper*, 26 June 2015, available at http://en.nhandan.com.vn/politics/domestic/item/3443302-supreme-people's-court-judges-appointed.html; and 'Judges, Deputy Chief Judges of Supreme Court Appointed', *Vietnamnet*, 22 June 2017, available at http://english.vietnamnet.vn/fms/government/180693/judges–deputy-chief-judges-of-supreme-court-appointed.html (both last accessed 11 July 2019).

97 Law No. 92/2015/QH13 dated 25 November 2015 coming into force as from 1 July 2016.

98 EVIPA, Art. 3.57(3).

period, the EVIPA provides that the investment award will be regarded as a foreign commercial arbitral award which will fall within the recognition and enforcement regime of the New York Convention.[99]

Vietnam has unfortunately become infamous for having a poor track record in the recognition and enforcement of foreign arbitral awards. Local judges tend to protect the local parties. Such protectionism would be heightened when the award debtor is the Government of Vietnam. Nevertheless, the award can theoretically still be enforced in any other member countries to the New York Convention wherever the Government of Vietnam has assets. Therefore, the procedure of recognition and enforcement of foreign arbitral awards in Vietnam can no longer be a safeguard for the Vietnamese government in evading their obligations under the award. However, to date, there has not been any investment arbitral award against the Vietnamese government where recognition and enforcement has been sought inside or outside the jurisdiction of Vietnam.

Furthermore, after the five transition years, Vietnam has to treat and enforce the award as if it were the local judgment of the Vietnamese court. In light of the inevitable, the Vietnamese government should prepare to face the increasing number of investment claims and their potential outcomes.

Additionally, the EVIPA also provides that final awards issued by the Tribunal or Appeal Tribunal shall be considered as arbitral awards and relate to claims arising out of a commercial relationships or transactions,[100] which will facilitate the enforcement of such awards in non-contracting states.

12.5.4 *Compatibility of Vietnamese Laws with the Commitment in the EVIPA*

According to a project by the Vietnam Chamber of Commerce and Industry (VCCI) reviewing the law of Vietnam relative to Vietnam's commitments under the EVIPA, the 2014 Law on Investment is surprisingly compatible with the provisions of the EVIPA save for a small number of provisions, definitions and the scope of application of some investment protection measures. These include the scope of application of investment liberation, National Treatment (NT), Most Favoured Nation Treatment (MFN), Treatment for Investment and Compensation for Losses.[101]

To streamline the process of fulfilling its obligations under the EVIPA, it is essential for Vietnam to close the gaps that exist between its domestic legislation and its obligations under the EVIPA through the amendment of the national investment law. In this regard, in order to ensure a friendly investment environment for foreign investors and equal business opportunities for Vietnamese enterprises, the VCCI suggested that the National Assembly promulgate a new law on the implementation of the EVIPA, providing specific guidance with respect to the incompatible areas of Vietnamese laws in comparison with the EVIPA.[102]

[99] Ibid., Art. 3.57(3).

[100] Ibid., Art. 3.57(7).

[101] Dr. Nguyen Thi Thu Trang (ed.), *Reviewing the Law on Investment of Vietnam in comparison with the Commitments under the EVFTA* (Industry and Trade Publisher, 2016) (in Vietnamese: Rà soát pháp luật của Việt Nam với các cam kết của Hiệp định thư ơ ng mại tự do Việt Nam – EU về Đầu tư), available at www.trungtamwto.vn/sites/default/files/tpp/attachments/3._dau_tu.pdf (in Vietnamese only); detailed review of provision by provision in English can be found at http://wtocenter.vn/sites/wtocenter.vn/files/event-education/attachments/Review%20Investment%20EVFTA%20-%20VCCI%20Eng.pdf (both last accessed 11 July 2019).

[102] 'Laws' Compatibility with EVFTA Commitments on Investment Reviewed', *Vietnamplus*, 16 March 2016, available at http://english.vov.vn/trade/laws-compatibility-with-evfta-commitments-on-investment-reviewed-314867.vov (last accessed 11 July 2019) – the Report on the Conference was held in Hanoi on 16 March 2016 to review Vietnam's legal framework against the commitments of the EVFTA on investment.

Furthermore, because the EVIPA opts for a modern but untested ITS, Vietnam should establish specific regulations on ISDS to ensure domestic compatibility with the regime. This task is predicted to cause difficulties for lawmakers.

12.5.5 *The Unusual Use of Arbitration Conducted under UNCITRAL Arbitration Rules in Vietnam*

Although Vietnamese laws support both institutional arbitration and ad hoc arbitration, the latter seems to be rarely used. According to the 'Preliminary Report on 04 Years of Implementation of the 2010 Law on Commercial Arbitration (LCA)' published by the Ministry of Justice (MOJ) in a conference on the same topic in September 2015,[103] in four years (from 2011 until mid-2015), arbitration centres in Vietnam enrolled 879 cases and rendered 586 arbitral awards. Furthermore, it is reported that to date, there has only been one ad hoc arbitration which has been conducted using the UNCITRAL Arbitration rules under the administration of the VIAC.[104] These figures indicate that Vietnamese parties still prefer institutional arbitration over ad hoc arbitration, and ad hoc arbitration is not familiar to the Vietnamese business community and judicial authorities. Thus, for both Vietnamese investors and the competent state authorities, investment arbitration conducted under the UNCITRAL Arbitration Rules is seen as a new territory, which may take time to adjust and adapt to.

12.5.6 *Newly Established Mediation Legislation*

Mediation in Vietnam is still in its infancy stages with the introduction of Decree No. 22/2017 on Commercial Mediation ('Decree on Commercial Mediation'), which was recently promulgated and came into effect early this year, and Chapter XXXIII on the Recognition of Results of Out of Court Mediation in the 2015 CPC. The business community as well as the Government of Vietnam are still unfamiliar with this method of alternative dispute resolution.

In addition, the Decree on Commercial Mediation suggests that the Government and the Supreme People's Court still harbour many concerns relating to mediation and have thus stipulated a number of policies and regulations to restrict the flexibility of mediation, such as requiring registration of ad hoc mediators with the Department of Justice, or necessitating high qualification standards for mediators. However, there is no explicit restriction on the nationality of the mediator except for the requirement for registration with the Department of Justice for ad hoc mediators. This regulation gives fair opportunity for foreign mediators to practise in Vietnam.

Additionally, the Decree on Commercial Mediation does not prohibit counsels from acting as ad hoc mediators or registering for a panel under a mediation centre in Vietnam. Nevertheless, while acting as a mediator, counsels must refrain from acting at the same time as the representative or consultant to one of the parties, and refrain from acting as an arbitrator

103 'Summary of 04 Years of Implementation of the Law on Commercial Arbitration', Web Portal of the Ministry of Justice, available in Vietnamese at http://bttp.moj.gov.vn/qt/tintuc/Pages/trong-tai-thuong-mai.aspx?ItemID=53 (last accessed 11 July 2019).

104 VIAC, 'Vietnamese Centre hosts first case under UNCITRAL rules', 2 August 2017, available at http://eng.viac.vn/viac.org.vn/Vietnamese-centre-hosts-first-case-under-UNCITRAL-rules-a462.html (last accessed 11 July 2019).

for the same dispute which is or was under mediation, unless otherwise agreed by the parties. Last but not least, it should be noted that Decree on Commercial Mediation does not govern mediations conducted under the EVFTA but only applies to investment disputes mediated pursuant to the 2014 Law on Investment.

Furthermore, there is much concern that mandatory mediation under the 2014 Law on Investment may prolong the dispute resolution process where the disputing parties are no longer on good terms and are unable to sit down for mediation. However, pursuant to the Decree on Commercial Mediation, either disputing party can refuse the request for mediation at the outset of the mediation process or at any time request for termination of the mediation. Hence, mediation will not delay other proceedings beyond the expectations of the disputing parties.

The enforceability of mediated settlement agreements has also received much attention. If the mediation was conducted under the 2014 Law on Investment and Decree on Commercial Mediation, the enforceability of the resultant mediated settlement agreement is guaranteed by Chapter XXXIII of the 2015 CPC. However, the recognition and enforcement of mediated settlement agreements under the 2015 CPC will not be applied for mediations conducted under the EVIPA.

Meanwhile, there is no provision providing for an enforcement mechanism of the mediated settlement agreement under the EVIPA despite the fact that both Vietnam and the EU have their own regulations to such effect, being the Directive 2008/52/EC of 21 May 2008 on certain aspects of mediation in civil and commercial matters for the EU and the 2015 CPC for Vietnam. This may cause disputing parties to be hesitant in choosing mediation to resolve their disputes. However, mediation is still regarded as a viable option where parties wish to avoid the transparency of ISDS proceedings under the EVIPA, as it still upholds the confidentiality principle.

12.5.7 *Limited Capable Human Resources that Specialize in ISDS*

Before the issuance of the Regulation 2014, Vietnam's authorities were not aware of the seriousness of being involved in investment disputes with foreign investors. As a result, the Government of Vietnam was very passive in dealing with investor–State disputes. The publication of the Regulation 2014 was believed to have remedied this situation by raising awareness of the relevant state agencies in coordinating and cooperating in resolving investment disputes following the MOJ's lead. However, being the permanent lead agency to handle ISDS, the MOJ should be more active and cooperative with other agencies, like the Ministry of Planning and Investment and Ministry of Foreign Affairs, in supervising and guiding other related agencies at all levels with respect to investment protection measures and prevention of investor–State disputes.

Furthermore, as investor–State disputes may arise from contractual claims between foreign investors and Vietnamese agencies, the Vietnamese government should also pay special attention to judiciary development. Vietnamese judges have very little knowledge and experience in investment disputes and there has been no official guidance provided to the judges on how to deal with such investment cases, which have characteristics distinctive from general commercial disputes. Hence, it is crucial to have projects, programmes, workshops and conferences to enhance the expertise of Vietnamese judges in the field of investment disputes.

Last but not least, the pool of lawyers, counsels and experts specializing in international investment disputes in Vietnam is extremely limited. In Vietnam, lawyers and legal counsels not only take part in the dispute settlement procedure but also provide legal opinions at the pre-dispute stages. Therefore, it is essential for legal practitioners to be well equipped with knowledge not only on Vietnamese laws but also on public international law, international investment law and dispute resolution.

Given the aforementioned analysis, an important responsibility of all levels of the Government of Vietnam is to build human resource capacity not just of persons who are directly involved in investment dispute resolution but also of judicial authorities and legal practitioners who take part in all stages of dispute management and prevention.

***

These challenges analysed earlier are only the most apparent ones, which can be foreseen in considering the accession of Vietnam to one of the world's most ambitious and comprehensive FTAs. Furthermore, these difficulties are only viewed from the investment perspective. There are still endless potential risks that can be pointed out from many other perspectives such as economy and trade. Playing in a large playground with giant partners, Vietnam should prepare to become acquainted with the difficulties and challenges, and be prepared to take steps to sustainably develop.

12.6 CONCLUSION

It is said that opportunities are always accompanied by challenges, and for Vietnam, participation in the most ambitious and comprehensive new generation of FTAs and investment protection agreements should herald a period of intense preparation to face of the plethora of challenges and difficulties, including the increase in number of investor-state disputes against the Government of Vietnam. At the moment, it seems that the Government of Vietnam is paying more attention to the opportunities that the EVFTA and EVIPA may bring, while underestimating the potential underlying risks.

Particularly, the ISDS regime under the EVIPA, with the establishment of the first ITS, presents many potential challenges for Vietnam not only in adapting to and implementing the regulations therein, but also in building human resource capacity to strongly and sustainably develop in such a new playground without any damage.

With the amendments to a number of important pieces of legislation, including the Law of Investment, the Civil Procedure Code and the Civil Code, Vietnam is showing positive progression toward integration into the global playground with giant partners. Diligent preparation is what Vietnam should aspire towards at the moment. Vietnam should make use of the time prior to entry into force of the EVIPA to be well equipped before entering the real battlefield.

As the new legislation and policy at both the domestic and international levels have still yet to be tested, it is worth looking forward to what the future may bring and the next steps that Vietnam will take to balance the opportunities and challenges, while sustainably developing and reaping the benefits from entering the new global playground.

13

Investment Rule-Making in Asia–European Union Relations

Legal and Policy Considerations

*Julien Chaisse and Xu Qian**

13.1 INTRODUCTION

States actively seek to attract foreign investment into their economies, since high levels of foreign investment have long been associated with increased economic growth and prosperity.[1] In the international legal sphere, the period since the North America Free Trade Agreement (NAFTA) entered into force has witnessed an explosion in the number of international investment agreements (IIAs),[2] in the form of both bilateral investment treaties (BITs) and free trade agreements (FTAs) involving all countries that were earlier part of the Soviet Union.[3] It was in the year 2000 that many Asian countries developed and reinforced their network of IIAs thereby making investment a key aspect of their economic pacts with third countries.[4] To put matters into the global context, the United Nations estimates that in 2017, the global inflow of foreign direct

* This research was supported by the General Research Fund (GRF) Project No. 14605915 of the Hong Kong SAR Research Grants Council (RGC). The GRC research projects are subject to a rigorous peer review process via the RGC's five subject panels supported by an international network of expert reviewers. The Author would like to thank Rahul Donde, Claudio Dordi, Mark Feldman, Shintaro Hamanaka, Sungjin Kang, Soo Kong, and Jun Xiao for comments on earlier drafts of this Chapter.

[1] Jeffrey Sachs, *The End of Poverty: How We Can Make It Happen in Our Lifetime* (London: Penguin Books, 2005).

[2] If, globally speaking, international investment law and policy have developed in the mid-1990s, it was essentially in North America and Europe. The path-breaking Chapter 11 (Investment) of the North American Free Trade Agreement 1994 ('NAFTA') embedded a full set of investment rules within the ambit of a trade architecture for the very first time.

[3] Investors, however, are free to invest where they choose, and without legal instruments and mechanisms to protect investments abroad, investors may be reluctant to invest their resources in a foreign state. As a consequence of concerns in respect of differences in legal systems and differences in the levels of legal infrastructure, over the past 25 years in particular, states have concluded more than 3,000 IIAs to regulate the treatment of foreign investors and investments and to provide a mechanism for the resolution of disputes between foreign investors and host states. In relation to investor–state arbitration, a number of organisations have formulated proposals for reform. For example, UNCITRAL, 'Possible future work in the field of dispute settlement: Reforms of investor-State dispute settlement (ISDS): Note by the Secretariat', *Report of the UNCITRAL Secretariat in the Fiftieth session (3–21 July 2017)*, UN Doc. A/CN.9/917, available at https://documents-dds-ny.un.org/doc/UNDOC/GEN/V17/023/69/PDF/V1702369.pdf?OpenElement (last accessed 11 July 2019); United Nations Conference on Trade and Development ('UNCTAD'), 'IIA Issues Note: Phase 2 of IIA Reform: Modernizing the Existing Stock of Old-Generation Treaties' (June 2017), UN Doc. UNCTAD/DIAE/PCB/2017/3, Issue 2.

[4] In terms of methodology, it is important to clarify that Asian countries are understood in this paper as being those states geographically located in the Asian region and which are also members of the Asian Development Bank. In total, 49 states belong to the Asian regional members category. Apart from North Korea, all states (regardless of their size, population and political regime) are considered in this study and their respective investment treaties are analysed.

investment (FDI) amounted to USD 1.8 trillion.[5] That figure represents capital moving from investors based in one State into investments located in another.

The European Union (EU) is by far the leading foreign investment power. At the end of 2016, the EU outward stock of FDI in Asia represented EUR 621 billion, which is equivalent to 19 per cent of all EU outward stock of FDI and is the amount of FDI affected by the change in FDI competence.[6] In parallel with the economic significance of foreign investment, the EU is emerging as an international actor in the regulation of foreign investment. The Treaty of Lisbon extended the Common Commercial Policy to FDI in 2009.[7] Albeit subject to unanimity, the EU competence, which is being implemented (and which is affecting all third countries) is broad and exclusive,[8] thereby enabling it to conceive what could be the main features of a new model of European investment agreement.

The shift from national to supranational level is, in itself, a major legal development. The EU is likely to leverage on its significant bargaining power when negotiating IIAs to improve, for instance, the standards of investment protection or to develop new forms of all-encompassing agreements.[9] In this regard, concluded treaties with Singapore and Vietnam and current EU investment negotiations with Asian countries are not only relevant for immediate participants but also for third countries, in particular in Asia where EU investors have a significant presence which will further increase.

This chapter delves into the evolving international regime for investment in Asia and comes at a crucial time for the EU when it is multiplying the number of treaty negotiations with Asian members. This naturally raises the question of whether this will lead to a reset or recalibration of Asian States' commitments to investment standards. The Asian regime for investment is not static but is instead very dynamic. It continues to grow and change, and will be affected by various factors in the coming months and years which relate to the rise of some new actors such as the EU, the regionalization of investment rule-making (illustrated by the

5 UNCTAD, *World Investment Report: Investment and the Digital Economy* (Geneva: United Nations, 2017), pp. 1–94.

6 Eurostat, European Commission, January 2017. In Asia, the most important destinations for outward stocks of EU-27 FDI were Singapore; Hong Kong, China; and Japan. Together, they accounted for half of the EU-27's positions in Asia in 2010. The relative importance of the PRC as a destination for EU-27 FDI has grown steadily in recent years, and outward FDI stocks in the PRC reached EUR 75.1 billion by the end of 2010, which was higher than in the Republic of Korea, India, and Indonesia, which are the next largest partners. Virtually, all these EU FDI in Asia (and FDI currently made) will see their legal protection modified as a result of current negotiations.

7 *See, e.g.*, European Commission, 'Treaty of Lisbon enters into force – Implications for the EU's trade policy', 1 December 2009, available at http://trade.ec.europa.eu/doclib/press/index.cfm?id=493 (last accessed 11 July 2019).

8 The EU now holds exclusive competence over FDI, which is interpreted to include the classical standards of investment protection. However, the absence of a definition of FDI in the Treaty still leaves scope for disagreement. For further discussion, *see* Julien Chaisse, 'Promises and Pitfalls of the European Union Policy on Foreign Investment – How Will the New EU Competence on FDI Affect the Emerging Global Regime' (2012) 15(1) *Journal of International Economic Law* 51.

9 The 'negotiation mandate' for EU FTAs with Canada, India, and Singapore was approved by the General Affairs Council on 12 September 2011. This confidential document confirms the trend that the EU will negotiate broad and encompassing FTAs to replace narrow and conventional BITs. Neither the 2008 Economic Partnership Agreement with the Caribbean Forum of African, Caribbean, and Pacific ('CARIFORUM') states, nor the 2010 signed agreement with the Republic of Korea addresses the core investment protection issues of minimum standards of treatment, expropriation and compensation. Nor do they provide recourse to investor–state arbitration procedures. The latter outcome reflects the legal situation prior to December 2009 and the shared competency, or 'mixed competence', between Member States and the EU in matters of investment regulation.

Comprehensive and Progressive Agreement for Trans-Pacific Partnership (CPTPP)) and the likely increase of litigation in Asia. In this fast-evolving context subject to multiple stimuli, this chapter attempts to assess the influence of the EU's proactive investment policy in Asia.

The chapter first provides a macro-analysis of Asian rule-making. This section helps to explain what the key characteristics of the Asian IIAs are (Section 13.2). Once the relevant IIAs have been identified, the chapter explores the details of these specific Asian IIAs. In doing so, the chapter provides a detailed micro-view of the Asian rule-making in investment (Section 13.3). That fundamental analysis will be complemented by a study of the mechanisms that govern the interplay of bilateral Asian IIAs with the rest of the world through regionalization and the application of the most-favoured nation (MFN) treatment clause (Section 13.4). Thereafter, there will be a thorough analysis of international investment litigation involving Asian parties (Section 13.5). Finally, this chapter concludes by answering the question of how EU investment policy is affecting the Asian regime for foreign investment (Section 13.6).

13.2 THE ASIAN MAP OF THE EUROPEAN INVESTMENT POLICY

Trade and investment dynamics might be boosted further by recent EU reforms. The Treaty of Lisbon came into force on 1 December 2009, amending the former EU and European Community (EC) treaties.

By abolishing the EC and replacing it with the EU, endowed with full legal personality,[10] the Treaty of Lisbon was key to improving the trade and investment dynamics. The new EU has the ambition to be a more prominent global actor, with the creation of a new European external relations service with EU delegations around the world and the EU's High Representative, which is assigned greater importance. The Treaty of Lisbon extends the scope of external trade policy to issues of investment.

For the EU and its trading partners, the extension of 'trade' policy to include investment is an important development and will impact the international investment regime. The most important change to benefit EU investors might be the shift from post-establishment to pre- and post-establishment rights granted to foreign investors, which represent the two main approaches to the admission of foreign investment that can be recognized in the BITs.[11] 'Entry' provisions erode the host State's control over the admission of foreign investment into its territory.[12] They may affect the capacity of the host State to prioritize certain investments over others, and undermine its negotiating power vis-à-vis new incoming investors, which in

[10] Prior to the entry into force of the Treaty of Lisbon on 1 December 2009, the EU did not have the legal capacity to sign up to international agreements. Articles 216–218 of the Treaty on the Functioning of the European Union (formerly the EC Treaty) amends this – Treaty of Lisbon (2008) *Official Journal of the European Union* C 115/1.

[11] As stated by the Commission, 'a comprehensive common international investment policy needs to better address investor needs from the planning to the profit stage or from the pre- to the post-admission stage. Thus, our trade policy will seek to integrate investment liberalization and investment protection.' *See* European Commission, *Communication from the Commission to the Council, the European Parliament, the European Economic and Social Committee, and the Committee of the Regions: Towards a Comprehensive European International Investment Policy* (Brussels, 7 July 2010), p. 5.

[12] In its 2010 communication, the Commission points out that the existing European BITs relate to the treatment of investors 'post-entry' or 'post-admission' only. This is perfectly true and implies that the Member States' BITs provide no specific binding commitments regarding the conditions of entry, neither from third countries regarding outward investment by companies of our Member States, nor vice versa. But the European Commission observes that '[g]radually, the European Union has started filling the gap of entry or admission through both multilateral and bilateral agreements at the EU level covering investment market access and investment liberalization', and illustrates this in a footnote because at the multilateral level the General

turn is crucial for negotiating terms and conditions that maximize the investment's contribution to sustainable development.[13]

13.2.1 *The Evolving Asian Regime for Investment*

Understanding Asian rule-making in international investment requires knowledge of the international treaties (in the form of bilateral investment treaties or preferential trade agreements with investment chapters) that involve at least one Asian country.[14] If at least one Asian country has signed such an investment pact, the host economy is likely to be affected by foreign investment, and in any case, its domestic investment policy is subject to the international obligations which are expressed in the investment agreement.[15]

The first methodological challenge lies in the fact that there is no international organization informed by Asian States of their international treaties. Also, not all Asian governments publish the results of their negotiations. As a result, one of the contributions of the current chapter is to provide a mapping of these Asian practices based on a survey on the main IIAs databases complemented by each national government's source of information.

In terms of substance, Asian investment treaty practice (as with all other national treaty practices in this regard) shows that virtually all treaties listed above which regulate foreign investment matters cover the following nine topics:[16] (1) definitions and scope of application; (2) investment promotion and conditions for the entry of foreign investments and investors; (3) general standards for the treatment of foreign investors and investments; (4) issues of monetary transfers; (5) expropriation (direct or indirect); (6) operational and other conditions; (7) losses from armed conflict or internal disorder; (8) treaty exceptions, modifications and terminations; and (9) dispute settlement.[17] These diverse provisions are important to reassure foreign investors that they will be able to reap the benefits of their investment, and no trend denies such an approach, although evidence on the extent to which investment decisions are influenced by investment treaties is mixed.[18] The following sections detail each of these provisions in light of Asian IIAs.

Agreement on Trade in Services ('GATS') provides for a framework for undertaking commitments on the supply of services through a commercial presence (defined as mode 3 in GATS Article I). At the bilateral level, the EU has concluded negotiations with the Republic of Korea on an FTA, which includes provisions on market access for investors and establishments.

13 Karl P. Sauvant, 'Reforming the International Investment Regime: Two Challenges' in Julien Chaisse, Tomoko Ishikawa and Sufian Jusoh (eds.), *Asia's Changing International Investment Regime: Sustainability, Regionalization, and Arbitration* (Springer, 2017), pp. 41–46.

14 Julien Chaisse, Tomoko Ishikawa and Sufian Jusoh, 'Introduction' in Julien Chaisse, Tomoko Ishikawa and Sufian Jusoh (eds.), *Asia's Changing International Investment Regime: Sustainability, Regionalization, and Arbitration* (Springer, 2017), p. 2.

15 For the divergence of international investment treaties and domestic regulations, specific example can be found in Julien Chaisse and Lisa Zhouyue Li, 'Shareholder Protection Reloaded: Redesigning the Matrix of Shareholder Claims for Reflective Loss' (2016) 52(1) *Stanford Journal of International Law* 51–94.

16 In order to review the Asian IIAs key investment provisions, I will address the key provisions (leaving for the last section the important issue of MFN) following the same methodology: what is the specific definition given in the TPP, what is the meaning and what lessons can be drawn from the IIAs orientations. The negotiators have to opt for either an admission clause or the pre-establishment rights, the definition of national treatment, the minimum standard of treatment, full protection and security and the indirect expropriation methodology. In another paper, these provisions have been analysed in the context of Asian IIAs.

17 Rahul Donde and Julien Chaisse, 'The Future of Investor-State Arbitration: Revising the Rules?' in Julien Chaisse, Tomoko Ishikawa and Sufian Jusoh (eds.), *Asia's Changing International Investment Regime: Sustainability, Regionalization, and Arbitration* (Springer, 2017), pp. 209–27.

18 The extent to which BITs actually attract increased flows of foreign direct investment is disputed. According to Salacuse and Sullivan, entering a BIT with the United States of America would nearly double a country's FDI inflows. However, entering BITs with other OECD countries had no significant effect on FDI. *See* Jeswald

The current section looks at the investment agreements concluded by the forty-nine regional Asian Development Bank (ADB) members. In total, ADB countries have concluded at least 1,194 BITS and 61 FTAs with an investment chapter since 1959.[19] Since approximately 3,300 BITs have been concluded worldwide over the same period of time, it means that Asian countries have taken part in no less than 40 percent of international rule-making.

13.2.2 *The Asian Economies Singled Out by the EU*

As part of the triad with North America and East Asia in investment matters, Europe is one of the most relevant sources and destinations for investment. Yet the EU is itself only just emerging as a player in investment matters. The EU Member States have shown a great keenness to retain national control over foreign investment, rather than see the same incursions into EU competence.[20]

One of the resulting consequences is that investment was covered by a plethora of BITs between individual EU Member States and third parties.[21] BITs were considered to be the single most important tool in investment relations between countries.

By proposing in 2006 a 'Minimum Platform on Investment' (MPoI), the Commission sent a signal that it wants to acquire all the competences needed to negotiate investment deals.[22] This 'MPoI' intended to serve – rather like national Model BITs – as a standardized negotiation proposal for ongoing and future Preferential Trade Agreement negotiations with third countries.

The Treaty of Lisbon extends the Common Commercial Policy to the second most important field of international economic relations, namely, foreign direct investment (Articles 206 and 207 of the Treaty on the Functioning of the European Union (TFEU)).

W. Salacuse and Nicholas P. Sullivan, 'Do BITs Really Work?: An Evaluation of Bilateral Investment Treaties and Their Grand Bargain'(2005) *Harvard International Law Journal* 46 at 67, 105–11. Another important study concludes that there is 'little evidence that BITs have stimulated additional investment'. Mary Hallward-Driemeier, 'Do Bilateral Investment Treaties Attract FDI? Only a Bit … and They Could Bite' (2003) World Bank Dev. Research Grp, Research Working Paper No. 3121, 22, http://elibrary.worldbank.org/content/workingpaper/10.1596/1813–9450-3121 (accessed 11 July 2019).

19 For the purposes of this Chapter, all reference to 'ADB members' will be relate to the 49 regional ADB members from within Asia and the Pacific. From 31 members at its establishment in 1966, ADB has since grown to encompass a total of 68 members, of which 49 are from within Asia and the Pacific and 19 outside: *see* Asian Development website, www.adb.org/about/members (last accessed 11 July 2019).

20 *Inter alia*, this was showcased at the Nice Summit (2000), where EU Member States agreed to amend Article 133 of the Treaty of Rome (which governs the Union's common commercial policy) by extending EU competence to a number of 'new' areas. In a few sensitive sectors such as audio-visual services (*e.g.*, *'l'exception culturelle'*) and investment, EU Member States did not agree on handing over 'shared' or 'mixed' competence to the EC. With the ratification of the Treaty of Nice, investment was one of a few most sensitive issues that remain subject to the rules and procedures of inter-governmentalism, as opposed to the 'community approach'. *See* Marcus Klamert and Niklas Maydell, 'Lost in Exclusivity: Implied Non-Exclusive External Competences in Community Law' (2008) 13 *European Foreign Affairs Review* 493–94.

21 Tomas Baert, 'The Euro-Mediterranean Agreements' in Gary Sampson and Stephen Woolcock (eds.), *Regionalism, Multilateralism and Economic integration – The Recent Experience* (New York: United Nations University Press, 2003), p. 116.

22 In November 2006 the Council of the European Union adopted the 'Minimum Platform on Investment' for EU FTAs with third countries (Minimum Platform on Investment, Council of the European Union, 15375/06, 27 November 2006). As explained at that time, the EU was already determined to expand its Common Commercial Policy powers to cover also investment issues. *See* Niklas Maydell, 'The European Community's Minimum Platform on Investment or the Trojan Horse of Investment Competence' in August Reinisch and Christina Knahr (eds.), *International Investment Law in Context* (The Hague: Eleven International Publishing, 2008), pp. 204–06.

However, in its 2/15 Opinion rendered in May 2017,[23] although the Court confirmed that the EU had exclusive competence over most of the EU–Singapore FTA, it also said that there is a shared competence over non-direct investment and Investor–State Dispute Settlement (ISDS). Despite the fact that the EU thus enjoyed competence to conclude the EU–Singapore FTA, the European Court of Justice (ECJ) came to the conclusion that the agreement required the involvement of the Member States in the ratification process.[24] This latest development might slightly complicate the political processes of negotiations and ratification (as some EU Member States might interfere in light of their interest), but should not affect the leadership of the EU in the investment policy-making.

The EU have already concluded trade agreements that include an investment chapter with both Singapore and Vietnam. In addition, as of July 2019, there are eight Asian partners with which the EU was negotiating new trade agreements which will reflect the recent changes in EU FDI competence, namely India, China, Japan, ASEAN as a bloc, but also bilateral discussions with Indonesia, Malaysia and Thailand. Almost all these countries are also involved in other investment negotiations: Malaysia, Singapore, and Japan signed the CPTPP, while ASEAN is leading the Regional Comprehensive Economic Partnership (RCEP) project.

13.3 THE ENDOGENOUS DETERMINANTS OF THE NEXT INVESTMENT TREATIES

This section looks at the investment agreements concluded by the forty-nine ADB developing member economies.[25] In order to facilitate the analysis of the huge number of treaties, four main groups of Asian countries are distinguished to reflect their respective role and importance in Asian investment rule-making. This section identifies the 'Asian Noodle Bowl' of IIA which represents the existing negotiated preferential treatment for investors that the EU will try to neutralize through current negotiations. It then identifies the various roles played by Asian countries and, in particular, by the eight partners already singled out by the EU. Third, the section looks at the quality of some existing Asian IIAs.

13.3.1 *Identifying the Asian Noodle Bowl of Investment Treaties*

In order to refine the contribution of ADB countries to international investment rule-making, it is necessary to narrow the analysis to these IIAs which have been concluded between Asian countries only. Indeed, many of the agreements presented above may have been concluded with leading capital exporting countries such as the United States or other Western countries, and this implies that the treaty might rather reflect the interest and bargaining power of the capital exporting countries. Narrowing the analysis to pure Asian IIAs also helps to identify the ADB countries that play a leading role in the development of investment rules in Asia.

[23] European Court of Justice, Opinion 2/15 of the Court (Full Court), EU-Singapore Free Trade Agreement, 16 May 2017, available at http://curia.europa.eu/juris/document/document.jsf?text=&docid=190727&pageIndex=0&doclang=EN&mode=lst&dir=&occ=first&part=1&cid=882092 (last accessed 11 July 2019).

[24] Ibid., paras. 244 and 292.

[25] Portions of this text draw updated tables earlier published as Julien Chaisse and Shintaro Hamanaka 'The Investment Version of the Asian Noodle Bowl: The Proliferation of International Investment Agreements' (April 2014) *ADB Working Paper Series on Regional Economic Integration No. 128*, available at www.adb.org/publications/investment-version-asian-noodle-bowl (last accessed 11 July 2019).

TABLE 13.1 *Current EU negotiations with Asian economies since 2009 to July 2019*

Asian country	Negotiating directives	Current status	Next steps
PRC	The Council authorized the Commission to initiate negotiations for a comprehensive EU-China investment agreement on 18 October 2013. The mandate to launch negotiations on a new Partnership and Cooperation Agreement with China was approved by the Council in December 2005.	Negotiations of a comprehensive EU-China investment agreement were formally launched at the EU–China Summit of 21 November 2013 in Beijing. The aim of this agreement is to remove market access barriers to investment and provide a high level of protection to investors and investments in EU and China markets. It will replace the twenty-six existing Bilateral Investment Treaties between twenty-seven individual EU Member States and China by one single comprehensive investment Agreement. The 14th round of negotiations took place in Brussels the week of 11 July 2017. In 2016 the EU and China negotiators reached clear conclusions on an ambitious and comprehensive scope for the EU–China investment agreement and established a joint negotiating text. The 21st round of negotiations took place in Beijing in the week of 10 June 2019. Separate negotiations with China for an upgrade of the 1985 Trade and Economic Cooperation Agreement were launched in 2007 but have been stalled since 2011 due to divergences between the mandates and expectations of the parties.	No date set for the next round.

India	Negotiating directives obtained in April 2007.	Negotiations for an ambitious and broad-based FTA were launched in June 2007 and, after twelve formal rounds and several technical meetings, were brought to a de facto standstill in the summer 2013 due to a mismatch of the level of ambitions. The EU remains committed to strengthening the economic partnership with India, and to a comprehensive and mutually beneficial India–EU FTA once there is sufficient mutual understanding on the scope and level of ambition thereof.	Both sides remain in regular contact in order to create the right conditions for resumption.
Singapore	Based on 2007 ASEAN negotiating directives.	Trade and investment negotiations with Singapore were launched in 2010 and completed in 2012, with the exception of provisions on investment protection, which were finalized in 2014 and subsequently amended in 2017 to bring them in line with the EU's new approach to investment protection and dispute resolution. Following the Court of Justice of the EU Opinion 2/15 (issued on 16 May 2017), the result of negotiations with Singapore was adjusted to create two standalone agreements: a Free Trade Agreement (FTA) and an Investment Protection Agreement (IPA). The draft trade and investment agreements were signed on 19 October 2018 and received the consent of the European Parliament on 13 February 2019.	Following the EP's consent, the FTA should enter into force once Singapore concludes its own internal procedures and both sides complete the final formalities. The IPA will further need to be ratified by all EU Member States according to their own national procedures before it can enter into force.

TABLE 13.1 *(continued)*

Asian country	Negotiating directives	Current status	Next steps
Malaysia	Based on 2007 ASEAN negotiating directives.	Trade and investment negotiations with Malaysia were launched in 2010 and, after seven rounds of negotiation, put on hold in April 2012 at the request of Malaysia.	Before resuming negotiations, it is important that the EU and Malaysia see eye-to-eye on the level of ambition of a future deal. The EU is looking for a comprehensive and ambitious agreement, equivalent to the ones it has reached with Singapore and Vietnam. A stocktaking exercise took place in 2016–2017 to assess prospects in this regard. The government that took office in Malaysia following the general elections of May 2018 has yet to take a position on the possible resumption of negotiations.

ASEAN	Negotiating directives obtained in April 2007.	Negotiations with a regional grouping of 7 ASEAN Member States started in July 2007. In March 2009, the 7th Joint Committee agreed to take a pause in the regional negotiations. In December 2009, EU Member States agreed that the Commission would pursue FTA negotiations in a bilateral format with countries of ASEAN. Negotiations with Singapore and Malaysia were launched in 2010, with Vietnam in June 2012 and with Thailand in March 2013. Negotiations with Philippines and Indonesia were launched in 2016. In March 2017 Ministers tasked the Senior Economic Officials to work out the parameters of a future ASEAN–EU region-to-region agreement and to report back to the next Ministerial meeting in 2018 under the Singapore chairmanship. In March 2018 in Singapore the Ministers took note of the progress done and tasked the Senior Economic Officials to continue their efforts in developing the future Framework, including through continued domestic consultations and engagements in experts' dialogues.	A group meeting taking place in July is to be confirmed.

TABLE 13.1 *(continued)*

Asian country	Negotiating directives	Current status	Next steps
Vietnam	Based on 2007 ASEAN negotiating directives.	Trade and investment negotiations with Vietnam were launched in 2012 and completed in December 2015. Following the Court of Justice of the EU Opinion 2/15, and in a similar way to what had been done with the EU-Singapore agreements, the result of negotiations with Vietnam was adjusted to create a Free Trade Agreement (FTA) and an Investment Protection Agreement (IPA). The trade and investment agreements were signed on 30 June 2019. The texts are available on DG Trade's website.	Following the signature of the agreements, both sides are carrying out their respective ratification procedures. On the EU side, the Council has seized the European Parliament for its consent. Once the European Parliament has given its consent, the FTA can be officially concluded by the Council and enter into force. The IPA will further need to be ratified by all EU Member States according to their own national procedures before it can enter into force.
Indonesia	Based on 2007 ASEAN negotiating directives.	The Council gave the Commission the green light to start negotiations for an FTA with Indonesia on 18 July 2016. The first round of negotiations took place in September 2016 in Brussels. The last round of negotiations took place in the week of 17 June 2019 in Jakarta.	The 9th round is scheduled to take place in the week of 30 September 2019 in Brussels.
Japan	Negotiating directives adopted on 29 November 2012.	The EU-Japan Economic Partnership Agreement came into force on 1 February 2019. The EPA removes the vast majority of duties paid by EU companies, which sum up to €1 billion annually, opens the Japanese market to key EU agricultural exports and increases opportunities in a range of sectors. It sets the highest standards of labour, safety, environmental and consumer protection, data protection, fully safeguards public services and has a dedicated chapter on sustainable development. For the first time, an agreement includes a specific commitment to the Paris climate change.	Negotiations continue separately for an Investment Protection Agreement (IPA) with Japan. While the substantive provisions have been agreed, the procedural ones (ICS) are still not accepted by Japan. The last discussions on the IPA took place on 20–22 March 2019 in Tokyo. The next discussions are planned for autumn 2019.

Thailand	Based on 2007 ASEAN negotiating directives.	The Council endorsed the launch of negotiations on an FTA with Thailand in February 2013. The talks were officially launched in March 2013 and four rounds took place with the last one held in April 2014. Since the military takeover in Thailand in May 2014 no further FTA rounds have been scheduled.	The EU remains committed to resuming negotiations with Thailand when the conditions are right to do so.
Philippines	Based on 2007 ASEAN negotiating directives.	Trade and investment negotiations with the Philippines were launched in December 2015. The first round of negotiations took place in May 2016 in Brussels and the second round was held in February 2017 in Cebu City (Philippines).	No date has been set yet for the next round of negotiations.
Myanmar/ Burma	Negotiating directives for an investment protection agreement adopted in March 2014.	The EU sent its text proposal in December 2014. Four rounds of negotiations have taken place so far: 9–12 February 2015, 25–29 May 2015, 21–23 September 2015 and 13–16 December 2016. Technical discussions were held on 26–27 April 2017, and good progress was made, but discussions will have to continue.	No date has been set yet for the next round of negotiations.

Source: EU, Trade Directorate Overview of FTA and other Trade Negotiations (updated July 2019).

In total, 208 IIAs have been concluded between two or more countries which are Asian. This great number of IIAs forms what is the core of the Asian Noodle Bowl of investment treaties. Out of the 208 IIAs, there are 146 BITs which are currently in force, whereas 41 BITs have been signed but have not yet entered into force. To these 187 BITs, one must add twenty-one FTAs with investment chapters, all of which have entered into force.

One may also discern certain patterns for each country. For instance, Singapore is a major user of FTAs to regulate investment as it already has seven such instruments. Next in line are New Zealand and Japan, with six FTAs covering investment issues. A majority of Asian countries have so far been reluctant to incorporate investment negotiations in their trade agreements. One can also observe that some countries have had difficulties in ratifying a BIT which was signed earlier. This is the case of Cambodia, Tajikistan, Vietnam and Malaysia, which have six BITs. At the top of this list is Pakistan which has signed eight BITs, all of which are yet to enter into force.

Basically, one key idea is that China has BITs or FTAs with almost all ADB countries except Nepal, and this makes China the Asian leader in investment rule-making.[26] China (thirty Asian IIAs) but also India (twenty-three Asian IIAs), Korea (twenty-two Asian IIAs), Vietnam (twenty-one Asian IIAs), Indonesia (twenty Asian IIAs) and Malaysia (nineteen Asian IIAs) are the ADB countries with the greatest number of IIAs in force which are also diverse in their forms (either BITs or FTAs). These are the big players which will be at the core of the substantive analysis in Section 13.3. These frontrunners' treaty practice is not only important in quantitative and qualitative terms, but it is also crucial in the light of one key IIAs provision, namely, the MFN treatment. This particular provision plays a role which increases in significance when a country is bound by a great number of investment treaties. The case of China is, in this light, very important as the MFN provision found in China's IIAs may, to some extent, represent an embryo of Asian multilateral agreements on investment.

This survey of IIAs concluded between Asian countries also helps to explain an important feature of Asian investment rule-making – the rise of FTAs to regulate investment matters. In total, twenty Asian FTAs with investment chapters have been concluded since 2001.[27]

13.3.2 *Quantitative Ranking*

First, there is a group of twelve ADB economies which had not concluded a single investment agreement as of January 2017. Bhutan, Cook Islands, Fiji, Kiribati, Maldives, Marshall Islands, the Federated States of Micronesia, Nauru, Palau, Samoa, Solomon Islands and Tuvalu have so far been reluctant to engage in international investment rule-making. Second,

[26] Leon E. Trakman, 'China's Regulation of Foreign Direct Investment' in Julien Chaisse, Tomoko Ishikawa and Sufian Jusoh (eds.), *Asia's Changing International Investment Regime: Sustainability, Regionalization, and Arbitration* (Springer, 2017), pp. 67–95.

[27] A list of Asian FTAs is as follows: New Zealand–Singapore FTA (1 January 2001); Japan–Singapore FTA (30 November 2002); China–Hong Kong FTA (29 June 2003); Singapore–Australia FTA (28 July 2003); Thailand–Australia FTA (1 January 2005); India–Singapore FTA (1 August 2005); Korea, Republic of–Singapore FTA (2 March 2006); Trans-Pacific Strategic Economic Partnership (Brunei Darussalam, Chile, New Zealand, Singapore) (28 May 2006); Japan–Malaysia FTA (13 July 2006); Pakistan–China FTA (1 July 2007); Japan–Thailand FTA (1 November 2007); Pakistan–Malaysia FTA (1 January 2008); Brunei Darussalam–Japan FTA (31 July 2008); China–New Zealand FTA (1 October 2008); Japan–Indonesia FTA (1 July 2008); Japan–Philippines FTA (11 December 2008); New Zealand–Malaysia FTA (1 August 2010); Hong Kong–New Zealand FTA (1 January 2011); Australia–New Zealand FTA ('ANZCERTA') (1 January 1989) (Investment Protocol 2011); ASEAN Comprehensive on Investment Agreement ('ACIA') (1 March 2012).

a group of nine ADB economies has signed a limited number of IIAs. Indeed, Tonga, Vanuatu, Afghanistan, Myanmar, Nepal, Papua New Guinea, Brunei Darussalam, Timor-Leste and New Zealand have each signed less than ten IIAs. Third, a group of fourteen ADB member economies has signed between ten and forty IIAs. This group comprises Hong Kong, China; Cambodia; Lao People's Democratic Republic (Laos PDR); Turkmenistan; Taipei, China; Japan; Australia; Kyrgyz Republic; Sri Lanka; Bangladesh; Georgia; Tajikistan; Armenia; and the Philippines.

Finally, there is a group comprising the frontrunners, which are the economies that have concluded more than forty IIAs: Thailand, Kazakhstan, Mongolia, Azerbaijan, Pakistan, Uzbekistan, Singapore, Vietnam, Indonesia, Malaysia, India, the Republic of Korea and, at the forefront, the People's Republic of China (PRC).[28] It is within this last group that most of our micro-analysis will be based. Logically, the great number of IIAs they have concluded reflects a very active investment diplomacy, which also means that there are bound to be a great number of third countries and rights granted to a great number of foreign investors. In this light, the EU has decided to negotiate investment with experienced Asian partners, including China, India, Malaysia, Vietnam, Singapore and Thailand, countries that are all in the Asian top tier. Only Japan, among the Asian partners negotiating with the EU, numbers fewer than forty IIAs.

If we limit the analysis to intraregional IIAs, some interesting observations can be made. One is that the PRC is the Asian leader in investment rule-making because it has BITs or FTAs with almost all ADB developing member economies except Nepal. The PRC (thirty Asian IIAs), India (twenty-three Asian IIAs), the Republic of Korea (twenty-two Asian IIAs), Vietnam (twenty-one Asian IIAs), Indonesia (twenty Asian IIAs) and Malaysia (nineteen Asian IIAs) have the greatest number of IIAs in force, which are also diverse in their forms. These are the big players that will be at the core of the substantive analysis in this section.

These frontrunners' treaty practice is not only important in quantitative and qualitative terms, but is also crucial in the light of one of the key IIAs provisions, that is, the provision which provides for MFN treatment. This provision plays a significant role when a country is bound by a great number of investment treaties. The practice of the PRC is very important because the MFN provision found in the PRC's IIAs may, to some extent, represent an embryonic Asian multilateral agreement on investment.

One may also discern some patterns for each country in terms of the distinction between BITs and FTAs. For instance, Singapore is a major user of FTAs to regulate investment because it already has seven such instruments. Next in line are New Zealand and Japan with six FTAs covering investment issues.[29] A majority of Asian countries have so far been reluctant to incorporate investment negotiations into their trade agreements. Virtually, all the FTAs concluded by India and the PRC disregard investment matters.

One can also observe that some countries have had difficulties in ratifying a BIT earlier signed. This is the case of Cambodia, Tajikistan, Vietnam and Malaysia, each with six BITs that have not yet come into force. On the top of this list is Pakistan, which has signed eight BITs that are yet to enter into force.

[28] Following the policy of opening implemented by the PRC more than 30 years ago and the admission of the PRC into the World Trade Organization, the PRC is now concluding a different generation of IIAs, the most recent granting full jurisdiction to International Centre for Settlement of Investment Disputes ('ICSID').

[29] For Japanese treaty practice, *see* Shotaro Hamamoto, 'A Passive Player in International Investment Law: Typically Japanese?' in Vivienne Bath and Luke Nottage (eds.), *Foreign Investment and Dispute Resolution Law and Practice in Asia* (London: Routledge, 2011), pp. 53–67.

TABLE 13.2 *IIAs signed by ADB member economies*

	Total IIAs	BITs	FTAs with investment chapters
China (People's Republic)	135	129	6
Korea, Republic of	97	92	5
India	84	83	3
Malaysia	70	67	3
Indonesia	64	63	1
Vietnam	59	58	1
Uzbekistan	49	49	0
Pakistan	48	46	2
Azerbaijan	45	45	0
Mongolia	43	43	0
Kazakhstan	42	42	0
Singapore	53	41	12
Thailand	41	39	2
Armenia	36	36	0
Philippines	36	35	1
Tajikistan	31	31	0
Bangladesh	29	29	0
Georgia	29	29	0
Kyrgyz Republic	28	28	0
Sri Lanka	28	28	0
Australia	28	23	5
Taiwan (Republic of China)	26	23	4
Lao People's Democratic Republic	23	23	0
Turkmenistan	23	23	0
Cambodia	21	21	0
Japan	27	18	9
Hong Kong, China	17	15	2
New Zealand	11	5	7
Brunei Darussalam	8	6	2
Myanmar	6	6	0
Nepal	6	6	0
Papua New Guinea	6	6	0
Timor-leste	3	3	0
Afghanistan	3	3	0
Vanuatu	2	2	0
Tonga	1	1	0

BIT = bilateral investment treaty; FTA = free trade agreement; IIA = international investment agreement.
Source: UNCTAD Database of Investment Agreements, WTO regional trade agreements database and National Ministries of Foreign Affairs public information.

13.3.3 *Qualitative Ranking*

All IIAs impose a series of obligations on the parties to ensure a stable and favourable business environment for foreign investors. These obligations pertain to the treatment that foreign investors are to be afforded in the host country by domestic authorities.

Meanwhile, such 'treatment' that encompasses many laws, regulations and practices from public entities also significantly affect foreign investors or their investments. Thus, analysis of the quality of investment treaties is important to provide a clearer view of their likely impact.[30] Not all investment treaties are drafted similarly and many of their provisions may vary significantly in terms of their scope of application and likely economic impact.[31]

The Bilateral Investment Treaties Selection Index (BITSel Index)[32] extends finely-detailed support to understand national treaty practices. In light of the great number of BITs in which different provisions and their different wordings would give birth to a broad kaleidoscope of legal obligations and, hence, regulatory effects, the BITSel Index, which is based on the eleven most important elements found in most existing BITs, provides guidance.[33] The BITSel Index has a scale from 1.0 (restrictive) to 2.0 (liberal). The data for the top five Asian frontrunners – Indonesia, Malaysia, India, the Republic of Korea and the PRC – have been extracted to shed light on the substance and quality of these respective treaties (Table 13.3).

The results are stunning because the strongest average quality indicator belongs to India (1.82), which is far more significant than those of countries with relatively weaker investment treaties such as Indonesia (1.57) and the PRC (1.58). Less surprisingly, the Republic of Korea ranks second (1.75) while Malaysia is third (1.62).

These average values are based on a relatively high number of treaties and confirm the significant gap between the top five in terms of rule-making: not all Asian investment treaties are similar. India is inclined to grant quite substantial rights to foreign investors, although it has signed fewer treaties than the PRC.[34] Conversely, the PRC has signed significantly more treaties, but their average quality is among the lowest of the top five.

Of course, these averages also depend on the partner countries. Treaties are, by definition, the result of negotiations and they reflect the consensus that the two sides have reached after exchanging their goals and visions. In view of this, we can take a closer look at the BITsel and see what treaties for each country in the top five stand at the extreme (most robust or weakest protection) of the national practice.

In the case of the PRC, the treaty with the greatest quality was concluded with Germany (1.90). This confirms the fact that the PRC truly entered a new generation of investment treaties, with greater rights and access to ISDS only after 2005, and thus the treaty with Germany represents a milestone. At the other extreme, the PRC concluded a series of relatively weak treaties with Bulgaria, Mexico, Colombia and Costa Rica. One can further fine-tune the

30 'While the treaties continue to govern the same key aspect of investment, they have morphed over the 40 year period to include different types of clauses. We need to take into account the heterogeneity in order to better understand the motivations of states': Srividya Jandhyala, Witolf J Henisz and Edward D. Mansfield, 'Pooling is a BIT Inappropriate: A Two Stage Model for Bilateral Investment Treaty Signing', Paper presented at the Annual Meeting of the American Political Science Association, Boston, 28–31 August 2008. 'While it should be recognized that a BIT could be an important commitment device, the nature of the commitment can vary enormously depending on the terms of the BIT. Too much attention has been placed on whether or not a BIT exists, than on the strength of the property rights actually being enshrined in these agreements': Mary Hallward-Driemeier et al., above n 19.

31 Julien Chaisse and Christian Bellak, 'Do Bilateral Investment Treaties Promote Foreign Direct Investment? Preliminary Reflections on a New Methodology' (2011) 3(4) *Transnational Corporations Review*, pp. 3–11.

32 BITSel, Bilateral Investment Treaties Selection Index, Version 4.30 (2016), available at www.cuhk.edu.hk/law/proj/BITSel (last accessed 11 July 2019).

33 These include: (i) the definition of investment; (ii) admission for foreign investment; (iii) national treatment; (iv) most-favoured nation; (v) expropriation and indirect expropriation; (vi) fair and equitable treatment; (vii) transfer of investment-related funds out of the host state provision; (viii) non-economic standards; (ix) investor–state dispute mechanism' (x) umbrella clause; and (xi) temporal scope of application.

34 Julien Chaisse and Debashis Chakraborty, 'The Evolving and Multilayered EU–India Investment Relations—Regulatory Issues and Policy Conjectures'(2014) 20 *European Law Journal* 385–422.

TABLE 13.3 *Sampling Asian treaties quality (BITSel quality indicator)*

	PRC	Rep. of Korea	India	Indonesia	Malaysia
BITSel number of IIAs	84	77	72	61	61
BITSel quality indicator: average	1.58	1.75	1.82	1.57	1.62
Strongest treaty and coefficient	Germany (1.90)	Vietnam (1.90)	Switzerland, Mauritius (1.90)	Germany (1.90)	Saudi Arabia (1.81)
Weakest treaty and coefficient	Bulgaria, Mexico, Colombia, Costa Rica (1.36)	Indonesia (1.36)	India (1.63)	Denmark (1.27)	Lebanon (1.36)
Coefficient of variation	0.31	0.23	0.20	0.30	0.29

IIA = international investment agreement; PRC = People's Republic of China.
Source: Data from BITSel Index, elaboration by the Author.

analysis and note that there is a significant difference between the IIAs concluded before and after 2005. In the wake of the PRC–Germany BIT, the PRC further negotiated treaties which were rather more favourable to foreign investors. This generation provides broader and more substantive obligations with regard to the treatment of foreign investment. Post-establishment national treatment – albeit with sectoral reservations in some cases – and no substantial restrictions on the ability of foreign investors to challenge host country measures in international arbitration are standard in this category. The PRC's 'new generation' of BITs concluded since the beginning of this century seems to belong in this category. As a result, these post-2005 IIAs obtained a score of 1.65, while those prior to 2005 scored only 1.55.

In the case of the Republic of Korea, the treaty with Vietnam is one of the highest scores (1.90). At the other extreme, there is the agreement between the Republic of Korea and Indonesia (1.36). India concluded more than a dozen treaties of a rather high quality, for example, the treaty with Switzerland and Mauritius earned a score of 1.90. On the other hand, a relatively poorer treaty was concluded between India and Mexico (1.63). Indonesia ranks fourth among Asian countries in terms of the number of investment treaties. However, it has a rather low average quality. In this light, it is interesting to note that the Germany–Indonesia treaty provides a very high level of protection (1.90), much higher than the Indonesian average. However, on the other hand, the Indonesia–Denmark treaty offers an example of a rather weak treaty (1.27). Last but not least, Malaysia, whose economic policy is deeply intertwined with politics, has concluded a relatively strong treaty with Saudi Arabia (1.81). However, the treaty between Malaysia and Lebanon scores poorly (1.36).

The next step is to calculate the coefficient of variation, which is a better measure of heterogeneity. The number itself expresses the relation of the standard deviation (a measure for the dispersion of the data) to their mean. If the coefficient of variation is lower than 0.5, the mean value is a good representation for all data. For Malaysia, it is 0.29. What does it tell us? Returning to our example, the 0.29 average for Malaysia means that the variation in the provisions is 29 per cent.

Because all the coefficients of variation are well below 0.5 for each BIT, the mean is a good representation for all the single BIT provisions. What does the coefficient of variation say in comparison to other countries? The one for the PRC is 0.31, so the heterogeneity of BITs is slightly larger for Chinese BITs than for Malaysian BITs. While the mean value of each country tells us how investor-friendly its BIT provisions are, the coefficient of variation tells us how heterogeneous they are. The key advantage of the coefficient of variation is that it is directly comparable across countries. If we have a coefficient of variation of country A at 30 per cent and country B at 60 per cent, we can say that the heterogeneity of country B is twice as large as that of country A.

At this stage, it is important to mention two lessons. Firstly, there is a significant discrepancy between Asian treaty practices and also between individual treaty practices for a particular country. Secondly, although this chapter focuses on the broad analysis of Asian investment treaties, it also underlines the need to look more carefully at the key provisions found in each investment treaty.

13.4 THE EXOGENOUS PARAMETERS OF THE CURRENT NEGOTIATIONS

The current negotiations on investment between the EU and Asian countries will also be affected by other exogenous parameters. Since the future treaties will be subject to existing MFN provisions, the meaning and implications of this legal provision must be reviewed. Secondly, the broader context of Asian investment integration through huge treaty negotiations (such as the TPP, RCEP and Triangular treaty) will be discussed. These ambitious pacts oblige the EU to negotiate at least comparable standards in order to maintain the competitive advantage of EU investors.

13.4.1 *The Most-Favoured Nation Treatment Principles in Motion*

The principle of national treatment prohibits discrimination on the grounds of nationality[35] and, more generally, any discrimination between investors and investments produced domestically and those from other countries.[36] Together with the MFN obligation, it forms the fundamental principle of non-discrimination in investment law.[37]

With regard to investments, the principle of the MFN treatment seeks to establish equal conditions of competition for all foreign investors, independently of their country of origin.[38]

[35] *Champion Trading Company and Ameritrade International, Inc. v. Arab Republic of Egypt*, ICSID Case No. ARB/02/9, Award, 27 October 2006, paras. 128 and 156.

[36] The Final Award in *Occidental Exploration v. Ecuador* stated that the purpose of national treatment is to protect investors as compared to local producers, and this cannot be done by addressing exclusively the sector in which the particular activity is undertaken. *Occidental Exploration and Production Company v. Republic of Ecuador*, LCIA Case No. UN3467, Final Award, 1 July 2004, para. 173.

[37] The scope and practical relevance of National Treatment is to a large extent dependent on the reading of the term 'like circumstances'. Its definition essentially sets the benchmark for national regulatory freedom to treat certain imported products differently from domestically produced ones. Indeed, '[o]ften the definition of national treatment is qualified by the inclusion of the provision that it only applies in "like circumstances" or "similar circumstances". As the situations of foreign and domestic investors are often not identical, this language obviously leaves room open for interpretation.' *See* Julien Chaisse, 'Exploring the Confines of International Investment and Domestic Health Protections – General Exceptions Clause as a Forced Perspective' (2013) 39(2/3) *American Journal of Law and Medicine* 332–61.

[38] Julien Chaisse, 'Changing Lanes – Trade, Investment and Intellectual Property Rights' (2014) 36(1) *Hastings International and Comparative Law Review* 101–48.

This principle allows investors covered by one IIA to claim equal benefits to those granted to investors by other countries, irrespective of whether those benefits are established in other IIAs, or in the actual regulatory practice of the host country.

While traditionally regarded as a standard clause without major implications, the MFN principle has, to say the least, recently gained attention in the ambit of international investment rule-making in the light of the application of this provision recently made by some arbitral panels.[39] The *Impregilo* v. *Argentina* tribunal majority diplomatically noted that the issues remain controversial and that the 'predominating jurisprudence which has developed is in no way universally accepted'.[40]

Article 9.5 of the CPTPP[41] investment chapter defined the MFN as follows:[42]

> '1. *Each Party shall accord to investors of another Party treatment no less favourable than that it accords, in like circumstances, to investors of any other Party or of any non-Party with respect to the establishment, acquisition, expansion, management, conduct, operation, and sale or other disposition of investments in its territory.*
>
> 2. *Each Party shall accord to covered investments treatment no less favourable than that it accords, in like circumstances, to investments in its territory of investors of any other Party or of any non-Party with respect to the establishment, acquisition, expansion, management, conduct, operation, and sale or other disposition of investments.*
>
> 3. *For greater certainty, the treatment referred to in this Article does not encompass international dispute resolution procedures or mechanisms such as those included in Section B.*'

The scope of most Asian IIAs MFN obligation, like any other substantial provision of the treaty, is limited not only by the overall coverage of the IIA, but also by the wording introduced in an IIA clause itself. Several aspects are relevant in this regard, as follows. Usually, whether the obligation applies to investments already established in the country, or whether it also applies to the ability of the investor to claim access to the host country (so-called pre-establishment rights). CPTPP MFN expressly extends the coverage of the MFN obligation to pre-establishment rights.[43] Usually, the language which allows the comparison between the treatment of investors from different countries may add specific conditions. The CPTPP MFN refers to the 'in like circumstances' which reflects typical wording of US

39 *Tza Yap Sum v. Peru* recognises the need to analyse the specific wording of each provision of a treaty in accordance with the established rules of international law; an *a priori* decision is not appropriate, *i.e.*, it is not possible to decide in general whether MFN clauses are efficacious in some sorts of situation while they are not in others; each MFN clause is a world in itself, which demands an individualized interpretation to determine its scope of application. See *Tza Yap Shum v. Republic of Peru*, ICSID Case No. ARB/07/6, Decision on Jurisdiction and Competence, 19 June, 2009, paras 196–98.

40 *See Impregilo S.p.A. v. Argentine Republic*, ICSID Case No. ARB/07/17, Award, 21 June 2011, para. 107.

41 The CPTPP is a separate treaty that incorporates, by reference, the provisions of the original Trans-Pacific Partnership ('TPP') as signed by Ministers on 4 February 2016 in Auckland, New Zealand. Under the CPTPP Agreement, signatories will implement the original TPP between them, with the exception of a limited number of provisions which will be suspended. Suspensions will remain in place until the Parties agree to end them, by consensus. The CPTPP treaty text should be read in conjunction with the text of the original TPP: *see* Australian Department of Foreign Affairs and Trade, 'TPP text and associated documents', available at https://dfat.gov.au/trade/agreements/not-yet-in-force/tpp/Pages/tpp-text-and-associated-documents.aspx (last accessed 11 July 2019).

42 Original TPP text, available, for example, on the website of the Office of the United States Trade Representative, available at https://ustr.gov/trade-agreements/free-trade-agreements/trans-pacific-partnership/tpp-full-text (last accessed 11 July 2019). The text of the investment chapter can be accessed at https://ustr.gov/sites/default/files/TPP-Final-Text-Investment.pdf (last accessed 11 July 2019).

43 *See* Julien Chaisse, 'The TPP as a NAFTA-related 'codification' and beyond' in N Jansen Calamita (ed.), *Current Issues in Investment Treaty Law – V* (London: British Institute of International and Comparative Law, 2014).

treaties and is very well known in NAFTA case law.[44] Finally, whether issues pertaining to investor–State dispute settlement procedures are covered by the MFN principle.[45] The CPTPP MFN clearly excludes in its third paragraph the ISDS clause.

As a result, the scope of the CPTPP MFN commitment is rather broad in order not to dilute advances made in future negotiations partners would conduct with third countries.[46] One can imagine that the CPTPP may apply to several third-party treaties with the possibility that the claimant may import substantive rights. For instance, the Tribunal in *MTD* v. *Chile* applied an MFN provision to accord an investment the fair and equitable treatment protections of other BITs.[47] The *Impregilo* v. *Argentina* Award recorded the claimant's contention that the requirement of 'full protection and security' in the Argentina–USA BIT was applicable through the MFN clause in the Argentina–Italy BIT.[48] Also, the *White* v. *India* Final Award held that the BIT's MFN clause, a substantive provision, reaches an 'effective means of asserting claims' provision contained in another of the respondent's BITs.[49] Finally, the *EDF* v. *Argentina* Award found that the applicable treaty's MFN clause permits recourse to the 'umbrella clauses' of third-country treaties.[50]

This should not be surprising. The principle of MFN treatment in the CPTPP is of paramount importance to the international investment regime. Non-existent in customary international law,[51] it constitutes the very foundation of treaty-based international investment

44 *Parkerings* v. *Lithuania* finds that for investors to be in like circumstances, three conditions must be met: the investor must be a foreign investor; they must be in the same economic or business sector; and the two investors must be treated differently. See *Parkerings-Compagniet AS* v. *Republic of Lithuania*, ICSID Case No. ARB/05/8, Award, 11 September 2007, para. 371.

45 Following to the arbitral decision in *Emilio Agustín Maffezini* v. *The Kingdom of Spain*, ICSID Case No. ARB/97/7), much attention has been drawn to the debate of whether provisions relating to the disputes settlement procedures enshrined in one IIA can be 'imported' into another IIA by virtue of the MFN clause. The question posed by the *Maffezini* decision ultimately addresses the general scope of the MFN principle and how the provision is crafted in each individual agreement. This leads us to last section of this chapter dealing with the TPP investor–state dispute mechanism.

46 One can first observe that the MFN provisions already existing in older IIAs will bring to them the benefits of TPP new chapter. Indeed, the commitments by TPP countries may have to be extended MFN, for instance, to Thailand (except dispute settlement), and China (except dispute settlement and obligations specific to existing FTA partners).

47 *MTD Equity Sdn. Bhd. and MTD Chile S.A.* v. *Republic of Chile*, ICSID Case No. ARB/01/7, Award, 25 May, 2004, paras. 104 and 197. This was later confirmed by the *Bayindir* v. *Pakistan* Award which applies an MFN clause to import the fair and equitable treatment standard from another treaty entered into after the treaty in question (*Bayindir Insaat Turizm Ticaret Ve Sanayi A.S.* v. *Islamic Republic of Pakistan*, ICSID Case No. ARB/03/29, Award, 27 August 2009, paras. 153–60), and ATA v. *Jordan* applies an MFN clause to import a fair and equitable treatment and treatment no less favourable than that required by international law clause (ATA *Construction, Industrial and Trading Company* v. *Hashemite Kingdom of Jordan*, ICSID Case No. ARB/08/2, Award, 18 May 2010, footnote 16).

48 However, the tribunal considers that having found a breach of the FET standard, it was unnecessary to examine whether there had also been a failure to ensure full protection and security. *Impregilo S.p.A.* v. *Argentine Republic*, ICSID Case No. ARB/07/17, Award, 21 June 2011, para. 334.

49 *White Industries Australia Limited* v. *The Republic of India*, UNCITRAL, Final Award, 30 November 2011, para. 11.2.

50 In doing so, the tribunal notes that it takes no position on the debate over the interaction of MFN clauses with jurisdictional and procedural requirements. *EDF International S.A., SAUR International S.A. and León Participaciones Argentinas S.A.* v. *Argentine Republic*, ICSID Case No. ARB/03/23, Award, 11 June 2012, paras. 930–36.

51 In *Asian Agricultural Products* v. *Sri Lanka*, the Dissenting Opinion of Samuel K.B. Asante, citing various publicists, noted that most-favoured-nation treatment does not derive from customary law. See *Asian Agricultural Products Limited* v. *Democratic Socialist Republic of Sri Lanka*, ICSID Case No. ARB/87/3, 27 June 1990, Dissenting Opinion of Samuel K.B. Asante, para. 40.

TABLE 13.4 *Non-applicability of the MFN principle to FTAs*

France 2006 Model BIT Art. 4	India 2003 Model BIT Art. 4	ASEAN comprehensive investment agreement 2012 Art. 6
This treatment shall not include the privileges granted by one Contracting Party to nationals or companies of a third party State by virtue of its participation or association in a free trade zone, customs union, common market or any other form of regional economic organization.	(3) The provisions of paragraphs (1) and (2) above shall not be construed so as to oblige one Contracting Party to extend to the investors of the other the benefit of any treatment, preference or privilege resulting from: (a) any existing or future customs unions or similar international agreement to which it is or may become a party, or (b) any matter pertaining wholly or mainly to taxation.	3. Paragraphs 1 and 2 shall not be construed so as to oblige a Member State to extend to investors or investments of other Member States the benefit of any treatment, preference or privilege resulting from: (a) any sub-regional arrangements between and among Member States; or (b) any existing agreement notified by Member States to the AIA Council pursuant to Article 8(3) of the AIA Agreement.

ASEAN = Association of Southeast Asian Nations; BIT = bilateral investment treaty; FTA = free trade agreement; MFN = most-favoured nation.
Source: Model BITs from national government websites.

regulation. The provision is constitutive of the system of a complex multi-layered governance for investment. Equally important in terms of future arbitration, the more IIAs that a country has, the higher the likelihood that MFN might play an important role in the future. Malaysia, Chile and Vietnam are in this regard, the CPTPP countries that should pay great attention to the CPTPP MFN, since these three have already granted rights to a great number of their party investors and investments.

The increase of Asian FTAs with investment chapters also raises an important issue in terms of connections with existing IIAs. Indeed, the MFN treatment provisions in existing treaties may give rise to the so-called free-rider issue that arises when benefits from customs unions, FTAs, or economic integration organization agreements are extended to non-members. In order to avoid this outcome, many IIAs exclude the benefits received by a Contracting State Party to a regional economic integration organization (REIO) from the scope of MFN treatment obligations through a REIO exception. Virtually all IIAs include a carve-out from the MFN principle (Table 13.4).

A considerable number of existing IIAs cover, at least, specific types of regional integration that are expressly mentioned in the agreement. But some countries extend the scope of the REIO exception to similar arrangements. For instance, the India model agreement[52] refers to 'any existing or future customs unions or similar international agreement to which it is or may become a party' (Article 4). The French model agreement refers to a 'free trade zone, customs union, common market, or any other form of regional economic organisation' (Article 4). Such provisions allow France or India to enter into new FTAs with investment chapters without the obligation to extend the benefits to countries with which

[52] Julien Chaisse, Debashis Chakraborty and Jaydeep Mukherjee, 'Deconstructing Service and Investment Negotiating Stance: A Case Study of India at WTO GATS and Investment Fora' (2013) 14 *Journal of World Investment and Trade* 44–78.

they were bound through a BIT. In this regard, one might also assume that some countries may be tempted to negotiate investment agreements in the context of an FTA so as to isolate the newly negotiated treaty from other BITs. Pakistan, for instance, seems to favour negotiations of investment within FTAs in order not to be subject to full MFN applicability under other BITs.

In light of this, the 2012 ACIA MFN exception is, logically, more limited. ACIA Article 6 applies only to 'any sub-regional arrangements between and among Member States; or (b) any existing agreement notified by Member States to the AIA Council pursuant to Article 8(3) of the AIA Agreement.' The effect of such a provision is to maintain the applicability of the basic MFN for the benefits of the members. Of course, in the context of a regional integration scheme, such as ACIA, members have an interest to be granted better treatment than one of them would grant of a third country, and this could be done through an IIA in the form of an FTA or a BIT.

13.4.2 *The Current Asian Negotiations on Investment: RCEP, Trilateral and TPP*

The rise of plurilateral agreements with wider scope is likely to produce greater economic effects while certainly spreading the basic principles of foreign investment protection to most Asian economies.[53] While the rise of plurilateral IIAs may alleviate the problems associated with the Noodle Bowl of IIAs, it may also intensify problems by creating more common-member agreements.

In this connection, three determinants are assessed to play a major role in Asian rule-making. Firstly, there are three Asian plurilateral agreements, either recently concluded or currently under negotiations, that deal with investment matters and illustrate the regionalization of investment law: ACIA[54]; RCEP; and the PRC–Japan–Republic of Korea Trilateral Investment Treaty. Secondly, the current CPTPP that was concluded on 23 January 2018 in Tokyo, Japan, may have resulted in one of the most ambitious investment treaties ever negotiated, which may have the potential to absorb all Asian investment treaties, once its investment chapter takes effect. Thirdly, an exogenous parameter is the EU decision to expand into investment negotiations and replace the negotiating role of EU Members States. Virtually all Asian countries presently bound with many of the twenty-seven EU Member States are going to be affected.

There has long been a debate between the PRC and Japan on the 'appropriate' membership of Asian economic cooperation bodies. The PRC prefers the ASEAN+3 framework (EAFTA), while Japan insists upon the inclusion of Australia, New Zealand, and India (CEPEA). To avoid being involved in the political rivalry between the two powers, ASEAN proposed the RCEP in 2011, under which the modality of economic interaction in East Asia could be discussed by going beyond membership problems. All partners that have FTAs or EPAs with ASEAN members – which include the PRC, Japan and the Republic of Korea, as well as Australia, New Zealand and India – are involved in RCEP.

53 Mark Feldman and Cristián Rodríguez Chiffelle, 'The Role of Pacific Rim FTAs in the Harmonization of International Investment Law: Towards a Free Trade Area of the Asia-Pacific' in Julien Chaisse, Tomoko Ishikawa and Sufian Jusoh (eds.), *Asia's Changing International Investment Regime: Sustainability, Regionalization, and Arbitration* (Springer, 2017), pp. 177–205.

54 Sufian Jusoh and Julien Chaisse, 'Ten as One? Explaining ASEAN Regulation on Foreign Investment' in Julien Chaisse, Tomoko Ishikawa and Sufian Jusoh (eds.), *Asia's Changing International Investment Regime: Sustainability, Regionalization, and Arbitration* (Springer, 2017), pp. 99–120.

Officially, the RCEP's aim is to create a liberal, facilitative, and competitive investment environment in the region.[55] Negotiations will cover the four pillars of promotion, protection, facilitation and liberalization. In this connection, the RCEP Working Groups in Goods, Services, and Investment were established by the ASEAN Leaders during the 19th ASEAN Summit to consider the scope of the RCEP and the ASEAN Economic Ministers have accepted their recommendations as detailed in the Guiding Principles and Objectives for Negotiating the RCEP. However, no progress had been made as of July 2013.

The ASEAN–PRC FTA came into force in 2005, while its investment chapter became effective in 2010. However, this is not an ambitious agreement, since it covers only the protection of investment. Meanwhile, Japan's EPAs with individual ASEAN members include relatively sophisticated investment chapters that cover both the protection and liberalization of investment. However, despite the Japan–ASEAN EPA being signed in 2008, its investment chapter is still under negotiation today. If Japan–ASEAN EPA's investment chapter simply consolidates Japan's EPA with individual ASEAN countries, it would become a relatively comprehensive one. However, there is a possibility that ASEAN as a bloc will exercise its bargaining power to lower the level of ambition. In any event, the modality of the future investment chapter for the Japan-ASEAN EPA will likely affect the investment chapter of RCEP.

Another important development that seems to have important implications for the investment chapter of RCEP is the PRC–Japan–Republic of Korea trilateral investment treaty, recently signed after nine years of negotiations. The trilateral investment treaty is not especially ambitious because it covers the protection of investment only (liberalization is not covered) and its list of prohibited performance requirement measures is limited. The dominant argument in Japan is that if the trilateral FTA between the PRC, Japan and the Republic of Korea is to be pursued, its investment chapters should be more ambitious.[56]

Thus, it is difficult to foresee at this stage the modality of the investment chapter of RCEP, mainly because of the disagreement between Japan and the PRC with regard to the level of ambition. Perhaps, from the Chinese perspective, the trilateral investment treaty is a done deal, upon which the investment chapter of a trilateral FTA should be based. From the Japanese perspective, however, upgrading the investment discipline is a necessary component of the trilateral FTA.

13.5 CONCLUSION

This chapter provides a framework of analysis for understanding investment rule-making in Asia and how EU investment policy is affecting the Asian regime for foreign investment. Viewed together, several important issues suggest that the EU factor only encourages a recalibration (rather than a reset) of the Asian regime for investment regulation. Firstly, as in the rest of the world, the regulation of international investment is a field of law, which has experienced major developments in Asia, especially during the last decade. Against such a fast-evolving canvass, the EU negotiations will both benefit from sound practice in

55 Junianto James Losari, 'A Baseline Study for RCEP's Investment Chapter: Picking the Right Protection Standards' in Julien Chaisse, Tomoko Ishikawa and Sufian Jusoh (eds.), *Asia's Changing International Investment Regime: Sustainability, Regionalization, and Arbitration* (Springer, 2017), pp. 141–62.

56 Shintaro Hamanaka, 'China-Japan-Korea Trilateral Investment Treaty: Implications for Future Investment Negotiations in Asia' in Julien Chaisse, Tomoko Ishikawa and Sufian Jusoh (eds.), *Asia's Changing International Investment Regime: Sustainability, Regionalization, and Arbitration* (Springer, 2017), pp. 121–40.

investment rule-making from partners but also encounter difficulties in adopting state-of-the-art provisions.

Secondly, there are currently 146 intraregional BITs in force, and there are 41 intraregional BITs that have been signed but have not yet entered into force. In addition, there are 21 intraregional FTAs in Asia that have investment chapters, which have all entered into force. Thus, in total, there are 187 intraregional IIAs in force (208 intraregional IIAs if 'signed but not yet in effect' IIAs are included). This large number of IIAs forms the core of the Asian Noodle Bowl of investment treaties.

Thirdly, out of the forty-nine Asian developing member economies, thirteen comprise a group of frontrunners that have concluded more than forty IIAs. This group consists of Thailand, Kazakhstan, Mongolia, Azerbaijan, Pakistan, Uzbekistan, Singapore, Vietnam, Indonesia, Malaysia, India, the Republic of Korea and the PRC. Last but not least, although investment rule-making has undergone profound changes in recent years (*e.g.*, 'treatification', legalization and proliferation); it is very likely to continue to evolve just as quickly. In this regard, a major trend of international investment rule-making is the increasing regionalization of negotiations, which will have an impact on Asian regulations. If the core of international investment regulations remains based on BITs and bilateral FTAs, it is important to underscore the importance of ongoing negotiations of broader pacts, which involve more than two countries and cover a number of economic areas. The rise of plurilateral agreements with a wider scope – such as ACIA, 'ASEAN plus' agreements, RCEP and TPP – is likely to produce greater economic effects while spreading the basic principles of foreign investment protection to most Asian economies. It also suggests that research and policy efforts should increasingly focus on these new instruments.

14

Reports of TPP's Death Have Been Greatly Exaggerated[*]

C. L. Lim

14.1 INTRODUCTION

In keeping with the book's focus, this chapter discusses the rebalancing of investor and investment protection in light of the regulatory concerns of the original twelve signatory countries to the Trans-Pacific Partnership's (TPP's) investment chapter (hereafter, 'TPP 12').[1] TPP's importance lingers notwithstanding claims in some quarters that the 'TPP is dead', following the Trump Administration's withdrawal from that treaty. In practice, treaty convergence – even sheer mimicry – occurs. One might think of that as being akin to procuring a live organ transplant. The analogy is not exact. Even long dead treaties can be organ donors and to the question how dead (or alive) a treaty organ donor needs to be the answer should be 'Who cares?'[2]

Thus seen, reports of TPP's death are not conclusive of its potential value as a model. They are inconclusive – even unreliable – evidence of any lack of prospect of TPP's design serving as just such a point of reference in future. Attention has in fact been drawn to TPP's potential in informing the design of the Regional Comprehensive Economic Partnership (RCEP) although little is known publicly at the time of writing of the investment provisions that could arise from those negotiations. Japan and Australia have proposed a 'high-standard' RCEP in the aftermath of the United States' withdrawal from TPP,[3] while for much of 2017 the remaining original signatories (hereafter, 'TPP 11') had been exploring ways to carry the treaty forward.[4] New Zealand was from the outset keen to forge ahead without the United States. The proposal was actively pursued throughout 2017 even if initially Japan and Vietnam had

[*] 'Mark Twain Amused', *New York Journal*, 2 June 1897 ('The report of my death was an exaggeration'). The erroneous version paraphrased here is the better-known.

[1] The United States, Canada, Mexico, Peru, Chile, Japan, Vietnam. Malaysia, Brunei, Singapore, Australia and New Zealand. For the background to the TPP negotiations, see generally C. L. Lim, Deborah Kay Elms and Patrick Low (eds.), *The Trans-Pacific Partnership Agreement: A Quest for a Twenty-First Century Trade Agreement* (Cambridge: Cambridge University Press, 2012). I say 'investor' and 'investment' protection in acknowledgement of the typical US-style clause which extends protection to 'investors'.

[2] 'Organ donor' was used in the author's presentation at the 24th General Council Meeting of the Pacific-Economic Cooperation Council under the Chairmanship of Vietnam, Hanoi, 15 May 2017.

[3] European Parliament Briefing Paper, European Parliamentary Research Service, May 2017, p. 5. The RCEP was signed on 15 November 2020 after this book went to press. The investor-State dispute settlement negotiations were previously suspended with a view to their future revival.

[4] The TPP 11 met in Chile in March 2017 for a high-level dialogue which included the participation of the Pacific Alliance, China and South Korea. See 'From TPP to New Trade Arrangements in the Asia-Pacific Region', ibid., p. 3.

demurred.[5] At the same time, nothing precludes bilateral deals based upon the TPP text and Peru had in fact proposed the 'bilateral adoption' of TPP.[6] Likewise, Japan has proposed bilateral negotiations with the United States. China, which had been invited to the high-level dialogue with the TPP 11 in Chile in March 2017, appears at least for now to have stuck to the RCEP and Beijing's proposal (first heard in the run-up to the APEC meeting in Qingdao in 2015) for a Free Trade Area of the Asia-Pacific (FTAAP).[7] By May 2017 TPP trade ministers meeting at the APEC Ministerial Meeting in Hanoi proclaimed a commitment to 'move forward',[8] Following the statement of the TPP 11 at the APEC Leaders' Meeting in Vietnam in November 2017, attention focused on the suspension of the application of a range of TPP provisions.[9] This the TPP 11 did eventually with the Comprehensive and Progressive Partnership for Trans-Pacific Partnership (CPTPP),[10] a TPP 11 configuration sans the United States which was signed on 8 March 2018 in Santiago, Chile. But this is not all. What is achieved with the CPTPP albeit presented as a near wholesale adoption of the TPP investment chapter – putting aside the 'suspension' of coverage of investment agreements and investment authorizations[11] – in a sense undermines in a significant way what TPP tried to achieve. Where TPP sought to counteract the wave of global opposition to investment treaties and investment arbitration and had sought to do so by rebalancing certain common investment treaty clauses which have been the source of special controversy, the CPTPP has – at least in the case of the treaty relationship between New Zealand and Australia, Brunei, Malaysia, Peru and Vietnam – excluded investor–State arbitration by way of side-letters. Thus, the CPTPP was not a mere adoption of TPP's investment treaty design. Rather – with the acceptance of New Zealand's rejection of investor–State arbitration by now no less than five of the TPP 11 – Saturn (the TPP 11) devours his son,[12] TPP's rebalanced provisions are rejected by a not insignificant group of its original signatories when it comes to New Zealand. The result sits uncomfortably with what the official narrative would have us think; namely the embrace by the TPP 11 of the TPP's investment treaty approach. Still, this chapter is not about the CPTPP. Rather, it is about TPP. To the extent that the CPTPP text was released, signed in quick succession,[13] and there is presently a febrile atmosphere surrounding it, it is mentioned as a necessary aside.

One thing is clear. The several options involving organ transplantation mentioned earlier, but for the curious example of the CPTPP itself, could if pursued lead to broader adaptation from and even adoption of the TPP's original design; even if the TPP itself ultimately fails to

[5] Ibid., pp. 3, 4. Japan, the Report notes, has warmed to the idea of TPP 11 since but the true explanation may lie in the fact that Japan is presented with a range of non-exclusive options – a bilateral deal with the United States, 'TPP 11' and 'TPP 12', among them.

[6] Ibid., p. 3.

[7] Ibid., p. 4. For FTAAP, see Collective Strategic Study on Issues Related to the Realization of the FTAAP (November 2016).

[8] European Parliament Briefing Paper, above n 3, p. 4.

[9] Trans-Pacific Partnership Ministerial Statement, 11 November 2017, available on the website of the Singapore Ministry of Trade and Industry at www.mti.gov.sg (last accessed 11 July 2019).

[10] For the text of the CPTPP, dated 21 February 2018, *see* the website of the New Zealand Ministry of Foreign Affairs www.mfat.govt.nz/en/trade/free-trade-agreements/free-trade-agreements-concluded-but-not-in-force/cptpp/comprehensive-and-progressive-agreement-for-trans-pacific-partnership-text/#chapters (last accessed 11 July 2019).

[11] To wit, the suspension of TPP Articles 9.1, 9.19.1 – a(i) B and C; b(i) B and C, and the chausette, 9.19.2, 9.19.3(b) (the phrase 'investment authorisation or investment agreement'), 9.22.5, 9.25.2 and Annex 9-L. Under TPP the latter carve-out – of investment authorizations – already existed as New Zealand, Canadian, Mexican and Australian carve-outs, in TPP Annex 9-H.

[12] Francisco Goya, *Saturn Devouring His Son*, 1819–1823, Museo del Prado, Madrid.

[13] 8 March 2018, Santiago, Chile.

come into being. Little compares, presently, to the attention which TPP's investment chapter, Chapter 29, has drawn. By now TPP's investment clauses are also, therefore, at least generally well-understood by investment treaty lawyers.

In short, notwithstanding the US withdrawal, the TPP model remains and it deserves close study for what it still reveals about a major initiative in the region to rebalance investment treaty commitments. The TPP's text can still be read as a search for a shared treaty vision aimed at accommodating social stability concerns alongside robust investment treaty protection and the device of investor–State arbitration. Tribunal awards on Asia-related or Asian-party disputes are still relatively few but controversy over some of these awards has already been felt from India to Indonesia. In this vein, a collective treaty vision, in a megaregional context, would facilitate a more coherent, principled treaty rebalancing exercise. The successes and failures of the TPP signatories' search has already been discussed earlier elsewhere,[14] and only the essential aspects bear repeating. 'Issue-specific' carve-outs are an example of a not wholly successful attempt to rebalance the obligations of host States, such as in the case of TPP's famous 'tobacco carve-out'. Here there exists a shared, principled public health vision which at the same time however was painfully narrow, highly issue-specific, and driven by external events.[15] Country-specific carve-outs are even less successful, in the form for example of Malaysia's limited carve-out of procurement disputes from investor–State dispute settlement, as others evidently did not share that vision.[16] New Zealand's latest carve-out of investor–State arbitration with five other CPTPP signatories is an example of a combination of both an issue- and country-specific carve-out.

Such examples are of incompletely shared social policy perspectives. They may be compared, however, to more comprehensive and cohesive treaty rule reformulations. In this vein, the TPP investment text also ushered in some fascinating new clauses which delegate to investor–State tribunals not only the task of resolving disputes, but also that of imagining, fashioning and applying appropriate standards of social protection. In an earlier paper, I have thus called TPP an exercise in 'prescriptive neutrality' as it stands in stark contrast with efforts to rewrite detailed investment treaty rules which will provide tribunals with little room to manoeuvre.[17] Of course, close prescription may be preferable in an ideal world, not least where the authority and legitimacy of arbitration tribunals is questioned. But in a world where social protection is only beginning to be built – and in a piecemeal, individual manner in various States, particularly in the developing world – one could hardly have hoped for close like-mindedness on how TPP should approach a range of social issues.[18] Still, TPP 12 had hewed together a fairly cohesive text according to a discernible and defensible design.

This chapter explores TPP's approach to regulatory autonomy safeguards as a rejection of a detailed, doctrinally focused approach to investment treaty rewriting. Rather, TPP's framers had abandoned bright line rules altogether where social issues were thought to be involved.

14 See C. L. Lim, 'Finding a Workable Balance between Investor Protection and the Public Interest in the Trans-Pacific Partnership' in Benedict Kingsbury, David Malone, Richard B. Stewart and Atsushi Sunami (eds.), *Contested Megaregulation: Global Economic Ordering After TPP* (Oxford: Oxford University Press, 2019).

15 That clause is peculiar for it allowed TPP parties to enter a carve-out immediately, but also for those which had not done so to do so at a later date after a dispute has emerged. See TPP Article 29.5. How this might affect the accrued rights, if any, of a private claimant in the context of investment arbitration is a fine question.

16 TPP, annex 9-K. Compare now New Zealand, which has sought to exclude investor-State dispute settlement altogether with some but not all CPTPP contracting states in the CPTPP context.

17 Lim, 'Finding a Workable Balance', above n 14.

18 I could say social protection is being 'rebuilt' into investment treaties. For a discussion of Ken Vandevelde's work in showing how embedded liberalism was once present in US FCN treaties, see Lim, 'Finding a Workable Balance', above n 14.

By way of a comparison, we do not see the EU–Canada Comprehensive Economic and Trade Agreement's (CETA's) detailed itemization of what can (and cannot) constitute a FET violation.[19]

In contrast, the TPP text is a pragmatic document. It is realistic in approaching the challenge of embedding investment norms in the social policies of the various TPP parties.[20] I would argue that this is part of an increasing acceptance by treaty makers and tribunals of a total absence of escape from investment treaty politics. TPP, however, is especially interesting as it is the latest break from a view once held that investment treaties contain rules with a fundamentally discoverable meaning, and that treaty law can somehow stand aloof from intense treaty politics.[21] Crafting more open-ended treaty rules may also present an alternate path to those who say that treaty-driven international law-making is exhausted in the modern age with the spectacular failures we have seen in multilateral treaty making in recent years.[22]

Because TPP's investment chapter is substantially a US-style investment treaty,[23] it should naturally be read against earlier attempts to rebalance successive US model BITs. In this regard, TPP's approach is not altogether new even if, as in some of the key examples I propose to discuss, it goes much further. In any event, TPP may be influenced by US treaties but is not solely modelled after them. Unlike the examples of NAFTA and the United States—CAFTA-DR, it is not a garden-variety regional treaty. Rather, it is intended to be a trans-regional treaty and had involved negotiations with a moderately large number of countries with substantially different approaches towards investment treaty design.

Notwithstanding the Trump Administration's withdrawal from TPP in the United States, the ensuing consternation over TPP's ultimate fate, and now that tragic creature which passes as the CPTPP's investment chapter, the intellectual contribution of TPP's investment chapter remains. TPP presents an approach to treaty rebalancing which is sufficiently distinctive, and which – who knows – could yet become dominant in the Pacific region not because of but *despite* the CPTPP.[24]

14.2 THREE CLAUSES (AGAIN) AS ILLUSTRATION

Observe three clauses in TPP's investment chapter. I have discussed these clauses in the earlier paper mentioned,[25] but will use them again as key exhibits to explain TPP's philosophy. For

19 CETA, Art. 8.10(2)(a)–(f).

20 This is a reference to 'embedded liberalism', on which see John Gerard Ruggie, 'International Regimes, Transactions, and Change: Embedded Liberalism in the Postwar Economic Order, (1982) 36*International Organisations* 379. See further, Andrew T. F. Lang, 'Reconstructing Embedded Liberalism: John Gerard Ruggie and Constructive Approaches to the Study of the International Trade Regime' in John Gerard Ruggie (ed.), *Embedding Global Markets: An Enduring Challenge* (Aldershot: Ashgate, 2008), pp. 13, 19.

21 For my earlier account, see Lim, 'Finding a Workable Balance', above n 14.

22 See Joel Trachtman, *Reports of the Death of Treaty are Premature, but Customary International Law May Have Outlived its Usefulness*, AJIL Unbound, 29 April 2014), at www.cambridge.org/core/journals/american-journal-of-international-law/article/reports-of-the-death-of-treaty-are-premature-but-customary-international-law-may-have-outlived-its-usefulness/8168FBD57CA3D393A8C83A8FF5BEB4D4 (last accessed 11 July 2019); and further, Joel Trachtman, 'The Growing Obsolescence of Customary International Law' in Curtis Bradley (ed.), *Custom's Future* (Cambridge: Cambridge University Press, 2016), p. 172.

23 See Wolfgang Alschner and Dimitriy Skugarievskiy, 'The New Gold Standard? Empirically Situating the TPP in the Investment Treaty Universe', Graduate Institute of Geneva and Centre for Trade and Economic Integration, Working Paper No IHEIDCTEI2015-08, p. 30.

24 At the time of writing, TPP signatories other than the United States have declared during at the APEC Economic Leaders' Meeting in Lima in November 2016 that they might yet find some way of pushing ahead with the deal.

25 See Lim, 'Finding a Workable Balance', above n 14.

present purposes, it may be useful also to revisit a well-known award – the *Methanex* Award,[26] which is now more than a decade old for the clues that it still offers to the thinking of TPP's American framers.

14.2.1 *Methanex and TPP's 'Like Circumstances' Test*

Recall *Methanex* v. *USA* then,[27] which was the very exemplification of controversy about over-broad protection given to foreign investors and investments. Indeed, *Methanex* is commonly viewed as a turning point in the debate about investment arbitration. Here I propose to use it only as a convenient illustration to demonstrate where the TPP's attempt to balance regulation against investor and investment protection would have drawn inspiration, and how the TPP model might therefore operate in practice.

The reader might also recall that the controversy in *Methanex* centred upon, inter alia, the application of NAFTA's National Treatment (NT) rule. Under that clause, a foreign investor's and investment's treatment ought to be compared to the treatment of domestic investors and investments only in cases where the two – domestic and foreign – are in 'like circumstances'.

It is noteworthy that the TPP text now says that this 'like circumstances standard' should take account of the existence of a national measure which is aimed at a legitimate public welfare objective.[28] In this way, TPP's 'Like Circumstances Clause' singles out a factor which is considered especially important and which it says a tribunal must consider. However, the treaty does not define the weight to be assigned to that factor. Furthermore, TPP does not tell us what aims should be considered to be 'legitimate public welfare' aims. This open-ended, pragmatic – legally realistic[29] – approach delegates to tribunals the task of assessing the legitimacy of such aims. I have chosen this clause especially to give the reader a foretaste of TPP's 'prescriptive neutrality'.

14.2.2 *Indirect Expropriation Will in 'Rare Circumstances' Only Be Found in the Face of a Legitimate Welfare Measure*

Methanex was, added to that, a case about indirect expropriation – what NAFTA Article 1110 terms a 'measure tantamount to expropriation'. However, under Annex 9-B, paragraph 3(b) of the TPP text (here dubbed the 'Rare Circumstances' Clause):[30]

> Non-discriminatory regulatory actions by a Party that are designed and applied to protect legitimate public welfare objectives, such as public health, safety and the environment, do not constitute indirect expropriations, except in rare circumstances.

The approach which TPP takes under this clause is to (again, as with the earlier example of TPP's Like Circumstances Clause) single out regulatory measures taken to protect legitimate public welfare objectives as a factor which must weigh with a tribunal. TPP does not specify

[26] *Methanex* v. *USA*, UNCITRAL (NAFTA), Final Award of the Tribunal, 7 August 2005; 16 ICSID Rep 40. *See further*, Kyla Tienhaara and Todd Tucker, 'Regulating Foreign Investment: Methanex Revisited', in C. L. Lim (ed.), *Alternative Visions of the International Law on Foreign Investment* (Cambridge: Cambridge University Press, 2016), p. 255.

[27] Ibid.

[28] TPP, Footnote 14.

[29] Lim, 'Writing Social Controversy', above Section IV. By which I mean American Legal Realism, see, e.g., William Twining, *Karl Llewelyn and the Realist Movement* (London: Weidenfeld & Nicolson, 1973).

[30] TPP, Annex 9-B, para 3(b).

how heavily this factor ought to weigh under the Rare Circumstances Clause. What TPP does, unlike the earlier Like Circumstances Clause, is to – at least – provide an illustrative list of 'legitimate public welfare measures'. I shall explain later why I believe this difference exists between the two clauses.

14.2.3 *On FET and Investor Expectations*

My final example is TPP's 'Mere Fact Clause', in which TPP addresses the doctrine of legitimate investor expectations in the tribunal jurisprudence on the fair and equitable treatment (FET) standard. This clause states that inconsistency with investor expectations alone is not a breach of the Minimum Standard of Treatment (MST), including FET. It is found in Article 9.6(4):

> For greater certainty, the mere fact that a Party takes or fails to take an action that may be inconsistent with an investor's expectations does not constitute a breach of this Article, even if there is loss or damage to the covered investment as a result.

Again, TPP singles out a factor, but this time – 'for greater certainty' – it prohibits a tribunal from placing sole reliance upon that factor in finding an FET breach. TPP does not identify what other factors might – indeed, will – also enter into the analysis.[31]

The three examples of TPP clauses which I have just provided are not the only provisions which show TPP's wariness of a bright-line rule approach. However, they are among the most interesting.[32] Importantly, they will suffice for the purpose of showing how TPP's framers have generally approached the investment treaty rebalancing exercise, which I now turn to

14.3 UNDERSTANDING PRESCRIPTIVE NEUTRALITY

I have mentioned that TPP maintains what I have called a 'prescriptively neutral' stance on the appropriate balance to be struck between social responsibility and the protection of foreign investors and investments. Let us come back to *Methanex*.

The essential facts, many will recall, are that a Canadian investor, the Methanex Corporation, and the United States were involved in an investor–State dispute under NAFTA Chapter 11. A third of the Methanex Corporation's production of methanol went towards the production of MTBE, a gasoline oxygenate employed as an additive in order to obtain lower fuel emissions. Research commissioned by the State of California had earlier recommended the phasing out of MTBE. However, a phase-out was denied by the US Environmental Protection Agency which favoured an outright ban. Methanex challenged that ban and a key issue arising under NAFTA was whether the ban – being an environmental measure – 'relate[d] to' an investor or investment.[33] Because ethanol production which has the same use had not been subjected to a similar ban, Methanex claimed that the United

31 Ibid.

32 TPP's many other innovative provisions include Article 9.16, the 'General Rebalancing Clause'. I have already mentioned TPP's carve-outs, be they country or issue-specific, only temporary or perpetual. At the same time, TPP's 'rebalancing clauses' (i.e. clauses which seek to assuage critics' demand for a more balanced trade and investment deal) include procedural refinements. As all these have been discussed elsewhere, on which see Lise Johnson and Lisa Sachs, 'Entrenching, Rather than Reforming, a Flawed System', CCSI Policy Paper, November 2015, and fall outside the focus of this chapter which is concerned with a distinctive non-bright line – what I have called 'Realist' – approach taken towards reform of substantive standards by the 12 original TPP parties, I leave them aside.

33 NAFTA, Article 1101.1. For an excellent discussion of *Methanex*, *see generally* Tienhaara and Tucker, 'Regulating Foreign Investment: Methanex Revisited', above n 26.

States had discriminated against Methanex in favour of Californian ethanol producers. That was how a claim under NAFTA's national treatment rule (under Article 1102) arose, as well as a claim of indirect or regulatory expropriation (under NAFTA Article 1110).

14.3.1 *NAFTA's 'Like Circumstances' Test and the Task of Assessing Legitimate Aims under TPP*

In *Methanex,* the claimant had advanced a broad reading of the term 'like circumstances' under NAFTA Article 1102's national treatment guarantee by equating the standard with that of 'like products'. The more broadly read the phrase, the more likely that a foreign and domestic investor or investment will be found to be in similar circumstances. The claimant had taken inspiration from the jurisprudence under Article 3 of the General Agreement on Tariffs and Trade (GATT) where the corresponding phrase was 'like products', which was clearly distinct from the NAFTA terminology. The GATT clause has been read broadly, albeit with careful attention to the structure of the GATT provision just mentioned, to encompass situations when two products show market substitutability.[34] In the context of the *Methanex* claim, this led Methanex to argue that the two markets for methanol and ethanol as oxygenates ought to be compared,[35] rather than drawing a narrower comparison between methanol producers in Canada and the United States.

Methanex's argument failed on textual grounds, given that the GATT was worded differently from NAFTA. What this meant – in the vernacular of trade lawyers – was that 'fine distinctions' drawn by a regulatory measure between a foreign and domestic investor, or between a foreign and domestic investment, may be valid notwithstanding the market substitutability of the products which a domestic and foreign investor produce.[36]

'Footnote 14' of the TPP investment chapter, the 'Like Circumstances Clause' states:

> ... whether treatment is accorded in 'like circumstances' under Article 9.4 (National Treatment) or Article 9.5 (Most-Favoured-Nation Treatment) depends on totality of the circumstances, *including whether the relevant treatment distinguishes between investors or investments on the basis of legitimate public welfare objectives*(emphasis added).

Viewed against the *Methanex* dispute, the intent of Footnote 14 becomes apparent. It focuses on whether a potentially fine distinction drawn in a regulatory measure is nonetheless drawn 'on the basis of legitimate public welfare objectives'. Footnote 14 does not say what such a legitimate public welfare objective might actually look like. Perhaps its framers felt they could not, and should not, pre-determine the issue. But in taking this path they have delegated decision-making to the tribunal. Implicitly, TPP endorses the exercise of strong tribunal discretion; indeed it has delegated the whole question of what objective would even qualify as a legitimate public welfare objective – what constitutes public welfare – to the investor–State tribunal. On such matters, TPP's framers remain wholly prescriptively neutral.

34 *See* Appellate Body Report, *Japan—Taxes on Alcoholic Beverages* (*Japan—Alcoholic Beverages*), WT/DS8/AB/R, WT/DS10/AB/R, WT/DS11/AB/R, adopted 1 November 1996.

35 This broad reading is not without precedent in the investment context, see *S.D. Myers, Inc.* v. *Government of Canada*, UNCITRAL, Partial Award, 13 November 2000; 8 ICSID Rep 18.

36 *See Methanex* v. *USA*, above n 26, Part IV, Chapter B, para. 28; *see further*, Howard Mann, 'The Final Award in Methanex v. US: Some Old Wine in New Bottles' (IISD, August 2005).

14.3.2 *Rarely Will Indirect Expropriation Be Found in the Face of a Legitimate Public Welfare Objective*

The *Methanex* dispute also involved a claim to indirect expropriation. Indeed, it was to become a crucial turning point in respect of claims of indirect expropriation. It takes pride of place in signalling the beginning of a contemporary movement towards the rebalancing of investment protection in order to better preserve the regulatory discretion of host States. In doing so, it was also a probable cause of a shift in emphasis in claimants' pleadings to breaches of FET rather than indirect expropriation. TPP's Like Circumstances Clause in Footnote 14 of Chapter 29, viewed in light of the host State's police powers, is only the latest evolutionary step of a treaty- and tribunal-driven[37] rebalancing process which gained momentum with the *Methanex* Award.[38]

Under TPP, all (direct or indirect) expropriation would be unlawful except where it occurs for a public purpose, in a non-discriminatory manner, on payment of compensation, and in accordance with due process.[39] As for indirect expropriation, specifically, TPP adopts the 2012 US Model BIT's 'three-part test'.[40]

The three-part test requires a tribunal to look to (1) the economic impact of the host State measure on the investment's value, (2) the extent to which the measure interferes with 'reasonable, investment-backed expectations',[41] and (3) the character of the host State measure.[42] TPP's 'Rare Circumstances Clause' for a case concerning indirect expropriation operates within this overall context:[43]

> Non-discriminatory regulatory actions by a Party that are designed and applied to protect legitimate public welfare objectives, such as public health, safety and the environment, do not constitute indirect expropriation, except in rare circumstances.

Observe, first, that unlike Footnote 14's Like Circumstances Clause which applies to claims for violation of the national treatment standard and whose textual language is absolutely silent on what 'police powers' States possess, the Rare Circumstances Clause provides an illustrative list of 'legitimate' public welfare measures i.e. measures taken for public health, safety and the environment. There is at least an apparent reason why this drafting difference exists.

In *Methanex* this question about what qualifies as a public welfare measure arose when the argument was raised that while health measures may qualify environmental measures will not.[44] The TPP's Rare Circumstances Clause puts this particular doubt to rest.

However – and this is a second observation – what might such 'rare circumstances' look like? Other treaties answer that question directly. The China–Canada BIT and China–Japan–Korea

[37] Tienhaara and Tucker, 'Regulating Foreign Investment: Methanex Revisited', above n 26, pp. 273–76 on the diversity of tribunal approaches; pp. 278 *et seq*, 285 *et seq*.

[38] Mann, 'Old Wine in New Bottles', above n 36, *p.* 6 *et seq*.; Tienhaara and Tucker, 'Regulating Foreign Investment: Methanex Revisited', n 26 above.

[39] TPP, Art. 9.8(1). TPP also clarifies that the concept of 'public purpose' is itself defined by customary international law, for which see TPP, Footnote 17.

[40] TPP, Annex 9-B, para. 3(a); *cf.* 2012 US Model BIT, Annex B, para. 4(a).

[41] Footnote 36 to Annex 9-B.3(a)(ii) offers closer guidance on the reasonableness of the investor's expectation, requiring weight to be given the existence of a written binding assurance, the nature and extent of the governmental regulation and the potential of governmental regulation in that sector.

[42] Annex 9-B, Para. 3(a).

[43] TPP, Annex 9-B, para. 3(b); *cf.* 2012 US Model BIT, Paragraph 4(b), Annex B. See also Footnote 37, which contains a non-exhaustive list of examples of 'regulatory action to protect public health'.

[44] *See* Mann, 'Old Wine in New Bottles', above n 36, p. 6 *et seq.*

Trilateral Investment Treaty both employ the three-part test.[45] In doing so, however, the 2012 China–Canada BIT looks to the severity of the measure and the existence of bad faith.[46] The China–Uzbek BIT also uses a severity test[47] and likewise with the China–Japan–Korea Trilateral Investment Treaty's own 'rare circumstances' test which turns on the 'severity' and 'disproportionality' of the measure.[48] In the case of TPP, considerations of fact and degree, such as 'severity', 'necessity' or 'proportionality' are already built into the 'three-part test' for assessing indirect expropriation.[49] No doubt, TPP's Rare Circumstances Clause is already shaped by TPP's definition of indirect expropriation, where one looks to the impact on the value of the investment, extent to which the measure or series of measures interferes with reasonable investment-backed expectations, and the character of the measure.[50]

Where investor expectations are at issue, one would look for the existence of a written binding assurance from the host government's relevant agency, and look to the nature and extent of the measure in addition to the potential for regulation in that sector in order to determine the reasonableness of the investor's expectation.[51]

But in clarifying that environmental measures qualify as police powers, TPP raises a further question: what other measures might qualify as well? What types of measures would be 'on par' with the paradigmatic examples of public health, safety and the environment? TPP does not clarify this, and in this regard, it begs the same philosophical question the *Methanex* tribunal faced in ultimately denying a finding of unlawful expropriation. The tribunal stated that as a matter of customary international law, 'a non-discriminatory regulation for a public purpose' which is 'enacted in accordance with due process' is not expropriatory (let alone

45 *See* China-Canada BIT, 9 September 2012, Annex B.10, para. 2; China-Japan-Korea Trilateral Investment Treaty, 13 May 2012, Protocol, para. 2(b). The new 2015 Indian Model BIT also employs a test which is similar to the three-part test. The new Indian test looks to the economic impact, duration and character of the measure as well as to 'whether a measure by a Party breaches the Party's prior binding written commitment to the investor whether by contract, licence or other legal document'; *see* 2015 India Model BIT, Art. 5.3.

46 China-Canada BIT, 9 September 2012, Annex B.10, para. 3 states that: 'Except in rare circumstances, such as if a measure or series of measures is so severe in light of its purpose that it cannot be reasonably viewed as having been adopted and applied in good faith, a non-discriminatory measure or series of measures of a Contracting Party that is designed and applied to protect the legitimate public objectives for the well-being of citizens, such as health, safety and the environment, does not constitute indirect expropriation.'

47 China-Uzbek BIT 13 March 1992, Art. 6(3) states that: 'Except in exceptional circumstances, such as the measures adopted severely surpassing the necessity of maintaining corresponding reasonable public welfare, non-discriminatory regulatory measures adopted by one Contracting Party for the purpose of legitimate public welfare, such as public health, safety and environment, do not constitute indirect expropriation.'

48 China-Japan-Korea Trilateral Investment Treaty, 13 May 2012, Protocol, para. 2(c): 'Except in rare circumstances, such as when an action or a series of actions by a Contracting Party is extremely severe or disproportionate in light of its purpose, non-discriminatory regulatory actions adopted by the Contracting Party for the purpose of legitimate public welfare do not constitute indirect expropriation.'

49 Annex 9-B, Para. 3(a).

50 For what might have otherwise been an illustrative case, *see Adel A Hamadi Al Tamimi* v. *Sultanate of Oman*, ICSID Case No. ARB/11/33, 27 October 2015 in which the three-part test is reflected in Annex 10-B 4(a) of the US–Oman FTA. As with the general design of the TPP's investment chapter, 'non-discriminatory actions by a Party that are designed and applied to protect ... the environment' would, likewise, be excluded from the scope of the US-Oman FTA's indirect expropriation rule. However, the *Al Tamimi* tribunal dismissed the expropriation claim on jurisdictional grounds. A more interesting comparison lies in the 2015 Indian Model BIT which, as we have seen, also employs something akin to a three-part test but unlike the case with TPP, the China-Canada BIT and the China-Japan-Korea Trilateral Investment Treaty, India does not favour a 'rare circumstances clause'. The Indian clause states only that 'Non-discriminatory regulatory measures by a Party or measures or awards by judicial bodies of a Party that are designed and applied to protect legitimate public interest or public purpose objectives such as public health, safety and the environment shall not constitute expropriation under this Article'; *see* 2015 India Model BIT, Art. 5.5.

51 Annex 9-B.3(a)(ii), footnote 36.

unlawful) and is therefore non-compensable in the absence of 'specific commitments' given to the putative investor.[52]

As for 'rarity', if a tribunal were to adopt a necessity or proportionality analysis,[53] TPP could suggest a generous assessment under not only the necessity, proportionality, or severity limbs of the analysis, but also the legitimacy of the measure's aim and of the connection or fit between aim and design. A future tribunal faced with a more unusual, even eccentric, aim is on its own. History has too often thrown up aims which have been political dynamite – Mexican agrarian reform, or a proletarian revolution – while today one might think of affirmative action policy, immigration policy, capital controls and other financial crisis measures such as Argentina's 'pesoization' policy.

14.3.3 *The Mere Fact Rule*

We turn finally to that head of claim which *Methanex*'s ruling on indirect expropriation probably caused to surge in popularity among claimants – breach of FET, on the presumptive basis that a FET claim may be easier to make out. I turn to TPP's Mere Fact Rule in its approach towards FET claims.

TPP's FET rule reflects the US Model BIT's rule. It is qualified by and linked to the customary international law minimum standard of treatment.[54] It is delinked from the breach of another provision of TPP or other international agreement.[55] The linkage to the customary international law rule sets a ceiling. This is made explicit by another sentence in TPP.[56] This is also true of TPP's FPS standard.[57]

Still, what the customary international law standard is, presents a difficult question. All we are told in TPP is that FET 'includes the obligation not to deny justice in criminal, civil or administrative adjudicatory proceedings in accordance with the principle of due process embodied in the principal legal systems of the world'. In other words, claims of denial of justice or breach of due process fall in, but then what else?

All of the above occupy the first three paragraphs of Article 9.6 of the TPP investment chapter. Then, the fourth paragraph states, as we have seen, that:

> . . . the mere fact that a Party takes or fails to take an action that may be inconsistent with an investor's expectations does not constitute a breach of this Article, even if there is loss or damage to the covered investment as a result.

We should separate uncertainty surrounding the customary international law standard and uncertainty over paragraph 4, the Mere Fact Clause, as a regulatory safeguard clause.

52 *See further Methanex Corp.* v. *USA*, *Final Award of the Tribunal on Jurisdiction and Merits*, UNCITRAL (NAFTA) Arbitration, 3 August 2005, para. IV.D.7. But see also Pedro J. Martinez-Fraga, *Public Purpose in International Law* (Cambridge: Cambridge University Press, 2010) pp. 84–85, criticizing the *Methanex* tribunal's application of the public policy doctrine.

53 See further, Caroline Henckels, *Proportionality and Deference in Investor-State Arbitration: Balancing Investment Protection and Regulatory Autonomy* (Cambridge; Cambridge University Press, 2015); Valentina Vadi, *Analogies in Investment Law and Arbitration* (Cambridge: Cambridge University Press, 2016), p. 203; Gebhard Bücheler, *Proportionality in Investor State Arbitration* (Oxford: Oxford University Press, 2015).

54 Art. 9.6(1) and (2), first sentence.

55 Art. 9.6(3).

56 Art. 9.6(2), second sentence.

57 Under Art. 9.6(2)(b), 'full protection and security' requires each Party to provide the level of police protection required under customary international law', and that standard is similarly subject to what has been said above about delinkage from the breach of another provision under TPP or a separate agreement, and the limitations imposed upon any search for an autonomous treaty meaning.

A customary standard has been applied by tribunals to protect investor expectations. In the famous *Metalclad* Award, there were already the beginnings of this, when the tribunal wrote that:[58]

> Mexico failed to ensure a transparent and predictable framework for Metalclad's business planning and investment. The totality of circumstances demonstrates a lack of orderly process and timely disposition in relation to an investor of a Party acting in the expectation that it would be treated fairly and justly in accordance with the NAFTA.

FET was used to fulfil expectations of a transparent and predictable framework for the investor's business planning and investment i.e. expectations of business and legal stability.[59] Today, there are other investor expectations, due in part to what Andreas Rigo Sureda views as 'unqualified reference[s] to the investor's subjective expectations'. This in turn has prompted tribunal warnings coming from the opposite direction,[60] but as the *Tecmed* v. *Mexico* tribunal put it in the licensing context:[61]

> The foreign investor ... expects the host State to act consistently, i.e. without arbitrarily revoking any preexisting decisions or permits issued by the State that were relied upon by the investor to assume its commitments as well as to plan and launch its commercial and business activities. The investor also expects the State to use the legal instruments that govern the actions of the investor or the investment in conformity with the function usually assigned to such instruments, and not to deprive the investor of its investment without the required compensation. In fact, failure by the host State to comply with such pattern of conduct with respect to the foreign investor or its investments affects the investor's ability to measure the treatment and protection awarded by the host State and to determine whether the actions of the host State conform to the fair and equitable treatment principle. Therefore, compliance by the host State with such pattern of conduct is closely related to the above-mentioned principle, to the actual chances of enforcing such principle, and to excluding the possibility that state action be characterized as arbitrary; i.e. as presenting insufficiencies that would be recognized '... by any reasonable and impartial man,' or, although not in violation of specific regulations, as being contrary to the law because:
> ... (it) shocks, or at least surprises, a sense of juridical propriety.

In *Saluka* v. *Czech Republic* the tribunal declared that:[62]

> The standard of 'fair and equitable treatment' is ... closely tied to the notion of legitimate expectations which is the dominant element of that standard.

And here is the NAFTA tribunal in *Thunderbird Gaming v. Mexico*:[63]

> Having considered recent investment case law and the good faith principle of international customary law, the concept of 'legitimate expectations' relates, within the context of the

58 *Metalclad* v. *Mexico*, ICSID Case No. ARB(AF)/97/1, Award, 30 August 2000, para. 84.

59 *See* Katia Yannaca-Small, 'Fair & Equitable Treatment Standard' in August Reinisch (ed.), *Standards of Investment Protection* (Oxford: Oxford University Press, 2008), p. 111.

60 A. Rigo Sureda, *Investment Treaty Arbitration: Judging Under Uncertainty* (Cambridge: Cambridge University Press, 2012), p. 77, citing *MTD Exports Sdn Bhd and MTD Chile SA* v. *Republic of Chile*, ICSID Case No. ARB/01/7, Decision on Annulment, 21 March 2007, para. 67 ('The obligations of the host State towards foreign investors derive from the terms of the applicable investment treaty and not from any set of expectations investors may have or claim to have').

61 *Tecnicas Medioambientales Tecmed S.A.* v. *United Mexican States*, Award, ICSID Case No. ARB(AF)/00/2, 29 May 2003, para. 154.

62 *Saluka* v. *Czech Republic*, UNCITRAL, PCA, Partial Award, 17 March 2006, para. 302.

63 *International Thunderbird Gaming* v. *Mexico*, UNCITRAL (NAFTA), Award, 26 January 2006, para. 147.

> NAFTA framework, to a situation where a Contracting Party's conduct creates reasonable and justifiable expectations on the part of an investor (or investment) to act in reliance on said conduct, such that a failure by the NAFTA Party to honour those expectations could cause the investor (or investment) to suffer damages.

Quite aside from the linkages, which tribunals have drawn,[64] with the legitimate expectations doctrine, the FET standard,[65] and indeed of the FPS standard,[66] are today seen to have themselves extended to an automatic assurance of a stable business and legal framework, and of a secure investment environment.

What TPP's framers must have held in mind in linking the MST/FET/FPS standard to international custom is the customary standard at the time of the famous *Neer Claim*.[67] There is too the assumption that a treaty FET rule has a fundamentally discoverable legal meaning. The well-known problem which, however, emerged from what originally was the NAFTA FTC's attempt to link the NAFTA and customary MST standards, is that we now have two lines of authority: the *Glamis Gold* line of authority, and the *Mondev* and *ADF* line of authority.[68] The former upheld the '*Neer* standard' of egregious, outrageous or shocking behaviour,[69] and rejected the idea that customary international law evolves through statements in arbitral awards. At best, awards only illustrate the application of custom where they do not involve what is purely treaty construction.[70] Against this, the *Mondev* Award stands for the contrary proposition that treaty practice has elevated the customary international law standard.[71]

The purpose of the Mere Fact Clause in TPP is to preclude sole reliance upon inconsistency with an investor's expectations as the basis for a tribunal finding of a FET violation. No positive weight is assigned to this sole factor. TPP merely states that whatever that weight, it is not conclusive. It could still be a weighty consideration, but this TPP's framers do not actually say. What they do say is that such weight which may be assigned to it is not all. Beyond that refrain, TPP's framers concede that tribunals should continue to enjoy wide latitude in making judgments of fact, degree and value. TPP's FET rule, unlike the indirect expropriation rule, says nothing about what to do with investor expectations beyond that.[72]

14.4 WRITING SOCIAL CONTROVERSY INTO INVESTMENT TREATY NORMS

It would be wrong not to see that the three clauses we have surveyed are also products of compromise. There is no coherent scheme beyond the singling out of factors – at times in a seemingly unconnected manner across the provisions – either as a mandatory factor or a factor defined negatively as one upon which sole reliance must not be placed. It is difficult

64 *Tecmed* v. *Mexico*, above n 61, para. 154.

65 *Occidental* v. *Ecuador*, LCIA No. UN 3467, Award, 1 July 2004, paras. 183–192.

66 *Azurix* v. *Argentina*, ICSID Case No. ARB/01/12, Award, 14 July 2006, para. 408.

67 4 RIAA, 60 (1926); 3 ILR, 213.

68 *Mondev* v. *USA*, ICSID Case No. ARB (AF)/99/2, Award, 11 October 2002, para. 125; *ADF* v. *USA*, ICSID Case No. ARB (AF)/00/1, Final Award, 9 January 2003, para. 179. *Contra Glamis Gold* v. *USA*, UNCITRAL (NAFTA) Arbitration, Award, 8 June 2009, paras. 600–01, 604; *International Thunderbird Gaming* v. *Mexico*, UNCITRAL (NAFTA), Award, 26 January 2006, para. 94; *Cargill Inc.* v. *Mexico*, Award, 18 September 2009, ICSID Case No. ARB(AF)/05/2, para. 272.

69 *Glamis Gold*, above n 68, para. 601. See also *Al Tamimi*, above n 50, in which the *Neer* standard was applied.

70 Ibid., para. 605.

71 *Mondev*, above n 68, para. 125.

72 *Contra* Annex 9-B.3(a)(ii), footnote 36.

to escape the view that tensions are being managed incompletely, and that there is much for the tribunal to do on its own.

One reason could be that suggested by a Principal-Agent Theory explanation – that this is all that the negotiators could achieve. Or worse, that when TPP is trumpeted as a rebalanced treaty, it is a bald lie. Both suggestions invite more careful consideration. Could the incompleteness of these rebalanced provisions not have been deliberate? Are we truly to take TPP as a lie and have that as the best construction we can place upon these provisions?[73]

US-style investment treaty clauses owe much of their liberal origins to the friendship, commerce, and navigation (FCN) treaties of the New Deal era. Ken Vandevelde, probably the foremost legal historian today of US BITs, has traced the modern US-style BIT to three commercial ideas – investment neutrality, investment security and market facilitation. These commercial principles, according to Vandevelde, mirror three political principles – liberty, the rule of law, and regulatory necessity.[74] Following the State's 'robust regulatory power' during the New Deal era, investment flows were reduced significantly. This ran counter to the notion of investment neutrality, which is the idea that 'investment flows should be guided by market principles',[75] that is, non-discriminatory market access. Consequently, even if discrimination was largely prohibited, market access itself was curtailed.[76] Neoliberalism, which the current backlash seeks to counter today, supports a second idea: investment security. And over time, pressure mounted to remodel FET and expropriation rules accordingly. This has corresponded with the evolution of successive US Model BITs.[77] However, the latest remodelling of treaty provisions, beginning in North America from about 2004, has aimed to strike a better balance with the host State's regulatory function i.e. in applying the principles of market facilitation and regulatory necessity.

The conceptual difficulty is that investment security and market facilitation exist in a state of perpetual tension.[78] Caught between binary, opposing demands the framers have elected prescriptive neutrality instead as their mode of treaty writing. They do so not necessarily because they are timorous, or because such an approach is simply a convenient way to close the deal (i.e. by way of deliberate constructive ambiguity). Rather, I suspect, because they well know that there is no science of treaty drafting that will provide abstract solutions for the practical controversies at hand – controversies which belong firmly in the political arena about liberty, the rule of law, and regulatory necessity.

TPP shows acceptance of the instability inherent in treaty-makers' assumptions about the guidance they can provide. It envisages a future in which tribunals increasingly resort to, or at least flirt with,[79] varieties of proportionality analysis and in so doing engage in some weighing and balancing (of their own) of competing public needs and private interests in politics and commerce. Some commentators have asked if a formal proportionality test is not even

73 See Johnson and Sachs, 'Entrenching, Rather than Reforming, a Flawed System', above n 32.

74 Kenneth J. Vandevelde, 'The Liberal Vision of the International Law on Foreign Investment' in C. L. Lim (ed.), *Alternative Visions of the International Law on Foreign Investment* (Cambridge: Cambridge University Press, 2016), pp. 43, 52 *et seq*.

75 Ibid., p. 52.

76 Ibid., pp. 52–53.

77 Ibid., pp. 53–59. *See further, generally*, Kenneth Vandevelde, 'A Comparison of the 2004 and 1994 US Model BITs' (2009) *Yearbook of International Investment Law and Policy* 2008–2009 283; Mark Kantor, 'Little Has Changed in the New US Model Bilateral Investment Treaty', (2012) 27 *I.C.S.I.D. Review* 335.

78 Vandevelde, 'The Liberal Vision', above n 74, p. 63.

79 See, e.g., the observations in Henckels, above n 53, pp. 124–25.

normatively desirable since tribunal analyses would assume – at least at the outset – that the host State's interest is an equally valid consideration. Proportionality analysis could require deference to host State policies under some form of margin of appreciation doctrine.[80] Admitting all this admits investment treaty politics and denies the view that the law is above politics.

TPP signals a retreat from the view that investment treaties are fundamentally discoverable in legal meaning and stand apart from actual political controversy as if such treaties were some brooding omnipresence in the sky.[81] It embraces what some have observed about the whole *Methanex* affair – namely, that it was simply a creature of the intense political controversy surrounding it.[82] Rather than to treat *Methanex* as an aberration, TPP's rebalancing act treats it (rightly) as the 'new normal' and would have the theory and practice of investment treaty protection evolve accordingly.

14.5 SATURN DEVOURS HIS SON

The CPTPP, which was recently unveiled had been mentioned at the outset of this chapter. The clauses (Footnote 14, the Rare Circumstances Clause and Mere Fact Clause) discussed earlier have all been retained. However, the TPP investment text had shown a remarkable 82 per cent degree of facial similarity with the United States-Colombia FTA.[83] In effect, the TPP text forms (in addition to forming a part of) a template; in this instance for other future Asia-Pacific agreements. Its conclusion was momentous for TPP is the first truly transcontinental 'mega-regional' concluded in midst of a still on-going global backlash against investment arbitration.[84] That backlash had spread from Latin America to South Africa, thence to India, Indonesia and Europe. TPP was to have been, and still could be, an answer to that backlash coming from the Asia-Pacific region, potentially forging a new 'Pacific' model investment treaty. The previous role of the United States and Japan in TPP among the TPP 12 as promoters of liberal investment rules could, alongside ongoing China–US bilateral investment treaty (BIT) negotiations, have offered the prospect of Sino–American–Japanese convergence in treaty policies; a coming together that is needed to forge a Pacific investment order driven by the world's three largest capital exporters. Such an investment order would be wider as a concept than that for which TPP stands, potentially stretching to include key RCEP economies such as India and Indonesia. It would have been a bulwark against a potentially very different European or Trans-Atlantic investment order.

TPP's innovations and refinements, some key examples of which have been discussed in this chapter, might be understood in such light but in essence they are refinements to preserve – not to abandon instead – some semblance of the investment treaty and investment arbitration regime while incorporating at least to some degree certain key lessons which have

80 See Yuval Shany, 'Toward a General Margin of Appreciation Doctrine in International Law?' (2005) 16 *European Journal of International Law* 907; and Stephan W. Schill, 'Deference in Investment Treaty Arbitration: Re-conceptualizing the Standard of Review through Comparative Public Law,' Society of International Economic Law Working Paper No. 2012/33. See also William W. Burke-White and Andreas von Staden, 'Private Litigation in a Public Law Sphere: The Standard of Review in Investor-State Arbitrations' (2010) 35 *Yale Journal of International Law* 283 at 285–86.

81 *Southern Pacific Company* v. *Jensen*, 244 U.S. 205, 222 (1917) (Holmes J., dissenting).

82 Tienhaara and Tucker, 'Regulating Foreign Investment: Methanex Revisited', above n 26, p. 258.

83 Alschner and Skugarievskiy, above n 23, p. 30.

84 See further, Michael Waibel, et al. (eds.), *The Backlash against Investment Arbitration* (The Hague: Kluwer, 2010).

been learnt since the explosion of investment arbitration in the 1990s beginning with the NAFTA and European Energy Charter arbitrations.

Some have said that signs of a backlash had emerged by 2004 with the remodelling of the US Model BIT, but whenever the backlash did begin, it remains in earnest. Contemporary official discontent outside North America since the emergence of investment treaty arbitration had first come into prominence with Bolivia's denunciation of the ICSID Convention under Article 71 of that treaty, and which took effect in November 2007.[85] Similar denunciations by Ecuador and Venezuela then came into effect in January 2010 and July 2012, respectively.[86] These Latin American developments were notable principally because criticism of investment treaty arbitration had hitherto been the province largely of non-governmental organizations not governments. Initially, these events had been limited to Latin America but that changed however when, in a new phase of the emerging *global* backlash against investment treaties and treaty arbitration, South Africa started in November 2012 to terminate its own BITs with successive European countries. At the same time, the backlash spread beyond simple withdrawals from the ICSID Convention and became focused on the substantive and procedural rules in existing BITs. In early 2014, Indonesia announced that it intended to terminate its BIT with the Netherlands. By March of 2015, India had released a new (then Draft) Model BIT. Thus began a new thread in the tale. There emerged a more moderate but nonetheless significant policy of replacing exiting BITs with reformulated treaties – treaty 'rebalancing' so-called. Indonesia is now reportedly revising its BITs, its earlier terminology of 'termination' having by now been firmly replaced by the new terminology of 'revision'. Elsewhere, in the context of the Trans-Atlantic Trade and Investment Partnership (TTIP) negotiations between the United States and the European Union (EU), the latter proposed a specialized investment court as a wholesale alternative to investor–State arbitration.[87]

Within the wider 'Indo-Pacific', India having issued its new Model BIT sent notices of termination for some fifty-eight BITs.[88] As I have already mentioned, a similar story is occurring in Indonesia.[89] However, countries like Malaysia took a different path and became a founding TPP signatory instead. Because of TPP and contrary to civil society protests in that country Malaysia – together with Singapore, Brunei and, at least for a moment, both Australia and New Zealand[90] – had emerged as a group of countries which had supported the reform

85 For the law on withdrawals, *see further*, Christoph Schreuer, 'Denunciation of the ICSID Convention and Consent to Arbitration' in Waibel et al., above n 84, p. 353.

86 Ben Bland and Shawn Donnan, 'Indonesia to terminate more than 60 bilateral investment treaties', Financial Times, London, 26 March 2014; Sergey Ripinsky, 'Venezuela's Withdrawal From ICSID: What it Does and Does Not Achieve', Investment Treaty News, 13 April 2012.

87 Such a mechanism already features in Article 12, Sub-Section 4, Chapter 8 of the EU-Vietnam FTA's agreed text as of January 2016. Likewise, see Articles 8.27 and 8.28 of the investment chapter of the EU-Canada FTA text concerning the new investment 'Tribunal' and 'Appellate Tribunal'. For materials and a discussion of the EU's position in the context of the wider backlash, see C. L. Lim, Jean Ho and Martins Paparinskis, *International Investment Law and Arbitration* (Cambridge: Cambridge University Press, 2018), pp. 479 *et seq* (esp. 504 *et seq.*). Currently discussions on a multilateral investment court are on-going in UNCITRAL Working Group III.

88 See, e.g., Alison Ross, 'India's BIT Terminations to Begin', Global Arbitration Review, 22 March 2017, available at https://globalarbitrationreview.com/article/1138510/indias-termination-of-bits-to-begin (last accessed 11 July 2019).

89 See further, Nicholas Lingard and Lexi Menish, 'Indonesia's BIT Terminations: Not the End of the Story', Global Arbitration Review, 1 November 2017, available at https://globalarbitrationreview.com/article/1148998/indonesia%E2%80%99s-bit-terminations-not-the-end-of-the-story (last accessed 11 July 2019).

90 Australian policy on the matter has been schizophrenic, and the story in New Zealand appears now to be, broadly speaking, similar. See, e.g., Edwina Kwan, 'Australia's Conflicting ISDS Approach: Where To From Here?', Kluwer Arbitration Blog, 4 June 2015, available at http://arbitrationblog.kluwerarbitration.com/2015/06/04/australias-conflicting-approach-to-isds-where-to-from-here (last accessed 11 July 2019); Amokura Kawharu and Luke

rather than abandonment of the investment arbitration regime. Likewise with Vietnam and Canada – they had both embraced the idea of an investment court with the EU while TPP was being concluded, yet both went on to sign TPP. Prior to the US withdrawal, TPP therefore had every appearance of promising to forestall a simmering Asia-Pacific revolt against investor–State arbitration.

Following the US withdrawal, however, the remaining eleven have not held the line well. One could argue that TPP's essential design has been undermined. While the CPTPP is being promoted as TPP in all but name – and one missing original signatory, the United States – it is, conceptually, distinct. It could be said that the CPTPP does the opposite of what TPP was meant to do in response to the global backlash against investment treaties. New Zealand's new centre-left Labour-led coalition has now, through its suite of side letters, excluded investor–State arbitration altogether in respect of investors from Australia,[91] Brunei, Malaysia, Peru and Vietnam; even if in some of these instances there is superfluous language permitting an investor–State claim if the host nation specifically consents to it.[92]

A contrary view would be that the same had previously been done between Australia and New Zealand when TPP was signed by the original TPP 12. In the case of the CPTPP, four of the TPP 11 have simply, therefore, followed Australia's lead previously in creating further flexibility for New Zealand. By employing five separate exchanges of side-letters, TPP 11 have moreover left the TPP text intact much in the same way that certain TPP clauses have been suspended in the CPTPP. A negotiator tasked to conclude some sort of interim treaty arrangement to keep the TPP on life support will see the logic of this contrary view, but in no way does the CPTPP commend itself as any sort of coherent treaty design or approach.

14.6 CONCLUSION

What might a TPP-inspired world have looked like? It would very likely have been (and could yet be, *notwithstanding* the CPTPP) a world in which tribunals assessing the legitimacy of host State public welfare measures might go on to replicate the deference which host State national courts will, typically, exhibit when scrutinizing their own governmental measures. In short, tribunals will be prompted to adopt some semblance of a general margin of appreciation doctrine in the international investment law context. Investment treaty standards could apply differently to different parties and situations, especially where complex social controversies are involved. The superstition that a treaty has a fixed, discoverable and invariable meaning across time, place and circumstance will be banished away. Rather than to admit that arbitral tribunals are not like national courts, the investment law literati might be drawn to take a closer look at what tribunals can and should be authorized to do; namely,

Nottage, 'NZ Renounces ISDS: Déjà Vu?', Kluwer Arbitration Blog, 6 December 2017, available at http://arbitrationblog.kluwerarbitration.com/2017/12/06/booked-luke-nottage/ (last accessed 11 July 2019).

91 With which a prior reciprocal agreement excluding investor–State dispute settlement is retained.

92 Superfluous because a host State can always agree to investor–State arbitration after the fact, although it must be added that this sort of 'opt-out-opt-in' clause one now finds in some of New Zealand's arrangements is reflective of the kind of investment treaty which provides for investor–State arbitration while apparently making that subject to further host State consent. For such a treaty clause, see *Churchill Mining Plc and Planet Mining Pty Ltd v. Indonesia*, ICSID Case No. ARB/12/14 and 12/40, 24 February 2014. The side letters are available at mfat.gov.nz (last accessed 11 July 2019).

some of what national courts do. Admittedly the public law analogy is controversial,[93] yet it is not difficult to imagine where TPP's design would tend to lead us.

It is precisely because recent events have put TPP in mortal jeopardy that we are free from some of the polarizing debate surrounding this treaty. We see it now for what it is, and all that it is, from an investment lawyer's viewpoint – an imperfect but still germane philosophy for the accommodation of capital and its discontents.

93 The analogy drawn between investment arbitration and public law reasoning, and the argument for greater adaptation of public law methods is controversial. Professor M. Sornarajah argues that with the advent of regulatory expropriation claims, tribunals embraced a proportionality test in applying pre -2000 BITs, but that the greater appearance of legitimacy sought to be produced would be no more than a facade; M. Sornarajah, *Resistance and Change in the International Law on Foreign Investment* (Cambridge: Cambridge University Press, 2015), pp. 376–77. For the contrary argument seeking to show how the proportionality doctrine, and more broadly public law methods, may be advantageous, *see, e.g.*, Benedict Kingsbury and Stephan Schill, 'Public Law Concepts to Balance Investors' Rights with State Regulatory Actions in the Public Interest—The Concept of Proportionality' in Stephan Schill (ed.), *International Investment Law and Comparative Public Law* (Oxford: Oxford University Press, 2010), p. 75. *See further*, Lim, 'Finding a Workable Balance', above n 14, Sect. IX.

PART V

Emerging Issues

15

The Due Diligence Expansion in International Investment Arbitration

Aloysius Llamzon and Jessica Beess und Chrostin[*]

15.1 INTRODUCTION

To mitigate the risks inherent in committing large amounts of capital into the developing world, foreign investors commonly partner with local elites who possess deep economic and political ties within that country. This is particularly true in developing Asia, where large and growing populations coupled with rising standards of living and an abundance of natural resources lead to vast amounts of foreign investment committed to the infrastructure and natural resources sectors; these areas of the economy, in turn, are often greatly aided by partnerships with entrenched local elites or subject to nationality restrictions outright. Joint ventures with local companies can help ensure an investment's success; but are not without peril, sometimes bringing about issues of potential illegality, including the fraudulent acquisition of concessions or contracts, misrepresentation of technical and financial capability, influence peddling, or bribery. While some of these offences can be committed by the investor alone, they are also often done at the instigation, or with the complicity, of the local partner, sometimes even without the investor's knowledge. It is therefore unsurprising that some of the most prominent cases in this area of international investment law have emerged from Asia, including *Fraport* v. *Philippines* and, more recently, *Churchill Mining* v. *Indonesia*.

These leading cases delineate much of the modern landscape on investor wrongdoing in international investment arbitration, particularly on the obligations of foreign investors to exercise diligence when deciding how and with whom they make their investments. The dividing line between the legitimate use of a local partner's social, economic, and political clout and outright illegal conduct is often difficult to discern, especially by a foreign investor who relies on that very same local partner to fall within the right side of the line. Such reliance cannot be done uncritically; independent of any national law obligations governing such partnerships, a norm appears to be emerging in international investment law that moulds over-arching principles of good faith and fair dealing into a specific requirement that foreign investors act with *due diligence*, not just with the investments they make, but with the local firms with which they partner. And that requirement of diligence has begun to expand to encompass not only the establishment or acceptance of the investment, but well after its inception – indeed, to its entire life-cycle.

[*] We are grateful to the editors, Mahdev Mohan and Chester Brown, as well as to Alexis Ang and Shalini Jayaraj. Any lack of diligence in this article is, of course, entirely our own.

That a due diligence requirement exists in international investment law may not itself be surprising – after all, no responsible foreign investor is likely to commit to a large-scale investment (and no bank would so finance that investment) unless the legality of an investment and the bona fides of a local partner who will help perpetuate that investment can be established to some degree. But there remains a large gap between what best practices are and what minimum requirements of 'due diligence' should be demanded of foreign investors as a rule or principle of public order. What 'due' diligence entails, for how long, and what the consequences of a failure to exercise such 'due' diligence should be, are all matters that remain in flux in international investment law, and will be explored in this chapter.

15.2 DUE DILIGENCE AS A HOST STATE OBLIGATION

'Due diligence' is a term that does not necessarily connote an obligation that resides only with the foreign investor. Indeed, in the early days of investment arbitration, due diligence was a term employed mostly to describe an obligation host States owed towards investors within the larger ambit of the full protection and security and fair and equitable treatment standards.

15.2.1 *Due Diligence as an Aspect of a Host State's Full Protection and Security Obligation*

The award of the very first case brought before the International Centre for Settlement of Investment Disputes (ICSID) under an investment treaty,[1] the 1990 *Asian Agricultural Products Ltd. (AAPL)* v. *Republic of Sri Lanka* award, identified an obligation of due diligence borne by host States, situating the principle within a bilateral investment treaty's (BIT) full protection and security standard as well as the minimum standard of treatment obligation under customary international law.

The claimant in *AAPL* v. *Sri Lanka* was a Hong Kong corporation which owned 48.5 per cent of Serendib Seafood Ltd., a Sri Lankan joint venture involved in the cultivation and export of shrimp. Shortly after Serendib commenced cultivation and export operations, a counter-insurgency operation of the Sri Lankan security forces resulted in the destruction of the shrimp farm and the deaths of twenty employees of the farm (fifteen of whom were claimed by Sri Lanka to be insurgents). AAPL filed an arbitration under the auspices of ICSID and the Sri Lanka–United Kingdom bilateral investment treaty claiming, *inter alia*, that the destruction of the shrimp farm breached the obligation to ensure full protection and security under the Sri Lanka–UK BIT.

In analysing the merits of AAPL's case, the tribunal (Dr Ahmed Sadek El-Kosheri, President; Prof. Berthold Goldman and Dr. Samuel K.B. Asante, co-arbitrators) considered the scope of a State's responsibility in cases of destruction resulting from anti-insurgency efforts. The tribunal concluded that 'there is an extensive and consistent state practice supporting the duty [of States] to exercise <u>due diligence</u>[.]'[2] Taking Prof. Brownlie's scholarship as a starting point, the tribunal found that:

[1] Derek Asiedu-Akrofi, 'Asian Agricultural Products Ltd. (AAPL) v. Republic of Sri Lanka' (1992) 86 *American Journal of International Law* 371('This decision is important because it is the first case submitted to arbitration under the auspices of the International Centre for the Settlement of Investment Disputes (ICSID) based upon a consent provision in a bilateral investment treaty.').

[2] *AAPL* v. *Sri Lanka*, para. 76, *citing* Ian Brownlie, *System of the Law of Nations, State Responsibility* – Part I (Oxford: Oxford University Press, 1986), p. 162 (emphasis added).

> [a]fter reviewing all categories of precedents, including more recent international judicial case-law, the learned Oxford University Professor arrived, not only to confirm that international responsibility arises from the mere 'failure to exercise due diligence' in providing the required protection, but also to note 'a sliding scale of liability related to the standard of due diligence[.][3]

This sliding scale ranged, according to the *AAPL* tribunal, from 'subjective' criteria such as 'the relatively limited existing possibilities of local authorities in a given context' towards an 'objective standard of vigilance in assessing the required degree of protection and security with regard to what should be legitimately expected to be secured for foreign investors by a reasonably well organized modern State'.[4]

The tribunal also took note of Prof. Freeman's writings on the subject of due diligence, finding that 'due diligence is nothing more nor less than the reasonable measures of prevention which a well-administered government could be expected to exercise under similar circumstances[.]'[5]

On the facts of the case, the tribunal ultimately concluded that Sri Lanka had violated its obligation to exercise due diligence in the protection of the claimant's investment. Key to this conclusion was the tribunal's finding that the Government of Sri Lanka should have tried to use peaceful channels of communication 'to minimise the risk of killings and destruction when planning to undertake a vast military counter-insurgency operation' in the area of the shrimp farm.[6] The obligation under the law on State responsibility was not one of strict liability, as the tribunal emphasised, but rather a question of what a *reasonably diligent State* could have been expected to do.[7] The case did not discuss any corresponding obligation of due diligence required of investors.

The State's obligations to exercise due diligence as an element of the full protection and security standard was again recognized in *Saluka Investments BV (The Netherlands)* v. *The Czech Republic*.[8] Saluka Investments B.V., a Dutch affiliate of the Japanese bank Nomura, owned 46.16 per cent of the shares of IPB, the third largest bank in the Czech Republic when, in June 2000, that State placed IPB under forced administration and shortly thereafter sold the bank to CSOB for the symbolic price of one Czech crown. Saluka commenced arbitration against the Czech Republic under the 1976 Arbitration Rules of the United Nations Commission on International Trade Law (UNCITRAL), arguing, among other things, that the State breached its obligation to afford Saluka's investment in IPB full protection and security under the Netherlands–Czech Republic bilateral investment treaty.

In assessing the meaning of the standard of full protection and security, the tribunal (Sir Arthur Watts KCMG QC, President; Maître L. Yves Fortier CC QC and Prof. Peter Behrens, co-arbitrators) considered that the 'full protection and security standard applies essentially when the foreign investment has been affected by civil strife and physical violence'.[9] Like the *AAPL* tribunal, the *Saluka* tribunal determined that the full protection and security standard does not imply strict liability, but rather requires the state to exercise due diligence.[10]

3 Ibid., para. 76 (citing Brownlie, *State Responsibility*, pp. 162 and 168).

4 Ibid., para. 77.

5 Ibid., para. 77 (citing Prof. Freeman, 1957 Lectures at the Hague Academy of International Law).

6 Ibid., para. 85.

7 Ibid.

8 *Saluka Investments B.V. (The Netherlands)* v. *The Czech Republic*, UNCITRAL, Partial Award, 17 March 2006.

9 *Saluka* v. *Czech Republic*, Partial Award, para. 483.

10 Ibid., para. 484 ('The standard does not imply strict liability of the host State however. The *Tecmed* tribunal held that "the guarantee of full protection and security is not absolute and does not impose strict liability upon the State that grants it". The host State is, however, obliged to exercise due diligence.').

To explain the context of the due diligence standard, the tribunal cited *Wena Hotels* v. *Egypt*, which in turn quoted from *American Manufacturing and Trading*:

> The obligation incumbent on the [host State] is an obligation of vigilance, in the sense that the [host State] shall take all measures necessary to ensure the full enjoyment of protection and security of its investments and should not be permitted to invoke its own legislation to detract from any such obligation.[11]

Likely mindful of its own admonition against imposing a standard of strict liability, the *Saluka* tribunal declined to find a violation of the due diligence requirement because, among other reasons, the State's actions were not 'totally devoid of legitimate concerns'.[12] Thus, on the facts before it, the tribunal did not find that the Czech Republic violated its obligation of due diligence and by extension, of full protection and security.

15.2.2 *Due Diligence as an Aspect of a Host State's Fair and Equitable Treatment Obligation*

The notion of due diligence found further recognition in investor–State arbitration as an element of the fair and equitable treatment standard.

In *Lauder* v. *Czech Republic*, the claimant invested in TV Nova, a Czech private television broadcaster, through a joint venture with a Czech business partner. After Mr. Lauder's local business partner withdrew from the venture, he brought suit against the Czech government, arguing that the Czech Media Council had unlawfully interfered with his investment. Lauder claimed that the State's conduct constituted a breach of the fair and equitable treatment and full protection and security standards incorporated in the United States–Czech Republic BIT.

In assessing the merits of Lauder's claim, the tribunal (Robert Briner, President; Lloyd Cutler and Bohuslav Klein, co-arbitrators) considered that 'fair and equitable treatment is related to the traditional standard of due diligence and provides a "minimum international standard which forms part of customary international law"'.[13] As with prior cases, the *Lauder* tribunal confirmed that the State's due diligence obligation was not one of strict liability, but rather required assessment of the specific facts and circumstances of the case at issue.[14] On the facts of the *Lauder* case, the tribunal held that there was no basis to find that the Czech Republic failed to exercise due diligence in its treatment of the claimant and his investment.[15]

The *Lauder* tribunal also held that the full protection and security standard 'obliges the Parties to exercise such due diligence in the protection of foreign investment as reasonable under the circumstances'.[16] Under the tribunal's analysis, both this substantive protection and fair and equitable treatment arose from the State's obligation to exercise due diligence in the treatment of investors and their investments.

11 Ibid., para. 484 (emphasis supplied).

12 Ibid., para. 490.

13 *Lauder* v. *Czech Republic*, Award, para. 292.

14 Ibid., para. 308 ('However, the Treaty does not oblige the Parties to protect foreign investment against any possible loss of value caused by persons whose acts could not be attributed to the State. Such protection would indeed amount to strict liability, which can not be imposed to a State absent any specific provision in the Treaty[.]').

15 Note that the *CME* v. *Czech Republic* case, which concerned the same facts and claims at issue in the *Lauder* case, found that the Czech Republic did, in fact, violate international law. *CME Czech Republic B.V. (The Netherlands)* v. *The Czech Republic*, UNCITRAL, Final Award, 14 March 2003.

16 *Lauder* v. *Czech Republic*, Award, para. 308.

The foregoing makes clear that while the obligatory nature of due diligence has long been recognized in investor–State arbitration, that principle was traditionally imposed and articulated as an obligation of the State, not the investor. It is only in recent years that a corresponding obligation on the part of the investor to exercise due diligence has begun to emerge.

15.3 DUE DILIGENCE AS AN INVESTOR OBLIGATION

As due diligence has increasingly been understood as an aspect of an investor's obligations when making and performing its investment, the obligation has taken two distinct modalities. First, an investor's due diligence obligation has been considered a check on its ability to hold a host State liable for substantive violations of investor protections under an investment treaty, particularly under the fair and equitable treatment standard. Second, due diligence is emerging as part of the corpus of obligation that an investor has to abide by the laws of the host State and to bring an investment into the host State in good faith, failing which that investor would be deprived of the ability to resort to investment arbitration at all, no matter what breaches of the investment treaty the host State might have committed.

15.3.1 *Investor Due Diligence as a Factor in Determining the Extent of Investor Protection Violations*

15.3.1.1 Due Diligence Before or At the Time the Investor Makes Its Investment

When ascertaining whether and to what extent the host State has violated the fair and equitable treatment standard, increasing emphasis has been placed over the years on the extent to which the investor itself engaged in diligence when it first made its investment or subsequently performed it. But initially, due diligence was demanded of an investor even before it made its investment, centring on the investor's pre-investment conduct, *i.e.*, his diligence leading up to the making of the investment.

Olguín v. *Paraguay* was a pioneer case that identified a due diligence requirement on the part of an investor that existed even at the preparatory (pre-investment) stage.[17] The dispute there arose out of the bankruptcy of a Paraguayan financial institution in which the claimant had made deposits of over US $1 million for the purpose of investing in a food production and distribution enterprise in Paraguay. The claimant, a dual national of Peru and the United States, brought an arbitration under the Peru–Paraguay BIT, claiming, among other things, that the Central Bank of Paraguay's endorsement of the credit instruments Mr Olguin received in exchange for his deposits and the Central Bank's subsequent negligence in supervising the activities of the financial institutions which had received the claimant's deposits resulted in the expropriation of his investment. The tribunal disagreed.

The tribunal (Rodrigo Oreamuno, President; Francisco Rezek and Eduardo Mayora Alvarado, co-arbitrators) held that information and assessments about investments that were provided by a State did not relieve the investor from making due inquiries, nor did it make the State a guarantor of the investment. Although the *Olguín* v. *Paraguay* tribunal did not expressly articulate this obligation using the term 'due diligence', its finding that the investor

[17] *Olguin* v. *Paraguay* (ICSID Case No ARB/98/5, Award of 26 July 2001).

should have taken further steps prior to making his investment effectively set out a due diligence requirement on the part of the putative investor.[18]

Similarly, in *Feldman* v. *Mexico*, the claimant was an American citizen who owned a Mexican company, CEMSA, whose business was the export of tobacco products from Mexico.[19] Mr. Feldman alleged that Mexico breached the North American Free Trade Agreement (NAFTA) by refusing to rebate excise taxes applied to cigarettes exported by CEMSA. The claimant maintained that Mexico's conduct violated, *inter alia*, NAFTA Article 1110 (Expropriation and Compensation).

In analysing whether Mexico's conduct constituted a breach of NAFTA, the tribunal (Prof Konstantinos D. Kerameus, President; Jorge Covarrubias Bravo and Prof. David A. Gantz, co-arbitrators) considered whether the requirements for obtaining the rebate (in relevant part, here, an invoicing requirement) were inconsistent with the claimant's rights under Article 1110. The tribunal noted, in particular, that the invoicing requirement under the relevant law had been in place for three years *prior* to Mr. Feldman's investment. This fact became fatal to Mr. Feldman's expropriation claim, because the tribunal considered on this basis that the investor's obligation to exercise due diligence in making his investment should have disclosed this requirement to him. In the words of the tribunal, 'the Claimant was or should have been aware at all relevant times that the separate invoice requirement existed, as there has been no *de jure* change in it at any time relevant to this dispute'.[20] As with *Olguin*, the tribunal did not expressly articulate a requirement of 'due diligence'; but the decision clearly placed the onus on the investor to know and understand the legal requirements applicable to his investment. Ultimately, the tribunal held that a State cannot be found liable for a circumstance that predated the investor's investment and of which a reasonably prudent investor ought to have known before it made the investment.[21]

The *MTD* v. *Chile* tribunal, by contrast, expressly pronounced a due diligence obligation on the part of the investor at the point at which the investment is made.[22] The claimants in *MTD* v. *Chile* were a Malaysian investment company and its Chilean subsidiary, who initiated arbitration against Chile under the Malaysia–Chile BIT. The claimants had invested in a project to develop a satellite city in the Chilean municipality of Pirque. The Foreign Investment Commission, a Chilean government body, signed a contract approving the investment, but after the claimants acquired the land on which the city was to be developed, the municipality refused to rezone the land to permit MTD to proceed with the development. On this basis, the claimants alleged several treaty breaches on Chile's part, including expropriation and breach of the fair and equitable treatment protection under customary international law. A key defence Chile presented was the argument that, if the investors had acted diligently, they 'would quickly have discovered that [their] Project was unfeasible[.]'[23]

The tribunal (Andrés Rigo Sureda, President; Marc Lalonde and Rodrigo Oreamuno Blanco, co-arbitrators) took a nuanced approach:

> Chile has argued that each organ of the Government has certain responsibilities, that it is not its function to carry out due diligence regarding the legal and technical feasibility of a project

[18] Ibid., para. 65(b).
[19] *Feldman* v. *Mexico* (ICSID Case No ARB(AF)/99/1, Award of 16 December 2002).
[20] Ibid., para. 128.
[21] Ibid., paras. 112–14, 128.
[22] *MTD* v. *Chile* (ICSID Case No. ARB/01/7, Award of 25 May 2004).
[23] Ibid., para. 127.

> for investors, and that this is the investors' responsibility. The Tribunal agrees that it is the responsibility of the investor to assure itself that it is properly advised, particularly when investing abroad in an unfamiliar environment. However, in the case before us, Chile is not a passive party and the coherent action of the various officials through which Chile acts is the responsibility of Chile, not of the investor. Whether the Claimants acted responsibly or diligently in reaching a decision to invest in Chile is another question.[24]

Thus, the *MTD* tribunal considered the affirmative actions of the respondent State vis-à-vis the investor and balanced the representations made to the investor with the investor's due diligence obligation, holding them to be separate obligations. In an often-quoted passage, the tribunal noted that:

> BITs are not an insurance policy against business risk and the Tribunal considers that the Claimants should bear the consequences of their own actions as experienced businessmen. Their choice of partner, the acceptance of a land valuation based on future assumptions without protecting themselves contractually in case the assumptions would not materialize, including the issuance of the required development permits, are risks that the Claimants took irrespective of Chile's actions.[25]

On balance, the tribunal held that Chile was culpable for making certain representations to the investors. But because the investors were also found to have failed to exercise the diligence of a reasonably prudent business investor, the tribunal decided to reduce the investors' damages by 50 per cent. The investors' lack of due diligence in the making of the investment was a significant damages issue, *i.e.*, the degree of due diligence affected the allocation of damages to which the investors were considered entitled.[26]

Plama v. *Bulgaria* was of a similar vein in its demand that the investor undertake due diligence at the time its investment is made.[27] The claimant there was a Cypriot company that had acquired shares in an insolvent refinery, Nova Plama AD, in Bulgaria with the consent of the Bulgarian Privatization Agency. Merely months after resuming operations, the refinery fell back into insolvency and was forced to shut down operations. Plama commenced arbitration against Bulgaria under the Energy Charter Treaty (ECT), alleging that Bulgaria had failed to provide fair and equitable treatment as well as constant protection and security because it did not create 'stable, equitable, favourable and transparent conditions' for investment.[28]

In its defence, Bulgaria claimed, in relevant part, that Plama had obtained the consent of the Bulgarian Privatization Agency through misrepresentations, which caused its investment to be void *ab initio* and thus incapable of protection under the ECT. The tribunal (Carl F. Salans, President; Albert Jan van den Berg and V.V. Veeder, co-arbitrators) held in favour of Bulgaria. It found that the claimant had indeed committed fraud in the making of its investment and was thus not entitled to protection under the ECT.[29]

In the process of dismissing Plama's claim, the tribunal identified an obligation of the investor to undertake reasonable due diligence in making its investment and understanding the applicable regulatory framework: '[I]t is clear to the Tribunal that Claimant, as the

24 Ibid., para. 164 (emphasis added).
25 Ibid., para. 178 (emphasis added).
26 Ibid., para. 246.
27 *Plama* v. *Bulgaria* (ICSID Case No. ARB/03/24, Award of 27 August 2008).
28 Ibid., para. 73.
29 Ibid., paras. 129, 133–35.

investor, was responsible for doing its due diligence regarding the tax consequences of debt reduction and for taking the necessary measures to deal with them'.[30]

Following *Plama*, an increasing tide of decisions has identified an obligation of due diligence on the part of the investor in the making of its investment. In *Anderson* v. *Costa Rica*, the claimants were 137 individual nationals of Canada with individual investments in Costa Rica, who together brought a claim against the Republic of Costa Rica.[31] The claimants 'alleged that Costa Rica, by failing to provide proper vigilance and governmental regulatory supervision over the national financial system, had injured their investments in violation of the [Canada–Costa Rica BIT] provisions regarding full protection and security, fair and equitable treatment, due process of law, and protection against expropriation'.[32] The tribunal held that prudent investment practice required that 'any investor exercise due diligence before committing funds to any particular investment proposal ... [and] an important element of such due diligence is for investors to assure themselves that their investments comply with the law. Such due diligence obligation is neither overly onerous nor unreasonable'.[33] The tribunal held that the claimants had not exercised proper due diligence in this regard, and that the respondent's objection on jurisdiction must therefore be sustained.

Finally, in *Lemire* v. *Ukraine*, the tribunal (Prof. Juan Fernández-Armesto, President; Jan Paulsson and Jürgen Voss, co-arbitrators) considered a claim by Joseph Charles Lemire, a national of the United States, against the Ukraine under the US–Ukraine BIT.[34] Lemire had invested in the radio broadcasting industry in Ukraine, after the government opened the sector to private investment. Lemire's company initially obtained some radio frequency licences, but between 1999 and 2008, Ukraine repeatedly denied Mr. Lemire's applications for further licences for radio frequencies and broadcasting channels in Ukraine. Lemire claimed that this constituted a breach of the US–Ukraine BIT's fair and equitable treatment provision, among other matters.

Similar to the prior cases discussed, in assessing whether Ukraine had violated the fair and equitable treatment protection, the tribunal held that the investor had a duty to perform an investigation before effecting an investment.[35] The majority of the tribunal, however, found no wrongdoing and held that Ukraine breached the fair and equitable treatment protection of the applicable treaty and consequently, Lemire was entitled to damages.[36]

15.3.1.2 The Requirement of Investor Diligence over the Life of an Investment

As these examples demonstrate, the emergence of the investor's obligation to exercise due diligence was traditionally focused on investigating and understanding the legal and regulatory environment prevalent before or at the time the investment was made. But that initial obligation at the commencement of the investment has now moved increasingly towards an investor being subjected to a constant duty of diligence in carrying out its investment. The decisions of the tribunals in *Biwater Gauff (Tanzania) Ltd.* v. *United*

30 Ibid., para. 268.
31 *Anderson* v. *Costa Rica* (ICSID Case No ARB(AF)/07/3, Award of 19 May 2010).
32 Ibid., para. 16.
33 Ibid., para. 58.
34 *Joseph Charles Lemire* v. *Ukraine* (ICSID Case No. ARB/06/18, Award of 28 March 2011).
35 *Joseph Charles Lemire* v. *Ukraine* (ICSID Case No. ARB/06/18, Decision on Jurisdiction and Liability of 14 January 2010), para. 285.
36 Ibid., para. 513; see also *Joseph Charles Lemire* v. *Ukraine* (ICSID Case No. ARB/06/18, Award of 28 March 2011).

Republic of Tanzania,[37] *Rusoro Mining Ltd.* v. *The Bolivarian Republic of Venezuela*,[38] and *Churchill Mining PLC and Planet Mining Pty. Ltd.* v. *Republic of Indonesia*[39] are pivotal in this regard.

The *Biwater* v. *Tanzania* dispute arose out of a disagreement between a British company and the Republic of Tanzania regarding a concession to operate the water and sewerage services in Dar es Salaam, Tanzania's capital. The parties had entered into a contract regarding water and sewerage operations, but Tanzania unilaterally determined that Biwater breached the contract and cancelled it to regain possession of the assets leased to Biwater under the agreement. The claimant brought two actions – a commercial case to determine the parties' rights and liabilities under the contract, and an investor–State arbitration under the auspices of ICSID and pursuant to the United Kingdom–Tanzania BIT. In the ICSID case, the investor claimed, *inter alia*, that Tanzania had failed to afford Biwater fair and equitable treatment.

In deciding whether Tanzania had breached the fair and equitable treatment protection, the *Biwater* tribunal (Bernard Hanotiau, President; Toby Landau and Gary Born, co-arbitrators) considered not only the conduct of the State, but also the conduct of the investor—both prior to and during the life of the investment. As the *Biwater* tribunal put it:

> In applying the general threshold [of customary international law fair and equitable treatment] as articulated (in particular) by the tribunal in *Waste Management* v. *Mexico (No. 2)*, the Arbitral Tribunal has also taken into account the submissions of the Petitioners, as summarised earlier, which emphasise countervailing factors such as the responsibility of foreign investors, both in terms of prior due diligence as well as subsequent conduct; the limit to legitimate expectations in circumstances where an investor itself takes on risks in entering a particular investment environment; and the relevance of the parties' respective rights and obligations as set out in any relevant investment agreement (here the Lease Contract).[40]

The above-quoted paragraph makes clear that the *Biwater* tribunal considered not merely pre-investment activities and diligence, but also the investor's subsequent conduct.

The pairing of 'prior due diligence' with 'subsequent conduct' constitutes an expansion of the investor's obligations. It becomes relevant in *Biwater* in the context of damages. Based on the facts before it, the tribunal held unanimously that Tanzania's conduct breached the investment treaty's fair and equitable treatment provision, the protection against unreasonable and discriminatory measures, and the full protection and security obligation. However, ultimately, the majority of the tribunal (Messrs. Hanotiau and Landau) held that while Tanzania's conduct may have constituted *prima facie* violations of certain protections under the treaty, the claimant had not established the necessary causal link. According to the majority, the State's conduct did not cause injury to the claimant's investment because the claimant's mismanagement of the investment had already deprived it of any value. Consequently, Tanzania's conduct had not injured Biwater or its investment.[41] The investor's own conduct throughout the life of the investment was thus determinative of the outcome.

37 *Biwater Gauff (Tanzania) Ltd.* v. *United Republic of Tanzania* (ICSID Case No. ARB/05/22, Award of 24 July 2008.)

38 *Rusoro Mining Ltd.* v. *The Bolivarian Republic of Venezuela* (ICSID Case No. ARB(AF)/12/5, Award of 22 August 2016.)

39 *Churchill Mining PLC and Planet Mining Pty. Ltd.* v. *Republic of Indonesia* (ICSID Case No. ARB/12/14 and 12/40, Award of 6 December 2016.)

40 *Biwater* v. *Tanzania*, Award, para. 601.

41 In a Partial Dissent, Mr. Born disagreed with the majority's conclusion that the claimant had failed to establish the causal link between Tanzania's breaches of the treaty and the claimant's injury. Mr. Born considered that a facial violation of the treaty automatically amounted to a compensable injury, meaning that the causal link was

Rusoro v. *Venezuela* concerned a dispute between a Canadian mining company and Venezuela regarding the latter's nationalization of the Venezuelan gold mining industry through presidential decree in August 2011. Rusoro initiated arbitration under the Canada–Venezuela BIT claiming, most notably, expropriation of its investments in Venezuela's gold industry. Rusoro sought roughly USD 2.3 billion plus interest in damages. One of the arguments Venezuela presented in its defence on the merits and damages, was that Rusoro was an inexperienced and inefficient gold mine operator.[42]

In assessing whether Venezuela's legislative nationalization of the gold industry amounted to a breach of the Canada–Venezuela treaty, the tribunal (Prof. Juan Fernández-Armesto, President; Prof. Francisco Orrego Vicuña and Judge Bruno Simma, co-arbitrators) considered it appropriate to engage in a balancing exercise in which it considered both the State's conduct as well as the investor's duty to perform due diligence before and during the investment:

> In evaluating the State's conduct, the Tribunal must balance the investor's right to be protected against improper State conduct, with other legally relevant interests and countervailing factors. First among these factors is the principle that legislation and regulation are dynamic, and that States enjoy a sovereign right to amend legislation and to adopt new regulation in the furtherance of public interest. The right to regulate, however, does not authorize States to act in an arbitrary or discriminatory manner, or to disguise measures targeted against a protected investor under the cloak of general legislation. Other countervailing factors affect the investor: it is the investor's duty to perform an appropriate pre-investment due diligence review and to show a proper conduct both before and during the investment.[43]

The *Rusoro* tribunal, like the *Biwater* tribunal before it, thus considered the due diligence obligation imposed on the investor to extend to conduct both pre- and post-making of the investment. The *Rusoro* tribunal took into account Venezuela's argument regarding the claimant's alleged inability to manage its gold mining operations effectively, but ultimately rejected this argument, stating that even if this were true *ad arguendem*, 'such situation would never justify an unlawful expropriation and would not impact on the "genuine value" of the investment (because the hypothetical buyer must be assumed to be a reasonable and diligent gold mine operator)'.[44] The tribunal ultimately held that Venezuela's conduct amounted to expropriation of Rusoro's investment in Venezuela and that the State was liable to pay close to US $1 billion in compensation.

15.3.2 *The Next Frontier: Due Diligence as a Consideration when Assessing Investor Wrongdoing*

Thus far, due diligence has been considered as a factor affecting the substantive rights and duties of investors and host States alike in international investment law. Due diligence has been employed to test the opposability of fair and equitable treatment and full protection and security – the ability (or inability) of an investor to show, for example, that it exercised diligence in trying to understand and comply with the regulatory regime that would govern

necessarily established. However, because the investment was worthless, the injury did not entitle the claimant to any damages because no actual injury was suffered.

42 *Rusoro* v. *Venezuela*, Award, para. 801.

43 Ibid., para. 525 (emphasis added).

44 Ibid., para. 801.

its investment would determine, to some extent, whether that investor actually had a legitimate expectation for fair and equitable treatment of its investment. Similarly, as to host States, their ability to claim that they met their full protection and security obligations rested to an extent on a showing that they exercised reasonable diligence in attempting to protect a foreign investor's property within their territory.

Recent cases have expanded the due diligence principle even further, bringing it within the corpus of rules on investor wrongdoing that affect the jurisdiction of investment treaty tribunals or the admissibility of claims made pursuant to BITs.[45] These are rules that demand of an investor that it not engage in fraud, corruption, or any other forms of illegal conduct under a multiplicity of norms – the national laws of the host State, transnational public policy, and public international law. But because investor wrongdoing can cover not only the acts of an investor itself but also those of its partners in the investment, as well as agents and employees (all of whom are often nationals of the host State), the due diligence requirement extends the realm of responsibility and accountability investors have to bear not only to their own actions, but also to the actions of those the investor works with in advancing the investment. How due diligence fits within this distinct aspect of international investment law is perhaps best articulated through a review of what has become the leading case on the matter: *Churchill Mining* v. *Indonesia*.[46]

In *Churchill* v. *Indonesia*, the claimants were a British company (Churchill Mining PLC) and an Australian company (Planet Mining Pty. Ltd.).[47] The claimants partnered with Ridlatama, a group of seven Indonesian companies, to invest in the East Kutai Coal Project (EKCP), which was to explore and then exploit a large coal deposit in the Regency of East Kutai, Indonesia. The claimants invested in EKCP by acquiring all shares of PT Indonesian Coal Development (PT ICD), a company registered in Indonesia. After the claimants acquired their investment, Ridlatama obtained mining licences for large areas in the EKCP. Ridlatama had agreements with PT ICD pursuant to which the latter would plan and perform all mining operations in exchange for 75 per cent of the revenue generated in the project.

In 2010, it became apparent that certain areas covered by the licences granted to Ridlatama overlapped with licences that had been granted to other companies in the area. The Regent of East Kutai revoked all licences belonging to the Ridlatama group. In response, the claimants filed for arbitration claiming, among other things, expropriation of their investment.

In its defence, Indonesia claimed that the Ridlatama group's concession licences were forged and therefore the claimants' claims were inadmissible. Indonesia argued that 'Ridlatama forged the disputed documents and that the Claimants were duped and that, even if they were unaware of the forgery, the Claimants bear the burden of engaging business relations with unreliable partners'.[48] Indonesia's secondary argument was that the claimants were actually aware of the forgery of the disputed documents. In either case,

45 See Aloysius Llamzon and Anthony Sinclair, 'Investor Wrongdoing in Investment Arbitration: Standards Governing Issues of Corruption, Fraud, Misrepresentation and Other Investor Misconduct' in A. J. van den Berg (ed.), *Legitimacy: Myths, Realities, Challenges: ICCA Congress Series No. 18* (Wolters Kluwer Law & Business, 2015), pp. 451–530.

46 *Churchill Mining PLC and Planet Mining Pty Ltd* v. *Indonesia* (ICSID Case No. ARB/12/40 and 12/14, Award of 6 December 2016.)

47 The claimants originally filed separate arbitrations, under the United Kingdom–Indonesia BIT and the Australia–Indonesia BIT, respectively, that were joined following the jurisdictional phases of the two arbitrations.

48 *Churchill* v. *Indonesia*, Award, para. 174.

according to Indonesia, the claimants' conduct evinced a lack of due diligence and even recklessness.[49]

The claimants denied any wrongdoing and pointed to two diligence reports they had commissioned, one by DNC Advocates at Work and a second report by Sondong, Tampubolon & Partners (STP), the latter of which had concluded that the mining licences were 'valid, unencumbered and legally enforceable[.]'[50] In all events, according to the claimants, 'a failure to investigate third-party wrongdoing does not automatically deprive an investor of treaty protection'.[51] Rather, the claimants argued that, because the acts of fraud and forgery were not their own, and because the claimants were *bona fide* investors, they should still be entitled to protection under the investment treaty.

On the facts before it, the *Churchill* tribunal (Gabrielle Kaufmann-Kohler, President; Albert Jan van den Berg and Michael Hwang, co-arbitrators) found that the licences were indeed forged, but that the record pointed to Ridlatama 'rather than the Claimants in relation to the forgery of the contentious documents'.[52] The operative question thus became what the consequence of a local partner's misconduct on the foreign claimants' arbitral claims should be, in a situation where the foreign investor did not participate in the misconduct.

To assess this question, the tribunal reviewed a series of cases addressing illegality in the making of an investment.[53] On the basis of these cases, the tribunal extrapolated the concept of the '"head-in-the-sand problem", also sometimes referred to as "Nelsonian knowledge", where a claimant knew or should have known of third-party wrongdoing in connection with an investment and still chose to do nothing (as opposed to just failing to take due care)'. The tribunal proceeded to note:

> Considering the specific circumstances of the present case, the Tribunal will assess the standard of <u>willful blindness</u> – also referred to as 'conscious disregard' or 'deliberate ignorance' – by focusing on the level of institutional control and oversight deployed by the Claimants in relation to the licensing process, whether the Claimants were put on notice by evidence of fraud that <u>a reasonable investor</u> in the Indonesian mining sector should have investigated, and whether or not they took appropriate corrective steps.[54]

The tribunal considered this a question of admissibility (rather than jurisdiction or the merits of the case) and concluded on the record before it that the claimants did not conduct extensive or exhaustive due diligence in verifying the authenticity of the disputed mining licences. In this context, the tribunal took note that the claimants were aware of the risks of investing in the Indonesian mining industry and were aware specifically of 'the risk of overlapping mining licenses'.[55] The tribunal considered that one would expect an investor who is aware of these risks 'to be particularly diligent in investigating the circumstances of its investment. Yet, the Claimants did not engage in proper due diligence in their dealings with their partners. In particular, they failed to exert due diligence when choosing Ridlatama ... and did not investigate the reliability of that company and its directors'.[56] Under these circumstances, the tribunal stated that one would expect the investor to exercise 'a heightened

[49] Ibid., para. 174.
[50] Ibid., para. 192.
[51] Ibid., para. 485.
[52] Ibid., para. 476.
[53] Ibid., paras. 488 *et seq*.
[54] Ibid., para. 504 (emphasis supplied).
[55] Ibid., para. 517.
[56] Ibid., para. 518.

degree of diligence',[57] and the claimants' failure to do so evidenced their lack of due diligence. The tribunal further considered that the claimants should have conducted due diligence once indications of forgery came to their attention, which they did not.

What is particularly remarkable about the tribunal's decision is that the investor had, in fact, conducted due diligence in advance of making its investment. The investor pointed to, and the tribunal acknowledged, the due diligence report of the Indonesian law firm STP, but the tribunal considered this due diligence insufficient as it was conducted in 2007, two years prior to the indications of forgery.[58] The tribunal thus expanded the investor's due diligence requirement to the life of the investment, *i.e.* the timeframe *after* the investor acquired the investment. It was the investor's failure to exercise due diligence not just at the outset of the investment, but particularly during the investment, that rendered the claimants' claims entirely inadmissible. The legal basis for an outcome of inadmissibility was also notable – instead of locating that consequence within the text of the BIT or the ICSID Convention, the tribunal agreed with Indonesia 'that claims arising from rights based on fraud or forgery which a claimant deliberately or unreasonably ignored are inadmissible as a matter of international public policy'.[59]

The holding of the *Churchill* v. *Indonesia* tribunal is at once reminiscent of and a departure from *Fraport AG Frankfurt Airport Services Worldwide* v. *Republic of Philippines*,[60] another case where both the extent of diligence conducted by the investor, as well as the wrongdoing of that investor and its local partner were put at issue.

The claimant in *Fraport* v. *Philippines* was a German airport operator who invested in a Philippine company, Piatco, which had won a concession to build and operate a terminal at the Ninoy Aquino International Airport in Manila. Six years after obtaining the concession, the Philippine Supreme Court declared the concession to be null and void, because Piatco had obtained it through fraud and deceit, and was not, in fact, a qualified bidder under Philippine law. Following the nullification of the concession, Fraport brought an arbitration against the Philippines alleging, among other things, that the Philippines had expropriated its investment.[61]

In the *Fraport I* award of 2007, the tribunal (Maître L. Yves Fortier, President; W Michael Reisman and Bernardo Cremades, co-arbitrators) dismissed the claimant's claim for lack of jurisdiction based on its determination that the investor had, in fact, made its investment in violation of Philippine law by entering into a 'secret shareholder agreement'[62] with its local partners in an attempt to establish indirect control over Piatco, knowingly circumventing Philippine 'anti-dummy' laws, which prohibited foreign control over a public utility (such as an airport terminal).[63] Of particular relevance was the fact that the investor's legal and financial due diligence included a warning from Philippine counsel that the structure of the investment, which would effectively give management and control to Fraport, would 'violate a serious provision of Philippine law,' and a determination from Fraport's board of directors (based on its financial experts' advice) that 'the only plausible way for its equity

57 Ibid., para. 519.

58 Ibid., para. 526.

59 Ibid., para. 508.

60 *Fraport AG Frankfurt Airport Services Worldwide* v. *Republic of Philippines* (ICSID Case No. ARB/11/12, Award of 10 December 2014) ('*Fraport II*'); *Fraport AG Frankfurt Airport Services Worldwide* v. *Republic of Philippines* (ICSID Case No. ARB/03/25, Award of 16 August 2007) ('*Fraport I*').

61 *Fraport I*.

62 Ibid., para. 125.

63 Ibid., paras. 327, 396–98.

investment to prove profitable was to arrange secretly for management and control of the project in a way which the investor knew were [sic] not in accordance with the law of the Philippines'.[64]

The *Fraport I* tribunal also made a temporal distinction on wrongdoing that is significant in relation to the subsequent *Churchill* decision. The tribunal clarified that the relevant time period to ascertain the legality of Fraport's investment, based on the language of the Germany–Philippines BIT, was the '*entry* of the investment and not the way it was subsequently conducted'.[65] 'Moreover,' the tribunal continued,

> the effective operation of the BIT regime would appear to require that jurisdictional compliance be limited to the initiation of the investment. If, at the time of the initiation of the investment, there has been compliance with the law of the host state, allegations by the host state of violations of its law in the course of the investment, as a justification for state action with respect to the investment, might be a defense to claimed substantive violations of the BIT, but could not deprive a tribunal acting under the authority of the BIT of its jurisdiction.[66]

The *Fraport I* award was subsequently annulled for other reasons, at which point Fraport filed a second arbitration based on the same facts and claims.

In the *Fraport II* award of 2014, the tribunal (Prof. Piero Bernardini, President; Stanimir A. Alexandrov and Albert Jan van den Berg, co-arbitrators) again dismissed the case on jurisdictional grounds. As with *Fraport I*, the *Fraport II* tribunal considered the financial and legal due diligence provided by Fraport's advisors, as well as Fraport's actions in light of that diligence at the time it made its investment. In a nutshell, the tribunal also found that Fraport had invested illegally, knowingly circumventing the limits on foreign investors' ownership and control of public utilities imposed by the Philippine anti-dummy law. The investor had received advice from its Philippine counsel QT that, due to Philippine law, 'arrangements other than mere equity investments ... must be considered carefully',[67] and yet a month later, had proceeded to negotiate and enter into a shareholders agreement with its local partner that would effectively hand over control of the management and operation of the concession to Fraport.[68] This knowing violation of Philippine law was found sufficient to deprive the arbitral tribunal of jurisdiction.

The tribunal also considered at length the Philippines' argument that Fraport's investment was not protected because, in addition to violating the State's anti-dummy laws, Fraport invested in Piatco knowing that the company had obtained its concession unlawfully. According to the Philippines, Fraport was aware when it made its investment that Piatco had misrepresented its qualifications to be a concessionaire and that Fraport's own consultants questioned the legality of the concession award.[69] The tribunal did not, however, query the propriety of assessing whether Fraport had undertaken sufficient due diligence of its local partner. Instead, *Fraport II* was aligned with the existing rule requiring the respondent to demonstrate that the foreign investor was complicit in any illegality the local partner may have committed (in this instance, alleged illegal payments made to obtain the concession and misrepresentations of financial and technical abilities), and that such illegality occurred at

[64] Ibid., para. 398.
[65] Ibid., para. 345.
[66] Ibid., para. 345.
[67] *Fraport II*, Award, para. 431.
[68] Ibid., paras. 432–36.
[69] Ibid., para. 489.

the time it made its investment, and not well before (or after) it did so. In the words of the tribunal: 'There is no basis in conflating PIATCO with Fraport and asserting that even if Fraport did not know of PIATCO's corruption, assuming such corruption is proven (which is not regarding the concession award), its investment "is unlawful and not protected by the BIT"'.[70]

Thus, the *Fraport II* tribunal found that even if it were true that the concession was obtained illegally, that illegality would not necessarily redound to Fraport in the absence of complicity or actual knowledge of that illegality at the time it made its investment.

15.4 IMPLICATIONS OF THE EXPANSION OF THE DUE DILIGENCE OBLIGATION

The obligation to undertake due diligence has undergone a significant evolution in scope and content over the past years in the context of investor–State arbitration. The brief survey this chapter undertook reveals 'due diligence' as a term capable of polyvalent meaning. Traditionally, due diligence was understood as part of an older branch of public international law concerning the protection of foreign property located within a host State – due diligence defined the State's obligation toward the foreign investor under the full protection and security and fair and equitable treatment principles. When used to identify the scope of a host State's obligations to provide those substantive protections, 'due diligence' forms part of either the customary international law governing the protection of foreign investment, or the law on State responsibility as it expounds upon the substantive protections found in bilateral and multilateral investment treaties.

More recently, 'due diligence' has been used to describe the scope of an investor's obligations towards a host State in relation to its investment. In this usage, 'due diligence' takes on a twin role: a *first*, and more established, role is as a qualification on the ability of an investor to advance its substantive claims (whether based on fair and equitable treatment, full protection and security, or others) based on how much effort it had taken to understand and comply with the legal and regulatory regime in place in that State. Due diligence here becomes one further manifestation of good faith and an aspect of legitimate expectations.

Second, the recent *Churchill Mining* award of December 2016 marks a potentially greater expansion of 'due diligence,' identifying the principle as a standalone obligation that engages an investor's responsibility not only for its own omissions or negligence, but also for the fraudulent, corrupt, or other illegal acts of its local partners, even when the investor had no knowledge (let alone complicity) in the wrongdoing of its co-venturer. As seen in juxtaposition to the *Fraport* cases, this is arguably a departure from the pre-existing rule that a local partner's wrongdoing cannot ordinarily be conflated with and attributed to the investor. Should *Churchill* endure, due diligence may eventually supplant the need to show an investor's complicity or actual knowledge of illegality of joint venture partners – all that

[70] Ibid., para. 480 ('There is a leap in the logic in alleging Fraport's corruption regarding events having taken place much before the time it made the Initial Investment or regarding payments to Datacenta made by PIATCO after the Concession had been obtained and still ongoing in March-June 1999 as "being the basis for awarding the concession." Even assuming Fraport knew of payment to Datacenta through PIATCO's project costs of 7 February 2002, this document is over two and a-half years after Fraport's initial investment. There is no basis in conflating PIATCO with Fraport and asserting that even if Fraport did not know of PIATCO's corruption, assuming such corruption is proven (which is not regarding the concession award), its investment 'is unlawful and not protected by the BIT.") (emphasis supplied).

needs to be shown is that the investor failed to exercise a reasonable level of diligence when vetting its local partner and *that partner's continuing activities*.

That final qualification is important. Through its expansion of the due diligence obligation, *Churchill Mining* upends a key aspect of the law on investor wrongdoing. Until that case, there had been a consistent body of case law that supported *Fraport I's* temporal limitation on investor wrongdoing, allowing it to be a jurisdictional issue only if the illegal acts occurred at the time the investment was 'made' (*i.e.*, established or admitted).[71] In *Hamester* v. *Ghana*, for example, the tribunal (referencing the Germany–Ghana BIT) stated unequivocally that 'the legality of the creation of the investment is a jurisdictional issue,' and 'the legality of the investor's conduct during the life of the investment is a merits issue'.[72]

Churchill Mining's subverts that apparent consensus: the *Churchill* tribunal refused to impose a temporal limit to the issue of illegality and on the investor's obligation to exert due diligence to ferret out that illegality. Instead of viewing illegality made over the course of an investment's performance a merits defence of the host State to be decided along with the claims of the investor, the tribunal viewed a failure to exercise due diligence well after the investment was made as a jurisdiction or admissibility issue. The tribunal did so without pointing to any specific textual basis for such a conclusion from any 'legality clause' found in the relevant BITs. Instead, the tribunal concluded that if an investor's claims arose from rights that were founded upon fraud or forgery, even if that forgery were committed by its local partner, a claimant's failure to exercise due diligence (or, in *Churchill's* words, to 'deliberately or unreasonably ignore[]' the local partner's illegality) renders all its claims inadmissible as a matter of 'international public policy'.[73]

This finding is a significant divergence from the logic of *Fraport I*, which viewed issues of illegality as ordinarily a matter for the merits of a case, and would only be considered as having jurisdictional consequences when explicitly said so in the relevant BIT.[74] Indeed, in *Yukos* v. *Russian Federation*, the tribunal considered and then rejected Russia's argument that the right to invoke the Energy Charter Treaty must be denied to an investor not only in the case of illegality in the making of the investment but also in its performance; the tribunal considered it to be contrary to the object and purpose of the treaty to deny an investor the right to a decision on the merits, especially when that question of illegality forms part of the dispute itself[75] (as arguably was the case with the validity of the licences themselves and their cancellation in *Churchill*).

[71] *See* Llamzon and Sinclair, 'Investor Wrongdoing', above n 45, pp. 500–02, *citing, inter alia, Inceysa Vallisoletana* v. *Republic of El Salvador* (ICSID Case No. ARB/03/26, Award of 2 August 2006), para. 242; *Quiborax S.A., Non Metallic Minerals S.A. and Allan Fosk Kaplún* v. *Plurinational State of Bolivia* (ICSID Case No. ARB/06/2, Decision on Jurisdiction of 27 September 2012), para. 266; *Teinver S.A., Transportes de Cercanías S.A. and Autobuses Urbanos del Sur S.A.* v. *The Argentine Republic* (ICSID Case No. ARB/09/1, Decision on Jurisdiction of 21 December 2012), para. 318; *Fraport I*, Award, paras. 401–04; *Metal-Tech Ltd.* v. *Republic of Uzbekistan* (ICSID Case No. ARB/10/3, Award of 4 October 2013), para. 193; *Saba Fakes* v. *Republic of Turkey* (ICSID Case No. ARB/07/20, Award of 14 July 2010), para. 119.

[72] *Gustaf F.W. Hamester GmbH & Co KG* v. *Republic of Ghana* (ICSID Case No. ARB/07/24, Award of 18 June 2010), para. 127.

[73] *Churchill* v. *Indonesia*, Award, para. 526.

[74] *Fraport I*, Award, paras. 344–45.

[75] *Hulley Enterprises (Cyprus) Limited, Yukos Universal Limited (Isle of Man) and Veteran Petroleum Limited (Cyprus)* v. *Russian Federation* (PCA Case Nos. AA226-228, Final Awards of 18 July 2014), para. 1355 ('If the investor acts illegally, the host state can request it to correct its behavior and impose upon it sanctions available under domestic law, as the Russian Federation indeed purports to have done by reassessing taxes and imposing fines. However, if the investor believes these sanctions to be unjustified (as Claimants do in the present case), it must have the possibility of challenging their validity in accordance with the applicable investment treaty. It would undermine the purpose and object of the ECT to deny the investor the right to make its case before an

On the other hand, *Churchill Mining's* treatment of due diligence as a continuing obligation on the part of the investor throughout the life of their investment has intuitive logic to it. A lack of due diligence is largely a sin of omission – the foreign investor should have but did not ask the right questions and conduct the appropriate investigations (including of its business partners) despite circumstances that would have caused a reasonable person to make those inquiries. Inaction, the argument goes, amounts to wilful ignorance or a head-in-the-sand approach, and a due diligence requirement is helpful in putting the onus on the foreign investor to continue to ensure, to the extent it reasonably can, that the acts of its partners, in addition to its own acts, do not cross into fraud, corruption, or other violations of the host State's laws. There is no cogent reason why such diligence should not be done on a continuing basis: investors who are charged with guarding against illegality at the inception of the investment – including through exercising due diligence – should continue to act reasonably and in good faith generally, and more specifically, to conduct themselves diligently throughout the life of their investment.

Imposing a dividing line between illegality as a jurisdictional or admissibility issue vs. one of the merits based on temporality – when an investment is made – thus has little sound basis in principle.[76] But a larger question arises: if due diligence should be a continuing obligation, should *Churchill's* identification of that principle as an issue of admissibility, and not merits, also be adopted?

It is on this key question that the authors part company with *Churchill*. There is significant doubt that questions of illegality in the performance of an investment should be considered an issue of jurisdiction, given the 'draconian' consequences of lack of jurisdiction or inadmissibility resulting from a violation of international public policy[77] – the claimant is deprived of an arbitral remedy (often its only realistic recourse) no matter how egregious the respondent's conduct may have been. The tendency to view issues of illegality in black-and-white, binary fashion – so that if illegality exists, it should immediately deprive an investment tribunal of jurisdiction, no matter what violations of international law the host State may have committed – can be dangerous. In the words of Prof. Cremades in *Fraport I*, '*[i]f the legality of the Claimant's conduct is a jurisdictional issue, and the legality of the Respondent's conduct is a merits issue, then the Respondent Host State is placed in a powerful position. In the Biblical phrase, the Tribunal must first examine the speck in the eye of the investor and defer, and maybe never address, a beam in the eye of the Host State*'.[78]

arbitral tribunal based on the same alleged violations the existence of which the investor seeks to dispute on the merits.').

76 Zachary Douglas, 'The Plea of Illegality in Investment Treaty Arbitration' (2014) 29 *ICSID Review—Foreign Investment Law Journal* 155 at 175 (In relation to the *Fraport* case, Prof. Douglas observed: 'This temporal dividing line between pleas of illegality that go to jurisdiction and to the merits has no sound basis in principle. The illegality discerned by the majority related to the execution of secret shareholders' agreements to ensure that Fraport could exercise managerial control over PIATCO in violation of the Anti-Dummy Law. These agreements were executed at the time that Fraport's direct and indirect shareholding interests in PIATCO were acquired and hence fell on the jurisdictional side of the dividing line. It would seem to follow that if those agreements had simply been executed after the shareholding interests were acquired, then this would be a problem for the merits. And yet the essence of the illegality would be identical.').

77 Ibid., at 176 ('It would appear that the category of violations that do not provoke a jurisdictional infirmity is expanding in the jurisprudence to avoid the draconian effects of the approach to the plea of illegality under consideration.') and 181 ('Tribunals must exercise care in their recognition of grounds of international public policy given the draconian consequences that follow the application of this doctrine.').

78 *Fraport AG Frankfurt Airport Services Worldwide* v. *Republic of Philippines* (ICSID Case No. ARB/03/25, Dissenting Opinion of Mr. Bernardo M. Cremades of 16 August 2007, para. 37. *See also* Douglas, 'Plea of Illegality'; Andrew Newcombe, 'Investor Misconduct: Jurisdiction, Admissibility or Merits' in C. Brown and K. Miles (eds.), *Evolution in Investment Treaty Law and Arbitration* (Cambridge: Cambridge University Press, 2012), p. 187.

That wise thought is particularly resonant with *Churchill's* expansion of the due diligence obligation. The practical consequence of that expansion is that if any kind of illegality is committed by the investor *or its local partner* at any point – whether pre- or post-investment – the absence of due diligence in discovering or preventing this illegality is alone sufficient to engage the responsibility and liability of the investor. That such liability would also become an issue of admissibility, and be enough to deprive the investor of the ability to obtain any relief in arbitration, should be considered carefully, and sceptically.

16

Combating Haze Pollution through the Enforcement of Investment Treaties and Human Rights

Robert McCorquodale and Mark Mangan[1]

16.1 INTRODUCTION

For many decades, Indonesia, Malaysia, Brunei, Singapore and Thailand have at times been covered in toxic air pollution called 'haze'. So frequent is the problem that there is now a 'haze season'. In 2019, the United Nations Children's Fund (Unicef) estimated that 10 million children in South East Asia were at risk from toxic air pollution due to wild forest fires.[2]

Transboundary haze pollution from forest and peat fires in Indonesia's Sumatra and Central Kalimantan, mainly used as a means to clear land, has impaired the health of millions of people in the region.[3] It also damages the regional economy. It has been suggested that the haze pollution in 2015 cost Singapore alone an estimated SGD 650 million.[4] Singapore's Foreign Minister, Vivian Balakrishnan, has described transboundary haze pollution as a 'man-made tragedy and crime'.[5] At the passage of the Transboundary Haze Pollution Act in Singapore two years earlier, Minister Balakrishnan said '[the Singapore government] must not allow companies to ignore the environmental and health impacts of their actions'.[6]

There have been a range of responses to transboundary haze pollution across the region. This has included action within Indonesia and by individual States, as well as by the Association of Southeast Asian Nations (ASEAN).[7] None have solved the problem of

1 This chapter is intended to provoke debate and does not necessarily reflect the final views of the authors or the organizations with which they work, and reflects the situation as at October 2019.

2 Unicef Report, 24 September 2019: www.unicef.org/press-releases/indonesia-10-million-children-risk-air-pollution-due-wild-forest-fires. See also, S. Koplitz et al., 'Public Health Impacts of the Severe Haze in Equatorial Asia in September–October 2015' (2016) 11 *Environmental Research Letters* 9.

3 On 27 July 2017, The Straits Times had reported that 'Dozens hospitalised in Indonesia as Haze Spreads', available at www.straitstimes.com/asia/se-asia/dozens-hospitalised-in-indonesia-as-haze-spreads (last accessed 12 September 2019). See also K. H Cheog, et al., 'Significant Association between Transboundary Air Pollution and Acute Myocardial Infarction' (2019) 73(9) *Journal of the American College of Cardiology* 248.

4 Yuan Lin et al., 'Singapore's willingness to pay for Mitigation of Transboundary Forest-Fire Haze from Indonesia' (2017) *Environment Research Letters* 12 02401, p. 7: https://iopscience.iop.org/article/10.1088/1748–9326/aa5cf6/pdf (last accessed 8 October 2019).

5 Reported in Today, 3 November 2015, *see* www.todayonline.com/world/asia/transboundary-haze-man-made-tragedy-and-crime-vivian-balakrishnan (last accessed 12 September 2019).

6 *Singapore Parliamentary Debates, Official Report* (4 August 2013) vol. 92 (Dr Vivian Balakrishnan, Minister for the Environment and Water Resources).

7 *See, e.g.*, A. Tan, '"Can't We Even Share Our Maps?": Cooperative and Unilateral Mechanisms to Combat Forest Fires and Transboundary "Haze" in Southeast Asia' in S. Jayakumar, T. Koh, R. Beckman and H. D. Phan, Transboundary Pollution: *Evolving Issues of International Law and Policy* (Elgar, 2015). *See also* H. Varkkey, 'Patronage Politics as a Driver of Economic Regionalisation: The Indonesian Oil Palm Sector and Transboundary

recurring haze pollution from forest fires. The aim of this chapter is to show that chronic and recurring haze pollution can violate human rights and be the subject of claims under applicable investment treaties.

The responses of Indonesia and South East Asian States to the haze pollution are considered first (Section 16.2). There follows an analysis of the responsibility of States to prevent transboundary pollution and to protect the human rights of those within their jurisdiction, as well as those residing in neighbouring States (Section 16.3). We consider how these obligations can be enforced under investment treaties (Section 16.4) and corporate responsibilities (Section 16.5).

16.2 REGIONAL RESPONSES TO HAZE POLLUTION

Indonesia has taken some steps to curb the traditional practice in rural areas of clearing land by fire. The Indonesian police reportedly arrested more than 450 individuals suspected of starting fires between January and September 2016.[8] There have been at least three convictions since 2015, including of a manager in a palm oil plantation company, who was sentenced to two years and a USD 75,000 fine for burning plantation crops, and against a pulpwood firm for setting fire to the land. The Indonesian Ministry of Environment and Forestry has also reportedly revoked the concessions of twenty-three Indonesian paper and palm oil companies accused of lighting illegal forest fires. Opaque property rights, however, make it difficult to determine who is responsible for the land upon which the fires are routinely set alight and the efficiency and integrity of the Indonesia court system has been called into question by Transparency International.[9]

The only State in the region to have enacted legislation directly to deal with the transboundary haze pollution is Singapore. In August 2014, the Singaporean parliament passed the Transboundary Haze Pollution Act (THPA).[10] The THPA imposes both civil and criminal liability[11] on companies domiciled in Singapore and overseas which cause or contribute to haze pollution in Singapore. Article 5(1) provides: An entity shall be guilty of an offence if –

(a) The entity –
   (i) Engages in conduct (whether in or outside Singapore) which causes or contributes to any haze pollution in Singapore; or
   (ii) Engages in conduct (whether in or outside Singapore) that condones any conduct (whether in or outside Singapore) by another entity or individual which causes or contributes to any haze pollution in Singapore; and

(b) There is haze pollution in Singapore at or about the time of that conduct by that entity.

By this legislation, companies or persons which cause or contribute to transboundary haze pollution in Singapore[12] can be subject to criminal liability. This can extend to companies

Haze' (2012) 53(3) *Asia Pacific Viewpoint* 314; Janice S. H. Lee et al., 'Towards Clearer Skies: Challenges in Regulating Transboundary Haze in Southeast Asia' (2015) 55 *Environmental Science & Policy* 87.

8 The information in this paragraph is from K. Ng, 'Transboundary Haze Pollution in Southeast Asia: The Effectiveness of Three Forms of International Legal Solutions' (2017) 10 *Journal of East Asia and International Law* 221 at 232–33.

9 Transparency International gives Indonesia a ranking of 38 out of 100, with zero considered highly corrupt and 100, very clean: Transparency International, *Global Corruption Index 2018*, available at www.transparency.org/cpi2018 (last accessed 8 October 2019).

10 Act 24 of 2014.

11 THPA, Sections 6 and 5 respectively.

12 Ibid., Section 4.

that condone this conduct, which could include parent companies. Civil penalties can be imposed for personal injury, property damage or economic loss in Singapore.[13]

The legislation creates a legal presumption that if there is haze pollution in Singapore and there is land or forest fire in the region from which smoke is moving in Singapore's direction, 'the haze pollution is caused by that land or forest fire'.[14] The THPA also empowers Singapore's National Environmental Agency (NEA) to issue 'preventive measures notices' to companies that are directly or indirectly involved in such conduct.[15] The NEA reportedly sent preventative measures notices to six Indonesian companies, under Section 9 of the THPA, requesting them to (i) deploy fire-fighting personnel to extinguish or prevent the spread of any fire on land owned or occupied by them; (ii) discontinue, or not commence, any burning activities on such land; and (iii) submit to the NEA any plan of action to extinguish any fire on such land or to prevent its recurrence.[16] These companies were suppliers for the Asia Pulp and Paper Group (a company which has a Singapore domicile). Two of them responded with explanations that the NEA accepted, after which it closed the cases against them. The other four did not respond.[17] NEA thereafter served APPCL in Singapore a notice pursuant to Section 10 of the THPA, seeking information from APPCL on the four subsidiaries, its related companies and suppliers in Singapore and Indonesia, as well as measures taken by its suppliers in Indonesia to put out fires in their concessions.[18] NEA found that APPCL had been opaque with the requested information for four of their suppliers. The NEA later served the director of one of the four companies with a notice to be interviewed by NEA when he entered Singapore. However, he failed to turn up and the NEA has since obtained a court warrant against him.[19] No criminal convictions have yet occurred, with only one charge brought against the said director.[20]

Singapore's actions taken under the THPA may have inspired the prosecutions, reportedly undertaken by the Indonesian government against Indonesian companies allegedly responsible for the haze.[21]

While there has been no legislation equivalent to the THPA promulgated in other South East Asian States, the ten ASEAN States reached an Agreement on Transboundary Haze Pollution in 2002, which entered into force in November 2003. Indonesia agreed to abide by its terms on 14 October 2014.[22] The Agreement requires the State parties to introduce prevention, monitoring and mitigation measures for transboundary haze pollution, to

13 Ibid., Section 6.

14 Section 8(1) THPA.

15 Section 9 THPA. Some companies have been issued with Preventative Measures Notices to provide information on their Singaporean and Indonesian subsidiaries, as well as what their suppliers are doing to fight fires in their concessions and mitigate haze pollution.

16 See M. Mohan, 'A Domestic Solution for Transboundary Harm: Singapore's Haze Pollution Law' (2017) 2(2) *Business and Human Rights Journal* 325; K. Ng, 'Transboundary Haze Pollution in Southeast Asia' above n8.

17 Audrey Tan, 'Haze-linked firm 'opaque with information', The Straits Times, 3 March 2017, available at www.straitstimes.com/singapore/environment/haze-linked-firm-opaque-with-information (last accessed 12 July 2019).

18 See Oral Reply by the Minister of the Environment and Water Resources in Parliament, on 4 October 2017: www.mewr.gov.sg/search?q=haze (last accessed 8 October 2019).

19 Audrey Tan, 'Haze-linked firm 'opaque with information', above n 17.

20 Ibid. No further information is available at this time.

21 Vaidehi Shah, 'Indonesia gets tough on companies responsible for haze', Eco-Business, 23 September 2015, available at www.eco-business.com/news/indonesia-gets-tough-on-companies-responsible-for-haze/; Francis Chan, 'Indonesia to sue another 10 firms over forest fires', The Straits Times, 7 January 2016, available at www.straitstimes.com/asia/indonesia-to-sue-another-10-firms-over-forest-fires (both last accessed 12 July 2019).

22 Indonesia sent its ratification to the ASEAN secretariat on 20 January 2015: *see* http://haze.asean.org/asean-agreement-on-transboundary-haze-pollution-2 (last accessed 12 July 2019). There have been meetings of SEAN ministers related to Transboundary Haze Pollution regularly, with the 21st meeting occurring in Brunei Darussalam on 6 August 2019:

respond to information requests made by affected States, and to provide mutual legal assistance to implement obligations under the Agreement.

The ASEAN Agreement on Transboundary Haze Pollution requires that any dispute as to the interpretation or application of the agreement shall be settled amicably by consultation or negotiation. It has no enforcement provisions. This seems to reinforce the view of 'a preference of ASEAN members for the 'ASEAN way' of resolving disputes based on extreme consensus'.[23] If there was to be a claim arising under this treaty, then it is unlikely that Indonesia would consent to jurisdiction of a court of arbitration body to resolve it.

Notwithstanding these regional measures, chronic haze pollution continues to be a recurring problem, with a return of the haze in September/October 2019.

16.3 STATE RESPONSIBILITY FOR HAZE POLLUTION

16.3.1 *Obligation to Prevent Activities Which Harm the Environment of Neighbouring States*

Under customary international law, a State will incur international responsibility for a breach of an international legal obligation where the act in question can be attributed to the State.[24] This has been codified by the International Law Commission (ILC) in its Articles on the Responsibility of States for Internationally Wrongful Acts.[25] Under these rules, a State is responsible for the actions and omissions of its executive, legislative, judicial and other State organs and officials, including police, military, immigration and similar officials.[26] This is the position even where those actions are committed outside the scope of the relevant body's apparent authority.

An arbitration tribunal as early as 1941 indicated that there is an international obligation on States to prevent transboundary environmental harm.[27] The International Court of Justice (ICJ) confirmed this obligation in the *Legality of the Threat or Use of Nuclear Weapons* Opinion:

> The existence of the general obligation of States to ensure that activities within their jurisdiction and control respect the environment of other States or of areas beyond national control is now part of the corpus of international law relating to the environment.[28]

http://haze.asean.org/2019/08/media-release-twenty-first-meeting-of-the-sub-regional-ministerial-steering-committee-on-transboundary-haze-pollution-21st-msc/ (last accessed 8 October 2019).

[23] S. Alam and L. Nurhidayah, 'The International Law on Transboundary Haze Pollution: What can we Learn from the Southeast Asian Region', (2017) *Review of European Comparative and International Environmental Law* 26, 243, 248.

[24] See, e.g., *Caire Claim (France* v. *Mexico)* (1929) 5 RIAA 516.

[25] International Law Commission, *Articles on the Responsibility of States for Internationally Wrongful Acts*, Report of the International Law Commission on the Work of its 53nd session, A/56/10, August 2001, UN GAOR. 56th Sess. Supp. No. 10, UN Doc A/56/10(SUPP) (2001) ('ILC Articles'). Note that the rules set out in the ILC Articles are considered by the ILC to be secondary rules of international law: *see* J. Crawford, *The International Law Commission's Articles on State Responsibility: Introduction, Text and Commentaries* (Cambridge: Cambridge University Press, 2002) ('ILC Commentaries'), p. 74.

[26] ILC Articles, Article 4. *See also Difference Relating to Immunity from Legal Process of Special Rapporteur of the Commission on Human Rights* (1999) ICJ Rep. 62, para. 62, where it is stated that this represents a rule of customary international law.

[27] *Trail Smelter Case (United States* v. *Canada)* (1941) 3 RIAA 1905 at 1965.

[28] *Legality of the Threat or Use of Nuclear Weapons* (1996) ICJ Rep. 226, para. 29. *See also Trail Smelter Case (United States* v. *Canada)* (1941) 3 RIAA 1905; *The Rainbow Warrior (New Zealand* v. *France)* (1990) 20 RIAA 215.

The ICJ expanded on this in 2010 in the *Pulp Mills Case (Argentine* v. *Uruguay)*:

> A State is thus obliged to use all means at its disposal in order to avoid activities which take place in its territory, or in any area under its jurisdiction, causing significant damage to the environment of another State. ··· [The State's duty of due diligence includes] a certain level of vigilance in their enforcement and the exercise of administrative control applicable to public and private operators . . . to safeguard the rights of the other party.[29]

This legal position has been confirmed by the ILC in its draft Articles on the Protection of the Atmosphere, with its current draft Guideline 3 providing:

> States have the obligation to protect the atmosphere by exercising due diligence in taking appropriate measures, in accordance with applicable rules of international law, to prevent, reduce or control atmospheric pollution and atmospheric degradation.[30]

It is therefore clear that a State can commit an internationally wrongful act if its activities within its jurisdiction or control, such as destruction of its forests and rural land, causes pollution to neighbouring States.[31]

16.3.2 *Obligation to Protect Human Rights*

Customary international law imposes an obligation on all States to take measures – such as by legislation and administrative practices – to control, regulate, investigate and prosecute actions by any persons or groups within that State, both State actors and non-State actors, which violate the human rights of those within the territory or jurisdiction of that State.[32] States are expected to exercise due diligence to protect the human rights of all persons in that State's territory or jurisdiction.[33] For example, in *Vélásquez Rodriguez* v. *Honduras*,[34] a case involving a disappearance of a person by a paramilitary group, the Inter-American Court of Human Rights held that:

> The State is obligated to investigate every situation involving a violation of rights under the Convention. If the State apparatus acts in such a way that the violation goes unpunished and the victim's full enjoyment of such rights is not restored as soon as possible, the State has failed to comply with its duty to ensure the free and full exercise of those rights to persons within its jurisdiction. The same is true when the State allows private persons or groups to act freely and with impunity to the detriment of the rights recognised in the Convention.[35]

Accordingly, States have been found to be in breach of their obligations of due diligence in relation to activities of non-State actors, including companies operating within or indeed outside their territory, because the acts or omissions of the State enabled the non-

[29] *Pulp Mills (Argentina* v. *Uruguay)* (2010) ICJ Rep. 14, paras. 101, 197. This was confirmed by the ICJ in *Construction of a Road in Costa Rica along the San Juan River (Nicaragua* v. *Costa Rica)* (2015) ICJ Rep. 665.

[30] ILC Draft Guidelines on Protection of the Atmosphere, 6 June 2018, UN Doc. A/CN.4/L.909.

[31] This is supported across the main writings in this field. See, e.g., P. Sands and J. Peel, *The Principles of International Environmental Law* (Cambridge: Cambridge University Press, 4th edition, 2018).

[32] See, e.g., *Ergi* v. *Turkey* (App. 23818/94) (1998) 32 EHRR 388; *Timurtas* v. *Turkey* (App. 23531/94) (2000) ECHR 221; *A* v. *UK* (App. 25599/94) (1999) 27 EHRR 611.

[33] See generally A. Clapham, *Human Rights Obligations of Non-State Actors* (Oxford: Oxford University Press, 2006).

[34] *Vélásquez Rodriguez* v. *Honduras*, (1989) 28 ILM 294.

[35] Ibid., para. 176.

State actor to act as it did.[36] This has been summarized by the UN Committee on Economic, Social and Cultural Rights ('ESCR Committee') as follows:[37]

> The extraterritorial obligation to protect requires States Parties to take steps to prevent and redress infringements of Covenant rights that occur outside their territories due to the activities of business entities over which they can exercise control, especially in cases where the remedies available to victims before the domestic courts of the State where the harm occurs are unavailable or ineffective …
>
> [I]t would be in breach of [the State's] obligations under the Covenant where the violation reveals a failure by the State to take reasonable measures that could have prevented the occurrence of the event. The responsibility of the State can be engaged in such circumstances even if other causes have also contributed to the occurrence of the violation, and even if the State had not foreseen that a violation would occur, provided such a violation was reasonably foreseeable.[38]

Furthermore, just as a State may be found liable for harming the environment of its neighbours (see earlier), a State may be held responsible for a violation of the human rights of those residing in neighbouring States.[39] Thus: '[w]here a state knows that its national's activities will cause, or are causing, harm to other States or peoples, it is consistent with this [general] duty that it should prevent such harm'.[40] As explained in the next section, haze pollution can violate the human rights to health and a clean environment.

16.4 INVESTMENT TREATIES

A State cannot be compelled to resolve a dispute against its will. In the words of the Permanent Court of International Justice (PCIJ):

> It is well established in international law that no State can, without its consent, be compelled to submit its disputes with other States either to mediation or to arbitration, or to any other kind of pacific settlement.[41]

Thus, a State must provide its consent in order for a claim to be pursued against it before any international court or tribunal, including for a breach of customary international law.

The ASEAN Agreement on Transboundary Haze Pollution (discussed earlier) reflects the 'ASEAN way', which focuses on unanimous and consent-based diplomacy, respect for national sovereignty and non-interference in other ASEAN State's domestic affairs.[42] It

[36] See, e.g., *Young, James and Webster* v. *UK* (App. 7601/76) (1982) 4 EHRR 38 (Labour Rights); *Social and Economic Rights Action Centre for Economic and Social Rights* v. *Nigeria* (2001) African Commission on Human and Peoples' Rights Decision 155/96 (Pollution); 1985–84; *The Mayagna (Sumo) Awas Tingni Community* v. *Nicaragua* (2001) IACHR Series C No 79 (Indigenous Rights).

[37] ESCR Committee, *General Comment No. 24 on State Obligations under the International Covenant on Economic, Social and Cultural Rights in the Context of Business Activities*, UN Doc E/C.12/GC/24 (2017).

[38] Ibid., paras. 30, 32–33.

[39] *Loizidou* v. *Turkey* (App. 15318/89) (1995) 20 EHRR 99 (Preliminary Objections), para. 62; S. Joseph, J. Schultz and M. Castan, *The International Covenant on Civil and Political Rights: Cases, Commentary and Materials* (Oxford: Oxford University Press, 3rd ed., 2013).

[40] M. Sornarajah, 'Linking State Responsibility for Certain Harms Caused by Corporate Nationals Abroad to Civil Recourse in the Legal Systems of Home States' in C. Scott (ed.), *Torture as Tort* (Hart, 2001), pp. 491, 507.

[41] *Status of Eastern Carelia (Finland* v. *U.S.S.R)* (1923) PCIJ Series B No. 5. Similarly, Article 36 of the Statute of the ICJ provides: 'The jurisdiction of the Court comprises all cases which the parties refer to it and all matters specially provided for in the Charter of the United Nations or in treaties and conventions in force'.

[42] See Ng, 'Transboundary Haze Pollution in Southeast Asia', above n 8.

therefore requires that the contracting States seek to resolve any disputes which arise under its terms 'by consultation or negotiation'.[43]

Investment treaties, however, typically incorporate a standing agreement by each State to resolve disputes arising under the treaty with qualifying foreign investors through international arbitration.

While each investment treaty stipulates its own qualifying criteria, broadly speaking the treaties protect nationals and companies of one State which is a party to the treaty (i.e., a Contracting State) which invest in another Contracting State. Qualifying investments are usually defined broadly as 'every kind of asset owned or controlled and invested by investors', including shares, movable and immovable property, intellectual property rights, and business concessions.[44]

Investment treaties provide significant protection. A typical treaty will protect a qualifying investor and its foreign investment against 'unfair or inequitable' treatment, arbitrary or politically motivated conduct by the government of the State hosting the investment, or a denial of justice by its judicial organs. They also typically guarantee 'full protection and security' as well as full, fair, and prompt compensation if its investment is expropriated. Another common protection is the right to be treated no less favourably than domestic investors (so-called 'national treatment') and investors from any other State (so-called 'most favoured nation treatment'). By way of illustration, Article 11 of the ASEAN Comprehensive Investment Agreement, to which all ten ASEAN States are party, provides that: 'Each Member State shall accord to covered investments of investors of any other Member State, fair and equitable treatment and full protection and security'.

Fair and equitable treatment extends to protecting an investor's legitimate expectations. One such expectation can be that a State will enforce its own laws. Thus, the tribunal in *Wena Hotels Ltd* v. *Arab Republic of Egypt* held that Egypt had breached the fair and equitable treatment standard by failing to prosecute persons responsible for damage caused to the investment property in question.[45]

Indonesia enacted Law No. 32 (Environmental Protection and Management) in 2009 which, in Article 69, expressly prohibits the clearing of land by burning. Violations are subject to a minimum three-year prison sentence and a fine capped at 10 billion rupiah.[46] Indonesian laws are to be interpreted in light of 'elucidations' which provide an official commentary to the law.[47] The elucidation to Law No. 32 provides that the prohibition against clearing by fire in Article 69 of Law No. 32 'shall take into account local wisdom'. Unfortunately from an environmental perspective, the 'local wisdom' is that each head of family may burn up to two hectares of land to be planted by plants belonging to local variety. It does not stipulate how frequently such clearing by each family may be done.

Indonesia has a rural population of approximately 110 million people, which in theory would be able to conduct significant State-sanctioned land clearing through burning. It has been estimated that Indonesia had 60,000 square km of forest cleared by burning in the ten-year period from the years 2000 to 2010.[48]

43 ASEAN Agreement on Transboundary Haze Pollution, Art. 27.

44 See Australia–Indonesia BIT (1992), Art. I.1(a).

45 ICSID Case No. ARB/98/4, Award, 8 December 2000, paras. 74, 94–95.

46 Environmental Protection and Management Act, Art. 100.

47 Indonesian Law Advisory, 'The Indonesian Legal System I', available at http://indonesianlawadvisory.com/ila2017/IndoLaw%20Law%20Overview%20Benny%20Tabalujan.aspx (last accessed 12 July 2019).

48 'Indonesia overtakes Brazil for Worst Deforestation Title', 30 June 2014, available at http://news.asiantown.net/r/38876/indonesia-overtakes-brazil-for-worst-deforestation-title (last accessed 12 July 2019).

Indonesia's apparent sanctioning of wide-scale clearing of land by fire pursuant to Law No. 32 needs to be considered in the context of its commitment to the protection of human rights. The Indonesian Constitution provides in Article 28H that every person has a right to live in physical and spiritual prosperity, to have a home and to enjoy a good and healthy environment. It is also noted in the recitals of Law No. 32: 'that a proper and healthy environment constitutes a human right of every Indonesian citizen as mandated in Article 28 of the Constitution of 1945'.

Customary international law requires States to respect and protect the human rights of their inhabitants. In the words of James Crawford: 'It is now generally accepted that the fundamental principles of human rights form part of customary international law, although not everyone would agree on the identity or content of the fundamental principles'.[49] Investors might be required to take such human rights obligations of States into account in their expectations of an investment.[50]

Indonesia for its part has ratified the International Covenant on Economic, Social and Cultural Rights (ICESCR) in 2006, Article 12 of which provides that: 'The States Parties to the present Covenant recognize the right of everyone to the enjoyment of the highest attainable standard of physical and mental health'. Indonesia also acceded to the Convention on the Rights of the Child in 1990, which recognizes the right of every child 'to the enjoyment of the highest attainable standard of health'.[51] Article 28H of the Indonesian Constitution further provides that every person has the right 'to enjoy a good and healthy environment'.

Thus, it is beyond dispute that respect for human rights forms a part of Indonesian domestic law as well as customary international law. A foreign investor operating in Indonesia may contend that it has a legitimate expectation that Indonesia would exercise due diligence to ensure the protection of human rights, including the right to health and a clean environment. Alternatively, Indonesia's obligation to provide 'full protection and security' under many of its investment treaties may require it to exercise sufficient due diligence in order to protect health and the environment.

Indeed, numerous international courts and tribunals have found that a State's failure to stop pollution can violate a person's human rights. In *Lopez Ostra* v. *Spain*, the European Court of Human Rights (ECtHR) held that Spain's failure to prevent a private company from discharging pollution from a waste treatment plant for leather tanneries violated Ms. Ostra's right to respect for her home (which was 12 metres from the waste treatment plant) and her private life in breach of Article 8 of the European Convention on Human Rights (ECHR):[52]

> [D]espite the margin of appreciation left to the respondent State, the Court considers that the State did not succeed in striking a fair balance between the interest of the town's economic well-being – that of having a waste-treatment plant – and the applicant's effective enjoyment of her right to respect for her home and her private and family life.

In other words, every State must strike the right balance between promoting a society's economic interests and the health of its inhabitants.

Similarly, in *Fadeyeva* v. *Russia*, the claimant suffered from air pollution from a steel factory (at which she herself was employed and within the vicinity of which she voluntarily

[49] J. Crawford, *Brownlie's Principles of Public International Law* (Oxford: Oxford University, 8th ed., 2012), p. 642.

[50] See *Urbaser S.A.* v. *Argentina*, ICSID Case No. ARB/07/26, Award (English), 8 December 2016, para. 624, where the Tribunal commented that '[t]he protection of [the] universal basic human right [to water] constitutes the framework within which [investor] Claimants should frame their expectations.'

[51] United Nations Convention on the Rights of the Child, Art. 24.

[52] *López Ostra* v. *Spain* (App. 16798/90) (1995) 20 EHRR 277, para. 58.

chose to live). It was the largest iron ore smelter in the former Soviet Union (now Russia), employing over 60,000 people. Notwithstanding those tangible economic benefits, and the fact that it had been emitting similar amounts of pollution since the 1960s, Russia was held liable for Ms. Fadeyeva's ill-health by the ECtHR. The Court noted: 'that the State's responsibility in environmental cases may arise from a failure to regulate private industry'.[53] It also found 'that the authorities in the present case were certainly in a position to evaluate the pollution hazards and to take adequate measures to prevent or reduce them'.[54]

As a result, Russia was found to have breached Ms. Fadeyeva's human rights despite: (a) a private company having operated the plant which emitted the pollution; (b) Ms. Fadeyeva choosing to work at the plant and live nearby; and (c) Ms. Fadeyeva being unable to establish with conclusive evidence that her ill-health was directly caused by the air pollution. It was enough in the eyes of the Court that expert evidence had demonstrated that the incidence of various illnesses, including neurological diseases she had contracted, had spiked because of the air pollution.

Therefore, a State's failure to strike the right balance between the attainment of its economic goals and the health of its inhabitants can be a breach of domestic and international laws which protect the environment and human rights.

While those affected can seek to enforce their rights through an action in the Indonesian courts, foreign investors operating in Indonesia have the potential for added protection if they qualify under one of Indonesia's existing investment treaties.[55] By way of illustration, a Canadian lawyer, Peter Allard, who owned a bird sanctuary in natural wetlands in Barbados, brought a claim against Barbados under the Canada–Barbados Bilateral Investment Treaty. The foreign investor alleged that Barbados failed to prevent the Barbados Water Authority from repeatedly discharging raw sewage into the wetlands, thereby undermining his bird sanctuary. Specifically, Mr. Allard alleged that Barbados failed to regulate the environment surrounding the wetlands in accordance with its assurances. In the result, the international arbitral tribunal rejected Mr. Allard's claim that Barbados had breached its obligation under the treaty to provide 'full protection and security' based on a finding that Barbados authorities had taken reasonable steps to prevent the pollution.[56]

In contrast, a claim against Indonesia for toxic air pollution in circumstances where it has legislation that expressly allows each rural family to clear two hectares of land through burning, potentially amounting to tens of thousands of hectares being burnt under State sanction, would need to be considered on its own facts. Indeed, the problem and its duration is of a scale vastly different to that faced by Mr. Allard's business. Haze pollution from land clearing in Indonesia has been recurring for more than forty years, and is estimated to have caused upwards of 100,000 deaths across Indonesia, Malaysia and Singapore.[57]

The bringing of an international law claim can help encourage a State to comply with its international and domestic law obligations. While Australia and New Zealand ultimately lost

53 *Fadeyeva* v. *Russia* (App. 55723/00) (2007) 45 EHRR 10 ('*Fadeyeva*'), para. 89.

54 Ibid., para. 96.

55 For a discussion of Indonesia's recent attempts to terminate its investment treaties following a spate of claims, see M. Mangan et al., 'How to protect investments in Indonesia despite the termination of its Bilateral Investment Treaties', Dechert, September 2015, available at https://info.dechert.com/10/5454/uploads/dechert-onpoint–how-to-protect-investments-in-indonesia-despite-the-termination-of-its-bilateral-investment-treaties–9–2015.pdf (last accessed 12 July 2019).

56 *Peter A. Allard* v. *The Government of Barbados*, PCA Case No. 2012–06.

57 See S. Koplitz and others, 'Public Health Impacts of The Severe Haze in Equatorial Asia in September–October 2015' (2016) 11 *Environmental Research Letters* 094023.

their claims against France for its testing of nuclear weapons on jurisdictional grounds, the object of the claims was achieved: France stopped testing nuclear weapons in the Pacific Ocean. Similarly, while Indian scholars complained forcefully[58] after an investment treaty tribunal found India liable for a nine-year delay in the review of an arbitration award by the Indian courts,[59] India later proceeded to enact new arbitration legislation designed to prevent such delays in the future.[60]

In this instance, the prospect of an investment treaty claim against Indonesia for its failure to prevent toxic haze pollution was first raised by Dechert lawyers in September 2015.[61] It was then reported in the local business[62] and international environmental[63] press. Following the reported threat of such claims and other pressure brought to bear on Indonesia, Indonesia finally accepted offers of outside assistance to help fight the blazing fires which, by that point, had been clearing vast tracts of land for months.[64] The Indonesian government subsequently expressed an interest in repealing the elucidation to Article 69(1)(h) of Law No. 32, which, as explained earlier, allows the burning of two hectares per rural family in accordance with 'local wisdom', although at least one commenter has argued for not only the retention, but the expansion of the role of 'local wisdom' in the management of Indonesia's forests.[65] Thus, the problem has still not been resolved and toxic haze returned to the skies over South East Asia again in 2019.

16.5 BUSINESS AND HUMAN RIGHTS

Companies may also face consequences for human rights violations. The key international document is the United Nations Guiding Principles on Business and Human Rights (UNGPs), adopted by the UN Human Rights Council in 2011.[66] The UNGPs are founded on three 'pillars': the State's duty to protect human rights, including from abuses by companies; the corporate responsibility to respect human rights; and the need for more effective

58 See S Kachwaha, 'The White Industries Australia Limited – India Bit Award: A Critical Assessment' (2013) 29(2) *Arbitration International* 275.

59 *White Industries Australia Limited* v. *The Republic of India*, UNCITRAL, Final Award, 30 November 2011, para. 11.4.19.

60 The Arbitration and Conciliation Act 1996 (as amended by the Arbitration and Conciliation (Amendment Act 2015), sections 11(13), 29A, 29B.

61 'Does the smoke haze over South East Asia violate international law?', *Dechert OnPoint*, September 2015, available at https://info.dechert.com/10/5575/september-2015/does-the-smoke-haze-over-south-east-asia-violate-international-law-(1).asp (last accessed 12 July 2019). Dechert Singapore has also been commended in the Financial Times Innovative Lawyer Awards Asia-Pacific 2017, noting 'A legal analysis showed that an investment treaty claim against the Indonesian government could be made in relation to toxic haze from forest fires in 2015. It was used by non-governmental organizations and others to put pressure on the Indonesian government and raise awareness': Financial Times, Friday, 2 June 2017.

62 Claire Huang, 'Investment treaties allow for claims against Indonesia for haze, says law firm', Business Times, 7 October 2015, available at www.businesstimes.com.sg/government-economy/investment-treaties-allow-for-claims-against-indonesia-for-haze-says-law-firm (last accessed 12 July 2019).

63 Mark Mangan and Henry Defriez, 'Does the haze over Southeast Asia violate international law?', Eco-Business, 8 October 2015, available at www.eco-business.com/opinion/does-the-haze-over-southeast-asia-violate-international-law/ (last accessed 12 July 2019).

64 Rahimah Rashith, 'Indonesia Finally Accepts Singapore's Help in Fighting Haze', Must Share News, 8 October 2015, available at http://mustsharenews.com/indonesia-accepts-help-haze/ (last accessed 12 July 2019).

65 R. Safa'at, 'A New Paradigm of Indonesia Forest Management Based on Local Wisdom' *Pertanika J. Soc. Soi & Hum.* 27(1): 571–84 (2019).

66 UNHCR, Guiding Principles on Business and Human Rights: Implementing the United Nations 'Protect, Respect and Remedy' Framework (Guiding Principles), UN Doc HR/PUB/11/04 (2011), available at www.ohchr.org/Documents/Publications/GuidingPrinciplesBusinessHR_EN.pdf (last accessed 12 July 2019).

access to remedies. While not a treaty, and thus not legally binding, the UNGPs have had strong influence in the development of international standards in this area. For example, it has directly influenced the revisions to the Equator Principles,[67] the International Finance Company's (IFC) Performance Standards,[68] the European Union (EU) Directive on Non-Financial Reporting[69] and the Council of Europe's Recommendations on Human Rights and Business,[70] as well as the Organisation for Economic Co-operation and Development (OECD) Guidelines for Multinational Enterprises 2011.[71] This section will consider primarily the responsibilities of companies in this area.

As noted earlier, States have an international legal responsibility for activities of all persons, including companies, domiciled in their territory or jurisdiction which violate human rights of either their inhabitants or those of neighbouring States. These could include the effects and impacts of haze pollution. As the UNGPs make clear:

> States must protect against human rights abuse within their territory and/or jurisdiction by third parties, including business enterprises. This requires taking appropriate steps to prevent, investigate, punish and redress such abuse through effective policies, legislation, regulations and adjudication.[72]

Thus, States must regulate and control all companies within their territory and jurisdiction in relation to their activities that have human rights impacts. This includes regulation and control of all companies 'domiciled' within the State,[73] which is understood to include companies registered in a State, as well as those with their principal place of business and headquarters there.[74] In addition, research has shown that States do have legal obligations where an action by a company within its territory has direct transnational effects, such as where the parent company directs a decision of a subsidiary located outside the parent company's jurisdiction as well as where the decisions by a company affecting its subsidiaries or business relationships has impacts transnationally.[75]

Companies also have legal responsibilities concerning human rights impacts that could lead to claims for redress. The UNGPs establish a two-part responsibility on companies:

67 The third edition of the Equator Principles or EP III is available at https://equator-principles.com/wp-content/uploads/2017/03/equator_principles_III.pdf (last accessed 12 July 2019).

68 International Finance Company 'Environmental and Social Performance Standards' (2012) and '2012 Guidance Notes', available at www.ifc.org/wps/wcm/connect/topics_ext_content/ifc_external_corporate_site/ifc+sustainability/our+approach/risk+management/performance+standards/environmental+and+social+performance+standards+and+guidance+notes (last accessed 12 July 2019).

69 Directive 2014/95/EU of the European Parliament and of the Council of 22 October 2014, amending Directive 2013/34/EU as regards disclosure of non-financial and diversity information by certain large undertakings and groups.

70 Council of Europe, Recommendation CM/Rec (2016) 3 of the Committee of Ministers to members States on human rights and business, adopted on 2 March 2016.

71 Available at www.oecd.org/daf/inv/mne/48004323.pdf (last accessed 12 July 2019).

72 Guiding Principle ('GP') 1.

73 GP 2.

74 EU Regulation 1215/2012 on Jurisdiction and the Recognition and Enforcement of Judgments in Civil and Commercial Matters (Brussels I Regulation Recast 2012), Art. 4.

75 *See* Jennifer Zerk, *Extraterritorial Jurisdiction: Lessons for the Business and Human Rights Sphere from Six Regulatory Areas* (2010), available at www.hks.harvard.edu/sites/default/files/centers/mrcbg/programs/cri/files/workingpaper_59_zerk.pdf (last accessed 12 July 2019); Nadia Bernaz, 'Enhancing Corporate Accountability for Human Rights Violations: Is Extraterritoriality the Magic Potion' (2013) 117(3) *Journal of Business Ethics* 493.

The responsibility to respect human rights requires that business enterprises:

(a) Avoid *causing or contributing* to adverse human rights impacts through their own activities, and address such impacts when they occur;
(b) Seek to *prevent or mitigate* adverse human rights impacts that are directly linked to their operations, products or services by their business relationships, even if they have not contributed to those impacts.[76]

This two-part responsibility means that a company that causes or contributes to a human rights impact through its own actions has a clear responsibility. A company may also be made responsible where it fails to use its 'leverage' over a third party, to which it has the ability to influence, which is engaging in wrongful practices.[77] The action that a company should take, according to the UNGPs, is to undertake human rights due diligence. This requires companies to identify the human rights impacts (usually through a human rights impact assessment), integrate these into their operations, track and communicate their actions,[78] and then remediate for any impacts. The UNGPs provide that human rights due diligence 'should be ongoing, recognising that the human rights risks may change over time as the business enterprise's operations and operating context evolve',[79] and not just be a once-off process. The UNGPs also make clear that 'business enterprises conducting such [human rights] due diligence should not assume that, by itself, this will automatically and fully absolve them from liability for causing or contributing to human rights abuses'.[80] However, it might be that undertaking reasonable human rights due diligence could be a possible defence, though this may only be possible where it is the third party which has caused or contributed to the human rights impact and not the company itself (as the company might have a no fault liability for its own actions much like a State does).[81]

This responsibility on a company to undertake human rights due diligence does not seem to be limited to actions within its own jurisdiction:

> Companies domiciled in the territory and/or jurisdiction of States Parties should be required to act with due diligence to identify, prevent and address abuses to Covenant rights by such subsidiaries and business partners, *wherever they may be located*. The Committee underlines that, although the imposition of such due diligence obligations does have impacts on situations located outside these States' national territories since potential violations of Covenant rights in global supply chains or in multinational groups of companies should be prevented or addressed, this does not imply the exercise of extraterritorial jurisdiction by the States concerned. Appropriate monitoring and accountability procedures must be put in place to ensure effective prevention and enforcement. Such procedures may include imposing a duty on companies to report on their policies and procedures to ensure respect for human rights and providing effective means of accountability and redress for abuses to Covenant rights.[82]

Indeed, legislation in a number of States specifically extends the scope of the UNGPs to the operations of companies, including subsidiaries, outside the territory of that State, where

76 GP 13 (emphasis added).
77 Commentary to GP 19.
78 GP 17.
79 GP 17(c). The Commentary to GP 12 notes that 'situations may change, so all human rights should be the subject of periodic review'.
80 Commentary to GP 17.
81 For a fuller discussion, *see* Jonathan Bonnitcha and Robert McCorquodale, 'The Concept of "Due Diligence" in the UN Guiding Principles on Business and Human Rights' (2017) 28(3) *European Journal of International Law* 921.
82 *See* ESRC Committee, General Comment, above n 37, para. 33.

there are human rights impacts.[83] For example, legislation passed in 2017 in France imposes a duty of care (*'devoir de vigilance'*) on certain parent companies in relation to subsidiaries over which they hold 'exclusive control', as well as in relation to its subcontractors and suppliers.[84] In addition, recent cases in Canada and the United Kingdom demonstrate that the scope of a parent company's duty of care can extend to the actions of its subsidiaries.[85] Hence, it is arguable that a company, even if not domiciled in Indonesia, could itself bear responsibility for activities that cause or contribute to transboundary haze pollution originating in Indonesia, for which there may be redress if there is necessary national regulation.

This is illustrated by human rights claims against a Thai company for the activities of its subsidiaries in Cambodia.[86] Specifically, in 2006, the Cambodian government granted some land in the Koh Kong Province to two sugar plantation companies which were subsidiaries of a Thai company, KSL. The land was cleared and they began sugar production. In the process it was alleged that 200 villagers were unlawfully and violently evicted from their land in violation of their human rights. The villagers brought a claim to the Cambodian courts, which, after five years, held that they had no jurisdiction. Separately, based on a claim before it by Thai nationals, the National Human Rights Commission of Thailand found that the two subsidiaries committed violations of human rights, particularly violations of the right to life and the right to self-determination.[87] The Commission decided that the Thai company, KSL, should take steps to ensure its subsidiaries returned the land and compensated the villagers because it had accepted the benefits of the plantation grant. The Commission concluded thus:

> [T]he International Covenant on Civil and Political Rights, the International Covenant on Economic, Social and Cultural Rights, the ASEAN Human Rights Declaration and the United Nations Guiding Principles on Business and Human Rights: Implementing the Protect, Respect, Remedy Framework (2013) Part 1 The State duty to protect human rights and Part 2, the corporate responsibility to respect human rights in particular Articles 16, 17 and 18, all affirm that member states such as Thailand have the clear duty to provide guarantees for human rights protection according to these international agreements. This duty includes prevention of transboundary human rights violations by companies located within each member state's territory or registered under each member state's jurisdiction.[88]

A case was also brought in the UK courts against Tate & Lyle for the tort of conversion on the basis that, by acquiring the sugar from KSL, Tate & Lyle had allegedly unlawfully deprived the claimants of their ownership, use and possession of their land, and converted it to its own

83 This is indirectly noted by the Commentary to GP 2: 'Some [states have adopted] domestic measures with extraterritorial implications. Examples include requirements on "parent" companies to report on the global operations of the entire enterprise; multilateral soft-law instruments such as the Guidelines for Multinational Enterprises of the Organisation for Economic Co-operation and Development; and performance standards required by institutions that support overseas investments. Other approaches amount to direct extraterritorial legislation and enforcement. This includes criminal regimes that allow for prosecutions based on the nationality of the perpetrator no matter where the offence occurs.'

84 Art. L. 225–102-4 and L.225–102-5 of the French Commercial Code.

85 See, e.g., *Choc* v. *Hudbay Minerals Inc.* 2013 ONSC 1414 (Canada); *Vedanta Resources plc* v. *Lungowe* [2019] UKSC 20. *See generally*, G. Skinner, *Parent Company Liability: Ensuring Justice for Human Rights Violations* (ICAR, 2015).

86 For a summary of the allegations, see www.clec.org.kh/web/images/Resources/Res_Koh%20Kong%20ASEAN%20Case%20Study%202013%20-%20ENG1374035991.pdf (last accessed 12 July 2019).

87 See www.earthrights.org/media/human-rights-violations-koh-kong-sugar-plantation-confirmed-thai-human-rights-commission (last accessed 12 July 2019).

88 Ibid., para. 6.

use.[89] A complaint was also made to the International Criminal Court against Cambodian officials,[90] and a claim was made to the US National Contact Point against ASR under OECD process.[91]

Therefore, returning to the haze pollution over South East Asia, a company which owns or operates on land in Indonesia, enables or allows the burning of the land, or contributes to it by not preventing it occurring, could be the subject of claims for abuses of human rights, depending on the national laws and court processes in which that company is domiciled. As information about haze pollution and its consequences are widespread, a company cannot plead lack of knowledge as part of its human rights due diligence processes. Instead, the UNGPs require that a company should have a human rights due diligence process to identify, prevent, mitigate and account for how it addresses its impacts on human rights, including human rights affected by environmental damage.

16.6 CONCLUSIONS

Preventing recurring haze pollution requires innovative solutions. It is clear that there are international legal obligations on States to prevent and remediate transboundary environmental pollution and human rights violations. There are limited means, however, to compel States to comply with international law.

This paper has explored two potential ways forward. A claim could be contemplated against a State which allows haze pollution to recur at dangerous levels under a relevant investment treaty if an investor's investment, including the human rights of its employees and other stakeholders, has been affected by the haze pollution. A claim could also potentially be brought against companies which have caused or contributed to human rights violations by their own actions or by actions of third parties with whom they have a business relationship.

89 *Song Mao* v. *Tate & Lyle Industries Limited*, Claim No. 2013, Folio 451, commenced in March 2013 and ongoing. See the Claimants' Particulars of Claim at http://business-humanrights.org/sites/default/files/media/documents/tate-lyle-particular-of-claim-28-mar-2013.pdf, and the Defendants' Defence and Counterclaim at http://business-humanrights.org/sites/default/files/media/documents/tate-lyle-defence-counterclaim-2-may-2013.pdf (both last accessed 12 July 2019). See also M. Mohan, 'The Road to *Song Mao* – Transnational Litigation from Southeast Asia to the United Kingdom' (2013) 107(4) *American Journal of International Law Unbound* 30.

90 See http://business-humanrights.org/en/cambodians-file-claim-before-intl-criminal-court-alleging-widespread-systematic-land-seizures-by-govt-govt-linked-businesses-amount-to-crime-against-humanity (last accessed 12 July 2019). This is ongoing.

91 See Complaint Under the OECD Guidelines For Multinational Enterprises, October 2012, Final statement: https://earthrights.org/wp-content/uploads/NCP-Final-statement.pdf (last accessed 8 October 2019).

17

Transparency in Investor–State Arbitration

Where Does Asia Stand?

N Jansen Calamita and Ewa Zelazna

Historically the resolution of claims under investment treaties has been confidential and private. Over the past fifteen years, however, there have been changes that require greater transparency in the arbitration of disputes between investors and States under investment treaties. The development with the potential to effect the greatest change in this regard is the recent work of the United Nations Commission on International Trade Law (UNCITRAL), through its promulgation of new Rules on Transparency in Treaty-based Investor–State Arbitration ('Rules on Transparency') and a Convention designed to give those rules wide application over existing investment treaties (the 'Mauritius Convention').

This chapter outlines the drivers of change regarding transparency in investor–State arbitration and asks critically about the role of Asian States in this process. While Asian States have been active in the development of treaty policy in a variety of substantive and procedural areas, they have been ambivalent at best with respect to developments on transparency. In the UNCITRAL negotiations, Asian States expressed considerable doubts about both the need for the Rules on Transparency and the Mauritius Convention. This chapter considers the arguments raised in that context, as well as current Asian State practice, and suggests that the unwillingness of States in Asia to undertake transparency obligations generally may severely curtail the promise of UNCITRAL's work.

17.1 INTRODUCTION

Claims arising under investment treaties concern challenges to the State's exercise of its sovereign power vis-à-vis foreign investors and their investments. While such challenges are substantively analogous to claims for administrative or constitutional review under domestic systems of public law, the resolution of claims under investment treaties has taken place historically according to procedures and principles associated with commercial arbitration, including with respect to the confidentiality and privacy of the proceedings. Thus, arbitral hearings have not been open to the public, there has been no general obligation to publish investor–State arbitral awards (or even to provide public notice that a particular dispute exists), and there has been little or no opportunity for third-party participation in investor–State proceedings.

As the treaty-based investor–State arbitration (ISA) regime has developed over the past fifteen years, however, there have been changes that require greater transparency. First, in the practice of Canada and the United States, following their experience as litigants under the

1994 North American Free Trade Agreement (NAFTA). Next, under the International Centre for Settlement of Investment Disputes (ICSID) rules, to a more limited degree, following a number of rule changes in 2006. And third, and most recently, through the work of UNCITRAL, and its promulgation of new Rules on Transparency[1] and the Mauritius Convention.[2] Taken together, the Rules on Transparency and the Mauritius Convention have established the most wide-ranging set of transparency commitments seen thus far in international practice. If given broad application, they will reshape the character of arbitration under both future and existing investment treaties.

This chapter outlines the developments underlying these changes to the approach to transparency in treaty-based ISA and critically enquires about the role of Asian States in this process. While Asian States have been active in the development of treaty policy in a number of substantive and procedural areas, with respect to current developments on transparency they have been ambivalent at best. The practices of individual Asian States have been inconsistent, with some States adopting transparency provisions in some treaties but not in others, and others rejecting transparency altogether. In the UNCITRAL negotiations, Asian States expressed considerable doubts both about the need for the Rules on Transparency and the Mauritius Convention. This chapter considers the arguments raised in that context and suggests that the unwillingness of States in Asia to undertake transparency obligations generally may severely curtail the promise of UNCITRAL's work.

17.2 THE VARIABLE MEANING OF 'TRANSPARENCY' IN INVESTMENT TREATY ARBITRATION

'Transparency' in the context of investor–State dispute settlement (ISDS) is an oft-used and ill-defined term.[3] Depending on the context in which the term is used, and who is using it, transparency may refer either (or both) to increased public information with respect to investor–State proceedings or increased public participation in the proceedings themselves. Thus, 'transparency' may refer to one or more of the following:

- publication with respect to the existence of an investor–State dispute, with or without publication of the notice of arbitration and subsequent pleadings;
- publication concerning the disposition of the investor–State dispute, with or without publication of the award itself;
- public access to hearings; and
- public participation in the dispute settlement process through *amicus curiae* or non-disputing party mechanisms.

This chapter uses 'transparency' broadly to refer to developments in treaty-making practice and arbitral rules addressing both public disclosure with respect to investor–State arbitration *and* mechanisms for non-party participation.[4]

[1] UNCITRAL Rules on Transparency in Treaty-based Investor-State Arbitration (effective date, 1 April 2014).

[2] *United Nations Convention on Transparency in Treaty-based Investor-State Arbitration*, opened for signature 17 March 2015, entered in force 18 October 2017 ('*Mauritius Convention*').

[3] This description and definition of 'transparency' is taken from N Jansen Calamita, 'Dispute Settlement Transparency in Europe's Evolving Investment Treaty Policy' (2014) 15 *Journal of World Investment and Trade* 645 at 649.

[4] In addition to mechanisms providing for public disclosure and public participation with respect to investor–State disputes, some conceptions of 'transparency' also include mechanisms for the participation of non-disputing state parties, that is, the party or parties to the treaty at issue in an investor–State arbitration which have not been named

17.3 WHY TRANSPARENCY IN TREATY-BASED ISA?

As the investor–State treaty regime has developed, and its wide scope of application has become more broadly appreciated, concern has grown about the 'lack of transparency' in investor–State arbitration, first in North America, and more recently in other regions around the world, especially in Europe. Calls for increased transparency have been put forward by States, international organizations, NGOs, and others. The arguments put forward in favour of increased transparency are straightforward and are briefly summarized below.

First, transparency in investor–State arbitration has been seen to promote the legitimacy of the investment treaty regime. A long-standing critique of investment treaty dispute settlement has been the lack of transparency in its operation, whether with respect to the existence of the disputes, the arguments made by the parties, the identities of arbitrators or the final disposition of claims.[5] Most recently, this criticism has been especially prominent in the context of the European Union's development of its international investment policy following the Lisbon Treaty.[6] Transparent public access to investor–State arbitration and free access to information about ISA proceedings addresses key factual arguments about the nature of the regime.

Second, expanding the scope of transparency in investor–State arbitration promotes accountable governance. While investment treaty arbitration often deals with issues of direct public concern, such as health, environment, and other social policies, even when it does not, it usually relates to some aspect of State governance and the exercise of sovereign power.[7] At issue is whether the State has discharged its international obligations under an investment treaty and whether those in government, acting for the State, have taken actions which expose the State to liability and require payment from the public purse. Accountable governance requires transparency, not only when the State deems it expedient to make matters public, but often precisely when it does not.

Third, transparency in investor–State arbitration serves the interests of States and investors by enhancing legal certainty. For example, the publication of arbitral awards contributes to the development of a public body of jurisprudence which allows both investors and host States to understand how particular investment agreements and their terms have been interpreted and applied in other instances. While awards in arbitrations are without formal precedential value, of course, knowledge of arguments raised and awards rendered allows

as respondent. Although important to investor–State arbitration, such mechanisms are not treated in depth in this chapter. Suffice it to note here that mechanisms like this appear to have originated in the North American Free Trade Agreement (NAFTA), Art. 1128, through which Canada, Mexico and the United States have each participated in many arbitrations to which they have not been named as respondent. More recently the practice has spread to states in other regions, and a mechanism to enable such participation is included in Article 5 of the new UNCITRAL Rules on Transparency.

5 See, e.g., UNCTAD, *Transparency, UNCTAD Series on Issues in International Investment Agreements II* (2012) p. 36.

6 In 2015, European Trade Commissioner Cecilia Malmström, observed that in order to address 'a fundamental lack of trust' by the European public in investor–State dispute settlement, Europe would need to reform its collective approach by, among other things, introducing full transparency in investor–State proceedings. See European Commission, Press Release, *Commission Proposes New Investment Court System for TTIP and other EU Trade and Investment Negotiations* (16 September 2015). Following the EU's decision to replace investor–State arbitration altogether with proceedings before treaty-based investment courts, transparency has continued to play a central role in this new process. See CETA, Art. 8.36; EU–Vietnam FTA, Ch. 8, Art. 20.

7 *Cf.* UN General Assembly Resolution 69/116, 'United Nations Convention on Transparency in Treaty-based Investor-State Arbitration', UN Doc GA/RES/69/116 (10 December 2014), chapeau ('*Recognizing* the need for provisions on transparency in the settlement of treaty-based investor-state disputes to take account of the public interest involved in such arbitrations. . . . ').

investors and host States to have a better understanding of how similarly-worded treaty provisions may be construed in future cases and allows them to adapt their conduct accordingly.[8]

Fourth, transparency addresses issues of fairness and equality in the resolution of investor–State disputes through arbitration. As currently structured, the lack of transparency in investor–State arbitration promotes information asymmetry between parties in arbitration. Because information about investor–State arbitrations is not made public, parties and their representatives often do not have the same knowledge of and access to recent and/or unpublished awards and decisions. This not only affects the parties' knowledge of the arbitral jurisprudence in general, but also their knowledge about arbitrators and their decision-making in prior cases. As a result, especially with respect to the appointment of arbitrators, the parties to an investment dispute often do not operate with the same or equal information.

17.4 DEVELOPMENTS RELATING TO TRANSPARENCY IN TREATY-BASED ARBITRATION

17.4.1 *Transparency Provisions in Investment Treaties*

Most international investment treaties currently in force do not contain express provisions addressing transparency in ISDS. Rather, the vast majority of treaties simply reference various types of arbitration available under the dispute settlement provisions and thereby incorporate the relevant arbitral rules.

That said, one can detect a trend in certain parts of the world towards including within the treaties themselves provisions which require transparency in investor–State arbitration, regardless of the system of arbitration chosen. Beginning with the practices of Canada, Mexico and the US under the NAFTA[9] and followed through in all of the BITs and FTAs concluded by Canada[10] and the US[11] in the years since, a 'North American approach' to transparency in investor–State arbitration has developed. Under this approach, transparency is mandatory as a matter of the treaty; it is a requirement of arbitration, not dependent on the disputing parties' agreement. Moreover, it is broad in its conception and application, usually requiring (1) publication of the notice of arbitration and subsequent pleadings; (2) publication of the disposition of the investor–State dispute, including the award; (3) public access to hearings; and (4) the opportunity for public participation in the dispute settlement process through *amicus curiae* or non-disputing party mechanisms.[12]

[8] See, e.g., European Parliament, *Resolution of 6 April 2011 on the Future European International Investment Policy*, 2010/2203 (INI), Official Journal C 296 E (2 October 2012), para. 15, preamble G & H.

[9] See NAFTA (1994), Arts. 1127, 1128, 1129, 1137.4. See also NAFTA Free Trade Commission, *Notes of Interpretation of Certain* Chapter Eleven *Provisions* (31 July 2001) (affirming the commitment of the NAFTA governments to the principle of transparency generally and created a presumption of public disclosure and openness); NAFTA Free Trade Commission, *Statement of the Free Trade Commission on Non-disputing Party Participation* (7 October 2003) (clarifying the NAFTA tribunals' discretion to accept third party submissions); NAFTA Free Trade Commission, *2004 NAFTA Commission Meeting: Joint Statement* (16 July 2004) (affirming the NAFTA parties' commitment to transparency and welcoming Mexico's support of open hearings).

[10] Canadian practice in these treaties is exemplified by the 2004 Canada Model BIT, Art. 38. The only variance on this practice is the 2012 investment treaty signed between Canada and China. See below n 12.

[11] US practice in these treaties is exemplified by the 2004 US Model BIT 2004, Art. 29 and the 2012 US Model BIT, Art. 29. The US Model BIT 2012 contains no changes on transparency from the 2004 version.

[12] The outlier in this practice is Canada's investment treaty with China. In that agreement Canada and China agree only to the mandatory publication of tribunal awards and to acceptance of *amicus curiae* submissions at the

More recently, this approach has been taken up by the European Union (EU). Following the transfer of competency for foreign direct investment to the EU in 2009, the European Commission has made the UNCITRAL Rules on Transparency its negotiating baseline.[13] Although the ISDS provisions in these treaties are not yet in force, for the Commission, acting on behalf of the Union's twenty-eight Member States, this is a revolutionary development. Almost uniformly, the more than 1,200 international investment treaties entered into by EU Member States in their own right do not contain *any* provisions providing for transparency in investor–State arbitration.[14] Now, in a stroke, the EU has cast aside the practice of its Member States and made Europe a global leader on investor–State arbitration transparency, at least with respect to Europe's future treaties.[15]

Elsewhere in the world, the trend in favour of increased transparency is not nearly as strong. In Latin America, for example, although a considerable number of investment treaties contain provisions requiring transparency as a result of treaties signed between Latin American States and Canada and the United States since 2004,[16] apart from these treaties there has been no general move towards transparency in the treaty texts of the States in the region. In Africa, similarly, there has been virtually no movement towards the inclusion of provisions on transparency in dispute settlement in treaty texts. Even the relatively recent Southern African Development Community (SADC) Protocol on Finance and Investment is silent on the issue.[17]

In Asia, to the extent that one can observe an acceptance of compulsory transparency in investor–State arbitration, it is principally because of the significant number of treaties signed between Asian States and Canada, the United States, Australia and New Zealand since 2004 (see Table 17.1). Outside of these treaties, Asian States have demonstrated little interest in including significant transparency provisions in their investment treaties. While agreements with Australia, Canada, New Zealand, the US (and now the EU) routinely

decision of the tribunal. Agreement Between the Government of Canada and the Government of the People's Republic of China for the Promotion and Reciprocal Protection of Investments (2012), Arts. 28–29. Article 28 permits, but does not require as other Canadian investment treaties do, public hearings and publication of pleadings and other documents produced in arbitration, only upon the agreement of the respondent state.

[13] See, e.g., Canada–European Union Comprehensive Economic and Trade Agreement (CETA) (signed 2016), Art. 8.36; Singapore-European Union Investment Protection Agreement, signed 19 October 2018 (not yet in force), Art. 3.16 and Annex 8; Vietnam-European Union Investment Protection Agreement, signed 30 June 2019, Art. 3.46.

[14] The exceptions to this uniform practice are several BITs entered into by Eastern European and Baltic Member States with Canada, which contain comprehensive transparency provisions, and a 2006 investment treaty between Mexico and the United Kingdom which provides for a minimal degree of transparency regarding the publication of arbitral awards. See Canada–Latvia BIT (2009), Annex C; Canada–Slovak Republic BIT (2010), Annex B; Canada–Czech Republic BIT (2006), Annex B; Canada–Romania BIT (2009), Annex C; and United Kingdom–Mexico BIT (2006), Art. 18(4).

[15] It is an open question as to whether Member States will act to bring transparency to their existing BITs which contain no transparency provisions. As noted below, EU Member States have been far from uniform in endorsing the Mauritius Convention for their existing bilateral agreements.

[16] See, e.g., Canada–Colombia FTA (2011), Art. 830; Canada–Panama FTA, (2013); Canada–Peru FTA (2009), Art. 835. Canada–Honduras FTA; United States–Peru Trade Promotion Agreement, (2009) Art. 10.21; United States–Colombia Trade Promotion Agreement (May 2012), Art. 10.21; United States–Uruguay BIT (2006), Art. 29; United States–Chile Free Trade Agreement (2004), Art. 10.20; Central America–Dominican Republic–United States Free Trade Agreement ('DR-CAFTA') (2004), Art. 10.21.

[17] Southern African Development Community (SADC) Protocol on Finance and Investment (2006). The only significant investment agreement in Africa to address issues of transparency is the now moribund Investment Agreement for the Common Market for Eastern and Southern Africa (COMESA) Common Investment Area. The COMESA Investment Agreement contains broadly applicable provisions on all aspects of transparency, including third-party participation. See, e.g., Art. 28. Although signed in 2007, the Agreement has not yet come into force and shows no signs of doing so any time soon.

TABLE 17.1 *Publication of arbitral documents under different Asian investment treaties*

Mandatory publication of award and arbitral documents, public hearings, and *amicus* participation.	Mandatory publication of award. Publication of other arbitral documents, and public hearings at discretion of respondent State. Varied *amicus*.
• Singapore–United States FTA (2004), Art. 15.20 • Korea–United States FTA (2012), Art. 11.21 • Taiwan–New Zealand ECA (signed 2013), Art. 25 & 27 • Korea–Australia FTA (2014), Art. 11.20–11.21 • Korea–Canada FTA (2015), Art. 8.35–8.36 • Singapore–European Union Investment Protection Agreement (signed 19 October 2018 (not yet in force), Art. 3.16 and Annex 8 • Vietnam–European Union Investment Protection Agreement (signed 30 June 2019), Art 3.46	• China–Australia FTA (signed 2015), Art. 9.17(2); Art. 9.16 (*amicus* upon agreement of disputing parties) • China–Canada BIT (2012), Art.28; Art. 29 (mandatory *amicus*)
Publication of awards at discretion of respondent State. Silent on other matters.	**Publication of all arbitral documents at discretion of defendant State. Silent on other matters.**
• ASEAN–Australia–New Zealand FTA (2009), Ch. 11, Article 26. • ASEAN Comprehensive Investment Agreement (2009), Art. 39 • India–Malaysia FTA (2011), Art. 10.14 • ASEAN – India Investment Agreement (2014), Art. 20	• Japan–Mongolia EPA (2015), Art. 10.13(19) • Japan–Mozambique BIT (2014), Art. 17(12) • Japan–Myanmar BIT (2014), Art. 18 • Japan–Uruguay BIT (2015), Art. 21(18)
Default publication of awards unless agreed by disputing parties. Silent on other matters.	
• China–Mexico BIT (2008), Art. 20(4) • Japan–Mexico FTA (2004), Art. 94	

require broad transparency, the most that Asian treaties with other States have been willing to do is to *allow* a limited range of disclosure at the election of the state party. For example, under the 2009 ASEAN Comprehensive Investment Agreement (ACIA), the public disclosure of tribunal awards and other tribunal decisions is permitted, but not required, by the defendant State.[18] Apparently the claimant investor does not have the same right. Recent Japanese treaties contain similar provisions,[19] as do the recent treaties signed by India with East Asian States.[20]

Another notable aspect of Asian treaty-making practice is that even where Asian States have entered into treaties requiring some degree of transparency, those States have not necessarily been consistent about adopting that treaty-making approach in subsequent treaties with other States. This appears to be true whether or not the transparency provisions previously adopted were of the broad variety found in treaties with States from North America and Oceania or the discretionary, 'transparency-lite' provisions also found in some Asian treaties. So, for example, with respect to ASEAN, while the 2009 ACIA permits the public disclosure of tribunal awards and other tribunal decisions by the disputing State,[21] the ASEAN–China Agreement on Investment, signed around the same time, contains no provisions on transparency at all. Similarly, Korea's free trade agreements with Australia in 2014, Canada in 2015 and the US in 2012 contain broad transparency provisions requiring publication of arbitral awards and other documents submitted in arbitration; public hearings; and *amicus* participation at the discretion of the arbitral tribunal.[22] Korea's investment treaties with other States, however, make no reference to transparency in investor–State arbitration at all.[23] Singapore's practice following its 2004 FTA with the United States[24] is similar.[25]

On 9 March 2018, Australia, Brunei Darussalam, Canada, Chile, Japan, Malaysia, Mexico, New Zealand, Peru, Singapore, and Vietnam signed the Comprehensive and Progressive Trans-Pacific Partnership (CPTPP), and this entered into force for Australia, Canada, Japan, Mexico, New Zealand, and Singapore on 30 December 2018, and for Vietnam on 14 January 2019.[26] The CPTPP incorporates by reference the text of the Trans-Pacific Partnership (TPP), originally signed by Australia, Brunei Darussalam, Canada, Chile, Japan, Malaysia, Mexico, New Zealand, Peru, Singapore, Vietnam, and the United States

18 The treaty contains no other provisions with respect to transparency. The approach in the ACIA is mirrored in the ASEAN–Australia–New Zealand Free Trade Agreement (AANZ FTA), signed in 2009. Like the ACIA, the AANZ FTA contains no provisions addressing non-disputing party participation, but simply allows the disputing state to disclose publicly all awards and decisions rendered. Chapter 11, Article 26. Both the ACIA and AANZ FTA contain further provisions qualifying this right of disclosure to account for protection of 'confidential information,' which is left undefined. Ibid., Ch. 11, Art. 26(2)–(3); ACIA, Art. 39(2)–(3).

19 See, e.g., Japan–Mongolia Economic Partnership Agreement (2015), Art. 10.13(19) (disputing state party may make documents available to the public); Japan-Mozambique BIT (2014), Art. 17(12) (same); Japan–Myanmar BIT (2014), Art. 18 (same); Japan–Uruguay BIT (2015), Art. 21(18) (same). But see Japan–Mexico Economic Partnership Agreement (2005), Art. 94 (either claimant or respondent may publicly disclose documents produced in arbitration).

20 India–Malaysia FTA (2011), Art. 10.14 (disputing state party may publish awards); ASEAN–India Investment Agreement (2014) (not yet in force), Art. 20 (same).

21 See above n 18.

22 Korea–United States FTA (2012), Art. 11.21; Korea–Australia FTA (2014), Art. 11.20–11.21; Korea–Canada FTA (2015), Art. 8.35–8.36.

23 Korea–Myanmar BIT (2014); Korea–China FTA (2015); Colombia–Korea FTA (2013); China–Japan–Korea Trilateral Investment Agreement (2014).

24 Singapore–United States FTA (2004), Art. 15.20. Thus, no Singaporean treaty since the US FTA until the recent FTA with the EU included any provisions on dispute settlement transparency.

25 See, e.g., Singapore–Russian Federation BIT (2010); Singapore–Costa Rica FTA (2013); Singapore–Colombia BIT (2013).

26 See Department of Foreign Affairs and Trade, 'Comprehensive and Progressive Agreement for Trans-Pacific Partnership', https://dfat.gov.au/trade/agreements/in-force/cptpp/Pages/comprehensive-and-progressive-agreement-for-trans-pacific-partnership.aspx (last accessed 9 July 2019). The final text of the CPTPP is available here, as well as at www.mfat.govt.nz/assets/CPTPP/Comprehensive-and-Progressive-Agreement-for-Trans-Pacific-Partnership-CPTPP-English.pdf (last accessed 9 July 2019) (hereinafter 'CPTPP').

on 4 February 2016,[27] but suspends the application of certain provisions of the TPP text[28] in order to account for the decision of the United States to withdraw from the TPP on 30 January 2017.[29] What is noteworthy about the final text of the CPTPP is that it reflects a willingness of the various States, including five Asian States, to agree to compulsory dispute settlement transparency modelled largely on the 2012 US Model BIT (even though the United States is no longer a party). Thus, the investment chapter requires investor–State arbitral tribunals to make hearings open to the public.[30] Moreover, it allows for non-disputing party *amicus curiae* submissions[31] and compels the tribunal to make such submissions publicly available, together with other documents associated with arbitral proceedings, including the notice of intent, the notice of arbitration, minutes and transcripts of hearings, orders, awards and decisions of the tribunal.[32] Although the CPTPP incorporates standard exceptions found in the 2012 US Model BIT,[33] it also includes additional language which increases the flexibility of investment tribunals in the application of transparency requirements. Article 9.24(5) provides that '... [t]he respondent should endeavour to apply ... [its laws on freedom of information] in a manner sensitive to protecting from disclosure information that has been designated as protected information'.[34] While some have suggested that this additional language may allow tribunals to prevent the release of information otherwise accessible under domestic freedom of information laws,[35] given the non-mandatory nature of the State's obligation ('*should endeavour*'), it is not clear that this is necessarily so.

17.4.2 *The Treatment of Transparency in Arbitral Rules*

In addition to developments in State treaty-making practice, there have been initiatives to increase transparency and clarify mechanisms for third-party participation through amendments to the arbitral rules most often referenced in investment treaties. In 2006 the ICSID Arbitration Rules were amended in an effort to address concerns about transparency. Although the amendments made modest changes to the treatment of transparency itself,[36] they introduced meaningful reform with respect to tribunal control of non-disputing party participation and *amicus* applications.[37]

27 CPTPP, Art. 1(1). The final text of the TPP as originally signed is available at www.mfat.govt.nz/en/about-us/who-we-are/treaties/trans-pacific-partnership-agreement-tpp/text-of-the-trans-pacific-partnership/ (last accessed 9 July 2019) hereinafter 'TPP Final Text').

28 CPTPP, Art. 2.

29 See Ltr. from Maria L. Pagan, Acting US Trade Representative to Trans-Pacific Partnership Depositary (30 January 2017), available at https://ustr.gov/sites/default/files/files/Press/Releases/1–30-17%20USTR%20Letter%20to%20TPP%20Depositary.pdf (last accessed 9 July 2019).

30 TPP Final Text, Art. 9.24(2). The same provision is present in 2012 US Model Bilateral Investment Treaty, Art. 29(2).

31 TPP Final Text, Art. 9.22(2) and 9.22(3). The same provision is present in 2012 U.S. Model Bilateral Investment Treaty, Arts. 28(2) and 28(3).

32 TPP Final Text, Art. 9.24(1); 2012 US Model Bilateral Investment Treaty, Art. 29(1).

33 TPP Final Text, Art. 9.24(4); 2012 US Model Bilateral Investment Treaty, Art. 29(4).

34 TPP Final Text, Art. 9.24(5).

35 Lise Johnson and Lisa Sachs, 'The TPP's Investment Chapter: Entrenching, Rather than Reforming, a Flawed System' (CCSI Policy Paper, November 2015), pp. 12–13.

36 See ICSID Arbitration Rule 48(4) ('The Centre shall not publish the award without the consent of the parties. The Centre shall, however, promptly include in its publications excerpts of the legal reasoning of the Tribunal'.). The terms of the ICSID Convention limit the degree of transparency which may be required of the parties short of amending the Convention. See ICSID Convention, Art. 48(5).

37 See, e.g., ICSID Arbitration Rule 37(2). See Lucas Bastin, 'The Amicus Curiae in Investor-State Arbitration' (2012) 1 *Cambridge Journal of International and Comparative Law* 208.

Far more wide-ranging, however, have been the developments with respect to the UNCITRAL Arbitration rules. Following completion of the 2010 revision of the UNCITRAL rules, UNCITRAL commenced work on the possibility of adopting special rules regarding transparency in treaty-based investor–State arbitration. After three years of work, the UNCITRAL Rules on Transparency in Treaty-based Investor–State Arbitration were adopted in 2013.[38] The adoption of the Transparency Rules was followed swiftly by the drafting of the Mauritius Convention, which opened for signature in 2015. The new Transparency Rules contain the most wide-ranging set of transparency commitments seen thus far in international practice and, as addressed in Section 17.6, the Mauritius Convention is an ambitious attempt to provide a platform for these Rules to the entire landscape of investment treaty arbitration.

17.5 THE UNCITRAL RULES ON TRANSPARENCY

The UNCITRAL Rules on Transparency bring about important changes to the process of treaty-based investor–State arbitration commenced under the UNCITRAL Arbitration Rules by embracing a degree of openness that has existed previously only under North American investment treaties. This section outlines the key provisions of the UNCITRAL Rules on Transparency and evaluates their effects on the investor–State arbitration process.

17.5.1 *Public Access to Documents and Hearings*

Under Article 2 of the Rules on Transparency, notice of arbitration triggers an obligation to 'promptly publish' the names of the disputing parties, the economic sector involved in the dispute and the identity of the treaty under which the claim is made. Publication is administered through a repository which as a default is the UNCITRAL Secretariat, although the parties may agree to another institution.[39] Following the issuance of the notice of arbitration, Article 3 of the Transparency Rules requires that other documents produced throughout the arbitration must be made public 'as soon as possible' subject to certain exceptions set out in Article 7. Identified in Article 3 for mandatory publication are:

(a) the notice of arbitration;
(b) the response to the notice of arbitration;
(c) the statement of claim;
(d) the statement of defence (and any further written submissions);
(e) a table listing all exhibits to any written submission as well as to expert reports and witness statements (but not the exhibits themselves);
(f) any written submissions filed by third parties or non-disputing parties;
(g) transcripts of hearings, where available; and
(h) orders, decisions and awards of the arbitral tribunal.[40]

[38] UN General Assembly, Resolution 68/109, *United Nations Commission on International Trade Law Rules on Transparency in Treaty-based Investor-State Arbitration and Arbitration Rules* (16 December 2013). The adoption of the Rules on Transparency was followed by a revision of the UNCITRAL Arbitration Rules in order to expressly incorporate the transparency provisions for the purpose of treaty-based investor–State arbitration.

[39] Ibid., Art. 8.

[40] UNCITRAL Rules on Transparency, Art. 3(1). The cost for making these documents available is borne by the parties, UNCITRAL Rules on Transparency, Art. 3(5). While expert reports and witness statements are not included in the list of documents subject to mandatory disclosure, Article 3 does provide that these documents shall be made available upon special request by any person: Art. 3(2). The cost of making expert reports and witness statements available is to be borne by the person granted access to those documents: Art. 3(5).

The Transparency Rules also address public access to arbitral hearings. Under Article 6, 'hearings for the presentation of evidence or for oral argument shall be public.' As with the provisions addressing publication of documents, the obligation in Article 6 is subject to certain exceptions set forth in Article 7.

17.5.2 *Exceptions to Public Access to Documents and Hearings under Article 7*

Article 7 sets out three principal exceptions to the obligations of transparency created in the rules: non-disclosure of 'confidential or protected information;'[41] non-disclosure of information which a respondent State 'considers to be contrary to its essential security interests;'[42] and non-disclosure in order to protect 'the integrity of the arbitral process'.[43] 'Confidential or protected information' is defined under Article 7 to consist of: (a) confidential business information; (b) information protected from disclosure under the relevant investment treaty; (c) information protected from disclosure by law; and (d) information the disclosure of which would impede law enforcement.[44] In applying Article 7, the arbitral tribunal is expressly granted the discretion to determine the mechanisms for protected disclosure of confidential or protected information.[45]

Article 7(6) addresses non-disclosure 'where the information, if made available to the public, would jeopardise the integrity of the arbitral process.' Article 7(7) makes clear that this is meant to be an 'exceptional' ground for non-disclosure. Thus, Article 7(7) identifies the circumstances under which non-disclosure may be permissible under this ground as being 'where such publication would jeopardise the integrity of the arbitral process because it could hamper the collection or production of evidence, lead to the intimidation of witnesses, lawyers acting for disputing parties or members of the arbitral tribunal or in comparably exceptional circumstances'.[46] This exception, it should be noted, is considerably more restricted than the approach taken by the tribunal in *Biwater Gauff* v. *Tanzania.* In that case, although the tribunal acknowledged as an initial matter that nothing in the ICSID rules 'expressly provides for the confidentiality of pleadings, documents or other information submitted by the parties during the arbitration',[47] it went on to effectively prohibit the disclosure of any documents (except the award and the instant procedural order) on the grounds that disclosure *in and of itself* might threaten the integrity of the proceedings or aggravate or exacerbate the dispute.[48] Such an approach would appear to be inappropriate under the Transparency Rules given the express provisions noted earlier for routinely making such (and even more extensive) disclosures.

41 Ibid., Art. 7(1).
42 Ibid., Art. 7(5).
43 Ibid., Art. 7(6).
44 Ibid., Art. 7(2).
45 Ibid., Arts. 7(3), (4).
46 Ibid., Art. 7(7).
47 See *Biwater Gauff (Tanzania) Ltd.* v. *Tanzania*, ICSID Case No. ARB/05/22, Procedural Order No. 3, 29 September 2006, para. 125.
48 Ibid., paras. 151–63 (prohibiting e.g., either party from disclosing 'the minutes or record of any hearings; any of the documents produced in the arbitral proceedings by the opposing party, whether pursuant to a disclosure exercise or otherwise; any of the Pleadings or Written Memorials (and any attached witness statements or expert reports); and any correspondence between the parties and/or the Arbitral Tribunal exchanged in respect of the arbitral proceedings.

17.5.3 *Participation by Third Persons*

The Transparency Rules also make provisions for the participation of third persons in investor–State arbitrations. For the purposes of the Transparency Rules, a 'third person' refers to 'a person that is not a disputing party, and not a non-disputing Party to the treaty'.[49]

Submissions by 'third persons' are addressed in Article 4. Under Article 4, the tribunal is given discretion to accept submissions by third persons, after consulting with the disputing parties, 'regarding a matter within the scope of the dispute'.[50] Applications for participation must be made in writing and must include a description of the third person (including its legal status, general objectives, nature of its activities and any parent organization); disclose any connection, direct or indirect, which the third person has with any disputing party; provide information concerning any financial or other assistance received by the third party in preparing the submission or any substantial assistance received by the third person in either of the two years preceding the submission; describe the nature of the interest the third party has in the arbitration; and identify the specific issues of fact or law in the arbitration on which the third party intends to make its submission.[51]

In determining whether to grant an application by a third person, Article 4 requires that the tribunal take into account whether the third person has a significant interest in the arbitral proceedings and the extent to which it believes the submission will assist the arbitral tribunal in deciding the claims before it.[52] In addition, Article 4 requires that the tribunal ensure that 'any submission does not disrupt or unduly burden the arbitral proceedings, or unfairly prejudice any disputing party'.[53]

17.5.4 *UNCITRAL Rules on Transparency – Application*

Early on in UNCITRAL's consideration of new rules on transparency for investor–State arbitration, it was recognized that the potential application of any future set of rules needed to be considered with respect to both treaties concluded before and treaties concluded after the new rules had been issued.[54] How should the rules apply? While many in the working group recognized that if the new transparency standards were given application only to treaties concluded after the Rules' effective date, it would fail to make a meaningful impact on the transparency of the investment treaty regime as a whole, it was also recognized that the simple enactment of a specialized set of rules on transparency for treaty-based investor–State

49 UNCITRAL Rules on Transparency, Art. 4(1). As noted at above n 4, the Transparency Rules also make provision for the participation of the other state parties to the investment treaty under which the arbitral tribunal has been appointed, but which have not been named as respondents. The Rules on Transparency refer to these participants as 'non-disputing parties' in Art. 5(1). The UNCITRAL nomenclature should not be confused with the nomenclature used in ICSID practice. In ICISD practice a 'non-disputing party' refers to an *amicus curiae* or what the UNCITRAL rules describe as a 'Third Person.' See ICSID Arbitration Rule 37(2) and UNCITRAL Rules on Transparency, Art. 4(1). There is no facility under the ICSID rules to allow a non-disputing state party to either the ICSID Convention or the underlying investment treaty to participate in a dispute to which it is not a disputing party.

50 Ibid., Art. 4(1).

51 Ibid., Art. 4(2)(a)–(e).

52 Ibid., Art. 4(3).

53 Ibid., Art. 4(5). See also Art. 4(6) (requiring that the tribunal ensure that the disputing parties are given a 'reasonable opportunity to present their observations on any submission').

54 At its 2011 summer meeting, the Commission confirmed for the Working Group that the question of the applicability of the rules on which it was working was part of the Working Group's mandate and a question of great significance, taking account of the high number of investment treaties then currently in existence. *See Official Records of the General Assembly, Sixty-sixth Session, Supplement No.* 17 (A/66/17), para. 200.

arbitrations under the UNCITRAL rules was an inopportune way to address conditions of transparency in the varied arbitral procedures provided for under the 2,500 or so investment treaties by then already in force.[55] Moreover, within the Commission, many States made clear that they did not wish to see the Transparency Rules given automatic application to existing (or, for some, even future) investment treaties providing for arbitration pursuant to the UNCITRAL Arbitration Rules. As a consequence, with respect to the application of the Transparency Rules, UNCITRAL took a conservative approach.

Pursuant to Article 1(1), the Rules on Transparency apply presumptively to all arbitrations conducted under the UNCITRAL Arbitration Rules pursuant to a treaty 'concluded on or after 1 April 2014,' unless the parties to the treaty have agreed otherwise.[56] The Transparency Rules may also be used in arbitrations conducted under other arbitral rules, such as those of ICSID, the Permanent Court of Arbitration, the Stockholm Chamber of Commerce, and others.[57] However, unlike arbitration under the UNCITRAL Rules pursuant to a treaty concluded on or after 1 April 2014, application of the new transparency provisions in arbitrations under these rules requires further agreement.[58]

17.6 THE MAURITIUS CONVENTION

Almost immediately upon finalizing the Rules on Transparency, UNCITRAL began working on a convention designed to give the Rules far broader application.[59] The goal of the

55 *See* United Nations Commission on International Trade Law, *Report of Working Group II (Arbitration and Conciliation) on the work of its fifty-third session (Vienna, 4–8 October 2010)*, UN Doc. A/CN.9/712 (20 October 2010), paras. 85–96. The possible application of the Rules on Transparency to existing investment treaties was a subject of frequent discussion in the course of negotiating and drafting the Rules.

56 Transparency Rules, Art. 1(1). The Transparency Rules do not define 'concluded' and it is not a term of art in the law of treaties. *But cf.* Vienna Convention on the Law of Treaties, Vienna, 23 May 1969, in force 27 January 1980, 115 UNTS 331, Art. 2(1)(a) (defining 'treaty' under the Convention as 'an international agreement concluded between States in written form and governed by international law, whether embodied in a single instrument or in two or more related instruments and whatever its particular designation'). A practical issue might well arise with respect to treaties signed prior to 1 April 2014 but coming into force after that date as to when the treaty has been 'concluded' for the purposes of the Transparency Rules. The best interpretation is that 'concluded' refers to treaties *signed* on or after 1 April 2014 rather than treaties *coming into force* on or after 1 April 2014. The former interpretation conforms to the intent of the Working Group in drafting Article 1. A consistent aim of the Working Group was to avoid having states become bound by the new transparency obligations under treaties negotiated and drafted without real or constructive knowledge of the Transparency Rules. *See* UNCITRAL, *Report of Working Group II (Arbitration and Conciliation) on the work of its fifty-fifth session (Vienna, 3–7 October 2011)*, UN Doc. A/CN.9/736, para. 20. As originally proposed, however, the text of Article 1(1) referred tentatively to an investment treaty '[which entered into force]' prior to the effective date of the Transparency Rules. See UN Commission on International Trade Law, *Report of Working Group II (Arbitration and Conciliation) on the Work of its fifty-fifth Session (Vienna, 3–7 October 2011)*, UN Doc. A/CN.9/736, paras. 18–24. The UNCITRAL Secretariat recognized that using the date of entry into force might have the unintended consequence of binding states to the Transparency Rules in treaties which had been negotiated, drafted and signed before the Transparency Rules' effective date. As a consequence, the reference to 'entering into force' was removed and word 'concluded' substituted. As the Secretariat noted, '[t]he word 'concluded' is proposed to be used . . . in replacement of the words 'entered into force' . . . as it is at the time of conclusion of the treaty (and not at the time of the coming into force of the treaty) that Parties may consent to the application of the transparency rules.' UN Commission on International Trade Law, *Note by the Secretariat, Settlement of Commercial Disputes: Preparation of a Legal Standard on Transparency in Treaty-based Investor-State Arbitration*, UN Doc. A/CN.9/WG.II/WP.169 (13 December 2011), para. 12.

57 Transparency Rules, Art. 1(9).

58 Ibid., Art. 1(9).

59 See UN Commission on International Trade Law, *Note by the Secretariat, Settlement of Commercial Disputes: Application of the UNCITRAL Rules on Transparency in Treaty-based Investor-State Arbitration to Existing Investment Treaties – Draft Convention*, UN Doc. A/CN.9/WG.II/WP.179 (1 August 2013).

convention is two-fold: (1) to facilitate the application of the Transparency Rules to investment treaties in force prior to the Rules' effective date; and (2) to provide a mechanism to give the Rules application not only to UNCITRAL investor–State arbitration, but to *all investor–State arbitration under a State Party's investment treaties.* As it has emerged, the Mauritius Convention is a highly ambitious treaty, which, if successful, will fundamentally change the way in which investor–State arbitration proceeds.

The broad sweep of the Convention's scope of application is made clear in Articles 1 and 2: mandatory transparency in all investor–State arbitration under treaties entered into before 1 April 2014.

> This Convention applies to arbitration between an investor and a State or a regional economic integration organization conducted on the basis of an investment treaty concluded before 1 April 2014 ('investor-State arbitration').[60]
>
> The UNCITRAL Rules on Transparency shall apply to *any investor-State arbitration, whether or not initiated under the UNCITRAL Arbitration Rules* ....[61]

The Convention provides two mechanisms for the application of this obligation: 'bilateral agreement' and 'unilateral offer.' 'Bilateral agreement' refers to the situation in which the respondent State and the investor's State are each parties to the Convention.[62] In that situation, assuming that neither State has entered a relevant reservation, the UNCITRAL Transparency Rules will apply to *any* investor–State arbitration brought under the relevant investment treaty, whether pursuant to the UNCITRAL rules or some other arbitral rules. 'Unilateral offer' refers to the situation in which the respondent State is a party to the Convention but the investor's State is not. In that situation, assuming no relevant reservation, the UNCITRAL Transparency Rules will apply only if the claimant investor agrees.[63]

The Convention provides three permissible reservations which States may make with respect to their acceptance of the Convention. First, a State may indicate specific investment treaties to which the Convention will not apply.[64] Secondly, a State may declare that the Transparency Rules will not apply to arbitrations conducted under rules other than the UNCITRAL Rules (e.g., ICSID, Stockholm Chamber of Commerce, etc.).[65] And, thirdly, a State may declare that the UNCITRAL Transparency Rules will not apply in investor–State arbitrations in which it is a respondent.[66]

The success of the Mauritius Convention will depend both on the willingness of States to become parties to the Convention and on their willingness to resist interposing widespread reservations. The Convention opened for signature on 17 March 2015, and entered into force on 18 October 2017, 'six months after the date of deposit of the third instrument of ratification, acceptance, approval or accession'.[67] As of this writing, the three States to have ratified the treaty are Canada, Mauritius and Switzerland. Nineteen other States have signed the Convention but not ratified it. Of these nineteen signatories, nine are from Europe, six

60 Mauritius Convention, Art. 1(1). Like the Transparency Rules, the Mauritius Convention does not define the term 'concluded.' See above n 56.

61 Ibid., Arts. 2(1) and 2(2) (emphasis added).

62 Ibid., Art. 2(1).

63 Ibid., Art. 2(2).

64 Ibid., Art. 3(1)(a).

65 Ibid., Art. 3(1)(b).

66 Ibid., Art. 3(1)(c).

67 Ibid., Art. 9(1).

from Africa, one from North America, one from Oceania, and two from the Middle East.[68] There are no signatories from Asia or Latin America.

17.7 TRANSPARENCY IN INVESTMENT ARBITRATION AND THE UNCITRAL INITIATIVE: UNDERSTANDING ASIAN NON-PARTICIPATION

Taken as a whole, UNCITRAL's work on both the Transparency Rules and the Mauritius Convention has the capacity to comprehensively reshape arbitration under both future and existing investment treaties. There is reason, however, to doubt if this will happen anytime soon. The lack of Asian participation is one reason why.

As noted in Section 17.4.1, there appears to be no consistent Asian position with respect to the inclusion of provisions on transparency in investment treaties. While some States in Asia appear unwilling to undertake transparency obligations altogether, many Asian States seem to view the issue as a matter for *ad hoc* consideration in the context of individual negotiations. Thus, where a negotiating counter-party seeks provisions on transparency, even States like China may be amenable to some mandatory provisions. Where, however, the negotiating counter-party does not place transparency on the agenda, Asian States have not indicated an interest at present to do so on their own accord. This suggests, of course, that transparency is not a policy priority for Asian States, but rather a bargaining chip that Asian States may be willing to trade in particular negotiations.

In the UNCITRAL debates in connection with the Rules on Transparency and the Mauritius Convention, Asian States made plain their misgivings about both the Rules and the Convention. For many Asian States, the objection appears to have been with transparency itself, or at least with the possibility of momentum developing internationally in support of mandatory rules requiring transparency in investor–State arbitration. In 2008, for example, China reported to the UNCITRAL Secretariat its view that '[g]iven the confidentiality of arbitration, we do not consider it appropriate to impose provisions of publicity and transparency on treaty-based settlement of investor-State investment disputes'.[69] Five years later, in the debates in the Commission with respect to what would become the Mauritius Convention, China objected that such a convention was inappropriate, as its mere existence might serve to put pressure on those States which chose not to adopt the Rules on Transparency, or the Convention itself.[70] Singapore offered similar arguments with respect to the Convention, arguing that the Commission should not draft a convention to give the Rules effect under existing treaties, because once such a treaty had been opened for signature it would place pressure on States which were not otherwise inclined to join it.[71] A similar comment was made by the Korean delegate, albeit in less forceful terms.[72]

68 The signatory states which have not ratified are: Australia, Belgium, Benin, Cameroon, Congo, Finland, France, Gabon, Germany, Iraq, Italy, Luxembourg, Madagascar, Netherlands, Sweden, Syria, United Kingdom, and the United States.

69 United Nations Commission on International Trade Law, Working Group II, *Settlement of commercial disputes: Transparency in treaty-based investor-State arbitration – Compilation of comments by Governments*, 53rd session, 4–8 October 2010, UN Doc. A/CN.9/WG.II/WP.159/Add.1, 12.

70 United Nations Commission on International Trade Law, *Forty-sixth Session (8–26 July 2013), Sound Recordings of the Meetings*, available at www.uncitral.org/uncitral/audio/meetings.jsp (10 July 2013) (last accessed 9 July 2019).

71 Ibid. (comments of Singapore delegate).

72 Ibid. (comments of Republic of Korea delegate). As a consequence of these concerns, which were not only expressed by Asian states, UNCITRAL made clear in its directions to Working Group II that it was being asked 'to prepare a convention that was intended to give those States that wished to make the Rules on Transparency

The general objections to transparency offered in these comments, and the concerns expressed about a developing global momentum in favour of transparency, reflect the complicated dynamic of Asian treaty-making on the issue. It seems evident that for many States in Asia, the prospect of broad, obligatory transparency in investor–State arbitration raises difficult, if not existential, issues of governance. While transparency in investment treaty arbitration holds the promise of systemic benefits for States individually and as an international community, agreeing to implement compulsory transparency in investment treaty arbitration requires courage, especially for States which are not accustomed to high levels of transparency in their domestic decision-making. For some States in Asia, therefore, obligatory transparency is still a non-starter. For other States, however, while there appears to be no great objection to transparency in individual treaties, there is as yet no appetite to commit to transparency as a general treaty policy. It may be that these States take the view that so long as transparency remains a key negotiating point for certain States, e.g., in North America and Europe, it does not make sense to give the point away for free.

A second set of arguments offered by some Asian States in opposition to the Mauritius Convention was that the UNCITRAL rules were 'new' and 'untested' and that to give them wide application so quickly after their adoption would be 'hasty'.[73] Singapore additionally noted that there were open questions with respect to the cost implications of the Rules on Transparency and suggested that the better approach for bringing the Rules into general application would be through bilateral arrangements.[74]

While it is true, of course, that the UNCITRAL Rules on Transparency were and are new, this argument is unconvincing. The principles underpinning the Rules, and many of the rules themselves, have clear antecedents in established state practice. For instance, transparency under the NAFTA has now been practiced for fifteen years, including the publication of documents, public hearings, and the admission of *amicus* submissions by tribunals. Similarly, there is over a decade of experience with respect to 'non-disputing party' practice under the 2006 amendments to the ICSID Rules. In other words, the application of rules on transparency is not the unknown proposition that it might once have been claimed to be. And, indeed, the UNCITRAL Rules in particular, far from being 'untested,' are the product of a multi-year process into which has fed virtually the entirety of state and tribunal experience in a host of cases under a wide variety of investment treaties. As for the issue of costs, it is true that the Rules largely place the costs of transparency on States, particularly the respondent State in a given arbitration. As a result, transparency obligations will have some effect of increasing the cost of arbitration. However, when one considers the overall cost for a State involved in defending an investment treaty claim, e.g., counsel fees, arbitrator fees, institution fees, increased costs as a result of transparency obligations are rather minor. Moreover, there is no reason why a successful State litigant cannot seek coverage of transparency-related

applicable to their existing investment treaties concluded before 1 April 2014 an efficient mechanism to do so, *without creating any expectation that other States would use the mechanism offered by the convention.*' *Official Records of the General Assembly, Sixty-eighth Session, Supplement* No. 17 (A/68/17), para. 127 (emphasis added). This language ultimately was also included in the General Assembly Resolution endorsing the Convention in December 2014. UN General Assembly Resolution 69/116, 'United Nations Convention on Transparency in Treaty-based Investor-State Arbitration' (10 December 2014).

73 United Nations Commission on International Trade Law, *Forty-sixth Session (8–26 July 2013)*, *Sound Recordings of the Meetings*, available at www.uncitral.org/uncitral/audio/meetings.jsp (10 July 2013) (comments of Republic of Korea delegate). See ibid. (comments of Philippines, China and Singapore delegates).

74 Ibid.

expenses in connection with a post-award application for costs. In any case, viewed in context, costs seems a rather insubstantial ground upon which to object to transparency.

It remains to be seen whether large, regional agreements like CPTPP, with comprehensive transparency provisions, will begin to change the approaches of Asian States to transparency or whether increasing numbers of parties to the Mauritius Convention will have the pressurizing, momentum-creating effect that many Asian States feared. In the meanwhile, the concerns raised about obligatory transparency from some Asian States seem firmly rooted, even if the motivation for these concerns seems grounded in the expedience of domestic control. Taken as a whole, UNCITRAL's work on the Transparency Rules and the Mauritius Convention has the capacity to comprehensively reshape arbitration under investment treaties, both future and existing. Adopted in a piecemeal fashion, however, it is likely instead to lead to an increasingly pronounced two-track system of investor–State arbitration: a transparent track and a non-transparent one. That too would be a change in the investment treaty landscape, although not the kind of systemic change that those who seek greater transparency are aiming for.

18

Third-Party Funding in Asia

Developments in Singapore and Hong Kong

Ingrid Coinquet and Siraj Shaik Aziz

18.1 THIRD-PARTY FUNDING: AN OVERVIEW

Third-party funding (TPF) is an arrangement whereby a third party finances the legal representation of another party involved in litigation or arbitration. The third party – referred to as a 'third-party funder – could be a bank, hedge fund, insurance company, a professional third-party funder or some other entity or individual which finances the party's legal representation in return for a profit. A third-party funder is an investor.

Most third-party funders are compensated by way of a success fee basis, most of the time a non-recourse fee. There are various ways to calculate the final share that the third-party funder receives as a compensation for its services. For instance, the share may be calculated as a multiple of the initial investment made by the funder, which is a multiple of the expenses paid on behalf of the funded party.[1] The remuneration may also be a percentage of sums recovered by the funded party, which varies between 10 and 50 per cent of the recovered amount. Sometimes, the success fee is a combination of those two options. The amounts that the third-party funder will receive may depend on time, because the client might be obliged to return, if successful, the amount invested by the funder plus interest (which may vary depending on the time elapsed).[2]

TPF is a relatively well-established way of funding judicial and arbitral proceedings in some jurisdictions, such as Australia and the United Kingdom,[3] and has existed for many years in international arbitration generally.[4] However, its growth in international investment arbitration is a more recent phenomenon. In 2012, a European gas company, Eurogas, announced that a Luxembourg fund would finance its 1 billion ICSID[5] claim.[6] In 2013, a

[1] Fox Williams, 'The New, New Thing: A Study of the Emerging Market in Third-party Litigation Funding' (15 November 2010), available at www.byfieldconsultancy.com/wp-content/uploads/TPF-report.pdf (last accessed 12 July 2019).

[2] Susanna Khouri, Kate Hurford and Clive Bowman, 'Third-party Funding in International Commercial and Treaty Arbitration—a Panacea or a Plague? A Discussion of the Risks and Benefits of Third-party Funding' (2011) 8 *Transnational Dispute Management* 3.

[3] For an overview, see Craig Miles and Sarah Zagata Vasani, 'Case Notes on Third-Party Funding' (2008) 3 *Global Arbitration Review* 35.

[4] See generally Marc J Goldstein, 'Should the Real Parties in Interest Have to Stand Up? – Thoughts About A Disclosure Regime for Third-Party Funding in International Arbitration' (2011) 8 *Transnational Dispute Management* 15–23.

[5] International Centre for Settlement of Investment Disputes.

[6] Wolfgang Rauball, 'EuroGas AG: European Investment-Fund Financed Billion-Lawsuit of EuroGas Group against the Slovak Republic', *BusinessWire*, 6 November 2012.

Canadian mining company made an agreement with a third-party funder to cover the costs of a multi-billion arbitration claim brought by its subsidiary against Bolivia.[7] In 2016, the European Union (EU) incorporated provisions addressing TPF in the Investor–State Dispute Settlement Provisions in their latest Free Trade Agreement with Canada (CETA) and in the EU–Vietnam BIT. Both instruments require the presence of TPF to be disclosed. The decision of the EU to address third-party funding in these treaties, particularly allowing for even not-for-profit funders may be influenced by the *Philip Morris* v. *Uruguay* case where a non-governmental organization voluntarily contributed funds towards the defence costs of the State.[8]

Given the above developments, it is inevitable then that TPF would be discussed in Singapore and Hong Kong. According to the survey conducted by the Queen Mary–White & Case 2015 International Arbitration Survey, Hong Kong and Singapore are amongst the top five most preferred and widely used seats for international commercial arbitration. Both jurisdictions are known for adopting competitive and innovative arbitration laws to promote themselves as leading seats of arbitration. Hong Kong and Singapore recently made significant strides towards formally permitting the use of TPF for international arbitration in their domestic arbitration laws, changing the legal landscape for all legal practitioners and parties, while adopting a slightly different approach to the new legislation on TPF. Indeed, Singapore abolished the tort and offence of champerty and maintenance, while Hong Kong introduced legislation which will permit TPF, taking steps to 'disapply' champerty and maintenance for arbitration proceedings alone, taking thus a more conservative approach,

This chapter examines the development of TPF in the field of investment arbitration in general and the challenges it poses (Sections 18.2 and 18.3). It will then study the unique position of Singapore and Hong Kong as the first Asian jurisdictions to expressly provide for TPF in their national laws (Section 18.4) and the flashpoint issues it will have to grapple with moving forward, namely the extent of disclosure, control and costs.

18.2 THE CASE FOR TPF IN INVESTMENT ARBITRATION

TPF may be sought by both investors and States for a variety of reasons. First, a party may not have the necessary financial means to engage in a costly and lengthy arbitration proceeding. It is not only the investor that may need financial assistance. Foreign investors often have economic muscle that can hardly be surpassed by many host States.[9] Today, some multinational enterprises have budgets far exceeding the budgets of many developing countries.[10] Already in mid-1990s, of the 100 largest economies in the world, fifty-one of them were corporations rather than countries.[11] Secondly, investors or States may be unwilling to allocate their own resources – public resources in the case of the latter – to finance long and onerous proceedings, and instead prefer to invest in other new opportunities within their normal business activities. Thirdly, the inherent uncertainty in effectively obtaining the

7 Leo Szolnoki, 'Miner secures funding for Bolivia claim', *Global Arbitration Review*, 28 May 2013.

8 *Philip Morris Brands Sàrl, Philip Morris Products S.A. and Abal Hermanos S.A.* v. *Oriental Republic of Uruguay*, ICSID Case No. ARB/10/7.

9 K.H. Boeckstiegel, 'Enterprise v State: The New David and Goliath?' (2007) 23 *Arbitration International* 93, 94.

10 See A.C. Habbard, 'The Integration of Human Rights in Corporate Principles in The Integration of Human Rights in Corporate Principles' in OECD, *OECD Guidelines for Multinational Enterprises Annual Report* (Paris: OECD, 2001), p. 99.

11 United Nations Conference on Trade and Development, World Investment Report 1995 (Geneva: UNCTAD, 1996).

requested compensation through the proceedings, and the substantial costs to potentially obtain such compensation, may financially justify a transfer of the risk of the proceedings to a third party.[12]

Concerns about TPF in the investment arbitration context have related to the proliferation of investment arbitration claims brought against States and a corresponding increase in the number of speculative or frivolous cases. Such criticism, as observed by the ICCA–Queen Mary Task Force Draft Report on Third-Party Funding in International Arbitration ('ICCA–QM Task Force Report'), would largely stem from a lack of understanding of the TPF model.[13] Indeed, the risk of funding a potentially frivolous case is low if the TPF is an established professional with a steady track record because of the extensive due diligence funders engage in as part of their decision about whether to invest into a case. Specifically, funders assess through either their own legal teams and experts or outsourced teams (i) the merits of the claim, (ii) the actual claim value, (iii) the jurisdictions(s) involved and the governing law, (iv) the prospects of recovery, (v) the level of investment required to fund the claim until a satisfactory recovery is reached and (vi) the overall financial risk, as the case may be. Professor Rogers noted the following about the manner in which funders conduct due diligence:

> In assessing claims, funders bring a level of sophistication and precision that is almost shockingly unknown and unmanageable by even large, sophisticated multi-national companies and the world's most sophisticated law firms.[14]

In the context of quantum in investment treaty claims, a distinction is usually drawn between 'sunk' investment costs and damages based on market-value assessments. Most third-party funders focus their due diligence on the former as a more reliable method of calculation and a more realistic one. Indeed, if a tribunal awards damages based on a market-value, such damages would usually be greater than expected profits.[15]

In the course of the due diligence process, it is reckoned that funders reject, on average, 80 per cent to 90 per cent of submitted claims for funding. Some claims can be rejected quickly whilst others may be superficially strong and attractive to invest in, only to become apparent that, for example, enforcement of an award will be problematic because the respondent's assets are difficult to trace. Funders tend to invest in claims with at least a 60 per cent prospect of success on the merits of the claim. The assessment of claims requires thorough analysis which can be costly. Such thoroughness should result in the rejection of hopeless and frivolous claims. The notion that funders deliberately support fictional claims in order to intimidate opponents into acceding to high settlement demands would be commercially counterproductive given the substantial financial risk, as well as the risk of reputational damage.[16]

Moreover, by front-loading the development of a case and identifying potential risks, funders are able to help shape a stronger case theory which can be run more efficiently for

12 Eric De Brabandere and Julia Lepeltak, 'Third-Party Funding in International Investment Arbitration' (2012) 27 (2) *ICSID Review* 379–98.

13 ICCA-QM Task Force Report, p. 161.

14 Catherine A Rogers, *Ethics in International Arbitration* (Oxford, Oxford University Press, 2014), p. 186.

15 Mick Smith, 'Mechanics of Third-Party Funding Agreements: A Funder's Perspective' in Lisa Bench Nieuwveld and Victoria Shannon, (eds.), *Third-Party Funding in International Arbitration* (Alphen aan den Rijn: Kluwer Law International, 2012), pp. 19–37.

16 James Clanchy, 'Third Party Funding in Arbitration: breaking down barriers and building bridges' (2016) 23 *Croatian Arbitration Yearbook* 2016 53–69.

the claimant; alternatively, if significant issues are identified, the wasted costs of pursuing a weak claim are often avoided. The involvement of a third-party funder's fresh pair of eyes triggers a 'reality check' for a claimant and can help the latter to develop strategies appropriate to the realistic prospects of a successful recovery.

18.3 CHALLENGES FOR TPF IN INVESTMENT ARBITRATION

Notwithstanding the clear need and opportunity for TPF in investment arbitration, there are unique challenges to utilizing TPF in such context.

18.3.1 *Jurisdictional Challenges*

Third-party funding has been met with jurisdictional challenges in investment tribunals. Such challenges have not succeeded.

The Tribunal of the Stockholm Chamber of Commerce (SCC) in *RosInvestCo UK Ltd.* v. *The Russian Federation* reasoned that an assignment from RosInvest 'to a funder of a different nationality than the funded party before the initiation of the arbitral proceedings does not affect jurisdiction' unless the relevant investment treaty states otherwise in clear language.[17] As a consequence, the tribunal concluded that financing for a claim does not affect jurisdiction for the arbitration. There is no difference in the outcome if the assignment took place after the initiation of proceedings. In *CSOB* v. *Slovakia*, CSOB assigned its claims to its home State. In concluding that it retained jurisdiction, the Tribunal reasoned that 'the transfer of rights after the institution of proceedings should not be taken into account at all, and consequently cannot affect jurisdiction'.[18]

The Respondents in *Teinver S.A.* v. *Argentine Republic* also challenged jurisdiction based on an assignment.[19] The Respondent argued that 'once the assignment is made, the assignor is replaced in the proceedings by the assignee, which has not been the case in this arbitration proceeding'.[20] Under this view, the funder, not the claimant, became 'the real party interested in this arbitration' after the assignment, a point supported by the fact that only the funder 'would seem to be potentially benefited in the case of a hypothetical award against Argentina in the instant case'.[21] In the final award, the ICSID tribunal found that the assignment was not for 'contentious claims' but rather for the 'proceeds from any award issued' and, therefore, in the eyes of the ICSID tribunal no assignment occurred that affected Claimants' standing in the proceedings.[22]

Based on those arbitral awards and in the absence of any new investment treaty provisions, the existing position in investment arbitration appears to be that TPF, regardless of the form, does not alter the national identity of a claimant and hence the jurisdiction of arbitral tribunals. This position is also consistent with the use of contingency and conditional fees, which in many respects are functionally equivalent to TPF, but likewise have not been asserted as a basis for challenging jurisdiction.

17 Jonas Von Goeler, *Third Party Funding in International Arbitration and Its Impact on Procedure* (Kluwer, 2016), p. 239.

18 Ibid., pp. 227–28.

19 *Teinver* S.A. v. *Argentine Republic*, ICSID Case No. ARB/09/1, Decision on Jurisdiction, 21 December 2012.

20 Ibid., para. 60.

21 Ibid.

22 *Teinver* S.A. v. *Argentine Republic*, ICSID Case No. ARB/09/1, Award, 21 July 2017, paras. 61–62.

18.3.2 *Enforceability of the Award*

Sovereign immunity poses a challenge to the enforcement of arbitral awards in the investment context and is thus an important consideration in selecting the forum for enforcement in cases being brought against a State or a governmental agency.[23] When a State invokes sovereign immunity from execution vis-á-vis located assets, the investor is left in the dark, trying to locate commercial assets and often leaving no stone unturned. However, this is costly and time-consuming. In this respect, Professor Schreuer opined that:

> [A]llowing plaintiffs to proceed against foreign States and then to withhold from them the fruits of successful litigation through immunity from execution may put them into the doubly frustrating position of having been lured into expensive and seemingly successful lawsuits only to be left with an unenforceable judgment plus legal costs.[24]

In satisfaction of their claims under the awards, some investors have sought to enforce awards against States by making applications to attach various classes of assets of the sovereign such as assets of a state-owned entity (e.g. *Benvenuti et Bonfat S.R.L* v. *Banque Commerciale Congolaise and Others*[25]), property of the central bank (e.g. *AIG Capital Partners* v. *Kazakhstan*[26]), fees and taxes due to a losing State and funds in the bank accounts of the embassy (e.g. *LETCO* v. *Liberia*[27]). Investors were unsuccessful in all of those cases as they could not displace the application of sovereign immunity from execution. This rate of success, coupled with the rising ICSID caseload, and economic crisis that diminishes States' ability to pay, the probability that the issue will persist is rather high. As such, TPF becomes a riskier proposition in the investor-State context.

A practical solution for investors may be to insist on waivers of sovereign immunity in contracts with States,[28] which is mostly possible if the investor has a strong bargaining position vis-à-vis the State. Such waivers can indeed often be found in transnational loan documents.[29] However, the reality is that often foreign private investors are in a 'David against Goliath' arrangement with the contracting State and pay more attention to the commercial terms than the dispute mechanism in a contract. Other longer-term measures include making changes to (1) international law; (2) domestic laws and (3) asking home States for assistance and perhaps multilateral pressure.[30]

18.3.3 *Escalating Costs in Investment Arbitration*

Escalating costs in investment arbitration will have implications for both investors and States on access to TPF. In an empirical study conducted by the Global Arbitration Review, average

23 Nigel Blackaby and Constantine Partasides QC, with Alan Redfern and Martin Hunter, *Redfern and Hunter on International Arbitration* (Oxford: Oxford University Press, 2009), p. 629.

24 Christopher Schreuer, *State Immunity: Some Recent Developments* (Cambridge: Grotius Publications, 1988), p. 125.

25 *Benvenuti and Bonfant Srl* v. *Banque Commerciale Congolaise*, France, Cour de cassation, 21 July 1987.

26 *AIG Capital Partners Inc & Anor.* v. *Kazakhstan* [2005] EWHC 2239 (Comm) (20 October 2005).

27 *Liberian Eastern Timber Corp.* v. *Government of Republic of Liberia*, 650 F.Supp. 73 (S.D.N.Y. 1986).

28 Giuliana Cane, 'The Enforcement of ICSID Awards: Revolutionary or Ineffective?' (2004) 15 *American Review of International Arbitration* 439.

29 Vincent O. Orlu Nmehielle, 'Enforcing Arbitration Awards under the International Convention for the Settlement of Investment Disputes (ICSID Convention)' (2001) 7 *Annual Survey of International and Comparative Law* 21 at 42.

30 See Andrea K. Bjorklund, 'Sovereign Immunity as a Barrier to the Enforcement of Investor-State Arbitral Awards: The Re-Politicization of International Investment Disputes' (2010) 21 *American Review of International Arbitration* 211.

party costs for claimants and respondents were found to have increased by 68 per cent and 13 per cent, respectively, since 2013, which corresponded to figures of USD 7.41 million and 5.19 million.[31]

The minimum cost of investor–State arbitration, that is, a bare-boned ISDS claim, was calculated by one international arbitration law firm to be approximately USD 1.3 million.[32] If funders tend to only consider the funding of cases where a multiple of the amount funded is expected for returns, many claimants may simply never have their day in court.[33]

On the flip side, respondent-side funding in investment treaty-based arbitrations is nearly non-existent. Since nearly all bilateral investment treaties (BITs) expressly protect investor rights, but not necessarily host State rights, it is unclear whether claims involving the host State's rights 'are within the scope of the consent of the parties' or whether counterclaims brought by the State are 'within the jurisdiction of the Centre'.[34] Several recent cases have dealt with this issue on a case-by-case basis but none of them have definitively resolved it. This asymmetry would create a situation where States are the sole payers in a system of TPF for investment treaty arbitration in which they are unable to enjoy a benefit equivalent to investors' benefits. If host States could become claimants against investor-respondents, or if arbitral tribunals determine that they have jurisdiction over host State counterclaims, then a funder would be paid from the investor-respondent's funds in the event a host State prevails. This would allow TPF in investment arbitration to achieve greater parity to its commercial counterpart.[35]

Finally, escalating costs will also have implications on funders particularly if they have to comply with adverse cost or security for cost orders. While such orders are not ubiquitous at present, greater use of them in the future could have a chilling effect on TPF if escalating costs remain unchecked.

18.4 SINGAPORE AND HONG KONG

Singapore and Hong Kong are the first Asian jurisdictions to explicitly regulate TPF in international arbitration on a State level. The reason for this is strongly linked to the fact that prior to these legislative changes, TPF of legal proceedings was altogether prohibited in those two States because of longstanding common law rules designed to protect vulnerable litigants and to prevent dispute resolution from becoming an area of speculative business ventures (based on the common law doctrines of maintenance and champerty). The volume of arbitration work that the region will see is likely to increase both as a result of the increased access to justice that permitting TPF will allow for, and the fact that the competitiveness of Singapore and Hong Kong as arbitral seats will continue its upward trajectory as a result of these amendments. As with Australia's experience introducing TPF (where related regulation

31 Matthew Hodgson and Alastair Campbell, 'Damages and Costs in Investment Treaty Arbitration Revisited', *Global Arbitration Review* (14 December 2017), available at www.allenovery.com/SiteCollectionDocuments/14-12-17_Damages_and_costs_in_investment_treaty_arbitration_revisited_.pdf (last accessed 12 July 2019).

32 'The Cost of Investment Arbitration: UNCITRAL, ICSID Proceedings and Third-Party Funding', Acercis Law (27 December 2017), available at www.acerislaw.com/cost-investment-arbitration-uncitral-icsid-proceedings-third-party-funding/ (last accessed 12 July 2019).

33 Ibid.

34 Victoria Shannon, 'The Structural Challenge of Investment Arbitration Viewed through the Lens of Third-Party Funding', Oxford University Press: Investment Claims Blog, 9 June 2015, available at http://oxia.ouplaw.com/page/491/the-structural-challenge-of-investment-arbitration-viewed-through-the-lens-of-thirdparty-funding- (last accessed 12 July 2019).

35 Ibid.

and legislation were varied and amended for almost three years between 2009 and 2012), it is likely that the legal regime in both Singapore and Hong Kong will similarly undergo a period of fine-tuning in their respective regulatory frameworks based on actual use and experience of TPF in each jurisdiction.

18.4.1 *Singapore*

On 10 January 2017, Parliament passed into law the Civil Law (Amendment) Bill that allows TPF for international arbitration and related proceedings before the Singapore courts. This will allow Singapore to stay competitive as a leading international arbitration hub, given that such funding is already available in other major arbitration centres around the world, including London, Paris and Geneva. Not to be outdone by Hong Kong, which first saw its Law Reform Commission pave the way for TPF in arbitration, Singapore joined the above jurisdictions in endorsing TPF.

In *Otech Pakistan Pvt Ltd* v. *Clough Engineering Ltd*,[36] the Court of Appeal held that the prohibition on champerty also applied to arbitration proceedings. In 2011, the Ministry of Law conducted a review of the International Arbitration Act and called for views on whether TPF would be appropriate in international arbitration. This marked a sea change in attitude from *Otech*. In the landmark decision of *Re Vanguard Energy Pte Ltd*, the Singapore High Court confirmed that litigation funding may, in the context of insolvency and under the appropriate circumstances, be permitted in Singapore.[37] This decision is significant insofar as it confirms the statutory power of a liquidator to sell a cause of action or its proceeds, against which the doctrine of maintenance and champerty has no application.[38]

While the scope of the Civil Law (Amendment) Bill only permits TPF for international arbitration proceedings and ancillary proceedings, it was indicated that the framework may be broadened in the future after a period of assessment, leaving the door open to TPF for domestic arbitration and litigation. It is for this reason that amendments have been made to the Civil Law Act rather than the International Arbitration Act. Its limited scope is deliberate so that the framework can first be tested within a limited sphere by parties of commercial sophistication.

The set of amendments pave the way for TPF in a few ways. First, the new Section 5A (2) of the Civil Law Act abolishes the common law tort of champerty and maintenance in Singapore. However, Section 5B does not remove the contractual bar to champertous arrangements which are void on grounds of being illegal and contrary to public policy.

Secondly, Sections 5B(3), read with 5B(8)(a) and 5B(10) of the Civil Law Act set out the qualifications for qualifying third-party funders. The third-party funder's principal business must be TPF and have at least SGD 5 million or the equivalent in paid-up capital or managed assets. Notably, the law does not require the funder to be based in Singapore. The third-party funder must have access to funds immediately within its control, including within a parent corporation or a subsidiary to fund dispute resolution proceedings in Singapore and said funds must be invested pursuant to a funding contract to enable the funded party to meet the costs of the proceedings. These requirements practically mean only established international professional funders will be able to provide TPF, which significantly diminishes the risk of frivolous litigation by less responsible funders. Pursuant to Section 5B(7) of the Civil Law Act,

36 *Otech Pakistan Pvt Ltd* v. *Clough Engineering Ltd* [2007] 1 SLR (R) 989.

37 *Re Vanguard Energy Pte Ltd* [2015] SGHC 156.

38 www.lexology.com/library/detail.aspx?g=ab41de8d-9d40-4642–9712-a14d6a7f231e (last accessed 12 July 2019).

the same funder would be required to continue performing its obligation under the funding agreement for the entirety of the proceedings. Funders who do not comply with requirements imposed on them will not be able to enforce their rights under the funding agreement. It is unclear whether any regulatory sanctions may also be imposed on non-compliant third-party funders in Singapore. As for the non-compliance by a third-party funder, it does not prejudice the rights of any other party to enforce the funding agreement against the third-party funder. This would leave funders with obligations but no rights; a deterrent to non-compliance with the above regulations. It was clarified that under Section 5B(5) and 5B(6), in the interest of fairness to funders, the Court or Arbitral Tribunal may grant relief to the funders on their application if the non-compliance was due to inadvertence or some other sufficient cause, or if it is just and equitable to do so. Section 5B(3) leaves the possibility open for further regulation of funders through subsidiary legislation.

The Legal Profession (Professional Conduct) Rules have also been amended to impose a duty on lawyers to disclose the existence of any TPF which their client is receiving.[39] The duty was placed on the lawyers as opposed to the funders because the latter would likely be out of Singapore's jurisdictional reach. This approach in fact mirrors the English position where similar obligations are to be found in Chapter 3 of the English Solicitors Regulation Authority Code of Conduct 2011. Those Rules are supplemented by the Law Society of Singapore's Guidance Note on TPF. This Note builds upon the Rules by discouraging lawyers from being jointly retained by both claimant and funder. It also encourages lawyers to provide advice on specific terms in the funding agreement which include (i) a funder's level of involvement in the decision making, (ii) dispute resolution procedures in the event of disagreement between client and funder, (iii) conditions for termination of the funding agreement and what obligations survive, (iv) advising the client on risks related to waiving legal privilege, and (v) the applicability of common interest privilege to documents disclosed to a funder.

Additional guidelines have been promulgated that apply not just to lawyers but extend to regulate the conduct of third-party funders and arbitrators. Issues such as conflicts of interest, control over proceedings and termination of the funding agreement are amongst those which are addressed in the guidelines.

The Singapore Institute of Arbitrators Guidelines for Third Party Funders largely mirror the Law Society Guidance Note but take the perspective of funders and covers areas including confidentiality and privilege, avoiding conflicts of interest, scope of funding, disclosure to Court/Tribunal of funding, and withdrawal of funding. It also requires funders to take all reasonable steps to ensure financial qualifications and requirements are met and continue to be met. The Singapore International Arbitration Centre (SIAC) Practice Note PN-01/17 on Arbitrator Conduct in Cases Involving External Funding requires arbitrators to disclose to the SIAC Registrar and parties any circumstances creating doubt as to their impartiality or independence, including direct/indirect relationship with a funder – arising before their appointment or at any point during proceedings.

The SIAC has also promulgated a set of Investment Arbitration Rules (SIAC IA Rules), which also addresses TPF. Notably, a 'Third-party funding arrangement' is not a defined term in the rules, and it remains to be seen how this provision is interpreted; that is, whether this will extend only to arrangements with formal TPF providers, or whether it will capture arrangements with insurance companies, banks and other third parties which achieve similar funding objectives. Under Rules 24(l) and 33.1 of the SIAC International Arbitration Rules,

[39] Legal Profession (Professional Conduct) Rules, Rules 49A and 49B.

the tribunal has the power to order parties to disclose TPF arrangements, the identity of the funder, and any other details which the tribunal deems necessary. The tribunal may also take into account any TPF arrangements when apportioning the costs of the arbitration.

Ultimately, the Singapore government has expressed a reticence for heavy-handed regulation in favour of industry-led 'soft law', echoing the Queen Mary– White & Case 2015 International Arbitration Survey wherein most respondents expressed a preference for the latter. The government's confidence in self-regulation also stemmed from its belief that the funding industry is a mature industry which has created its own emergent industry standards and practices. After debating on whether TPF can be extended to an internationalized domestic court such as the Singapore International Commercial Court (SICC'), the Supreme Court of Judicature (Amendment) Bill No. 47/2017 was passed on 9 January 2018 and confirms that the SICC, being a division of the High Court, 'has jurisdiction to hear any proceedings relating to international commercial arbitration that the High Court may hear and that satisfy such conditions as the Rules of Court may prescribe'.[40] This recent legislation has the effect of permitting TPF in some of the proceedings before the SICC. Chief Justice Sundaresh Menon indicated that Singapore may widen TPF to all cases before the SICC. The SICC being an international forum with a bench of judges with extensive experience in international commercial disputes, having little or no connection with Singapore, is a natural forum to allow TPF.

Singapore faces strong competition from London and other major commercial dispute centres. If it wishes to become a jurisdiction of prime choice, it has to offer the same advantages as those in mature and sophisticated jurisdictions for third-party funding. The United Kingdom and Australia, both common law jurisdictions, abolished the tort of champerty fifty years ago,[41] and have today a mature approach to litigation funding as well as an abundance of judicial and regulatory experience. The recent opening for the SICC to hear matters funded by third parties is the first step in the right direction and it may not be long before the Singapore Courts follow the example of their arbitration colleagues and admit its introduction. Already, on 14 March 2017 the Dubai International Financial Centre (DIFC) Courts issued 'Practice Direction 2 of 2017 – TPF in the DIFC Courts' (PD 2/2017) forming part of the Courts' procedural rules. PD2/2017 in short requires a party using TPF in respect of litigation in the DIFC Courts to disclose the fact of the funding by giving notice to the other parties. While there are no obligations imposed by PD 2/2017 on third-party funders, it reaffirms the DIFC Courts' existing power to make costs orders against non-parties, including funders, where appropriate.

18.4.2 *Hong Kong*

Until recently, Hong Kong did not permit TPF on account of the doctrines of maintenance and champerty, which sought to prevent '(...)gambling in litigation, or of injuring or oppressing others by abetting and encouraging unrighteous suits, so as to be contrary to public policy (...)'.[42] Notwithstanding this, judicial pronouncements in Hong Kong have not foreclosed the use of TPF in the context of arbitration. A landmark case which considered

40 Supreme Court of Judicature (Amendment) Bill No. 47/2017, s 2.

41 For example, *Criminal Law Act 1967* (UK), s 14; *Civil Liability Act 2002* (NSW), Sch 2 cl 2; *Wrongs Act 1958* (Vic), s 32.

42 Hong Kong Consultation Paper, referring to *Ram Coomar Coondoo* v. *Chunder Canto Mookerjee* [1876] 2 App Cas 186 at para. 210.

TPF in the context of arbitration was *Cannonway Consultants Ltd* v. *Kenworth Engineering Ltd*.[43] The court held that the prohibition did not apply to arbitration in Hong Kong. It did not consider it appropriate to extend the doctrine of champerty to arbitration as 'it would be extending champerty from the public justice system to the private consensual system which is arbitration'.[44] In a more recent decision, *Unruh* v. *Seeberger*, the court left open the question as whether maintenance and champerty applied to agreements regarding arbitrations taking place in Hong Kong.[45] In the case of *Re Cyberworks Audio Video Technology Ltd*, it was held that the assignment of a cause of action by a liquidator or a trustee as part of a funding agreement is an exception to the prohibition on maintenance and champerty and therefore lawful.[46] The reason for this was that a cause of action is a chose in action (which a liquidator has the power to sell by virtue of the Hong Kong Companies Ordinance section 199(2)(a)) coupled with the right of a liquidator to assign the proceeds of a successful prosecution of a cause of action. Having considered such right, the court found that such arrangements fall into the third exception in *Unruh*. The court in the 2011 case of *Geoffrey L Berman (In His Capacity as Trustee of The Lender Trust)* v. *Spf Cdo I, Ltd And Others* held that the central question to be answered by the court when assessing the assignment of a chose in action is whether there is a proper commercial purpose to the transaction, which does not give rise to a risk of corruption of the judicial and litigation process.[47]

The Law Reform Commission issued two reports after consultations, in October 2015 and October 2016, which culminated in the landmark Arbitration and Mediation Legislation (Third Party Funding) (Amendment) Ordinance 2017 on 23 June 2017 ('Amendment Ordinance'). These amendments, like their Singapore counterpart, provide that of the torts of maintenance and champerty do not apply in arbitration proceedings, in that it ensures 'that third party funding of arbitration is not prohibited by particular common law doctrines'.[48] In contrast to Singapore's focus on international proceedings, the Hong Kong proposal involved allowing TPF for domestic, as well as international, arbitrations in Hong Kong. It also permits TPF in circumstances where legal services are being provided in Hong Kong for arbitrations which are seated elsewhere.[49]

The new law does not include regulations to which third-party funders must adhere. Hong Kong's approach involves the introduction of a Code of Practice setting out the practices and standards for third-party funders to follow.

The regulation will be implemented in stages. During the first three years, Hong Kong will follow a self-regulating approach through implementation of this code. Amongst other obligations, third-party funders will be required to (1) submit an annual financial return to the Hong Kong Advisory Body (the HKAB) and (2) provide the HKAB with any other information reasonably requested. After the initial three-year period, the HKAB will issue a report setting out recommendations about how TPF should be implemented and regulated in the future; this could take the form of a revised Code or the establishment of a statutory regulatory body.[50] On 7 December 2018, the Secretary of Justice published the Hong Kong

43 [1995] 1 HKC 179.

44 [1995] 1 HKC 179, 190.

45 [2007] 2 HKLRD 414, para. 78.

46 [2010] 2 HKLRD 1137.

47 HCMP1321/2010 (Decision of 14 March 2011).

48 Arbitration and Mediation Legislation (Third Party Funding) (Amendment) Ordinance 2017, s 98E.

49 Hong Kong Arbitration Ordinance, section 98N.

50 Law Reform Commission of Hong Kong, Consultation Paper: Third Party Funding for Arbitration (October 2015), Ch. 5, para. 5.2, p. 52, states that the responses put forward regarding this issue were 'fairly evenly split

Code of Practice for Third Party Funding in Arbitration (HK Code) which came into effect on 1 February 2019.[51] The provisions of the HK Code are binding on all parties and 'appl[y] to any funding agreement', in contrast to its English counterpart, which is voluntary and is only to be followed by members of the Association of Litigation Funders.[52] Failure to comply with the HK Code does not render any person liable to any judicial or other proceedings, but any non-compliance would only be used as evidence in subsequent court or tribunal proceedings.[53] The HK Code includes requirements for third-party funders to take reasonable steps to ensure that a funded party is made aware of the right to seek independent legal advice on a funding agreement before entering into it, maintain access to a minimum HKD20 million of capital at all times to ensure the capacity to pay all debts when they become due, and to maintain effective procedures for managing any conflict of interest that arises in relation to the activities undertaken by the funder for the duration of the funding agreement.

These developments in Hong Kong have since spread to mainland China. On 1 October 2017, the Investment Arbitration Rules of the China International Economic and Trade Arbitration Commission (CIETAC Rules) entered into force, marking the first time a Chinese arbitral institution has adopted a set of rules specifically designed for resolution of international investment disputes. These Rules are meant to support Chinese companies 'going out' in furtherance of China's Belt and Road initiative,[54] and signal China's evolution from an 'observer' to an important 'participant' in the contemporary international investment regime.[55] The CIETAC Rules expressly permit TPF. Article 27 of the Rules requires that parties receiving funding disclose in writing, 'without any delay', the existence and nature of the arrangement, together with the particulars of the funder(s) to the other disputing party, the arbitral tribunal, and the CIETAC Commission.[56] The tribunal may also specifically request such disclosure.[57] When deciding on costs for the arbitration, the tribunal may take into consideration the existence of a TPF arrangement, and whether the concerned party complied with the disclosure requirements.[58]

18.5 CONSIDERATIONS WITH THIRD-PARTY FUNDING

Going forward, various ethical considerations will feature in, what is expected to be, growing arbitrations in Singapore and Hong Kong, testing the operation of their existing rules.

between supporting statutory regulation (45 per cent) and supporting self-regulation (43 per cent) with 12 per cent supporting both'.

51 Hong Kong Code of Practice for Third Party Funding in Arbitration ('HK Code'), available at www.info.gov.hk/gia/general/201812/07/P2018120700601.htm (last accessed 23 September 2019).

52 HK Code, para. 1.2.

53 Arbitration and Mediation Legislation (Third Party Funding)(Amendment) Ordinance 2017, sections 98S(1) and S(2)(a).

54 China's One Belt, One Road (OBOR) initiative is a combination of two complementary proposals: A twenty-first-century Silk Road economic belt that passes through Central Asia and connects two of the world's largest economies, China and Europe, and a maritime Silk Road that connects Europe and China via Southeast Asia, South Asia, the Middle East and East Africa. It involves the undertaking of construction and infrastructure projects spanning across at least sixty countries.

55 CIETAC Explanatory Note Regarding the CIETAC Investment Arbitration Rules (26 September 2017).

56 CIETAC Investment Arbitration Rules, Art. 27(2).

57 Ibid.

58 CIETAC Investment Arbitration Rules, Article 27(3).

18.5.1 *Extent of Disclosure about Third-Party Funding*

One issue to be decided is whether TPF arrangements should be disclosed, and if so, the scope of such disclosure. It is now generally accepted in ICISD jurisprudence, particularly the *South American Silver*,[59] *Eurogas*,[60] and *Muhammet Çap & Sehil* cases,[61] that funded parties have to disclose the identity of a third-party funder to allow arbitrators to satisfy themselves that there is no conflict of interest. However, there is yet to be a consensus on whether additional funding information beyond the funder's identity needs to be disclosed to ensure security for costs. Different tribunals have reached different conclusions on its appropriateness in this context. In the procedural decision of *South American Silver Limited (Bermuda)* v. *Bolivia*,[62] it was held that 'there is basis to order the disclosure of the name of the third-party funder, but not to order the disclosure of the agreement entered into with the third-party funder'; while in the procedural decision of *Muhammet Çap & Sehil Inşaat Endustri ve Ticaret Ltd. Sti.* v. *Turkmenistan*, the claimant was ordered to disclose the 'name or names and details of the third-party funder(s), and the nature of the arrangements concluded with the third-party funder(s), including whether and to what extent it/they will share in any successes that the claimants may achieve in this arbitration'.[63] The tribunal in the latter case concluded that disclosure would allow an assessment of whether it was necessary to order the funded party to provide security for costs, as it sympathized with the respondent's concern that if it were successful in this arbitration, the claimants would be unable to meet these costs and the third-party funder would likely have disappeared (not being a party to the arbitration). The tribunal in the former case reached the opposite conclusion on the basis that '[t]he fact of having financing alone does not imply risk of non-payment', and that ordering security every time that TPF is established would 'increase the risk of blocking potentially legitimate claims'.[64]

Rule 24 of the SIAC IA Rules reflects this state of law. It grants tribunals the express authority to require the disclosure of any TPF arrangements and empowers them to 'order the existence of a Party's TPF arrangement and/or the identity of the third-party funder and, where appropriate, details of the third-party funder's interest in the outcome of the proceedings, and/or whether or not the funder has committed to undertake adverse costs liability'. Article 44 of the 2018 Hong Kong International Arbitration Centre (HKIAC) Administered Arbitration Rules and Article 98U of the Hong Kong Arbitration Ordinance, by contrast, require funded parties to disclose the existence or termination of a funding agreement as well as the identity of their funder at the outset of the arbitration. A disclosure of the content of the funding agreement is not required. While Singapore and Hong Kong have both adopted a mandatory disclosure rule, it is interesting to observe the different approaches in which the two jurisdictions have implemented that rule. It remains to be seen whether Singapore's approach in placing the obligation to disclose on counsel, rather than on the parties, will be more effective. Under the current regime in Singapore, it would appear that funding arrangements of parties who are not represented by lawyers subject to the Conduct Rules

59 *South American Silver Limited (Bermuda)* v. *Bolivia* (Procedural Order No. 10 of 11 January 2016).

60 *EuroGas Inc. and Belmont Resources Inc* v. *Slovak Republic* (ICSID Case No. ARB/14/14, Procedural Order No. 3 of 23 June 2015).

61 *Muhammet Çap & Sehil Inşaat Endustri ve Ticaret Ltd Sti* v. *Turkmenistan* (ICSID Case No. ARB/12/6, Procedural Order No. 3 of 12 June 2015.)

62 *South American Silver Limited (Bermuda)* v. *Bolivia* (Procedural Order No 10 of 11 January 2016), para. 84.

63 *Muhammet Çap & Sehil* v. *Turkmenistan* (ICSID Case No ARB/12/6, Procedural Order No. 3 of 12 June 2015) para. 13.

64 *South American Silver* v. *Bolivia* (Procedural Order No 10 of 11 January 2016), paras. 75–77.

would not be disclosable, even if the funding arrangements relate to Singapore-seated arbitrations. This could create a double standard where foreign counsel are not subject to the ambit of Singapore's TPF legislation. Moreover, this could put Singapore-registered counsels in multi-jurisdictional counsel teams in a difficult position, as their mere involvement would trigger the disclosure obligations under the Singapore Legal Profession (Professional Conduct) Rules.

The approaches in Singapore and Hong Kong also somewhat differ from the UK Association of Litigation Funders Code (ALF Code), which does not require 'automatic' disclosure of the existence of TPF. The approaches are, however, consistent with the most recent edition of the International Bar Association's Guidelines on Conflicts of Interest, which holds parties responsible for disclosing any relationship between the arbitrator and the parties, including those with a 'direct economic interest in the award to be rendered in the arbitration, such as an entity providing funding for the arbitration'.[65]

It is debatable whether disclosure of the existence of TPF is beneficial to any party to the arbitration. To some extent, the disclosure may assist the claimant in avoiding frivolous challenges during the arbitration proceedings, frequently raised by a respondent seeking to frustrate such process. Indeed, as challenges to arbitrators on the grounds of impartiality and independence are fairly common in international arbitration, disclosure of the existence of TPF at the onset of proceedings may assist in preventing a possible later challenge by a party, especially at the enforcement stage.[66] While some institutions such as the ICCA have guidelines that require an arbitrator to disclose multiple appointments by a single party, the arbitrator would be unable to follow such requirements unless a third-party funder or claimant voluntarily disclosed the existence of the funding agreement.[67]

Disclosure may also provide an opportunity for the parties to better assess their claims and the dispute as a whole.[68] The disclosure of TPF may affect how an opposing party wishes to proceed in arbitration.[69] For example, once notified of the existence of a third party, an opposing party may be more willing to settle, instead of proceeding with the case, because the opposing party may view the third-party funder as raising the probability of success for the other side and not surrendering to litigation fatigue.[70] Many users of TPF are well-capitalized, solvent corporations and financial institutions who are willing to disclose their use of TPF and the identity of the funder, seeing it as evidence of the strength of their position in the dispute at hand, essentially seeing the benefit of a 'positive bias' when the existence of TPF is disclosed.

TPF information is also often sought in the context of a contemplated security for costs application against the deep pockets of funders. The desirability and implications of a cost order will be discussed in Section 18.5.3.

65 IBA, IBA Guidelines on Conflicts of Interest in International Arbitration, Explanation to General Standard 7, para. (a) (October 2014).

66 A. Trusz, 'Full Disclosure? Conflicts of Interest Arising from Third-Party Funding in International Commercial Arbitration' (2013) 101 *Georgetown Law Journal* 1649 at 1667.

67 See William W. Park and Catherine A. Rogers, *Third-Party Funding in International Arbitration: The ICCA Queen-Mary Task Force*, Legal Studies Research Paper No 42–2014, p. 7.

68 Paula Hodges and Christian Leathley, *Publication of New IBA Guidelines on Conflict of Interests in International Arbitration – the key changes*, HSF Notes, 4 December 2014, available at https://hsfnotes.com/arbitration/2014/12/04/publication-of-new-iba-guidelines-on-conflict-of-interests-in-international-arbitration-the-key-changes/ (last accessed 12 July 2019).

69 Ibid.

70 Ibid.

18.5.2 *Control of Proceedings*

The extent of the control exercised by the third-party funder in relation to the conduct of the arbitration, in particular, in relation to any compromise of the dispute, is another area that can be fraught with difficulty. Generally speaking, the funder and the funded party have autonomy to agree on the extent of control to be exercised by the funder. In England, the ALF Code merely provides that the agreement should 'state whether and if so how the funder may provide input to (...) decisions in relation to settlements'.[71] Singapore has adopted an approach similar to that taken in England, recognizing that control of the proceedings 'is something that should be dealt with in the funding agreement'.[72] The proposed Hong Kong Code mirrors the ALF Code in that it will prohibit the funder from 'seeking to influence the funded party's legal representative to cede control or conduct of the arbitration to the third party funder', and from '[taking] any steps that cause or are likely to cause the funded party's legal representative to act in breach of professional duties'.[73] However, the Hong Kong Code takes the obligation one step further by prohibiting the funder from seeking to 'control or direct the funded party as to the conduct of the arbitration, including, without limitation, as to the negotiation and conclusion of any settlement'.[74] This more stringent approach reflects concerns which have been expressed by the Hong Kong courts concerning the potential for third-party funders to influence the conduct of the proceedings.[75]

The ICCA-QM Task Force Report noted a divergence of opinion on the matter amongst funders. Some funders report that, after careful initial assessment, they function only as distant and detached monitors who are entitled to receive regular updates.[76] Others argue that a relatively high degree of control would be important for funders to be able to protect their investment and ensure that a case is prosecuted consistent with the assumptions and analysis that facilitated the funding in the first place. This view has effectively been endorsed by the Court of Appeal in *Excalibur Ventures LLC* v. *Texas Keystone Inc and others*, in where Lord Tomlinson observed:

> I should also comment on the suggestion of the ALF that 'to avoid being fixed with the conduct of the funded party, the funder would have to exercise greater control over the conduct of the litigation throughout and that this runs the risk that the funding agreement would be champertous'. I understand why this concern is raised but I consider that it is unrealistic (...) What the judge characterised as 'rigorous analysis of law, facts and witnesses, consideration of proportionality and review at appropriate intervals' is what is to be expected of a responsible funder – as the ALF to some extent acknowledges and as did some of the funders in this case in their evidence presented to the judge – and cannot of itself be champertous. I agree that, rather than interfering with the due administration of justice, if anything such activities promote the due administration of justice.[77]

It has also been observed that such an aversion to control is at odds with how, in Singapore and Hong Kong, competent adults may give control over their affairs to others through a power of attorney, and yet could not give control over their litigation/arbitration to a

[71] AFL Code, 11.1.

[72] Singapore Parliamentary Debates, Official Report (10 January 2017) vol. 94 (Indranee Rajah, Senior Ministry of State for Law).

[73] HK Code, 2.11.

[74] Ibid.

[75] *Akai Holdings Ltd.* v. *Ho Wing on Christopher* [2009] 5 HKLRD K2; *Re Co. A* [2015] HKEC 2089; *see also* Law Reform Commission of Hong Kong, *Report: Third Party Funding for Arbitration* (October 2015), para. 6.

[76] Jonathon Molot, 'Theory and Practice in Litigation Risk' (Burford, 2015), available at www.burfordcapital.com/wp-content/uploads/2015/01/Booklet-Theory-and-Practice.pdf (last accessed 12 July 2019).

[77] *Excalibur Ventures LLC* v. *Texas Keystone Inc and others* [2016] EWCA Civ. 1144, para. 31.

professional, fulltime, expert litigation manager such as a funder if they wished to do so.[78] For many clients, dispute resolution management services from a professional provider removes a significant burden and distraction from their shoulders by shielding them from a drain of time and resources in management.[79] Funders can also assist the claimant to shape its strategy and prepare a well-grounded claim, which can even be decided on pre-judicial stage through settlement.[80] In this regard, the involvement of funders in the proceedings is moving away from a control/no control dichotomy towards a collaborative model.

18.5.3 *Costs and Third-Party Funding*

18.5.3.1 Allocation of Costs

The existence of TPF raises a number of issues with respect to the allocation of costs between the parties. Should a funded party that has prevailed in the arbitration be able to recover costs where these costs have been funded by a third party? Should a funded party that has prevailed in the arbitration be able to recover outcome-dependent payments made to the third-party funder? The ICSID jurisprudence points towards the negative. The tribunal in *Ioannis Kardassopoulus & Ron Fuchs* v. *Georgia*[81] held that it 'knows of no principle why any such third-party financing arrangement should be taken into consideration in determining the amount of recovery by the Claimants of their costs'. *Ron Fuchs* v. *Georgia* has been followed in the subsequent cases of *RSM Production Corporation* v. *Grenada*[82] and *ATA Construction, Industrial and Trading Company* v. *Jordan*.[83] In *Quasar de Valores* v. *Russia*,[84] the SCC tribunal held that there was 'no legal duty on the part of the Claimants to hand over any recovery on account of costs' because the respondents had a 'total free ride'. These views were echoed more recently by the ICCA–QMUL Task Force on TPF in International Arbitration in its Subcommittee Draft Report 1 on Security for Costs and Costs of 1 November 2015. This line of reasoning is generally in line with the *inter partes* effect of contractual agreements and the limited jurisdiction of international investment tribunals, which clearly do not cover TPF agreements. In addition, TPF agreements usually contain their own dispute settlement clauses and are subject to a different applicable law.

However, an English court has recently taken the opposite view in the context of third party litigation funding. In *Essar Oilfields Services Limited* v. *Norscot Rig Management Pvt Limited (Essar Oilfields)*,[85] a challenge had been brought on the basis the arbitrator exceeded his powers pursuant to section 68(2)(b) of the English Arbitration Act. The arbitrator had held that the Respondent was entitled to the costs of litigation funding, which included not just lawyers' costs but also sums due to the funder under the funding agreement; having interpreted third-party funding under the head of 'other costs'. The court held that 'the arbitrator's interpretation of 'other costs' was correct, in that it extended in principle to the costs of

78 Oliver Gayner and Susanna Khouri, 'Singapore and Hong Kong: International Arbitration Meets Third Party Funding' (2017) 40 *Fordham International Law* 1033, 1044.
79 Ibid.
80 C R Flake, 'In Domestic Arbitration: Champerty or Social Utility?' (2015) 2 *Dispute Resolution Journal* 70 at 115–17.
81 *Ioannis Kardassopoulus & Ron Fuchs* v. *Georgia* (ICSID Case No. ARB/07/15, Award of 3 March 2010), para 691.
82 *RSM Production Corporation* v. *Grenada* (ICSID Case No. ARB/05/14, Order of the Committee Discontinuing the Proceeding and Decision on Costs of 28 April 2011), para. 68.
83 *ATA Construction, Industrial and Trading Company* v. *Jordan* (ICSID Case No. ARB/8/02, Order Taking Note of the Discontinuance of the Proceeding of 11 July 2011), para. 34.
84 *Quasar de Valores* v. *Russia* (SCC) (Award of 20 July 2012), paras. 223–24.
85 [2016] EWHC 2361 (Comm).

obtaining third party legal funding. Whether then to award it is a matter of discretion'.[86] The facts in *Essar Oilfields* were extreme in that the arbitrator specifically found that Essar had deliberately engaged in a concerted attempt to deprive Norscot of the ability to pursue its claim and that Norscot was able to continue with its claim only with the aid of litigation funding. However, one might argue the door is now ajar for claimants to recoup commissions due to a funder from their opponent. The authors submit that the *Essar Oilfields* ruling should be treated as English authority for arbitrations seated in London under the English Arbitration Act and the English 'indemnity rule'.

In any event, the SIAC IA Rules, has tackled the issue of costs and TPF. Rule 33.1 gives the tribunal the power to take TPF arrangements into account when deciding on the apportionment of costs. Rule 35 states that:

> The Tribunal shall have the authority to order in its Award that all or a part of the legal or other costs of a Party be paid by another Party. The Tribunal may take into account any third-party funding arrangements in ordering in its Award that all or a part of the legal or other costs of a Party be paid by another Party.

In light of these developments, it remains to be seen how *Essar Oilfields* will be treated in arbitrations seated in Asia.

18.5.3.2 Security for Costs

The ability of an arbitral tribunal to grant security for costs has taken a different perspective with the existence of TPF. Indeed, it is questioned whether arbitral tribunals should take into account the existence of a TPF arrangement when assessing applications for security for costs. For instance, is the existence of a TPF agreement, or particular terms in such agreement, relevant in ascertaining whether a particular claimant is impecunious? In *RSM* v. *Saint Lucia*,[87] the respondent's request for security for costs was granted. The fact that the claimant admittedly did not have sufficient financial resources itself and that it admitted its funding from an unknown third party suggested to the ICSID Tribunal that the claimant might not be financially able to comply with a possible costs award rendered in favour of the Respondent.[88] However, it was later noted in the ICSID case of *EuroGas Inc. and Belmont Resources Inc.* v. *Slovak Republic*[89] that *RSM* v. *Saint Lucia* was likely an outlier in light of the exceptional factual matrix, as 'the claimant was not only impecunious and funded by a third party, but also had a proven history of not complying with cost orders'.[90] Indeed, it was questioned whether the presence of TPF had a decisive impact on the outcome or if it would have been reached nevertheless. The *Eurogas* Tribunal also found that the existence of TPF does not 'necessarily constitute per se exceptional circumstances justifying that the Respondent be granted an order of security for costs',[91] a view echoed by the tribunal in *South American Silver Limited (Bermuda)* v. *Bolivia*[92] and the Task Force Report on Security for Costs.

86 Ibid., para. 70.

87 *RSM* v. *Saint Lucia* (ICSID Case No. ARB/12/10, Decision on Saint Lucia's Request for Security for Costs of 13 August 2014).

88 Ibid., paras. 83–86.

89 *EuroGas Inc. and Belmont Resources Inc.* v. *Slovak Republic* (ICSID Case No. ARB/14/14, Procedural Order No. 3 of 23 June 2015).

90 Ibid., para. 122.

91 Ibid., para. 123.

92 *South American Silver* v. *Bolivia* (Procedural Order No. 10 of 11 January 2016), paras. 76–78.

It remains unclear whether States have a protected right to security for costs under the ICSID Convention. While the ICSID Convention provides that each party must abide by and comply with the terms of the award,[93] execution of the award is left to the national applicable law.[94] The Tribunal in *Eskosol S.P.A. in Liquidazione* v. *Italian Republic* (*Eskosol*) [95] noted that 'there is something analytically curious about the notion that an ICSID tribunal, while not empowered to protect a claimant's ability to collect on a possible merits award, nonetheless should intervene to protect a State's asserted 'right' to collect on a possible costs award'. While the ICSID Tribunal in *Eskosol* decided not to address this matter as the respondent had failed to demonstrate that the security for costs request was urgent even assuming that the State had a protectable right, it went on to observe that:

> The Tribunal accepts that respondent States have genuine concerns about their ability to enforce an eventual costs award against unsuccessful claimants, and some States are starting to raise the possibility of reforms to the ICSID system to protect themselves more systematically. But at the same time, such States would be unhappy to see a similar argument about a right to effective relief used against them, for example by claimants worried about collection risk associated with any final merits award of compensation.[96]

The response from the funding community has been mixed, as observed in the ICCA-QM Task Force Report. Some funders have argued that security for costs does not have a place in arbitration generally. Under this view, the risk of an unenforceable award (including an unenforceable award for costs) is like any litigation risk, and should not be treated differently in the investment context. Systematic issuance of security for costs orders will simply raise the cost of TPF for investors, which may translate into restrictions on the availability of funds. Either scenario, it is argued, will reduce the ability of genuinely aggrieved investors to access justice. Other funders have argued that they are rather agnostic about the imposition of security for costs because any costs added by such an order can simply be added into the funding agreement. The greater problem, under this view, is uncertainty about whether security for costs will be granted. Such uncertainty can be mitigated by the purchase of an 'After the Event' (ATE) insurance to provide for coverage in the event a claimant is liable for adverse costs.[97] Indeed, in *Eskosol S.p.A.* v. *Italy*, the ICSID tribunal found that Italy's request for security for costs was not urgent because the claimant had purchased ATE insurance.[98]

In any event, tribunals should continue with the common tradition that security for costs should be granted with the 'greatest reluctance', even in cases involving TPF.[99] A great increase in orders for security for costs may carry the risk of opposing parties automatically applying for security for costs as a strategy to draw out proceedings.[100] It also risks stifling meritorious claims if tribunals automatically grant security for costs and the third-party funder does not agree to pay on the part of the claimant.[101] The development in this area of law

93 ICSID Convention, Art. 53(1).

94 Ibid., Art. 54(3).

95 *Eskosol SpA in Liquidazione* v. *Italian Republic* (ICSID Case No. ARB/15/50, Procedural Order No 3 of 12 April 2017), para. 35.

96 Ibid., para. 34.

97 *Eskosol SpA in Liquidazione* v. *Italian Republic* (ICSID Case No. ARB/15/50, Procedural Order No 3 (Decision on Respondent's Request for Provisional Measures) of 12 April 2017).

98 Ibid.

99 William Kirtley and Koralie Wietrzykowski, 'Should an Arbitral Tribunal Order Security for Costs When an Impecunious Claimant is Relying upon Third-Party Funding?' (2013) 30 *Journal of International Arbitration* 17, 19.

100 Ibid., at 22.

101 Ibid.

remains to be seen. The Singapore government has concluded that this issue is 'best left to the parties and tribunals'. In Hong Kong, the October 2016 report by the TPF for Arbitration Sub-Committee expressed some enthusiasm for imposing adverse cost orders on third-party funders. However, this has not been reflected in the legislative amendments in Hong Kong.

18.5.3.3 Costs Orders against Third-Party Funders

With the advent of TPF in arbitration, it has been debated if arbitral tribunals could render costs orders directly against third-party funders. The conventional position is succinctly articulated in the Task Force Report on Security for Costs and deserves reproduction in full:

> In principle, a tribunal will lack jurisdiction to issue a costs order against a third-party funder. The third-party funder is not typically party to the arbitration agreement, and has no involvement in the underlying dispute between the two parties in an arbitration. While funders may be involved in the proceedings, this cannot readily be interpreted as consent to arbitrate. The sub-committee is not aware of any arbitral award ordering a funder to pay adverse costs.[102]

In the context of third-party litigation funding, the English courts have been able to make costs orders against third-party funders. In *Excalibur Ventures*, it was held that the derivative nature of a commercial funder's involvement should ordinarily lead to it being required to contribute to the costs on the basis upon which they have been assessed against those whom it chose to fund. That is not to say that there is an irrebuttable presumption that that will be the outcome, but rather that that is the outcome which will ordinarily, in the nature of things, be just and equitable. It remains to be seen whether a similar equitable approach could be adopted in the context of arbitration. A contractual approach could be taken as suggested by the Hong Kong Law Reform Commission suggested that the funder could contractually submit to the Tribunal's jurisdiction on a case by case basis. In the alternative, might it be possible, in particular cases, to award costs against third-party funders by binding non-signatories to the arbitration agreement? In any event, funders will likely adapt the terms of their funding agreements to reflect the risk of cost orders against them.

18.6 CONCLUSION

The embrace of TPF in Singapore and Hong Kong, jurisdictions which already have a strong arbitration framework underpinned by a supportive legislature and judiciary, is a welcome step in the right direction, particularly in dire economic times where affordability of the arbitral process is a significant barrier to its utilization and by extension access to justice. However, the devil is in the details. As funders and the arrangements they make are as amorphous as the funded parties and the funding agreement they enter into, any oversight, be it legislation or soft law will need to be nimble so as to adapt quickly to the realities and practicalities of litigation funding. Ultimately, regulation must be principled and proportionate to the actual risks in question as excessive regulation inhibits growth. Singapore and Hong Kong have demonstrated such careful calibration in the past and will likely continue to do so going forward with TPF in investment arbitration.

102 ICCA-QMUL Task Force on TPF in International Arbitration, Subcommittee on Security for Costs and Costs, Draft Report, 1 November 2015.

19

Settling Investment Disputes through Mediation

Possibilities and Limitations

Jaemin Lee

19.1 INTRODUCTION

Since the first Investor–State Dispute Settlement (ISDS) provision was included in an International Investment Agreement (IIA) in 1969, such provisions have become a core element of these international agreements. ISDS provisions offer a unique international dispute settlement mechanism in the form of an arbitration between a foreign investor on the one hand and the government of the host State on the other hand. Having dealt with more than 900 cases so far, the ISDS regime is now faced with growing global criticisms concerning the consistency of awards, cost and duration, and independence and impartiality of arbitrators, to name a few. Robust discussions are currently taking place in multiple forums to improve and reform the existing ISDS regime. The United Nations Commission on International Trade Law (UNCITRAL) tasked one of its Working Groups (Working Group III) to explore possible options to reform the present ISDS in July 2017, and the Working Group just completed its fifth round of discussions in October 2019.[1] The International Center for the Settlement of Investment Disputes (ICSID) began its own project to amend the rules relating to ISDS in 2015, and proposed new rules in August 2018.[2] There are other forums that are looking into these issues as well.

A wide range of issues are being discussed at these forums. One of them is to explore and facilitate an amicable, non-binding dispute resolution mechanism, in addition to the current system of ISDS by binding arbitration. This would not replace the existing ISDS regime, but would rather supplement it by offering another route of settling disputes. The prevailing consensus seems to be that the ISDS provisions which provide for the arbitration of claims are still essential in IIAs, either by *ad hoc* arbitration or through a permanent body. So, a legally binding dispute settlement mechanism is and will be an essential component of IIAs. That said, there also seems to be a desire among States for a non-binding dispute settlement mechanism in IIAs as a subsidiary or perhaps an alternative means to settle international investment disputes.

1 See United Nations Information Service, *Successful Conclusion of the UNCITRAL Meeting in Vienna on the Reform of Investor–State Dispute Settlement (ISDS)*, UNIS/L/285 (21 October 2019).

2 See Alexander G. Leventhal, 'The 2018 Proposals for Amendments of the ICSID Rules: ICSID Enters the Era of Trump, Populism, and State Sovereignty', (2018) 22(15) *American Society of International Law Insights*, available at www.asil.org/insights/volume/22/issue/15/2018-proposals-amendments-icsid-rules-icsid-enters-era-trump-populism (last visited on 25 October 2019).

Notably, this development is in line with a new trend of international dispute settlement mechanisms. States have realized the usefulness and utility of Alternative Dispute Resolution (ADR) proceedings in settling their own State-to-State disputes.[3] Private entities also look to the ADR proceedings as an effective means to settle their own international disputes.[4] Preferences for ADR are prompted by the efficiency and effectiveness these non-binding dispute settlement proceedings can provide. Often times, though not always, a party (be it a State or a private entity) seems more willing to accommodate the views of the other party or a compromise proposal from a third party, derived from a less contentious, non-judicial, non-binding proceeding, where preservation of a long-term relationship is valued. The same could equally apply to settle investment disputes. As much as ISDS has become so contentious and sensitive, seeking an amicable resolution instead may turn out to be an effective and efficient alternative.

Needless to say, some disputes do require a legally binding proceeding by nature, and those disputes can only be resolved through one. Other disputes, on the other hand, are more susceptible to reaching a resolution through candid discussion and mutually supportive interaction. Investment disputes are no exception. It follows that some recent IIAs purport to establish and facilitate non-binding dispute settlement proceedings between investors and host States. These ADR proceedings can take different forms. They can be consultation between disputing parties, deployment of an official to hear grievances from an investor (such as an ombudsman), or engagement of a third party hearing from both parties and suggesting a solution (mediation). This chapter examines mediation in this regard.

This chapter is structured as follows. Section 19.2 provides an overview of mediation together with a new trend of systematization and elaboration. Section 19.3 analyses the possibility of mediation as a means of settling investment disputes, including its merits and benefits. Section 19.4 looks into limitations and challenges associated with mediation in settling investment disputes. Section 19.5 then concludes.

19.2 RENEWED ATTENTION – MEDIATION AS A MEANS TO SETTLE INTERNATIONAL DISPUTES

ADR seeks an amicable resolution of a dispute, setting aside a formal judicial settlement proceeding for a moment. Mediation is one of the ADR options. Mediation involves an active participation of a third party (mediator) who hears from the disputing parties, examines the facts and proposes solutions to the parties.[5] As one would put it, mediation represents 'efforts by third parties to prevent the eruption or escalation of destructive conflict behavior and to facilitate a settlement that makes renewed destructive behavior unlikely'.[6] In fact, objective opinions of a mediator could considerably facilitate compromises between the disputing

[3] See Rachel Chiu, *Arbitration, Mediation, and the Singapore Convention on Mediation* (dated on 5 August 2019), Thomson Reuters, available at http://arbitrationblog.practicallaw.com/arbitration-mediation-and-the-singapore-convention-on-mediation/ (last visited on 25 October 2019).

[4] See Joseph Mante, Issaka Ndekugri and Nii Ankrah, *Resolution of Disputes Arising from Major Infrastructure Projects in Developing Countries* (dated on January 2011), available at www.irbnet.de/daten/iconda/CIB_DC24504.pdf (last visited on 25 October 2019).

[5] See J.G Merrills, *International Dispute Settlement* (Cambridge University Press, 5th ed, 2011), 26; Francisco Orrego Vicuña, 'Mediation', in Rüdiger Wolfrum (ed.), *Max Planck Encyclopedia of Public International Law* (December 2010), para. 1.

[6] Kjell Skejelsbaek and Gunner Fermann, 'The UN Secretary General and the Mediation of International Disputes', in Jacob Bercovitch (ed.), *Resolving International Conflict: The Theory and Practice of Mediation* (Lynne Rienner Publishers, 1996), p. 76.

parties more than in direct bilateral negotiations.[7] At the same time, it could also avoid the situation where litigation ruins the relationship between parties.[8] The process is subject to a strict confidentiality requirement and, most notably, the proposals of concessions or the final outcomes are not binding.[9] Conciliation is similar to mediation in terms of the process, except that the former tends to involve more formalistic features such as a formal composition of a panel and adoption of procedural rules.[10] Conventional views distinguish the two proceedings by nature, noting that mediation usually involves more pressure for a peaceful solution on an on-going dispute, while conciliation presupposes suspension of hostilities and proceeds under a stronger will for a settlement between the two parties, thus taking a more formalistic approach.[11] That said, even these conciliation procedural rules and the panel's terms of reference are more flexible than legally binding proceedings.[12] Increasingly, however, the terms conciliation and mediation are used interchangeably, and the term mediation is apparently being used more consistently to cover both.[13] This chapter uses the term mediation in this broad sense.

Furthermore, mediation is getting renewed attention with the signing of the *United Nations Convention on International Settlement Agreements Resulting from Mediation* ('Singapore Convention') in August 2019.[14] This convention applies to mediation from commercial disputes by parties.[15] States can adopt reservation (declaration) if it wishes to exclude its own disputes from the application of the convention.[16] Stated differently, without such reservation, States' disputes can still be covered by Singapore Convention as long as the disputes are commercial in nature. The fact that as many as fifty-three States have signed the convention so far points to the fact that the international community has started to look to mediation as a critical method of dispute settlement.

19.2.1 *State-to-State Mediation*

Mediation as an effective ADR method equally applies to disputes between two sovereign States. As a matter of fact, mediation was frequently utilized in the nineteenth century in various international disputes.[17] Some recent examples include the one by Algeria in the US diplomat hostage crisis between Iran and the United States in 1980,[18] and the one by the Organization of American States (OAS) regarding a dispute between El Salvador and Honduras in 1969. The OAS also mediated conflicts involving the situations in Belize in 2002, and in Honduras in 2009.[19]

7 Ibid.

8 See Claire Huang, 'Mediation: Solutions that Save Relationships', *Business Times* (3 October 2015), www.businesstimes.com.sg/consumer/mediation-solutions-that-save-relationships (last visited on 25 October 2019).

9 Ibid.

10 See Merrills, above n 5, 58.

11 'Conciliation', in Rüdiger Wolfrum (ed.), *Max Plank Encyclopedia of Public International Law*,

12 See e.g. Korea–EU FTA Chapter 13 (Trade and Sustainable Development), at Article 13.15 (dispute settlement proceedings) together with Chapter 14 (Dispute Settlement) & Annex 14-B.

13 See Justice M. Jagannadha Rao, *Concepts of Conciliation and Mediation and their Differences*, http://lawcommissionofindia.nic.in/adr_conf/concepts%20med%20rao%201.pdf (last visited on 25 October 2019).

14 United Nations Convention on International Settlement Agreements Resulting from Mediation (New York, 2018) ('Singapore Convention'), opened for signature 7 August 2019, available at https://uncitral.un.org/en/texts/mediation/conventions/international_settlement_agreements (last visited on 9 November 2019).

15 Singapore Convention, Article 1.

16 Singapore Convention, Article 8, para. 1

17 Orrego Vicuña, 'Mediation', above n 5, para. 22.

18 Ibid., para. 25.

19 Ibid.

On its part, the Gulf Cooperation Council (GCC) (which consists of the United Arab Emirates (UAE), Bahrain, Saudi Arabia, Oman, Qatar, and Kuwait) has been mediating disputes since its creation in 1981. For example, Kuwait is reportedly stepping in as a mediator for a dispute between Saudi Arabia, UAE, Oman and Bahrain on one hand and Qatar on the other hand, which has been evolving since 2017.[20] Sometimes, the GCC takes up a more active role. Its Charter of the GCC contains a provision establishing the Commission for the Settlement of Disputes (Article 6), through a decision of the Supreme Council (Article 10, Section 1), when a dispute, left unattended, may lead to the erosion of trust among GCC members. This is an *ad hoc* commission reporting to the Supreme Council, the highest decision- making body of the organization comprising the heads of States of the six Member States (Article 7). Given that the Commission for the Settlement of Disputes is not an adjudicative entity rendering a legally binding decision, but instead issues a recommendation based on a third party's flexible consideration of various circumstances, the process can also be regarded as a particular method of mediation.

19.2.2 *Mediation Experiments in Recent Treaties – More Systematization*

In light of this renewed attention to mediation as a mechanism to settle State-to-State disputes, some recent treaties began to adopt new provisions in this regard. For instance, the Korea–EU FTA[21] and the Korea–China FTA[22] both adopt a non-binding mediation mechanism to deal with disputes involving Non-Tariff Barriers (NTBs).[23] As of the time of writing, these are the first FTAs to include mediation as a means to settle NTB disputes. Provisions in these two FTAs do not merely refer to mediation in an abstract manner; they set forth detailed steps to implement the proceeding.[24] This new experiment is the reflection of the two facts: (i) NTBs have become one of the most controversial and complex issues in recent FTAs; and yet, (ii) existing dispute settlement mechanisms (DSMs) with binding panel decisions are not always suitable to handle these disputes. In this respect, navigating through the web of laws and regulations, both written and unwritten, is sometimes like walking down the labyrinthine streets of an old city. The unpredictable exercise of discretion and invisible regulatory restriction couched in vague terms unfortunately neutralize the benefits from the tariff elimination of the FTAs. The identification and elimination of NTBs have thus become critical in implementing FTAs. Having realized the inherent limitations of the existing DSMs in dealing with disputes of NTBs, this new scheme of mediation has been introduced as a flexible alternative wherein parties are more likely to accept and implement a decision of a third party (mediator).

At the same time, mediation takes on the trend of more systematization. The relevant provisions do not simply recommend mediation in abstract but offer it in a serious manner with detailed provisions. The Korea–EU FTA and the Korea–China FTA offer good examples by setting forth detailed provisions for mediation to deal with disputes of NTBs.[25] In the Korea–EU FTA, Annex 14-A sets rules for the mediation mechanism, especially for non-tariff measures. Given the time-consuming nature of a formal dispute settlement procedure, the two

20 Mohammed Nuruzzaman, 'Gulf Cooperation Council (GCC), Qatar and Dispute Mediations: A Critical Investigation' (2015) 8(4) *Contemporary Arab Affairs* 535.

21 Korea–EU FTA, signed on 6 October 2010(entered into force (provisionally) on 1 July 2011).

22 Korea–China FTA, signed 1 June 2015 (entered into force on 20 December 2015).

23 Korea–EU FTA Annex 14-A; Korea–China FTA Article 20.5, paragraph 4.

24 Ibid.

25 Ibid.

parties agreed for a more 'comprehensive and expeditious procedure' helped by a mediator on market access issues relating to NTBs.[26] One of the notable characteristics of this procedure is the encouraged timeline. Consent for launching a mediation should be given within fifteen days of the request being submitted by another party,[27] and the appointment of the mediator should be completed within thirty days at most.[28] The mediation process is encouraged to be concluded within sixty days of the date of the appointment of the mediator.[29] In other words, the whole process is designed to be completed in approximately 100 days. Compared to the time consumed in a more typical dispute settlement procedure, the resort to mediation could be very effective in solving NTB disputes concerning market access. Additionally, the mediation process in the case of NTBs ensures diplomatic flexibility. In Article 5, the rules of the procedure set out the authority of the mediator in deciding on a method of mediation,[30] and the mediator can only provide an 'advisory opinion' in which the mediator is not to consider 'whether the measure at issue is consistent or not' with the FTA.[31] As the solution is not binding, much authority given to the mediator would also be less of a burden for the parties, even if they were unable to agree on the proposed solution.[32] Moreover, this mediation procedure is established as an independent option apart from the formal dispute settlement mechanism. The parties can still bring about a formal dispute on the issue tackled in mediation.[33] However, the information revealed or relied on in the mediation process cannot serve as a basis for the dispute settlement procedure.[34]

Article 20.5 of the Korea–China FTA also reflects the governments' intention to promote the utilization of alternative dispute resolution mechanisms, including good offices, conciliation and mediation. These processes can be embarked on voluntarily.[35] Particularly, recourse to mediation is encouraged to solve conflicts regarding NTB issues.[36] The basic principles of the mediation process, which, among others, are to proceed in an expeditious way,[37] to act in good faith in implementing any mutually agreed solution,[38] and to commit on reserving confidentiality of information discussed during mediation are also outlined in this Agreement.[39] The general nature of the intended mediation process seems to be similar to the one set out in the Korea–EU FTA, but the Korea–China FTA lacks any specific rules on the specific time frame of the procedure, on the appointment of a mediator, or on the ways to terminate and conclude the procedure.

Indeed, these NTB mediation-specific provisions are not the only ones in FTAs. As a general matter, many FTAs include provisions relating to ADR in their Dispute Settlement Chapter, of which mediation constitutes an integral part. The Korea–EU FTA and the Korea–China FTA also contain general provisions of ADR including mediation. As an example of these general ADR provisions, Article 19.7 of the Korea–New Zealand FTA reads:

26 See Korea-EU FTA, Annex 14-A, Article 1.
27 Ibid., Article 3.2.
28 Ibid., Article 4.1.
29 Ibid., Article 5.3.
30 Ibid., Article 5.2.
31 Ibid., Article 5.3.
32 Ibid., Article 5.5.
33 Ibid., Article 7.2.
34 Ibid., Article 7.1.
35 See Korea–China FTA, Chapter 20, Article 20.5.1.
36 Ibid., Article 20.5.4.
37 Ibid., Article 20.5.5.
38 Ibid.
39 Ibid., Article 20.5.6.

Article 19.7 Goods Offices, Conciliation or Mediation

1. The Parties may at any time agree to good offices, conciliation or *mediation*. They may begin at any time and be terminated at any time.
2. Proceedings involving good offices, conciliation and *mediation*, and in particular positions taken by the Parties during these proceedings, shall be confidential and without prejudice to the rights of either Party in any further proceedings.[40]

Likewise, the Korea–Vietnam FTA[41] and the Korea–Colombia FTA[42] stipulate good offices, conciliation and mediation.[43] FTAs between Japan and Singapore,[44] between Japan and Thailand,[45] and Japan and Switzerland[46] have similar provisions.[47] China's recent FTAs also follow suit.[48] Recent mega FTAs such as the CPTPP[49] and the TTIP[50] also have similar provisions on mediation.[51] While specific wordings vary, the core elements of these provisions share commonalities: State parties may initiate or terminate mediation at any time; discussions statements made during mediation should remain confidential and cannot be referred to in any other future proceedings; and parties reserve their rights to proceed to binding dispute settlement proceedings after mediation. In short, maximum flexibility is sought in these mediation proceedings.

19.3 MEDIATION AS AN ALTERNATIVE TO ISDS BY ARBITRATION

The same rationale in favour of mediation could equally apply to the regime for ISDS. An argument can be made that the international community might want to seek an alternative route of dispute settlement to deal with investment disputes which are politically sensitive and legally complex: if anything, sometimes a non-binding mechanism in investment dispute settlement proceedings seems to offer a viable solution. This is especially the case as the current approach to ISDS is often to focus on the parties' rights and obligations, rather than to find a common ground by enhancing mutual interest.[52] In addition, the ISDS regime is currently in a fluid state, with a significant overhaul expected in the coming years. Efforts to

40 Korea–New Zealand FTA, Art 19.7 (emphasis added).

41 Korea–Vietnam FTA, signed on 5 May 2015 (entered into force on 20 December 2015).

42 Korea–Colombia FTA, signed 21 February 2013 (entered into force on 15 July 2016).

43 See Article 15.5 of the Korea–Vietnam FTA; Article 20.6 of the Korea–Colombia FTA.

44 Japan–Singapore Economic Partnership Agreement, signed in January 2002 (entered into force on 30 November 2002).

45 Japan–Thailand Economic Partnership Agreement, signed 3 April 2007 (entered into force on 1 November 2007).

46 Japan–Switzerland Economic Partnership Agreement, signed 19 February 2009 (entered into force on 1 September 2009).

47 See Article 141 of the Japan–Singapore Economic Partnership Agreement; Article 161 of the Japan–Thailand Economic Partnership Agreement; Article 118 of the Japan–Vietnam Economic Partnership Agreement; Article 140 of the Japan–Switzerland Economic Partnership Agreement.

48 Article 61 of the China–Pakistan FTA; Article 187 of the China–New Zealand FTA; Article 15.6 of the Australia–China FTA.

49 Comprehensive and Progressive Agreement for Trans-Pacific Partnership (entered into force on 30 December 2018) (CPTPP).

50 Transatlantic Trade and Investment Partnership (not in force) (TTIP).

51 See Article 28. 6 of the CPTPP; Article 4 of the TTIP's Government-Government Dispute Settlement (GGDS) Chapter. Article 4 of Chapter on GGDS, EU negotiating texts in TTIP, available at http://trade.ec.europa.eu/doclib/press/index.cfm?id=1230#rules (last visited on 25 October 2019).

52 The four options that are potentially available for investors seeking to resolve disputes under IIAs are arbitration, conciliation, fact-finding and direct negotiation. As has been explained, 'Arbitration is binding and rights-based. Conciliation as it exists under ICSID or UNCITRAL is non-binding but still rights-based. Fact-finding is

reform the existing system began with a transparency issue in early 2010s leading to the adoption of the 2014 UNCITRAL Rules on Transparency and the conclusion of the 2014 United Nations Convention on Transparency in Treaty Based Investor–State Arbitration (known as the 'Mauritius Convention').[53] These efforts have also led to a full blown discussion on ISDS reform at UNCITRAL starting from November 2017.[54] As the entire ISDS system is being re-examined with a critical eye on the existing regime, non-binding mediation may sometimes prove to be more pertinent and effective to the extent it seeks to find common ground between an investor and a host State rather than an all-out confrontation through international arbitration.

Interestingly, mediation has been only rarely used in settling investment disputes. In fact, there have been only eleven known conciliations – a procedure equivalent to mediation – recorded by ICSID as of March 2019.[55] An even smaller number of tribunals have encouraged parties to try mediation.[56] Nevertheless, some specific actions have been taken realizing that this trend does not reflect the demand from the market. In 2012, the International Bar Association (IBA) adopted a distinct set of rules for investor–State mediation and there has been an increasing number of bilateral and multilateral trade agreements that recently integrated provisions for investor–State mediation into their respective frameworks.[57] Recent examples include the EU–Canada Comprehensive Economic and Trade Agreement (2016),[58] the EU–Singapore Investment Protection Agreement (2018),[59] the CPTPP (2018),[60] and the Indonesia–Australia Comprehensive Economic Partnership Agreement (2019).[61] The Dominican Republic–Central American–United States Free Trade Agreement (CAFTA) also contains similar provision in Article 10.15 which reads that 'the claimant and the respondent should initially seek to resolve the [investment] dispute through consultation and negotiation, which may include the use of non-binding, third-party procedures such as conciliation and mediation'.[62] Likewise, the Investment Agreement for the COMESA Common Investment Area, in Article 26, requires a six-month cooling off period, during which the parties 'shall seek the assistance of a mediator of non-disputing parties'.[63]

ostensibly neutral on the rights/interests divide but inevitably emphasizes the facts relevant to a connected rights-based process. While negotiation is an interest-based process, it is also unstructured and prone to failure in particularly complex disputes. On the other hand, mediation, with the help of a mediator who would facilitate discussion to understand parties' interests and find a more optimal solution to their problem, would offer a process that is more structured and interest-based, with a problem-solving orientation': Note, 'Mediation of Investor-State Conflicts' (2014) 127(8) *Harvard Law Review* 2543, 2552–53.

53 See Shahla Ali and Odysseas Repousis, 'Investor-State Mediation and the Rise of Transparency in International Investment Law: Opportunity or Threat?' (2018) 45 *Denver Journal of International Law and Policy* 229, 238.

54 Crina Baltag, 'An Update on the ISDS Reform: the 37th Session of the UNCITRAL Working Group III Investor-State Dispute Settlement Reform' (2 May 2019), *Kluwer Arbitration Blog*, available at http://arbitrationblog.kluwerarbitration.com/2019/05/02/an-update-on-the-isds-reform-the-37th-session-of-the-uncitral-working-group-iii-investor-state-dispute-settlement-reform/ (last visited on 25 October 2019).

55 Daniel Weinstein, 'Making Mediation More Attractive for Investor-State Disputes' (26 March 2019), *Kluwer Arbitration Blog*, available at http://arbitrationblog.kluwerarbitration.com/2019/03/26/making-mediation-more-attractive-for-investor-state-disputes/ (last visited 25 October 2019).

56 Ibid.

57 Ali and Repousis, above n 53, 238.

58 EU–Canada Comprehensive Economic and Trade Agreement, signed on 30 October 2016 (entered into force on 21 September 2017).

59 EU–Singapore Investment Protection Agreement, signed on 19 October 2018, Art 3.4 (not yet in force).

60 CPTPP, signed on 8 March 2018, Art. 9.18 (entered into force 30 December 2018).

61 Indonesia–Australia Comprehensive Economic Partnership Agreement, signed 4 March 2019, Art. 14.23 (not yet in force).

62 DR-CAFTA, signed on 5 August 2004, Art. 10.15 (entered into force on 1 March 2006).

63 Investment Agreement for the COMESA Common Investment Area, signed on 23 May 2007 (not yet in force).

In 2016, the Energy Charter Conference also unanimously endorsed the 'Guide on Investment Mediation' which is an explanatory document that encourages States and investors to actively consider mediation for investor–State disputes.[64] This Guide is especially significant as it focuses specifically upon investor–State treaty-based mediation, by providing detailed rules on mediation for investment disputes.[65]

Mediation provisions can take many different forms. For example, Belgium/Luxembourg–United Arab Emirates BIT (2004) provides in Article 12.1 that 'as far as possible, the Parties shall endeavour to settle the dispute amicably through negotiations, if necessary by seeking expert advice from a third party, or by conciliation between the Contracting Parties through diplomatic channels, by way of an ad hoc joint commission'.[66] The China–EU Bilateral Investment Treaty, being negotiated as of this writing, is also reported to reflect this trend by introducing detailed provisions on mediation.[67] China and the EU have reportedly collectively noted the importance of mediation as a means to settle investment disputes and included detailed provisions for mediation.[68]

Most notably, ICSID is about to adopt detailed rules on mediation.[69] In 2018, ICSID began work on a new set of mediation rules. The rules aim to settle investment disputes through mediation at all stages. The rules, comprising of twenty-one articles, set forth detailed provisions for a wide range of mediation proceedings. Once approved by ICSID Member States, their availability will assist Member States to implement their international investment agreement provisions offering investment mediation.

Investment disputes have unique features that may make mediation more appealing to the disputing parties. First, the highly political nature of an investment dispute makes it difficult for both an investor and a host State government to come up with an amicable solution, as this would come across as confessing to a weak legal position. The confidential nature of mediation can ensure that disputing parties can engage in a candid discussion for a solution.[70] Second, the host State and investor often enjoy a 'symbiotic relationship' and it would be important that the dispute resolution does not sour their relationship. Arbitration could easily harm the relationship but mediation does not.[71]

64 See Esme Shirlow, 'The Rising Interest in the Mediation of Investment Treaty Disputes, and Scope for Increasing Interaction between Mediation and Arbitration' 27 September 2016), in *Kluwer Arbiration Blog*, available at http://arbitrationblog.kluwerarbitration.com/2016/09/29/the-rising-interest-in-the-mediation-of-investment-treaty-disputes-and-scope-for-increasing-interaction-between-mediation-and-arbitration/ (last visited on 25 October 2019).

65 Ibid.

66 Agreement between the United Arab Emirates, on the one hand, and the Belgian–Luxembourg Economic Union, on the other hand, on the Reciprocal Promotion and Protection of Investments (entered into force on 22 November 2007).

67 Chunlei Zhao, 'Investor State Mediation in a China-EU Bilateral Investment Treaty: Talking about Being in the Right Place at the Right Time' (2018) 17 *Chinese Journal of International Law* 111, 113 (para. 3), Sections IV.A and IV.B.

68 Ibid.

69 ICSID, *Proposals for Amendment of the ICSID Rules: Working Paper No.* 3 (2019), available at https://icsid.worldbank.org/en/Documents/WP_3_VOLUME_1_ENGLISH.pdf (last visited on 9 November 2019).

70 For example, Note, 'Mediation of Investor-State Conflicts', above n 52, 2556.

71 Shahla Ali and Odysseas Repousis, 'Investor-State Mediation and the Rise of Transparency in International Investment Law: Opportunity or Threat?' (2018) 45 *Denver Journal of International Law and Policy* 248. In only a limited number of cases (e.g. *CME* v. *Czech Republic*), have funds recovered through investment arbitration been reinvested in the host state. See Kluwer Arbitration Blog available at http://arbitrationblog.kluwerarbitration.com/2019/03/26/making-mediation-more-attractive-for-investor-state-disputes/; Eunice Chua, 'A contribution to the conversation on mixing the modes of mediation and arbitration: Of definitional consistency and process structure', (2018) *Transnational Dispute Management*, at 12 (last visited on 25 October 2019).

Third, investment arbitration entails a long-term process spanning several years including enforcement proceedings.[72] Mediation, if successfully concluded, usually does not bring with it such logistical burden. Finally, mediation would permit a policy scheme of the host State to continue by avoiding going through an international review process and being officially impugned by arbitrators.[73] This is particularly meaningful when the policy aims to achieve legitimate social objectives.

Among others, the most notable benefit of mediation seems to be the impact on 'cost and duration'. In practice, 'cost and duration' is a real concern for States participating in ISDS proceedings. Strong consensus has been formed to introduce a new system where litigation costs can be reduced and the length of the proceedings shortened. 'cost and duration' gets more serious attention because ISDS disputes deal with sovereign States' authority to regulate.[74] Obviously, the problem of 'cost and duration' raises a particular concern for developing States that have difficulty in defending themselves against foreign investors.[75]

First, litigation cost is a huge concern for a State.[76] A 2017 study illustrates the financial burden for parties participating in ISDS proceedings. According to the study, an average claimant-investor assumes a total litigation cost of USD 6,019,000, while an average respondent State faces a total litigation cost of USD 4,855,000. In addition to these party costs, the organization and administration of an average arbitration tribunal require additional costs of USD 933,000.[77] So, taken together, the total average cost for an ISDS proceeding stands at USD 11,807,000.[78] As a respondent State is supposed to take up half of the tribunal cost, a State usually looks at a total spending of USD 5,321,500 on average, which is arguably a significant financial burden for the State. Undeniably, the burden becomes more acute for a developing State. It should be also borne in mind that this is just the cost for one proceeding: in the case of multiple proceedings, the cost increases proportionately.

A surge of the cost has led to yet another new phenomenon of third-party funding, i.e., a financing method in which an outside private entity agrees to finance an ISDS proceeding for an investor in anticipation of remuneration once the investor prevails in the proceedings.[79] This funding scheme certainly helps destitute investors to finance their

72 Ali and Repousis, above n 53, 248; Leonard M. Kessler, 'Using Mediation to Resolve Construction Disputes' (27 September 2017), LexisNexis, available at www.lexisnexis.com/lexis-practice-advisor/the-journal/b/lpa/posts/using-mediation-to-resolve-construction-disputes (last visited on 26 October 2019).

73 Ibid.

74 Anthea Roberts, 'Clash of Paradigms: Actors and Analogies Shaping the Investment Treaty System' (2013) 107 *American Journal of International Law* 45–94, 58–63.

75 David Riesenberg, 'Fee Shifting In Investor-State Arbitration: Doctrine And Policy Justifying Application of The English Rule' (2011) 60 *Duke Law Journal* 977–1013, 1107 *et seq*. See also UNCTAD, 'Reform of Investor-State Dispute Settlement: In Search of a Roadmap', *International Investment Agreement Issues Note (No. 2)* (June 2013), 4.

76 See David Gaukrodger and Kathryn Gordon, 'Investor-State Dispute Settlement: A Scoping Paper for the Investment Policy Community', *OECD Working Papers on International Investment* 2012/03 19 (OECD Publishing, 2012).

77 Matthew Hodgson and Alistair Campbell, 'Damages and Costs in Investment Treaty Arbitration Revisited', Allen & Overy (14 December 2017), available at www.allenovery.com/SiteCollectionDocuments/14-12-17_Damages_and_costs_in_investment _treaty_arbitration_revisited_.pdf (last visited on 25 October 2019).

78 Ibid.

79 See Lisa Nieuwveld and Victoria Sahani, *Third Party Funding in International Arbitration* (2nd ed., 2017); Duarte Henriques, 'Third-Party Funding: A Protected Investment?', (2017) 30 *Spain Arbitration Review* 100,115.

ISDS litigation and ensure their access to justice.[80] At the same time, third party funding may also bring into question the very integrity of an ISDS proceeding by commercializing ISDS claims.[81]

Secondly, duration of a case is also a major practical concern for a State. One recent study found that the average duration of ICSID ISDS proceedings is calculated as 3.75 years, or 1,370 days (with median of 1,266 days).[82] In the case of UNCITRAL ISDS proceedings, the average duration stands at 3.96 years, or 1,446 days (with median of 1,246 days).[83] In 2011, the Arbitration Institute of the Stockholm Chamber of Commerce (SCC) reported the average length of an investment case under its rules as 21 months.[84] The average four-year duration for the ICSID and UNCITRAL proceedings, which take up a majority of ISDS proceedings, means that governmental agencies and officials of a respondent State have to be involved in and follow up an ISDS proceeding for a lengthy period of time. This obviously causes a significant logistical burden for the State.

If anything, mediation, with its shortened time frame and non-adversarial nature, may help both States and investors alleviate this logistical burden. Mediation does not seek to explore the myriad of legal issues hidden in IIAs, an increasingly common feature in ISDS proceedings; rather it seeks to find a mutually acceptable common ground. One of the viable options to deal with concerns over cost and duration in the present ISDS proceedings certainly seems to be mediation.

19.4 LIMITATIONS AND REMAINING QUESTIONS

At the same time, this new attempt also raises novel questions, both in terms of policy and legal aspects. The success of mediation as an effective tool to settle investment disputes hinges on how to deal with these questions.

19.4.1 *Relationship with ISDS Proceedings*

The most immediate question is the new system's coordination and alignment with the existing one. Since the introduction of mediation does not mean the abolishment of the present ISDS mechanism, the two should be coordinated and aligned in IIAs.

80 J Goeler, *Third Party Funding in International Arbitration and its Impact on Procedure* (Kluwer Law International, 2016), 82–83; Henriques, above n 79, 127–28.

81 M Stoyanov and O Owcarzek, 'Third-Party Funding in International Arbitration: Is It Time for Some Soft Law Rules?', (2015) 2 *BCDR International Arbitration Review* 171. For an overview of some notable conferences dedicated to the issue see S. Seidel, 'Third-Party Investing in International Arbitration Claims' in Bernardo Cremades and Antonias Dimolitsa (eds.), *Third Party Funding in International Arbitration* (ICC Publication No. 752E, 2013) 18; Nadia Darwazeh and Adrien Leleu, 'Disclosure and Security for Costs or How to Address Imbalances Created by Third Party Funding' (2016) 33 *Journal of International Arbitration* 125, 127–29 ; Goeler, above n 80, 87–88; Nieuwveld and Sahani, above n 79, 16.

82 Jeffery Commission, 'How Long Is too Long to Wait for an Award?', *Global Arbitration Review* (18 February 2016); Jeffrey Commission, 'How Much Does an ICSID Arbitration Cost? A Snapshot of the Last Five Years', *Kluwer Arbitration Blog*, (29 February 2016); and Jeffrey Commission, 'The Duration Costs of ICSID and UNCITRAL Investment Treaty Arbitrations, in Vannin Capital, *Funding in Focus Report Three* (July 2016), available at www.vannin.com/downloads/funding-in-focus-three.pdf (last visited on 16 March 2019). The study is based on an analysis of 138 ICSID arbitrations between 2011 and 2015.

83 Ibid.

84 SCC Statistics (2011), p. 4, available at https://sccinstitute.com/statistics/statistics-2008–2016/ (last visited on 25 October 2019).

19.4.1.1 Utilization of Mediation Materials in ISDS Proceedings

One of the practical questions in this regard is the treatment of statements and materials made or submitted during a mediation proceeding in a future ISDS proceeding. In order to facilitate candid discussion and robust pursuit of the middle ground, recent mediation proceeding provisions stipulate that all statements and submissions made during mediation remain confidential and are not to be submitted or referred to in future proceedings, most notably legally binding DSMs.[85] Likewise, admission to some facts or proposal for settlement cannot be introduced in subsequent legally binding proceedings.[86] Some recent IIAs introducing mediation for investment disputes contain similar provisions.[87]

Arguably, however, these provisions are largely skeletal and do not account for specific circumstances where this issue may arise in an actual dispute. In other words, chances are, parties would have to submit the same argument and same positions in a subsequent ISDS proceeding to be held after a failed mediation, because the underlying governmental measure is the same. It follows that in a prospective ISDS proceeding parties may end up discussing and disputing the scope of this provision.

Therefore, in future discussions taking place at various forums, States and interested parties might wish to clarify the extent to which they can submit their statements and documents in a new submission after they have failed to settle their disputes through mediation; in other words, although they are not permitted to submit the same submission (i.e. recycling) in future ISDS proceedings, they can and should be permitted to submit new submissions that contain core elements of law and facts that have been previously submitted in mediation proceedings. The boundary between recycling or resubmission which is prohibited and new submission which should be permitted should be carefully and clearly drawn. This line is not entirely clear in present provisions. In practice, distinction between the two may be far from easy as oftentimes the same documents and arguments are implicated for the same governmental measures at issue. A blurred line may trigger disputes at ISDS proceedings, which may in turn jeopardize the utilization of mediation.

19.4.1.2 Another Procedural Layer Leading to Binding DSMs

One possible downside of a mediation proceeding is that it can be simply another additional procedure before a dispute proceeds to arbitration. In other words, disputing parties are bound to proceed to arbitration anyway, and mediation may become a way station in the process. An example can be found in 'consultation' proceedings of the WTO's DSM.[88] Consultation was included in the WTO's DSU as a mandatory procedural requirement, because it was believed that States could settle their dispute through this mechanism. As it currently stands, WTO's DSU consultation procedure has largely become an additional and ceremonial proceeding that eats up important time and cost for the disputants, and has now turned into a topic of whether the procedure can be dispensed with in future DSU proceedings.[89] Should that phenomenon be repeated in IIAs, it would be a fatal procedural defect: reducing 'cost and duration' of ISDS proceedings is one of the paramount objectives of the recent reform discussions.

85 See Korea–EU FTA, Annex 14-A, Article 7. 1; Korea–China FTA, Article 20.5, para. 6.

86 Ibid.

87 See the EU proposal for TTIP.

88 See WTO DSU, Article 4.

89 See WTO DSU Amendment Negotiation.

In addition, it is also feared that mediation itself may invite another set of its own disputes. For instance, disqualification of mediators due to alleged conflict of interest or misconduct in the course of mediation, interpretation of the mediation result, or enforcement of the completed mediation can be raised by a party or parties when mediation is robustly carried out. These mediation-related disputes may further prolong a mediation proceeding. Assuming an ISDS proceeding follows, a lengthy mediation would mean a longer lead time before a dispute proceeds to ISDS.

Therefore, architects of future ISDS proceedings would have to be mindful of the experience of the WTO in this regard, so that they can introduce a workable and practical mediation. This objective can only be achieved when mediation has its own benefits on its own accord, and States become cognizant of such benefits, independent of existing, conventional DSMs.

19.4.1.3 Post-ISDS Mediation Proceeding

At the same time, it is not entirely clear either whether disputing parties, after having completed their conventional ISDS proceedings, can still initiate a mediation proceeding. If parties want to pursue such an option for whatever reason, they may agree to come to mediation after an unsuccessful or unsatisfactory outcome at an ISDS proceeding. At that stage, the parties may suspend an enforcement proceeding pending mediation. It is also possible that parties have continuing disputes under other IIAs at other fora and tribunals after the conclusion of the ISDS proceeding, and thus may agree to mediation for the resolution of all pending disputes.

The question then is whether IIAs may or should permit States to pursue such an option. It is one thing that the parties of an IIA can choose mediation instead of ISDS. It is another whether the disputing parties can proceed to mediation *after* the completion of an ISDS proceeding due to the dissatisfaction with a decision from the proceeding. Mediation at this stage may seem a de facto appeal procedure. This aspect does not seem clear in the current IIAs. Mediation's relationship with the present ISDS should preferably be more carefully contemplated and clearly stipulated in future IIAs.

19.4.2 *Procedural Due Process*

Given its inherent flexibility, mediation is arguably not amenable to procedural due process, at least not at the level of court proceeding or arbitration. For instance, mediation rules do not necessarily prohibit *ex parte* communication or contain rules of evidence.[90] Mediators are accorded a wide latitude of discretion. However, as much importance is now being attached to the proceeding, a guarantee of procedural due process apparently becomes more critical. IIAs may need provisions that aim to regulate specific conduct of mediation proceedings. These provisions should address parties' oral statements and written submissions. Conflict of interest should also be dealt with. Mediators' greater levels of intervention in the process, something that is not to be seen in arbitration or court proceedings, should also be carefully contemplated in fine-tuning the provisions. In crafting these procedural elements, due process will remain a constant concern.

90 For instance, mediation proceedings of Korea–EU FTA and Korea–China FTA do not have provisions to regulate these issues in mediation proceedings.

This is a dilemmatic situation for mediation. Its beauty lies in flexibility. But efforts to facilitate its utilization entail more systematization, which in turn invites concerns over procedural due process. Enhanced focus on procedural due process would in turn erode the very strength of mediation – flexibility. This is a vicious circle. How procedural due process can be assured in future mediation is an open question.

19.5 CONCLUSION

Some scholars view mediation as a future structure of decision-making processes for international issues.[91] They note that in the decentralized international regime the voluntary nature of mediation will lead to an increase of compliance and decrease of the free rider problem. They claim that the problem-solving techniques associated with mediation get to the heart of issues, which ensure more reasonable agreements and subsequent compliance. In addition, robust two-way communication during mediation to find the common ground over an issue in dispute helps ensure not only the settlement of the immediate dispute at hand but also the cultivation of a long-term relationship, which may in turn reduce disputes in the future. In addition, mediation is sometimes a useful tool to deal with sensitive claims relating to national regulatory authority. This unique trait of mediation will apply to investment disputes with equal force. The international community has realized possible benefits and contributions of mediation in settling investment disputes. Discussions to introduce and facilitate mediation in addition to or in lieu of present ISDS proceedings are taking place in various fora including UNCITRAL and ICSID.

More generally, the merits and demerits of the ISDS proceeding with legally binding force and strict confinement of governing law have prompted States to look into the benefit of flexible and non-binding dispute settlement proceedings for investment disputes. Sometimes, it may be the case that these non-legally binding dispute settlement proceedings help States settle their disputes more effectively and efficiently. However, this is not to replace the ISDS regime with these non-binding mechanisms. Rather, it is only to supplement the existing system.

With the risk of over-generalization, Asian countries have been regarded as more receptive of harmonious resolution of disputes and less litigious in settling disputes.[92] In many ways, this traditional legal culture stands in line with the renewed focus on mediation as means of settling international disputes and, in particular, international investment disputes. It has turned out that some investment disputes can be better dealt with through mediation by dint of their political sensitivity, ambiguous legal texts and the importance of long-term relationship. Mediation can help settle these investment disputes in an effective and amicable manner. States have realized this possibility and included mediation as one of core topics in ISDS reform discussions. With the traditional culture and experience, this seems to be one of the areas where Asian countries can contribute.

91 See Carrie Menkel-Meadow, 'Case for Mediation: The Things that Mediators Should be Learning and Doing' (2016) 82 *International Journal of Arbitration, Mediation, and Dispute* 22; John Dryzek and Susan Hunter, 'Environmental Mediation for International Problems' (1987) 31 *International Studies Quarterly* 100.

92 See e.g. Zhao, above note 67, 124 (para. 32), 125 (para. 35); Joel Lee and Teh Hwee Hwee, 'An Asian Perspective on Mediation', Singapore Mediation Centre/Singapore Academy of Law, Academy Publishing (2009), 4–6; Yujun Feng, 'Legal Culture in China: A Comparison to Western Law', (2010) 16 *Revue Juridique Polynesienne* 115, 120. In case of the low rate of litigation rate in Japan in the 1990s, see Tom Ginsburg and Glenn Hoetker, 'The Unreluctant Litigant? An Empirical Analysis of Japan's Turn to Litigation' (2006) 35 *The Journal of Legal Studies* 31.

20

The Singapore Convention on Mediation

Origins and Application to Investor–State Disputes

Nadja Alexander and Shouyu Chong

20.1 INTRODUCTION

The Singapore Convention on Mediation is a multilateral treaty which provides a legal framework that facilitates the circulation of international mediated settlement agreements ('iMSAs') across national borders. Neither a contract nor a consent arbitral award, iMSAs falling within the scope of, and that satisfy the conditions within, the Singapore Convention enjoy a unique status. It may be said that the Singapore Convention elevates iMSAs to the status of a new type of legal instrument recognized in international law. As outlined further, the Convention establishes a system for the recognition and enforcement of commercial iMSAs. This chapter provides an analysis of the key features of the Convention and comments on its application to, and potential impact upon, investor–State dispute settlement.

20.2 BACKGROUND

At the 51st Session of the United Nations ('UN') Commission on International Trade Law ('UNCITRAL') on 25 June 2018, the final draft of the Convention on International Settlement Agreements Resulting from Mediation[1] (the 'Singapore Convention') was recommended for submission to the UN General Assembly's review. At the same session, the UNCITRAL Model Law on International Commercial Mediation and International Settlement Agreements Resulting from Mediation, 2018 (the '2018 Model Law') was adopted.[2] A resolution to name the Convention the 'Singapore Convention on Mediation' was also approved.[3] This concluded three years of rigorous debate in UNCITRAL Working Group II (Dispute Settlement) which involved the participation of more than ninety UN Member States and thirty-five international governmental and non-

[1] United Nations Convention on International Settlement Agreements Resulting from Mediation, GA Res 73/198, adopted at the United Nations General Assembly, 73rd Session (20 December 2018) (the 'Singapore Convention').

[2] UNCITRAL Model Law on International Commercial Mediation and International Settlement Agreements Resulting from Mediation (amending the UNCITRAL Model Law on International Commercial Conciliation, 2002) GA Res 73/199, adopted at the United Nations General Assembly, 73rd Session (20 December 2018).

[3] Beate Czerwenka, Chairperson of the 51st session of the United Nations Commission on International Trade Law, address to the Sixth Committee of the General Assembly (15 October 2018), p. 2.

governmental organizations.[4] Subsequently, the UN General Assembly adopted the Convention on 20 December 2018.[5]

The signing ceremony of the Singapore Convention took place in Singapore at the Shangri-La Hotel on 7 August 2019 where the Convention was opened for signature, attended by seventy official State delegations, and signed by forty-six.[6] At the time of writing, seven more States have signed the Convention, increasing the total number of signatory States to fifty-three. Five States have ratified it, and one has approved it.[7] In accordance with Article 14, the Singapore Convention entered into force on 12 September 2020.[8]

Notwithstanding the perceived difficulty of enforcing a settlement agreement, we believe the Singapore Convention creates an international regime for enforcing international settlement agreements arising from mediation, which is not unlike how the 1958 Convention on the Recognition and Enforcement of Arbitral Awards[9] (the 'New York Convention') facilitates the enforcement of arbitration awards.[10] This comports with the observations of a 2014 survey conducted of members of the international business and legal communities where 74 per cent of respondents indicated that they believed a multilateral instrument providing for the international enforcement of settlement agreements that result from international commercial mediation would result in an increase in the number of such mediations in their home jurisdictions.[11] In the same vein the 2019 SIDRA international dispute resolution survey suggests that users of Arb-Med-Arb and other hybrid dispute resolution procedures are drawn to such multi-tiered procedures in part because of the promise of expedited enforceability of outcomes.[12] At the same time, users seek mediation because of its many advantages, in particular the opportunity to preserve business relationships.[13] It follows that the enforceability mechanism offered by the Singapore Convention is likely to increase the attractiveness of mediation as a standalone international dispute resolution procedure.

4 Deborah Masucci, 'Singapore Mediation Convention' (*International Mediation Institute*), www.imimediation.org/2018/06/27/singapore-mediation-convention/ (last accessed 25 November 2018).

5 United Nations General Assembly, *Resolution Adopted by the General Assembly on 20 December 2018: Seventy-third Session* (A/RES/73/198) (11 January 2019); 'Press Release: General Assembly Adopts the United Nations Convention on International Settlement Agreements Resulting from Mediation' (UNIS/L/271) (21 December 2018).

6 Nadja Alexander and Shouyu Chong, 'UN Treaty on Mediation Signed in Singapore' (2019) 23(2-3) *Nederlands-Vlaams tijdschrisft voor Mediation en conflictmanagement* 71; see also Singapore Convention, Article 11.

7 See, e.g., United Nations Treaty Collection, Chapter XXII, available at https://treaties.un.org/Pages/ViewDetails.aspx?src=TREATY&mtdsg_no=XXII-4&chapter=22&clang=_en (last accessed 14 December 2020).

8 Singapore Convention, Article 14; see also Nadja Alexander and Shouyu Chong, '12 September 2020: The Singapore Convention on Mediation Comes into Force', *Kluwer Mediation Blog* (12 September 2020).

9 Convention on the Recognition and Enforcement of Arbitral Awards, opened for signature 10 June 1958, 330 UNTS 3 (entered into force 7 June 1959) ('New York Convention').

10 Khory McCormick and Sharon SM Ong, 'Through the Looking Glass: An Insider's Perspective into the Making of the Singapore Convention on Mediation' (2019) 31 *Singapore Academy of Law Journal* 520, paras. 68–69.

11 Stacie Strong, 'Use and Perception of International Commercial Mediation and Conciliation: A Preliminary Report on Issues Relating to the Proposed UNCITRAL Convention on International Commercial Mediation and Conciliation' (2014) *University of Missouri School of Law Legal Studies Research Paper No. 2014–28*, 45, available at SSRN https://papers.ssrn.com/sol3/papers.cfm?abstract_id=2526302 (last accessed 25 November 2018).

12 Nadja Alexander, Janet Checkley, Shouyu Chong et al., 'International Dispute Resolution Survey: Currents of Change' (Singapore International Dispute Resolution Academy Preliminary Report, 2019).

13 Adrian Tan, 'A Kinder, Gentler way to Settle Disputes, Named after Singapore', *The Straits Times* (Singapore, 26 July 2019).

20.3 HOW DOES THE SINGAPORE CONVENTION WORK?

In most cases, once parties have concluded an iMSA, they comply with their obligations. Where this is not the case, the Singapore Convention provides parties to iMSAs that fall within its scope (Article 1) with the possibility to proceed to a relevant court of a State to seek enforcement relief (Article 3(1)). The party seeking relief will file an application before that court and submit as evidence the iMSA containing parties' signatures and an attestation by the mediator or mediation institution that the settlement resulted from mediation (Article 4).[14] Provided the iMSA does not fall foul of any of the grounds for refusal defined in Article 5, it will be directly enforced. Alternatively, issues resolved and contained in the iMSA may be administered as a complete defence to the commencement of litigation or arbitral proceedings where parties seek to contest issues already resolved and contained in the iMSA (Article 3(2)). Key to the direct enforcement method is that there is no requirement for an iMSA to undergo a review process at the place where it was concluded (the State of origin). In other words, there is no 'seat' of mediation in the sense that there is a 'seat' of arbitration. Court review in terms of the Convention only occurs in the State of enforcement.

20.3.1 *Key Provisions of the Singapore Convention*

Building upon the overview offered in the previous section, here we will explore the significant provisions of the Singapore Convention.

20.3.1.1 Which Forms of Mediated Settlement Agreements Fall Within the Scope of the Convention?

This issue may be examined in two parts. First, we will discuss the scope of the Convention in relation to international agreements resulting from mediation, which we will refer to as international mediated settlement agreements or 'iMSAs' throughout this chapter. Secondly, we will discuss the kinds of iMSAs which have been explicitly excluded by the Convention.

The Convention applies to the recognition and enforcement of international settlement agreements arising from mediation[15] which have been concluded in writing[16] by parties to resolve a commercial dispute.[17] A meticulous consideration of these key terms, 'international', 'commercial' and 'mediation' is imperative. The 'in writing' requirement is examined in the next section, where the form requirements for iMSAs are considered.

Only mediated settlement agreements with an *international* character may be recognized and enforced under the Singapore Convention. This accords with UNCITRAL's mandate, which has a cross-border focus, and the Commission's desire not to intervene with the domestic law of enacting States.[18] Article 1(1) generally defines what constitutes an international dispute, where:

14 Article 4 further provides that other forms of suitable evidence may be submitted in the absence of the mediator's signature on the iMSA or an attestation by the mediator or mediation institution that the settlement agreement resulted from mediation.

15 Singapore Convention, Article 1(a)–(b).

16 Ibid., Article 1.

17 Ibid., Article 1.

18 United Nations Commission on International Trade Law, Working Group II (Dispute Settlement), *Report of Working Group II (Arbitration and Conciliation) on the Work of Its Sixty-third Session* (Vienna, 7–11 September 2015), (A/CN.9/861) (2015), paras. 36–39.

(a) At least two parties to the settlement agreement have their places of business in different states;

or

(b) The State in which the parties to the settlement agreement have their places of business is different from either:

(i) The State in which a substantial part of the obligations under the settlement agreement is performed; or

(ii) The State with which the subject matter of the settlement agreement is most closely connected.[19]

Where parties have more than one place of business, the relevant place of business for the purposes of defining the international character of the iMSA concerned will be – according to Article 2(1)(a) – benchmarked at the place which bears the closest relationship to the dispute resolved by the 'settlement agreement, having regard to the circumstances known to, or contemplated by, the parties at the time of the conclusion of the settlement agreement'. It is noteworthy that the relevant place of business must be determined with regard to the circumstances known to, or reasonably contemplated by, the parties *at the time of the conclusion of the settlement agreement*.[20] Where a party to the iMSA is a natural person (i.e. he or she does not have a 'place of business' per se), reference will be made to that party's habitual residence, according to Article 2(1)(b).

It is necessary to provide a functional definition of what constitutes an 'international' dispute in the Articles of the Convention, owing to the fact that there is no concept of a seat of mediation,[21] in the sense that there is a seat of arbitration.[22] Whereas the internationality of a *foreign* judgment or arbitral award enforced under prevailing instruments such as the

[19] Singapore Convention, Article 1(1).

[20] This caveat is important in situations where parties migrate their businesses from one jurisdiction into another, or when parties merge or become acquired by another business from outside of jurisdiction. For deeper analysis, see Nadja Alexander and Shouyu Chong, *The Singapore Convention on Mediation: A Commentary* (Wolters Kluwer, 2019), paras. 2.03–2.04.

[21] Shouyu Chong and Nadja Alexander, 'Singapore Convention Series: Why is there no Seat of Mediation?' *Kluwer Mediation Blog* (1 February 2019); Shouyu Chong and Felix Steffek, 'Enforcement of International Settlement Agreements Resulting from Mediation under the Singapore Convention: Private International Law Issues in Perspective' (2019) 31 *Singapore Academy of Law Journal* 448, para. 15.

[22] As an aside, one should note that the relevance of the seat is fundamental in international arbitration because it is crucial in the determination of whether the award sought to be enforced is a foreign or domestic award (see the New York Convention, Article I). Secondly, it is commonly understood that the courts of the seat of arbitration have been traditionally entrusted with the powers by the drafters of the New York Convention through Article V (1)(e) of the Convention to engage in a principal review of awards made by the tribunal (see Nadia Darwazeh, 'Article V(1)(e)', in Herbert Kronke, et al. (eds.), *Recognition and Enforcement of Foreign Arbitral Awards: A Global Commentary on the New York Convention* (Kluwer Law International, 2010), 327; for further information on how the seat of arbitration is determined and a perusal of the function of courts at the seat, see AJ Bělohlávek, 'Seat of Arbitration and Supporting and Supervising Function of Courts' (2015) 5 *Czech (and Central European) Yearbook of Arbitration* 21) before it is taken abroad for enforcement. It is usual for the courts at the seat to examine whether rules of natural justice have been breached by the arbitral tribunal during the determinative process and set it aside if any breach has occurred: for instance, the court may examine whether the parties have been sufficiently appraised of the justifications by arbitrators when rendering their award (see *TMM Division Maritima SA de CV* v. *Pacific Richfield Marine Pte Ltd* [2013] 4 SLR 972, para. 99). It follows that there is simply no need to discern the seat of mediation as it is not a determinative process as is arbitration: the nature of the natural justice considerations is fundamentally different, because in mediation, parties are not compelled to arrive at their dispute resolution outcome. Accordingly, the power of the competent authority of the signatory State to refuse to enforce an iMSA based on the fairness of the mediation process resulting in an iMSA is strictly confined to cases where mediator misconduct is so egregious that it materially influences parties to enter into it inadvertently (see the Singapore Convention, Article 5(e)–(f)).

Hague Convention of 30 June 2005 on Choice of Court Agreements ('HCCCA') and the New York Convention respectively is evident on the face of it,[23] the internationality of a mediated settlement agreement has to be defined, for it is a non-starter to describe that agreement as 'foreign' when there is no such concept of a seat in mediation:[24] in other words, there would be no basis upon which the mediated settlement agreement may be compared as 'foreign' in respect to. Hence it is only meaningful to refer to mediated settlement agreements to be of 'international' character, in contrast to those of 'domestic' character (which would fall outside of the Article 1(1) definition).

Circumscribing the applicability of the Singapore Convention to commercial disputes resolved at mediation is the result of two factors, namely that commercial matters have traditionally fallen within the mandate of UNCITRAL, and that non-commercial subject matters are more likely to cause internal conflict with public policies that are specific to legal cultures and domestic circumstances. Interestingly, the term 'commercial' is not defined in the Convention. However, a definition has been provided in footnote 1 of the 2018 Model Law which was drafted alongside the Convention – this definition may be of use to jurisdictions without a discrete body of commercial law:

> The term 'commercial' should be given a wide interpretation so as to cover matters arising from all relationships of a commercial nature, whether contractual or not. Relationships of a commercial nature include, but are not limited to, the following transactions: any trade transaction for the supply or exchange of goods or services; distribution agreement; commercial representation or agency; factoring; leasing; construction of works; consulting; engineering; licensing; investment; financing; banking; insurance; exploitation agreement or concession; joint venture and other forms of industrial or business cooperation; and carriage of goods or passengers by air, sea, rail or road.[25]

This quote demonstrates that commercial relationships include 'investment' transactions. Furthermore, the UNCITRAL Working Group II's proposal to limit the scope of the Singapore Convention to 'commercial agreements between businesses only'[26] was not accepted by the delegates, and it is evident that States may be parties to mediated settlement agreements under the Convention, in the absence of a reservation to the contrary.[27]

Consistent with the focus on 'commercial', consumer disputes 'for personal, family or household purposes', and disputes in relation to 'family, inheritance or employment law' are excluded by Article 1(2).

[23] For example, Art I of the New York Convention provides, 'This Convention shall apply to the recognition and enforcement of arbitral awards made in the territory of a State [i.e. the 'seat'] *other than the State where the recognition and enforcement of such awards are sought* [. . .]' (emphasis added).

[24] Chong and Alexander, 'Singapore Convention Series: Why is there no Seat of Mediation?', above n 21; Chong and Steffek, above n 21; also see United Nations Commission on International Trade Law, Working Group II (Dispute Settlement), *Report of Working Group II (Arbitration and Conciliation) on the Work of Its Sixty-third Session* (Vienna, 7–11 September 2015), (A/CN.9/861) (2015), para. 35.

[25] UNCITRAL Model Law on International Commercial Mediation and International Settlement Agreements Resulting from Mediation, 2018 (amending the UNCITRAL Model Law on International Commercial Conciliation, 2002) GA Res 73/199, adopted at the United Nations General Assembly, 73rd Session (20 December 2018), footnote 1.

[26] Cf. United Nations Commission on International Trade Law, Working Group II, *Note by the Secretariat on Comments received from States on the Settlement of commercial disputes: Enforceability of settlement agreements resulting from international commercial conciliation/mediation – Revision of the UNCITRAL Notes on Organizing Arbitral Proceedings* (New York, 2–6 February 2015), (A/CN.9/WG.II/WP.188) (2015), p. 3.

[27] McCormick and Ong, above n 10, para. 31. Note that the relevant reservation may be found in Article 8(1)(a) of the Singapore Convention: this will be discussed later in this chapter.

'Mediation' is defined broadly under Article 2(3) of the Singapore Convention to be:

> a process, irrespective of the expression used or the basis upon which the process is carried out, whereby parties attempt to reach an amicable settlement of their dispute with the assistance of a third person or persons ('the mediator') lacking the authority to impose a solution upon the parties to the dispute.[28]

The earlier definition has been adapted from the definition of 'conciliation' provided by Article 1(3) of the UNCITRAL Model law on International Commercial Conciliation (2002) into one for 'mediation'. As such, it encompasses a diversity of facilitative and advisory dispute resolution processes, but not determinative processes such as arbitration and adjudication.[29]

Such a broad definition reflects a recognition of the diversity in cross-border mediation practices across the world. Notably, the provision in Article 1(3) is a functional one, focusing on the *nature* and *substance* of the dispute resolution process rather than the label.[30] This means that parties do not need to pedantically refer to the term 'mediation' when describing what led to the conclusion of their iMSAs for the Convention to apply.[31] Therefore processes such as neutral evaluation and mini-trial could conceivably fall within the broad definition of mediation. In the near future, as and when technology advances so as to enable artificial intelligence algorithms to be administered to provide mediation services, it is hoped that the broad definition provided of 'the mediator' in the Singapore Convention would be shaped accordingly with the necessary nuances to accommodate contemporary innovations, especially if we start to conceive of the possibility of granting legal personality to artificial intelligence software systems.[32]

The Singapore Convention endeavours to fill gaps in the cross-border enforcement regimes of iMSAs. However, its drafters were mindful to avoid overlaps in the enforcement regimes for foreign judgments,[33] foreign arbitral awards[34] and iMSAs.[35] Hence, the following notable exclusions feature in Article 1(3) of the Convention, which expressly excludes settlement agreements that:

(a) have been approved by a court or have been concluded in the course of court proceedings; and are enforceable as a judgment in the state of that court; or

28 Singapore Convention, Article 2(3).

29 Chong and Steffek, above n 21, para. 17.

30 Nadja Alexander and Shouyu Chong, 'An Introduction to the Singapore Convention on Mediation – Perspectives from Singapore' (2018) 22(4) *Nederlands-Vlaams tijdschrisft voor Mediation en conflictmanagement* 37, 41.

31 Chong and Steffek, above n 21, para. 17. Take for instance, a mediated settlement agreement which carries the label of a 'Memorandum of Understanding' will still, in substance, be recognized as a settlement agreement which was procured as a result of mediation (see *Ram Niranjan* v. *Navin Jatia and others and another suit* [2019] SGHC 138).

32 Alexander and Chong, 'An Introduction to the Singapore Convention on Mediation – Perspectives from Singapore', above n 30, 41, citing P. Čerka, J. Grigienė & G. Sirbikytė, 'Is It Possible to Grant Legal Personality to Artificial Intelligence Software Systems?' (2017) 33 *Computer Law & Security Review* 685.

33 Notably, the Hague Convention of 30 June 2005 on Choice of Court Agreements (30 June 2005; entry into force 1 October 2015), as well as the Hague Convention of 2 July 2019 on the Recognition and Enforcement of Foreign Judgments in Civil or Commercial Matters (2 July 2019), which has been adopted by the Hague Conference on Private International Law on 2 July 2019 but not come into force at the time of writing (only Uruguay and Ukraine have since signed on to the Convention).

34 Notably, the New York Convention.

35 Natalie Y. Morris-Sharma, 'Constructing the Convention on Mediation – The Chairperson's Perspective' (2019) 31 *Singapore Academy of Law Journal* 487, para. 45. See also UNCITRAL, *Report of Working Group II (Disputes Settlement) on the Work of Its Sixty-third Session* (Vienna, 7–11 September 2015) (A/CN.9/861) (17 September 2015), p. 6.

(b) have been recorded and are enforceable as an arbitral award.[36]

The carve- out provisions in Article 1(3) were inserted to deconflict the administration of the Singapore Convention with other prevalent international instruments, such as the New York Convention and the HCCCA, which already provide mechanisms that specifically facilitate the enforcement of those aforementioned forms of settlement agreements.[37] As Morris-Sharma reports:

> Specifically, the purpose was to avoid overlaps between the Singapore Convention and the Hague Convention on Choice of Court Agreements, the Judgments Project of the Hague Conference on Private International Law ('the Judgments Project') [which later materialised into the Hague Convention of 2 July 2019 on the Recognition and Enforcement of Foreign Judgments in Civil or Commercial Matters] and the New York Convention. This was, in many ways, *the main preoccupation* of delegations for this issue. It was, in many ways, a function of the fact that a number of the most interested delegations in the UNCITRAL process were also active in the Judgment Project discussions. They were therefore able to keenly appreciate the various permutations and combinations of how the outcomes of the UNCITRAL discussions and the anticipated output of the Judgments Project could interact.[38]

In this regard, the purpose of the Convention is akin to a 'gap-filler'. It endeavours to provide a recognition and enforcement remedy to parties in circumstances where those other instruments are otherwise inapplicable: for instance, where out-of-court settlements are not brought back into the courtroom for judicial approval with the object of enforcement under the HCCCA regime, and consequently do not qualify as a 'judgment' for the purposes of such enforcement. At this juncture, it bears reiterating that the Singapore Convention's main endeavour is in relation to the cross-border recognition and enforcement of iMSAs that result from commercial mediation processes, whether institutional or ad hoc in nature, provided the resulting iMSAs are not internationally enforceable under the alternative aforementioned mechanisms. Nevertheless, it should also be noted that in any case of conflict, Article 7 of the Singapore Convention, which serves as a 'more-favourable-right' clause, preserves the right of parties to enforce their iMSAs under another enforcement regime outside of the Singapore Convention, if a more favourable result ensues.[39] The 'more favourable' enforcement regime may be encompassed in domestic law or in another treaty.

20.3.1.2 How Does Enforcement Operate under the Convention?

Here we shall analyse the recognition and enforcement mechanism of the Singapore Convention, as well as set out the formal and evidentiary conditions necessary to enforce

[36] Singapore Convention, Article 1(3).

[37] Consider, for instance, the Hague Convention of 30 June 2005 on Choice of Court Agreements, Article 12. Additionally, it should be noted that the applicability of the Singapore Convention must also be de-conflicted with the Hague Convention of 2 July 2019 on the Recognition and Enforcement of Foreign Judgments in Civil and Commercial Matters , when it comes into force in due course (see Francisco J Garcimartín Alférez and Geneviève Saumier, *Fourth Meeting of the Special Commission on the Recognition and Enforcement of Foreign Judgments 24–29 May 2018, Judgments Convention: Revised Preliminary Explanatory Report* (May 2018)).

[38] Morris-Sharma, above n 35, para. 45 (emphasis added).

[39] Alexander and Chong, *The Singapore Convention on Mediation: A Commentary*, above n 20, para. 7.02; and McCormick and Ong, above n 10, para. 30.

an iMSA under the Convention. It should first be noted that the Convention provides latitude and autonomy to the contracting State Parties to adhere with their Convention obligations by not stipulating a specific mode of enforcement.[40] Contracting State Parties to the Singapore Convention may, in accordance with domestic law, determine their own rules of procedure in relation to the recognition and enforcement of iMSAs, provided they comply with the conditions laid down by the Convention in respect to scope (as examined earlier), form and evidence (analysed subsequently).[41] For convenience, we will refer to the recognition and enforcement mechanism of the Singapore Convention collectively as one of enforcement, to avoid tedious repetition.

It may be useful to study the operation of the enforcement mechanism under the Convention by applying the metaphors of a 'sword' and 'shield'.[42] Article 3(1) establishes that iMSAs may be applied as a 'sword', in the sense that parties may commence proceedings in the courts of a Party to the Convention to compel performance of another party to it, and in the process enforcing the obligations encapsulated therein, if the requirements set out in the Convention are fulfilled and no grounds for refusal under Article 5 may be proven. Article 3(2), establishes that parties may administer an iMSA as a 'shield', compelling the courts of a Party to the Convention to functionally 'recognize' the discrete issues already resolved by themselves at mediation, which have been reflected in their concluded *written* iMSA,[43] and dismiss (or strike out) those issues 'already resolved' if they were raised for a second time in court.[44]

Although the Singapore Convention does not explicitly refer to the term 'recognition' (in the private international law sense) in relation to iMSAs in the same way as the New York Convention refers to the recognition of foreign arbitral awards, Article 3(2) describes functionally the aspects of recognition. This carefully-drafted wording reflects the debate and compromise reached within the Working Group as to how the use of the term 'recognition' may impact civil procedural rules in certain jurisdictions (particularly those from non-common law traditions) and whether other terms such as 'binding' might be more appropriate.[45] As interpreted by lawyers trained in non-common law traditions, private international law 'recognition' would not embrace dispute resolution outcomes procured outside of litigation and arbitration, which engender a '*res judicata* effect'.[46] Instead of remaining deadlocked on terminology, the Working Group was able to bridge the fundamental differences in understanding of private international law 'recognition' from various conflicting domestic lenses. Rather than rely on labels taken from the realm of private international law which might be interpreted differently in different legal systems, the

40 Singapore Convention, Article 3.

41 For the applicable conditions, see the Singapore Convention, Articles 1, 2 and 4.

42 The metaphors were helpfully applied by Schnabel in Timothy Schnabel, 'The Singapore Convention on Mediation: A Framework for the Cross-Border Recognition and Enforcement of Mediated Settlements' (2019) 19 *Pepperdine Dispute Resolution Law Journal* 1, 35 *ff*.

43 Cf. *Jumaiah bte Amir* v. *Salim bin Abdul Rashid* [2019] SGHC 63.

44 This also assumes if the conditions set out in the Convention are met and no grounds for refusal under Article 5 can be proven.

45 Timothy Schnabel, 'The Singapore Convention on Mediation: A Framework for the Cross-Border Recognition and Enforcement of Mediated Settlements' (2019) 19 *Pepperdine Dispute Resolution Law Journal* 1, 35 *ff*; Morris-Sharma, above n 35, para. 40.

46 Morris-Sharma, above n 35, para. 39.

conflict was overcome with the provision of a functional description of what they intended into the draft of Article 3(2).[47]

Parties endeavouring to enforce an iMSA under the Singapore Convention are simply required to produce the *written* iMSA signed by the parties; and provide evidence that it was procured as a result of a mediation process.

In other words, Parties to the Convention may simply legislate that iMSAs are *prima facie* enforceable, in accordance with domestic procedural rules and conditions.

The precise form requirements for enforceable iMSAs are minimal under the Convention. The iMSA is to be in writing[48] and signed by the parties.[49] There are no further formalities such as notarization, requirements to use the services of locally-licensed mediators or the like. The 'in writing' requirement for an iMSA is easily satisfied 'if its content is recorded in any form [...] [including] an electronic communication if the information contained therein is accessible so as to be useable for subsequent reference'.[50] Notably, this opens the possibility of disputes settled through a diversity of online dispute resolution (ODR) forums administered through various channels of electronic communication (including text messaging, email, online conference calls and dedicated ODR platforms)[51] to be amenable to enforcement under the Singapore Convention, so long as the parties are able to conclude their iMSA by endorsing it with a recognized electronic signature,[52] and provide the enforcement authority with evidence that the iMSA was a result of mediation.[53]

It is to be remembered at this juncture that the Singapore Convention does not apply to settlement agreements negotiated and concluded outside of a mediation process. For this reason parties seeking to enforce an iMSA are additionally required to produce evidence that the settlement resulted from mediation.[54] To prove that the settlement resulted from mediation, parties *may* produce a mediation agreement,[55] the mediator's signature on the settlement agreement, a separate document signed by the mediator confirming that mediation was carried out in respect to the settlement agreement concerned or an official attestation by the institution or dispute resolution service provider administering the mediation.[56]

Furthermore, there is a 'catch-all' clause (Article 4(1)(b)(iv)) which provides the competent authority of the Party to the Singapore Convention with the autonomy to decide what other forms of evidence may be furnished as proof that the iMSA sought to be enforced had arisen from mediation.[57]

47 Ibid., para. 40.
48 Singapore Convention, Article 1.
49 Ibid., Article 4(1)(a).
50 Singapore Convention, Article 2(2).
51 Consider as an example the e-negotiation and e-mediation services available under the recently constituted Singapore Employment Claims Tribunals online filing module; whilst it is acknowledged that employment law claims are excluded under the Singapore Convention's scope, the electronic platform tools may be transferable in future to resolving small-scale cross-border commercial disputes. See Joanna Seow, 'New Employment Claims Tribunals portal allows users to have disputes mediated online' *The Straits Times* (4 January 2019).
52 Singapore Convention, Article 4(1)(a) read with Article 4(2).
53 Ibid., Article 4(1)(b).
54 Ibid., Article 4(1)(b).
55 United Nations Commission on International Trade Law, Working Group II (Dispute Settlement), *Report of Working Group II (Arbitration and Conciliation) on the Work of Its Sixty-third Session* (Vienna, 7–11 September 2015), (A/CN.9/861) (2015), para. 68.
56 Singapore Convention, Article 4(1)(b)(i)–(iii).
57 Ibid., Article 4(1)(b)(iv).

20.3.1.3 When Can a Court Refuse to Enforce an iMSA?

Article 5 of the Singapore Convention sets out exhaustively the possible exceptions to enforcement of iMSAs which would otherwise fulfil the Article 4 conditions. The relevant competent authority *may*[58] refuse to grant enforcement relief if one of these grounds are proven. It is worth noting that Article 5(1) of the Singapore Convention requires parties to furnish proof to the relevant competent authority that one or more grounds for refusal under that provision may exist, whilst Article 5(2) provides that the relevant competent authority may by its own volition find that such grounds for refusal under that provision may exist, without – technically – first having parties furnish them with such proof. The grounds for refusal to grant relief may be examined in four categories: contract-related grounds for refusal, mediator conduct-related grounds for refusal, public policy justifications and where the subject matter is incapable of settlement by mediation. Of all the Articles in the Singapore Convention, Article 5 was subject to the most robust debate and took the longest time to achieve consensus. The following introduction to the various grounds for refusal and accompanying remarks will not do justice to the rich complexity of Article 5. Nevertheless, we hope that our subsequent observations will spark impulses for deeper research and discussion.

(A) CONTRACT-RELATED GROUNDS FOR REFUSAL Article 5(1) of the Singapore Convention provides seven grounds for refusal of enforcement of iMSAs founded in contract law. The competent authorities of Parties to the Convention may refuse to enforce an iMSA if:

(a) a party to it was under some form of incapacity at its conclusion;[59]
(b) it is null and void, inoperative or incapable of being performed according to the applicable law;[60]
(c) it is not binding, or is not final, according to its terms;[61]
(d) it has been subsequently modified;[62]
(e) the obligations in it have been performed;[63]
(f) the obligations in it are not stated clearly or comprehensibly;[64] or
(g) granting relief would be contrary its terms.[65]

58 It is in theory within the prerogative of the competent authority to exercise its discretion and, nevertheless, enforce the iMSA even if one or more of the Article 5 grounds were proved. As to theories behind how such discretion may be exercised, see Jonathan Hill, 'The Exercise of Judicial Discretion in Relation to Applications to Enforce Arbitral Awards under the New York Convention 1958' (2016) 36 *Oxford Journal of Legal Studies* 304. Hill has observed, albeit in the arbitration context, that such a discretion is likely applied within circumscribed circumstances: 'As a general rule, if a defence to enforcement [...] is established, enforcement will be (and should be) refused. [However, to] this general principle, there is a limited number of exceptions [...], which are based on intelligible legal principles, rather than the court's perception of what would be fair in all the circumstances.' This is an area which should be left for further research in another article, in the cross-border mediation context.

59 Singapore Convention, Article 5(1)(a).

60 Ibid., Article 5(1)(b)(i).

61 Ibid., Article 5(1)(b)(ii).

62 Ibid., Article 5(1)(b)(iii).

63 Ibid., Article 5(1)(c)(i).

64 Ibid., Article 5(1)(c)(ii).

65 Ibid., Article 5(1)(d).

First, the incapacity defence applies to parties that are natural or legal persons. The term 'incapacity' must be understood in the appropriate context, with reference to the governing law of the iMSA.[66] This is because civil and common law traditions approach the concept of incapacity from different perspectives.[67] The governing law of an iMSA should broadly be determined by an express choice of law agreed upon by the parties. If no express choice of law were made, or if the express choice were invalid,[68] courts may generally determine that the law governing the iMSA would be that which is most-closely connected with the dispute.[69] Other choice of law techniques, such as the 'validation principle' and *renvoi*, may also be considered.[70] Normally, the incapacity defence may be relevant when parties integral to the conclusion of iMSAs are minors, natural persons with intellectual disabilities or deficits, or legal persons that are not validly represented.

Secondly, the defence available when an iMSA is null and void, inoperative or incapable of being performed under the applicable law may be further examined in three separate parts. iMSAs which are 'null and void' contain defects at the moment in time when they are concluded. Having determined the governing law of the iMSA, the competent court may apply the following contract defences, to determine if an iMSA were null and void: misrepresentation, fraud, duress, undue influence or unconscionability.[71] Defects which arise subsequently should not render the iMSA 'null and void'.[72] Instead, iMSAs which are considered 'inoperative' may become ineffective due to circumstances transpiring at or after the point of contractual conclusion:[73] this may occur as a result of poorly drafted iMSAs containing inherently contradictory or self-defeating clauses that intrinsically cancel each other out, rendering it sterile of any effect to begin with.[74] Alternatively, an iMSA may be inoperable due to subsequent agreements to waive all rights to pursue remedies under it.[75] iMSAs which are 'incapable of being performed' are (or become) impossible to execute or enforce, perhaps owing to supervening occurrences transpiring after its

66 Chong and Steffek, above n 21, para. 46.

67 For instance, the capacity of natural persons in civil law jurisdictions is generally governed by the law of their nationality, while the capacity of natural persons in common law jurisdictions is governed by the law of their domicile: Gary Born, *International Commercial Arbitration* (Wolters Kluwer, 2nd ed., 2014), pp. 3489–90.

68 For instance, when conflicting express choices of law were made: see *Dubai Electricity Co and ors* v. *Islamic Republic of Iran Shipping Lines (The Iran Vojdan)* [1984] 2 Lloyd's Rep 380, 385.

69 Take for instance, courts in the European Union are bound by the Regulation (EC) No. 593/2008 of the European Parliament and of the Council of 17 June 2008 on the law applicable to contractual obligations (Rome I), which generally provides a framework for the determination of the law of closest connection governing contracts with cross-border elements in the EU.

70 Chong and Steffek, above n 21, paras. 65–67. At this juncture it should be noted that the administration of the 'validation principle' and *renvoi* remains in a state of flux at this point in time. The 'validation principle' has recently been rejected by the Singapore High Court: *BNA* v. *BNB* [2019] SGHC 142, paras. 52–66. Furthermore, the 'pro-enforcement bias' underpinning the "validation principle" is subject to much criticism in practice and theory, as it could potentially compromise party autonomy. But the UK Supreme Court has appeared to apply it when determining the governing law of an arbitration agreement: *Enka v Chubb* [2020] UKSC 38, [108]. *Renvoi* is a difficult concept to grasp, and also administer: David Alexander Hughes, 'The Insolubility of '*Renvoi*' and Its Consequences' (2010) 6 *Journal of Private International Law* 195.

71 Chong and Steffek, above n 21, para. 69.

72 Alexander and Chong, 'An Introduction to the Singapore Convention on Mediation – Perspectives from Singapore', above n 30, 45. See also George Bermann, 'Recognition and Enforcement of Foreign Arbitral Awards – The Interpretation and Application of the New York Convention by National Courts' in George A Bermann (ed.), *Recognition and Enforcement of Foreign Arbitral Awards – The Interpretation and Application of the New York Convention by National Courts* (Springer, 2017), 23.

73 Alexander and Chong, 'An Introduction to the Singapore Convention on Mediation – Perspectives from Singapore', above n 30, 45; see also Bermann, above n 72, 23.

74 Bermann, above n 72, 24.

75 Consider *Apple & Eve LLC* v. *Yantai N Andre Juice Co* 610 F Supp 2d 226 (ED NY, 2009).

conclusion,[76] or poor drafting.[77] The competent court would, with reference to the appropriate governing law, take reference to private law defences relating to contractual impossibility, frustration or other related defences.[78]

Thirdly, iMSAs which are not binding, or are not final, according to their terms may be refused enforcement. Such iMSAs may contain terms and conditions which expressly or implicitly provide that they have no final or binding effect.[79] Reference to the governing law of the iMSA is also imperative. For instance, if Singapore law governed the iMSA, where it resolves social and domestic disputes flowing from a family business, a legal presumption that parties do not intend to create legal relations has to be rebutted in order to prove the binding effect of that agreement.[80]

Fourthly, if the terms of an iMSA have been validly modified (according to the applicable governing law), the original settlement agreement will be rendered ineffectual, due to the subsequent conclusion of that variation agreement which should revoke the effect of the earlier terms. Consequently, only the modified iMSA shall be enforced. It follows logically that the original iMSA must be refused enforcement.

Fifthly, if the obligations within an iMSA have already been performed (according to the applicable governing law), it logically follows that courts must refuse enforcement of that iMSA, since those obligations have been discharged by performance. This avoids the making of doubled claims by parties.

Sixthly, if the iMSA is not drafted in clear or comprehensible terms, courts may refuse to enforce it. It bears emphasis that meticulous drafting is essential. Undoubtedly, key terms and obligations (such as price to be paid in a specified currency, or consideration due from one party to another in exchange for carefully or precisely defined performances) must be elucidated with conscientiousness and precision. The drafters of an iMSA should ideally provide for the precise steps or measures expected or demanded of parties, especially when the obligations flowing from a compromise at mediation do not involve a monetary transaction. For instance, if a party to a mediation has agreed to apologize to another, the terms of the iMSA may be provided as such:

> Mia Pte Ltd shall publish the following words: 'We unconditionally and sincerely express our deepest apologies to Janet AB and their associates for any embarrassment resulting from the words our employees have caused to be published on the *FunTube*, which is a popular video sharing site, and on their behalf offer to rescind those embarrassing statements made,' on the front pages of the relevant local newspapers, *The Fun Times* and *The Cheerful Nightly*, and on

[76] Alexander and Chong, 'An Introduction to the Singapore Convention on Mediation – Perspectives from Singapore', above n 30, 45; see also Bermann, above n 72, 24.

[77] See *Polish Supreme Court (Sqd Najwyzszy) Civil Chamber Division, Case No. V CSK 231/14 of (5 February 2015)* (Reported in English in the *Czech (and Central European) Yearbook of Arbitration* (2015), 214–16). Also see Aldo Frignani, 'Interpretation and Application of the New York Convention in Italy' in George Bermann (ed.), *Recognition and Enforcement of Foreign Arbitral Awards – The Interpretation and Application of the New York Convention by National Courts* (Springer, 2017), 568: a curious example was reported in this publication, where a party from Italy and one from Syria agreed that 'any dispute arising [. . .] shall be settled by a sole arbitrator [. . .]. [T]he arbitrator shall be an expert in Swiss law and in the production of Arabic bread'. However, this agreement was determined by courts to be incapable of being performed for no arbitrator satisfying both conditions may be identified.

[78] Chong and Steffek, 'Enforcement of International Settlement Agreements Resulting from Mediation under the Singapore Convention: Private International Law Issues in Perspective', above n 21, para. 70.

[79] Ibid., para. 48.

[80] *Ram Niranjan v. Navin Jatia and others and another suit* [2019] SGHC 138, para. 84. Readers unfamiliar with Singapore law should note that the presumption is easily rebutted; but the High Court caveats that 'the facts, context and circumstances in each case must be carefully considered'.

their social media platforms (such as *FunBook* and *Fun-gram*), as a form of apology to Janet AB, in return for Janet AB's application to discontinue Suit No. XYZ/2019 and Suit No. ABC/2019.

To conclude an iMSA by getting parties to agree to simplistically drafted terms (e.g. that 'Mia Pte Ltd shall apologise to Janet AB') might risk producing an iMSA that is too unclear and imprecise for enforcement under the Singapore Convention.

Seventhly, an iMSA may be refused enforcement if granting relief would be contrary to its terms. For example, when conditions precedent or conditions subsequent contained in an iMSA have not been satisfied, courts may refuse its enforcement, because the obligations in it do not accrue at the point in time when enforcement is being sought.[81] This provision accommodates for the possibility for parties to opt out of the application of the Singapore Convention entirely.[82] It also gives effect to *force majeure* clauses: where a contractually stipulated supervening event transpires and the terms of the iMSA accommodates for a discharge of obligations accordingly, courts may refuse its enforcement under this provision as it would be contrary to its terms to do so.

(B) MEDIATOR CONDUCT-RELATED GROUNDS FOR REFUSAL Next, Article 5(1) of the Singapore Convention provides for two mediator conduct-related grounds for refusal. First, the courts of Parties to the Convention may refuse to enforce an iMSA where there was 'a serious breach by the mediator of standards applicable to the mediator or the mediation *without which breach that party would not have entered into the settlement agreement*'.[83] Parties relying on this ground must prove that not only was there *egregious* conduct breaching mediator standards when the affected iMSA was concluded – with reference to the proper standards[84] governing that mediation (e.g. a mediator who is susceptible to the 'Code of Conduct for Mediators'[85] under the Singapore Law Society's Mediation Scheme must abide dutifully by that code of conduct) – the breach must also be shown to have *caused or influenced* them to enter into that settlement agreement. Proving the element of causation is imperative for this defence to succeed.[86]

The second mediator conduct-related ground for refusal is essentially a narrower illustration falling within the scope of the first ground, where:

> [t]here was a failure by the mediator to disclose to the parties circumstances that raise justifiable doubts as to the mediator's impartiality or independence and *such failure to disclose had a material impact or undue influence on a party* without which failure that party would not have entered into the settlement agreement.[87]

81 United Nations Commission on International Trade Law, Working Group II (Dispute Settlement), *Report of Working Group II (Dispute Settlement) on the Work of Its Sixty-eighth Session* (A/CN.9/934) (New York, 5–9 February 2018), para. 57.

82 Schnabel, 'The Singapore Convention on Mediation: A Framework for the Cross-Border Recognition and Enforcement of Mediated Settlements', above n 45, 56ff; Hal Abramson, 'New Singapore Convention on Cross-Border Mediated Settlements: Key Choices', in Catharine Titi and Katia Fach-Gomez (eds.), *Mediation in International Commercial and Investment Disputes* (Oxford University Press, 2019), 14.

83 Singapore Convention, Article 5(1)(e) (emphasis added). Note that this aligns with Articles 6(4), 6(5) and 7(3) of the 2018 Model Law on International Commercial Mediation.

84 For a closer examination on how the proper standards governing a mediation may be determined, see Alexander and Chong, *The Singapore Convention on Mediation: A Commentary*, above n 20, paras. 5.99–5.102.

85 See generally, The Law Society of Singapore, 'Mediation Scheme Handbook' (2017) www.lawsociety.org.sg /Portals/0/ForThePublic/PDF/LSMS%20Handbook.pdf (last accessed on 25 October 2018).

86 Alexander and Chong, *The Singapore Convention on Mediation: A Commentary*, above n 20, para. 5.88.

87 Singapore Convention, Article 5(1)(f) (emphasis added). Note that this aligns with Articles 6(4), 6(5) and 7(3) of the 2018 Model Law on International Commercial Mediation.

In the same way, parties must demonstrate that the mediator misconduct here has *caused or influenced* them to conclude the challenged settlement agreement, to successfully argue that this ground for refusal may be applied. Specifically, parties must provide real and credible evidence that the mediator's misconduct was one in relation to his or her ability to be impartial or independent at the mediation table leading to justifiable doubts of their abilities. Consequently, there must have been a duty for the affected mediator to disclose their compromised circumstances to the parties at mediation; where he or she fails to do so, parties seeking relief from enforcement must *additionally* demonstrate that they were subject to undue influence[88] to accept the terms of the iMSA, or that there was some other material influence as a result of the mediator's compromised circumstances – which may have manifested itself as a misrepresentation as to the terms of the iMSA, a material non-disclosure of facts and circumstances,[89] or an unconscionable[90] action amidst an unfortunate set of circumstances – swaying the outcome of the iMSA.

(C) PUBLIC POLICY AS A GROUND FOR REFUSAL Article 5(2)(a) of the Singapore Convention provides that a court may, on its own initiative,[91] refuse to enforce an iMSA that is 'contrary to the public policy'[92] of the State in which enforcement is sought. It bears emphasizing that the public policy exception should be considered in light of prevailing private international law rules, which contemplates a scrutiny of *both* domestic and international conditions.[93] Whilst the domestic public policy of the State where enforcement is pursued must be accorded with due regard, it has to be applied 'in a manner that is consistent, insofar as possible, with the objectives of the Convention and the public policies and interests of other Contracting States'.[94] Consequently, the competent enforcing authorities should only under *highly exceptional circumstances* exercise their discretion to refuse to enforce

88 See generally *Chan Gek Yong v Violet Netto (practising as L F Violet Netto) and another and another matter* [2018] SGHC 208, where a party to a mediated settlement agreement attempted to challenge its validity owing to duress, some of which was allegedly attributed from the mediators; also see, for a case summary, Nadja Alexander and Shouyu Chong, 'Singapore Case Note: What happens when a party to an MSA has a change of heart?' *Kluwer Mediation Blog* (17 October 2018).

89 As to what may constitute a material non-disclosure of facts and circumstances which could sway the outcome of a mediated settlement agreement, see the Singapore case of *Ram Niranjan* v. *Navin Jatia and others and another suit* [2019] SGHC 138, paras. 75–79.

90 The definition of unconscionable action by parties to a contract during the process of contract formation which may result in the avoidance of some contractual obligations has been clarified in the Singapore Court of Appeal recently in *BOM* v. *BOK* [2018] SGCA 83: see para. 142 *et seq*. An instance of an unconscionable action which may vitiate contractual obligations may be illustrated by the facts in *BOM* v. *BOK* [2018] SGCA 83: where a wife takes advantage of the immense grief suffered by her estranged husband, whose mother had passed away suddenly and violently in a murder, to compel him to sign away *the entirety* of his multi-million dollar inheritance and put it on trust in favour of their infant child, this could be viewed by the Singapore courts as an unconscionable action which engenders vitiation of contractual obligations tainted by the wife's conduct.

91 Alexander and Chong, *The Singapore Convention on Mediation: A Commentary*, above n 20, para. 5.113; Schnabel, 'The Singapore Convention on Mediation: A Framework for the Cross-Border Recognition and Enforcement of Mediated Settlements', above n 45, 42. Of course, parties remain free to plead for the public policy defence to apply and submit evidence into court accordingly.

92 Singapore Convention, Article 5(2)(a).

93 Chong and Steffek, 'Enforcement of International Settlement Agreements Resulting from Mediation under the Singapore Convention: Private International Law Issues in Perspective', above n 21, para. 55; cf. Gary Born, *International Commercial Arbitration* (Wolters Kluwer, 2nd ed., 2014), p. 3652.

94 Born, above n 94, 3655; although taken out of context (i.e. Born's words refer to the Convention on the Recognition and Enforcement of Foreign Arbitral Awards (330 UNTS 3) (10 June 1958; entry into force 7 June 1959)), the phrasing of the words apply with equal logical force to the Singapore Convention on International Settlement Agreements Resulting from Mediation as well. See *Renusagar Power Co Ltd* v. *General Electric Co* [1994] AIR 860, para. 63.

iMSAs by reason of public policy,[95] as it is trite that in the realm of private international law, the public policy exception functions as an 'escape mechanism'.[96]

It is useful to consider a recent example where a dispute resolution outcome was not enforced based on the public policy exception: in *Daiichi Sankyo Co Ltd* v. *Malvinder Mohan Singh*,[97] the High Court of New Delhi exercised its discretion on public policy grounds to refuse to enforce part of an international arbitral award, because it bound young children (who were between the ages of eight and twelve when the arbitration was conducted) to be jointly and severally liable to pay the equivalent of more than £400 million in damages, awarded by an arbitral tribunal seated in Singapore.[98] It does not take a stretch of imagination to consider the rendering of such a large sum of damages against minors objectionable on both domestic and international levels of public policy. It is likely that similar considerations would apply when the courts in India – a Party to the Singapore Convention – are presented with an iMSA binding young children for enforcement under the Singapore Convention.

(D) SUBJECT MATTER OF THE DISPUTE IS NOT CAPABLE OF SETTLEMENT BY MEDIATION Article 5(2)(b) of the Singapore Convention provides that the competent authorities may, on their own initiative,[99] refuse to enforce iMSAs if the 'subject matter of the dispute is not capable of settlement by mediation under the law of that [State]'.[100] Here, although the choice of law provided in the Article appears to trigger the *lex fori* of the competent authority, the court should apply and interpret it with similar private international law considerations as the 'public policy' exception, just as it has been discussed and asserted in the previous paragraphs. The subject matter defence is another exceptional 'escape mechanism' defence.[101] Whilst the enforcing court may consider according to its own domestic rules that some subject matter

95 Chong and Steffek, 'Enforcement of International Settlement Agreements Resulting from Mediation under the Singapore Convention: Private International Law Issues in Perspective', above n 21, para. 55; see also Tiong Min Yeo, 'Statute and Public Policy in Private International Law: Gambling Contracts and Foreign Judgments' (2005) 9 *Singapore Yearbook of International Law* 133. The Singapore Court of Appeal has described exceptional circumstances as those which would 'shock the conscience' or be 'clearly injurious to the public good or [. . .] wholly offensive to the ordinary reasonable and fully informed member of the public', or violate 'the forum's most basic notion of morality and justice' (*PT Asuransi Jasa Indonesia (Persero)* v. *Dexia Bank SA* [2007] 1 SLR(R) 597, para. 59).

96 Consider *IPCO Nigeria Ltd* v. *Nigerian National Petroleum Corp* [2005] EWHC 726, para. 13, where in the context of refusing to enforce arbitral awards under the New York Convention by reason of the relevant public policy exception, Gross J warned that 'considerations of public policy, if relied upon to resist enforcement of an [arbitral] award, should be approached with extreme caution[. . .] [the public policy exception] was not intended to furnish an open-ended escape route for refusing enforcement of New York Convention awards'.

97 *Daiichi Sankyo Company Limited* v. *Malvinder Mohan Singh and ors.* (2016) O.M.P.(EFA) (Comm.) 6/2016.

98 Also see *BAZ* v. *BBA and others and other matters* [2018] SGHC 275, especially at para. 169 *et seq*, for a deeper perusal of the facts of this case. Here, the Singapore High Court ruled on an application to set aside the arbitral award. Unusually, the judgment of the New Delhi enforcement proceedings, which were concurrently initiated with the setting aside proceedings in Singapore, was delivered first, before the setting aside proceedings were concluded. If the Singapore judgment had been delivered before the New Delhi proceedings were concluded, the public policy issue raised in the New Delhi court may be rendered moot, as the Singapore High Court eventually also ruled to set aside the award against the children for public policy reasons.

99 Alexander and Chong, *The Singapore Convention on Mediation: A Commentary*, above n 20, para. 5.113; Schnabel, 'The Singapore Convention on Mediation: A Framework for the Cross-Border Recognition and Enforcement of Mediated Settlements', above n 45, 42. Of course, parties remain free to plead for the public policy defence to apply and submit evidence into court accordingly.

100 Singapore Convention, Article 5(2)(b).

101 Alexander and Chong, *The Singapore Convention on Mediation: A Commentary*, above n 20, para. 5.110; Alexander and Chong, 'An Introduction to the Singapore Convention on Mediation – Perspectives from Singapore', above n 30, 49; Schnabel, 'The Singapore Convention on Mediation: A Framework for the Cross-Border Recognition and Enforcement of Mediated Settlements', above n 45, 55.

areas are not susceptible to mediation (for instance, some jurisdictions may consider some intellectual property disputes as not capable of being resolved at mediation),[102] they ought to also appraise the extent to which the subject matter has a sufficient nexus to the forum, before categorically imposing domestic conditions unto the iMSA.[103] In private international law disputes, Born has persuasively argued with the support of precedents (albeit in the context of international commercial arbitration, but this may be justifiably analogized to the international commercial mediation context) that the courts ought to avoid parochialism when administering the 'subject matter' exception.[104] Instead, courts may administer the law of closest-connection to the dispute.[105]

(E) DISCRETION TO REFUSE ENFORCEMENT Finally, we have previously noted, the relevant competent authority *may* refuse to grant enforcement relief if one of the grounds for refusal under Article 5 is proven. This means that the competent authority possesses residual discretion to enforce iMSAs, even if one or more of the grounds for refusal under Article 5 is proved. This wording appears to be drawn from the New York Convention on arbitration and reflects the stance taken in international commercial arbitration.[106] Following conventional practice in arbitration, it is likely that the discretion available in the context of enforcing iMSAs under the Singapore Convention would similarly be exercised within narrow circumstances.[107] There is fertile ground for deeper analysis (going beyond the analogy with arbitration) into the exercise of judicial discretion in relation to the enforcement of iMSAs under the Singapore Convention, as more examples of iMSA enforcement (or challenges to its enforcement) under the Convention are reported in the years after it is signed in Singapore and ratified accordingly into national laws across jurisdictions.

20.3.1.4 Can a Party to the Convention Declare Any Reservations?

Article 8 of the Singapore Convention provides for only two permissible reservations.[108] The first permissible reservation under Article 8(1)(a) broadly permits Parties to the Convention to provide that the Convention does not apply to iMSAs of which it is a party, or of which its government agencies or any person acting on behalf of its govern-

102 For instance, under South Korean law, some intellectual property disputes which touch on validity of intellectual property rights are not capable of settlement at mediation, as it is the orthodox view that such disputes must fall within the exclusive jurisdiction of the Korean Intellectual Property Office: see Gyooho Lee, Keon-Hyung Ahn and Hacques de Werra, 'Euro-Korean Perspectives on the Use of Arbitration and ADR Mechanisms for Solving Intellectual Property Disputes' (2014) 30 *Arbitration International* 91, 104.

103 Chong and Steffek, 'Enforcement of International Settlement Agreements Resulting from Mediation under the Singapore Convention: Private International Law Issues in Perspective', above n 21, para. 75.

104 Born, above n 94, 3702.

105 Take the hypothetical scenario where under the laws of Country X, commercial tax disputes are subject matters incapable of settlement at mediation. The forum of Country X is presented with an iMSA that was concluded in Country Y, of which the choice of law for that settlement points to the laws of Country Z (noting that under the rules of Y and Z tax disputes are susceptible to mediation). If the mediated dispute has *no connection* whatsoever to Country X, the courts of Country X should not refuse relief owing to their convention obligations to enforce dispute resolution outcomes – see Born, above n 94, 606 and 3700.

106 For example, Julian Lew, Loukas Mistelis and Stefan Kröll, *Comparative International Commercial Arbitration* (Kluwer Law International, 2003), paras. 26–68.

107 For example, Hill, above n 58, 333.

108 Singapore Convention, Article 8(2).

ment agency is a party.[109] This reservation may be made if Parties to the Convention wish to carve out civil immunities for their respective government or government agencies, insofar as the Convention applies, possibly for national security or fundamental domestic public policy reasons. However, it should be noted that Parties to the Convention may not exclude the Convention's applicability to state-owned enterprises under this reservation.[110]

The second permissible reservation under Article 8(1)(b) permits Parties to the Convention to reverse the default application of the Convention, by providing for an 'opt-in' regime instead.[111] If a State makes the second reservation, obligations under the Convention would not apply in that State, unless parties to an iMSA have expressly (i.e. in their concluded settlement agreement) agreed that the Singapore Convention would apply as such, thereby opting-in to its regime. When this reservation is made, the 'opt-in' regime will *only* apply in respect of the competent authority where relief is sought; there will be no reciprocal effect on the treatment of iMSAs in other jurisdictions.

At the signing ceremony of the Singapore Convention in August 2019, reservations were made by Belarus (invoking Article 8(1)(a) of the Singapore Convention)[112] and Iran (invoking Article 8(1)(a) and 8(1)(b)).[113] Reservations must be made in accordance with the procedures stated in Article 8(3)–(4) of the Singapore Convention. States are not bound to make all-or-nothing reservations: this means that for the first reservation, States may, for instance, choose which of the three types of entities (i.e., the State itself, its government agencies and persons acting on their behalf) would benefit from this reservation. Article 8(3) permits Parties to the Convention to make reservations at any time. But in any case, Article 8(5) permits Parties to the Convention which have lodged reservations to withdraw them at any time, by lodging a withdrawal notice and depositing it at the depositary.

109 Ibid., Article 8(1)(a).

110 See Intervention of Singapore, in Audio Recording: Working Group II, Sixty-Third Session (United Nations 2015), 8 September 2015, 09:30–12:30, www.uncitral.org/uncitral/audio/meetings.jsp (accessed 20 May 2019). Also see Alexander and Chong, *The Singapore Convention on Mediation: A Commentary*, above n 20, paras. 8.15–8.16.

111 Singapore Convention, Article 8(1)(b).

112 *Reservation made upon signature:*

> In accordance with [A]rticle 8 of the Convention, the Republic of Belarus shall not apply this Convention to settlement agreements to which it is a party, or to which any governmental agencies or any person acting on behalf of a governmental agency is a party.

113 *Declaration made upon signature:*

> The Government of the Islamic Republic of Iran seizes the opportunity at this moment of signing 'the United Nations Convention on International Settlement Agreements Resulting from Mediation', to place on the record its 'understanding' in relation to provisions of the Convention, bearing in mind that the main objective for submitting this declaration is the avoidance of eventual future interpretation of the following articles in a manner incompatible with the original intention and previous positions or in disharmony with national laws and regulations of the Islamic Republic of Iran.
>
> It is the understanding of the Islamic Republic of Iran as well as reservations that:
>
> - [T]he Islamic Republic of Iran has no obligation to apply this Convention to settlement agreements to which it is a party, or to which any governmental agencies or any person acting on behalf of a governmental agency is a party, to the extent specified in the declaration;
> - The Islamic Republic of Iran will apply this Convention only to the extent that the parties to the settlement agreement have agreed to the application of the Convention;
> - The Islamic Republic of Iran may have the choice to make reservations upon ratification;
> - The Islamic Republic of Iran, in accordance with the relevant provisions of the Convention, reserves the right to adopt laws and regulations to co-operate with the States.

20.4 HOW THE SINGAPORE CONVENTION MAY IMPACT DISPUTE RESOLUTION IN INVESTOR–STATE ARRANGEMENTS

As noted elsewhere in this volume,[114] a discernable increase in dissatisfaction with investor–State arbitration is emerging, fuelled by concerns about the cost and length of proceedings as well as the unpredictability of outcomes and problems with compliance.[115] Moreover the European Court of Justice has recently held that EU bilateral investment treaties are incompatible with EU law,[116] a decision which sent shock waves through the investor–State dispute settlement community and the impact of which is still unfolding.[117] Accordingly investor–State dispute settlement finds itself at a turning point and in search of reform options. The signing of the Singapore Convention on Mediation has drawn significant international attention to the role that mediation may play in the international dispute resolution arena. Deliberations about reform of investor–State dispute settlement in UNCITRAL's Working Group III canvass mediation as one of numerous reform options. In his contribution to this volume, Lee highlights the increasing incorporation of mediation provisions in treaties and other international instruments to deal with investment-related disputes. For example, he examines the Korea–EU FTA[118] and Korea–China FTA[119] which both adopt mediation mechanisms to deal with disputes involving Non-Tariff Barriers.[120]

Mediation is attractive as a dispute resolution option, because it provides a flexible dispute resolution procedure with the capacity to address the interests of diverse stakeholders in evolving and complex disputes, comprising political, economic, social, legal and multiple other dimensions. Mediation's procedural agility offers opportunities to design dispute resolution systems that can accommodate needs to preserve the business/investment relationships and balance requirements for confidentiality and transparency in dealing with investment disputes involving States and public interest issues.[121] However, a major critique of mediation in this context is the absence of an expedited enforcement mechanism for

[114] See, e.g., Jaemin Lee, Chapter 19 in this volume.

[115] See Rachel L. Wellhausen, 'Recent Trends in Investor-State Dispute Settlement' (2016) 7 *Journal of International Dispute Settlement* 117, 134.

[116] *Slovak Republic v Achmea B.V.* (Case C-284/16). To briefly summarise, the European Court of Justice (ECJ) ruled that clauses in bilateral investment treaties which establish a mechanism for EU Member State-parties to that treaty to settle disputes between that State-party and an investor *may* run contrary to Article 344 – read with Article 267 – of the Treaty on the Functioning of the EU (TFEU), as it could prevent disputes arising from that investor-State relationship from being resolved in a manner that affords parties the full effectiveness of protections under EU law. Yet, it should be noted that the ECJ caveated, '[A]n international agreement providing for the establishment of a court responsible for the interpretation of its provisions and whose decisions are binding on the institutions, including the Court of Justice, is not in principle incompatible with EU law [...] provided that the autonomy of the EU and its legal order is respected'. (at para. 57).

[117] ASA Board, *The Cost of Achmea* (2018) 36 ASA *Bulletin* 553; Clément Fouchard, 'The Judgment of the CJEU in *Slovak Republic* v. *Achmea* – A Loud Clap of Thunder on the Intra-EU BIT Sky!' *Kluwer Arbitration Blog* (7 March 2018).

[118] Korea–EU FTA, signed on 6 October 2010 (entered into force (provisionally) on 1 July 2011).

[119] Korea–China FTA, signed 1 June 2015 (entered into force on 20 December 2015).

[120] See Jaemin Lee, Chapter 19.

[121] However, also consider the criticisms of how degrees of confidentiality engendered at the mediation or conciliation forum may run contrary to various policies of state: see Susan Frank, 'Reconsidering Dispute Resolution in International Investment Agreements' in Karl P Sauvant (ed.), *Appeals Mechanism in International Investment Disputes* (Oxford University Press, 2008), p. 179.

international mediated settlement agreements.[122] This factor has certainly limited the use of mediation in investor–State disputes.[123]

Empirical evidence indicates that users of dispute resolution procedures for whom expedited enforceability is of critical importance gravitate towards arbitration in relation to their international disputes.[124] However, where relationship preservation is also considered critical, there is a marked shift towards the use of multitiered dispute resolution procedures combining both mediation and arbitration, especially in relation to complex and long-term projects in fields such as energy, construction and investment.[125] In many multiiered procedures, mediated settlement agreements can be recorded as consent arbitral awards; in this form they are said to fall within the scope of the New York Convention on Arbitration.

While it is still early days, the Singapore Convention with its promise of an expedited enforcement regime for mediated settlement agreements, has the potential to change the dispute resolution game in the international investment context.[126]

As indicated earlier, the Singapore Convention focuses on international commercial settlements resulting from mediation. There has been some discussion as to whether the term 'commercial' extends to investor–State matters.[127] The broad definition of 'commercial', examined earlier, suggests that the Convention could indeed apply. Working Group II had drafted the Singapore Convention sufficiently broadly, providing generous latitude for dispute resolution outcomes resulting from investor–State disputes.[128] There appears to be no reason to exclude mediated settlement agreements arising out of investor–State disputes from its application, unless a reservation applies (see Article 8 of the Singapore Convention) to exclude such mediated settlement agreements where the State's government or government agencies are parties. In regards to the term 'commercial', the United States delegate to UNCITRAL Working Group II, Timothy Schnabel, has argued that it could 'include *at least*

122 Chang-Fa Lo, 'Desirability of a New International Legal Framework for Cross-Border Enforcement of Certain Mediated Settlement Agreements' (2014) 7 *Contemporary Asia Arbitration Journal* 119. In any case, one should also consider, whereas the current enforceability mechanisms for dispute resolution outcomes in international arbitration (vis-à-vis the 1958 New York Convention) and litigation (vis-à-vis the 2005 Hague Convention on Choice of Court Agreements or the 2019 Hague Convention on the Recognition and Enforcement of Foreign Judgments in Civil or Commercial Matters) rely heavily on the availability of judicial sanctions (owing to judicial recognition and enforcement of that dispute resolution outcome, *e.g.*, arbitral award or foreign judgment), the ultimate effect as to whether that outcome would be honoured, or if in contrast it would merely remain as a 'paper tiger', remains elusive. Nonetheless it is widely accepted that the threat of judicial sanctions *must compel* parties to honour the dispute resolution outcome to a high degree: such is the extent of conclusiveness of dispute resolution outcomes which enforceability mechanisms promise.

123 Interestingly, this is in spite of widely-accepted knowledge that 'the chances of the parties reneging on their obligations and not performing according to the agreed terms and conditions [of a mediated settlement agreement] is limited': Chang-Fa Lo and Janice Lee, 'A New Approach for the Settlement of Regional Disputes to Maintain Dynamic Stability – A Selective Elaboration of the Draft Agreement of the Establishment of the Asia-Pacific Regional Mediation Organization' (2018) 13(1) *Asian Journal of WTO & International Health Law and Policy* 27, 40–41.

124 See generally, Alexander, Checkley, and Chong et al., above n 12.

125 Consider the Singapore Infrastructure Dispute-Management Protocol, which was recently launched in 2018 (see Janice Heng, 'Singapore launches new dispute management protocol for mega infrastructure Projects' *The Business Times* (23 October 2018)). The Protocol adopts a proactive dispute prevention approach by requiring parties to appoint the Dispute Board from the beginning of the project, instead of only after a dispute has occurred; the Protocol may provide for a range of methods which could assist parties with addressing the said dispute.

126 Christine Sim, 'Conciliation of Investor-State Disputes, Arb-Con-Arb, and the Singapore Convention' (2019) 31 *Singapore Academy of Law Journal* 670.

127 Ibid.; Surya Kapoor, 'How does the Singapore Mediation Convention Affect International Dispute Resolution? – ISDS perspective' *Kluwer Mediation Blog* (November 2019).

128 McCormick and Ong, above n 10, para. 31.

some investor-State disputes in the areas such as construction or natural resource extraction'.[129] Furthermore, Schnabel notes that had the drafters of the Singapore Convention intended to exclude the coverage of investor–State dispute resolution outcomes, they would have provided for it, just as the Hague Conference on Private International Law had done in the Hague Convention of 2 July 2019 on the Recognition and Enforcement of Foreign Judgments in Civil or Commercial Matters, under which judgments arising out of 'administrative matters'[130] are expressly excluded by Article 1(1).

To date the investor–State community has responded positively to the Singapore Convention: by way of example, the ICSID Mediation Rules specifically anticipate that that the Singapore Convention, once in force, will apply to settlements reached in the context of investment disputes[131] As Sim observes:

> The ICSID, currently the institution with the world's largest caseload in administering investor–State arbitration, has already referred to the possibility of using the Singapore Mediation Convention in its 2018 reform of the ICSID Conciliation Rules. The ICSID amendments to the ICSID Conciliation Rules have been drafted in a manner to allow such an agreement to fall within the purview of the [. . .] Singapore Mediation Convention on enforcement of mediated [settlement agreements].[132]

20.5 CONCLUSION

The Singapore Convention promises to leave a significant impact on international dispute resolution practices and, beyond that, on trade and investment flows.[133] It has the capacity to enhance the attractiveness of mediation within regional initiatives, such as the Belt and Road Initiative,[134] and to support the regulatory robustness of cross-border online dispute resolution initiatives.[135] This capacity will, in turn, enhance access to justice and the efficacy of dispute resolution for users across borders. Disputes of an investor–State nature are not marginalized

[129] Schnabel, 'The Singapore Convention on Mediation: A Framework for the Cross-Border Recognition and Enforcement of Mediated Settlements', above n 45, 22–23.

[130] Here Schnabel's working assumption would be that subject matters as to an investor–State relationship flowing from an international investment agreement between States and other States or investors would be more appropriately and substantially be framed as issues governed by administrative law.

[131] 'Annex E: (Additional Facility) Mediation Rules', in ICSID Secretariat, *Proposals for Amendment of the ICSID Rules – Working Paper* (Volume 3) (2 August 2018), p. 748ff.

[132] Sim, above n 127, para. 44. For further examples see Jaemin Lee's Chapter 19.

[133] For example, Sussman has observed that the Singapore Convention has so far inspired "the proposed changes to the ICSID rules on conciliation [which] specifically suggests that the parties sign a settlement agreement [which may be embodied in a conciliation Report] so that parties in ICSID conciliation proceedings can benefit from the enforcement regime for mediated settlements contemplated by the Singapore Convention" (Edna Sussman, 'The Singapore Convention – Promoting the Enforcement and Recognition of International Mediated Settlement Agreements' (2018) 3 *ICC Dispute Resolution Bulletin* 42, at 54, citing ICSID Secretariat, *Proposals for Amendment of the ICSID Rules – Synopsis*, Volume 1 (2 August 2018), para. 95).

[134] According to the World Bank, the Belt and Road Initiative (BRI) is an effort initiated by China to improve regional cooperation and connectivity between continents, endeavouring to build robust infrastructure, trade and investment ties between China and at least 65 other countries which, together, account for over 30 per cent of global Gross Domestic Product (GDP), 62 per cent of the world's population, and 57 per cent of known exploited energy reserves. See the World Bank website at www.worldbank.org/en/topic/regional-integration /brief/belt-and-road-initiative (Accessed 3 March 2019).

[135] See, for example, the proposed APEC-wide ODR framework that is set to provide access to commercial justice for micro, small and medium enterprises (MSMEs) in cross-border B2B disputes. APEC is the Asia-Pacific Economic Cooperation. See *APEC Draft Collaborative Framework for Online Dispute Resolution of Cross-Border E-Commerce Business to Business Disputes* (2018).

from the Convention's purview, but this is subject to whether Parties to the Convention have made the relevant reservations under Article 8(1)(a).[136] From a user perspective, the Singapore Convention offers a risk management mechanism accessible in terms of its flexibility and affordability to cross-border business players, whether they are States, multinational corporations, publicly listed corporations, traditional incorporated limited entities, sole traders or start-ups.

[136] McCormick and Ong, above n 10, para. 31. Take for instance, Belarus and Iran have made the Article 8(1)(a) reservation, as discussed earlier in the chapter.

PART VI

What Lies Ahead?

21

Reconciling Public Interests with Private Interests in International Investment Arbitration and Securing Effective Remedy for Investment–Related Human Rights Violations

Surya P Subedi, QC[*]

21.1 INTRODUCTION

The law of foreign investment has developed over several centuries in response to changing political and economic events. It has evolved in response to the challenges brought about by the industrial revolution during which the people of the industrial world ventured out to new territories to invest in the acquisition of exotic products and raw material; the wave of independence of the Latin American colonial territories, seeking to assert economic sovereignty, and to re-write the law of foreign investment following their political independence; the challenges brought by the Russian revolution to foreign-owned property in that country; the attempts made by the Asian, African and Latin American States in the immediate aftermath of the Second World War when these States were seeking to assert full economic and permanent sovereignty over their natural resources; the attempts made by the developing countries to bring about fundamental changes to the law on international economic relations under the notion of the New International Economic Order, and the subsequent wave of expropriations and nationalization in the 1960s and 1970s; the end of the Cold War, the collapse of the old political order and the ideological triumph of the West; and the excesses of foreign investors undermining the very State authority that accorded them their protection in the first place. After witnessing various upheavals in the past fifty years or so, the law of foreign investment appears to be going through a particularly interesting phase in its development at this juncture and this phase is characterized by the tension between public interests with private interests in international investment arbitration and the perceived need to secure effective remedy for investment-related human rights violations.[1]

[*] An earlier version of this chapter was presented as a keynote speech at an International Seminar on 'Regulation and Investment Disputes: Asian Perspectives' at Singapore Management University, Singapore, 4 August 2016. In this chapter, the author also draws on his earlier paper, Surya P Subedi QC, 'International Law Response to Land Grabbing in Asia', in Connie Carter and Andrew Harding (eds.), *Land Grabs in Asia: What Role for the Law?* (Abingdon: Routledge, 2015), pp. 24–34.

[1] See generally, M. Sornarajah, *The International Law on Foreign Investment* (Cambridge: Cambridge University Press, 2010); G van Harten, *Investment Treaty Arbitration and Public Law* (Oxford: Oxford University Press, 2007); S Montt, *State Liability in Investment Treaty Arbitration: Global Constitutional and Administrative Law in the BIT Generation* (Oxford: Hart Publishing, 2011); UNCTAD, *Investor–State Disputes: Prevention and Alternatives to Arbitration* (UNCTAD Series on International Investment Policies for Development, United Nations, New York and Geneva, 2010); Campbell McLachlan et al., *International Investment Arbitration: Substantive Principles* (Oxford: Oxford University Press, 2007); R. Dolzer and C. Schreur, *Principles of International Investment Law* (Oxford: Oxford University Press, 2008); P. Muchlinski et al., *The Oxford Handbook of International Investment Law* (Oxford: Oxford University Press, 2008); Campbell McLachlan et al., *International Investment Arbitration:*

The tension that has been witnessed in recent years between the law of foreign investment which guarantees investors' protections and legitimate expectations, on one hand, and the need not to unduly restrict the right of host governments to implement their public policy, including the protection of the environment and human rights, and the promotion of social and economic justice within the host country, on the other, is the result of the growing concern about the trend in jurisprudence in this area of law, about the gradual dissatisfaction with the investor–State dispute settlement (ISDS) mechanism itself and the gradual rejection of the institution of bilateral investment agreements (BITs) or international investment agreements (IIAs).[2]

The issues relating to the need to reconcile public interests with private interests within international investment law has in recent years received attention far beyond the confines of a small group of investment negotiators, practitioners and academics, as well as the sporadic involvement of non-governmental organizations. Different stakeholders from various walks of life are increasingly interested in investment law matters, especially the ISDS mechanism. The main concerns for these stakeholders seem to be with the ISDS mechanism due to the alleged or apparent inconsistencies in arbitral decision-making, insufficient regard by some arbitral tribunals to the host State's right to regulate in interpreting IIAs, BITs or free trade agreements (FTAs), charges of bias of the system in favour of foreign investors, concerns about the lack of independence and impartiality of arbitrators, and the absence of an appellate mechanism to harmonize their decisions.[3]

The very States which decided to constrain their policy space by entering into BITs have now decided to reverse their decision and started to reject such treaties. This is partly because some international investment tribunals started according a meaning to certain provisions in the treaties that differ significantly in scope and breadth from what the States had originally

Substantive Principles (Oxford: Oxford University Press, 2007); I. Tudor, *The Fair and Equitable Treatment Standard in International Foreign Investment Law* (Oxford: Oxford University Press, 2008); P. Muchlinski (eds.), *Multinational Enterprises & the Law* (Oxford: Oxford University Press, 2007); JW Salacuse, *The Law of International Investment Treaties* (Oxford: Oxford University Press, 2010); Christina Binder et al., (eds.), *International Investment Law for the 21st Century: Essays in Honour of Christoph Schreuer* (Oxford: Oxford University Press, 2009); A. F. Lowenfeld (eds.), *International Economic Law* (Oxford: Oxford University Press, 2008); M. Sornarajah, *Resistance and Change in the International Law of Foreign Investment* (Cambridge University Press, 2015).

2 See for example UNCTAD, 'Reforming the international investment regime: an action menu' (June 2015), http://unctad.org/en/PublicationChapters/wir2015ch4_en.pdf (last accessed 23 September 2019); UNCTAD, 'World Investment Report 2015' (2015) available at http://unctad.org/en/PublicationsLibrary/wir2015_en.pdf (last accessed 23 September 2019); M. Waibel, et al., (eds.), *The Backlash Against Investment Treaty Arbitration: Perceptions and Reality* (Kluwer 2010); G. Van Harten, 'A case for an international investment court' (Presentation at Society of International Economic Law Conference 2008) available at http://papers.ssrn.com/sol3/papers.cfm?abstract_id=1153424 (last accessed 23 September 2019); J. Kalicki and A. Joubin-Bret (eds.), *Reshaping the Investor-State Dispute Settlement System* (Brill, 2015); N. Hachez and J. Wouters, 'International investment dispute settlement in the 21st century: does the preservation of the public interest require an alternative to the arbitral model' (2012) Leuven Centre for Global Governance Studies, Working Paper No. 81, available at https://ghum.kuleuven.be/ggs/publications/working_papers/new_series/wp81-90/wp-81-hachez-wouters-iil-arbitration-and-the.pdf last accessed 23 September 2019); and S. Schill, 'Editorial: Towards a Normative Framework for Investment Law Reform', (2014) 15 *Journal of World Investment and Trade* 795.

3 Some of the most famous examples of such inconsistent decisions include *CME* and *Lauder* (*CME Czech Republic B.V.* v. *Czech Republic*, Ad hoc – UNCITRAL Arbitration Rules, Partial Award of 13 September 2001 and IIC 62 (2003), Final Award of 14 March 2003 and *Lauder* v. *Czech Republic*, Final Award, 3 September 2001 (Ad hoc – UNCITRAL Arbitration Rules)) as well as the SGS cases (*SGS Société Générale de Surveillance S. A.* v. *Islamic Republic of Pakistan* ICSID Case No. ARB/01/13 (2003) 42 ILM 1290 and SGS *Société Générale de Surveillance S.A.* v. *Republic of the Philippines* ICSID Case No. ARB/02/6 (2004)). For academic commentary of inconsistencies see for example S. Franck, 'The Legitimacy Crisis in Investment Treaty Arbitration: Privatizing Public International Law through Inconsistent Decisions' (2005) 73 *Fordham Law Review* 1521.

intended to mean. The view was that by being creative and adopting an expansive approach in treaty interpretation, these tribunals were encroaching upon the policy space of States.[4] The issues of legitimacy, accountability, transparency and fairness associated with the workings of such tribunals, the propriety of the selection process of the arbitrators and their integrity as well as the absence of an appeal mechanism against their decisions have contributed to the growing opposition to the ISDS mechanism.[5]

Some commentators have gone further and have challenged the compatibility of the current ISDS mechanism with the notion of human rights or the rule of law. For instance, the UN Independent expert on the promotion of a democratic and equitable international order, Alfred de Zayas, stated in his report submitted to the UN Human Rights Council in September 2015 that the ISDS mechanism 'has mutated into a privatized system of "justice", incompatible with Article 14(1) of the International Covenant on Civil and Political Rights, whereby three arbitrators are allowed to override national legislation and the judgments of the highest national tribunals, in secret and with no possibility to appeal. This constitutes a grave challenge to the very essence of the rule of law'.[6]

The growing opposition to BITs or ISDS is partly due to the confidence that many largely democratic countries in the developing world such as India, Indonesia and South Africa have in their own national legal and judicial systems. They appear to imply that foreign investors should be comfortable with the protection of the right to property under their individual constitutions and under the international human rights treaties ratified by them. Compounding this confidence is their deep dissatisfaction with some of the rulings of ICSID panels, both initial and annulment, and other UNCITRAL arbitration panels in the face of their ostensible failure to balance private interests with public interests and between competing principles within international law in general and international investment law in particular.[7]

It is not only developing countries, but also the developed countries that have become growingly vigilant about the ISDS mechanism. This trend engendered an increasing appreciation for the need to protect the regulatory freedom of host States and limit arbitral discretion. A number of cases have been brought against developed States themselves, including the United States, Canada, Australia and Germany. Indeed, some high-profile regulatory disputes, like Germany being sued over its decision to phase out nuclear power and

[4] E. Neumayer and L. Spess, 'Do Bilateral Investment Treaties Increase Foreign Direct Investment to Developing Countries?' (2005) 33 *World Development* 1567; H. Mann and K. von Moltke, 'A Southern Agenda on Investment? Promoting Development with Balanced Rights and Obligations for Investors, Host States and Home States' (2005) IISD and K. Sauvant and L. Sachs, *The Effect of Treaties on Foreign Direct Investment: Bilateral Investment Treaties, Double Taxation Treaties and Investment Flows* (USA: Oxford University Press, 2009); E. Aisbett, 'Bilateral Investment Treaties and Foreign Direct Investment' in K. Sauvant and L. Sachs (eds.), *The Effect of Treaties on Foreign Direct Investment* (OUP, 2009); L Poulsen 'The Importance of BITs for Foreign Direct Investment and Political Risk Insurance: Revisiting the Evidence' in K Sauvant (eds.), *Yearbook on International Investment Law and Policy* (OUP, 2010); J Yackee, 'Do Bilateral Investment Treaties Promote Foreign Direct Investment? Some Hints from Alternative Evidence' (2010) 51 *Virginia Journal of International Law* 397; C. Peinhardt and T. Allee, 'Failure to Deliver: The Investment Effects of US Preferential Economic Agreements' (2012) 35 *The World Economy* 757, and S Jandhyala and R Weiner, 'Institutions Sans Frontieres: International Agreements and Foreign Investment' (2014) 45 *Journal of International Business Studies* 649.

[5] G. Van Harten, 'Private Authority and Transnational Governance: The Contours of the International System of Investor Protection' (2005) 12 *Review of International Political Economy* 600.

[6] Report of the UN Independent expert on the promotion of a democratic and equitable international order: UN Doc A/HRC/30/44 of 14 July 2015.

[7] Catharine Titi, 'Investment Arbitration in Latin America: The Uncertain Veracity of Preconceived Ideas' (2014), 30 (2) *Arbitration International* 357–86.

Australia being sued over its tobacco packaging regulations, have made capital exporting countries themselves cautious about the ISDS mechanism in its current form.

A growing number of new model BITs or IIAs themselves have started to include provisions designed to admit non-compensable regulatory expropriation. The 2012 Model BIT of the United States is an example. Another example of State practice in this direction is the 2011 India–Nepal BIT which defines in Article 5(2) the nature and scope of regulatory expropriation. The definition of regulatory expropriation in this BIT is an attempt to reconcile the law on foreign investment protection with other competing principles of international law.[8]

It respects the sovereignty of States and enables them to fulfil their commitments flowing from other international treaties or to pursue bona fide economic, environmental, health and safety-related policies in the greater interest of the native residents in the host countries. If the trend of accepting legitimate or bona fide governmental measures undertaken in a non-discriminatory manner for good environmental, health or safety causes as non-compensable regulatory expropriation continues, bona fide governmental measures to protect core human rights will soon be subsumed under the definition of regulatory expropriation as well.

Since the trend emerging in the jurisprudence of international investment tribunals is to extend BIT protection to companies affected negatively by investment contracts, albeit under narrowly defined conditions, it could be argued that the real victims of the activities of foreign investors which undermine human rights and the environment should also be given access to international investment tribunals to present their cases under narrowly defined conditions and especially in cases of gross violations of human rights and massive degradation of the local environment. A few attempts have been made to sue foreign companies in domestic courts for polluting the local environment. However, under the existing international legal framework the real victims of the violations of human rights and the degradation of the local environment have no effective legal remedy before international courts and tribunals against the perpetrators of such violations. The real victims of the Bhopal gas disaster did not have any legal remedy against the Union Carbide company before any international tribunal. They were at the mercy of the federal Indian government to pursue the case on their behalf against the company. However, if Union Carbide had been severely negatively affected by the activities of the people or the Government of India, the company could have brought a claim before an international tribunal.

Most of the IIAs impose obligations on States, define their responsibilities and provide protection to foreign investors. This is basically a one-way traffic. It is in this context that this chapter examines some possible options designed to reconcile public interests with private interests in international investment arbitration and to secure an effective remedy for investment-related human rights violations globally in general and in Asia in particular. In doing so, this chapter will focus on the human rights issues raised by economic and other land concessions in many developing countries and various options for remedy for those adversely affected by such concessions.

8 Article 5(c) of the 2011 Indo–Nepal BIT reads as follows: 'Non-discriminatory regulatory measures by a Contracting Party that are designed and applied to protect legitimate public welfare objectives including the protection of health, safety and environment do not constitute expropriation or nationalization; except in rare circumstances, where those measures are so severe that they cannot be reasonably viewed as having been adopted and applied in good faith for achieving their objectives. (d) Actions and awards by judicial bodies of a Contracting Party that are designed, applied or issued in public interest including those designed to address health, safety and environmental concerns, do not constitute expropriation or nationalization.' See Surya P Subedi QC, 'India's New Bilateral Investment Promotion and Protection Treaty with Nepal: A New Trend in State Practice' (2013) 28 (2) *ICSID Review: Foreign Investment Law Journal* (Oxford: Oxford University Press), 384–404.

21.2 HUMAN RIGHTS FOUNDATIONS OF INTERNATIONAL INVESTMENT LAW

One of the principal objectives of the early international human rights treaties was to protect the right to property of natural and juridical persons investing their capital abroad. When people speak of business and human rights the business community often gets jittery about it, believing that the agenda is to lay blame at the doors of the business organizations for violations of human rights by their activities. The coin of the agenda of business and human rights has two sides to it. The other side of the coin is to promote human rights in such a manner that the regime of protection of foreign investors becomes more robust. For instance, as the UN Special Rapporteur for human rights for Cambodia, the present author focused his first substantial report on the reform of the judiciary in the country with a view to enhancing the independence and capacity of the judiciary to dispense impartial, speedy and efficient justice to all.

He went on to great lengths to persuade the government to buy the idea that the more robust the judiciary was and was seen to be robust the more the confidence the international community would have in investing serious money in Cambodia. The government finally heeded the message and enacted three fundamental laws to reform the judiciary in order to make it more independent, robust, and resourceful. Therefore, a way forward would be to locate IIAS and investment protection within broader human rights framework underpinned by international human rights treaties adopted under the auspices of the UN. The better the situation of human rights in a given country the better the protection foreign investors would have in the country regardless of the existence of an IIA or BIT.

Even if the current regime of investment protection through BITs were to be phased out, international human rights standards will remain applicable.[9] The concepts such as the denial of justice under regional and international human rights treaties and the rule of law in its broadest sense are likely to be invoked by foreign investors to sue host governments for compensation for their failings in protecting foreign investors under these human rights standards.[10] Supposing that the ICSID were to cease to exist, there is nothing to prevent foreign investors from suing host governments before other human rights mechanisms, such as the European Court of Human Rights, or to national courts themselves in the host countries.[11]

Indeed, invoking the right to property under the European Convention on Human Rights and especially its Option Protocol 1, some foreign investors have gone to the European Court of Human Rights against some governments whose financial decisions have had a detrimental impact on the investment of foreign investors.

Individual human rights such as property rights and the right to equality have long been relied upon to seek protection for foreign investors. However, now it seems that the very law of foreign investment could limit the attempts by host States to promote workers' rights and other labour rights if they interfere with the activities of foreign investors. Therefore, the need

[9] For example see the Bingham Centre for the Rule of Law and Investment Treaty Forum, 'Risk and Return: Foreign Direct Investment and the Rule of Law' (2015), 17 and Surya P Subedi QC, 'The Universality of Human Rights and the UN Human Rights Agenda: The Impact of the Shift of Power to the East and the Resurgence of the BRICS' (2015) *Indian Journal of International Law* 177.

[10] Jan Paulsson, *Denial of Justice in International Law* (Cambridge: Cambridge University Press, 2005).

[11] See generally, Uche E Ofodile, 'Foreign Investment in Land and the Clash of Regimes: Mapping the Role of International Law and International Human Rights Law' (2013) 7 *Human Rights and International Legal Discourse* 56.

is to make a contribution to the development of international investment law in a manner which regards this body of law as part of a wider family of public international law that is capable of reconciling competing principles and interests.

21.3 PROTECTION OF LAND RIGHTS AND INVESTMENT PROTECTION

One important area of business or international investment in which the protection of human rights has remained weak is economic or other land concessions in which a host government allows foreign investors to use land in the country for commercial activities for a long period of time with a view ostensibly to generate the revenue needed for economic development of the country. However, serious human rights issues arise when the government in the country concerned evicts people from their land to make way for economic land concessions. A land concession is a contract between the government and a state or private actor that gives that actor specific rights (e.g. exclusive rights to manage and harvest the land) normally for a long period of time, but not ownership.[12] This phenomenon is known as land-grabbing in many developing countries of Asia, Africa and Latin America.

The main method used for land-grabbing or land acquisition in these countries in transition has been economic land concessions and other land concessions (generally referred to as 'land concessions') includes not only acquisition of land for agro-industry (e.g. rubber, sugar, acacia, and cassava plantations), but also for mining, oil and gas, forestry and for the purposes of tourism, property development, and large scale development projects, such as hydropower dams.

It should be recognized that as developing countries these countries in transition may wish to utilize their land and natural resources in order for the country to develop and become more prosperous. Nevertheless, the problem arises when land concessions are not granted and managed within a sound legal and policy framework, with due consideration for and consultation with those who will be affected, and with the sustainable use of natural resources in mind.

This is because the human cost of many such concessions has been high and the poorest of the poor have suffered the most. It is not clear how many of the people in these countries have actually benefitted from land concession and many such concessions often have a dimension of corruption because they operate behind a veil of secrecy. There are far too many land disputes associated with economic or other land concessions that remain unresolved and they are having a negative impact on the lives and livelihood of the rural and urban poor, the indigenous people, and other traditional communities.

[12] See generally L. Cotula et al., Land Grab or Development Opportunity? Agricultural Investment And International Land Deals In Africa (IIED/FAO/IFAD, 2009); K Barney, A Note on Forest Land Concessions, Social Conflicts, and Poverty in the Mekong Region proceedings: International Conference on Poverty Reduction and Forests (Proceedings of the International Conference on Poverty Reduction and Forests, Bangkok, 2007); S.M. Borras et al., 'Towards a Better Understanding of Global Land Grabbing: An Editorial Introduction' (2011) 38 *The Journal of Peasant Studies* 209; O. De Schutter, 'How Not to Think of Land-Grabbing: Three Critiques of Large-Scale Investments in Farmland' (2011) 38 *The Journal of Peasant Studies* 249; Ruth Hall, 'Land grabbing in Southern Africa: The Many Faces of the Investor Rush' (2011) 38 *Review of African Political Economy* 193; Food and Agricultural Organization, *Voluntary Guidelines on the Responsible Governance of Tenure of Land, Fisheries and Forests in the Context of National Food Security* (2012); A. Zoomers, 'Globalisation and the Foreignisation of Space: Seven Processes Driving the Current Global Land Grab' (2010) 37 *The Journal of Peasant Studies* 429.

In spite of the gravity of the problem of land-grabbing across Asia and some other countries in Africa and elsewhere and its impact on the people in society, the response to this problem in law, both national and international, has remained weak. There is no specific 'hard law' instrument in international law to deal with the challenges posed by land-grabbing. What we have is only an assortment of provisions in various 'soft-law' instruments which touch on certain aspects of the problem of land-grabbing.

What is at stake with regard to the problem of land-grab is the right to property itself. The Magna Carta, the English Bill of Rights, and American and French Revolutions were inspired by the people's right to property against state interference. This right is at the heart of the rule of law, democracy and human rights. Under international law, the right to property (especially of foreigners or foreign investors) has been protected for a long time. The land belonging to individuals can be taken by the State only under certain conditions recognized in international law. The conditions for the acquisition, expropriation or nationalization of land are as follows:

- Compensation must be given.
- It must be carried out in a non-discriminatory manner.
- It must be carried out with due process of law.
- It must be for a bona fide public purpose.

The Universal Declaration of Human Rights (UDHR) recognized all individuals' right to property. However, the Cold War politics resulted in the International Bill of Human Rights (International Covenant on Civil and Political Rights (ICCPR) and International Covenant on Economic, Social and Cultural Rights (ICESCR)) not guaranteeing the right to property. Since UDHR has now been widely regarded to have acquired customary international law character the rights embodied in it are regarded as binding on all States. When the 192 UN nations met in 2005 in New York they agreed that the UDHR is a binding legal document. This is a clear endorsement of the UDHR's legal and binding nature. Across Asia, land is typically divided into four categories:

- State public land – land which is protected by law and difficult to encroach upon
- State private land – land which the state can sell off to individuals and companies
- Private land – land owned by private individuals
- Community land – land owned by indigenous or other peoples, which the state cannot encroach upon.

In many countries, state public land is being converted to state private land. State public land belongs to the people but when it is reclassified as state private land, legal protection is stripped from the land and the state obtains the power to sell the land. Problems also arise when governments sell off land with national parks, wildlife sanctuaries, protected areas, multiple-use areas, national heritage sites, marine parks and biosphere resources on them. Pursuant to international conventions on the protection of such lands, States do conserve large tracts of them. Since demand is growing, there is a tendency to encroach on and reclassify these lands. This is happening across Asia. However, there is no hard law instrument to guide States on how to harness their land resources and there is no effective dispute resolution mechanism either for individuals seeking legal redress. When disputes arise, foreign investors can sue the host government before an international tribunal. However, this facility is not available to individuals. National mechanisms are not strong enough because the right to property is not well protected in national legal systems.

21.4 BUSINESS AND HUMAN RIGHTS FRAMEWORK WITHIN THE UN SYSTEM

Within the UN human rights system, none of the nine or ten treaty bodies is competent to deal with issues related to land grabbing. None of the 130 international human rights instruments has a clear mandate to deal with land grabs. UN Special Rapporteur reports have submitted recommendations to governments through the UN Human Rights Council but, from experience, in the absence of a proper follow up mechanism, these recommendations are not translated into law.

The United Nations Declaration on the Rights of Indigenous Peoples[13] is a major 'soft law' instrument which provides an international normative foundation for the legal framework on the recognition and registration of indigenous peoples and their right to collective land title. The adoption of the Declaration was the result of culmination of decades of advocacy for indigenous peoples' rights and explicitly lays out rights to land, culture, livelihood and consultation, among other things.

Another instrument of significance is the Basic Principles and Guidelines on Development based Displacement and Evictions of 2007, developed by the Special Rapporteur on adequate housing. It provides a baseline standard related to the relocation of people affected by land concessions.[14] The Guidelines recommend States to explore all possible alternatives to evictions and to ensure full consultation and participation of affected communities throughout the entire process, as well as provide adequate compensation and restitution.[15]

An international instrument of major significance is the Guiding Principles on Business and Human Rights (Guiding Principles) adopted unanimously by the United Nations Human Rights Council in June 2011.[16] While not a legally binding document, this endorsement established the Guiding Principles as the authoritative global reference point, clarifying business accountability and the responsibilities of the State. It should be noted that the concept of business and human rights includes efforts of corporate social responsibility but international standards impose obligations that are neither voluntary nor ad hoc.[17]

The Guiding Principles are grounded in recognition of States' existing obligations to respect, protect and fulfil human rights and fundamental freedoms. The Guiding Principles apply to all business enterprises, both transnational and others, regardless of their size, sector, location, ownership and structure.[18] Therefore, *all* businesses involved in

[13] UNGA Res 61/295, UN Doc A/61/PV.107 (13 September 2007).

[14] Basic Principles and Guidelines on Development-Based Evictions and Displacement, A/HRC/4/18: Annex 1 of the report of the Special Rapporteur on adequate housing as a component of the right to an adequate standard of living.

[15] The Office of the United Nations High Commissioner for Human Rights in Cambodia published in December 2009 the 'United Nations Commentary and Guidelines on Eviction and Resettlement'(which was reprinted in June 2013), available at http://cambodia.ohchr.org/en/content/united-nations-commentary-and-guidelines-eviction-and-resettlement (last accessed 23 September 2019).

[16] See UN HRC, 'Human Rights and Transnational Corporations and other Business Enterprises' (UN Doc A/HRC/17/L.17/Rev.1 (15 June 2011)). The Guiding Principles on Business and Human Rights are contained in the annex to the 'Report of the Special Representative of the Secretary-General on the Issue of Human Rights and Transnational Corporations and other Business Enterprises' (UN Doc A/HRC/17/31 (21 March 2011)), available at www.ohchr.org/Documents/Issues/Business/A-HRC-17-31_AEV.pdf (last accessed 23 September 2019); see also 'Guiding Principles on Human Rights: Implementing the United Nations' Protect, Respect and Remedy' Framework', available at www.ohchr.org/Documents/Publications/GuidingPrinciplesBusinessHR_EN.pdf (last accessed 23 September 2019).

[17] Ibid.

[18] See generally, Nadia Bernaz, *Business and Human Rights* (Routledge, London, New York, 2016).

land concessions in the host State, including businesses operations from foreign countries (the home States) bear the responsibility to protect against human rights violations.

The Guiding Principles are a set of thirty-one standards to support the implementation of the United Nations 'Protect, Respect and Remedy' policy framework.[19] They are the product of six years of research and extensive consultations involving governments, businesses enterprises and associations, civil society, affected individuals and communities, and investors. They highlight what steps States should take to foster businesses' respect for human rights, providing a standard for stakeholders to monitor and assess these steps, and show how businesses can become aware and demonstrate to others that they respect human rights and reduce the risk of causing or contributing to human rights harm. They also stipulate what both States and business enterprises should do to enhance access to effective remedies for those whose rights have been harmed.

There are a myriad of other standards that set out the international legal obligations of States for addressing environmental and social impact of economic or other land concessions. Business enterprises are internationally obliged to carry out 'due diligence', that is to identify, prevent, mitigate, and account for how they address their adverse human rights impacts.[20] Not only do businesses have this responsibility, but it is the duty of the State to ensure proper management and monitoring of this function. As noted earlier, States have the duty to protect against human rights abuses by third parties in their country or area of jurisdiction. Moreover, they are obligated in their international human rights obligations to exercise adequate oversight when they contract with or legislate for business enterprises.

The process for both States and businesses should include assessing the actual and potential human rights impacts, integrating and acting upon the findings, tracking responses, and communicating how such impacts are addressed. This applies to all State and donor-operated projects and to all business enterprises, regardless of size (whether transnational corporations, conglomerates, or small and medium owned enterprises), sector, structure, ownership, or country of domicile or operation (national or foreign). In the context of land concessions, it may refer directly to the environmental and social impact – carrying out assessments with good faith participation of all those affected.

Moreover, the assessment of the impact should be participatory and development planning should be inclusive of all those potentially affected. The International Covenant on Civil and Political Rights and on Economic, Social and Cultural Rights both recognize the right of all individuals and peoples to 'freely pursue their economic, social and cultural development'. The United Nations Declaration on the Right to Development[21] laid the foundation for participation and consultation in development processes, which was complemented by references in the United Nations Declaration on the Rights of Indigenous Peoples, which

19 The 'Protect, Respect and Remedy' policy framework was unanimously welcomed in 2008 by the United Nations Human Rights Council: Human Rights Council, 'Protect, Respect and Remedy: a Framework for Business and Human Rights: Report of the Special Representative of the Secretary-General on the Issue of Human Rights and Transnational Corporations and other Business Enterprises' (UN Doc A/HRC/8/5 (7 April 2008)); Human Rights Council, 'Report of the Special Representative of the Secretary-General on the Issue of Human Rights and Transnational Corporations and other Business Enterprises: Addendum – Summary of Five Multi-Stakeholder Consultations' (UN Doc A/HRC/8/5/Add.1) (23 April 2008).

20 'Guiding Principles on Human Rights: Implementing the United Nations' Protect, Respect and Remedy' Framework', 17–24, available at www.ohchr.org/Documents/Publications/GuidingPrinciplesBusinessHR_EN.pdf (last accessed 23 September 2019).

21 UNGA Res 41/128 (UN Doc A/RES/41/128 (4 December 1986)). Article 1 states that everyone is 'entitled to participate in, contribute to, and enjoy economic, social, cultural and political development'.

upholds free, prior, and informed consent.[22] In addition to the international human rights obligations of States and businesses, there are practical, operational and logistical reasons for incorporating these requirements in business and development activities, and many governments have incorporated these standards into their national laws and policies, and companies into their standard operations.[23]

With regard to access to an effective remedy, there are several non-judicial and quasi-judicial mechanisms for dispute resolution, including the various levels of the cadastral system. However, the time-consuming administrative and procedural burden, financial costs associated with submitting a complaint (although there are no official fees, as with courts, transportation, lost wages, legal assistance, and so on, can prove costly for individuals), and a lack of faith in the system means that these mechanisms are being used inconsistently. What is more, experience has demonstrated that decisions by such bodies are inconsistent, irregular, and subject to political interference.

Most of the countries in transition have no independent national human rights institution. Owing to an uneven application of the relatively well-developed legal framework governing land rights, and an inadequate access to remedies, communities are becoming increasingly frustrated and disillusioned by formal judicial and administrative processes. Demonstrations and protests by affected communities are increasing and have become more violent. The proliferation of displays of discontent around the countries related to land disputes point to inadequate consultation and negotiation with those affected. Early and inclusive consultation can address the tensions before they escalate and contribute to preventing disputes. The United Nations Guiding Principles on Business and Human Rights promotes the use of 'operational-level' grievance mechanisms to facilitate addressing disputes early and directly. These mechanisms should be accessible directly to individuals and communities who may be adversely impacted by business activities, and are typically administered by business enterprises alone or with the collaboration of local authorities and civil society organizations.[24] Some concession companies have set up procedures to deal with local level disputes and complaints, which can be an effective way of directly addressing misinformation and addressing tensions before they escalate.

The majority of the challenges in the countries in transition with regard to the granting and management of economic and other land concessions derive from a failure to properly apply the domestic legal framework – that is, the laws, policies and regulations that the government itself has developed. The granting and management of economic and other land concessions in these countries suffer from a lack of transparency and adherence to existing laws and there is no robust

22 UNDRIP, A/RES/61/295 (13 September 2007) Article 32(2). For a practical guide on FPIC, see Oxfam, 'Guide to Free, Prior and Informed Consent' (27 July 2010).

23 For commentaries on the utility of human rights policies for businesses, see Business and Human Rights Resource Centre, 'Commentaries on human rights policies', available at www.business-humanrights.org /ToolsGuidancePortal/Policies/Commentaries (last accessed 23 September 2019) and for a list of companies which have incorporated human rights into their statements, see 'Company Policy Statements on Human Rights', available at www.business-humanrights.org/en/company-policy-statements-on-human-rights (last accessed 23 September 2019).

For a list of member companies of the Global Business Initiative on Human Rights, see www.global-business-initiative.org/Members.html (last accessed 23 September 2019). Of these members, at least Chevron, Sime Darby, General Electric, Unilever, Coca Cola, Novo Nordisk and Total operate in Cambodia.

24 'Guiding Principles on Human Rights: Implementing the United Nations' Protect, Respect and Remedy' Framework', 28–31, available at www.ohchr.org/Documents/Publications/GuidingPrinciplesBusinessHR_EN .pdf (last accessed 23 September 2019).

system of monitoring compliance by governments and local councils of the standards set out earlier.

21.5 MANAGING ECONOMIC AND OTHER LAND CONCESSIONS WITHIN A LEGAL FRAMEWORK

The response of international law to the challenges posed by land-grabbing is weak and inadequate. Therefore, there is a need for negotiation and the eventual adoption of a sector specific binding international legal instrument to address the challenges posed by land-grabbing which can consolidate and strengthen the provisions to be found in some of the international 'soft law' instruments examined earlier and develop new principles vis-à-vis land grabbing and protection of the rights of the people evicted from their land or facing the threat of eviction. This would make States accountable for failures to comply with international law standards. Such an instrument should require consultation, participation and environmental and social impact assessments before granting land to national and international investors. There should be a dispute resolution mechanism for affected individuals. There should be a complaints mechanism where individuals can petition UN treaty bodies, other UN bodies or other international bodies.

Changes to national law will take time as each country has its own political cycle. International law has always been the guiding body of law for national law. If an international legal instrument is adopted it is likely to bring about change in the behaviour of governments in many States. Therefore, there is a need for an international treaty to govern land grab with a provision for a separate treaty body empowered to receive individual petition from people affected by land grabs.

The very existence of an international legal instrument would give advocates a language to speak and to use it so that governments cannot keep denying as is the case in many countries at the moment. Such an instrument will empower domestic courts to invoke it when providing remedy to the victims of land grab. The judiciaries of India, Pakistan and the Philippines have led the way in giving force to soft law instruments, although in doing so they have been criticized for judicial activism.

Until such as a treaty dedicated to addressing human rights issues arising from land-grabbing is concluded, the UN Human Rights Council should consider appointing a special rapporteur with a global mandate to report on human rights violations resulting from economic and other land concessions and other forms of land-grabbing by governments in various countries and to make recommendations to the governments concerned and to the international community and to develop a binding legal instrument designed to address these issues. The main function of the UN Special Rapporteurs for human rights is to monitor the situation of human rights in a certain country and report publicly to the UN. It is about holding governments accountable for violations of human rights by asking sensible and often difficult questions to probe into the situation. The endeavour is to induce governments towards compliance with their international human rights obligations flowing from the treaties ratified by the country and to assist them to travel along the road to a stronger democracy, genuine rule of law and greater respect for human rights and to building their capacity to achieve this.[25]

[25] See generally Philip Alston, 'Hobbling the Monitors: Should U.N. Human Rights Monitors Be Accountable?' (2011) 52 *Harvard International Law Journal* 561, 563–649; David Weissbrodt, 'The Three "Theme" Special Rapporteurs of the UN Commission on Human Rights' (1986) 80 *American Journal of International Law* 684, 685–99; Helena M. Cook, 'The Role of the Special Procedures in the Protection of Human Rights: The Way

In practice, the Special Rapporteurs perform a supervisory, consultative, advisory, or monitoring function, rather than one of enforcement. They are a special UN mechanism of a quasi-judicial nature. The Special Rapporteurs have been crucial in promoting and protecting human rights through not only monitoring and fact-finding, but also standard-setting. They have significantly influenced the elaboration, interpretation, and implementation of international human rights law and have brought the human rights work of the UN to ordinary men and women around the globe. Therefore, the appointment of a special rapporteur with a global mandate to report on human rights violations resulting from economic and other land concessions and other forms of land-grabbing by governments in various countries would be well placed to develop a binding legal instrument designed to address these issues which could include an international mechanism for settling such land disputes between foreign investors and the communities affected by economic and other land concessions. Once such a legally binding document is in place, it would be easier for international investment tribunals to take into account its provisions when adjudicating upon investment disputes.

Another possibility would be for the International Law Commission (ILC) to formulate or develop draft articles concerning human rights and business like the 2001 draft articles on State Responsibility or the 1978 draft articles on MFN clauses[26] it did in in the past. The investment legal landscape is dominated not only by BITs or IIAs, but also by State–investor contracts. Therefore, without ensuring responsible State–investor contracts the reform of the BIT or IIA regime would not bring about the desired results. Responsible contracting would entail dispensing with traditional contract templates or standard form contracts and incorporating human rights into such contracts. The Ruggie Principles, or the UN's Guiding Principles on Business and Human Rights, do offer certain guidelines for responsible contracts. If there was general consensus on the part of the investment-exporting and investment-receiving States to harmonize the law and practice, they could revise the investment or State contracts that exist among themselves to reflect the changes that have been taking place in this area. If foreign investors and the host States concerned were to come to the view that both of these sides have a duty to uphold the human rights and environmental values, they have a number of options including: amending the investment contracts; inserting provisions to this effect into the contracts; concluding supplementary contracts to complement the original contracts; or amending the relevant provisions in the original contracts.

Investment contracts could extend this notion to require that foreign investors must subject their major investment projects to environmental, human rights and other social impact assessment in the host country concerned. In addition, an international agency could be entrusted with the task of verifying the content of an investment agreement or contract below a certain threshold and certifying that it meets the international human rights or environmental standards applicable to such an agreement. What is more, a system similar to the Inspection Panel of the World Bank could be created to receive complaints against serious

Forward After Vienna' (1993) 50 *Review of the International Commission of Jurists* 31; Marc J. Bossuyt, 'The Development of Special Procedures of the United Nations Commission on Human Rights' (1985) 6 *Human Rights Law Journal* 179; Surya P Subedi QC, 'Protecting Human Rights Through the Mechanism of UN Special Rapporteurs' (2011) 33 *Human Rights Quarterly* 201.

26 Text adopted by the International Law Commission at its 30th session, in 1978, and submitted to the General Assembly as a part of the Commission's report covering the work of that session (at para. 74). The report, which also contains commentaries on the draft articles, appears in *Yearbook of the International Law Commission* (1978) vol II, part two.

violations of human rights or international environmental standards by foreign investors in the countries where they conduct their business.

21.6 THE ASIAN APPROACH TO BUSINESS AND HUMAN RIGHTS

Having come out of either a colonial past such as India or a semi-colonial past[27] such as China, most of the Asian States have remained ambivalent about their wholesale subscription to international law perceived as a euro-centric system in its origin or the use of international judicial mechanisms.[28] This ambivalence has made them largely rule takers rather than rule shakers or rule makers until recently. Owing to their focus on economic development, these States have not been enthusiastic supporters of the UN human rights agenda focused initially on civil and political rights. This is the case even with the countries with a democratic system of government such as India. The country has its own human rights problems, whether concerning separatist or secessionist movements or Maoist insurgency or other law and order problems, to deal with, be it in Kashmir or Bihar or far flung places such as those bordering Burma. By getting involved with other States internal affairs the Indians seem to fear that others will interrogate theirs. That is why India's role has been limited in the promotion and protection of human rights internationally.[29]

The story of States with a socialist system of government such as China and Vietnam or with a socialist past such as Cambodia is of course a different one.[30] Even some other Asian States without a socialist system or a socialist past have autocratic tendencies and adherence to the international rule of law and human rights has not been their priority. Consequently, the Asian States have not been enthusiastic rule shakers or rule makers in the international arena until recently.

However, the equation seems to be changing especially with regard to trade and investment law matters. Asian States such as China and India have been increasingly assertive in developing the rules concerning international trade and investment and using the dispute settlement mechanism for disputes in such matters.[31] For instance, according to Moynihan, since China became a member of the WTO, 'it has been a respondent in 39 disputes (the third-highest number of all 164 members), and has initiated 15 cases itself (putting China in the top 10 initiators of cases before the WTO). China has also been active as a third party, intervening in 136 Cases'.[32]

Although the first-generation of BITs and FTAs concluded by China did not include a provision for international investment arbitration, the more recent ones have included it and China has already been a party to a number of investment arbitration cases. It is likely to be a party to an increasing number of such investment arbitration as China has become a major investor country around the globe and is busy negotiating and concluding many BITs

27 See generally Prabhakar Singh, 'Sino-Indian Attitudes to International Law: of Nations, States and Colonial Hangovers', the Chinese Journal of International Law (September 2015).

28 See for an interesting analysis of Asia's approach to international law: Simon Chesterman, 'Asia's Ambivalence about International Law & Institutions: Past, Present and Futures' (2016) 27 *European Journal of International Law* 945.

29 Surya P Subedi QC, 'The Universality of Human Rights and the UN Human Rights Agenda: The Impact of the Shift of Power to the East and the Resurgence of the BRICS' (2015) 55 *Indian Journal of International Law* 177.

30 Surya P Subedi QC, 'China's Approach to Human Rights and the UN Human Rights Agenda' (2015) 14 *Chinese Journal of International Law* 437.

31 Harriet Moynihan, 'China's Evolving Approach to International Dispute Settlement' Chatham House Briefing, March 2017).

32 Ibid., p. 6.

and FTAs. Moreover, with its ambitious 'One Belt, One Road' programme China's investment abroad is likely to grow and with it the number of investment disputes involving China. India too has been a party to a number of disputes before the WTO Dispute Settlement Mechanism and has taken a lead in developing rules on the regulation of foreign investment. It has adopted an innovative and far-sighted Model BIT which is likely to place India at the centre of new developments in international investment law.

Since most of the Asian States are in transition of some kind, whether politically or economically, they have faced many more challenges than their counterparts in the Western world and the challenges raised by economic land concessions and the harsh treatment meted out to the populations in these countries by their governments is a case in point. Since the right to property is not traditionally strong in these States, the victims of deprivation of their right to property do not seem to get a fair treatment from their governments in these countries. Therefore, as the Asian countries such as China and India become global economic and political powers and engage in more trade and investment matters with the rest of the world with a better provision for the protection of the property of their citizens abroad and eventually with international dispute resolution mechanisms, especially those relating to trade and investment disputes, they can be expected to offer better protection of rights, including the right to property to the citizenry in general at home.

Those Asian States with a social past have a long way to go to protect the property rights of their citizens and Cambodia is an example. In one of the cases of economic land concessions in Cambodia involving a company Union Development Group Company in Botum Sakor National Park, Koh Kong province serves as an example. Concessions granted in Botum Sakor National Park in Koh Kong Province were established by a Royal Decree and classified as a natural park (an area reserved for nature and scenic views, which was to be protected for scientific, educational and entertainment purposes). It was later designated as a protected area under the 2008 Protected Areas Law. Nevertheless, since that time, the Government granted land concessions within the national park to at least nine private companies for the planting of agro-industrial crops (e.g. acacia, palm oil and rubber), as well as for eco-tourism, commercial developments, water reservoirs and hydropower dams. The concessions were granted through the issuance of sub-decrees to reclassify protected areas into sustainable use zones, which raised issues with compliance with the legal framework for the conservation of protected areas. In May 2008, the Government, represented by the Minister of Environment, signed a long-term lease contract of ninety-nine years with Union Development Group Company, Ltd. for the construction of a commercial development zone and resort to attract tourists and further investment over 36,000 hectares in the Kiri Sakor and Botum Sakor districts. The contract was signed by the Minister for Environment, approved by the Minister of Economy and Finance, and witnessed by the Minister of Commerce. Under the contract, Union Development Group was authorized to develop infrastructure that would support the tourism sector, including casinos, condominiums, apartments and resorts. The company was authorized to clear forest area while undertaking its development, per the master plan, but was liable to pay royalties should it log trees with any economic value. But the villages affected by the project had been in existence for generations. The community members had settled in the area before the Sihanouk regime in the 1960s, who relocated during or after the Khmer Rouge regime, and who arrived in the 1980s (after the fall of the Khmer Rouge). More families moved there later following private purchase of land plots. The government formally recognized these villages in the 1990s following the end of the civil war.

According to the district officials involved in the assessment of the occupied land, the project could affect 1,163 families inhabiting residential land and tending to orchards in the area. But the affected communities were reportedly not consulted about the project and its potential impacts, but had noticed company representatives and governmental officials travelling throughout their communes and measuring land before the signing of the contract in 2008. The communities were reportedly officially informed of the project, including a promise for compensation, for the first time during a visit in November 2009 to the Kiri Sakor district by officials of the Ministry of the Environment, Royal Cambodia Armed Forces, the Koh Kong provincial government and representatives of Union Development Group. In total, 1,163 families, and at least one primary school and three Buddhist pagodas had to be relocated. A decision was implemented to relocate these communities away from their traditional land without their consent and without them being offered a satisfactory package of compensation.[33] What was witnessed in this case is not unique. Many governments in socialist countries or with a socialist past in Asia have been evicting people from their land to make way for new development projects in breach of their own national laws and international standards.

21.7 CONCLUSIONS

In response to the expropriation in all its forms by host States, the developed countries have been trying to strengthen the position of their foreign investors by restricting a host country's ability to control and regulate foreign investment through, both bilateral and multilateral, treaties. International tribunals have followed suit and been quick to deliver judgments to strengthen the position of foreign investors. Regional economic co-operation treaties and a number of bilateral investment treaties sought to accord protection to foreign investors greater even than those accorded under customary international law. Various arbitral awards which relied on the terms and conditions of regional and bilateral treaties appeared to go as far as to restrict the right of host States to adopt regulatory measures or exercise their 'police power'.

The irony is that none of the major international instruments yet impose any corresponding duties and obligations on foreign investors. In other words, foreign investors have on the whole no environmental and social obligation towards their host countries under most of the BITs or IIAs or FTAs. There are, of course, various 'soft' law instruments and self-regulatory codes of conduct which call upon foreign investors in general and the multinationals in particular to have due regard to the environment and respect human rights in the countries where they have their business. But what goes on around the globe on the ground presents a very disappointing picture with regard to compliance with such 'soft law' principles and voluntary codes of conduct by the multinationals.

During the formative years of the law of foreign investment the notion of laissez-faire provided the philosophical underpinning for this body of law. This traditional notion gradually gave way to the neo-liberal concept of regulation of foreign investment in order to achieve the higher goals of humanity. The law of foreign investment became part of the attempt to create a global order supported by international law. But this attempt gave rise in

33 Surya P Subedi QC, 'A Human Rights Analysis of Economic and Other Land Concessions in Cambodia' (UN Doc A/HRC/21/63/Add.1 (25 September 2012)).

due course to a divided world where the interests of developed and developing countries came to clash.

It was the developing countries who sought in the 1960s, 1970s and 1980s to regulate foreign investment through one international instrument rather than leaving the matter to customary international law. However, in the 1990s these countries became reluctant to support the idea of regulation of foreign investment under the auspices of the WTO because their governments believed that they would have to accept the standards of the developed world through such an instrument. Fortunately, at present, the interests of both developed and developing countries seem to be converging gradually towards the adoption of one international agreement to regulate foreign investment. In the absence of a concerted effort to balance the law of foreign investment with other competing principles of international law such as the protection and preservation of the environment and human rights the world may witness more chaos and confusion in this area of law in the years to come.

Many developing countries which have opposed the adoption of an international treaty on investment within the WTO are waking up to the fact that they have been forced to accept the pro-developed country or pro-investment standards through the decisions of arbitration tribunals. It is better for the developing countries too to have an internationally negotiated treaty than accept the often unbalanced and controversial dicta of such tribunals of ad hoc character. The time has come for the UN to reassert its role and take an appropriate initiative in this direction. This could be one possible and sensible way forward to reconcile public interests with private interests in international investment arbitration and to secure an effective remedy for investment-related human rights violations globally in general and in Asia in particular. Responsible business organizations would see that the longer term benefits of respecting human rights in the countries where they do their business would outweigh the costs of compliance. In the absence of effective access to legal remedy, communities affected by human rights violations by business organizations have taken to the streets and some of the demonstrations have resulted in violence and loss of lives. Therefore, the way forward for all sides would be to have faith in the system of human rights and develop international investment law in a manner that is conducive to reconciling public interests with private interests in international investment arbitration and to securing effective remedy for investment-related human rights violations around the globe. This will contribute to building a fairer society for all underpinned by the principles of the rule of law and greater respect for human rights in pursuing prosperity.

22

Rebalancing Investment Treaties and Investor–State Arbitration in the Asian Region

Luke Nottage[*]

22.1 INTRODUCTION

Foreign direct investment (FDI) has been accelerating into Asia, which is also emerging as a major source of outbound FDI.[1] This inflow, together with the proliferation of investment treaties with investor–State dispute (ISDS) provisions, has led to investor–State arbitration claims being lodged against Asian host States. Yet the volume of such cases is comparatively low. A significant number of them are only against a few States – notably, Vietnam and Indonesia – with very few adverse awards. Investors within Asian States such as Singapore, Malaysia and recently India, are also starting to use treaty-based ISDS provisions to protect their outbound investments by filing arbitration claims.[2] In addition, standalone bilateral investment treaties (BITs) are increasingly being supplemented or displaced by investment chapters in broader free trade agreements (FTAs) on a regional basis,[3] which further entrenches ISDS-backed treaty protections.

Thus, Asian economies continue to walk a tightrope as they seek to (re)balance their interests in supporting more outbound investment, preserving appropriate regulatory autonomy while attracting inbound investment, and maintaining an attractive environment for

* Parts of this chapter elaborate, with permission, on L. Nottage, 'Rebalancing Investment Treaties and Investor-State Arbitration: Two Approaches' (2016) 17 *Journal of World Investment and Trade* 1015. The chapter also draws on support from an Australian Research Council Discovery Project (DP140102526) for 2014–2017 on international investment dispute management, jointly with Dr Shiro Armstrong and Professors Jurgen Kurtz and Leon Trakman. I thank Prof. Julien Chaisse for helpful feedback on an earlier draft and Kirsten Gan for excellent editorial and research assistance.

1 V. Bath and L. Nottage, 'Asian Investment and the Growth of Regional Investment Agreements' in C. Antons (ed.), *Routledge Handbook of Asian Law* (Abingdon, England: Routledge, 2017), pp. 182–99; V. Bath and L. Nottage, 'International investment Agreements and Investor-State Arbitration in Asia" in J. Chaisse, L. Choukroune and S. Jusoh (eds), *Handbook of International Investment Law and Policy* (Springer, Singapore, 2020) 1-36. .

2 L. Nottage and S. Thanitcul, 'International Investment Arbitration in Southeast Asia' (2017) 18 *Journal of World Investment and Trade* 767.

3 S. Cho and J. Kurtz, 'The Limits of Isomorphism: Global Investment Law and the ASEAN Investment Regime' (2016) 17 *Chicago Journal of International Law* 341; V. Bath and L. Nottage, 'The ASEAN Comprehensive Investment Agreement and "ASEAN Plus" – the Australia–New Zealand Free Trade Area (AANZFTA) and the PRC–ASEAN Investment Agreement' in M. Bungenberg, J. Griebel, S. Hobe and A. Reinisch (eds.), *International Investment Law* (Oxford: Hart, 2015), pp. 283–303; L. Nottage, 'The TPP Investment Chapter and Investor-State Arbitration in Asia and Oceania: Assessing Prospects for Ratification' (2016) 17(2) *Melbourne Journal of International Law* 313; S. Schacherer, 'TPP, CETA and TTIP Between Innovation and Consolidation – Resolving Investor-State Disputes under Mega-regionals' (2016) 7(3) *Journal of International Dispute Settlement* 628.

foreign investors. To understand the issues and likely future trajectory for international investment law in the region, it is first important to understand the broader dynamics and features of past treaties. A useful starting point is a comprehensive study by Lauge Poulsen, focusing on the experiences of developing countries world-wide but including analyses of several Asian States (as outlined in Section 22.2).[4] Despite marshalling powerful arguments and evidence for manifestations of 'bounded rationality' in BIT negotiations and drafting, some limits to his theory are suggested by a closer analysis of various Southeast Asian countries (Section 22.3). Accordingly, it seems premature to abandon altogether the ISDS-backed treaty protection regime.[5] Nonetheless, a combination of new approaches is worth considering under both existing treaties and with respect to future negotiations (Section 22.4).[6]

22.2 BOUNDED RATIONALITY BY DEVELOPING COUNTRIES IN INVESTMENT TREATY NEGOTIATIONS

Poulsen's extensively researched but succinctly written study begins with a brief preface, titled the 'curious case of Pakistan', describing the bemusement of its top two senior legal officers upon receiving notification in 2001 about Pakistan's first treaty-based ISDS claim.[7] Yet Poulsen emphasizes that the South Asian nation's experience was not unique: 'only few developing country governments realized that by consenting to investment treaty arbitration, they agreed to offer international investors enforceable protections with the potential for costly and far-reaching implications'.[8] Poulsen goes on to highlight the key puzzle addressed by the book: 'why did practically all developing countries suddenly rush to sign largely identical treaties, which significantly constrained their sovereignty? Why did they expose themselves to expensive investment claims and give such a remarkable degree of flexibility to private lawyers to determine the scope of their regulatory autonomy?'[9]

Poulsen's response is that this pattern aligns with theories of 'bounded rationality' derived from behavioural psychology and economics. In particular, he contends there are three biases commonly observed in decision-making that seemed to be at work in the uptake and design of BITs.[10] First, policy-makers employed 'motivated reasoning' which meant they *wanted* to believe that BITs would lead to more inbound foreign investment.[11] This was akin to 'confirmation bias' – where parties tend to give more weight to data that supports their pre-

4 L. N. S. Poulsen, *Bounded Rationality and Economic Diplomacy: The Politics of Investment Treaties in Developing Countries* (Cambridge: Cambridge University Press, 2015).

5 *See also generally* C. Campbell, S. Nappert and L. Nottage, 'Assessing Treaty-Based Investor-State Dispute Settlement: Abandon, Retain or Reform?' (2014) 11(1) *Transnational Dispute Management*, available at: www.ssrn.com/abstract=2280182 (last accessed 12 July 2019); L. Trakman and D. Musaleyan, 'The Repudiation of Investor-State Arbitration and Subsequent Treaty Practice: The Resurgence of Qualified Investor-State Arbitration' (2016) 30 *ICSID Review—Foreign Investment Law Journal* 194.

6 Cf. also, e.g., J. Kalicki and A. Joubin-Bret (eds.), *Reshaping the Investor-State Dispute Settlement System* (Leiden, The Netherlands: Brill, 2015).

7 *SGS Société Générale de Surveillance S.A. v. Islamic Republic of Pakistan*, ICSID Case No. ARB/01/13.

8 See above n 4, Poulsen, *Bounded Rationality*, xv–xvi.

9 Ibid., 5.

10 Ibid., Poulsen, *Bounded Rationality*, 17–19, 26–27.

11 Cf. also T. Harford, 'Why forecasters failed to predict Trump's victory', Undercover Economist, Financial Times Magazine (23 November 2016); G. Mayraz, 'Wishful Thinking' (2013) *University of Melbourne Research Paper*, No. 1172, available at: www.fbe.unimelb.edu.au/data/assets/pdf_file/0008/796967/1172.pdf (both last accessed 12 July 2019).

conceived views.[12] Secondly, host States exhibited 'salience bias' by underestimating the risks of being held liable for breaching substantive treaty commitments such as non-discrimination, expropriation, or fair and equitable treatment (FET), until they were faced with the initial ISDS claims brought by foreign investors. Thirdly, policy-makers displayed 'status quo' bias by 'satisficing' rather than optimizing treaty drafting. In particular, they had agreed to and maintained BITs based on the shorter and ubiquitous models developed by major European capital-exporting States rather than the more elaborate US model.

Poulsen further argues that this combination of biases is likely to be particularly apposite for developing countries for multiple reasons. First, he suggests that public officials in such States were more likely to underestimate risks given that so few had any specialist expertise in international investment law during the 1980s and 1990s.[13] Secondly, Poulsen contends that salience-inducing bias was exacerbated by 'the high turnover in many developing country bureaucracies'. Thirdly, an absence of expertise and experience arguably influenced the status quo bias, with 'generalist bureaucrats ... much less likely to opt out of default treaty designs' adopted by predecessors.[14]

Poulsen nonetheless charts 'a difficult beginning' for BIT programmes. This was initiated from around 1960 – particularly by Germany and then the largest capitol exporter in Europe – the United Kingdom – to protect investments overseas. The cause for concern arose from the unlikelihood of multilateral treaty protections being achieved by the fledgling Organisation for Economic Cooperation and Development (OECD) and the World Bank through its new International Centre for the Settlement of Investment Disputes (ICSID). For instance, the 1965 ICSID Convention[15] was drafted without any substantive protections but only provision of an ISDS procedure where further consent was separately provided by the host State – be it by national law, investment contracts, or further treaties. This was due to opposition from South American States, who in the tradition of the Calvo Doctrine, insisted that foreign investors be limited to remedies through domestic law and courts. The United Kingdom, as well as the Netherlands, France and Belgium, then began seeking to include consent to ICSID arbitration in their treaties from the late 1960s. However, even for the United Kingdom, the ISDS provision was a 'desirable but not essential' element of their model. Overall, by the late 1970s, only 165 BITs had been successfully concluded, and negotiations were rarely sophisticated. Assertions from developed countries that treaties would promote more inbound investment were most often rejected; where accepted, it was based on political preferences of the developing country, rather than empirical analysis. Furthermore, the key ISDS enforcement mechanism was rarely even considered.[16]

From the 1980s however, a new era began for promoting investment. Sovereign debt crises increasingly led developing countries to reform economies to receive debt relief and foreign aid from international financial institutions, especially the World Bank.[17] ICSID encouraged further developed countries to include ISDS clauses in their BITs and began developing a negotiation handbook, all the while encouraging developing countries to agree to treaties to

[12] See generally, e.g., R. Thaler, *Misbehaving: The Making of Behavioural Economics* (London, England: Penguin, 2016), p. 172.

[13] As mentioned further, however, this could well have been true also of officials in developed countries that had not yet confronted ISDS claims.

[14] See above n 4, Poulsen, *Bounded Rationality*, 44–45.

[15] Convention on Settlement of Investment Disputes Between States and Nationals of Other States, Washington, 18 March 1965, in force 14 October 1966, 4 ILM 532.

[16] Ibid. Poulsen, *Bounded Rationality*, 65, 69–70.

[17] This is illustrated by a case study of Ghana: *See ibid*, Poulsen, *Bounded Rationality*, 99–102.

attract more investment. The new Multilateral Investment Guarantee Agency assisted this effort through general policy advice (directly and then through the Bank's Foreign Investment Advisory Services) rather than withholding political risks insurance to foreign investors in States lacking BITs.[18] Western countries, especially the United States, also accelerated the promotion of BITs directly as well as via these international organizations. This occurred partly through numerous (often aid-funded) private consultants dispatched to Central and Eastern Europe after the collapse of the Iron Curtain,[19] exemplified by the Czech Republic, which then rushed to conclude many BITs.[20]

Interestingly, the United Nations Conference on Trade and Development (UNCTAD) adopted a very pro-BIT stance, especially after negotiations collapsed for a Multilateral Agreement on Investment (MAI) through the OECD. Notably, between 1999 and 2004, UNCTAD promoted numerous BIT facilitation rounds and signing ceremonies (in Geneva and elsewhere) for groups of countries. As investment treaty arbitrations emerged, UNCTAD turned to assisting developing countries in managing and avoiding disputes, often bringing in private law firms as consultants.[21] Zimbabwe was an example of a developing country shifting to signing BITs as part of a programme of liberalizing and attracting foreign investment, with UNCTAD assistance.[22] However, Zimbabwe accepted the view that BITs led to more investment, at face value. It did not appreciate risks over the 1990s despite ISDS claims starting to be brought against other countries, and it did not significantly adjust BIT wording from European templates – either to limit risks or to become more pro-investor to attract investment compared to neighbouring African countries.

In addition to such qualitative analysis of past treaty negotiations, Poulsen presents some aggregate quantitative evidence for a less-than-rational competition among States. When an econometric study by Elkins and others was redone with updated data,[23] the statistics showed that BIT adoption rates by host States were not significantly related to adoptions by competitor States. This was observed even for the 1990s period, when developing countries started to initiate BIT negotiations and offer more ISDS protections. Also, contrary to Elkins and others, Poulsen found no significant additional adoptions when States signing BITs appeared to generate more FDI.[24] More qualitatively, he could not discern major changes in BIT content overall in competing for more investment,[25] such as adding pre-establishment rights or prohibitions on performance requirements.[26] Poulsen then illustrates these patterns by way of case studies from the 1990s across Latin America (focusing on Mexico, Argentina and Chile), Asia (Pakistan, Thailand and Turkey) and Africa (Ethiopia and Nigeria). However, Poulsen acknowledges that 'if there was no information about the potency of the treaties at the

18 Ibid, Poulsen, *Bounded Rationality*, 71–81.

19 Ibid., 81–87.

20 Ibid., 102–06.

21 Ibid., 91–99.

22 Ibid., 106–09.

23 Z. Elkins, A. Guzman & B. Simmons, 'Competing for Capital: The Diffusion of Bilateral Investment Treaties, 1960–2000' (2006) 60(4) *International Organisation* 811.

24 See above n 4, Poulsen, *Bounded Rationality*, 110–14.

25 Ibid., 114–17.

26 The latter may not be such a good test, however, given some were introduced for all World Trade Organisation members particularly under the Trade-Related Investment Measures Agreement of 1994, albeit enforced through inter-state dispute settlement. Nonetheless, performance requirements remain pervasive and arguably have not yet been effectively disciplined under that multilateral regime: H. Hestermeyer and L. Neilsen, 'The Legality of Local Content Measures under WTO Law' (2014) 48 *Journal of World Investment and Trade* 553.

time they spread rapidly, it would not necessarily have been unreasonable to avoid spending time and scarce resources to find out whether they had an impact on investment flows'.[27]

Accordingly, Poulsen considers whether sufficient information was indeed available, by tracking the rise of investment treaty arbitration. The first treaty-based ICSID claim came in 1987, followed by two more in the late 1990s, after a few others under other arbitration rules that were not made public. Poulsen also points to the contemporaneous North American Free Trade Agreement (NAFTA) claim by the US Ethyl Corporation against Canada's restrictions on a fuel additive.[28] This resulted in a settlement that became highly politicized as impeding regulatory autonomy.[29] Poulsen concludes, rather ambitiously from these few examples, that by then 'the potency of the [ISDS] regime should have been crystal clear for anyone caring to seek relevant information'.[30] Yet he argues, from a further econometric analysis with updated data from work with Emma Aisbett,[31] that it was only when each State was subjected to its own first ISDS claim that risks seem to have significant impact – specifically, a reduction of BIT signings by 35 per cent.[32] Such impact, and other mostly incremental responses including somewhat less pro-investor wording in subsequent BITs, are then illustrated again by multiple brief country studies. These range across Latin America (adding Ecuador), Asia (adding India) and Africa (adding Kenya, and later a detailed study of South Africa).[33]

Nonetheless, Poulsen is careful to acknowledge some exceptions to such 'narcissistic learning' only after ISDS claims.[34] For example, Costa Rica did not agree to BITs haphazardly, so as to demonstrate some 'achievement' from high-level diplomatic missions. Instead, Costa Rica had a small but highly skilled team for negotiating BITs, which pressed for more restrictive provisions in light of the growing number of claims against Argentina. The latter was aware of the potential potency of ISDS clauses in the 1990s, even if surprised by the extent of claims. Likewise, Lebanon's key negotiator had experience in international arbitration and also concluded BITs more carefully. Most relevantly for the present chapter, Poulsen concedes that China's treaty practice evolved to accept more scope for ISDS as it emerged as a major outbound investor.[35]

27 See above n 4, Poulsen, *Bounded Rationality*, 134.

28 North American Free Trade Agreement, 17 December 1992, in force 1 January 1994, 32 ILM 289; *Ethyl Corporation* v. *The Government of Canada*, UNCITRAL, Award on Jurisdiction, 24 June 1998.

29 Although it might be added that the measure discriminated in favour of local suppliers.

30 See above n 4, Poulsen, *Bounded Rationality*, 141.

31 L. Poulsen and E. Aisbett, 'When the Claim Hits: Bilateral Investment Treaties and Bounded Rational Learning' (2013) 65(2) *World Politics* 273.

32 See above n 4, Poulsen, *Bounded Rationality*, 141–6. It could also be instructive to assess the impact of ISDS claims based on consent contained in investment contracts (or, much more rarely, domestic laws) rather than just treaties. Host states (including developing countries in Asia: L. Nottage, 'The TPP Investment Chapter') were quite often subject to the former categories of claims before the latter. Other empirical studies into ISDS patterns tend to combine both categories (e.g. T. Schultz and C. Dupont, 'Investment Arbitration: Promoting the Rule of Law or over-empowering Investors? A Quantitative Empirical Study' (2014) 25 *European Journal of International Law* 1147). Admittedly, experiences with contract-based ISDS arbitrations may be even more unlikely to have impacted on BIT signing; but they could have led to (rational) changes in investment contract drafting – although this would need to be tested instead by qualitative research, likely also to be constrained by confidentiality provisions.

33 See also, e.g., E.C. Schlemmer, 'An Overview of South Africa's Bilateral Investment Treaties and Investment Policy' (2015) 31(1) *ICSID Review—Foreign Investment Law Journal* 167.

34 See above n 4, Poulsen, *Bounded Rationality*, 156–60.

35 See, e.g., V. Bath, 'China' in F. Morosini and M. Ratton Sanchez Badin (eds.), *Reconceptualizing International Investment Law from the Global South* (Cambridge: Cambridge University Press, 2017), pp. 1–46.

Finally, Poulsen revisits the South African strategy since 2010 – replacing BITs with national legislation – as one way that developing countries might promote reform of the current treaty-based ISDS regime. The immediate practical impact is admittedly limited due to 'survival' or sunset clauses that extend treaty protection for existing investors. However, he argues that 'as long as they make it painstakingly clear that their exit is not opportunistic and they still protect property rights of foreign investors, it is questionable just how harshly international markets would react'.[36] Poulsen reiterates that foreign investors may still seek protection in other ways, for example by negotiating individual investment contracts with host States. However, it should also be added that the transaction costs will be high compared to even a careful treaty negotiation, especially for smaller developing countries.

As an alternative less extreme than outright 'exit' from the treaty-based ISDS regime, Poulsen further argues that developing countries should not underestimate their 'voice' to promote reform. As well as joining coalitions with stakeholders in developed countries, such as NGOs, they might 'consider exploiting the salience bias by mounting campaigns in international media' in relation to cases such as *Ethyl* (which helped scuttle the MAI) and recently the '*Phillip [sic.] Morris* claim [against Australia over tobacco plain packaging law, which has] contributed to growing European resistance' towards ISA in agreements with Canada and the US.[37] Poulsen also suggests that a broader lesson from his book is to 'be careful of the status quo bias', although again without expressing any strong normative view. Governments might go 'beyond incrementalism' by considering treaty wording that allows for multiple alternatives. These include counterclaims by host States, inter-State interpretations that are binding on tribunals, a requirement for the exhaustion of domestic remedies before an ISDS is commenced, innovations such as a permanent investment court for arbitration claims by investors, or perhaps even just inter-State arbitration.[38] In addition, Poulsen briefly canvasses practical measures to improve expertise and experience of treaty negotiators from developing countries, such as more specialization and an advisory centre on international investment law. He also acknowledges that past lapses in rational decision-making do not excuse developing countries from existing treaty commitments, but suggests that this history may influence tribunals required to interpret the treaties.[39]

22.3 LIMITS TO BOUNDED RATIONALITY: A CLOSER LOOK AROUND THE ASIAN REGION

In general, Poulsen's arguments are mostly persuasive and certainly thought-provoking. His combination of quantitative and qualitative methods is admirable and well-executed, and usually only achieved by entire teams of researchers.[40] In addition, bounded rationality

36 See above n 4, Poulsen, *Bounded Rationality*, 202. Nonetheless, for example, World Bank data on annual net inbound FDI into South Africa shows a considerable drop over 2010–15 compared to 2007–9: see the World Bank, 'Foreign Direct Investment, Net Inflows', available at https://data.worldbank.org/indicator/BX.KLT.DINV.CD.WD?locations=UZ (last accessed 23 September 2019).

37 See above n 4, Poulsen, *Bounded Rationality*, 201.

38 Ibid., pp. 196–200.

39 Ibid., pp. 192–95.

40 See, e.g., S. Armstrong, J. Kurtz, L. Nottage and L. Trakman, 'The Fundamental Importance of Foreign Direct Investment to Australia in the 21st Century: Reforming Treaty and Dispute Resolution Practice', *Sydney Law School Research Paper*, No. 13/90 (2014), available at www.ssrn.com/abstract=2362122; and related project publications so far, see 'Publications Listing – ARC Grant on International Investment Dispute Management', *Japanese Law and the Asia Pacific Blog*, 19 February 2016, available at https://japaneselaw.sydney.edu.au/2016/02/publications-listing-arc-grant-on-international-investment-dispute-management-2 (both last accessed 12 July 2019).

paradigms have been deployed effectively to explain developments in other legal fields too, including other aspects of international law.[41] However, some biases can cut both ways. For example, some earlier work on the Philip Morris arbitration suggested that 'availability bias' (similar to 'salience bias') may result in *over-estimating* risks, to the detriment of sound policy-making.[42] Indeed, even though that tobacco company's claim was subsequently dismissed on jurisdictional grounds in 2015,[43] it is now indelibly imprinted on the public discourse over ISDS in Australia – and probably beyond.[44]

In addition, while the book's country studies appear convincing, a few doubts arise upon a closer analysis of several States in the Asian region. In the case of Thailand for example,[45] its first BIT was signed with Germany in 1961, then with the Netherlands in 1972 and the United Kingdom in 1978. All these BITs excluded ISDS, despite the general British preference for including ISDS provisions in that era – as Poulsen himself notes. Furthermore, from the 1980s, Thailand either excluded ISDS altogether in its BITs, or allowed for it only if both parties were party to the ICSID Convention – which Thailand signed in 1985, but has never ratified. This continued all the way to 1993, until a BIT it has entered into with Romania. The exclusion of an ISDS unless both States were parties to ICSID persisted in some BITs signed through to 1997 (with Switzerland) and 2000 (with Egypt). This meant that ISDS was effectively unavailable with such States. It is at least plausible that someone within the Thai government intentionally negotiated such wording to limit liability exposure.[46]

More consistently with Poulsen's thesis, from 1993 most BITs also allowed the option of ISDS under ad hoc arbitration rules. On 18 February 2000, Thailand even signed seven BITs (with Egypt and six other States).[47] However, some within the Thai government may have considered that liability exposure was still limited by the requirement for covered investments to be specifically approved in writing. Even Thailand's FTA practice from 2004 adopted this feature by further incorporating various pro-host-State provisions, indirectly influenced by US

[41] See, e.g., S. Kozuka, 'The Myth of the Careful Consumer: Law, Culture, Economics and Politics in the Rise and Fall of Unsecured Lending in Japan' in J. Niemi-Kiesilainen, I. Ramsay and W. Whitford (eds.), *Consumer Credit, Debt and Bankruptcy: Comparative and International Perspectives* (Oxford: Hart, 2009), p. 199; T. Broude, 'Behavioural International Law' (2015) 163 *University of Pennsylvania Law Review* 1099.

[42] L. Nottage, 'Investor-State Arbitration Policy and Practice after *Philip Morris Asia v. Australia*' in L. Trakman and N. Ranieri (eds.), *Regionalism in International Investment Law* (Oxford University Press, 2013), p. 452 (shorter version available at www.ssrn.com/abstract=2041680 (last accessed 12 July 2019)).

[43] *Philip Morris Asia Limited (Hong Kong) v. The Commonwealth of Australia*, PCA 2012–12, Award on Jurisdiction and Admissibility, 17 December 2015. See generally J. Hepburn and L. Nottage, 'A Procedural Win for Public Health Measures' (2017) 18 *Journal of World Investment and Trade* 307.

[44] L. Nottage, 'Investment Treaty Arbitration Policy in Australia, New Zealand – and Korea?' (2015) 25 *Journal of Arbitration Studies* 185, manuscript available at www.ssrn.com/abstract=2643926 (last accessed 12 July 2019). *See also generally* L. Nottage, 'International Arbitration and Society at Large', in A. Bjorklund, F. Ferrari and S. Kroell (eds.), *Cambridge Compendium on International Arbitration* (Cambridge University Press, forthcoming).

[45] The following paragraphs summarise a detailed analysis in L. Nottage and S. Thanitcul, 'The Past, Present and Future of Investment Arbitration in Thailand', *Sydney Law School Research Paper*, No. 16/31 (2016), available at www.ssrn.com/abstract=2770889 (last accessed 12 July 2019).

[46] Of course, it is also possible that (a) the wording that limited scope for ISDS claims (by requiring both states to be party to the ICSID Convention) was derived from an early counterparty's template and then replicated in Thailand's subsequent treaties without appreciating the consequence, and (b) the implication of signing the ICSID Convention without then ratifying it was not considered either. This alternative seems more implausible, but further qualitative research should be addressed to this question.

[47] Some of the latter six were represented at UNCTAD 'BIT facilitation rounds', although no round is listed by Poulsen for that date, or otherwise as formally involving Thailand.

treaty practice.[48] After all, the issue had come up in the first (and only) ISDS claim against Myanmar under the 1987 Association of Southeast Asian Nations (ASEAN) Agreement for the Promotion and Protection of Investments, as well as the first ICSID claim against Malaysia.[49]

Thailand also raised this point in contesting jurisdiction after being subjected to its first-ever claim lodged in 2005 by Walter Bau's liquidator under a revised 2002 BIT with Germany (which, unlike the original treaty, allowed for ISDS). That BIT, plus earlier UK-influenced Thai BITs, also impacted on Thailand's Model BIT of 2002 . It was developed in the wake of greater parliamentary scrutiny of executive action under the People's Constitution of 1997, but did remain somewhat pro-investor. However, after Thailand lost the Walter Bau case in 2009,[50] it developed a less pro-investor Model BIT in 2012 and withdrew partly from FTA practice.[51] In parallel, Thailand continued to vigorously resist enforcement of the ad hoc arbitration award in favour of Walter Bau across multiple jurisdictions.[52] Through this strategy, it could draw on longer experience in resisting contract-based arbitration claims by foreign investors.[53] Thailand's 'incremental' approach to improving its ISDS and investment treaty practice now has at least an 'intended rationale' given the State became a net FDI exporter in 2011,[54] while losing attractiveness for foreign businesses compared to the other major Southeast Asian economies.

Turning next to Indonesia, the largest economy in ASEAN, a recent study highlights the care that it devoted to negotiating even early BITs in the 1960s and 1970s. It also suggests that letting present treaties lapse since 2014, but leaving in place or negotiating new FTAs with investment treaties, is a careful approach. In addition, some legislative initiatives envisaged future treaties allowing still for ISDS provisions.[55]

As for Singapore, a major regional hub for FDI, Alschner notes how its BIT with China in 1995 already included an innovative Article 11 on 'Prohibitions and Exceptions':

> 'The provisions of this Agreement shall not in any way limit the right of either Contracting Party to apply prohibitions or restrictions of any kind or take any other action which is directed to the protection or its essential security interests, or to the protection of public

[48] For the texts of almost all of Thailand's investment treaties: UNCTAD, 'International Investment Agreements Navigator', *Investment Policy Hub*, available at https://investmentpolicy.unctad.org/international-investment-agreements/countries/207/thailand (last accessed 12 July 2019).

[49] M. Sornarajah, 'Review of Asian Views on Foreign Investment Law' in V. Bath and L. Nottage (eds.), *Investment Law and Dispute Resolution Law and Practice in Asia* (London: Routledge, 2011), pp. 242, 246–47, discussing respectively *Yaung Chi Oo Trading Pte Ltd. v. Government of the Union of Myanmar* (ASEAN ID Case No. ARB/01/1, Award of 31 March 2003); and *Philippe Gruslin v. Malaysia* (ICSID Case No. ARB/99/3, Award of 27 November 2000.

[50] *Werner Schneider, acting in his capacity as insolvency administrator of Walter Bau Ag (In Liquidation)* v. *The Kingdom of Thailand* (Award of 1 July 2009).

[51] However, Thailand did so without signing any further BITs (as opposed to FTAs) since 2008.

[52] See, e.g., R. Klager, '*Werner Schneider (Liquidator of Walter Bau Ag) v Kingdom of Thailand*: Sovereign Immunity in Recognition and Enforcement Proceedings under German Law' (2014) 29(1) *ICSID Review—Foreign Investment Law Journal* 142.

[53] However, Cabinet Resolutions since 2004 have required prior approval before public authorities can enter into certain contracts: V. Sucharitkul, 'From *Walter Bau* to *Hopewell*: Pathways to Bangkok Don Muang Airport' (2015) 1 *Asia-Pacific Arbitration Reporter* 309.

[54] *See* World Bank, 'Foreign direct investment, net outflows', available at: https://data.worldbank.org/indicator/BM.KLT.DINV.CD.WD (last accessed 23 September 2019).

[55] A. Crockett, 'The Termination of Indonesia's BITs: Changing the Bathwater, but Keeping the Baby?' (2017) 18 (5–6) *Journal of World Investment and Trade* 836. Indonesia's FTA signed with Australia in 2019 includes ISDS, albeit unusually allowing the host state to force the investor into mandatory mediation before arbitration: see Ana Ubilava and Luke Nottage, 'Novel and Noteworthy Aspects of Australia's Recent Investment Agreements and ISDS Policy: The CPTPP, Hong Kong, Indonesia and Mauritius Transparency Treaties' in Luke Nottage et al (eds), *New Frontiers in Asia-Pacific International Arbitration and Dispute Resolution* (Wolters Kluwer, 2021) chapter 5.

health or the prevention of diseases and pests in animals or plants or the protection of its environment.'

A similar general exceptions clause, much broader than Article XX of the multilateral General Agreement on Tariffs and Trade (requiring measures to be necessary and non-discriminatory),[56] then spread through Mauritius into the BIT practice of many African States so that 'at the turn of the century, African countries were at the forefront of global efforts to balance public interest regulation and investment protection'.[57] More recently, Singaporean negotiators showed their sophistication by agreeing to some substantive provisions, based on the recently developed EU model in their FTA concluded in 2014; but initially not the innovative two-tier permanent investment court system for investor–State disputes (as agreed in the EU's subsequent two FTAs with Vietnam and Canada).[58]

Overall, treaty-making by ASEAN Member States has tended to involve more 'rule-making' than 'rule-taking', at least as measured by consistency of the investment treaty provisions obtained against various counterparties relative to per capita GDP of each Member State.[59] Nor had any ASEAN Member State ever paid out on an adverse treaty-based ISDS award, although Thailand recently did so (after exhausting appeals through German courts in the Walter Bau saga outlined earlier[60]), some treaty-based ISDS claims have been settled, and for example Indonesia was subject to a small adverse ICSID Convention award based on consent in an investment contract.[61] Meanwhile, Southeast Asia has benefitted from a large inflow of FDI.

Furthermore, in India, econometric research shows a significant and positive effect on inbound FDI due to the accumulation of its investment treaties.[62] In addition, there have been significant improvements in arbitration law and practice in India. This was brought about by the Most Favoured Nation (MFN) clause in the Australia–India BIT which was at issue in *White Industries Australia Ltd v India*. When an adverse award was rendered in

56 Accessible at www.wto.org/english/docs_e/legal_e/gatt47.pdf (last accessed 12 July 2019).

57 W. Alschner, 'Diffusion of Public Policy Exceptions in Investment Treaties – How Africa turned from Innovator to Imitator', *Mapping BITs Blog*, 29 June 2016, available at: http://mappinginvestmenttreaties.com/blog/2016/06/african-innovators/ (last accessed 12 July 2019). More recently, treaties by African seem to have more like 'rule takers' than 'rule makers', adopting differently formulated exceptions clauses. On the potentially narrow scope of WTO-like general exceptions, see also J. Chaisse, 'Exploring the Confines of International Investment and Domestic Health Protections – Is a General Exceptions Clause a Forced Perspective?' (2013) 39 *American Journal of Law and Medicine* 332.

58 M. Mohan, 'Singapore and its Free Trade Agreement with the European Union: Rationality "Unbound"?' (2017) 18 *Journal of World Investment and Trade* 858. Generally, on the EU's proposals for a permanent investment court and broader developments in its evolving treaty practice, *see* C. Titi, 'International Investment Law and the European Union: Towards a New Generation of International Investment Agreements' (2015) 26 *European Journal of International Law* 639; A. Reinisch, 'The European Union and Investor-State Dispute Resolution: From Investor-State Arbitration to a Permanent Investment Court', *CIGI Investor-State Arbitration Series Paper*, No. 2 (March 2016), available at www.cigionline.org/sites/default/files/isa_paper_series_no.2.pdf (last accessed 12 July 2019).

59 Nottage and Thanitcul, 'International Investment Arbitration in Southeast Asia', above n 2, Figure 7, derived from Figure 4 in W. Alschner and D. Skougarevskiy, 'Mapping the Universe of International Investment Agreements' (2016) 19(3) *Journal of International Economic Law* 561.

60 On 6 November 2016, the German Supreme Court (BGH, case I ZB 13/15) gave its judgment finally upholding the 2009 award. This paves the way for payment to be made to the German award creditor out of Thai government funds in Germany paid into escrow to allow release of the airplane of the Crown Prince (soon new King) of Thailand that had been seized by German court order in 2011: see Nottage and Thanitcul, 'Investment Arbitration in Thailand', above n 45.

61 *Amco Asia Corporation and others v. Republic of Indonesia*, ICSID Case No. ARB/81/1. See Figure 8 and the Appendix in Nottage and Thanitcul, 'International Investment Arbitration in Southeast Asia', above n 2.

62 As outlined further in Section 22.4.2.

a claim under that BIT by White Industries, it triggered an obligation under the subsequent India–Kuwait BIT to provide effective means for enforcing commercial arbitration awards. Subsequent improvements to domestic law and practically have arguably been for the benefit of Indian as well as foreign companies.[63]

Thus, on a rough cost-benefit analysis, offering ISDS-backed investment treaty commitments has worked out quite well – so far, at least – for a variety of significant Asian economies, including developing countries. Conversely, Poulsen's theory of bounded rationality may better fit a *developed* country like Australia. Specifically, an ICSID tribunal decided that Australia's early BIT with Indonesia was intended (like several other Australian BITs) not to provide advance consent to ICSID arbitration, although it upheld jurisdiction instead, on the basis of a mining licence issued by Indonesian authorities.[64] More likely, such a severe limitation on access to ISDS was an irrational drafting error on the Australian side.[65] The mistake was arguably repeated in several subsequent treaties due to status quo bias, exacerbated by the Australian government never making Cabinet-approved BIT templates public.

Furthermore, there was only marginal public discussion about the potential risks of ISDS provisions – drawing on North American experience rather than European influence. But not only were such considerations absent in the Australia–US FTA of 2004, the analysis was also cursory. It was only from 2011 when a few earlier fears about ISDS were confirmed by Philip Morris' initiation of its ISDS claim about tobacco packaging law, that the then-Gillard Government departed from longstanding policy by eschewing ISDS in all future treaties – even with developing countries. However, since 2014, the Coalition Government has reverted back to agreeing to ISDS after case-by-case assessments.[66]

Overall, these further partial case studies tend to go against Poulsen's thesis. Nonetheless, he still marshals much other supporting evidence for bounded rationality, and the analysis also squares quite well with other emerging quantitative research. For example, one recent econometric study focusing on *renegotiated* treaties finds that a significant trigger was a State's direct experience of ISDS claims, rather than a generalized increase in claims worldwide.[67] Related work shows that overall, renegotiations have so far led to *more* access to ISDS (except

[63] See *White Industries Australia Ltd.* v. *The Republic of India*, UNCITRAL, Final Award, 30 November 2011; H. K. Sathyapalan, 'Indian Judiciary and International Arbitration: A BIT of a Control?' (2016) 33 *Arbitration International* 503.

[64] *Churchill Mining PLC* v. *Republic of Indonesia*, ICSID Case No ARB/1214 and 12/40, Decision on Jurisdiction, 24 February 2014; *Churchill Mining v. Indonesia*, Award, 6 December 2016; 'In New Award, Tribunal Finds that Fraud During 'Performance' Phase of Investment Renders BIT Claims Against Indonesia Inadmissible', Investment Arbitration Reporter, 7 December 2016, available at www.iareporter.com/articles/in-new-award-tribunal-finds-that-fraud-during-performance-phase-of-investment-renders-bit-claims-against-indonesia-inadmissible (last accessed 12 July 2019).

[65] For a critique, see L. Nottage, 'Do Many of Australia's Bilateral Treaties Really Not Provide Full Advance Consent to Investor-State Arbitration? Analysis of *Planet Mining v Indonesia* and Regional Implications' (2015) 15 (1) *Transnational Dispute Management*, updated and elaborated in L. Nottage, 'The Limits of Legalisation in Asia-Pacific Investment Treaty Arbitration' in J. Chaisse and T-Y. Lin (eds.), *International Economic Law and Governance: Essays in Honour of Mitsuo Matsushita* (Oxford University Press, 2016), p. 153. Why would the Australian government have wanted to curtail ISDS with respect to Indonesia but not Hong Kong, with a contemporaneous BIT using different wording to clearly indicate advance consent to ISDS, even though Hong Kong had the much more reliable and familiar local legal system for protecting Australian outbound investors?

[66] J. Kurtz and L. Nottage, 'Investment Treaty Arbitration "Down Under": Policy and Politics in Australia' (2015) 30 *ICSID Review—Foreign Investment Law Journal* 465.

[67] Y. Haftel and A. Thompson, 'When Do States Renegotiate International Agreements: The Case of Bilateral Investment Treaties' (2015) (unpublished manuscript under review and on file with the author).

if one or more States are from the Americas),[68] which does not seem very rational. A separate quantitative project counters earlier research by concluding that, overall, being hit by an ISDS claim does not lead to significant innovations in treaty design.[69] Other preliminary qualitative research finds it hard to discern rational patterns among developing and middle-income countries in terms of implementing dispute management or prevention strategies in the wake of investment claims.[70]

However, although such behaviour may not seem optimal in retrospect, we should take another leaf out of the social psychologists' books and beware also of 'hindsight bias'.[71] In addition, even if bounded rationality has been pervasive in the past, there is the possibility of better learning – reinforced by better information – with respect to future design and application of investment treaties. Ironically, this is owing to the growing volume of ISDS claims. In any event, both developed and developing countries are now more likely to enjoy greater scope for regulatory autonomy thanks to the diffusion of US-style treaty-drafting over the last decade, at least across many parts of the Asia-Pacific region.[72] The United States not only updated its Model BIT in 2004 in light of experiences with claims under NAFTA but went on to use that template for negotiating FTA investment chapters. Of course, whether this illustration of a new status quo bias[73] is good or bad will depend on the observer, and the possible alternatives – including the emerging EU model, which may well still prove to be an attractive compromise in the wider Asia-Pacific region.[74]

At the very least, since other quantitative research shows that arbitral case law has a more pronounced influence on treaty drafting,[75] it seems worth taking fuller advantage of that mechanism to seek further improvements in international investment treaty law, before abandoning ISDS altogether or adopting some of the more radical proposals sketched towards the end of Poulsen's book. After all, patterns for ISDS cases have been shifting since the turn of the century. One recent empirical study identifies pro-State orientations in tribunals generally since around 2002, connecting this to a shift in arbitrator behaviour triggered by increasing terminations of investment treaties, decreasing numbers of new

68 T. Broude, Y. Haftel and A. Thompson, 'Who Cares About Regulatory Space in BITs? A Comparative International Approach' in A. Roberts (ed.), *Comparative International Law* (Oxford: Oxford University Press, 2018), 527. manuscript available at www.ssrn.com/abstract=2773686 (last accessed 12 July 2019). However, their ongoing research will examine whether this greater exposure to claims may be tempered by renegotiated substantive provisions that are less pro-investor.

69 W. Alschner and D. Skougarevskiy, 'Consistency and Legal Innovation in the BIT Universe', *Stanford Public Law Working Paper*, No. 2595288 (2015), available at www.ssrn.com/abstract=2595288 (last accessed 12 July 2019).

70 M. Sattorova, 'Reassertion of Control and Contracting Parties' Domestic Law Responses to Investment Treaty Arbitration: Between Reform, Reticence and Resistance' in A. Kulick (ed.), *Reassertion of Control over the Investment Treaty Regime* (Cambridge University Press, 2016), p. 14, manuscript available at:www.ssrn.com /abstract=2767014 (last accessed 12 July 2019) (discussing the possibility that responses may be due to an assessment that the experience in defending claims was quite successful, and/or support from international organizations like UNCTAD).

71 Cf. generally, e.g. Thaler, Misbehaving, above n 12, pp. 21–22.

72 See, e.g., W. Alschner and D. Skougarevskiy, 'The New Gold Standard? Empirically Situating the TPP in the Investment Treaty Universe' (2016) 17(3) *Journal of World Investment and Trade* 339.

73 Cf. generally W. Alschner, 'The Impact of Investment Arbitration on Investment Design: Myth Versus Reality' (2016) 42 *Yale Journal of International Law* 1 available at: www.ssrn.com/abstract=278152 (last accessed 12 July 2019).

74 L. Nottage, 'US vs EU vs Other Models for Investment Treaties in the Asia Region', *Japanese Law and the Asia-Pacific Blog*, 10 June 2016, available at http://blogs.usyd.edu.au/japaneselaw/2016/02/publications_listing_arc2 .html; A. Kawharu and L. Nottage, 'Models for Investment Treaties in the Asian Region: An Underview', *Sydney Law School Research Paper*, No. 16/87 (2016), Part 6, available at: www.ssrn.com/abstract=2845088 (both last accessed 12 July 2019).

75 W. Alschner, 'The Impact of Investment Arbitration on Investment Design: Myth Versus Reality', above n 73.

treaties signed, and pro-State 'signals' sent by influential States such as the United States which released interpretive notes under NAFTA and new Model BITs.[76] Another empirical study observes more claims being brought against developed countries since the late 1990s, paralleled by a move away from ISDS claims, seeking primarily to impose an international standard for the rule of law in developing countries in individual cases. Instead, there is shift towards ISDS claims serving to enhance overall predictability for cross-border investments.[77] In addition, it is possible that ratifying investment treaties or being exposed to treaty-based ISDS claims may trigger improvements in overall governance within host States, especially developing countries. However, this remains a 'complex empirical question',[78] dependent on domestic political and institutional dynamics.

22.4 TWO PATHWAYS FORWARD

Given that the evidence of bounded rationality in investment treaty negotiations and drafting is grounded in an earlier era and with major apparent exceptions, what can and should be done now? Section 22.4.1 teases out some normative implications when it comes to interpreting the large numbers of existing treaties, while Section 22.4.2 focuses on pending or future treaty negotiations.

22.4.1 *Interpreting Existing Treaties*

First, arbitrators (and counsel) interpreting existing treaties should be wary about assuming too much rationality on the part of treaty negotiators: the core lesson to be drawn from Poulsen's study, but also perhaps from developed countries in the Asian region such as Australia.[79] But they should also not underestimate the rationality of treaty negotiators from particular developing countries (such as Thailand).

Secondly, in support of such nuanced interpretations of existing treaties, as well as with other logistics involved in defending ISDS claims, there is much merit in calls by Poulsen and previously others for an advisory centre on international investment law – perhaps along the lines of the very successful Advisory Centre on World Trade Organisation (WTO) Law.[80] This idea of reform has been around for a decade,[81] but it has recently attracted powerful

76 M. Langford and D. Behn, 'Managing Backlash: The Evolving Investment Treaty Arbitrator?' (2016) 29(2) *European Journal of International Law* 551, manuscript available at www.ssrn.com/abstract=2835488 (last accessed 12 July 2019).

77 T. Schultz and C. Dupont, 'Investment Arbitration: Promoting the Rule of Law or over-empowering Investors? A Quantitative Empirical Study' (2014) 25 *European Journal of International Law* 1147.

78 K. Gordon and D. Gaukrodger, 'Investor-State Dispute Settlement: Public Consultation 16 May – July 2012', *OECD Investment Division Scoping Paper*, p. 12, available at www.oecd.org/investment/internationalinvestmentagreements/50291642.pdf (last accessed 12 July 2019). *See also, e.g.*, M. Sattorova, 'International Investment Treaties and the Promise of Good Governance', *European Society of International Law Conference Paper Series*, No. 11/2014 (2014), available at: www.ssrn.com/abstract=2546404 (last accessed 12 July 2019).

79 On the broader politics and related anomalies in Australia's investment treaty programme, see also L. Nottage, 'Investor-State Arbitration Policy and Practice in Australia' (2016) 6 *CIGI Investor-State Arbitration Series*, available at www.cigionline.org/publications/investor-state-arbitration-policy-and-practice-australia (last accessed 12 July 2019).

80 See Advisory Centre on WTO Law, available at www.acwl.ch/ (last accessed 12 July 2019).

81 E. Gottwald, 'Leveling the Playing Field: Is It Time for a Legal Assistance Centre for Developing Nations in Investment Treaty Arbitration?' (2007) 22(2) *American University International Law Journal* 237; L. Nottage and K. Miles, '"Back to the Future" for Investor-State Arbitrations: Revising Rules in Australia and Japan for Public Interests' (2009) 26(1) *Journal of International Arbitration* 25.

support through the World Economic Forum.[82] In the meantime or in parallel, large law firms experienced in ISDS claims should be encouraged to provide their services especially to developing countries on a pro bono or reduced-rate basis. Already there is anecdotal evidence of this happening, perhaps because these law firms perceive the educational implications of training up their younger lawyers, and marketing potential for their arbitration practices associated with assisting host States in increasingly public ISDS proceedings. Empirical evidence shows generally the importance of good legal advice in terms of ISDS outcomes,[83] and this seems to be corroborated by the record of Southeast Asian host States in defending ISDS claims mostly very successfully.[84]

Thirdly, when interpreting substantive commitments under existing investment treaties especially when the challenge involves regulation introduced to maintain public health or the like, more attention should be paid to notions of proportionality and deference to host State decision-making, as propounded recently by Henckels.[85] The proportionality test, derived from administrative law in Germany, has since influenced public law in many other countries as well as various areas of public international law. It involves scrutinizing a government measure in terms of (i) the legitimacy of its objective, (ii) its suitability (or effectiveness) in achieving the objective, (iii) its necessity in light of available alternatives, and (iv) the importance of the objective balanced against the harm caused to the protected right or interest ('proportionality *stricto sensu*'). The first and especially last stages are often more controversial, because they implicate value judgements, compared to the fact-oriented inquiries into suitability and necessity of impugned measures.[86]

As for the standard of review that might be applied at each of these four stages, this is rarely detailed in treaty texts, but Henckels argues that tribunals can set it based on inherent powers and perhaps rules on evidence, given the impact on the burden and standard of proof. The main theoretical ground for tribunals deferring to the host State as primary decision-maker is normative and/or empirical (factual) uncertainty, combined with 'the desirability of regulatory autonomy and decision-making by actors that are proximate to or embedded in the national polity, and the practical advantages of relying on the decisions of actors with greater institutional competence or expertise'.[87] However, that desirability is arguably less convincing, outside the field of normative uncertainty over value judgments, than the practical advantages. Henckels also acknowledges that in principle tribunals might apply more deference where the host State had less institutional capacity or, more controversially, democratic legitimacy.[88] This might make her approach more attractive particularly in cases involving developing countries, bearing in mind potential 'bounded rationality'.

When assessing legitimate objective, suitability, and necessity, Henckels is critical of 'strict approaches' taken by some (often earlier) tribunals in favour of investors, and then identifies and proposes more nuanced alternatives. Regarding legitimate objectives for example, she argues that some tribunals seem to have been overly deferential in approving measures with

[82] K. Sauvant, 'The Evolving International Investment Law and Policy Regime: Ways Forward', *International Centre for Trade and Sustainable Development (ICTSD) and World Economic Forum E15 Task Force on Investment Policy – Policy Options Paper* (2016), part 3.4, pp. 31–33.

[83] S. Franck and L. Wylie, 'Predicting Outcomes in Investment Treaty Arbitration' (2015) 65(3) *Duke Law Journal* 459.

[84] Nottage and Thanitcul, 'International Investment Arbitration in Southeast Asia', above n 2, Appendix.

[85] C. Henckels, *Proportionality and Deference in Investor-State Arbitration: Balancing Investment Protection and Regulatory Autonomy* (Cambridge: Cambridge University Press, 2015).

[86] Ibid., 23–29.

[87] Ibid., 36.

[88] Ibid., 41–43.

discriminatory motivations, contrary to the treaty. However, Henckels supports tribunals that do vary the standard of review based on how widespread the measure is, apart from using common practice across countries to confirm the legitimacy of the measure. In contrast, at the suitability stage, she concedes that greater international consensus or harmonization can be seen as illustrating less normative or empirical uncertainty, so the argument for deference being accorded to significantly divergent States is arguably weaker. However, Henckels argues that this factor should still not be decisive,[89] which may provide some comfort, for example to developing States that are still out of step with global standards for a variety of possible reasons. For necessity testing, Henckels approves of recent tribunals that have required an alternative measure to be equally effective and/or acknowledges the actual possibility of the government adopting it, and some that permit more discretion to States by allowing them to show that alternatives had in fact been considered.

In short, under her approach:

> ... tribunals would afford a measure of deference on the basis of regulatory autonomy and proximity concerns when evaluating the legitimacy of a measure's objective, and would use this stage of proportionality analysis only to identify cases whether states were acting with discriminatory or other impermissible objectives. They would apply the suitability test in a way that takes account of any empirical uncertainty, and would permit states to adduce evidence to demonstrate that a measure would be expected to achieve its objective in future. They might afford a measure of deference even where states have, acting in good faith, made mistakes. Tribunals would also permit states to rely upon any relevant institutional competence and expertise in demonstrating the necessity of the challenged measure in light of possible alternatives .... Tribunals might also afford deference on the basis that states have thoroughly investigated alternative options before promulgating the measure in question or carefully balanced the interests at stake.[90]

Henckels' approach seems particularly promising for developing countries, including those within the Asian region. In some respects, however, it may be somewhat too ambitious. Compared to deference in the standard of review, proportionality testing may not be so easily transplanted, as it lacks many specific 'hooks' in current treaty wording. Indeed, another commentator now argues that the potential for enhanced proportionality testing with respect to fair and equitable treatment is constrained by a tendency for States to constrain arbitrator discretion by spelling out more specific obligations with respect to transparency of laws, administrative decision-making, access to courts, and anti-corruption.[91] Nor can it easily filter in from national law via state practice, as an element of customary international law, or as an identifiable general principle of law. Thus, for now, proportionality testing mostly relies on arbitrators drawing broader analogies from other legal regimes.[92] Nonetheless, a few recent treaties even in the Asian region make express reference to proportionality with respect to measures adopted by the host State, particularly in the context of determining indirect expropriation.[93]

89 Ibid., 133–38, 144–45.

90 Ibid., 171.

91 M. Moranis, 'Between Power and Procedure: The Changing Balance of Investment Treaty Protections' (2015) 31 *Arbitration International* 81 at 107–08 (with references to the earlier work by Kingsbury and Schill).

92 See generally V. Vadi, 'The Migration of Constitutional Ideas: The Strange Case of Proportionality in International Investment Law and Arbitration' (2015) 35 *Northwestern Journal of International Law & Business* 557.

93 Cf., e.g., Korea–Australia Free Trade Agreement, Seoul, 8 April 2014, in force 12 December 2016, Annex 11-B: Expropriation, fn 53: 'For Korea, a relevant consideration could include whether the investor bears a *disproportionate* burden such as a special sacrifice that exceeds what the investor or investment should be expected to endure for the public interest' (emphasis added).

Admittedly, investment treaty arbitrators often refer to other tribunal decisions, as well as academic writings,[94] so the emergent case law and its detailed analysis (as helpfully now elucidated by Henckels) may gather momentum.[95] However, States themselves are now paying closer attention to the development of arbitral case law as well.[96] Further, arbitrators appointed on an ad hoc basis still mostly come from a background in commercial law rather than public international law,[97] where broad standards and balancing tests are arguably more common. By contrast, Henckels shows that more robust applications of proportionality and deference instead have emerged – even without much textual foundation – in fields of international law where adjudicators can gain greater confidence and legitimacy by serving on permanent courts. Those include the European Court of Human Rights and the Court of Justice of the EU, in contrast to the dispute settlement system under the WTO where only the Appellate Body, which reviews decisions of ad hoc panels, comprises tenured 'members'. This point of comparative institutional design highlights the potential significance of the permanent investment court system promoted by the EU in its recent investment treaties.[98] Although the system will rely on building up a body of (possibly partly overlapping) investment court judges, treaty-by-treaty, already there are calls to develop a multilateral mechanism.[99]

In other respects, Henckels' approach may prove to be not ambitious enough. She concludes that investment tribunals should not carry out proportionality analysis *stricto sensu* because of the major legitimacy implications for certainty and regulatory autonomy. Yet Henckels herself acknowledges that others have presented quite convincing arguments that such analysis may be permissible – at least in exceptional circumstances – and that there are a few applications by the European Court of Human Rights and the Court of Justice of the EU. For example, Kingsbury and Schill are interpreted as allowing such review to be discharged procedurally or with a 'margin of appreciation'.[100] In my view, it may also become more readily justifiable as investment treaty provisions are increasingly folded into mega-

94 See, e.g., K. Gordon and J. Pohl, 'Investment Treaties Over Time – Treaty Practice and Interpretation in a Changing World', *OECD Working Papers on International Investment*, 2015/2, 13–14, available at www.oecd-ilibrary.org/finance-and-investment/investment-treaties-over-time-treaty-practice-and-interpretation-in-a-changing-world_5js7rhd8sq7h-en (last accessed 12 July 2019).

95 See also, e.g., Y. Taniguchi and T. Ishikawa, 'Balancing Investment Protection and Other Public Policy Goals: Lessons from WTO Jurisprudence' in J. Chaisse and T-Y. Lin (eds.), *International Economic Law and Governance: Essays in Honour of Mitsuo Matsushita* (Oxford University Press, 2016), p. 68.

96 *See* A. Roberts, 'Subsequent Agreements and Practice: The Battle over Interpretive Power', in G. Nolte (ed.), *Treaties and Subsequent Practice* (Oxford University Press, 2013); J. Lee, 'Taming Investor-State Arbitration?' in J. Chaisse and T-Y. Lin (eds.), *International Economic Law and Governance: Essays in Honour of Mitsuo Matsushita* (Oxford University Press, 2016), p. 131 (with particular reference to recent Asia-Pacific developments).

97 J. Pauwelyn, 'The Rule of Law without the Rule of Lawyers? Why Investment Arbitrators are from Mars, Trade Adjudicators are from Venus' (2015) 109(4) *American Journal of International Law* 761. *See also generally* M. Hirsch, *Invitation to the Sociology of International Law* (Oxford University Press, 2015), pp. 136–53.

98 Cf. generally S. Schill, 'Editorial: US versus EU Leadership in Global Investment Governance' (2016) 17(1) *Journal of World Investment and Trade* 1, 3, warning that: 'A permanent [EU-style investment] court could, much more than [ad hoc investor–State] arbitration, develop its own institutional dynamics and become even more independent from government influence than is currently the case with arbitration. The courts in Luxembourg and Strasbourg are perfect examples for the unexpected dynamics permanent international courts can develop.'

99 G. Kaufmann-Kohler and M. Potesta, 'Can the Mauritius Convention serve as a model for the reform of investor-State arbitration in connection with the introduction of a permanent investment tribunal or an appeal mechanism? Analysis and Roadmap', *Paper for CIDS – Geneva Center for International Dispute Settlement*, 3 June 2016, available at www.uncitral.org/pdf/english/commissionsessions/unc/unc-49/CIDS_Research_Paper_-_Can_the_Mauritius_Convention_serve_as_a_model.pdf (last accessed 12 July 2019).

100 See above n 85, Henckels, Proportionality and Deference, p. 166; B. Kingsbury and S. Schill, 'Investor-State Arbitration as Governance: Fair and Equitable Treatment, Proportionality, and the Emerging Global

regional FTAs, even if not yet as institutionalized as the EU system, especially if adjudicators start to become permanently appointed judges rather than ad hoc arbitrators.

In addition, empirical research from social psychology tends to confirm the jurists' intuition that 'procedural justice' matters; parties are more likely to accept the result, even if having lost the case, if the preceding procedure is perceived as fair.[101] Where a tribunal has already upheld the host State's arguments at the first three posited stages of proportionality testing, if it extends significant deference at the fourth stage of proportionality *stricto sensu* but nonetheless rules in favour of the investor who is exceptionally disadvantaged, it will be hard for the host State to complain too vociferously.

22.4.2 *Negotiating New Treaties*

There is also significant scope to apply lessons from Poulsen's study into bounded rationality when it comes to negotiating new treaties. First, there needs to be more and better background policy-oriented research in order to provide guidance to politicians and officials as to what is truly important when negotiating increasingly complex and wide-ranging treaties. For example, when discussing 'motivated learning', Poulsen rightly queries the ready assumption, on the part of developing countries and international organizations like UNCTAD, that offering investment treaties would lead to significantly more cross-border FDI. Although this has theoretical plausibility, it is ultimately an empirical question. Yet research remains sparse and results have been varied.

Indeed, in 2010 the (traditionally quite laissez-faire) economists in the Australian government's Productivity Commission seized on a few studies suggesting that, on an aggregate (world-wide) basis, ISDS-backed treaty provisions had not significantly increased investment flows, in order to recommend that Australia cease agreeing to ISDS provisions in any future treaties.[102] Yet a recent econometric study by Armstrong and Nottage casts doubt on that observation.[103] It found instead positive and significant impacts from ISDS provisions on FDI outflows from OECD countries over 1985–2014, using a Knowledge-Capital Model with a dynamic panel indicator (effectively addressing the problem of endogeneity in variables, since FDI might lead to treaties being signed, as well as vice versa). This impact on FDI flows was found from ISDS provisions on their own (especially in treaties signed or promptly ratified with non-OECD or less developed countries), and also when combined with the MFN provision (as a key and indicative substantive treaty commitment to foreign investors).

Administrative Law' in A. van den Berg (ed.), 50 *Years of the New York Convention* (Alphen aan den Rijn: Kluwer, 2009), p. 5; B. Kingsbury and S. Schill, 'Public Law Concepts to Balance Investors' Rights with State Regulatory Actions in the Public Interest – The Concept of Proportionality' in S. Schill (ed.), *International Investment Law and Comparative Public Law* (Oxford University Press, 2010), p. 75. However, considering that this aspect of proportionality analysis may inflame rather than address investment treaty law's legitimacy crisis, J. Paine, 'The Project of System-Internal Reform in International Investment Law: An Appraisal' (2015) 6 *Journal of International Dispute Settlement* 332, still tends towards Henckels' preference not to allow proportionality *stricto sensu*.

101 See, e.g., T. Tyler, *Why People Obey the Law* (New Jersey: Princeton University Press, 2006).

102 Australian Government Productivity Commission, 'Bilateral and Regional Trade Agreements', *Research Report* (2010), available at www.pc.gov.au/inquiries/completed/trade-agreements/report/trade-agreements-report.pdf (last accessed 12 July 2019).

103 S. Armstrong and L. Nottage, 'The Impact of Investment Treaties and ISDS Provisions on Foreign Direct Investment: A Baseline Econometric Analysis', *Sydney Law School Research Paper*, No. 16/74 (2016), available at: www.ssrn.com/abstract=2824090 (last accessed 12 July 2019).

Nonetheless, counter-intuitively and importantly for negotiators of future treaties, positive FDI impact was even larger for *weaker-form* provisions. This could be due to investors historically having been impressed by a broader 'signalling' effect from States concluding investment treaties. Yet the impact from ISDS provisions also seems to be diminishing since 2001, when ISDS claims started to pick up world-wide and therefore investors (or at least legal advisors) could have begun to pay more attention to the details of ISDS and other treaty provisions. Reduced impact since 2001 may be related to more efforts from host States to *unilaterally* liberalize and encourage FDI. However, it could also be due to a saturation effect (as treaties began to be concluded with less economically important partner States), or indeed due to less pro-investor provisions being incorporated into investment treaties (influenced by more recent US practice, partly in response to ISDS claims[104]).

Further variables impacting on FDI (such as double-tax treaties) could be investigated, as can regional differences. Data limitations also remain, as there is now considerable FDI outflow from non-OECD countries. Nonetheless, this baseline study suggests that it has been and still may be risky to eschew ISDS provisions altogether. In particular, results indicate a strong positive effect on FDI flows from ratified investment treaties overall even from 2001. States would have missed out on that if they had insisted on omitting ISDS, and this then became a deal-breaker for counterparty States.

Focusing more specifically on Asia, econometric research through at the Indian Council for Research on International Economic Relations[105] suggests that India was correct not to abandon ISDS provisions altogether in its revised Model BIT finalized in December 2015 (and to retreat from an even less pro-investor earlier draft of the Model BIT[106]). Results from Jaivir Singh (using instead a gravity-type model) find that although the signing of individual BITs had an insignificant impact on FDI inflows into India, the *cumulative* effect of signing BITs is significant and so is the coefficient associated with the signing of FTAs. Since almost all of India's investment treaties provide for full ISDS protections, these preliminary results suggest that ISDS can have a positive influence on investment, albeit in a non-obvious compound manner.[107]

In addition, a recent econometric study of Chinese outbound FDI (measured instead by numbers of both greenfield and M&A projects, rather than investment value) finds a significant positive impact on outflows from 2003 to 2014 due to China's investment treaties, coded using the composite BITSel index to measure the overall extent to which treaties are favourable to foreign investors.[108] However, the impact instead became negative for Chinese FDI into the subset of upper-higher-income host States. Desbordes and others therefore speculate that Chinese investors 'may feel confident to invest in countries whose political-

[104] Alschner and Skougarevskiy, 'Mapping the Universe of International Investment Agreements', above n 59.

[105] See Indian Council for Research on International Economic Relations, available at www.icrier.org/ (last accessed 12 July 2019).

[106] J. Dalhquist and L. E. Peterson, 'Analysis: In Final Version of its New Model Investment Treaty, India Dials Back Ambition of Earlier Proposals – But Still Favors Some Big Changes', Investment Arbitration Reporter, 3 January 2016, available at www.iareporter.com/articles/analysis-in-final-version-of-its-new-model-investment-treaty-india-dials-back-ambition-of-earlier-proposals-but-still-favors-some-big-changes/ (last accessed 12 July 2019).

[107] Jaivir Singh, "Indian Investment Treaty Practice: Qualitatively and Quantitatively Assessing Recent Developments" in Luke Nottage, Shahla Ali, Bruno Jetin and Nobumichi Teramura (eds), *New Frontiers in Asia-Pacific International Arbitration and Dispute Resolution* (Wolters Kluwer, 2021) chapter 12.

[108] On BITSel, see generally J. Chaisse and C. Bellak, 'Navigating the Expanding Universe of International Treaties on Foreign Investment: Creation and Use of a Critical Index' (2015) 18(1) *Journal of International Economic Law* 79; www.cuhk.edu.hk/law/proj/BITSel/ (last accessed 12 July 2019).

economic environment shares strong similarities with the one they face at home'.[109] Even more interestingly, and potentially relevant for Chinese negotiators of future investment treaties, this econometric study found no statistically significant effect on outbound investment numbers from including ISDS provisions in the relevant treaties. The positive impact on outbound FDI came instead from four other sets of provisions that also make up the composite BITSel index: provisions related to treaty scope (such as the definition of investment), market access (such as pre-establishment commitments), MFN and national treatment, expropriation and FET.[110] Future research may reveal different results if the ISDS provisions are further differentiated as strong (full) or weak (qualified), as in the study of world-wide FDI flows undertaken by Armstrong and Nottage applying some underlying coding of the treaties used to generate the BITSel index.

So far, this econometric analysis of Chinese outbound FDI patterns suggests that traditional ISDS provisions may be a less important component of investment treaties than has generally been assumed. However, this could be due to the unusually strong support on the part of the Chinese government for its outbound investors, making it easier to mobilize (informally) inter-State dispute settlement mechanisms. In particular, it is only in recent years that private companies in China, but still along with State-Owned Enterprises, have become major sources of outbound FDI.[111]

Indeed, another more recent econometric study based on similar methods finds that for BITSel-coded intra- and extra-Asian investment treaties (a large proportion of the total recorded by UNCTAD) over 2000–2016, there is a significant positive impact on the cumulative number of FDI projects not only with respect to such investment treaties overall, but also with respect to their component ISDS provisions. In fact, when the *marginal* effects on FDI are analysed, ISDS is the *only* provision having a significant positive influence from among the five components, meaning that 'the most important provision in BITs is access to international arbitration'.[112]

Such studies reinforce the need to be careful about abandoning ISDS provisions in investment treaties, especially in the Asian region, even while taking care not to indulge in 'motivated learning'. Moreover, to minimize the risk of 'status quo' bias and unthinkingly perpetuating past treaty drafting practices, countries in the Asian region should consult more widely with a view to developing and publicizing model treaties (or at least provisions) as a basis for future negotiations. This may be particularly important for developing countries, which otherwise may end up too readily acceding to templates proposed by larger counterparties, as evidenced perhaps by Cambodia signing a BIT in 2016 with India that adopts almost verbatim the latter's new Model BIT.[113] Yet it is also preferable for countries like Australia, not least to minimize scope for further infelicities in drafting being replicated

109 C. Azemar, J. Chaisse, R. Desbordes and I. Wooton, 'Do Bilateral Investment Treaties Influence Chinese Outward FDI? More Than a BIT', *Paper presented at the Asian Investment Forum II conference, Chinese University of Hong Kong* (29–30 November 2016, on file with the present author), p. 13 (discussing results in their Table 3).

110 Ibid., p. 14 (Table 4).

111 On broader trends in China's cross-border FDI and investment treaty practice, including implications for several major negotiations with Asia-Pacific partner countries, see J. Chaisse, 'China's International Investment Policy: Formation, Evolution, and Transformation(s)' in J. Chaisse and L. Nottage (eds.), *International Investment Treaties and Arbitration Across Asia* (Brill, 2018), pp. 544–78.

112 Asian Development Bank, *ASEAN Economic Integration Report 2016*, p. 163 (with reference to Tables 6.28 and 6.29).

113 R. Weeramantry, 'International Investment Law and Practice in the Kingdom of Cambodia' (October 2016 manuscript, on file with the present author). In contrast, in 2016, Laos began developing its own Model BIT.

across multiple treaties.[114] However, to avoid simply mimicking others' models or entrenching one's own, these should be regularly reviewed, or possibly stated in the form of general principles for negotiators (along the lines of the current EU approach).

Furthermore, partly to minimize the effects of 'salience bias' associated with initial (or potentially other high-profile) ISDS claims, States should seriously consider moving away from the traditional approach of each disputing party freely appointing arbitrators on an ad hoc basis, whose awards are not reviewable even for serious error of law. An EU-style two-tier investment court, with judges nominated by the treaty partner States for a roster, is only one possible alternative. One can conceive of various other combinations of appellate review mechanism, roster or standing panels,[115] and codes of conduct for arbitrators. Indeed, some variants are already emerging in recent Asia-Pacific investment treaties.[116] Ironically, given impediments to including ISDS mechanisms in EU treaties, highlighted by a recent decision of the Court of Justice of the EU with respect to its FTA with Singapore,[117] it may instead be intra-Asian investment treaties that lead the way in experimenting with 'EU-style' permanent courts or other new hybrid forms of ISDS.

Lastly, as such attempts at recalibrating investment treaties begin to emerge in the region, particular care needs to be taken with 'mega-regional' agreements, such the Regional Comprehensive Economic Partnership (RCEP or ASEAN+6) FTA.[118] After all, inter-State commissions that might otherwise, for example, agree on interpretations of treaty provisions, binding future (and possibly even current) arbitral tribunals,[119] are less likely to be able to play such roles effectively (compared to bilateral or smaller-scale treaties), if the commissions require agreement of representatives from many Member States. It may also be much more difficult to reach a mutual agreement to terminate such mega-regional agreements, in order to 'reset' on a new basis as economic and political circumstances evolve. A further impediment to such recalibration arises as States, such as Australia and now seemingly Indonesia, seek to replace standalone BITs with comprehensive FTAs.

Acknowledging the role of bounded rationality in an increasingly complex world, future treaty negotiators may need to consider mechanisms that could make it easier to conclude, renegotiate or terminate investment chapters within FTAs, especially mega-regional agreements. On the one hand, negotiators may be tempted to go 'back to the future' and negotiate standalone BITs, so that opposition to particular provisions (such as ISDS) does not jeopardize the conclusion of FTAs. On the other hand, this strategy may make it harder to trade off divergent interests to reach agreement at all. Alternatively, it may risk watering down BITs despite significant econometric and other evidence for their usefulness; and potentially FTAs themselves especially if other controversial chapters end up being omitted, even though comprehensive regional agreements better fit the contemporary economic reality of regional

114 Nottage, 'Investor-State Arbitration Policy and Practice in Australia', above n 79.

115 See generally L. Trakman and D. Musaleyan, 'Arguments for and against Standing Panels of Arbitrators in Investor-State Arbitration Evidence and Reality' (November 2016, manuscript on file with the present author).

116 Kawharu and Nottage, 'Models for Investment Treaties', above n 74, Part 6.B.

117 M. Mohan, 'Singapore and its Free Trade Agreement with the European Union: Rationality "Unbound"?' (2017) 18(5–6) *Journal of World Investment and Trade* 858.

118 See Kawharu and Nottage, 'Models for Investment Treaties', above n 74, especially Part 5. See also generally, noting the recent signing of RCEP without for now ISDS (or India) but that most pairs of signatory States have ISDS-backed commitments through other treaties anyway: Luke Nottage and Bruno Jetin, 'New Frontiers in Asia-Pacific Trade, Investment and International Business Dispute Resolution' in Luke Nottage et al (eds), *New Frontiers in Asia-Pacific International Arbitration and Dispute Resolution* (Wolters Kluwer, 2021) chapter 1.

119 See generally, e.g., Lee, 'Taming Investor-State Arbitration?', above n 95, pp. 137–38.

and global value chains.[120] However, it still makes sense to think more carefully about provisions, particularly in mega-regional FTAs such as the RCEP, that could allow for re-assessments and even more ready termination of component parts such as investment chapters.

22.5 CONCLUSION

To know where to go next, we should check where we have come from. A useful roadmap is provided by Poulsen's recent study of investment treaty making by developing countries (Section 22.2). Yet a closer analysis of his 'bounded rationality' thesis reveals some limits, at least for some countries in the Asian region (Section 22.3). Accordingly, we should focus on various further possible reforms to the international investment treaty system, rather than abandoning it altogether, beginning with ISDS provisions as a key procedural mechanism. For existing treaties, for example, arbitrators and counsel should consider applying more principled approaches to proportionality testing and deference to host State decision-making (Section 22.4.1). For future treaties (Section 22.4.2), we need better background policy research (including into the important issue of whether and how ISDS-backed investment treaties promote cross-border FDI), as well as more public consultation to consider developing model investment treaties or provisions.[121] Procedural innovations, including but not limited to an EU-style permanent investment court, deserve to be trialled. In any event, thought should be given to making it easier to adjust and even terminate investment provisions, especially within mega-regional FTAs, to balance the significant roles they can play in this new current era of globalization against the cognitive, informational and increasingly political challenges facing those negotiating investment treaties.

[120] R. Baldwin, *The Great Convergence: Information Technology and the New Globalisation* (Cambridge, Mass.: Harvard University Press, 2016).

[121] Australia has recently begun reviewing its remaining standalone BITs, a useful approach that may generate model provisions: see Luke Nottage, 'Submission to DFAT consultation on "Review of Australia's Bilateral Investment Treaties"', Erga Omnes blog (14 September) <https://erga-omnes.sydney.edu.au/2020/09/submission-to-dfat-consultation-on-review-of-australias-bilateral-investment-treaties/> (accessed 12 December 2020).

Index

For EU product safety concerns, contact us at Calle de José Abascal, 56–1°,
28003 Madrid, Spain or eugpsr@cambridge.org.

www.ingramcontent.com/pod-product-compliance
Lightning Source LLC
LaVergne TN
LVHW060018210926
848481LV00013B/3736